German History since 1800

German History since 1800

EDITED BY
MARY FULBROOK
Professor of German History, University College London

ADVISORY EDITOR
JOHN BREUILLY
Professor of Modern History, University of Birmingham

A member of the Hodder Headline Group
LONDON • NEW YORK • SYDNEY • AUCKLAND

First published in Great Britain in 1997 by
Arnold, a member of the Hodder Headline Group
338 Euston Road, London NW1 3BH
175 Fifth Avenue, New York, NY 10010

Distributed exclusively in the USA by
St Martin's Press, Inc.
175 Fifth Avenue, New York, NY 10010

British Library Cataloguing in Publication Data
A catalogue record for this book is available from the British Library

Library of Congress Cataloging-in-Publication Data
German history since 1800 / edited by Mary Fulbrook.
    p.   cm.
Includes bibliographical references and index.
ISBN 0-340-69199-9 (hb).—ISBN 0-340-69200-6 (pb)
1. Germany—History—1789–1900.   2. Germany—History—20th century.
I. Fulbrook, Mary. 1951–
DD203.G47   1987
943—dc21   96-52707

ISBN 0 340 69199 9 (hb)
ISBN 0 340 69200 6 (pb)

Typeset in 10/13pt Plantin by Phoenix Photosetting, Lordswood, Chatham, Kent
Printed and bound in Great Britain by The Bath Press, Bath

Contents

Part I   1800–1870

Part II   1871–1918

List of figures

List of maps

List of illustrations

List of tables

Acknowledgements

Editing a substantial volume with a large number of authors is no easy undertaking. The Editor would like to thank the UCL Centre for Interdisciplinary Research in the Arts and Humanities for a grant towards the running costs of a workshop which helped greatly to coordinate the coverage of chapters and to impose a degree of intellectual coherence on the project. The Editor would also like to thank Sue Jones of the UCL German Department for her invaluable assistance in administration and coordination.

The editors and publisher would like to acknowledge the following for the use of visual materials for the illustrations: AKG Photo, London, for illustration numbers 7.1, 8.1, 17.1, 18.1, 18.2, 20.1, 22.1 and 25.2; AP Photo/Michael Probst for 27.2; Bildarchiv Preussischer Kulturbesitz, Berlin, for 3.1, 3.2, 4.1, 12.1, 27.1 and 27.2; the British Film Institute, London, for 21.1 and 21.2; Colindale for 13.1; the British Library, London, for 13.1; Bundesarchiv, Koblenz, for 14.3, 15.1, 15.2, 16.1, 19.1, 19.2, 20.2 and 22.2; Kölnisches Stadtmuseum for 5.2; Kunsthalle Bremen for 10.1; Neue Pinakothek München for 5.1; Rijksinstituut voor Oorlogsdocumentatie, Amsterdam, for 16.2 and 17.2; the Royal Institute of British Architects, London, for 10.2; Städtische Kunsthalle, Mannheim, for 14.3; and Ullstein Bilderdienst, Berlin, for 11.1.

I

Introduction

Mary Fulbrook

In 1800, there was no 'Germany' as we think of a unitary nation state today. The centuries-old pattern of a multiplicity of states – some tiny, barely larger in size than a knight's castle on a hill-top, or a modest prince-bishopric, others large and complex, scattered territories united under personal rule – was still nominally held together under the framework of the Holy Roman Empire. Nevertheless, its political shape and boundaries were in flux, under the influence of the Napoleonic Wars; in 1815, a new, more streamlined Confederation took its place. 'Germany' was at this time a largely rural land, the large tracts of forest, heath and farmland interspersed with small towns and hamlets, and a few more important urban centres. The population was much sparser than today, communications more rudimentary: no railways, no metalled roads, no cars, aeroplanes, telephones, or mass media of communication. Regional variations were great, in economic, political and cultural respects. Not only were there massive differences between, say, the system of serfdom on feudal estates east of the Elbe compared to the peasant smallholdings in the southwest; or between cities whose mark was stamped by a prince or bishop compared to the merchant and patrician culture of a Hanse city like Hamburg; the linguistic watersheds between Bavarian, Swabian or Frisian, the religious chasms between Protestants and Catholics, served to render Germany a place of pattern and great variety. At the same time, however, above the vast majority of the labouring population whose horizons were largely local and regional, there was an educated minority who felt that, for all the regional differences of dialect and culture, for all the variants of socioeconomic and political structure, there were common elements of a Geman culture which served to render the Germans a *Kulturnation*, a nation defined by its culture.

In the following two centuries, Germany went through massive transformations. In the nineteenth century, quickening processes of industrialization, urbanization, and population growth radically altered the very face of the country; and, for all the political upheavals which followed, the German economy has remained a formidable powerhouse in central Europe. In the later nineteenth and early twentieth centuries, the formation of a unitary state and political centralization within that state started to erode, although never entirely erase, the regional differences inherited from the past and sustained – in some areas even strengthened – in the Confederation. The political cataclysms and upheavals of the twentieth century, with two World Wars unleashed from German soil, and with the purposeful mass murder of six million people in the Nazi genocide, dramatically affected the whole of European and indeed world history. With its apparently 'belated' unification in 1871, its slide from democracy into dictatorship and the arguably unparalleled atrocities of the Nazi period, its extraordinary division into two opposing states in the Cold War and its subsequent reunification, modern German history has aroused the most virulent controversies and debates over conflicting interpretations.

I German identity and diversity

Observers of Germany have often sought to identify specific features which may account for its apparently peculiar patterns of development. Older notions of a putative 'national character' were often merely replaced by apparently more acceptable culturalist explanations, pointing the finger, for example, at traditions from Luther, through Kant and Hegel, to the failure of Germans to resist Nazism. Although such long-term culturalist approaches have fallen into widespread disfavour among historians in recent decades, they have never entirely faded away (one recent variant may be found in the study of the Holocaust by American historian Daniel Goldhagen).[1]

As a number of chapters below show (but particularly Chapter 27 by John Breuilly), the definition of what it means to be 'German' is not some essence, a Holy Grail to be defined and enshrined, but rather a sociocultural construction, the subject of controversy, political negotiation and change. As Whaley and Clark point out (Chapters 2 and 3), in the early nineteenth century the meanings of local and national identities could be cross-cutting, with divided loyalties and no predetermined drive towards the kind of small-German state that was to emerge under Bismarck. Regional diversity in Germany – against an older Prusso-centric view – is emphasized too in the chapters on nineteenth-century economic and social developments (see particularly Chapters 4 and 9). Moreover, as Karin Friedrich points out in Chapter 5, nineteenth-century German culture shared in more general European intellectual trends, shaped by the specific, decentralized character of German politics. A variety of routes out of the pre-nineteenth-century pattern of *Kleinstaaterei*, with its rich variety of political forms based in the main on dynastic, hereditary or religious principles, might have been conceivable.

In the later eighteenth and through the nineteenth centuries, new principles began to develop alongside these older forms. In particular, notions of nationhood became, at least among vociferous and educated minorities, more salient. At first such notions were couched in purely cultural terms; it was only later that the idea that cultural and political entities should be coterminous began to gather political support. The connections between the emergence of nationalist movements and nation states in the era of industrialization and modern capitalism have puzzled and intrigued many scholars.[2] In retrospect, however, it is important to remember how contingent the specific outcomes of these general developments were. Identity definition and construction could be attached to a region, a locality, a broader focus; how these processes actually worked out historically – what became a candidate for 'nation state-ness' and what did not – was more often a matter of power politics than of any 'natural' entity in some way 'realizing itself'. Had it not been for the specific ways in which Austria failed in certain of its projects, Bavaria, for example, could as well have become part of an expanded Catholic Habsburg state as part of a Prussian- and Protestant-dominated German Empire. Detailed historical and political analysis must take the place of essentialist and teleological views in recounting the actual course of German history.

Diversity has remained a feature of twentieth-century German history. Even the growth of commercialized mass culture in the Weimar Republic was not sufficient to homogenize German culture across all regions and classes, as Elizabeth Harvey points out in Chapter 14. The definition of a homogenous national identity became something very different with Hitler's notion of an ethnically pure *Volksgemeinschaft* (national community), and with the divergent and diverse reactions against this in the democratic and Communist states which replaced the Third Reich. Even within one state, the Federal Republic, there were tensions between different polarities, different conceptions of German national identity, as Erica Carter points out in Chapter 21. Moreover, political division between East and West in the post-1945 period assisted in the formation of two very distinct variations on the long-running theme of social, economic and regional diversity in German history (see Chapter 20). Reflecting more broadly on the course of modern German history, one is perhaps most struck by the inappropriateness of many long-held myths about Germany: and most of all by the myth that one could define a single German national character, culture, identity or essence.

From the later 1960s culturalist or essentialist approaches were in part displaced by a variety of attempts to explain Germany's history by dislocations in aspects of its social and political development. Notions of the 'belated nation', of archaic political forms coexisting with dynamic and changing socioeconomic structures, of authoritarian legacies in a modern world, began to proliferate in the historical scene. Works such as Hans-Ulrich Wehler's deliberately provocative theses on Imperial Germany stimulated a prolific spate of detailed research into aspects of Germany's social structure and political culture in a period of rapid economic modernization.[3] The type of societal history often associated with what has become known as the 'Bielefeld School' provided rich new perspectives on complex patterns of sociopolitical development within Germany. These historiographical developments also brought new perspectives to bear on questions – such as the origins of the First World War, first opened up in the

Fischer controversy of the 1960s – which had previously been treated primarily in terms of international relations and high politics rather than in the light of domestic social tensions.

In reaction to the often overly structuralist character of some of these approaches, in the course of the later 1970s and 1980s new interest began to focus on culture defined in the broad, anthropological sense, and on the experience of everyday life (see Chapter 23 by Stefan Berger, and Chapter 24 by Jürgen Kocka, below). Nor did the more general assumptions behind the *Sonderweg* approach go unchallenged. As many commentators have pointed out, notions of 'distortion' or 'belatedness' are essentially predicated on a view of what is 'normal'. This view of peculiarity and normality, when examined more closely, quickly unravels: all 'national histories' are in some ways unique combinations of different variables, formed and shaped perhaps by common trends (such as industrialization) but also open to the influence of individual actions and accidental conjunctures.

There is, in other words, no 'normal' national history, against which German history is to be measured (and found wanting). This is not to say that comparative history is impossible: rather, that it should be undertaken analytically, teasing out similarities and differences in complex patterns of development, without prioritizing any one particular – and historically unique – pattern as 'normal'. In this respect, the notion of a *Sonderweg*, or special path to modernity, however untenable in its fundamental assumptions, has in fact been heuristically rather fruitful: it has stimulated, not only major theoretical and interpretive controversies, but also a wealth of detailed empirical research into key aspects of modern German history. Many of the fruits of these debates will be found in the chapters which follow.

II   German history in an international context

The apparently 'normal' units of analysis in modern European history, namely nation states, are themselves to a high degree the products of, as well as the actors within, a broader international system. The changing international context is crucial to understanding German history; the very shape, location and borders of 'Germany' were intimately affected by broader trends and a changing location within wider systems.

The loose pattern of the Holy Roman Empire, described by Joachim Whaley in Chapter 2, proved sufficiently flexible to allow the persistence of a multiplicity of tiny, medium and larger territories, with a wide variety of political systems, to persist over centuries within the broader juristic and political framework of the Empire. Warfare, dynastic politics and marriage constantly served to redraw boundaries between individual territories or to change the rulership of particular states within the Empire.

Napoleonic expansion in post-revolutionary France was the prime catalyst of the collapse of the Holy Roman Empire and the redrawing of central European boundaries. In 1815, the emergence of a larger, economically more powerful and more western-orientated Prussia was part of an attempt to create a stronger buffer between France and Russia. The Confederation, with its delicate balance between Prussia and Austria, provided a framework within which newer and older forms and principles coexisted uneasily. Dynastic principles were increasingly challenged by the growth of constitutional liberalism and emergent nationalism (in a variety of political colours), although, as Wolfram Siemann shows in Chapter 6, popular unrest in 1848 had more to do with protest and reaction against modernization than with liberal demands for constitutional reform and national unity. At the same time, economic developments relating intimately to developing industrial capitalism began to erode territorial boundaries through new institutional forms (such as the customs union) and the increased mobility of a rapidly growing population (see Chapters 3 and 4).

But, as John Breuilly shows in Chapter 7, it was less any 'organic' emergence of a unified Germany based in developing economic organization and population movement or a growing sense of a common 'national' culture than the military successes of Prussia, orchestrated by the opportunistic political genius Bismarck, which effected the creation of the Prussian-dominated 'small-German' Second Empire of 1871–1918. Even in the Empire, as Kathy Lerman shows in Chapters 8 and 11, tensions still persisted between older dynastic and newer 'national' principles. These included the predominance of Prussia (with the Prussian army) and the ambiguities in the power structure of Imperial Germany; and the uneasy and unstable compromises between the personal will of the Emperor and his close advisers, on the one hand, and the emerging expression of a more democratic participation through parliamentary parties with a growing voice but without real power, on the other.

Again, however, domestic conflicts were played out within a specific international constellation. It was in the broader context of a late nineteenth- and early twentieth-century competition among European powers for imperial territories and markets that this domestic configuration played its tragic role in unleashing the First World War. Germany may have borne prime responsibility for the specific timing and sparking of the conflagration: but the First World War erupted in an unstable international system characterized by the formation of opposing alliances, the race for military preparedness and superiority, and the unstable resolution of periodic flashpoints and crises over preceding years. The settlement embodied in the Versailles Treaty sought, like the Vienna settlement a century earlier, to provide a pan-European solution to the 'German question'.

In some respects, the Second World War shows clear lines of continuity with the First. Widespread belief in the 'stab in the back legend', a sense of national humiliation and rejection of the terms of the Treaty of Versailles, played a role in the willingness of many (though never an absolute majority of) Germans to countenance and acquiesce in the rise of Adolf Hitler and the NSDAP (see Chapters 12 and 15). There was no inevitability about this, but the degree of freedom of manouevre, with respect to economic policy, for example, was circumscribed (see the discussion by Niall Ferguson in Chapter 13). With the Nazis came new tones: Hitler's megalomaniac aspirations to world domination went way beyond the more moderate aims of the traditional conservative military elites, whose break with their would-be puppet and eventual master was too little and too late; by the time of the 1944 July Plot, the *Götterdämmerung* of mass destruction and genocide unleashed by the Third Reich had advanced too far. And, for all the common elements to be found in eugenic and racial theories in the late nineteenth and twentieth centuries, the translation of racism into mass genocide was unprecedented, unparalleled. Hitler's foreign policy successes during the peacetime years of 1936–9 were certainly made possible by the non-intervention or acquiescence of the great powers, for a variety of reasons. But with Hitler, German history profoundly affected European and world history in a conscious act of political will which no amount of geopolitical theorizing can conjure away (see Chapter 26).

The wider, underlying instability of the European state system was dramatically altered by the radical changes of the period after 1945. Having been dragged, belatedly, into two World Wars, the United States of America finally gave up its isolationist stance and became, after 1945, policeman and protector of the Western world – a political role which harmonized nicely with its economic interests in the expansion of its overseas markets. At the same time, twice invaded and militarily savaged, the Soviet Union erected a buffer of 'satellite states' along its western flank. The Cold War between the two world superpowers, with their opposing ideologies and political-economic systems, took precedence as the decisive parameter of the international context. Within Western Europe, conflict between states was replaced by emphasis on harmony and increasing cooperation and integration. Eastern European states were brought, with a degree of coercion, under the control of the Soviet Union. Germany itself was divided, and two very different political systems, bearing the imprint of the two superpowers, were imposed – with a degree of domestic cooperation on the part of different German elites on each side – in the ruins of defeated Nazi Germany (see Chapters 18 to 21).

For all the undoubted contributions made by those who came out to march and demonstrate in East German towns and cities in autumn 1989, it was the end of the Cold War – the effective capitulation of Gorbachev's USSR, its admission that it could no longer economically or politically sustain the arms race – that proved crucial in bringing about the end of German division, as Jonathan Osmond points out in Chapter 22. Once again, international and domestic factors intertwined: West Germany, in the person of Helmut Kohl, seized the historic opportunity to power forwards with plans for the unification of the divided states, while a majority of East Germans, faced with the rapid collapse of their economy once exposed to the chill winds of Western competition and spiralling unemployment, voted willingly for their incorporation into an enlarged Federal Republic.

Germany at the end of the twentieth century finds itself in a radically changed international environment from that of the preceding half century. Gone are the cold certainties of the Cold War years: in their place are new conflicts and turmoils. The 'lesson' of German history, if such a thing there be, is that no one factor can serve to explain or predict the outcome of such conflicts. Political and cultural will, on the basis of given resources, are key determinants of the balance of forces in any given constellation; but the role of contingency, of accident, of unexpected actions and developments, is always a key, if uncertain, factor in the unfolding of historical events.

III   Approaches to German history

One book cannot cover everything; nor can it even aspire to adumbrate all relevant aspects of a topic or period. This book is intended to be read in conjunction with more detailed narratives of German history, covering the whole or part of the period (see the Select Bibliographies for each chapter). The chapters which follow seek to address some of the major themes and developments of each period, and to register and take issue with recent historiographical shifts.

Many of the following chapters address the range of debates and approaches to the particular period or issue covered. History is not just a question of supplying a simple chronological narrative of events: even the most apparently naive narrative incorporates principles of selection, attributes causality and accords different weightings to different factors in the account. But most historians go beyond the notion of 'recounting the story as it actually happened' and seek to theorize more explicitly about their subject. Theoretical differences become apparent at a number of levels.

Historians develop and employ different general models of the period with which they are dealing. Different aspects are highlighted, different contextual connections are adduced, depending on the model chosen. To take a few examples from the chapters which follow: discussion of Imperial Germany, as Kathy Lerman shows in Chapters 8 and 11, has spawned a variety of different concepts seeking to capture the hybrid character of this state, which combined dynastic and national/constitutional principles in an uneasy and unstable compromise. The character of Nazi Germany, as Ian Kershaw and Nick Stargardt show (Chapters 16 and 17), has been interpreted in the light of a variety of theoretical models, ranging from totalitarianism through fascism to a racial state which was arguably *sui generis*. Similarly, as Mark Allinson points out in Chapter 19, the GDR is now the subject of heated controversies over the nature of the dictatorship and its comparability or otherwise with the Third Reich. In some contrast, as Mark Roseman points out in Chapter 18, the historiography of the Federal Republic of Germany is not as yet as clearly crystallized around specific models and debates. No doubt, however, with increasing distance – as the old West Germany appears increasingly remote – this period will also become the object of more clearly delineated controversies.

History is, of course, not only a matter of theorizing, and theoretical models cannot be plucked out of thin air with no reference to empirical material on the ground. But, very often, the particular topics which historians choose to research, and the specific questions in the light of which they actively interrogate the evidence or remnants of the past, depend on prior assumptions about the nature of that which is under investigation. There is an interactive process between theory and empirical enquiry, in which both mutually inform and modify the other. Many of the chapters in this book seek to capture the current state of this productive interplay, to convey the current state of debates and research in their area. A certain level of familiarity with the period in question may be assumed; although relevant details are incorporated into each account or essay as they arise in the context of the argument, there is no pretence of exhaustive coverage or empirical saturation.

There is also the issue of selection of topic. Decisions have to be made about scope and space for particular issues within the general chronological framework. The Holocaust – to take a key example – is such a central event in modern German and world history, and is the subject of so much emotional heat and pain, as well as theoretical controversy, that it seemed essential to devote a whole chapter to this. Moreover, while it is vital to analyse particular periods in detail, sometimes important broader trends and wider interpretive questions can get lost without a more panoramic and thematic approach. Again, not every possible topic can be covered: there are many well-defined particular areas in which contemporary historical research is producing highly interesting and stimulating results (such as the history of crime and punishment, or the history of science and medicine), which are not included. Part V concentrates, however, on a selection of more general questions which are central to a broad understanding of modern German history as sketched in this Introduction.

Stefan Berger (Chapter 23) analyses the changing paradigms and frameworks within which Germans have conceptualized and written their own history. Jürgen Kocka (Chapter 24) addresses the crucial issue, from the perspective of the late twentieth century, of the conditions for the emergence of civil society, while Ute Frevert (Chapter 25) focuses on the degrees of social and historical malleability of an apparent biological given, the construction of gender. Charles Maier (Chapter 26) engages with approaches to one of the central questions of modern German history, the conditions for war and peace. Finally, in Chapter 27, John Breuilly returns to a question which has dogged Germans and observers of Germany for generations, the question of what it is to be German, and presents a differentiated analysis of the ways in which different conceptions of German national identity have been constructed and propagated over the last two centuries.

Taken as a whole, the chapters which follow characterize and reflect on key issues in the controversial course of modern German history. They do not cumulatively represent a single line of argument or a coherent new paradigm in German historiography; rather, they reflect the diversity and liveliness of the field, and provide informed and informative points of entry to key issues and debates with which all students and scholars of the period must engage.

Notes:

1. Daniel Goldhagen, *Hitler's Willing Executioners. Ordinary Germans and the Holocaust* (London: Little, Brown and Co., 1996).
2. See for example: Benedict Anderson, *Imagined Communities* (London: Verso, 1983); John Breuilly, *Nationalism and the State* (Manchester: Manchester University Press, 2nd edn., 1993); E. Gellner, *Nations and Nationalism* (Oxford: Blackwell, 1983); E. J. Hobsbawm, *Nations and Nationalism since 1789* (Cambridge: Cambridge University Press, 1991); Anthony Smith, *National Identity* (Harmondsworth: Penguin, 1991).
3. See Hans-Ulrich Wehler, *The German Empire* (Leamington Spa: Berg, 1985).

Part I

1800–1870

Introduction to Part I: 1800–1870

John Breuilly

The essays dealing with the period from 1800 to the formation of the German Second Empire cover a variety of subjects. The concern is mainly political in the contributions by Whaley, Clark, Siemann and Breuilly. Lee considers social and economic aspects while Friedrich focuses on culture. In this brief introduction I will make two basic points.

First, Germany did not exist as a national state until the end of the period covered by this section. Even then a major part of pre-1871 Germany, the German part of the Habsburg Empire, was excluded from the new state. Not only were there many states in 'Germany' but these states were themselves subject to territorial alteration through processes of war and diplomacy as well as undergoing considerable institutional and social change. One should also draw attention to the great regional variations within the larger states. Sometimes there were different institutional and legal arrangements in different parts of the same state. Inhabitants of one Prussian province had little contact with those of other provinces. Catholic culture differed enormously from Protestant culture; social divisions were much greater than today; life in east Germany was very different from that of west Germany; town and countryside were almost different worlds. One could multiply such examples of variation, difference and distance. Conversely, Germans in border regions often had closer contacts with non-Germans in the same region than with Germans in other regions, for example Rhenish Prussians with Belgians. Even how we make a judgement on that depends on whether we define a German as a native speaker of German or as a subject of a German state. All this makes the terms 'Germany' and 'German' problematic and this is a point one will encounter frequently in the various essays and which needs to be constantly kept in mind.

Second, it is quite impossible to cover every aspect of the history of Germany in this period. The essays by Clark and Friedrich touch upon religion, philosophy and popular literature but it was simply impossible to provide a full survey either of the history of ideas or of popular culture. Instead the focus is upon organized religion, the work of philosophers which had a contemporary social or political significance, and upon the development of a new and distinctive culture associated with the bourgeoisie. War was a major feature of the Napoleonic period and the period between 1854 and 1871 and was also important in 1848–9. However, there is little military history in these essays which focus rather upon the state as a political arena, a policy-making agency and an administrative apparatus, taking war into account more as something which happens to these states than a matter for detailed investigation (see, however, Chapter 26 on the subject of war by Charles Maier).

Nevertheless, the essays cover a great deal of ground and provide much detail. There is perhaps a danger that the reader will lose sight of the 'big picture'. Some historians would dispute such an idea and suggest that this simply means imposing some preconceived idea of what is important on the period. However, I do think there are certain major transformations in German history in this period that underpin much of the detail. Most obviously, by 1871 Germany had been brought under the control of a single state, that of Prussia. Germans moved around their country much more by 171 than before (and many more of them also emigrated abroad). Furthermore, that movement was now largely from east to west. From mid-century urban population growth outstripped that of the countryside. The imagination of contemporaries was captivated by the rapid expansion of railways, coal, iron and steel. By 1871, compared to 1800, Germans were more prosperous, more mobile and far more conscious of being Germans. Not only had a national state been formed but the elements of a national economy, society and culture were much more clearly visible than at the beginning of the century.

Of course, one should not exaggerate how far this had gone or imagine that what had happened was inevitable. The essays constantly point to underlying continuities and the extent to which 'Germany' remained a land of diverse regions, cultures and possibilities throughout this period. Still, it is much easier to write something called 'Germany history' by the end of this period than it was at the beginning.

2

The German lands before 1815

Joachim Whaley

In the decades before 1815 the German lands underwent a process of revolutionary change, but there was no revolution as such, nothing to compare with events in France in 1789. Yet contemporaries experienced this period as one of profound and rapid transformation. Most obviously, the map of Germany in 1815 looked very different from what it had been in, say, 1780. The Holy Roman Empire had ceased to exist after a thousand-year history; a bewildering patchwork of several hundred quasi-independent territories had been replaced by 41 sovereign states in a loose confederation. This 'territorial revolution' was accompanied by other equally profound changes: the transformation of political and legal institutions; a new relationship between church, state and society in the Catholic regions; new social and economic structures resulting from the massive transfer of Catholic ecclesiastical property; new cultural attitudes and novel perceptions of what 'Germany' and the very identity of the Germans was or might be; a new political vocabulary and new concepts with which Germans described the world in which they lived. The sheer magnitude and pace of change struck many contemporaries as the major characteristic of their age. The Gotha bookseller and publisher Friedrich Perthes (1772–1843) expressed the sense of many when he reflected in 1818 that while previous periods in history had been characterized by gradual change over centuries, 'In the three generations alive today our own age has, in fact, combined what cannot be combined. No sense of continuity informs the tremendous contrasts inherent in the years 1750, 1789 and 1815; to people alive now . . . they simply do not appear as a sequence of events.'[1]

Much of this complexity was lost in the classic accounts of this period by German historians of the later nineteenth and early twentieth centuries. They constructed a narrative which showed the inevitability of the emergence of a Prussian-dominated nation state in 1871. For Treitschke and others, German history was Prussian history. The Holy Roman Empire was portrayed as decayed and moribund, the German territories as backward and corrupt. When challenged by the ideas and the armies of the French Revolution, German political institutions, both imperial and territorial, collapsed. Yet out of Napoleon's humiliation of the Germans, according to the traditional view, a new sense of German destiny arose. Prussia, which had emerged as a great power under Frederick the Great, became the focus of a new national movement, while the Prussian reforms after 1806 supposedly embodied the German answer to 1789. Most leading historians, like Friedrich Meinecke (1862–1954), held that Stein and Hardenberg transformed Prussia into a bastion of the German national movement, the driving force in the Wars of Liberation which defeated Napoleon and finally expelled the French from Germany.

Elements of the traditional view survive even in some recent surveys. Thomas Nipperdey's account of Germany in the nineteenth century (published in 1983) opens with the words: 'In the beginning was Napoleon'.[2] Nipperdey cannot be accused of being an exponent of the '*kleindeutsch*' tradition of Prusso-centric history. Yet his portrayal of Napoleon as the 'creator' echoes the teleological ideology of the nationalist historians. German nationalism is presented as a response to French domination characterized by a reaction against French ideas (the 'ideas of 1789'), the problematic inception of modernity in Germany.

Tradition dies hard, but in the last few decades virtually every aspect of the period before 1815 has been the subject of revision. Some scholars have explored the 'modernization' of Germany in this period. Others, working primarily from an early modern perspective, have found continuity as well as change. Above all much recent research has sought to investigate alternatives to the Prusso-centric view of German history. The insistence that the emergence of the Prussian-German nation state in 1871 was not inevitable has focused attention on other options, such as a Holy Roman Empire or the Confederation of the Rhine. This has in turn shed new light on the history of nationalism and on the significance of reform movements outside Prussia, particularly in south and west Germany. At the same time a growing emphasis on lines of continuity, from enlightened absolutist reform before 1789 to the bureaucratic reforms after 1800, has challenged the view that the modernization of the German states, including Prussia, was purely defensive. Furthermore, in the European context, it appears increasingly that revolutionary France rather than reforming Germany was the exception. Some aspects of this tendency to 'normalize' German history before 1815 may be as much reflections of the *Zeitgeist* of the Federal Republic of the 1980s and 1990s as the Prusso-centric view was of the political ideology of Germany between 1871 and 1945. Yet recent research has done much to undermine the view that German history between 1780 and 1815 represents a stage in a straightforward progression towards the nation state, still less a *Sonderfall* with disturbing implications for the history of the later nineteenth and twentieth centuries.

I   The Holy Roman Empire in the eighteenth century

The Prussian-German tradition viewed the Holy Roman Empire as inadequate because it failed to become a nation state. Modern scholars, by contrast, argue that the system worked effectively. Under the Emperor as *Schutz- und Schirmherr* (protector and guardian), the Reich fulfilled a vital role after 1648 in the areas of law, defence and peace in central Europe. As a *Friedensordnung* (a peace-preserving order), it both guaranteed the peace and stability of Europe as a whole and ensured the survival of the myriad small German territories, none of which, except Prussia, were capable of survival as independent units in the competitive world of European powers. As a *Verteidigungsordnung* (a system of defence), the Reich ensured protection from external threat. As a *Rechtsordnung* (a legal system), it provided mechanisms to secure the rights both of rulers and, more extraordinarily, of subjects against their rulers. Its institutions, such as the imperial courts in Wetzlar and Vienna, provided legal safeguards for many of the inhabitants of the German territories.

Conditions varied enormously amongst the territories which made up the Reich. Some were characterized by corruption, mismanagement and stagnation. Many of the smaller south German Imperial Cities, the miniature territories of imperial knights or

Illustration 2.1   The functioning of the Holy Roman Empire: a banquet for the Kaiser and the Electors in the Römer (town hall), Frankfurt am Main, 1758. The Empire came to an end in 1806 under the influence of Napoleon

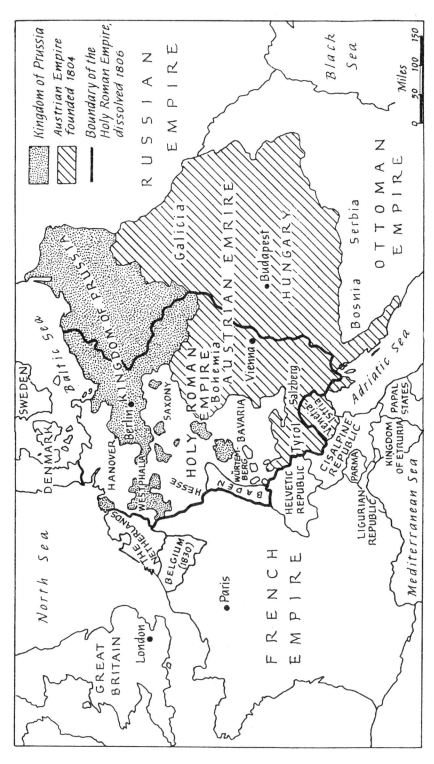

Map 2.1 Germany and the Austrian Empire, 1800–6

independent abbeys and the like, were incapable of significant innovation even if the will to change was there. In many territories, however, the decades after 1750 saw significant changes. Inspired by enlightened rationalism and driven by the need for revenue, particularly acute in the economic crisis which followed the end of the Seven Years War in 1763, many German princes embarked on ambitious reform programmes. Even in the ecclesiastical territories, commonly regarded as anachronisms by the end of the eighteenth century, wide-ranging reforms were introduced in education, poor relief and administration generally. Other states saw the beginnings of codification of law and a rationalization of fiscal administration. As the term 'enlightened absolutism' indicates, the process was initiated by the princes, but it was driven and implemented by a growing army of educated officials. For many of them the reforms represented the first stage of the emancipation of society that formed a central ideal of the German Enlightenment (*Aufklärung*). In the upheavals after 1800 the inherent contradiction between absolutism and emancipation became glaringly apparent. Yet in this first phase there was periodic tension but little conflict. The German educated classes were not composed of disaffected intellectuals, but of active and often enthusiastic participants in the reform process.

There were, of course, limits to what could be achieved by even the most ambitious enlightened prince. The most significant constraint was the imperial system itself. The German princes were not sovereign rulers: their power was qualified by a feudal subordination to the Reich which guaranteed the status quo, especially the rights of estates and corporations which in many territories impeded the imposition of rationalized central control. This limitation was only seriously challenged in the Habsburg lands and in Prussia, with fundamental implications for the future of the Reich and for the subsequent history of German lands.

From the early eighteenth century, Habsburg policy was characterized by a growing tension between dynastic interests and imperial duties. The succession crisis of 1740 underlined the need to consolidate the Habsburg inheritance, a collection of territories which straddled the southeastern frontier of the Reich. The creation of a Habsburg unitary state meant removing the western Habsburg lands from the Reich. In Austria, therefore, enlightened reform aimed to construct a closed unitary state. Under Joseph II from the late 1770s that involved policies hostile to the Reich, in particular a plan to exchange Bavaria for the Netherlands (with or without the consent of the Bavarian estates). Joseph only succeeded in uniting the Reich against him, but the idea of 'rounding off' a consolidated Habsburg state in southeastern Europe, including Bavaria if possible, remained an *idée fixe* in the corridors of the Hofburg even after his death.

A similar tension between Reich and territorial state characterized Brandenburg-Prussia. The construction of a formidable administrative and military machinery began before 1700 and reached a peak in the reign of Frederick William I (1713–40). The reform process was energetically promoted by Frederick II (1740–86) and shaped by his enlightened precepts. It culminated after his death in the publication of a general legal code in 1794 (*Allgemeines Landrecht*), significant for the way in which, technically illegally, it transcended imperial law to provide a unitary legal framework for the Prussian territories. At the same time Prussia's geopolitical position, straddling the Reich's northeast frontier, was similar to that of Austria. Her rulers were not, however, constrained by imperial obligations, and Frederick II in particular used this freedom to exploit every weakness in the Habsburg position. As significant as his military annexation of Silesia in 1740 was the virtuosity with which he manipulated the imperial constitution thereafter, becoming a kind of 'anti-Emperor' in the Reich.

It has often been argued that the power struggle between Austria and Prussia after 1740 doomed the Reich. It is, however, anachronistic to speak of Austria's 'departure' from Germany in the eighteenth century or of Prussia's extension of hegemony over it. Despite being torn in other directions, both states remained deeply wedded to the Reich. Their mutual antagonism was carried out through the mechanisms of the Imperial constitution: not by outright confrontation but through a constant jockeying for position in the Reich's representative institutions.

Furthermore, the other territories were not merely pawns in the larger game. The response of what became known as the 'third Germany' (the smaller territories and ecclesiastical principalities of the south and west) was a series of initiatives to reform the Reich after the 1760s. This new *Reichspatriotismus* (imperial patriotism) failed to generate a renewal of the Reich. The League of Princes (Fürstenbund) of 1785, its one concrete result, did not prove durable or effective in promoting the interests of the smaller territories, formed in opposition to Joseph II's aggressive policies. It foundered in 1788 because it fell into the undertow of Prussian policy. Despite this, the reform initiatives demonstrate three important points: first, the continuing interest in the Reich of many of its members, for whom it fulfilled a vital function; second, the inability of either Austria or Prussia to subvert the Reich against the determined resistance of the other territories; but third also the inability of the Reich to reform itself. In the last resort its durability derived from the fact that it was securely bedded into the old European state system. It was only when that international system itself was plunged into crisis in the 1790s that the Reich was acutely threatened. Once the buttresses were removed the ancient imperial edifice rapidly began to show the effects of the disintegrative tendencies that had so far been held in check.

II   The impact of the French Revolution on Germany

The French Revolution of 1789 transformed the German political landscape. The revolutionary slogan of 'liberty, equality, fraternity' created a new context for German politics, while the revolutionary wars after 1792 unleashed forces which led directly to the dissolution of the Reich in 1806 and to the emergence of a new constellation of reformed German states. There was no German revolution, but the way in which the German territories responded to the revolutionary challenge and adapted to the ideas of 1789 shaped the development of German politics and society into the twentieth century.

The first response of most German commentators to the events of 1789 was over-whelmingly positive. Figures as diverse as Kant, Herder, Hegel and Fichte hailed the news from France as the dawn of a new age of freedom for mankind, a watershed of world historical significance. In many German towns in 1790 clubs were formed and liberty trees planted, while journals and newspapers carried enthusiastic reports of the progress of events in France. At the same time, however, there was a strong feeling that the revolution had specifically French causes and a conviction that Germany did not need a revolution because conditions were better there. Some argued that the Reformation had effected a kind of 'pre-revolution' in Germany, which the *Aufklärung* had built upon to bring about a society capable of peaceful change. Others argued that the French monarchy was simply more despotic and hopelessly corrupt than anything to be found in the Reich. The consensus was clear: Germany did not need to emulate the French Revolution because many of its ideals and objectives could be, indeed were being, achieved by evolutionary means. As the revolution became more radical, so the distinction made between France and Germany became more emphatic. After the execution of the king in January 1793 and the emergence of Robespierre's reign of terror the enthusiasm of the early years largely dissolved. Some held on to the ideals of 1789, explaining that the revolutionary regime had betrayed them. Others turned against both the *Aufklärung* and its reforming ideals and rediscovered the virtues of 'German liberty' in the world of the traditional estates, and by 1800 at the latest the debate had been 'internalized' and revolved not around the French example but around variations on the 'German way'.

The reaction of intellectuals alone cannot explain the lack of a German revolution. More significant was the fact that the preconditions of the explosion in France were quite simply absent in Germany. The nobility, the educated classes and the lower clergy, all of whom played a key role in the French crisis, were in one way or another integrated into the machinery of the state in Germany. The middling classes in the Imperial Cities were deeply conservative. Rural conditions were either not so bad (west of the Elbe over 90 per cent of peasants owned some land, compared with 35 per cent in France) or rigidly under noble control (east of the Elbe). Lacking a powerful capital city, the decentralized Reich, with its legal conflict resolution mechanisms, was able to absorb more minor shocks than the unwieldy centralized French monarchy.

These structural factors inhibited a serious revolutionary crisis. Widespread unrest in the Rhineland in 1789 and 1790, uprisings of artisans in Hamburg and elsewhere in north Germany remained localized. Substantial peasant uprisings in Saxony in 1790 and in Silesia in 1792–3 were brutally put down by military force. The most colourful revolutionary episode, the attempt to establish a republic in Mainz after Custine's occupation of the city in 1792, was a short-lived farce conducted by a small number of 'Jacobins' without popular support. If the Mainz radicals were leaders without a following, the problem elsewhere was the lack of real revolutionaries. Individuals such as the Liepstadt rope-maker Benjamin Geißler, who proclaimed a genuinely revolutionary programme inspired by French ideas in Saxony, remained an exception.

Few of the German Jacobins were in fact committed to revolutionary change. The agitation of the 1790s had, however, two important results. First, among many rulers and thinkers the unrest, compounded by increasingly alarming news from France, provoked a fierce reaction. In Prussia (after 1793) and Austria (particularly after the discovery of a 'Jacobin conspiracy' in Vienna in 1794) this stifled the last impulses of the enlightened reform process. In many other areas the unrest generated demands for participation often coupled with a growing criticism of princely absolutism. In many areas of south and west Germany this was manifest in the renewed vigour and stridency of the representatives of the estates in the territories. In other areas enlightened officials and non-revolutionary 'Jacobins' pressed more urgently than ever for reform before it was too late, echoing the maverick (and sometime alleged Jacobin) Freiherr von Knigge's exhortation to the princes: 'While there is yet time, O princes, lend your own helping hands for the improvement that is needed!'[3]

III The French Revolutionary Wars and the end of the Holy Roman Empire

Knigge was wrong: the German princes did not have time. After 1792 the Reich became embroiled in the revolutionary wars which led to its dissolution, to the dispossession of many princes and independent rulers, and to the reorganization of the territories that remained. The crisis revealed that the Reich lacked the capacity to defend itself against armed force. Neither Austria nor Prussia showed any desire to coordinate and lead a sustained defence of the Reich. Indeed both pursued policies which explicitly undermined the very principles on which the Reich was founded and both contributed as much as France to its dissolution in 1806.

A divergence between the interests of the Reich on the one hand and the concerns of Austria and Prussia on the other became apparent as early as 1789–90. The abolition by the French revolutionaries of feudal rights and the confiscation of church property represented an attack on both German secular princes who held lands in Alsace and Lorraine and on those prince bishops whose dioceses extended into French territory. These actions struck at the very foundations of the Reich: the inviolability of feudal principles and the continued existence of the ecclesiastical states which formed its core. The radical implications of the French actions were immediately clear to the German rulers of the Rhineland and the southwest.

Yet nothing was done. The smaller territories were incapable of acting alone. Neither Austria nor Prussia moved to support their cause, for each was motivated by other concerns and preoccupied with larger strategies. Both Vienna and Berlin viewed the Revolution as a purely domestic problem. It was also felt that the French troubles might bring about a welcome absence of France from the European stage. The mutual distrust between Austria and Prussia persisted, but in 1790 pragmatic considerations dictated a reconciliation sealed by the Convention of Reichenbach.

For the Reich the new Austro-Prussian *détente* was ominous. First, in entering into an alliance with Prussia the Emperor had apparently abandoned his own imperial role as impartial mediator. Second, the reconciliation revived Austrian plans to exchange the Netherlands for Bavaria, this time potentially with Prussian consent. Third, as the tension with France escalated in 1791 it became clear that neither Austria nor Prussia would fight without territorial compensation. Hardly surprisingly the smaller states viewed the situation with alarm. As the Bishop of Würzburg told the Austrian envoy in December 1791: 'If Austria and Prussia agree then the Reich will be finished.'[4] In fact the only immediate result of the new Austro-Prussian understanding was to bring them both into conflict with France. Their declaration of solidarity with Louis XVI inflamed the radicals in the National Convention and led directly to the French declaration of war in April 1792.

Initially the Reich remained neutral. The German princes only agreed to enter the war with an independent imperial army in March 1793 after the French had advanced to the Rhine and occupied Mainz. The decision was made with reluctance: it was rightly pointed out that Austria and Prussia alone were to blame for the war, and that it was not being fought to defend the interests of the Reich. The anxieties expressed in the Reichstag proved amply justified. In military terms the princes gained nothing. The hopes raised by a successful campaign against the French in 1793 were dashed the following year when the revolutionary armies reoccupied the Rhineland, this time permanently. Nor did their entry into the war win them the gratitude of the two major protagonists, who remained wedded to their own objectives. In Vienna grandiose and unrealistic schemes for a reorganization of the Reich proliferated. By contrast, Prussia rapidly lost even formal interest in developments in the west. The opportunity to acquire territory in Poland in 1793 diverted troops and money to the east, and the conflict with France became an unjustifiable expenditure with no prospect of reward.

The failure of the 1794 campaign, undermined in part by the half-hearted participation of the Prussian military, generated a widespread desire for peace. Even that was, however, frustrated by renewed antagonism between Austria and Prussia, by Austria's determination not to give in to the French, and by a deepening mistrust on the part of many German princes of the motives of the imperial court. Prussia alone withdrew in 1795 after signing the Peace of Basel with France which deferred all territorial issues until a future settlement between France and the Reich. In the meantime Prussia agreed to cease hostilities and to recognize the legitimacy of the revolutionary government. In additional secret clauses, however, Prussia accepted French occupation of the left bank of the Rhine, in return for which she was to be compensated by territory on the right bank. Prussia also agreed to seek to secure the withdrawal from the war of all the north German territories, while the French undertook to respect the neutrality of the Prussian sphere of influence.

The treaty effectively divided the Reich by removing most of Germany north of the Main from the war for the next 10 years. Prussia's 'treachery', rapidly emulated by her neighbours, forced the territories south of the Main to turn to Vienna. They needed the Emperor's protection more than ever, against the French armies and against the spectre of domestic revolution. Yet Austrian protection had its price. The Austrians were not slow to present their bills to their protegés. Furthermore, the very proximity of Austrian troops both threatened the independence of the smaller territories and generated anxiety in Bavaria, whose estates remained acutely aware of Austria's annexationist ambitions. The position was the more threatening now that Austria's northern rival, so often the protector of the smaller territories in recent decades, basked in the safety of French-guaranteed neutrality. Attempts by Baden, Württemberg and Bavaria to hedge their bets only made matters worse. In 1796, fearing the renewed failure of the Austrian army, each concluded a secret agreement with France recognizing the loss of the left bank of the Rhine to France in return for compensation with secularized ecclesiastical property. When the Archduke Charles then defeated the French at Amberg and Würzburg, the south Germans were treated like a defeated enemy.

Austria's behaviour towards those she was supposedly protecting ensured that the Emperor gained no moral advantage from shouldering the full burden of the war against France. Furthermore her own position was soon undermined by defeat at the hands of Napoleon in Italy. Forced to conclude peace at Campo Formio in 1797, Austria followed Prussia and the three larger south German territories by agreeing (in secret clauses) to French annexation of the left bank of the Rhine in return for compensation on the right bank. As a reward Austria was promised the archbishopric of Salzburg and parts of eastern Bavaria.

If the willingness of Baden, Württemberg and Bavaria to abandon the Reich had been exposed by Austria, the intention of Prussia and Austria to do likewise was only revealed at the Rastatt conference convened in December 1797 to draw up terms for a general peace with France, though negotiations broke down in April 1799 once the secret clauses of Basel and Campo Formio became known. Perhaps the most significant outcome of Rastatt was a new French policy towards the German territories, for the conference exposed the potential isolation of Austria and Prussia. In November 1799 the Directory clearly recognized that the German princes were more promising allies than German republicans: ideological aggression waned as the Directory adopted the traditional Bourbon policy of dividing and ruling in southwest Germany.

Austria's attempts to resume the war merely resulted in less favourable terms being dictated to her by Napoleon at Lunéville in 1801: she was obliged to accept all of the concessions of the Campo Formio settlement without any of the rewards. Now, however, the majority of the princes, who had latterly scarcely been able to conceal their lack of enthusiasm for the Austrian cause, agreed with alacrity to conclude peace. Indeed several went further and concluded individual peace treaties with France which guaranteed them territorial enlargement. Acutely aware of Austria's isolation in Germany, the Emperor refused to preside over a conference to reorganize the Reich: indeed by now he and his advisers were simply concerned to secure sufficient compensation from France in return for relinquishing the imperial crown. As a result, the Reichstag itself appointed a commission which in March 1803 produced the *Reichsdeputationshauptschluß* (final constitutional law). This re-drew the map of

Germany along lines dictated by France (with the agreement of Russia, the third guarantor power of the Reich). The changes were massive: the left bank of the Rhine was formally ceded to France; on the right bank three electorates, 19 bishoprics and 44 abbeys disappeared; in all about 10,000 square kilometres of land and some three million people were incorporated into new territories. The major winners were Prussia (in the Rhineland), Baden, Württemberg and Bavaria. The disappearance of the ecclesiastical states gave the Protestant princes a majority for the first time, a further threat to the Habsburg position in the Reich.

Further changes soon followed. In 1804 Francis II assumed the title of Emperor of Austria, anticipating his abdication as Holy Roman Emperor in 1806 after another disastrous defeat and humiliating peace at Pressburg in December 1805, which also recognized the full sovereignty of Bavaria and Württemberg as kingdoms and of Baden and Hesse-Darmstadt as grand duchies. Even before the final dissolution of the Reich on 6 August 1806, 16 south and west German princes abandoned it by joining the Confederation of the Rhine. Another wave of changes began in 1806. Prussia's fatal decision to resume hostilities with France after 10 years of neutrality resulted in her crushing defeat at Jena and Auerstedt in October. Most of her recent territorial acquisitions were incorporated into new Napoleonic satellites: the kingdom of Westphalia and the grand duchies of Berg and Warsaw. In south Germany some 70 further minor territories were either secularized or 'mediatized', i.e. Imperial Cities and the lands of imperial knights were incorporated into the new sovereign states. By the end of 1807 the territory of the former Reich was divided into three fairly distinct areas: the left bank of the Rhine under France; the states of the Confederation of the Rhine (Rheinbund) under French influence and control; Austria and Prussia, both diminished in size and 'excluded' from Germany.

The main driving force in the dissolution process was clearly the success of the French armies. The eventual outcome was, however, shaped by the reactions of many of the German rulers. Since the early 1790s both Austria and Prussia had aimed at aggrandizement, which could only succeed at the expense of the smaller territories. Military inferiority, but also vacillation, deceitfulness, blindness and woeful miscalculations ensured by 1807 that neither achieved anything. The same ambition pursued after 1795–6 by the three largest south German territories led to success because they worked with Napoleon rather than against him. Of course they had little choice in that; even so, spectacular rewards fell into their tied hands.

Nationalist historians reserved harsh judgements for those who swam vigorously with the French tide. Recent scholars have adopted a more balanced view. Ambition and greed were clearly strong motives. The newly promoted rulers of Baden, Württemberg and Bavaria were determined to survive as independent sovereigns. On the other hand, idealism and a desire to rescue something from the Reich also played a part in the 'third Germany'. Some hoped that Napoleon might be persuaded to become head of a new reformed Reich. The driving force behind many of these ideas was Karl Theodor von Dalberg, Elector of Mainz and Imperial Archchancellor. His

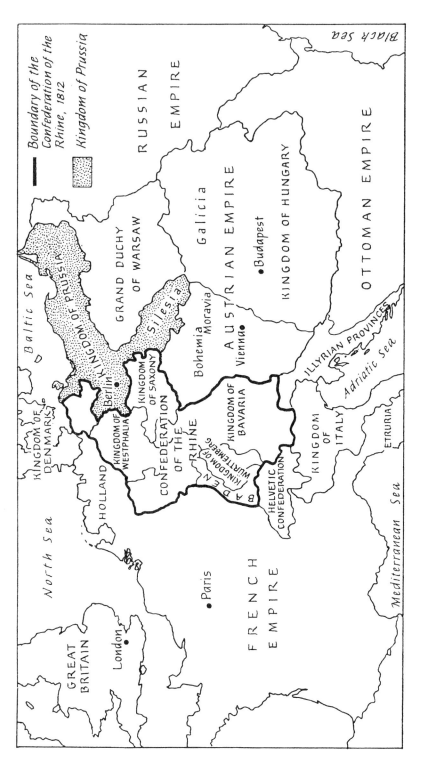

Map 2.2 Germany and the Austrian Empire, 1812

self-interest is clear. While other ecclesiastical princes were dispossessed, Dalberg managed to have himself translated to Regensburg in 1803, made apostolic administrator of the whole Rhineland in 1805 with the title of Prince-Primate, made nominal head of the Rheinbund in 1806 and created Grand Duke of Frankfurt in 1810. Yet he too was captivated by the idea that a new Reich might be forged out of the old, with Napoleon as the new Charlemagne at its head.

Dalberg was not an isolated visionary. His ideas were echoed in the lively periodical literature devoted to the Rheinbund and found support among leading constitutional theorists such as Joseph Görres. Indeed in 1808 concrete proposals were made to transform the Rheinbund into a kind of national state of the Germans. It failed to become anything of the kind because of the opposition of Bavaria and Württemberg and above all because Napoleon himself had no interest in anything other than a loose federation which might serve his own military ends. His position as 'protector' of the Rheinbund was stronger than it might have been as ruler of a coherent German state capable of turning against him.

Though it ceased to exist in 1813, the Rheinbund was of exceptional importance. Its federal constitution looked both forward and backward. The central institutions envisaged in its constitution (though never in fact implemented) translated many of the representative mechanisms of the Reich into a modern idiom. At the same time the sovereign status of its 39 members marked a clear break with the past. It was, in fact, neither a reformed Reich nor a nation state. On the contrary it provided the framework for the creation of a new type of reformed sovereign territorial state in Germany.

IV   Reform and renewal in the German states

The nature and extent of the changes which took place in the so-called 'German reform era' have been the subject of intensive research in recent decades. Nationalist historians concentrated on the 'German' or 'organic' reforms in Prussia, as opposed to the allegedly superficial 'rationalist' reforms elsewhere, either imposed by Napoleon or at least derivative of French models. More recently, however, it has been recognized that the Rheinbund states made significant progress towards modernization in this period. At the same time it is still debated whether the reforms represented a 'defensive modernization', a 'revolution from above' forced on the German states by Napoleon, or whether they represented the continuation of an indigenous reform process begun in the 1770s and 1780s.

Despite regional differences, the reforms had many common features. The question of why the absolutist state collapsed in the face of the French armies was as acute in Baden and Bavaria as it was in Prussia. The answer too was broadly similar. Enlightened absolutist reform had created a gulf between state and society, the significance of which was driven home by the triumph of the new French nation of *citoyens*. This dictated that participation and representation, emancipation in the broadest sense, became a major theme of the reforms, though the remedies proposed ranged from traditional forms of representation based on estates to modern constitutional models. At the same time the reform process was shaped by more practical necessities. The new sovereign states, enlarged by secularization and mediatization, had to integrate new territories and mould them into a coherent governable whole: the new duchy of Nassau, for example, was made up of no less than 23 previously independent entities. Secularization meant that the state had to take up the functions previously exercized by the churches, which ensured that educational reform, with particular emphasis on the universities, was as central in south Germany as it was in Prussia. Confessionally uniform territories gave way to confessionally mixed states with complex legislation that guaranteed religious freedom and that tended to separate church and state.

At the same time long years of war and occupation financially exhausted many of the German territories, and the problems were exacerbated as the new states assumed the debts of the territories they took over. The result was a 'financial revolution' of the German states: the creation of state budgets, centralized financial administration, the distinction between public and dynastic finances. The sheer scale of the task ensured that the post-1806 reforms were not carried out by enlightened princely dilettantes but by experts and bureaucrats. Württemberg was exceptional in that the reforms there were implemented, against all opposition, in a fit of late absolutism by King Frederick I (1754–1816). In general, however, one of the most significant results of reform was the creation of the bureaucratic state, even in Württemberg. The problem of participation and representation was nowhere satisfactorily resolved before 1814–15, but everywhere the 'enlightened reform state' gave way to 'bureaucratic state absolutism'. The leading reformers embodied continuity between the two forms. Montgelas (Bavaria), Reitzenstein (Baden), Marshall von Bieberstein (Hessen) Barckhausen and Du Thil (Nassau), Hardenberg (Prussia) and the like, for all their differences, were the intellectual heirs of the enlightened princes of the 1780s. In the 1790s they had perceived the limitations of enlightened reform. The events of 1806 provided the opportunity to implement the remedies they had formulated in the light of the lessons taught by France since 1789.

The scope and intensity of reform was varied. In many smaller middle and north German states the impact was minimal. In some, the nobility frustrated all attempts at change. In others, the territorial reorganization had less impact and there was consequently less incentive and less perceived need to change. Austria was another, more important, exception. Here the catastrophic political failure of Joseph II's state absolutism, combined with the crises of the 1790s, revived the alliance between crown and nobles, a reassertion of the traditional status quo. This reinvigorated *ancien régime* undermined efforts to reform the Austrian monarchy after the collapse of 1806. Neither Sinzendorff's French-inspired modernization plans nor the Stadion brothers' conservative programme (inspired by Herder) for the revival of the traditional estates made any significant impact. Johann Philipp Stadion succeeded in introducing universal conscription and in forming a Landwehr (territorial militia) in 1808. But his programme collapsed with Austria's renewed defeat by Napoleon in 1809. His successor, Metternich, saved the Austrian monarchy by accommodating himself with Napoleon and by restoring sound financial management. Survival for Austria in 1809 meant making the old status quo work.

The significance of Austria's failed reform, and the gulf that opened up between her and the other German states, becomes apparent when set beside the reforms elsewhere. Four areas and types of reform may be distinguished: the left bank of the Rhine; the Napoleonic satellites of Westphalia, Berg and Frankfurt; the south German states; and finally Prussia.

In the first two areas, French influence was clearly paramount. The left bank of the Rhine was integrated into the French *département* system in 1802. After ten years of often brutal occupation, exploitation and military activity, the introduction of the Code Napoleon and the French administrative system brought a measure of relief. Furthermore, the sale of former church lands, often to prosperous town dwellers, seems to have loosened the social structure more effectively than it did elsewhere, while local industry profited from the continental blockade. As a whole the changes in these areas – legal, institutional and social – were profound, and were recognized as such by the new governments after 1815, which ensured the Code Napoleon remained in force until 1900. Ironically, that was not the fate of the reforms undertaken in the satellite states of Westphalia (under Napoleon's brother Jerôme) and Berg (under Murat until 1808, then under Napoleon as regent for his nephew Napoleon Louis). Their 'model' status was undermined because they were ruthlessly exploited: their finances were milked and state demesne used to provide rewards for the new Napoleonic nobility. Thus the Westphalian constitution of November 1807 (the first German constitution ever) was never fully implemented and like most of the changes effected during the French period was swept away when the kingdom of Westphalia was dissolved in 1815. The same fate befell the French reforms in the duchy of Frankfurt and grand duchy of Warsaw, and the occupied areas of northern Germany (e.g. Hamburg).

The reforms in the new sovereign states of Baden, Württemberg and Bavaria together with Hesse-Darmstadt and Nassau were more durable. In Bavaria, for example, Montgelas implemented a programme which he had outlined in his 'Ansbach memorandum' of 1796. Some measures were introduced as early as 1799, but the major reform drive began in 1806. Montgelas set about reforming the central administration, creating a new state bureaucracy, consolidating all state debts and setting state finances on a secure footing, marking out a distinction between state and dynasty. At the same time the secularization process required the state to take over the universities and schools, as well as other former ecclesiastical institutions. Montgelas's vision of a state based on the equality of all before the law led to an assault on noble privileges and to the promulgation of a constitutional edict which envisaged a representative system.

It is significant that Montgelas resisted French pressure to introduce the Code

Napoleon. Where he borrowed from the French model, for example in devising regional divisions based on the *départements*, it was for pragmatic reasons, in this case the erosion of traditional loyalties and of local noble power bases. Equally important, however, were the limitations. Most obvious was the enormous accumulated debt and Napoleon's continuing financial demands: Bavaria was at war almost continuously throughout the reform period and was obliged by her French alliance to maintain an over-large army. Second, noble resistance to the reforms was strong and thwarted the full implementation either of peasant emancipation (until 1848) or of a representative constitution (until 1818).

Reform had its limits. On the other hand the fact that a constitutional movement did prevail in south Germany (including Württemberg) after 1815 has prompted a re-evaluation of the Rheinbund reforms in recent years. They are now viewed as an extension of *Aufklärung* reforms of the 1780s, the more revolutionary for the fact that they were based on the idea of *bürgerliche Freiheit* (bourgeois freedom), with all that implied for the limitation of royal power and the participation and representation of the individual.

If constitutionalism, or at least the introduction of a constitution soon after 1815, is taken as the ultimate criterion of successful modernization, then Prussia must be regarded as a failure. Some have argued that this reflected the complete triumph of the bureaucracy, which resisted constitutionalism because it regarded itself as a kind of representative body. Others emphasize the entrenched nature of the noble opposition to the reform process as a whole, and argue that Hardenberg held back on the constitutional question for tactical reasons. The debate underlines the continuing importance of Prussia in German historiography: the question about Prussia's 'delayed' constitutional history inevitably raises larger questions about later German history as a whole.

Prussia experienced a different pattern of reform within a different institutional and social context and with some different motivations. For one thing Prussia already had a kind of constitutional law in the form of the *Allgemeines Landrecht* of 1794 (a framework of rights as well as a code of law). Second, many historians emphasize the theoretical and philosophical sophistication of the Prussian reform movement which contrasts strikingly with the pragmatic late-Enlightenment rationalism of south German reformers. In economic terms the reforms were characterized by a systematic and rigorous application of the principles of Adam Smith. The reformers aimed to liberate the economic potential of man. This involved both relaxing trade and craft restrictions and dismantling the constrictive feudal agrarian order. The emancipation of 1807 gave little to the peasant, though he now had the freedom to realize his potential if he could. The estate owners, by contrast, profited immediately since it now became possible to intensify the agricultural production process. Other areas of activity (education, military reform) were also characterized by a distinctive philosophical inspiration. Nipperdey has argued that Prussian reforms transcended the *Aufklärung*; they embodied the new post-Kantian philosophical idealism which aspired to enable man to achieve ultimate freedom. Certainly the influence of Kant on the Prussian bureaucracy was profound, and the Prussian reform is characterized by the involvement in many different areas of individuals who were highly gifted theoreticians as well as practitioners. Humboldt in education, Scharnhorst, Gneisenau and Boyen in the army, are merely the best known of a whole phalanx of philosophically minded protagonists of change.

Prussian reform was also the product of humiliating military defeat and, in many minds, motivated by the desire for revenge. Nationalist historians believed this gave the movement a profound moral dimension and a higher 'national' purpose. They regarded Stein as the central figure: a conservative romantic nationalist who aimed to make Prussia into the foundation of a Germany capable of withstanding Napoleon.

This myth obscures two important points. First, as elsewhere, the origins of reform ideas in Prussia lie in the 1780s and 1790s: defeat in 1806 provided the reformers with their opportunity but not with their agenda. Second, recent research has tended to emphasize the significance of Hardenberg. Stein's period of office was short (he was dismissed in November 1808 after only 14 months in office); Hardenberg was *Staatskanzler* from 1810 until 1822. Their ideas also differed fundamentally. Stein *was* a nationalist who dreamt of an uprising of the Germans against French tyranny. He was also a conservative. In his view the only conceivable form of representation was that based on property, i.e. the traditional estates. The mobilization of society, Stein believed, meant the reinvigoration of historically grown forms of participation and representation. If Stein wished to 'reorganize' the Prussian state, Hardenberg aspired to 'revolutionize' it. Stein's 'Nassau memorandum' (1806) concentrated exclusively on administration; Hardenberg's 'Riga memorandum' (1807) spoke of 'unleashing' all abilities, of bringing about a 'revolution' which would lead to the 'great end of the ennoblement of mankind, through wise government and not through violent force either from within or from outside'. The most appropriate form for the 'current *Zeitgeist*', he declared, was 'democratic principles in a monarchical system'.[5] Hardenberg's emphasis on the *Zeitgeist* indicates that he saw no going back: 1789 marked the start of a new era in human history; the task of all wise politicians was to adapt to it successfully. Military reform played a central role in the programme. 'All inhabitants of the state are born defenders of the same', Scharnhorst wrote; 'the government must enter into an alliance with the nation' in order to bolster its independent spirit.[6] Gneisenau declared that the state must be established on the 'threefold foundation of arms, education and constitution'.[7]

If there are many elements of similarity between Prussia and, say, Bavaria, the obstacles to success were much greater in Prussia. Financial ruin in 1806 dictated that much of the reform process was driven by fiscal needs rather than by constitutional ideals. The resistance of the nobility to change was formidable. Military reformers were denounced as 'Jacobins' because they wanted to arm the peasantry. Any hint of constitutional plans aroused intense opposition, even amongst many bureaucrats. Like Montgelas, Hardenberg was a virtuoso tactician and combined his philosophical convictions with wily pragmatism. The reformers succeeded in their fiscal, economic, administrative and educational measures. The military reform represented a compromise; the constitutional issue remained in suspension. The outcome was a bureaucratic absolutism serviced by a sophisticated educational system which presided over an economic system shaped by the spirit of Adam Smith and a traditional society still dominated by the nobility. The tensions inherent in that formula were only later revealed, in particular when the system was overtaken by the effects of the dramatic demographic explosion of the decades since 1740.

It is tempting to see the diminution in the number of German territories from over 1000 to around 40 as part of a long-term progress of integration, another stage in the delayed progress of the Germans towards a nation state under Prussian leadership. The point is apparently reinforced by the similarities generated by the reform process between many of the new states and by Austria's failure to reform. This ignores, however, one of the central characteristics of the thinking and language of most leading reformers. They were concerned with the nation, but primarily with the Bavarian or the Prussian nation, rather than the German nation. When Montgelas wrote that elementary schools must help shape the *Nationalgeist*, he meant the Bavarian national spirit.[8] When Hardenberg wrote of 'stamping a single "Nationalcharakter" upon the whole', he meant a sense of national identity for the whole Prussian state.[9] The similarities between the reforms cannot obscure the fact that they were explicitly intended to create differences between the new sovereign states. This immediately raises important questions about the origins of German nationalism in this period. If *Nationalgeist* pertained to the new sovereign states, what did *die deutsche Nation* mean at this time?

V   The Wars of Liberation and German nationalism

In traditional historiography the most important feature of the Napoleonic period was the birth of German nationalism. Napoleon's defeat and humiliation of Prussia, it was argued, generated a sense of German national resentment against French tyranny; ideas developed in Prussia by men such as Fichte, Arndt and Jahn provided the inspiration for a national uprising of the Germans led by Prussia. In this view the Wars of Liberation (1813–15) were interpreted as the first collective action of the German nation, its first violent rite of passage in an ordeal by fire. In fact this 'birth myth' of the German nation was an artificial construct of nationalist ideology. Later Prussian nationalism wrote its own history and then declared it to be the history of Germany as a whole (see Chapter 24, below). From an eighteenth-century perspective, however, the development of German nationalism appears much more diffuse. It leads neither to a single coherent ideology nor to a firm political or state orientation by 1815.

Since the 1760s there had been a growing preoccupation among many German intellectuals with questions of patriotism and German identity. There was no single movement, rather a variety of lines of development. One strand led to the *Reichspatriotismus* of the 1780s and then on to the debate over reform of the Reich around 1800. Another strand can be identified in the tradition of lyric poetry from

Klopstock to Hölderlin, in which the quasi-religious identification with a German fatherland forms a persistent theme. Related to that was the so-called 'German movement' of the 1770s and 1780s: young *Sturm und Drang* writers and their successors whose interest in 'Germany' formed part of their rebellion against society in the name of freedom. The main emphasis was on the 'cultural nation', 'Germany' defined by language and a common literary and philosophical culture. Yet this 'cultural nationalism' was not unpolitical: its tendency was anti-absolutist and democratic.

In the 1790s Herder's notion of the individuality of all peoples took on a new meaning in the context of the German response to the French Revolution. The argument that Germany did not need a revolution formed part of a world historical perspective in which the Germans, from medieval freedom through revolutionary Reformation to *Aufklärung*, emerged as the nation of true freedom as opposed to anarchic French liberty. The idea of the unique mission of the Germans was central to this view: as Schiller put it in 1797, their day had yet to come; it would be the last day, the final and highest stage in the development of human freedom. Parallel to this some writers of the 1790s, often associated with early Romanticism, renewed older poses against French cultural imperialism in literature, once more emphasizing the gulf between 'Germany' and France. A revived literary patriotism responded to the French threat. In areas such as the Rhineland this also connected with the bitter experience of invasion and occupation, and a deep popular resentment against the exploitative and militantly secular French revolutionary authorities.

In so far as any of these diverse preoccupations with 'Germany' were anchored on a political system they were focused on the Reich (even though constitutionally the 'nation' of the Reich only included the higher nobility). The Reich manifestly failed from the mid-1790s. Yet the sense of the functions that it had served was still strong, and there was a wide sense of the need to find something that would replace it. The Reich's dissolution in 1806 created a new situation since it left 'the German nation', however defined, without any institutional framework. Nationalist historians argued that the 'nation state' led by Prussia stepped into the breach. The reality is more complex. In south and west Germany much 'national' thinking focused on the Rheinbund, sometimes with Napoleon envisaged as the new Emperor of the Germans. That vision soon lost credibility, but arguments for some form of equivalent to the Reich played an important part in discussions right up to 1815.

The reaction against Napoleon elsewhere had no coherent political programme, no clear ideology, no clear preference for the leadership of the German nation. The anonymous pamphlet *Deutschland in seiner tiefen Erniedrigung* (May 1806), generally regarded as the first blast of the anti-Napoleonic movement in Germany, was deeply critical of both Austria and Prussia, particularly for having abandoned the German people. Indeed much of the patriotic literature after 1806 contains many echoes of the anti-absolutist rhetoric of the 1780s and 1790s.

Inevitably, however, the 'German' patriots gravitated towards Vienna, Dresden and Berlin outside the sphere of direct French control. Vienna attracted conservative patriots, Romantic political theorists of the reaction, Catholics or converts to Catholicism, and others who wanted to revive the old Reich (now idealized as an Arcadia of traditional politics and religion). After 1805 intellectuals such as Friedrich Schlegel, Adam Müller, Friedrich Gentz (the 'German Burke') and Heinrich von Kleist (significantly, a Brandenburg nobleman disillusioned by Prussian neutrality before 1806) provided the ideological foundations for Stadion's conservative reform programme for the Austrian monarchy. In Berlin the movement was more diffuse. Military reformers drew up plans for a *levée en masse*. Stein propagated the idea of a conservative estates-based nation state version of the old Reich. The literary patriotism of Arndt, Jahn and Theodor Körner drew on pietist traditions in propagating a religious identification with a German fatherland, calling for an uprising of the German *Volk* and a fight to the death against France. Fichte appealed for a new *Nationalerziehung*, necessary because the princes had betrayed the *Volk*. Romantic conservatism combined with 'national democratic' tendencies in a broad church united only by a common desire to end the French tyranny.

One should be wary of overestimating the contemporary significance of this flood of patriotic literature. The 'national' interests of Prussia and Austria were not submerged in the German cause, though both governments exploited the ambiguity of the 'national' idea. In Berlin, Stein, inflamed with hatred for 'French filth' and infuriated by the admiration for Napoleon of young Romantics such as Tieck, actively coordinated the activities of the patriotic writers, promoting journals and offering financial inducements. In Austria too Stadion coordinated a literary campaign which provided the ideological dimension to the Austrian rebellion against Napoleon in 1809. Inspired by the Spanish insurrection, the Stadion faction persuaded the Emperor to appeal to all Germans to rise up against the French. The appeal failed and after an initial triumph at Aspern in May 1809, the Austrian army was decisively crushed at Wagram in July. Indeed the whole affair revealed a deeply ambivalent attitude to the whole concept of popular insurrection: when the Tyrolean peasants rebelled and triumphed over the French under the charismatic Andreas Hofer the Austrians failed to support them.

Austria under Metternich had no more truck with patriotic uprisings. The case of Prussia is more complex. Fundamentally, of course, Napoleon was brought down by the progressive collapse of his empire after 1810. The disastrous Russian campaign of 1812 was the final straw. Furthermore, when Prussia joined forces with Russia in December 1812, it was the result of the deeply conservative Yorck von Wartenburg's rebellious defiance of the king's orders: not a national patriotic uprising but an insurrection of the reactionary East Prussian nobility. None the less Yorck forced the king's hand and allowed the reformers in Berlin to implement their plans for a people's army. The king's call to arms 'An Mein Volk' (significantly directed at 'Brandenburger, Preußen, Schlesier, Pommern, Litthauer!' not Germans) unleashed a ferocious patriotic wave.[10]

Many did give 'gold for iron'; the military reforms allowed the formation of an army of 280,000 with impressive speed; some 28,000 volunteers joined up. How decisive all this was is another matter. Soon after the battle of Leipzig (16–19 October 1813) it became clear that the future of Germany would not be decided by German patriots but by the particularist interests of the sovereign states. Bavaria had left the Rheinbund just before Leipzig. Württemberg, Baden, Hesse-Darmstadt and Hesse-Kassel left just after. The plans of Stein and his secretary Arndt for a strong German national imperial state served only as a useful foil in the complex negotiations over the future of the German lands which were dominated by Hardenberg and Metternich, both at root sceptics on the 'national' issue.

VI Conclusion

Heinrich Heine later wrote that the Germans had become patriots and defied Napoleon because their princes ordered them to. That fails to do justice to the strength of anti-Napoleonic sentiment in many parts of Germany by 1813–14. But there was no 'national uprising' or 'national crusade'. There remained a world of difference between the nationalism of some intellectuals and the 'nation' they aspired to lead. Heine's comment also underestimates the ambivalence of contemporary governments towards the very idea of arming the peasantry for an uprising of the *Volk*, as envisaged by the likes of Arndt or Jahn. In the excitement of victory the issues became confused, and later the veterans of 1813 constructed a myth of the Wars of Liberation that bore little relation to reality. That mythology, formed around the canon of patriotic writing of the period 1806–15, is an important legacy of the period. It provided the foundation for later nationalist ideology which increasingly drew on everything but the democratic tenor of the first phase: the image of the French *Erbfeind* (hereditary enemy); the glorification of the *Volk*; Germany as the nation which had defeated the ideas of 1789 and which had developed its own superior 'idea'; the myth of a strong Reich.

Little of that could, however, have even been imagined in 1815. Far from celebrating the birth of the German nation, men such as Arndt and Jahn were bitterly disappointed. The Vienna settlement reflected not their ideas but the process of evolution and adaptation that had occurred since the late eighteenth century. Secularization, mediatization and the dissolution of the Reich had removed the obstacles to the emergence of fully sovereign states to replace the feudal patchwork of the past. What emerged at Vienna in 1815 was a confederation which placed the seal on the emergence of the German sovereign territorial states. Prussia was strengthened by the acquisition of the Rhineland; Austria was to an extent diverted by her position of strength in Italy; but both remained leading players in Germany. The settlement created a balance of power designed to maintain peace and stability, and led to the competition between Austria and Prussia ending in stalemate.

More important than anything else in 1815 was the fact that many of the new sovereign states were in one way or another 'reformed'. The path from the Reich to the German Confederation was characterized by a complex adaptation to the challenges posed by the French Revolution and the Napoleonic regime. Reformers reacted to what they perceived were the limitations of the enlightened state by reforming its structure and by aiming to overcome the gulf between the state and its subjects. Financial necessity drove a reform process which created the bureaucratic state. On the other hand, ambivalence and noble opposition undermined first attempts to mobilize the population or to secure their representation. The result in many German states was a dissonant mixture: a strong, 'modernized' state grafted on to a traditional society. Nowhere did the reformers achieve complete success. Even so, their collective efforts brought about fundamental and irrevocable changes. They ensured that for the next generation at least most politically active Germans would be preoccupied not with the national issue but with the implications of the German 'revolution from above'.

Notes:

1. Quoted by Hans-Ulrich Wehler, *Deutsche Gesellschaftsgeschichte*, Band 1: *1700–1815* (Munich, C. H. Beck, 1987), p. 546.
2. Nipperdey, Thomas, *Deutsche Geschichte 1800–1866. Bürgerwelt und starker Staat* (Munich, C. H. Beck, 1983), p. 11.
3. Quoted by Horst Möller, *Fürstenstaat oder Bürgernation. Deutschland 1763–1815* (Berlin, Siedler Verlag, 1989), p. 531.
4. Quoted by Karl Otmar von Aretin, *Vom Deutschen Reich zum Deutschen Bund* (2nd edn, Göttingen, Vandenhoeck and Ruprecht, 1993), p. 61.
5. The memorandum is printed in Georg Winter, ed., *Die Reorganisation des Preußischen Staates unter Stein und Hardenberg* Teil 1. Band 1 (Leipzig, S. Hirzel, 1931), pp. 302–63; quotation from pp. 305–6.
6. Quoted by Nipperdey, *Geschichte*, pp. 51, 53.
7. *Ibid.*, p. 51.
8. Quoted in Max Spindler, ed., *Handbuch der bayerischen Geschichte,* 4 vols. (Munich, C. H. Beck, 1967–1975), vol. I, pt. I, p. 7.
9. Winter, *Reorganisation*, pp. 319–20, 325.
10. Printed in Hans-Bernd Spies, ed., *Die Erhebung gegen Napoleon 1806-1814/15* (Darmstadt, Wissenschaftliche Buchgesellschaft, 1981), pp. 254–5.

Select bibliography

Aris, R., *History of Political Thought in Germany from 1789 to 1815* (London: Frank Cass, 1936).

Beiser, Frederick C., *Enlightenment, Revolution, and Romanticism. The Genesis of Modern German Political Thought, 1790–1800* (Cambridge, MA: Harvard University Press, 1992).

Blanning, T. C. W., *The French Revolution in Germany: Occupation and Resistance in the Rhineland, 1792–1802* (Oxford: Oxford University Press, 1983).

Breuilly, John, *The Formation of the First German Nation-State, 1800–1871* (London: Macmillan, 1996).

Gagliardo, John G., *Reich and Nation. The Holy Roman Empire as Idea and Reality, 1763–1806* (Bloomington: Indiana University Press, 1980).

Gooch, G. P., *Germany and the French Revolution* (London: Frank Cass, 1920).

Hughes, Michael, *Early Modern Germany* (London, Macmillan, 1992).

Schroeder, Paul W., *The Transformation of European Politics, 1763–1848* (Oxford: Oxford University Press, 1994).

Sheehan, J. J., *German History, 1770–1866* (Oxford: Oxford Unversity Press, 1989).

Vann, J. A. and Rowan, S., eds, *The Old Reich: Essays on German Political Institutions 1495–1806* (Brussels: Les Editions de la Librairie Encyclopédique, 1974).

Walker, Mack, *German Home Towns: Community, State, General Estate, 1648–1871* (Ithaca, NY: Cornell University Press, 1971).

3

Germany 1815–1848: Restoration or pre-March?

Christopher Clark

The period discussed in this chapter fell between two great European upheavals: the revolution of 1789 with its Napoleonic aftermath and the revolutions of 1848. Inevitably, this has influenced the way we think about the era. The term 'Restoration', often used for the years until 1830 or 1840 and sometimes for the period as a whole, evokes the struggle to reverse the effects of the French Revolution and underlines the reactionary, backward-looking character of the age. The term 'pre-March', generally used for the years from 1830 or 1840, is forward-looking; it suggests a prelude to upheaval, specifically to the Revolutionary unrest of the 'March days' of 1848. Both terms are problematic, since they encourage us to think of this era either as a reconstruction of the past or as a rehearsal for the future.

'Should the half-dead forms of the old regime, which still contain so much of the beautiful life of the past, be maintained?' Leopold von Gerlach asked himself in 1813. 'Or should they be boldly destroyed to make way for the new?'[1] As Gerlach himself was aware, the answers history gives to such questions are always composite and provisional, never absolute. There was no thorough-going 'restoration' of the old regime after 1815, nor, on the other hand, were traditional structures and allegiances entirely destroyed 'to make way for the new'. But the period covered by this chapter was one of heightened political and social conflict that often turned on the question Gerlach had asked. Guilds, corporate privilege, feudal tenure, dynastic particularism – all these not-so-dead forms inherited from the old regime had their defenders and detractors. It was conflict over these and related issues that made the years between 1815 and 1848 an 'epoch of polarization' across a broad range of fronts.

The conflict between modernity and tradition in its various manifestations forms the central theme of this chapter. The chapter does not provide a chronological narrative but examines five areas in turn. The first sub-section deals with that unloved institution, the German Confederation, which provided the outer framework for German political life throughout and beyond the period covered by this chapter. We then turn to the bureaucratic state, which has often been seen as the most important 'modernizing' force in early nineteenth-century German society. There follows a discussion of the various forms of political mobilization that were so characteristic of the period. A section on the mass poverty and economic dislocation of the 1830s and 1840s attempts to identify what was modern and what was not about the 'social question' that so preoccupied contemporaries. This is followed by a discussion of the religious revival of the 1820s and 1830s that did much to galvanize political debate, but was also a formidable social force in its own right. Each of these topics has been the subject of extensive recent debate in the historiography of the period, and each will help to bring us nearer to what was distinctive about the decades between 1815 and 1848.

I The German Confederation

In the eighteenth century, German Europe had been divided into some 300 territories. After the secularizations and territorial resettlements of the Napoleonic period and the readjustments made at the Congress of Vienna, only 38 sovereign states (39 after 1817) remained. These were joined in a loose association of independent sovereign entities known as the 'German Confederation'. The largest and most significant were the Austrian Empire and the Kingdom of Prussia, with 9.3 and 8.1 million Confederal subjects respectively (Prussia's easternmost provinces and Austria's non-German lands were excluded from the Confederation, as they had been from the old Reich). The remaining member states ranged in size and significance from the most powerful middle states, Bavaria, Baden, Württemberg and Hanover, all of which had made substantial territorial gains since the dissolution of the Reich, to the little Duchy of Liechtenstein, with a population of only 5,000. As in the old Reich, the small states outnumbered the large. In 1818, there were only seven German states with populations in excess of one million; 21 had fewer than 100,000 inhabitants.

The Confederation managed to get by on a minimum of institutions and personnel. It had only one statutory body, the Federal Diet (*Bundesversammlung*), which met in Frankfurt. The Diet was effectively a permanent congress of diplomatic representatives who were appointed and instructed by their respective governments. The supreme executive organ of the Confederation was the Inner Council (*Engerer Rat*); all the states were represented on this body, but only Austria, the kingdoms of Prussia, Bavaria, Württemberg, Saxony and Hanover, Electoral Hesse, the grand duchies of Baden and Hesse-Darmstadt, Denmark (on account of Holstein) and the Netherlands (on account of the Grand Duchy of Luxemburg) had the right to a full individual vote; the remaining states were organized by size in groups of between two and nine members, each of which had one vote. The Inner Council dealt with the regular administration of the Confederation; if matters arose that touched on the Confederal constitution or on the function and status of its institutions, these had to be dealt with by the Plenary Diet (*Plenum*), in which each state spoke and voted for itself. But even here, the pri-

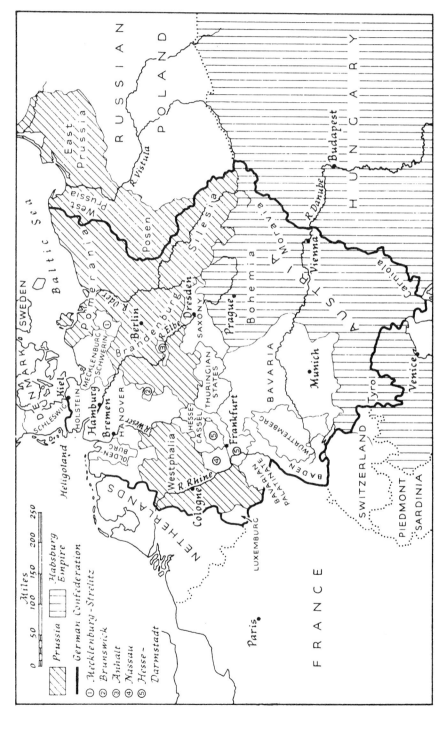

Map 3.1 The German Confederation in 1815

macy of the greater states was guaranteed by allocation of votes; with four votes each, Austria and the five kingdoms could combine to veto any unwelcome initiative from a smaller state.

The Confederation does not enjoy a good reputation. It was a bitter disappointment to those federalists and nationalists who had hoped for a more cohesive organization of the German territories and it has been much criticized since. One historian has recently described it as 'a prediluvian monster' that had no place in the age of the emergent nation state, another as an 'incarnation of illiberality and oppression'. These reproaches reflect two distinct, though related, lines of argument that have often been advanced against the Confederation.

It is certainly true that the Confederation failed to create genuinely 'national' institutions. The Act of 1815 had left open a number of important issues, including joint defence policy, the creation of a unified economic area within the Confederation, the legal status of the Jews and constitutional reform. These were to be subject to subsequent debate and deliberation by the Confederal Diet. It was thus plausible, in 1815, to believe that the following years would see the gradual extension of the central powers and responsibilities of the Confederation, and perhaps even the emergence of a genuinely 'federal' German authority.

In the event, these hopes were not fulfilled. Power remained firmly in the hands of the individual sovereigns. The promised Confederal regulation of the status of Jewish residents was not forthcoming. Instead, Jews remained subject to a bewildering variety of regional legal codes – 33, for example, in the Kingdom of Prussia alone. The question of constitutional reform was likewise left to the discretion of the individual states. Attempts to reach an agreement on customs in the German states foundered on Austrian opposition. The failure of the Diet to take the lead in organizing a German customs union was to prove highly significant, since it enabled Prussia, which had already effected a union in its own territories, to seize and retain the initiative in this area. The German customs union which emerged in 1834 was not motivated by Prussian desire to found a small German nation state, nor did it represent an irreversible step towards the emergence of such a state. But to the Austrian government, which remained excluded from the *Zollverein*, its strategic significance as a means by which Prussia might exert influence on the lesser states was clear.

National defence was one area in which the Confederation did have some limited success in establishing federal institutions. Under Article 2 of the 'Final Act' (*Wiener Schlussakte*) of 1820, a revised version of the earlier Federal Act of 1815, the Confederation was to exist as 'a community of independent states' in its domestic affairs, but as a 'politically unified, federated power in its external relations'. The 'military constitution' accepted in its final form after long debate in July 1822 provided for a single wartime army under unified command. In fact, however, the 'federal army' never became a cohesive body. Its various contingents rarely served together, there was very little common planning or policy-making, and the great royal armies, such as the Austrian and the Prussian, clung to their particularist traditions. The fact was that after

1815, the states of the Confederation had very diverse defence priorities. The small states were concerned above all to avoid any move that might subordinate their interests to those of a more powerful partner. In the event of conflict with France, the south German states were first in the line of fire; in times of crisis they drew together and looked to Prussia for support. Austria, by contrast, saw the southwest German states as a buffer zone (and possible battlefield) between France and the Austrian heartland; it was more concerned to protect its vulnerable Italian possessions. The absence of a coordinated Confederal defence policy became painfully evident during the French war scares of 1830 and 1840–1.

In marked contrast with its half-hearted efforts at reform was the vigour with which the Diet set about suppressing political dissent within the Confederation. In 1819, after the assassination of the reactionary publicist Kotzebue by the nationalist student Karl Sand, the Confederation began to acquire new powers of censorship and surveillance. The 'Karlsbad Decrees', initiated by Chancellor Metternich and passed by the Diet in September 1819, called for closer supervision of the universities throughout the Confederation, the dismissal of subversive teaching staff, as well as the establishment of a press commission for the enforcement of censorship throughout the German states and of the 'Mainz Central Investigative Commission' for dealing with persons involved in 'revolutionary agitation'. These new federal responsibilities were enshrined in the 'Final Act' of 1820, Article 26 which stipulated that the Confederation had the right to intervene in the internal affairs of a member state in order to suppress unrest and restore order, even if the government of that state were 'rendered unable to request help'.

In July 1832, shortly after the Hambach Festival (see p. 51 below), the Diet introduced new and stronger censorship regulations, forbade public assemblies and festivals, as well as the foundation of political clubs, organized new forms of surveillance over travellers and 'conspicuous' persons, and established procedures for the extradition of political suspects. In the aftermath of an attack by ex-student activists on the garrison buildings in Frankfurt in 1833, the Diet even founded a new political intelligence-gathering institute, the Frankfurt Investigation Authority. The new body was intended to collate information on political malefactors through informants, surveillance and interrogation, but like its predecessor in Mainz, it tended increasingly to act preventatively against those merely suspected of subversive activity. The most important Confederal powers involved the use of armed force on the territory of a member state. In October 1830, following the revolutionary unrest of that year, new laws were introduced by the Diet permitting armed intervention within member states with or without the prior request or permission of the relevant governments. This was more than a paper threat; a Confederal force intervened in revolutionary Luxemburg in 1830 and against the Free City of Frankfurt in 1833 (after the above-mentioned attack on the garrison buildings). There were also cases in which the mere threat of armed intervention was sufficient to coerce governments into following the line set out by the Diet. When Baden, for example, introduced liberal press laws and

Der Mann der Zeit

Die Preßfreiheit.

Illustration 3.1   The curtailment of liberty: (left) a caricature on the Karlsbad decrees of 20 September 1819, introducing measures for the suppression of 'demagogic agitation'; (right) 'The man of the times': a comment on restrictions on the freedom of the press

abolished internal censorship towards the end of 1831, the Diet successfully used the threat of 'federal action' (*Bundesexekution*) to reassert the validity for all territories of the Press Laws of 1819.

That the Confederation was illiberal and oppressive is impossible to deny. That it was an anachronism, a 'prediluvian monster', is a more complex claim that may require some qualification. There is no doubt that the Diet was out of tune with nationalist aspirations. The war scare of 1840–41, when loose talk by the Thiers government in Paris prompted fears that France would push her borders forwards to her 'natural frontier' on the Rhine, generated a wave of nationalist 'Rhine songs' by poets and poetasters across the German states. But it is important not to overestimate the power or homogeneity of German nationalism as a political force during this period. German nationalism as a mass phenomenon tended to be reactive, erupting in response to perceived threats (especially from France) and then subsiding again. It is true that nationalist organizations such as the Gymnasts' Movement (*Turnbewegung*) grew at an impressive rate in the mid-1840s – there were 90,000 gymnasts in 300 clubs by 1847 – but attachments to individual states and dynasties remained strong. And as the experiences of 1848 were to show, confessional allegiances divided Catholic enthusiasts for a German nation under Habsburg captaincy from Protestant 'small-Germans' who envisaged a narrower federation under Hohenzollern leadership.

Recent studies have tended to reject the teleology implicit in the nationalist critique, and to focus on the Confederation's 'forward-looking' characteristics. It was an association of sovereign entities with a commitment to the maintenance of peace and the provision of justice through interstate arbitration; in these respects, it 'anticipated' modern supranational entities such as the United Nations and the European Union. Moreover, the Confederation succeeded in reconciling a robust and peaceful solution of the 'German question' with the need to meet the security needs of the European great powers in the then-foreseeable future. Viewed from the perspective of our own day, this was a formidable achievement.

II The modernizing state

The major German states all emerged from the years of war and internal reform with larger, better organized, and more powerful bureaucracies. Supreme executive power remained with the sovereign, but his authority was increasingly mediated through state officials. This can be seen in the changing balance of fiscal power. While revenues raised personally by the sovereign through loans or from royal domains – once staple sources of public finance – dwindled in significance, those collected by officials in taxes, tolls and tariffs accounted for an increasing portion of state income. For G. W. F. Hegel, Professor of Philosophy at the University of Berlin from 1818 whose writings profoundly influenced the thinking of generations of Germans, these were developments of the most fundamental importance. Hegel saw the rationalized, bureaucratized state as the highest form of government. As a 'universal caste' distinct from civil society, the bureaucracy was uniquely capable of providing informed and disinterested administration for the good of all.

Following in this tradition, a number of historians have seen in the emergent *Beamtenstaat* (civil service state) of the post-war decades the single most important motor of social and economic modernization. There is something to be said for this view. In Prussia, for example, one could cite the bureaucratic achievements of the era of reform discussed in the previous chapter. Bureaucrats played a crucial role in the establishment of a Prussian customs union in 1818, forerunner of the German customs union (*Zollverein*) negotiated in 1834. In Württemberg, Bavaria and Baden, bureaucrats helped to draw up 'national' constitutions (see below). One could find further evidence for the modernizing role of the state in the area of educational provision. Prussia was the first major German state to introduce compulsory primary schooling. By 1848 the state provided systematic teacher-training in 49 purpose-designed institutions. Rates of school attendance and general literacy far outstripped those in France and Britain.

Important as these achievements are, the thesis of the modernizing state requires some qualification. A distinction has to be drawn between the political and the economic spheres. The state was not, generally speaking, a *politically* progressive institution. Even Hardenberg, one of the great modernizers of the Prussian bureaucracy, took an extremely illiberal line on political dissent. Indeed, one historian has described the Prussian bureaucracy in this period as an 'agency of domination' which acted to control and contain public and even domestic life through the routine administration of violence. This contrast between political reaction and economic modernity led Thomas Nipperdey to speak of the 'Janus-head' of the Prussian state after 1815.[2]

But even in the economic sphere, the state's achievements were ambivalent. The most recent studies have tended to relativize the longer-term impact of the reform undertaken during the Napoleonic era. In Prussia, it has been argued that a resurgence of conservative forces resulted in the modification or disabling of key legislative initiatives and a 'victory for traditional society'.[3] And throughout the post-war decades, state bureaucracies did little to help and much to hinder economic development. The Prussian financial bureaucracy opposed the foundation of joint-stock companies, and thus hindered the concentration of funds necessary to facilitate investment. Moreover, government credit policies tended to favour agriculture, with the result that money was drawn away from industrial and commercial investment. In this and many other areas, government policy reflected the still formidable political power of the landed nobility. The government did attempt to promote industry by sponsoring various technical experiments and innovations, but its approach was haphazard and its successes modest.

Detailed studies of individual sectors of the economy have revealed a similarly negative picture. Mining entrepreneurs in the Ruhr valley region, for example, found their freedom of action constrained by the government's insistence on managing the industry through its own bureaucratic 'experts'. Mine-owners frequently complained of overregulation and red tape. In 1842, a water-pump had to be removed from the 'Crown Prince' mine in the Ruhr because the owner had not obtained a permit from the *Bergamt* before installation; while the machine was out of commission the mine flooded and had to be abandoned. The state's most significant contribution to the later industrialization of Prussia probably lay in the area of infrastructure (especially roads and waterways) and technical education.

State bureaucracies remained small by modern standards. It is true that after 1815 a growing percentage of government spending went into administrative costs and bureaucratically administered social services, but the lion's share still went to the military, as in the eighteenth century. Many German states were heavily indebted by the end of the wars and large payments in debt-service put pressure on bureaucratic budgets. As a consequence, the overall number of government officials remained low or gradually declined. In 1846, there were only 7.1 government employees in Prussia for every thousand subjects and only a very small proportion of these were administrative bureaucrats proper. Policemen were particularly thin on the ground, a fact which substantially qualified the state's capacity to impose day-to-day control. Indeed, one historian has spoken of a 'trickling away' of the state's power in rural areas, where the shortage of officials was most keenly felt.[4]

The situation was different in the south of Germany, where bureaucracies tended to be larger. In Württemberg, for example, the number of persons employed in 'public service' in 1821 stood at 53,849: about one in three adult males not working on the land was working for the government. In the south German states, the bureaucracy became the dominant political force, not only through its administrative functions, but also through the involvement of officials in parliamentary politics. Bureaucrats had a vital role to play in homogenizing the diverse administrative districts of the recently expanded south German states. Their special status was recognized in the state constitutions, where the public standing and function of the civil servant were formally set down and guaranteed.

However, greater size did not necessarily entail heightened effectiveness. There were practical limitations to the bureaucracy's ability to impose reforms; in Bavaria, measures taken in support of industry and manufacture proved sporadic and ineffective. The laws introduced by the Bavarian government to raise agricultural productivity foundered on the inertia and conservatism of the agrarian sector. A comprehensive reform of Bavarian agriculture was not introduced until the 1850s. In Württemberg, despite the draconian penalties meted out to those who dared to impugn the civil service, there were frequent complaints of the wasteful 'surfeit of scribbling' (*Vielschreiberei*) that so burdened public finances, and recent economic surveys have tended to confirm that the diversion of public money into the large southern bureaucracies harmed, rather than helped, economic growth and development.

Many contemporary observers were less concerned with the economic than with the social impact of bureaucratic reforms. In the south German states and to a lesser extent in Prussia, the nobility emerged from the era of wartime reforms with its privileges and political standing diminished. In this context, it is easy to understand why conservative noblemen railed in the immediate post-war years against the new 'administrative despotism, which eats up everything like vermin'.[5] But it is also important not to underestimate the continuing power and social dominance of the nobility, despite the upheavals of the reform era. In some areas, such as Bavaria and East-Elbian Prussia, nobles retained their traditional policing and judicial rights after well-organized campaigns against the modernizing bureaucrats. In Prussian Silesia, they even managed to cling on to their feudal rights until 1848. In the kingdom of Saxony, likewise, the old feudal agrarian system remained intact, though this changed after 1830, when feudal tenure was abolished in the wake of widespread social unrest. Nobles continued to dominate the agrarian sector in their capacity as large landowners – in Prussia, many estate owners bought up the smallholdings of their emancipated peasants and became successful agrarian entrepreneurs. Moreover, throughout and beyond the period covered by this chapter, nobilities dominated the political, administrative and military institutions of most of the German states: the parliaments, provincial Diets, bureaucracies and armies.

III   Political mobilization

There had been talk at the Congress of Vienna of harmonizing the various political systems within the new German Confederation: in fact, however, the individual states took matters into their own hands and the result was a diverse array of constitutional arrangements that makes any generalization problematic. Broadly speaking, one can distinguish between those states – the Free City of Lübeck, Hanover, Electoral Hesse, Mecklenburg, Saxony, Prussia and other small north German states – in which the old corporate representative bodies retained all or much of their power and those – Nassau, Württemberg, Bavaria, Baden and several of the small Thuringian states – which issued formal constitutions providing for the convocation of bicameral representative assemblies.

The constitutions of the southern states created a completely new institutional context for political participation in Germany. For the first time, parliaments became partners in the legislative process. No law, no budget, could be passed without their approval. It is important, however, not to exaggerate the 'modernity' of these new political arrangements. Almost all of the constitutions were 'issued' by sovereigns; there was no prior negotiation with constituent assemblies. The monarch remained the supreme executive with decisive powers of veto and emergency decree. Moreover, governments did what they could to prevent parliaments from becoming a focus of partisan political activity. Deputies were forbidden, for example, to choose their seats in the chamber; instead, places were pre-assigned or drawn by lot in order to prevent the coalescence of like-minded factions. The German constitutions enshrined various 'human rights', such as equality before the law, freedom of confession and of conscience and the security of property, but political rights, such as freedom of association and assembly or freedom of the press, were either not granted at all or were hedged in by conditions permitting their curtailment by law or decree. Moreover, the upper chambers of the south German parliaments, whose agreement was also required for the passing of any law, were dominated by princes of the ruling family, members of the high nobility and appointed notables.

Until 1848, elections for the lower chambers were subject to numerous restrictions. Suffrage was limited to males who met certain legal and economic qualifications and voting was indirect – enfranchised citizens voted for a college of electors drawn from the social elite, who then selected the deputies; these were themselves required to satisfy stringent economic criteria. In Baden, for example, often regarded as the most liberal of the south German polities, 17 per cent of the population were entitled both to vote and to stand for the college of electors, but only 0.5 per cent were entitled to become deputies if elected. In Bavaria and Württemberg, traces of the old corporate representation remained, even in the lower chambers, where people voted under separate franchise regimes according to occupation and social group.

Despite these and other measures designed to limit the impact of the political process on the public, the parliaments of the south German states did manage to function as the focus for a political opposition of sorts. In 1823, for example, a narrow majority of deputies in the lower chamber of the Baden parliament succeeded in blocking the government's new budget. In the early 1830s, a dispute raged between Duke William of Nassau and his parliament over the sovereign's right to dispose of the ducal domains. When the government refused in 1832 to comply with the demands of the liberal parliamentary majority, the entire lower chamber, excluding five loyalist deputies, resigned *en masse* in a public gesture of disgust. The unequal distribution of constitutional and coercive power meant that governments generally had little difficulty overcoming such opposition. They could stock the upper chambers with loyalist appointees, shift the focus of decision-making away from the legislature into government committees, dissolve uncooperative parliaments, or employ intimidation in order to prevent the re-election of opposition deputies. One example is the Heidelberg bookseller Christian Friedrich Winter, who had led the anti-budget 'faction' in the Baden parliament in 1823. The college of electors in his Heidelberg constituency were informed by the government that if they re-elected Winter their beloved university would be moved to another town.

The unevenness of the contest between sovereigns and elected deputies sometimes had the effect of moving the focus of political opposition out of the parliaments altogether. But in spite of these frustrations and setbacks, it is striking how significant the representative assemblies remained as forums of political dispute and argumentation. In Hesse-Darmstadt, a protracted struggle between the opposition and the reactionary Grand Duke Ludwig II during the early and mid-1830s resulted in the emergence of a liberal faction under the able leadership of Ludwig von Gagern; he and his movement were to win an impressive victory in the parliamentary elections of September 1847. In 1843, liberal deputies in the Baden parliament began to sit together, thereby declaring their willingness to work together under a single programme. The vote of no confidence passed by the lower chamber in the same year represented a further important milestone in the development of parliamentary politics in Germany. Even the very modest provincial assemblies of neo-absolutist Prussia, which were intended to function solely as advisory bodies, gradually became centres of liberal opposition to government policy.

What did 'liberal' mean in the context of early nineteenth-century Germany? This question is less easy to answer than one might expect. Although the term was in widespread use by the early 1830s, its meaning remained imprecise. There was no single liberal 'party' or organization with a monopoly of liberal doctrine. Generally speaking, liberals were opponents of despotism and defenders of liberty. They demanded that the power of the state be bounded by laws and constitutions and they opposed privilege by birth. Their attitude to the state was ambivalent. Many opposed the incursions of state bureaucracies; the castigation of 'paper government' was one of the stock themes of south German liberalism. But many looked upon the strong constitutional state with favour as the chief guarantor of law and order, especially in periods of heightened social unrest. Many liberals favoured free trade, but some did not: 'economic liberals' called for the removal of constraints on the free operation of markets; 'cameral liberals' (the categories are those of the German historian Dieter Langewiesche) sought the implementation of liberal policies through agencies of the state.

Early nineteenth-century German liberals were far from being democrats in the modern sense. They saw themselves as representatives of 'the people', by which they generally meant the educated, property-owning elite. Liberals tended to distinguish between those whose education and economic standing justified their participation in the political process, and the 'mob' (*Pöbel*), though there were widely diverging views on where exactly the line should be drawn. Their political preferences and cultural outlook were those of the emergent *Bürgertum*: professionals, academics, men involved in commerce and manufacture. But it would be a mistake to see liberalism as confined to the 5 per cent of the population who belonged to the commercial and educated bourgeoisie. Many distinguished liberals were noblemen, such as Heinrich von Gagern in Hesse-Darmstadt and Theodor von Schön in Prussia, and it is clear that liberalism also enjoyed considerable support among the self-employed in trade, manufacture and services.

Thanks to economic restrictions on the franchise in the constitutional German states, the upper reaches of the *Bürgertum* tended to be overrepresented in the liberal parliamentary factions. But liberal political activity was not confined to representative institutions. There were liberal 'factions' in many of the German bureaucracies. This was certainly the case in Prussia, where it has been argued that senior officialdom functioned as a kind of 'surrogate parliament'. Although historians no longer argue that the Prussian bureaucracy as a whole was liberal it is clear that there were significant groups of liberal officials, though their influence on policy appears gradually to have waned after 1820. In Baden, liberal officials played an important role in mobilizing public opinion against the government after the reactionary ministry of Freiherr von Blittersdorf tried to prevent them from taking up seats in parliament by restricting civil service leave allowances in 1839; there were similar campaigns by civil servants in the other southern states.

Political opposition in Restoration Germany was not, of course, limited to these forms of 'institutional' dissent. A variety of extra-parliamentary groups emerged in the immediate post-war years, of which the most important was a small but active student movement organized around university fraternities known as *Burschenschaften*. The *Burschenschaftler* were romantic nationalists who hoped by the creation of a pan-German student movement to overcome the narrow confines of the dynastic polities. The political implications of the students' nationalism remained unclear. Some saw their task in terms of education and culture, others were willing to contemplate a more activist political agenda. In October 1817, members of the movement congregated to hold a political festival on the Wartburg. Here, at the castle where Luther had produced his translation of the Bible, students gathered to hear speeches exhorting them to take up the cause of the nation. It is important not to exaggerate the impact of the student movement; there were fewer than 500 students on the Wartburg in 1817, and probably no more than 1,000 *Burschenschaftler* in all. The festival's importance lies more in the emotional and theatrical character of its politics. In addition to hearing and giving speeches, the students burnt reactionary books and objects held to symbolize despotism, among them an officer's cane and a French corset. They wore jackets and hats intended to evoke the traditional 'German costume'; their colours (black, red and gold) were those of the patriotic volunteers who had fought in the Wars of Liberation. 'Festivals' of this kind, in which specific political appeals were blended with the emotive use of symbol and spectacle were henceforth to play an important role in the development of nationalist and radical movements in Germany.

The *Burschenschaft* movement suffered a serious setback in 1819 when a student from its most radical wing stabbed to death a reactionary publicist employed by the Russian legation in Mannheim. The assassination prompted a dramatic change in the political mood. The governments of the German states, egged on by the Austrian chancellor, Metternich, introduced a package of laws known as the 'Karlsbad Decrees' (see above, p. 42) to tighten controls on political activity throughout the Confederation. The student movement was banned, as was the 'old German costume', and fraternity members were hounded by the police. A censorship regime was introduced and the right to form voluntary associations was narrowly circumscribed.

Despite these constraints, the decades of the Restoration era saw the emergence of a widespread and increasingly differentiated network of voluntary organizations whose tone was predominantly liberal. In the 1820s, for example, a wave of support for the Greek uprising against the Ottoman Empire led to the formation of a dense network of 'Greek clubs' concentrated especially in the southwest of Germany. The *Griechenvereine* attracted volunteers from an unprecedentedly broad social spectrum ranging from the *Bürgertum* to urban and rural labourers. The clubs were not overtly 'political' in their aims, but they developed innovative techniques of public mobilization such as the mass distribution of posters and pamphlets and used political festivals and monuments to encourage public 'participation' in the campaign.

In 1830, the July Revolution in Paris combined with widespread shortages and price rises caused by poor harvests to produce a political crisis in several German states. The main centres of civil unrest in the autumn of 1830 were Saxony, Braunschweig, Hesse-Darmstadt and Electoral Hesse. In Braunschweig, there was open rebellion; the ducal residence was set on fire on 7 September and the duke himself forced to flee. Although the motivations for these episodes of unrest had little to do with high politics – more important was the failure of respective administrations to meet social needs – they had lasting political consequences. Constitutions were subsequently granted in all four states. Throughout the German Confederation and especially in the southwest, the events of 1830 raised the political temperature. Factional politics in the parliaments became more confrontational. There was an unprecedented flood of political pamphlets and a proliferation of new dissenting organizations. Among the best known of these was the Patriotic Club in Support of the Free Press ('Press Club'), founded in 1832 to protest against the reactionary policies of the Bavarian government and specifically its restrictive press laws. Members were distributed across 116 auxiliary associations in Bavaria and neighbouring states. Whereas the printed propaganda of the Press Club tended to focus on constitutional issues and to reflect the world-view of the commercial and academic *Bürgertum*, the speeches of individual agitators often focused on social issues and adopted a more radical tone. In this way, Press Club publicity reflected increasingly divergent standpoints within German liberalism.

Press Club agitation culminated in a political festival at the ruined castle of Hambach near Neustadt. The *Hambacher Fest* attracted at least 20,000 participants and has rightly been described as 'the first political demonstration in modern German history'.[6] Once again the internal tensions within the opposition were manifest; the extremism of some of the speeches far exceeded the intentions of the organisers. This did not escape the attention of the watchful Austrian chancellor, Prince Metternich: 'Liberalism has given way to radicalism', he commented in a letter to the Austrian ambassador in Berlin.[7] In June and July 1832, new laws were issued under the authority of the German Confederation forbidding 'festivals' and large assemblies and tightening censorship controls.

Those 'radicals' who stood to the left of liberalism placed more emphasis on social and economic reform as a precondition for the exercise of political liberties; they were likely to be republican, whereas most liberals were constitutional monarchists. They favoured a greatly enlarged or even universal male franchise – voting for women was not on the agenda. The dividing line between radicals and liberals was only gradually clarified, but the widespread unrest of the early 1830s was a crucial milestone in the emergence of a distinctive radical milieu. Radicals distinguished themselves less by their political programmes than by their greater willingness to carry out or condone attacks upon authority. They directed their appeals above all to artisans, peasants and labourers. Radical agitation among these strata was not entirely without success. A network of activist cells and small associations emerged, most of them dominated by urban artisans, and radical factions began to crystallize in some of the parliaments, but in general there was little public sympathy for radical politics. In April 1833, for example, when a small gang of ex-student and artisan activists stormed the police station in Frankfurt am Main, the stolid burghers of the city looked on with interest but offered nothing in the way of support. Radical activism was marked by amateurishness and dilettantism – 'professional revolutionaries' of the legendary type were few and far between. Meanwhile, on the socialist and communist far left, there were attempts to establish a sound theoretical basis for a revolutionary agenda. By the late 1840s, Karl Marx was emerging as an influential figure. The brilliance – and savagery – of the polemical essays in which Marx defended his views and demolished the arguments of his various rivals were to ensure him a central place in the nascent labour movement. For the moment, however, Marx and the communist left played at best a marginal role in the political experience of most German labourers and artisans.

By comparison with liberalism and radicalism, conservative politics have until recently attracted relatively little attention. Though it is clear that the states of the German Confederation often adopted reactionary policies, it is important not to conflate conservatism with the centres of government power. As often as not, conservatives found themselves in opposition to the state. In Prussia, for example, conservative political circles formed among sections of the nobility in opposition to the reforming measures of government bureaucrats. And within the bureaucracy itself, a conservative faction fought with considerable success to wrest control over policy-making from liberal senior officials. In Baden, conservative nobles rejected the constitution offered by the Grand Duke and boycotted the parliament, preferring instead to lobby the Confederal authorities in Frankfurt. The *Evangelische Kirchenzeitung*, founded in 1827 by the theologian Ernst Wilhelm Hengstenberg in Berlin was the chief organ of north German conservative opinion in the late 1820s and 1830s, but it, too, opposed the Prussian government on various issues, especially in the area of church policy. The *Berliner Politische Wochenblatt* founded by ultraconservatives in 1831, conceived of itself as a loyalist organ directed against the subversive forces unleashed by the July Revolution, but even this newspaper was subject to constant obstruction from government censorship authorities. The public resonance of such journals was modest, but they bore witness to a growing willingness among conservatives to 'organize' for the purpose of influencing opinion. Generally speaking, conservative political theory used organic metaphors and religious argumentation to legitimate an idealized 'traditional order'. Historically given, 'natural' social relations based on paternalistic and localized structures of authority were opposed to the levelling, homogenizing thrust of bureaucratic modernization. It was not until the late 1840s, with the rise to prominence of the legal theorist Friedrich Julius Stahl, that a middle road was found between modern constitutionalism and the provincial, nostalgic politics of the old conservatives.

IV The social question

Public discussion and debate in Germany during the last decade before the revolutions of 1848 were characterized by a growing awareness of social issues. Books such as Lorenz Stein's *History of Social Movements in France from 1789 to Our Own Day* (1842) and Friedrich Engels' *Condition of the Working Classes in England* (1845) raised public awareness of the 'social question' by focusing on the plight of factory workers and artisans. In 1841, when Bettina von Arnim published her two-volume work *This Book is for the King* in Berlin, readers were less interested in the book's political arguments than in its long appendix documenting the appalling living conditions that prevailed among industrial and manufacturing workers in Berlin. The 'social question' embraced a complex of different issues: working conditions within factories, the problem of housing in densely populated areas, the dissolution of corporate entities (e.g. guilds, estates), the vicissitudes of a capitalist economy based on competition, the decline of religion and morals among the emergent 'proletariat', the fear of revolutionary upheaval. In other words, the social question was also a political question, which turned on divergent evaluations of economic liberalism and its consequences. But the central and dominant issue was 'pauperization', the progressive impoverishment of the lower social strata. The 'pauperism' of the pre-March era differed from traditional forms of poverty in a number of important ways. It was a mass phenomenon, collective and structural, rather than dependent upon individual contingencies, such as sickness, injury or crop failures. It was permanent rather than seasonal. And it showed signs of engulfing social groups whose position had previously been relatively secure, such as artisans (especially apprentices and journeymen) and smallholding peasants. 'Pauperism', the *Brockhaus Encyclopaedia* noted in 1846, 'occurs when a large class can subsist only as a result of the most intensive labour'. The key problem was a decline in the value of labour and its products. This affected not only unskilled labourers and those who worked in the craft trades, but also the large and growing section of the rural population who lived from various forms of cottage industry.

Inevitably, the causes of mass poverty were extremely complex; generalizations are difficult, since conditions varied according to occupation and locality. The older historical literature on this subject tended to focus on state-sponsored processes of modernization, particularly industrialization, arguing that more efficient modes of production had a drastic effect on older forms of manufacture. But, as we have seen, this view is founded on on a misapprehension of the power and ambitions of the state. Industrialization had made only very modest advances in the German states by the time revolution broke out. German society remained overwhelmingly rural; in the 1840s, over 70 per cent of the population still worked on the land. There were a few sectors (such as cotton-printing, typesetting and nail-making) in which mechanized production posed a serious threat to manual labour by the late 1840s, but in the great majority of manufacturing trades, various kinds of skilled and unskilled manual labour still predominated. In 1846, for example, when there were at least 55,000 male workers in Berlin, the city could boast only 75 steam engines. In Prussia as a whole, industrial workers proper accounted for no more than 3.9 per cent of the population.

The most fundamental cause of mass impoverishment was probably demographic growth. In 1816, the population of the German Confederation, including the three provinces of Prussia outside its borders, was about 32.7 million. By 1865 this figure had risen by 60 per cent to 52.2 million. The reasons for this rapid growth are still debated and they cannot be dealt with here (see further Chapter 4 below, pp. 63–9). However, it is important to remember that the impact of demographic growth was socially very uneven. It was above all a rural phenomenon. In Prussia, for example, the population increased by 56 per cent from 10.3 million in 1816 to 15.9 million in 1846, while the percentage of the population living in cities rose only from 26 per cent to 28 per cent. A few cities, particularly Berlin, did experience dramatic growth, but the overall picture was one of stasis. Both in the cities and on the land, moreover, the effects of population growth were most apparent among the least economically secure social groups. On the land the abolition (by liberal bureaucrats) of marriage restrictions and the extension of land under cultivation raised nuptiality and fertility among the 'sub-peasant strata' (*unterbäuerlichen Schichten*), especially families on subsistence holdings and landless rural labourers. In Minden-Ravensberg, for example, the ratio of families living from the wages of hired labour to full-time peasants (*Vollbauern*) was 149/100 in 1800; by 1846, the ratio had risen to 310/100. Such families earned an increasingly marginal living from a combination of agrarian labour and various forms of domestic piece-work for merchants who dealt with supra-regional markets. Rural labourers of this kind spent most of their income on food; they were vulnerable not only to rises in the cost of agrarian produce, but also to fluctuations in the business cycle which could depress demand for the goods – especially textiles – they helped to manufacture.

There was a similarly disproportionate growth in the number of artisans. This becomes clear if we consult figures for Prussia during the period 1816–46, when, as we have seen, the population as a whole rose by 56 per cent. The number of master artisans rose by 70 per cent during the same period. Much more dramatic was the rise (156 per cent) in the number of assistants and apprentices. A similarly dramatic growth in this sector can be observed for the same period in the German Confederation as a whole.

In a buoyant, elastic economy, such changes may have been sustainable; in the stagnant conditions of the 1830s and 1840s, however, the growth in the labour supply was not matched by a corresponding demand for manufactured products. The result – leaving aside the dramatic differences between regions and sectors – was a continual net decline in the living standard of those involved in craft trades and rural proto-industrial manufacture. From the 1830s, the Poor Office in Cologne dedicated a special category of charity to master craftsmen who had fallen on hard times. A contemporary statistical survey suggested that between 50 and 60 per cent of the Prussian population were living on a subsistence minimum. The striking combination of rising population and mass poverty may lead us to suspect that the social crisis of this era was the result of a 'Malthusian trap', where the needs of the population exceeded the available supply of agricultural produce. However, it is important to remember that during the period covered by this chapter technical improvements (artificial fertilizers, modernized animal husbandry and the three-field rotation system) and an increase in land under cultivation had doubled the productivity of German agriculture. In other words, the food supply increased at about twice the rate of population growth in the German Confederation. The problem was not, therefore, chronic underproduction. But large agricultural surpluses could also have a harmful effect on manufacturing, since they depressed the prices of agricultural produce. The result was a collapse in agrarian incomes and a corresponding decline in the demand for goods from the overcrowded manfacturing sector.

More importantly, food supplies remained vulnerable despite the impressive growth in total agricultural production, because natural catastrophes – poor harvests, cattle epidemics, crop diseases – could still turn the surplus into a drastic shortfall. This is what happened in the winter of 1846, when harvest failures sent food prices up to double and even triple the normal average. The crisis was compounded by a downturn in the business cycle and a crop disease that wiped out the potato harvests upon which many regions had become dependent. The rise in prices was accompanied by a heightened frequency of civic unrest. In Prussia alone, 158 food riots – marketplace riots, attacks on stores and shops, transportation blockades – took place during April/May 1847, when prices were at their highest. Interestingly enough, the geography of food riots did not coincide with that of the most acute shortage. Extremely hard-hit areas like upper Silesia, where some 50,000 people are thought to have died from diseases related to malnutrition, remained riot-free. Riots were more likely to occur in areas which produced food for export, or in transit areas with high levels of food transportation. Such protests should certainly not be seen as 'rehearsals' for revolution; they were generally pragmatic attempts to control the food supply, or to 'remind' the authorities of their traditional obligations to provide for afflicted subjects. Rioters did not act as members of a 'class', but as representatives of a local community whose right to justice had been denied. The human targets of their wrath were likely to be 'outsiders': merchants who dealt with distant markets, customs officials, foreigners or Jews.

We have seen that despite considerable improvements in the cultivation of land and livestock German societies remained vulnerable to sudden disruptions in the agrarian sector. This primacy of agriculture led Eric Hobsbawm to describe the European crisis of the late 1840s as 'the last, and perhaps the worst, economic breakdown of the *ancien régime*'. But this view requires some elaboration: harvest cycles and climate fluctuation remained crucial as they had been in traditional societies; in this sense, certainly, the German crisis of the 1840s was a crisis 'of the old type'. But the dramatic growth and internal restructuring of the labour force in the manufacturing sector was new. It generated new social groups, who were exposed to poverty in different ways and through more complex mechanisms than the smallholding peasants and traditional artisans of the *ancien régime*. This helps to explain not only the heightened sensitivity of these groups to fluctuations in supply and demand, but also the chronic character of mass poverty in pre-March society.

V   Religion

Throughout the period covered by this chapter, politics and religion were closely intertwined. We must be wary of applying anachronistic assumptions based on the relatively marginal and specialized role of religion in modern public life. Political views were often articulated in religious language and religious disputes and allegiances could easily take on political character. This was apparent, for example, in the case of those Prussian noble families – Gerlachs, Thaddens, Senfft von Pilsachs, Kleist-Retzows, Belows, Oertzens and others – whose conservatism drew upon religiously motivated opposition to government church policy. In Bavaria, likewise, conservative Catholics in Würzburg formed a 'Literary Society' whose aim was to oppose the secularizing reforms of the ministry under Montgelas. Some historians have seen this organization as a forerunner of the Centre Party. Political and religious milieux tended to overlayer each other: in Prussia, for example, conservative political mobilization remained a largely Protestant domain. In the predominantly Catholic Rhineland, conservative newspapers were rarely read outside the Protestant 'ghetto'. Even the political rhetoric of pre-March radicalism, with its evocations of brotherly love, justice, spiritual renewal and utopian prospects, was saturated with the language of the gospels.

Religious allegiances also influenced contemporary responses to social problems. The efforts by Protestants to alleviate social need among the impoverished often focused on the need to reconcile the conditions of modern manufacture with the maintenance of a strict ethical code founded on providential religion and the sacralization of labour. Typical of this tendency were the 'spinning houses' established by Baron Kottwitz in Silesia and Berlin in the 1810s, or the orphanage complex built up by Count von der Recke near Düsseldorf in the 1820s, where prayer and elementary instruction were combined with work in a variety of manufactures. By contrast, socially minded Catholics tended to be more fundamental in their criticism of economic liberalism and the modern industrial system. In their place, Catholic theorists offered corporatist solutions: the philosopher Franz von Baader – the first writer in Germany to use the term 'proletarian' (1835) – called for obligatory corporations of workers led by priests with the right to political representation in the parliaments. Others called for state controls on the ownership of property, protective tolls, laws against long working hours and child labour, and marriage restrictions to prevent further overpopulation. The intention was to reverse the 'decorporation' and atomization characteristic of modern capitalist society. These responses doubtless reflected the fact that Catholics and Catholic regions were less involved in the modernization of manufactures and industry than their Protestant counterparts – Protestants were greatly overrepresented, for example, in the early industrial enterprises of the Catholic Rhineland.

It is important, however, not to see religion merely as a fund of language and argumentation for various forms of political discourse, or as a passive 'milieu' that coloured the public life of German communities. The dynamism of religion as an autonomous social force was arguably greater during this era than at any time since the late seventeenth century. In the Protestant north of Germany, the early decades of the nineteenth century brought a widespread and socially differentiated Christian revival movement. 'Awakened' Christians emphasized the emotional, penitential character of faith in a language reminiscent of eighteenth-century pietism; their religious commitment often found expression outside the institutional confines of the church. Characteristic for this period was the proliferation of voluntary Christian societies with a variety of purposes: the distribution of charity, the housing and 'betterment' of 'fallen women', the moral improvement of prisoners, the care of orphans, the printing and distribution of bibles, the provision of subsistence labour for paupers and vagrants, the conversion of Jews and heathens. Most of these societies were supported by networks of auxiliaries throughout northern Germany. In Prussia, they generally enjoyed the patronage of 'awakened' nobles, and in many cases, of the sovereign and his family; the auxiliary groups in smaller communities were often dominated by pious master artisans.

German Catholicism also entered a phase of revival during the period covered by this chapter. It is important to remember that the church had been the foremost victim of the secularizations carried out during the Napoleonic era. The ecclesiastical principalities of the old Reich had been dissolved and absorbed into new or enlarged secular states, some with a Protestant majority. The revival of religion among the mass of the Catholic faithful and the tightening of clerical control over popular religious life characteristic of the Restoration era have to be seen against this background. Catholic revival reflected a larger trend away from rationalism towards a greater emphasis on emotion, mystery and revelation – in this sense at least, Catholic and Protestant revival were cut from the same cloth. But it also offered a means of compensating for the church's traumatic loss of resources and political autonomy. Whereas the Protestant awakening was dominated by lay initiatives, Catholic revivalism tended to be clerically led. In Bavaria from the 1820s, the clergy used liturgical innovations, pilgrimages and processions to encourage and deepen public participation and to replace the rationalist ethics of the Catholic Enlightenment with a respect for mystery and miracle. In the Rhineland, the 1840s saw the emergence of a new style of pilgrimage characterized by mass participation – 400,000 went to view the Holy Robe at Trier in 1844 – and a high level of clerical discipline. The untidy, festive mobs of the traditional pilgrimage were replaced by ordered groups under strict clerical supervision.

Closely associated with the phenomenon of Catholic revival was the rise of ultramontanism. Ultramontanes were those who argued that the strict subordination of the church to papal authority was the best way of protecting it from state interference.

They perceived the church as a strictly centralized but international body. Until around 1830, Catholic conservatives were concerned above all with 'inner'.religious renewal; thereafter the focus of their activity shifted to strengthening the ties with Rome. Inevitably, the rise of ultramontanism led to increasing tension between church and state. In Bavaria, a dispute broke out in 1831 over the education of children in Catholic–Protestant mixed marriages. The ultramontanes moved on to the offensive and liberal publicists depicted the debate as a struggle between the forces of darkness and light. Six years later, a much more serious fight broke out over the same issue in Prussia, in the course of which the authorities arrested and imprisoned the ultramontane archbishop of Cologne. Such conflicts helped to accelerate the emergence of an increasingly confident and aggressive 'political Catholicism'. The *Historisch-Politischen Blätter für das katholische Deutschland*, founded by Joseph Görres in Munich in 1837, became the chief organ of this tendency. It favoured the political consolidation of the traditional corporate social bodies and the return to a Habsburg-led German Reich.

In Protestant Germany, there was a similar shift away from the 'awakening' of the early decades, with its romantic and ecumenical overtones, towards a more narrowly confessional revivalism. In 1830 the three-hundredth anniversary of the Confession of Augsburg, one of the founding texts of Lutheran Protestantism, was greeted with celebrations by Lutherans throughout northern Germany. In Saxony, it was the refusal of the Catholic sovereign to permit Lutheran celebrations that unleashed the first protest demonstrations of that troubled year. In Prussia, revived Lutheranism found itself in direct conflict with the government. Since 1817, King Frederick William III had been effecting a gradual union of the Calvinist and Lutheran Confessions in Prussia. But from 1830 an 'Old Lutheran' movement emerged in Silesia that openly rejected the Church of the 'Prussian Union'. The government responded with fines, surveillance, arrests and imprisonment, in the hope that the beleaguered Lutherans would relinquish their separatism and return to the Union. Instead, the Old Lutheran movement steadily grew; by 1840, when Frederick William died, there were some 10,000 known active separatists in Prussia. A further 2,000 had emigrated to Australia and North America to escape persecution. The conflict was only defused when Frederick William IV offered a general amnesty and granted the Lutherans the right to establish themselves within Prussia as an autonomous 'church society'.

Both Protestant and Catholic revivalism were, as we have seen, closely affiliated with conservatism. But these movements did not remain unchallenged within the two confessional communities. The 'German Catholic' movement, founded in Leipzig in 1845, called for a severing of ties with Rome and a movement of enlightened spiritual renewal which would abandon the straitjacket of traditional dogma and create the foundation for a German, Catholic–Protestant, 'national church'. Two years later, the movement had acquired 250 congregations with a total membership of some 60,000, of whom about 20,000 were converts from Protestantism. There were close ties with Germany's leading political radicals. Among the foremost supporters was Robert Blum, who used his *Vaterlandsblätter* to combine anti-Roman polemic with attacks on bureaucracy, police and censorship. Another was the radical Gustav von Struve, who was to lead the ill-fated Badenese uprising of 1849. The connection between religious critique and political radicalism was equally clear in the case of the Protestant movement known as the 'Friends of Light' (*Lichtfreunde*). Like the German Catholics, the Friends of Light combined rationalist theology with a presbyterial-democratic organizational culture in which authority was devolved on to the individual congregation and its elected elders. The movement was particularly successful in attracting poor urban and rural artisans, especially in Saxony, the most industrialized state in the German Confederation. Both the Friends of Light and the German Catholics were concentrated among social strata and in areas which later became centres of radical democratic activity: Silesia, Saxony, Electoral Hesse, Baden, Vienna. Located halfway between sect and party, these movements offer dramatic evidence of the intimate relationship between religion and politics in the pre-March era.

VI Conclusion

The fascination of the period 1815–48 for students of German history lies partly in its transitional character. The bureaucratic state was larger and stronger than it had been before 1806, but not as strong as it would later become. Parliamentary factions, political 'festivals' and mass demonstrations coexisted with corporate noble-dominated estates – a reminder that modernity was born in Germany long before the old regime had died. The result of the overlap, as we have seen, was a heightened tension between restorative inertia and the progressive movement that was briefly to win the day in 1848.

But 'transition' is in some ways an inadequate metaphor for the developments we have discussed. The mass poverty and social dislocation of the 1840s were not the consequence of a transition from a traditional agrarian to a modern industrial society. Not all movements were progressive and forward-looking, nor, as we have seen, were the forces of Restoration purely backward-looking. Revivalist religion generated a new and dynamic social force that was neither entirely reactionary, nor entirely modern. The political Catholicism that emerged in the 1830s was to play a decisive role in the public life of the Wilhelmine Empire, the Weimar Republic and, later, of the German Federal Republic. Rather than combing through the 'pre-March' for the first signs of 1848, we should remember that this era, like all eras, contained the seeds of many futures.

Notes:

1. Diary of Leopold von Gerlach, Breslau, February 1813, Bundesarchiv Abteilungen (BA) Potsdam, NL von Gerlach 90 Ge 1 (transcript), B1.45.
2. Nipperdey, T., *Deutsche Geschichte 1800–1866. Bürgerwelt und starker Staat* (1983), p. 333.
3. Nolte, Paul, *Staatsbildung als Gesellschaftsreform. Politische Reformen in Preußen und den süddeutschen Staaten 1800–1820* (1990), p. 105.

4. Kocka, J., 'Preußischer Staat und Modernisierung im Vormärz', in B. Vogel, ed., *Preußische Reformen 1807–1820* (1980), pp. 49–65; here p. 58.

5. Gerlach, Leopold von, 1 May 1816, BA Potsdam, NL von Gerlach, 90 Ge 2, Bl. 9.

6. Heuss, Theodor, cited in H. Schulze, *Der Weg zum Nationalstaat. Die deutsche Nationalbewegung vom 18. Jahrhundert bis zur Reichsbründung* (1985), p. 78.

7. Metternich quoted in J. J. Sheehan, *German History 1770–1866* (1989), p. 613.

Select bibliography

Anderson, M. L., 'Piety and Politics: Recent Work on German Catholicism', *Journal of Modern History*, 63 (1991).

Beck, H., 'The Social Policies of Prussian Officials: The Bureaucracy in a New Light', *Journal of Modern History*, 64 (1992).

Billinger, R. D., *Metternich and the German Question. State Rights and Federal Duties 1820–1834* (1991).

Botzenhart, M., *Reform, Restauration, Krise. Deutschland 1789–1847* (1985).

Diefendorf, J., *Businessmen and Politics in the Rhineland, 1789–1834* (1980).

Lee, L. E., *The Politics of Harmony. Civil Service, Liberalism and Social Reform in Baden 1800–1850* (1980).

Lee, W. R., 'Economic Development and the State in Nineteenth-Century Germany, 1815–1870', *Economic History Review*, 2nd series, 41 (1988).

Lüdtke, A., *Police and State in Prussia 1815–1850* (1989).

Lutz, H., *Zwischen Habsburg und Preussen: Deutschland 1815–1866* (1985).

Nipperdey, T., *Deutsche Geschichte. Bürgerwelt und starker Staat* (1983).

Schulze, H., *The Course of German Nationalism: From Frederick the Great to Bismarck*, trans. S. Hanbury-Tenison (1990).

Sheehan, J. J., *German History 1770–1866* (1989).

Sperber, J., *Popular Catholicism in Nineteenth-Century Germany* (1984).

Sperber, J., 'State and Civil Society in Prussia: Some Thoughts on a New Edition of Reinhart Koselleck's *Preußen zwischen Reform und Revolution*'. *Journal of Modern History*, 57 (1985).

4

'Relative backwardness' and long-run development

Economic, demographic and social changes

Robert Lee

Any discussion of Germany's economic development during the decades of the nineteenth century prior to political unification in 1871 is still influenced by a series of hypotheses stemming from the Gerschenkronian paradigm of 'relative backwardness'.[1] On the basis of this analysis, Germany's apparent economic backwardness and the persistence of market imperfections enhanced the role of special institutional factors, such as banks and the state, and generated a more rapid rate of industrialization with a greater emphasis on producer goods, large plant size and up-to-date technology. The creation of a unified internal market with the establishment of the customs union (*Zollverein*) in 1834 and the elimination of internal tariffs and customs barriers was a 'significant step forward', and the role of the state was equally evident in the official encouragement of railway construction and extensive improvements in educational training. Recent research, however, has begun to question some, if not all, of these traditional explanations. This chapter will therefore attempt to explore the extent to which our understanding of the pattern of economic and social change in nineteenth-century Germany prior to political unification in 1871 has now been altered or modified.

I The 'relative backwardness' of Germany in the late-eighteenth century

A key question, in this context, is whether Germany (or the different states that constituted Germany) was actually 'backward' in the late eighteenth or early nineteenth centuries, and to what extent? Recent views on the level and nature of economic activity at the start of this period vary considerably in terms of their interpretation of the available data. On the one hand, although there were certain well-established manufacturing centres, output levels were low and development was hindered by restricted markets and an inadequate transport infrastructure. Urban guilds constituted a major obstacle to economic growth, political divisions within the German Confederation hindered the development of both trade and industry, and specific sectors, such as the iron and steel industry, were slow to introduce more modern methods of production. In Prussia in the early 1800s over 70 per cent of the population either lived or worked in the countryside, agriculture continued to attract the lion's share of net investment and the production of capital goods was very limited. In addition, capital accumulation remained a major problem as a result of the relative backwardness of the economy and German agriculture, even by the 1840s, was apparently amongst the most backward in Europe.

Recent research, on the other hand, has helped to create a more differentiated picture of Germany's economic position at the end of the eighteenth century. The expansion of proto-industrial production, particularly in such regions as Silesia, Saxony and the Rhineland, fostered important changes in the regional division of labour and contributed to an increasing diversification in urban function. Minimal regulation in rural areas kept labour costs low and encouraged the long-term territorialization of handicraft production, so that even in Bavaria over 50 per cent of all holdings were probably dependent on some form of non-agricultural income by 1752–60. Similarly in the Kurmark Brandenburg more than half of all agricultural holdings in 1755 were held by day labourers or domestic craftsmen. In some regions, such as Lower Saxony, the expansion of rural handicrafts did not immediately threaten existing urban production, but many city guilds continued to oppose this trend. However, substantial population growth from the mid-eighteenth century onwards, together with price inflation and increased accessibility to markets, provided important incentives for a general expansion of industrial production.

The eighteenth century also witnessed the development of larger units of centralized production (*Manufakturen*) whether in Bavaria, the electorate of Mainz or Schleswig-Holstein, often as a result of direct state initiatives reflecting a concern to reduce unemployment and to promote the sale of luxury goods. In line with cameralist principles, for example, 150 new *Manufakturen* were first registered in Saxony between 1793 and 1800. It is not surprising, therefore, that many individual towns and cities had developed a respectable manufacturing and trading profile: if approximately one-third of all households in Krefeld were engaged in the linen and silk trades in 1750, the proportion had risen to over 46 per cent by the end of the eighteenth century. Despite a long tradition of city states and a substantial number of cities, Germany only had a low level of urbanization in the early eighteenth century. By 1800, however, there had been significant changes: new industrial and commercial centres had developed in the Rhine and Ruhr regions, with expanded regional capitals (such as Cologne and Frankfurt am Main); Saxony was increasingly dominated by Dresden and Leipzig, and Silesia by Breslau and Lemberg. The growth of administrative cities (*Residenzstädte*) was spectacular, with demographic growth reflecting policies which openly encouraged immigration, in contrast to the more restrictive controls retained on urban in-migration by the older German home towns.

At the same time there are indications of significant primary sector growth, including an expansion of plough land and a reduction in the extent of fallow. Further confirmation of this trend can be found in the dissemination of improved cultivation patterns (for example, the Holstein *Koppelwirtschaft*); the introduction of new crops (including clover, esparto grass, potatoes and lucerne); and buoyant grain exports, particularly from the eastern territories. Certainly by the late eighteenth century specialist areas of production had already emerged, with different field systems and cultivation patterns; for example, by 1800 almost 30 per cent of the cultivable area of Lower Saxony was devoted to flax. Moreover, the expansion of rural craft production, together with the proliferation of smallholdings had already stimulated regional specialization in the primary sector. In various regions of Germany there were clear signs of increased agricultural prosperity: higher dowry values in rural communities, a fall in the frequency of enforced sales of agricultural holdings, and a more commercial approach to market opportunities by certain types of peasant, such as the dairy farmers of Neuholland.

II   Rates of growth in the nineteenth century

It is generally accepted that the industrialization of Germany took place in three distinct phases. From the 1780s onwards there were clear signs of economic growth, but only in certain regions such as the Rhineland, Saxony and Silesia. The years after 1815 witnessed the reintroduction of restrictive guild regulations in such states as Hesse-Kassel, Hanover and Oldenburg, and a collapse of agricultural prices in the 1820s which led to indebtedness and depression in many rural communities and a fall in aggregate demand. Many rural industries in Prussia, for example, suffered from a lack of suitable markets during these years. The period between the 1840s and the early 1870s, on the other hand, was characterized by a significant acceleration in the pace of industrialization, associated with the expansion of heavy industry and extensive railway construction. In Prussia the 1840s can be seen as a watershed which marked the final acceptance by élite groups of the inevitability of industrial development and a recognition after 1848 that the private sector, rather than the state, should control the forces of production. The central decades of the nineteenth century therefore marked the beginning of Germany's industrial revolution, in line with the Gerschenkronian model that specifies a big spurt discontinuity in the growth rates of relatively backward national economies. This was then followed by a second phase of industrialization in the late nineteenth century associated with the successful development of the chemical and electricity industries (see below, Chapter 9).

However, such an interpretation of Germany's economic performance is not based on firm quantitative evidence and seriously underplays the extent and dynamic nature of economic growth in the earlier decades of the nineteenth century. In the first instance, existing estimates of the trend in agricultural output, despite certain limitations, confirm the relatively positive performance of the German primary sector during this period (Table 4.1). Within Prussia the highest growth in agricultural output in the period 1816 to 1855 was registered in Posen, Saxony, Silesia and West Prussia. In terms of total population employed in the primary sector, the rate of change in the period 1816 to 1849 was as fast as during the later period from the mid-nineteenth century to 1883. In Württemberg the rise in output more than kept pace with the increase in population, and in good years the primary sector generated a noticeable surplus. Grain output in Bavaria, for example, increased by an estimated annual rate of 4.2 per cent between 1810 and 1864, whereas total population only rose by 0.6 per cent per annum. Indeed, for Germany as a whole, the estimated rate of growth in agricultural output was higher in the first half of the nineteenth century up until 1861–5, than in the following three decades. In general, there was an improvement in yields, a significant expansion in the cultivation of potatoes and root crops, as well as a selective shift to dairy produce. The rise in arable output, however, was largely achieved through an expansion in the cultivable area and, particularly in the eastern provinces of Prussia, through continuous increments in labour supply. Undoubtedly the liberal agrarian reforms of the early nineteenth century, such as the Prussian legislation of 1807, 1811 and 1821, modified land distribution, farm organization and agricultural production, particularly within a regional context, even if their contribution to economic development has frequently been exaggerated. But the estimated increase in annual agricultural output in the 1820s and 1830s of 1.32 per cent and 2.58 per cent respectively (in comparison with an equivalent figure of 0.12 per cent between 1840 and 1850) also reflected a positive response to rising levels of aggregate demand and the buoyancy of export markets after an initial decline in the Danzig grain trade. With the revival in agricultural prices in the 1830s peasant production increased signifi-

Table 4.1   The development of agricultural production per unit of labour input (LI) in Germany, 1800–50 on the basis of grain values

Period	Production in 1,000 tons					
	Arable	Livestock	Total	Labour force (1,000)	Tons per LI	Index
1800–10	14,500	7,555	22,055	9,525	2.32	100
1811–20	15,660	7,332	22,992	9,530	2.41	104
1821–25	19,140	8,100	27,240	10,100	2.70	116
1826–30	20,010	8,787	28,797	10,300	2.80	120
1831–35	22,910	11,205	34,115	10,600	3.22	139
1836–40	24,795	12,262	37,057	11,057	3.35	144
1841–45	26,825	13,719	40,544	11,662	3.48	150
1846–50	29,000	14,874	43,874	11,425	3.84	165

Note: Index shows the relative growth in output (tons per LI) from the base line of 1800–10.
Source: G. Franz, 'Landwirtschaft, 1800–1850', in H. Aubin and W. Zorn, eds, *Handbuch der deutschen Wirtschafts- und Sozialgeschichte*, vol. 2 (Stuttgart, 1976), p. 313.

cantly: the growth in rape seed and sugar beet cultivation was symptomatic of a stronger commercial approach to agriculture by the peasantry and a willingness to respond positively to market demands.

Second, new estimates of trends in industrial investment, specifically in the case of Baden, and total net capital formation in Prussia have revealed evidence of substantial growth in the post-Napoleonic period. Industrial enterprises in a number of states showed early signs of development, and the Prussian tariff of 1818, by treating pig-iron imports as a raw material, provided an important impulse for the long-term development of the iron and steel industry. Trade in Saxony increased noticeably throughout the 1820s and various industries in and around Berlin registered substantial growth during the 1830s and early 1840s. During the first half of the nineteenth century the highest annual growth rate in textile production, in particular of cotton and woollen goods, was registered in the period 1831–40. It is not surprising, in this context, that the changes in occupational structure in the western provinces of Prussia were just as extensive during the period 1816 to 1849 as in the later nineteenth century. Moreover, the traditional periodization of German economic development has been further undermined by a re-estimation of the available data on net domestic product. On this basis the overall performance of the economy during the 1840s, which has often been viewed as the starting point for Germany's industrial revolution, was weaker than predicted, with a significant increase in growth rates only occurring from the 1850s onwards. Industrialization, therefore, was not characterized by extensive discontinuities and economic development in Germany was essentially a cumulative long-term process with significant changes taking place in the pre-1840 period.

In terms of the overall structure of employment, agriculture retained its predominant role throughout this period. Although its relative position declined as a result of the disproportionate growth of employment opportunities in the secondary and tertiary sectors, it still accounted for 49.3 per cent of total employment in 1871. Indeed, because of the continued dependency on labour-intensive methods of production, approximately two million more individuals were now employed in the primary sector than had been the case in 1800. Although the 1850s and 1860s witnessed a substantial expansion in the output of capital goods industries (such as iron and steel production, coal-mining, and machine construction), textiles (including the leather and clothing industries) still remained the largest component in the secondary sector. Even in 1875 just over 37 per cent of the 'industrial' workforce in Germany was employed in textiles, in comparison with approximately 14 per cent in the second largest sector – metal production and manufacture. Moreover, until the mid-nineteenth century textile production, in particular cotton-spinning, led the way in terms of factory organization and management. Indeed, despite the significant changes that took place during this period in specific sectors of German industry, the general nature of industrial organization did not alter substantially. Certainly in the case of Prussia, employment levels in craft production increased two-fold between 1816 and 1861: the number of master craftsmen grew at a rate well above that of total population, but the number of registered journeymen rose on average

Illustration 4.1   Despite some mechanization of agriculture – represented here by a steam-driven threshing machine – the sector remained labour-intensive and by 1871 employed two million more workers than in 1800

by 3 per cent per annum. As a result the average enterprise size increased from 1.6 to 2.0 people. The introduction of freedom of trade in certain states may well have led to an initial fall in the overall number of craftsmen, but the expansion of many trades in the 1820s and 1830s gave rise to a growing concern over excess labour supply, the proliferation of unskilled and untrained workers, and the decline in income levels of master craftsmen. By the early 1840s only 407 of the 2,812 registered shoemakers in Berlin earned enough income to be liable to the *Gewerbesteuer* (trade tax), and the situation in Elberfeld and Barmen was considerably worse. But the continuing growth in the number of bakers, tailors, shoemakers, joiners and masons also reflected a long-term expansion of consumer demand which required skills that remained relatively unaffected by new techniques of production. Moreover, the construction industry in Prussia (providing employment for masons, painters, roofers, carpenters and stonemasons) underwent an even more remarkable process of expansion between 1816 and 1858, particularly in the period 1831 to 1846: there was an almost five-fold increase in the number of journeymen and a three-fold expansion in average enterprise size which reflected a significant degree of concentration within this sector as it responded to favourable economic conditions.

Unfortunately, there is little reliable information on German foreign trade prior to the creation of the customs union in 1834, but the available data reveal further evidence of a long-term growth process. Although the depression of the early 1820s can-

Illustration 4.2   Poor cobbler's family (from a drawing by Theodor Hosemann, 1845)

not be denied, as the decline in the merchant fleet both in Hamburg and Bremen reveals, the value of Saxony's imports and exports nevertheless grew by 8 per cent throughout that decade. Grain exports from Prussia, via the Baltic ports of Elbing, Lübeck, Rostock, Königsberg, Stettin and Stralsund, also expanded by approximately 21 per cent between 1825 and 1831. For those states within the *Zollverein* the value of imports and exports between 1837 and 1855 rose by 4.6 per cent and 4.5 per cent annually. The estimated export surplus increased from 37.6 million taler in 1834 to 65 million in 1845 and over 101 million by 1860. Shipping capacity increased four-fold between the end of the 1820s and 1850, at a time when German merchants were establishing themselves extensively in both North and South America, as well as in other parts of the world. Although Germany's foreign trade performance in the second half of the nineteenth century was even more impressive, the process of development before 1850 was nevertheless considerable.

This interpretation is reinforced by demographic evidence. Population growth in the second half of the eighteenth century was already substantial, but this continued to be the case during the early decades of the nineteenth century (Table 4.2). Between 1816 and 1864 high rates of population growth were registered in the eastern agricultural provinces of Prussia, including East and West Prussia, Pomerania and Brandenburg, slightly lower but significant growth rates in the developing industrial centres of Saxony, the Rhineland and Westphalia, and markedly lower rates in the southern states of Baden, Bavaria and Württemberg. Indeed many German territories recorded peak population growth rates during this period, which were not exceeded until the end of the nineteenth

Table 4.2   General rates of population growth (per annum): 1816–64, 1864–1910

Province/state	1816–64			1864–1910		
	Absolute increase (000s)	%	% p.a.	Absolute increase (000s)	%	% p.a.
East Prussia	875	98.75	2.05	303	17.20	0.37
West Prussia	682	119.43	2.48	451	35.99	0.78
Berlin	435	219.69	4.57	1,438	227.17	4.93
Brandenburg	898	82.68	1.72	2,109	106.30	2.31
Pomerania	755	110.54	2.30	279	19.40	0.42
Posen	704	85.85	1.78	576	37.79	0.82
Silesia	1,609	84.59	1.76	1,715	48.84	1.06
Saxony	848	70.84	1.47	1,044	51.05	1.10
Schleswig-Holstein	302	43.32	0.90	622	62.26	1.35
Hanover	316	19.62	0.40	1,016	52.75	1.14
Westphalia	601	56.37	1.17	2,458	147.45	3.20
Hesse-Nassau	430	44.88	0.93	833	60.01	1.30
Rhineland	1,462	76.54	1.59	3,749	111.09	2.41
Hohenzollern	10	18.18	0.37	6	9.23	0.20
Total (Prussia)	9,873	72.01	1.50	16,583	70.32	1.52
Bavaria	1,168	32.38	0.67	2,112	44.23	0.96
Saxony	1,143	95.72	1.99	2,470	105.69	2.29
Württemberg	337	23.88	0.49	689	39.41	0.85
Baden	436	43.33	0.90	711	49.65	1.07
Mecklenburg-Schwerin	245	79.54	1.65	87	16.32	0.35
Gross-Sachsen	87	45.07	0.93	137	48.92	1.06
Mecklenburg-Strelitz	27	37.50	0.78	7	7.07	0.15
Oldenburg	80	34.18	0.71	169	53.82	1.17
Braunschweig	67	29.64	0.61	201	68.60	1.49
Saxe-Meiningen	57	47.10	0.98	101	56.74	1.23
Saxe-Altenberg	46	47.91	0.99	74	52.11	1.13
Saxe-Coburg-Gotha	53	47.32	0.98	92	55.75	1.21
Anhalt	73	60.83	1.26	138	71.50	1.55
Schwarzburg-Sonderhausen	21	46.66	0.97	24	36.36	0.79
Schwarzburg-Rudolstadt	20	37.03	0.77	27	36.48	0.79
Waldeck	7	13.46	0.28	3	5.08	0.11
Lippe	30	37.03	0.77	40	36.03	0.78
Elsass-Lothringen	366	30.04	0.62	290	18.30	0.39
Hesse	255	45.37	0.94	465	56.91	1.23
Total (excl. the three Hansa towns)	14,559	58.62	1.22	25,534	64.82	1.40

Source: Compiled from official sources.

century. Debate continues over the causal factors behind this trend, and the relative contribution of changes in nuptiality, fertility or age-specific mortality to long-run population growth. In most German states crude birth rates remained relatively high and easily exceeded contemporary mortality levels, except during the 1816–17 famine and the major cholera epidemics of 1831–2, 1848–50 and 1852–5, and the further fall in the death rate from the mid-nineteenth century has been attributed to a decline in the variability of mortality. However, health conditions in many cities were far less favourable than in rural areas and until the 1880s mortality was positively correlated with city size. In the five largest cities of Prussia (Berlin, Breslau, Cologne, Magdeburg and Königsberg) crude mortality rates rose from the early nineteenth century onwards. Urban population growth therefore depended to a large degree on the in-migration of craftsmen and domestic servants, who frequently came from surrounding rural areas or adjacent towns. Infant mortality remained a major component of total mortality, particularly in the south German states of Bavaria and Württemberg, and it continued to rise in most parts of Germany until the 1870s. To some extent, this may have been the result of a failure to breastfeed infants at a time when poverty and environmental factors heightened the risks associated with artificial feeding. But child mortality, at least in Prussia, had certainly fallen by the 1860s, perhaps as a result of the earlier introduction of smallpox inoculation or the reduced virulence of specific childhood diseases. The gains in life expectancy for older age groups, on the other hand, were much more limited.

It is important to note, however, that overall population density rose from 45.9 inhabitants per square kilometre in 1816 to 75.9 by 1871. Indeed such was the extent of population growth in the early nineteenth century that a number of states, including Baden, Bavaria and Württemberg, imposed legal restrictions on marriage, while Doctor Weinhold from Halle advocated infibulation as a means of restricting procreation. The legislation in Bavaria was not repealed until 1862–8, although its precise impact in terms of contemporary trends in illegitimate fertility is difficult to substantiate. A more immediate reaction to the problems created by high rates of population growth was the increase in emigration (Table 4.3). In the first wave of mass migration between 1845 and 1858, approximately 1.3 million individuals left Germany to seek a better life overseas and between 1864 and 1873 a further million followed a similar path. Particularly during the 1830s and 1840s, overseas migration was a direct result of relative overpopulation, as measured in terms of employment opportunities, as well as rising prices and harvest failure.

III Regional variations in development

The inherent unevenness of German economic development has been highlighted by recent research. By the late eighteenth century iron and steel production was concentrated on both sides of the Rhine, in the Siegerland and Hesse, to the west in the Eiffel, in Silesia, as well as in a few other regional centres. Industrial production was particularly concentrated in Berlin, Saxony, Silesia and the Ruhr. The Grand Duchy of Berg

Table 4.3 German overseas emigration, 1816–1934

Period	Emigrants (000s)	Immigrants to USA (000s)	%	Annual average emigration rate[a]
1816–19	25.0			2.7
1820–24	9.8	1.9	19.4	1.0
1825–29	12.7	3.8	29.9	1.2
1830–34	51.1	39.3	76.9	2.2
1835–39	94.0	85.5	91.0	2.6
1840–44	110.6	100.5	90.9	2.4
1845–49	308.2	284.9	92.4	4.5
1850–54	728.3	654.3	89.8	9.0
1855–59	372.0	321.8	86.5	4.3
1860–64	225.9	204.1	90.4	2.5
1865–69	542.7	519.6	95.7	3.6
1870–74	484.6	450.5	93.0	2.3
1875–79	143.3	120.0	83.7	0.7
1880–84	864.3	797.9	92.3	3.8
1885–89	498.2	452.6	90.9	2.1
1890–94	462.2	428.8	92.8	1.8
1895–99	142.4	120.2	84.4	0.5
1900–04	140.8	128.6	91.3	0.5
1905–09	135.7	123.5	91.0	0.4
1910–14	104.3	84.1	80.6	0.3
1915–19	4.1	1.0	24.4	0.0
1920–24	242.3	150.4	62.1	0.8
1925–29	295.3	230.1	77.8	0.9
1930–34	88.1	62.1	70.6	0.3

Note: [a]Based on the population of the areas affected by emigration.
Source: W. Köllmann and P. Marschalck, *German Emigration to the United States. Perspectives in American History*, vol. 7 (1974), p. 518; F. Burgdörfer, 'Die Wanderungen über die deutschen Reichsgrenzen im letzten Jahrhundert', *Allgemeines Statistisches Archiv*, 20 (1930), p. 189 *et seq.*; W. Mönckmeier, *Die deutsche überseeische Auswanderung* (1912), p. 14.

was one of the most advanced areas on the continent and individual towns, such as Krefeld, had become important manufacturing and trading centres well before the end of the eighteenth century. On the other hand, the increasing emphasis on export-orientated grain monoculture in the eastern provinces of Prussia hindered economic diversification as the profitability of rye exports reinforced the region's relative dependency on primary sector production. At the same time there was a greater distribution of craftsmen (*Handwerker*) in the south than in the north, which, in turn, recorded a better level of provision than the east. Particularly in the case of Prussia there is clear evidence of significant regional divergence by the early nineteenth century between the eastern and western provinces, in terms of estimated per capita income, selective income proxies, and relative levels of urbanization.

The extent to which economic development in the period between 1815 and 1871 modified or aggravated the degree of pre-industrial regional economic divergence is still a subject of considerable debate and the evidence is not unambiguous. By and large, however, this period witnessed an accentuation of regional divergence. The increasingly regional concentration of industrial production in west, southwest, northwest and central Germany was accompanied by a greater emphasis on agricultural employment in other areas. This was the case in the eastern provinces of Prussia, as well as in the southern states of Baden, Bavaria and Württemberg, which became more agricultural relative to the national average. Furthermore, even within the primary sector, there is evidence of increasing regional divergence during this period – a trend that was reinforced by the selective impact of peasant emancipation legislation and reform 'from above'. The eastern provinces of Prussia (East and West Prussia, as well as Pomerania), for example, were increasingly characterized by extensive cereal production, primarily for export, and the growing emphasis on grain monoculture was accompanied by a continuing reliance on traditional cultivation methods. By contrast, there was a perceptible shift towards intensive cultivation in the western regions of Germany, with an emphasis on commercial crops and the dairy–livestock sector. In those regions of Germany where domestic textile production, particularly linen manufacture, had developed in response to growing export opportunities, flax cultivation had become widespread, whereas other agricultural areas, such as the Magdeburger Börde, had concentrated on sugar beet production as a result of official tax incentives. Regional specialization was also increasingly evident in relation to viticulture and livestock–dairy farming, although it would be false to overstate the extent of such trends during this period. Moreover, because of the ability of established landed élites to resist institutional change, agrarian reforms affected more backward regions with a noticeable time lag or not at all, thereby reinforcing existing regional differentials.

Urbanization also affected the trend towards increased regional divergence: it spread out from Saxony and Berlin at the start of the nineteenth century to the industrializing areas of the Rhineland, Westphalia and Silesia by the 1850s. Although there was only a marginal increase in the level of urbanization in Prussia between 1816 and 1871 (from 27.9 to 32.5 per cent of total population), the average size of cities in the west was already noticeably greater than in the east, and whereas urbanization levels rose slightly in the western provinces before 1840, they actually fell in the East. Moreover, there was a clear difference in the components of urban growth: in the west urban centres developed through a combination of in-migration and natural increase; eastern towns remained almost solely dependent on in-migration. In general, both age at marriage and the proportion remaining single were higher in urban areas, but fertility was often lower than in rural areas. However, during the final period of increasing urban mortality levels during the 1860s and 1870s, it was primarily cities in eastern Germany, such as Elbing, Frankfurt (Oder), Stralsund and Görlitz, that registered a disproportionate rise in both male and female mortality. By contrast, during the 1850s some of the developing industrial cities in the Ruhr, such as Mönchen-Gladbach, had a higher migration intensity (in terms of in-, and out-migration per 1,000 inhabitants) as Berlin, and the population of Essen expanded almost exponentially from just over

4,000 in 1811 to over 180,000 by the end of the century as a result of the development of the Krupp works in the town. It is instructive to note, however, that even in 1871 almost 83 per cent of the population of the German Confederation still lived in communities with less than 10,000 inhabitants.

Further evidence of trends in regional differentials can be obtained from demographic data. Within Prussia, for example, the crude death rate throughout this period was consistently higher in the eastern provinces than in the west. Infant deaths remained a major component of total mortality throughout this period: the infant mortality rate rose perceptibly during the central decades of the nineteenth century and remained disproportionately high in the southern states of Bavaria and Württemberg, as well as in the eastern provinces of Prussia. The high variance in the infant mortality rate became even more accentuated towards the end of the nineteenth century and was still visible, although to a lesser extent, in the age group 1–15. A significant rise in the number of illegitimate births in the south, particularly in Bavaria (Table 4.4), reinforced this trend, given the higher mortality rates of illegitimate offspring. Regional differences, however, were not so prominent in relation to adult death rates as life table evidence confirms. At a disease-specific level, tuberculosis mortality also displayed a pronounced east–west gradient, reflecting, in all probability, differential nutritional levels and labour intensity. Equally in terms of fertility-related indices, regional differentials remained clearly visible in the nineteenth century, both in terms of the birth rate and the practice of family limitation.

Table 4.4   Illegitimate births in Bavaria (per 100 live births), 1835–60 to 1872

Period	Illegitimacy rate
1835–60	21.1
1860–68	22.2
1868–69	17.9
1869–70	16.4
1871	15.2
1872	14.4

Source: Die Bewegung der Bevölkerung des Königreichs Bayern im Jahre 1877, *Zeitschrift des kgl. Bayerischen Statistischen Bureaus*, Jahrgang 11 (Munich, 1879), p. 259.

IV The role of the state

It is generally accepted that the state was heavily involved in the industrialization process in Germany, whether in responding to the problems generated by relative backwardness and market imperfections, or in clearing away many of the obstacles hindering economic development. Indeed it is often argued that the state played a critical role in providing the preconditions for successful industrialization, specifically through the abolition of the feudal agrarian regime, the dismantling of guild controls and the introduction of more liberal trade policies, as well as through the provision of an appropriate legal framework for capitalist production. Even if political reform was strenuously avoided, the state effectively promoted economic development through financial and administrative reforms. Taxation policy, for example, showed a clear bias in favour of industrial interests and capital formation and direct government support was important in the creation of social overhead capital, particularly in the case of railway construction. The state, however, also played a more selective interventionist role by providing direct subsidies to individual sectors, such as sugar beet production, steam-engine construction or specific branches of the textile industry. In Upper Silesia, for example, the retention of the *Direktionsprinzip* until 1864 contributed to the efficiency of the mining and metallurgical industries, where expansion to a large degree was state-induced. Indeed the state was often directly involved in production. In Prussia, the *Seehandlung* (Overseas Trading Corporation), originally created as a state salt monopoly in 1772, had become a major economic force by the early 1820s, running its own enterprises (such as flour and paper mills, chemical works, and river steamers) and providing capital investment to the private sector. Finally, state support for education, it has been argued, was probably the most important contribution to industrial development, with tangible benefits in terms of technology transfer, technical training and the inculcation of appropriate attitudes within the German working class as a whole. Even during the 1860s and early 1870s, when more liberal policies tended to prevail, state intervention in the economy remained durably persistent. Many of the leading entrepreneurs of the early nineteenth century, such as Harkort and Mevissen, had advocated government action to correct the abuses of industrialization, and the idea of state intervention, whether in the form of subsidies, monopoly grants, tariff concessions or special treatment of key industries, was always congenial.

More recently, however, the view that German industrialization was ultimately achieved with the support of state power has been challenged. It has been argued that state priorities in terms of economic policy were often inappropriate. The exercise of state power, by increased regulation, might have contributed to economic efficiency at the margin, but the lifting of traditional restrictions on trade was not a prerequisite for industrial expansion. Prussia had achieved this objective as early as 1807–11, but the absence of trade liberalization in Saxony until 1861 did not adversely affect its position as one of the most dynamic areas of economic growth during this period. The trade policy (*Gewerbepolitik*) of some of the south German states, such as Baden and Bavaria, attempted to maintain small-scale handicraft production based on a traditional concessionary system, although such policies militated against large-scale industrialization. In the case of Württemberg such a policy contributed to a general opposition to factories in the period before 1848 and in Schleswig-Holstein trade policy was concerned primarily with the maintenance of existing privileges, rather than the promotion of economic development. The efficiency of the administrative apparatus in coordinating the separate economic functions of the state has also been questioned, as well as the net contribution of government intervention in individual sectors. Even in relation to the official commitment to improved educational provision, it has been argued that the needs of industry were often neglected; the curriculum of the elementary schools (*Volksschulen*) was inadequate; trade schools remained fee-paying; and secondary education, particularly in Prussia, was characterized by a continuing conflict between classicism and modernism and limited social mobility. It is not surprising, therefore, that certain historians view the role of the state in promoting industrialization as having been circumscribed, with economic growth during this period primarily a function of growing intra-German and international competition, indigenous resource endowment, the expansion of foreign trade and the interplay of market forces.

V   Redefining the state

It is commonly agreed that the state, building on cameralist and mercantilist principles, showed a high level of interest in economic affairs between the late eighteenth century and 1871. However, the persistence of a national consensus in German economic history and the tendency to view Prussia as the paradigm of the modern German state has prevented a rigorous exploration of its role. By 1815 the complex territorial configuration of the Holy Roman Empire of the German nation had been substantially transformed, but there were still 39 federal states, ranging from Prussia with over eight million inhabitants, to minor principalities, such as Liechtenstein (7,000 inhabitants), and the free cities of Bremen, Frankfurt am Main, Hamburg and Lübeck (Table 4.5). With few exceptions, there was general support within Germany for the federal idea, which remained dominant both in the constitution of 1848–9, at the foundation of the Norddeutsche Bund in 1867, and in the Bismarckian constitution of 1871. Unfortunately there are very few modern studies of the economic history of individual German states for the period between 1815 and 1871, and even fewer historians have attempted to examine aspects of economic policy in a comparative context. In

Table 4.5   The German federal states in 1816

State	Population	Area (in km²)	Population (per km²)	%
A Empire and Kingdoms				
1 Austria[1]	9,482,227	195,228.44	48.6	31.15
2 Prussia[2]	8,042,562	185,460.25	43.4	29.59
3 Bavaria[3]	3,560,000	76,395.75	46.4	12.19
4 Hanover[4]	1,328,351	38,568.43	34.4	6.15
5 Württemberg	1,410,327	19,506.66	72.3	3.11
6 Saxony	1,192,789	14,958.15	79.7	2.39
B Grand duchies and duchies				
7 Baden	1,005,899	15,307.23	65.7	2.44
8 Mecklenburg-Schwerin	308,166	13,260.65	23.2	2.12

9 Holstein-Lauenburg[5]	360,000	9,580.44	37.6	1.53
10 Hesse-Kassel[4]	567,868	9,567.78	59.4	1.53
11 Hesse-Darmstadt	587,995	8,414.82	69.9	1.34
12 Oldenburg	221,399	6,339.06	34.9	1.01
13 Nassau[4]	301,907	4,765.44	63.4	0.76
14 Braunschweig	225,273	3,729.21	60.4	0.60
15 Saxe-Weimar[6]	193,869	3,640.57	53.3	0.58
16 Mecklenburg-Strelitz	71,764	2,724.92	26.3	0.43
17 Luxemburg[7]	154,000	2,587.82	59.5	0.41
18 Saxe-Meiningen[6]	115,000	3,549.28	45.1	0.41
19 Saxe-Gotha[6,8]		1,422.75		
20 Saxe-Coburg[9]	111,989	586.39	55.7	0.32
21 Saxe-Altenburg[6]	95,855	1,330.80	72.0	0.21
22 Anhalt-Dessau[10]	52,947	894.17	59.2	0.14
23 Anhalt-Bernburg[10]	37,046	827.55	44.8	0.13
24 Anhalt-Köthen[10]	32,454	662.92	49.0	0.11
C Principalities				
25 Waldeck-Pyrmont	52,557	1,202.51	43.7	0.19
26 Lippe-Detmold	78,900	1,129.83	69.8	0.18
27 Hohenzollern -Hechingen[11]	50,060	1,148.00	43.6	0.18
28 -Sigmaringen[11]				
29 Schwarzburg -Rudolstadt[6]	53,937	958.04	56.3	0.15
30 -Sondershausen[6]	45,125	852.33	52.9	0.14
31 Reuss Junior Line[6]	69,333	834.16	83.1	0.13
32 Schaumburg-Lippe	24,000	443.23	54.2	0.07
33 Reuss Senior Line[6]	30,293	345.78	87.6	0.06
34 Hessen-Homburg[4]	23,000	262.09	87.8	0.04
35 Liechstenstein[7]	7,000	159.67	43.8	0.03
D Free Cities				
36 Lübeck	36,000	364.50	100.4	0.06
37 Hamburg	146,109	351.83	415.3	0.06
38 Bremen	50,139	263.19	190.5	0.04
39 Frankfurt am Main	47,850	100.76	474.9	0.02
Total	30,174,590	626,725.40	48.1	100.0

[1] Only those areas belonging to the Deutsche Bund.
[2] Excluding the provinces of West and East Prussia, and Posen, which did not belong to the Deutsche Bund.
[3] Including the Pfalz which ceased to belong to Bavaria after 1920–45.
[4] Annexed by Prussia in 1866.
[5] Acquired by Prussia in 1866.
[6] Merged with Thuringia in 1920.
[7] Independent since 1866 and the dissolution of the Deutsche Bund.
[8] Acquired by Coburg in 1826 following the inheritance apportionment contract of Hildburghausen.
[9] Joined with Bavaria in 1920.
[10] After the demise of the Köthen line (1847) and the Bernburg line (1863), the dukedoms were united with Anhalt.
[11] Joined to Prussia in 1849.
Source: Kiesewetter, H., Industrielle Revolution in Deutschland 1815–1914 (Frankfurt am Main, 1989) pp. 308–9.

order to explore further the role of the state in German economic development during this period, three points need to be emphasized.

First, the continuing fragmentation of political power directly affected the role of the state. Many of the states that emerged from the Napoleonic period were both 'modern', in that a central authority exerted control throughout the entire kingdom, and economically important. Bavaria, for example, with a total population of 4.5 million by 1849 was the third largest state in the German Confederation after Austria and Prussia. Even in 1816 five German states, in addition to Prussia, already had a total population in excess of one million (Baden 1.3; Bavaria 3.5; Hanover 1.3; Saxony 1.7; Württemberg 1.4). Given that approximately 60 per cent of Germany's population experienced a change in ruler during the Napoleonic period, it is not surprising that many of the states, such as Hesse-Darmstadt and Hanover, pursued a 'narrow particularism' in the period after 1815. Bavaria and Württemberg, for example, constantly emphasized their uniqueness and school books were explicitly redesigned to create a separate sense of 'national' identity. Although a number of banks, such as the Badische Bank in Mannheim or the Sächsische Bank in Dresden, were founded with outside capital participation, most state banks during the first half of the nineteenth century had a conservative policy in terms of capital provision and supply. They had a particular responsibility to promote local infrastructural improvements or to cater for 'national' needs, as in the case of Saxony's Landrentenbank which was the first state credit agency founded in Germany in 1832. Although capital supply frequently extended over state boundaries, the majority of firms operated within a narrowly defined local institutional framework. This was the case in Saxony and the Rhineland-Palatinate, where industrial enterprises were almost entirely supported by indigenous capital. Indeed, even in terms of money supply, policy differences continued to exist. Most states permitted the use of a wide variety of currencies (including foreign banknotes), but Württemberg, for example, only issued silver coins during this period.

Individual states generally fought for their own narrow interests and often pursued different approaches to specific issues, such as the development of the railway network, the introduction of freedom of trade, tariff policy or the maintenance of handicraft-based production. Tax policy is an instructive example, in this context, as it remained the responsibility of the federal states throughout the nineteenth century and beyond. Tax reforms were widely implemented in the post-Napoleonic period, but individual states frequently adopted a different approach which reflected local needs and divergent traditions. Baden, as a result of its substantial territorial expansion by 1815, was faced by a multiplicity of tax regimes and opted for a relatively simple tax system based on land values that could be applied without additional administrative costs. On the other hand, Württemberg consolidated its existing land tax based on net yield, and Bavaria retained an assessment system based on gross production until 1855. Indirect taxes continued to provide a significant proportion of government revenue in most states, but the actual balance between direct and indirect taxation varied considerably.

Prussia failed to develop a uniform tax system: urban communities remained subject to indirect taxation, whereas direct taxes were levied in rural areas.

At the same time, there were noticeable differences in the overall distribution of the tax burden. In the case of Baden the more flexible system of tax liability assessment introduced in 1848, together with the retention of an unmodified trade or occupation tax (*Gewerbesteuer*) between 1815 and 1854, encouraged increased capital investment in the secondary sector throughout the first half of the nineteenth century. Württemberg's system of taxation also promoted economic growth by providing explicit benefits for rural manufacturing, housing construction and recipients of high incomes, as well as encouraging the replacement of labour by machinery. As a result, the specific configuration of individual tax regimes in the federal states affected a range of economic variables in a differentiated manner, including the relative balance between consumption and investment, capital accumulation, technological change, and the spatial location of manufacturing production.

In a number of policy areas, including the gradual introduction of protective employment legislation or the establishment of local craftsmen's associations, federal states often followed a common strategy. For example, there were clear similarities in the legislation adopted by Prussia in 1836 and by Bavaria in 1842 relating to the establishment of local associations of craftsmen and merchants. This reflected not only the impact of general processes of change and increasing economic integration, but also an element of competitive rivalry between the individual states and a recognition of the need to emulate policy initiatives developed in other parts of Germany. But in most other areas of policy-making, as the example of taxation policy indicates, the federal states maintained a particularist approach. In general, the overall timing, direction and extent of government intervention varied significantly and this, in turn, affected the process of economic development and industrialization in the separate federal states.

Second, the existence of numerous federal states with well-defined provincial, administrative structures facilitated both the emergence of interest groups and their articulation of economic demands. In large nation states, as Olson has demonstrated, substantial resources are frequently required to influence government policy, whereas interest groups operating within the federal state framework of nineteenth-century Germany would have had lower operational costs and greater organizational powers for collective action. On the one hand, the initiative to develop corporate industrial structures had frequently been taken by the state, whether in Prussia or Bavaria (see above), although the establishment of extended merchant corporations in the eastern ports of Danzig, Memel, Stettin and Tilsit in the 1820s followed the Danish model based on the *Kammerkollegium* (Revenue Board) which had been adopted in Altona in 1738. Corporate organizations played an increasingly active role at the federal level in registering specific demands and in exercising lobbyist functions, whether over the ruinous effect of increased taxes on small traders in Buxtehude, or the promotion of the south German cotton industry. On the other hand, the continued fragmentation of state power after 1815 allowed an effective prioritization of local issues in the federal states. In many cases a narrow policy of self-interest characterized the attitudes of both town and country members of state parliaments, but the federal structure of Germany after 1815 allowed a more effective articulation of lobbyist interests than might otherwise have been the case within the framework of a larger nation state. It also contributed, as was the case in Baden, to a provincial atmosphere that reinforced the impression of a closer proximity between the rulers and the ruled.

As a result, economic policy at the level of the federal state often reflected local needs. In Saxony, for example, the political influence of business and industry increased perceptibly after 1830 and economic development was promoted by the state through a range of administrative and financial reforms. Industrialists and businessmen were particularly active in advocating tariff protection, specifically for the textile industry, and the state helped to reshape the institutions of an industrializing society by responding effectively to their demands. The state provided considerable support for the development of the railway network and other infrastructural improvements: it subsidized the expansion of the machine-construction industry, and paid particular attention to the provision of educational and training facilities. From a modern perspective it is clear that economic policy in Saxony during this period suffered from considerable weaknesses: policy initiatives were often selective and inconsistent, and the state authorities failed to develop a long-term concept for financing industrial enterprises. Nevertheless, the localized framework of economic policy-making, within a political context that allowed entrepreneurs and industrialists considerable influence, enabled the state to adopt a more supportive approach to contemporary development issues.

On the other hand, the fragmentation of political power within a federal structure and the existence within individual states of a strong tradition of provincial representation also allowed traditional élites in relatively backward regions to maintain their position by blocking necessary reforms and by maintaining unresponsive economic institutions. This was particularly the case in relation to the agrarian reforms of the early nineteenth century. Considerable emphasis used to be given to the capacity-widening effects of these structural reforms 'from above', on the basis that they facilitated more efficient arable cultivation as well as the partition and enclosure of common lands. In contrast to eighteenth-century reforms, they made possible, in theory, the development of a free rural population, owning landed property. However, longer-term processes of structural change were evident in the German countryside well before the end of the eighteenth century and the exact nature of agrarian reform legislation differed in many respects in individual German states. In most cases peasant emancipation was only achieved as a result of extensive compromises with the local aristocracy and estate-holders, whose preferential treatment directly affected the level of compensation payments and the extent of land redistribution. Traditionally a clear distinction existed between western areas of Germany, characterized by peasant cultivation and hereditary tenure (*Grundherrschaft*) and the eastern territories dominated by extensive seigneurial estates with a dependent and largely servile peasantry

(*Gutsherrschaft*). To a large extent, the specific impact of the reform legislation reflected this distinction, as well as the relative power of the provincial nobility and regional political élites. Within Prussia reform legislation reinforced the role of the Junker estate owners and large-scale peasant cultivators in the east, with their increasing dependency on an export-orientated grain monoculture, whereas land compensation in many western territories benefited a wider spectrum of peasants and further encouraged agricultural diversification. Whereas serfdom was finally abolished in Mecklenburg in 1820, the continued influence of the landed aristocracy in Baden meant that feudal rights were only terminated when revolution was imminent in 1848. Agrarian reforms, therefore, only affected more backward regions, such as eastern and southern Germany, with a noticeable time-lag, or not at all. The ability of traditional élites to resist structural change, in such cases, only served to reinforce existing regional differentials.

Third, in assessing the nature and impact of economic policy during the first half of the nineteenth century it is always important to establish how state power was constituted. Particularly at the federal level, state economic policy was often determined by the bureaucracy (for a fuller discussion, see Chapter 2, above). The expansion of the bureaucratic apparatus was a precondition for the growth of state power and most German states witnessed a significant increase in administrative personnel in the period under consideration. In Prussia, for example, the number of civil servants (including both central and local officials) rose annually by 1.4 per cent between 1846 and 1880, in contrast to an annual rise of 0.8 per cent in total population. Primarily because of the limited electoral franchise throughout Germany, bureaucrats increasingly determined state policy. In Baden, for example, a group of officials sharing a common educational and social background assumed national leadership; in Prussia civil servants felt superior to the emerging entrepreneurial class; and in Bavaria there were growing complaints against what was perceived in some quarters as civil service absolutism. Moreover, the development of an extensive state administrative apparatus preceded the creation of modern representative bodies which, in turn, tended to be dominated by civil servants. They constituted approximately 50 per cent of the federal parliament (*Landtag*) in Baden in the early nineteenth century and almost 64 per cent of the deputies in the North German parliament in 1867.

In this context, the state bureaucracy was uniquely placed to influence economic policy. In certain cases its contribution was significant. In Saxony, for example, liberal-minded bureaucrats helped to reshape the institutions of an industrializing society; civil servants in Baden during the 1830s were committed to liberal objectives, such as free trade, transport improvements and wider educational facilities; and state officials in Prussia also pursued selective policies conducive to industrial development. On the other hand, the continuing recruitment of higher civil servants in northern Germany from the landed aristocracy undoubtedly encouraged a more conservative approach to contemporary issues, just as the fusing of the old social order with the new service hierarchy in the form of the Prussian *Landrat* (or rural administrative officer) in the eastern provinces had a negative impact on government policy-making.

VI The role of the banks

It is traditionally accepted that Germany, as a result of its relative backwardness, depended on banks far more than other Western economies (such as Britain) for both investible funds and entrepreneurial initiative. In the first half of the nineteenth century the development of an appropriate banking infrastructure was constrained by insufficient demand and an absence of commercial concentration. Although there were a number of prominent private banking houses, such as the Rothschilds and Bethmanns in Frankfurt am Main, and Bleichröder and Mendelsohn in Berlin, they were primarily concerned with government loans and state bonds. In Württemberg, for example, the main function of the Hofbank (founded in 1817) was to meet the capital requirements of the crown and private banking firms, such as the Gebrüder Benedict and Stahl und Federer, restricted their activities to mortgage lending or exchange transactions. There were very few stock exchanges: in Frankfurt am Main, as elsewhere, activities were confined to dealing in government securities and the stock exchange in Berlin was not geared to large-scale industrial transactions. Furthermore, the activity of savings banks (except in Bremen, Hamburg and Saxony) remained restricted. Initial attempts to develop a network of savings banks (*Sparkassen*) were initiated in Bavaria (1816) and Württemberg (1822), primarily as a means of enabling domestic servants and day labourers to achieve a limited degree of economic independence. However, by the mid-1830s there were only 281 savings banks throughout Germany and it was only after Prussian legislation in 1838 that their number increased significantly. It was not until the foundation of the first credit banks, such as the Schaafhausen Bankverein (1848) and the Diskonto-Gesellschaft (1851) that an effective basis was laid for the direct promotion of industrial investment and development.

In complete contrast with this situation, historians have argued that the *Kreditbanken* (or universal banks), particularly from the 1850s onwards, helped to finance risky investments, facilitated mergers and the formation of cartels, and contributed to the stabilization of the business cycle. By the mid-1860s there is evidence of increased capital mobility: Berlin banks provided loans to Baden and 'national' bank consortia were formed in individual states to negotiate government loans. The Bank für Handel und Industrie in Darmstadt (founded in 1853), in this context, served as a proto-type: it was created as a joint-stock enterprise, provided current account facilities to several industrial firms and was involved from the outset in small-scale industrial promotion. Developments in the banking infrastructure, therefore, helped to remove traditional barriers that had restricted the flow of capital to German manufacturers. Joint-stock banks, in particular, played a major role in supporting the expansion of heavy industry and railway construction at a time when capital investment in the German textile industry also rose significantly.

However, capital supply does not appear to have been a major problem in the first half of the nineteenth century: capital costs were generally low; interest rates continued to fall, partly as a result of the liquidation of state debts; and entrepreneurs were able to employ a variety of strategies to limit short-term capital requirements. Even if capital markets remained imperfect and long-term credit was seldom available, the cost of technical innovation, particularly in agriculture, was not high during this period. Although the capital market, particularly in Prussia, had a pronounced regional character, the number of banks in Cologne with links to industrial enterprises was already considerable by 1830. This was specifically the case in relation to Rhenish textile firms, although extensive connections with enterprises operating in the Ruhr only became evident after 1850. Even before the end of the eighteenth century, Cologne merchants had financed the development of the mining industry in the Siegerland, and prior to the crisis of 1848 the Schaaffhausen Bank had acted as the mainstay of at least 170 factory enterprises with approximately 40,000 workers. Indeed, even in relation to the later nineteenth century there are continuing doubts concerning the precise role of the *Kreditbanken* in terms of their sectoral concentration on heavy industry and the specific nature of bank–industry relations. Although the Cologne banks played an important role in the formation of joint-stock companies in the Ruhr's iron and steel industry from the early 1850s onwards, their range of activity had a limited geographical radius and new banking initiatives were inevitably pro-cyclical. The marked involvement of the *Kreditbanken* in heavy industry was counterbalanced by a more limited, or even minimal, role in the development of the chemical, machine construction and electrical engineering industries. Nor is it possible to construct a uniform model of bank–industry relations: existing micro-level studies of specific enterprises confirm the continued predominance of self-financing and the important role of the credit banks in promoting industrial concentration in the late nineteenth century effectively weakened the influence of any one bank on the business activity of individual industrial enterprises. To this extent, even in the late nineteenth century, the banking system may well have played a 'permissive' rather than a 'causative' role in German industrial development and it is important not to overestimate the role of the banks in the first phase of German industrialization.

VII The *Zollverein*

As an example of enlightened state policy, the foundation of the *Zollverein* in 1834 is frequently accorded a major role in German economic development. Friedrich List even argued that the *Zollverein* and the railway system were 'Siamese twins', contributing to Germany's emergence as the focal point for intra-European trade. In the late eighteenth century there were approximately 1,800 customs frontiers in Germany and it was only between 1807 and 1812 that the three southern states of Bavaria, Württemberg and Baden finally eliminated their internal customs dues. According to Henderson, Germany's industrial development was 'undoubtedly . . . stimulated' by the creation of the *Zollverein*, as the persistence of numerous customs barriers had only served to cripple trade and encourage smuggling. On this basis, the development of the customs union demolished internal trade barriers; intensified inner-German economic links; contributed to the formation of a 'national' market and a unified commercial law; provided supportive tariff protection for infant industries (particularly following the tariff of 1844); facilitated a major improvement in internal communications as a function of railway construction; and fostered increased optimism throughout the whole of Germany. The creation of the *Zollverein*, therefore, represented a significant step forward. It consolidated the achievements of the Prussian customs law of May 1818, stimulated Germany's industrial revolution, and provided substantial benefits for participating states, such as Baden, Bavaria and Saxony.

More recently, however, the role of the *Zollverein* as a key factor in German development has been subject to reappraisal. As Dumke has shown, both the immediate and longer-term welfare gains of the *Zollverein* were relatively small. Although there was an improvement in the terms of trade for the south German states through their membership of the customs union, it only accounted for a 1.5 per cent increase in national income. In the case of the three Hesse states (Kurhessen, Hesse-Darmstadt, and Nassau), *Zollverein* membership did generate some significant benefits, particularly in terms of increased competition, but it failed to promote rapid industrialization and could not prevent the serious socio-economic dislocations of the 1840s. As far as most other states are concerned, poor data quality for assessing contemporary trade flows continues to preclude a more rigorous analysis of this issue, although the economic impact of membership was almost certainly highly differentiated, depending on the overall structure of 'national' economies, as well as the extent and sectoral configuration of industrial production. Moreover, the motives behind the establishment of the *Zollverein* were primarily fiscal and not economic, as individual states sought simultaneously to maximize revenue gains from a more efficient customs system and to minimize the possibility of budgetary control by nascent parliamentary institutions. Most German states in the early nineteenth century were too small to establish an independent border tax system as an efficient source of government revenue, but this situation was radically transformed through the creation of the customs union. Bavaria's customs receipts, for example, virtually doubled in 1834 as a result of its membership of the customs union. At the same time, the creation of the *Zollverein* post-dated significant developments in the German economy (see above): the long-term growth in German trade can be traced back to the 1820s and inner-German trade links were already well established before 1834. Macroeconomic factors, therefore, including rising British demand for German primary produce and increased aggregate demand within Germany itself as a result of high rates of population growth, may have played a more critical role than the *Zollverein* in stimulating industrial development in the first half of the nineteenth century. Indeed, the economic unification of Germany had still not been achieved by 1871: it was not until 1881 and 1888 respectively that the Empire's two premier ports, the city states of Hamburg and Bremen, finally became members of the customs union.

VIII Railway development

Traditionally, the development of a railway network has been seen as a factor that critically shaped German industrialization. In particular, from the 1840s to the late 1860s the increased demand generated by railway construction had a very positive effect (via backward linkages) on heavy industry, specifically in relation to iron and steel production and coal-mining, constituting what is often known as a leading sector complex in the German economy. Indeed, proponents of such a view have been able to mobilize a substantial amount of evidence. During this period railway construction accounted for approximately one-third of net investment and therefore directly affected the development of the business cycle; it generated an unprecedented increase in demand from heavy industry; and encouraged significant progress in terms of import substitution. For example, Germany was virtually self-sufficient as far as locomotive construction was concerned by the late 1840s. The expansion of the railway network undoubtedly contributed to a substantial reduction in transport costs; it facilitated a greater degree of market integration and industrial concentration within Germany; improved the speed and regularity of communications; extended the area of supply for perishable goods; and narrowed the gap between producers and consumers. Indeed, in line with the Gerschenkronian paradigm, railway development was also directly assisted by the state. By guaranteeing a minimum rate of return on private investment in individual railway lines, the federal states were able to boost construction and simultaneously encourage the development of the capital market. Indeed, in Bavaria the first railway line was built with state funds in 1836 and the Baden authorities right from the start of railway development in 1838 were committed to the construction of a 'national' network. Direct state investment in such cases therefore represented an enforced transfer of resources via taxation in a manner that would have promoted economic growth.

Certainly within the period 1852 to 1874 railway construction was probably the most important sector in the German economy, particularly in terms of relative growth rates (estimated at 13.6 per cent per annum), intersectoral linkages, and its contribution to unbalanced growth. However, even in this case recent research has contributed to a process of reappraisal. Within the provinces of Prussia price data for rye reveal an extensive degree of market integration by the early 1820s, and little evidence of any further improvements before 1865. From a spatial perspective, the long-term process of concentration of economic activity preceded the onset of railway construction, and urban growth was not dependent on railway development. At best, it would appear to be the case that the most important pre-railway cities only obtained short-term gains from the development of the railway network, although railways played an important role in serving cities, such as Chemnitz, which were not directly located on existing waterways. Specific regions clearly benefited from railway development which encouraged, for example, the mining and use of raw materials in the Westerwald that were previously discounted as commercial propositions because of high transport costs. On the other hand, the surge in coal production in the Saarland from the early 1850s was not a result of railway development, given existing canal links with the Rhine and Main. Indeed, it should not be forgotten that during the period 1816 to 1870 a further 1,400 kilometres of canals were added to the German network. State intervention could also be counterproductive, as in the case of Baden where government officials opted for a non-standard gauge which meant that the track had to be rebuilt after a number of years. Furthermore, even by the turn of the nineteenth century the estimated social savings generated by the railway system constituted no more than 5 per cent of German GNP, although this was a slightly greater contribution than was the case in some other European states.

IX Education and human capital

Finally, it is often stated that state support for improved educational training was a key factor in the long-term development of the German economy. The nineteenth century witnessed an increased level of state support for educational provision in all German states, which reflected not only common political objectives, but also a systematization process that was hierarchically determined. Many states showed an early commitment to the introduction of compulsory primary education, as was the case in Prussia with the decree of 1763–5, or saw improved educational provision as a means of creating a 'national' identity following the territorial changes of the Napoleonic period. In Prussia approximately 50 per cent of all children between the ages of 5 and 14 were attending elementary schools (*Volksschulen*) by the end of the eighteenth century, and by 1816 attendance rates had risen to 60 per cent. Similarly, there was general recognition of the need to widen the base of secondary education beyond the established structures of the grammar school (*Gymnasium*), in order to satisfy the more practical needs of the emergent commercial and industrial classes. This resulted in the creation of more modern secondary schools with a greater emphasis on science and languages (*Realschulen, Bürgerschulen*), as well as more specialized town schools. Vocational education was also expanded considerably during this period, which saw the development of continuation schools for various trades and businesses, the establishment of agricultural high schools (as at Hohenheim, 1818), and weaving schools in Elberfeld in 1844. In particular the promotion of technical education and training has been singled out as indicative of the positive contribution of the German state to economic development. Technical education was clearly meant for application: it was symptomatic of a close connection between education and business, and may well have contributed to technological innovation (as has been argued in the case of Baden). In 1821 a technical school was created in Berlin. By 1850 Prussia had approximately 20 provincial trade schools (*Gewerbeschulen*) primarily serving local needs, and the 1850s and 1860s, in particular, witnessed a general expansion of technical training opportunities throughout Germany. Finally, there was a disproportional expansion of higher education, at least in terms of government funding, which represented a considerable subsidy for upper income families. During the early nineteenth century university enrolment increased substantially, although student numbers slumped during the 1830s and did not rise again until after 1870. At the same time, this period saw the creation of a number of specialized institutions – the forerunners of the technical high schools – which were primarily concerned with the application of science for practical and technological purposes. To this extent many German states, such as Prussia, had succeeded by the 1860s in creating a 'modern' education system which functioned relatively effectively even in the rapidly expanding urban communities of the Rhineland and the Ruhr.

However, although the importance of education was widely recognized throughout Germany during this period, noticeable differences persisted in terms of state educational policy and training provision. On the one hand, the overall level of state funding for schools and universities was already relatively high by the early 1860s: in Bavaria and Prussia it accounted for 18 per cent of total expenditure. On the other hand, per capita expenditure on higher education, science and technology varied considerably, with Baden, Württemberg and Bavaria achieving a greater level of provision than Saxony and Prussia throughout the 1850s and 1860s. Bavaria, in particular, appears to have underperformed in most aspects of primary education. The reform movement of the early nineteenth century was gradually emasculated by a conservative reaction. Although a comparatively favourable pupil–teacher ratio of 1:64 was recorded by 1860–1, Bavaria had the poorest school attendance rate of all German states. Indeed, it was only in the early 1870s that it finally passed the 80 per cent figure that Prussia had already achieved in the 1830s. It may well be the case that educational reforms in the period before 1871 followed a relatively similar pattern in most German states, reflecting a general process of institutional convergence, but the timing of legislation, as well as the extent of improved educational provision, remained very uneven. This was the case in relation to both teacher-training and technical education. Even in terms of school supervision and quality control, practice also continued to vary. There was substantial hostility in many German states, such as Bavaria, to any change in the confessional framework for primary and secondary education, but both Baden and Hesse-Darmstadt had successfully introduced non-confessional schools by the end of this period.

It is not surprising, therefore, that there should be some doubt over the precise contribution of the educational system to Germany's economic development in the pre-unification period. Certainly there was a noticeable increase in literacy rates and it is reasonable to infer that the cumulative impact of greater educational provision at virtually every level would have led to improvements in the quality of human capital as a factor of production. However, the actual extent of reform should not be exaggerated. Elementary education was largely provided in large, single classes with an emphasis on religious instruction and morality rather than practical training; the curriculum continued to reflect the standards of a pre-modern society and in states such as Bavaria it was only gradually modernized. Moreover, a considerable number of children below the age of 14 were only taught in half-day or holiday schools (*Halbtagsschulen* or *Feiertagsschulen*). Secondary education was also characterized by rigid compartmentalization: there were no significant changes to the curriculum between the 1830s and 1880s; science training in the grammar schools was still deficient and failed to meet the 'demands of the present'; recruitment remained class-based; and private funding for secondary education continued to play an important role. There was no significant correlation between technical high school enrolment and industrial production, even in the later nineteenth century, and certain aspects of technical training were subject to 'continuous academization'. Although the larger universities were already highly specialized by the early 1860s, it was only after this period that expenditure levels on higher education increased significantly. Indeed, despite the early development of a public education system in Germany, its net contribution to economic growth remains questionable, even in the late nineteenth century. In Prussia quality improvements in labour as a factor of production, according to a recent estimation, only contributed 2 per cent to the recorded rate of growth in total output between 1864 and 1911.

X   Conclusion

Many of the issues raised in this chapter cannot be viewed in isolation. Long-term processes of economic change and adjustment were evident well before the end of the eighteenth century, as well as after political unification (see below, Chapter 9). At the same time, there is clearly a need to rethink traditional explanatory models. Economic growth in the nineteenth century was to a large degree a regional phenomenon, and it is important to analyse the dualistic nature of development and its costs, as well as the impact of specific factors, within a regional context. The pattern of regional development, in turn, was an interdependent process which reflected the role of different economic, social and political factors.

In particular, Germany's economic development prior to unification in 1871 can only be understood within an appropriate political framework. The state was heavily involved in the industrialization process and in the promotion of economic growth, but any discussion of the precise role of the state and the impact of state policy needs to be refocused, given the continuing federal structure of the German state: the fragmentation of political power, the local impact of lobbyist groups, and the disproportional role of the federal state bureaucracy in formulating economic policy.

Such an approach, however, places in doubt the continued applicability of the Gerschenkronian paradigm as a means of explaining Germany's long-run development. Germany was not uniformly backward, even in a relative sense, at the end of the eighteenth century; economic growth was more continuous than previously thought, particularly in the earlier decades of the nineteenth century; and the impact of key factors, such as the banks, the *Zollverein*, railway development or educational provision, was more muted than previously imagined.

This reappraisal of economic development in the pre-unification period, however, has broader implications. In recent years the focus of a great deal of research on European economic development in the nineteenth century has been on the role of regions and the unevenness of economic growth. In the case of Germany, however, such an approach is even more relevant, because the long-run development process was directly affected by political forces and social institutions that continued to operate at the level of the federal state. Indeed, after 1871 (see below, Chapter 9) regional economic divergence became even more accentuated and political power, to a large extent, remained fragmented within the federal framework of the Bismarckian constitution.

Notes:

1. On the basis of a detailed analysis of a number of European states in the nineteenth century, Alexander Gerschenkron put forward a number of hypotheses to explain the overall pattern of industrialization. According to the Gerschenkronian paradigm the relative backwardness of a country affected not only the rate of growth of industrial production, but the emphasis on producer rather than consumer industries. The more backward the country, the more active was the role of institutional factors, such as the banks or the state, and the greater the pressure on consumption levels in order to facilitate capital formation. For a fuller discussion of these issues, see Richard Sylla and Gianni Toniolo (eds.), *Patterns of European Industrialization. The Nineteenth Century*. London and New York, 1991, pp. 1–28.

Select bibliography

Brose, E. D., *The Politics of Technological Change in Prussia* (Princeton, NJ: Princeton University Press, 1993).

Dumke, R. H., 'Tariffs and Market Structure: The German *Zollverein* as a Model for Economic Integration', in W. R. Lee, ed., *German Industry and German Industrialization. Essays in German Economic and Business History in the Nineteenth and Twentieth Centuries* (London and New York: Routledge, 1991), pp. 77–115.

Henderson, W. O., *The Rise of German Industrial Power, 1834–1914.* (London: Temple Smith, 1975).

Lee, W. R., 'Germany', in Lee, ed., *European Demography and Economic Growth* (London: Croom Helm, 1979), pp. 144–95.

Olson, M., *The Rise and Decline of Nations. Economic Growth, Stagflation and Social Rigidities* (New Haven: Yale University Press, 1982).

Tilly, R., 'Germany', in R. Sylla and G. Toniolo, eds., *Patterns of European Industrialization. The Nineteenth Century* (London and New York: Routledge, 1991), pp. 175–96.

5

Cultural and intellectual trends

Karin Friedrich

> Intellectual education is perfect in Germany, but everything there passes into theory ...
> the government is the real instructor of the people, and public education itself, however
> beneficial, may create men of letters, but not citizens, warriors, or statesmen. In Germany,
> a man who is not occupied with the comprehension of the whole universe has really
> nothing to do.[1]

This judgement on German higher education by Madame de Staël, the daughter of
Louis Necker, Louis XVI's unfortunate finance minister, sums up the prevailing view
on the unpolitical and escapist nature of intellectual life in nineteenth-century
Germany, which regards early nineteenth-century Romantic Idealism as the first step
toward the intellectual German *Sonderweg* ('special path') that led to the totalitarianism and irrationalism of the Nazi regime. Although this paradigm has been persuasively challenged in many areas of German social, economic and political history
during the last decade, it still pervades many works on German cultural and intellectual history before and after the foundation of the Empire in 1871. The weakness and
backwardness of the bourgeoisie, the main pillar of political reform in other European
countries, has been blamed for the unpolitical, elitist and esoteric nature of most nineteenth-century German cultural and philosophical trends, which stood in stark contrast to Germany's rapid economic growth and the development of its natural and
technical sciences.

The territorial divisions of Germany and a confusing diversity of intellectual, religious and artistic movements complicate the task of assessing the political and social
achievements of German cultural life in the nineteenth century. Its main trends, which
accompanied the social and intellectual changes from the end of the Holy Roman
Empire to the foundation of the Kaiserreich under Prussian leadership show, however,
that in no other area more than in the arts, literature and philosophy was the transformation of German society so clearly influenced and shaped by the middle classes.

What Thomas Nipperdey called the 'defeudalization' of the arts in Germany was a
process guided by the effective improvement of education on the primary, secondary

and university level. As Christopher Clark and Robert Lee show in preceding chapters (Chapters 3 and 4, above), the early introduction of compulsory elementary education and the growing diversity of school types contributed to an increase in literacy rates among the whole German population. It was the German bourgeoisie (*Bürgertum*) which benefited most from educational reforms. From the point of view of the political authorities, however, education proved a double-edged sword. The encouragement of critical and independent thinking among the educated fitted ill with the unconstitutional government of the Restoration period and the repression of the 1848 revolution. The complexity of the German *Bürgertum* and its internal political and social divisions complicate the assessment of bourgeois cultural responses to the Restoration periods following 1815 as well as 1848. On the one hand, the quiet 'philistine' world of Biedermeier, to which many Germans turned as a result of political frustration and harsh repression, proved the most persistent of all German bourgeois art styles; on the other hand, its seemingly unpolitical nature often served as an efficient cover for satire and tentative political criticism without provoking the censor. Moreover, in the second half of the nineteenth century, Biedermeier and Realism triggered an elitist response from a new avant-garde, itself deeply rooted in the *Bürgertum*, which felt alienated from the established political and social order – possibly more so than in other countries. Thus the elitism and high abstraction of much of German art and philosophy, particularly in the last decades of the century, was indirectly the result of the involvement of the bourgeoisie, and not, as the *Sonderweg* theory suggests, its absence or weakness.

I The transformation of the German education system

When Madame de Staël published her famous work *De l'Allemagne* in 1813, wide-ranging military, administrative and educational reforms were in full swing in most German states. As part of these reforms, Berlin University had been founded in 1810. It seemed an odd moment for the Prussian king, facing occupation by Napoleon's armies at the time, to invest in an institution of higher learning. Yet the decision resulted from an intense debate about the purpose of scholarship and the relationship between science, research and teaching, which had preceded the Napoleonic wars.

Academic opinion was divided between governmental reformers such as Karl Freiherr vom Stein and Carl August von Hardenberg, who had deprived the universities of their old corporate status and favoured a utilitarian approach to the education of the administrative elite on the one hand, and supporters of Wilhelm von Humboldt's (1767–1835) neo-humanist concept of philosophical and scientific activity on the other. Humboldt's university was meant to combine teaching with research in an environment in which professors and students could form an intellectual and moral community, striving for the moral and material improvement of the human condition. 'Solitude and freedom' became the motto of the scholarly ideal of the post-Enlightenment period. Neo-humanists strove to educate morally responsible citizens, conscious of their political freedom, through intellectual pursuit for its own sake. This

Idealist approach was opposed by reformers guided by the pedagogical ideas of the Swiss educator Johann Heinrich Pestalozzi (1746–1827), who saw more need to foster vocational and practical skills among the young in schools and academies which produced citizens 'useful' to the state. The difference between the two camps, however, has often been overemphasized. Although non-utilitarian in nature, Humboldt's concept of the university as an institution open to all talents was still influenced by Enlightenment ideas and driven by the political purpose of improving education firmly under the control of the state.

German patriots of the post-Napoleonic period, however, reacted with suspicion to Humboldt's classicist and universalist values. The Idealist philosopher Johann Gottlieb Fichte (1762–1814), whose historical work is explored by Stefan Berger (see Chapter 23, below), advocated a system of national education based on Johann Gottfried Herder's *Volksgeist* (national spirit), which was opposed to the 'emptiness of the Enlightenment'. The Romantic Lutheran theologian and philosopher Friedrich Schleiermacher (1768–1834), like Fichte, professor at Berlin University and a strong advocate of German cultural unity, argued that a Prussian university should play a more pragmatic role in the formation of the country's social and political elite. In 1810, a compromise was struck between Humboldt, who was head of the section for religion and public instruction in the Prussian Ministry of the Interior (a predecessor of the Ministry of Education), and the followers of Pestalozzi over the future shape of the reformed university in Berlin. The neo-humanist ideal of 'general human education' assured an emphasis on autonomous research, while a close pedagogical supervision sought to transform students into useful members of their community and loyal subjects of their monarch.

The universalism advocated by Humboldt, who was inspired by a social conscience shaped by the ideas of the French Revolution as well as the late eighteenth-century fascination with Greek antiquity, also prevailed in secondary and primary schools. A strict separation between vocational schools and general education at the *Gymnasium* prevented the early specialization of pupils destined by their talent for university. In 1812, university entrance was regulated in Prussia by an edict making the *Gymnasium* diploma, the *Abitur*, compulsory on the basis of a curriculum dictated by the ministries of education and culture in each state, many of which remodelled their requirements along Prussian lines. Candidates who passed the *Abitur* then had complete freedom of choice of any subject at any German university. The popularity of these reforms was reflected in the number of students entering German universities: between 1819 and 1830, enrolment more than doubled from 7,378 to 15,838 students, while general school attendance in Prussia rose from about 60 to over 90 per cent by 1864.[2] The multidisciplinary preparation of future university students and a generally meritocratic approach opened up some, albeit not unlimited, opportunities for social advancement beyond the university, into state service.

Examination regulations were accompanied by great improvements in the formation of future schoolmasters, for whom the obligation to study theology was replaced with a free choice of academic subjects. Neo-humanist ideals remained wedded to a strict control by the state and its department of culture over teacher-training. Teachers were employed by the government and became civil servants bound to obedience by an oath to their state. The overwhelmingly positive impression which elementary and higher education made on foreign observers in the first half of the nineteenth century suggests that German schooling was regarded as more liberal and modern than the educational system in countries with more liberal and parliamentary constitutions than the German states. The liberal Rhenish industrialist Friedrich Harkort (1793–1880), an admirer of the British parliament, condemned English schools as 'a barbarian colony rather than enlightened parts of a civilised Christian state', while the American John Quincy Adams observed that, in contrast to their American and English counterparts, Prussian teachers 'not merely load the memory of their pupils with words, but make things intelligible to their understanding; to habituate them to the use of their own reason'.[3]

After a promising start, however, the promotion of a secular, well-organized education system with rigorous teacher-training lost its impetus during the Restoration period, particularly after 1848. Undoubtedly, regional differences existed within Germany. Although Winfried Speitkamp has recently tried to diminish the importance of Prussia's leadership in political and educational reform, it is uncontested that literacy and school attendance were poorer in rural areas in states such as Bavaria, where the reforms of the Montgelas government were reversed by the Catholic Church's reaffirmation of control over education in the 1820s. In Prussia, the clampdown came later. Frederick William IV blamed the revolution on the fostering of a 'rebellious spirit' in schools and universities, and attacked primary schoolteachers for their supposed radicalism. The expulsion of teachers with republican preferences, the tightening of censorship, and the return to teacher-training dominated by religion under the regulations of the 1854 decree by Ferdinand Stiehl, then councillor in the Ministry of Education, once more reinforced the image of a strictly controlled, uninspiring school environment worthy of an absolutist, militaristic state. Stiehl banned the reading of Goethe and Schiller in teacher-training colleges, while philosophical and scientific pursuits were replaced by the mechanical memorization of Biblical texts and the Catechism. Low pay and the low social prestige of primary schoolteachers contributed to their sinking morale. The end of the Restoration period and the foundation of the German National Teachers' Association in 1861 slightly improved their fortunes and consequently the quality of elementary education. Nevertheless, in 1870, the narrow focus of German *Gymnasia* on the creation of an administrative elite, and the failure of the reforms to open up schooling for all social groups and classes in German society, was reflected in Harkort's criticism:

> Like the Hindu caste system, we too impress on the lower social classes the seal of lifelong servitude through the lack of education. Our learned schools do not relate to the people. Only the well-off can attend the more advanced schools and private institutes on account of their considerable costs.[4]

Except on the primary level, where boys and girls were educated together in village schools, female education lagged behind. From 1804, Bavaria provided the first college for female teachers, but until 1866 women were taught only 'practical' subjects, aimed at preparing girls for housework and motherhood. Education reformers and ministries considered 'noble womanhood' unsuited for higher education and intellectual pursuit; women's destiny was to lead a 'quiet and domestic life, unburdened by difficult mental work'. In 1837, the Berlin *Gymnasium* director Johann Heinrich Schulz wrote that teaching brought out in women the most 'pedantic, unattractive and nasty' character, prone to irrational reactions, while a man, even in rage, still kept his 'titanic and imposing authority'.[5] It was again in Berlin, however, that the first association for women teachers was founded in 1869, following the establishment of Louise Otto-Peters' General German Women's Association of 1865.

Not all social groups benefited from the tripartite system of primary schools, practical and vocational schools (*Realschule*) and the *Gymnasium*. The survival of high standards and a humanist orientation in the German *Gymnasium* were crucial to the development of a widening split between an intellectual meritocracy among the German bourgeoisie serving the state in civil and military offices, and an industrial, trade and craft-oriented German middle class educated in vocational and technical schools. Measured against the long-term growth of German industrialization, however, it seems that the persistence of neo-humanist ideals at least did not obstruct the development of the natural sciences and technical innovation in Germany.

II Religious and philosophical trends

Despite the attempt of many German state governments to introduce complete control over school education, confessional schools and the influence of the Protestant and the Catholic churches on public education survived the reform period of the 1810s and gathered strength after the failed revolution of 1848. The reaction against the French Enlightenment and Revolution, as well as against Kantian rationalism and its emphasis on the critical abilities of human reason, has traditionally been held responsible for a religious revival that went hand in hand with the emotional appeal of German Romanticism.

Recently, however, Nicholas Riasanovsky has argued that far from being a mere condemnation of the Enlightenment, early German Romantic writers such as Novalis (Friedrich Leopold von Hardenberg, 1772–1801), Friedrich Schlegel (1772–1829) and Ludwig Tieck (1773–1853) were influenced by an Enlightenment-inspired pantheism which filled the religious vacuum left by the French Revolution. For intellectuals and the educated, secularized *Bürgertum*, Romantic art, music, philosophy and science took on religious qualities and replaced or complemented religion in the spiritual life of the nineteenth century. Novalis's belief that 'now on earth men must become Gods' was paralleled by Schlegel's plan to create a new human religion: 'God is I'.[6] Belief in salvation in this life instead of after death was taking root as there was, in the words of the poet Georg Büchner (1813–37), 'more of heaven on this side of the grave'. Thomas Nipperdey accurately pointed at the religious contents adopted by German cultural life in the first half of the nineteenth century: philosophy and the arts were transformed into the substitute religion of the post-Enlightenment era, which found expression in a cult of ultimate subjectivity that needed no church. True atheism, however, only took hold among a small intellectual avant-garde in the later nineteenth century, when the belief in the existence of a spiritual and transcendental realm was increasingly challenged by the rising natural and social sciences and the influence of materialist and nihilist philosophy.

The Christian faith even found vociferous defenders among the Romantic movement. The diatribe by the Protestant theologian Schleiermacher against Enlightenment intellectuals who 'disdain religion' set the Romantic tone against the rationalist definition of man and the 'paganism' of Weimar classical culture. Man could never be defined by reason alone. The religious emotionalism preached by the late eighteenth-century Pietists had emphasized the personal relationship between the individual and God. The Romantics went further and accepted their mystical, Romantic God as part of their human nature. Although Schleiermacher stressed that human longing for the infinite could be fulfilled before death, in this world, he was not a pantheist. Moreover, his Protestant devotion separated him as much from the more mystic branches of Romanticism, as from the strongly anti-Enlightenment Pietists in Prussia and Pomerania, and from the sceptics among Protestant theologians, such as Johann David Strauß, who questioned in his *Life of Jesus* (1835) the historical existence of Jesus Christ and tried to explain miracles with natural science.

Soon, however, Schleiermacher's Romantic theology was superseded by a secularized, rationalist religiosity among the Protestant *Bürgertum*. After 1848, the growing consensus within the German Protestant Church against political and social revolution forged an alliance between the Restoration governments and the orthodox Lutheran leadership in most Protestant states, especially in Prussia. Friedrich Julius Stahl (1802–61), the main ideologue of the Prussian state in the pre-March period (and paradoxically a baptized Jew from Bavaria), set the agenda in his work *The Christian State*, which justified divine-right rule with Luther's teaching of obedience towards secular powers and a national, state-dominated church. The changing focus of the popular Luther festivals between 1817 and 1863 closely mirrored the political changes in Germany during this period: in the early decades of the century, the depiction of Luther as a sympathetic fighter for religious and political freedom and national unity coincided with the hopes of the liberal movement of the *Vormärz* to win constitutionally guaranteed civic liberties and national unity. After 1848, however, Luther festivals started celebrating either a *bürgerlich* figure, in a cosy home with his wife and children, displaying the virtues of an unpolitical and obedient member of bourgeois society, or a useful representative of the *Bildungsbürger* establishment, with a doctorate and an academic post.

A similar process transformed German Catholicism, which in the first half of the century played a major role in the general religious revival that accompanied Romantic literature and philosophy. Several writers, such as Friedrich Schlegel and Adam Müller, converted to Catholicism in the early nineteenth century in search of the emotionality which they missed in orthodox Lutheranism. A favourite Romantic theme was the quest for an idealized image of the German Middle Ages. It is no coincidence that the first Romantic novella was published in 1797 under the title *An Art-Loving Friar Pours Out His Heart*. The rediscovery of the Middle Ages and the Gothic as a 'typically German' art style also played a role in the Romantic project of completing the unfinished medieval cathedral in Cologne. The nationalist writer Joseph Görres (1776-1848), another convert to Catholicism, spoke of it as a symbol of national greatness uniting Germany not only politically but also across religious divides, as a 'home for all Germans'. Since Frederick William IV, however, personally oversaw the funding of its construction and, as the 'patriarch of the nation', became the protector and patron of the cathedral project, it lost its predominantly Catholic character. The 1842 and 1848 festivals that celebrated the continuation of building work on the cathedral were therefore not dominated by a religious but a national and dynastic agenda. These public events found the enthusiastic support of the liberal *Bildungsbürgertum* represented in the parliament of the Frankfurt Paulskirche. The presence of school classes, fraternities, associations and choir societies performing patriotic chorus works in front of the king, the assembled officialdom and the archbishop of Cologne, lent the cathedral fes-

Illustration 5.1   Building the future on the past: the figure of Germania celebrating the completion of Cologne Cathedral. *Germania Holds the Laurel Wreath* by Toni Avenarius

tivals a popular tone, increasingly marginalizing the religious cause of the city's Catholic community.

Unlike Protestantism, and with the exception of the reformist splinter-groups of the *Deutschkatholiken* (German Catholics), the Catholic Church in Germany remained generally sceptical of patriotic and national activities. The creation of political Catholicism and the ultramontane movement, analysed earlier by Clark (Chapter 3, above), centred around journals such as *Eos*, published in Munich, or *The Catholic* in Mainz, and in a social movement among artisans. In 1845 the Kolping Association (Adolf Kolping, 1813–65) for Catholic workers was founded, followed by the Pius Association and the Boniface Association in 1848 and 1849 respectively. After 1850, the growing strength of Catholicism was also reflected in the increase of the numbers of monasteries and convents: Bavaria had 27 monasteries in 1825, but 441 in 1864, which included charitable institutions connected with monastic establishments.

Romantic religion, and the subsequent pseudo-religious character of national festivals, was one response to the growing uncertainties of the industrial age; Romantic philosophy was another. The towering figure of German Idealism was Georg Wilhelm Friedrich Hegel (1770–1831), whose real significance for German intellectual development revealed itself only in the decades after his death, through the influence he exerted on such heterogeneous figures as Ludwig Feuerbach (1804–72), Karl Marx (1818–83), Arthur Schopenhauer (1788–1860) and Friedrich Nietzsche (1844–1900).

Hegel comprehended history as a dialectical process led by the 'world spirit', perfecting itself in several stages from the Orientals, the Greeks and the Romans to the Germans through a process of achieving ever higher levels of freedom. Hegel's ideas of political or constitutional freedom were not those of the liberals. In his *Phenomenology of the Spirit*, Hegel defined the condition of progress as 'reason that governs the world, and, therefore, in world history things have come to pass rationally'. The state was the embodiment of this worldly reason, the 'actually existing realized moral life', the 'divine idea as it exists on earth'. This and the formula that 'everything that is real is reasonable, and everything is reasonable because it exists', have often been criticized as a justification of the repressive institutions of the Prussian state.[7]

More important than Hegel's support for the authoritarian state, however, were the two main schools formed after Hegel's death, the 'Right Hegelians' and the 'Left Hegelians', of which the latter transformed Hegel's dialectical principle into a revolutionary theory. In Hegel's view of life, where all things real were determined by a dialectical process involving the human will as the highest expression of freedom and 'objective' institutions, the state and society, and not individual morality and a transcendental God, occupied the supreme place. Inspired by Hegel's philosophy, Bruno Bauer (1809–82) thus asked: 'why does hell concern us?' and formulated the atheist world-view further elaborated by Feuerbach and Marx. In rebellion against Hegel's 'world spirit', Feuerbach concluded that in a materialist world ('man is what he eats') God is a human invention, a mere projection of human desires and hopes. In his critique of the failure of the 1848 revolution, Marx called religion 'the opiate of the people', whose sedating effect prevented the proletariat from feeling the pain of its social misery: only if Christianity was got rid of could they be convinced of the necessity of popular revolution.

The writings of Marx and Feuerbach had little immediate impact. Atheism only began to affect German intellectual life more widely when the social and natural sciences, in particular anthropology and the theory of evolution, further undermined religious revelation as a source of certainties about the meaning of life. At the same time, the quest for more worldly knowledge itself adopted sometimes quasi-religious qualities: as the physician Rudolf Virchow wrote in 1865, 'science became our religion'. This development prepared a fertile ground for the success of Darwinism, while the wave of cultural pessimism and religious nihilism that followed the 'death of God' was embodied in the philosophy of Arthur Schopenhauer (1788–1860). He was convinced that all human life was built on the will to survive, a will that was in itself evil and destructive. Man could only reach moral superiority by liberating himself from this will in an individual and aesthetic act of art. With this apotheosis of Romantic and atheistic ideas, and his interest in non-Christian cultures and religions, Schopenhauer remains the thinker most closely conforming to the stereotype of German Romantic 'irrationalism' before Nietzsche.

III Literature, music and the arts: Romanticism to Realism

The growing importance of speculative philosophy to the Romantics has often been attributed to the tendency in the German national and cultural character towards exaggeration, irreality and unpolitical abstraction: 'that peculiarly German sense of inwardness and remoteness from reality'.[8] Comparisons with other European Romantic movements and an interdisciplinary analysis have, however, led to the revision of this one-sided picture, decisively formed by the poet Heinrich Heine (1797–1856) and his caricature of German Romanticism, *The Romantic School* (1838).

The relationship between art and social, political and historical reality was more complex. The search for the infinite – as seen in the landscape paintings of Caspar David Friedrich (1774–1840) – the 'blue flower' of Romantic love, pantheism and the mysticism of natural philosophy with an ever more immanent God, the revival of medieval culture, the rediscovery of folklore in music and literature, the enchantment with deep, dark forests and sunny landscapes, the urge to travel the world, most aptly expressed in Joseph von Eichendorff's (1788–1857) poems and novellas - all these themes are also present in French, Russian and English Romanticism. The mutual inspiration of the English and Scottish Romantic movement led by Byron, Coleridge, Shelley, Carlyle and Scott, and German Romantics, such as E. T. A. Hoffmann (1776–1822), Schlegel and Friedrich Hölderlin (1770–1843), Novalis and Jean Paul (Johann Paul Friedrich Richter, 1763–1825), and the influences of German Romanticism on Balzac, Poe and Dostoevsky are well known.

Even though English and French Romantic literary heroes tend to be more politically active, this does not mean that German writers shunned political issues. Moreover, there was no political – liberal or conservative - consensus among them. First inspired by the French Revolution, but subsequently appalled by Napoleon's conquests, writers such as Fichte and Ernst Moritz Arndt (1769–1860), and poets such as Heinrich Kleist (1777–1811) and Theodor Körner (1791–1813), engaged in patriotic myths of the Germanic past and a pronounced Gallophobia. Other Romantics accepted a role in the political establishment: Schlegel became a supporter of Metternich's Restoration policy, Eichendorff was a councillor in the Prussian education ministry, and the Jacobin Joseph von Görres (1776–1848) turned into a Catholic defender of the Bavarian monarchy.

Without Idealism and Romanticism, the rebellious and highly politicized literary movement of Young Germany, would have been unthinkable. Emancipatory and socialist ideas, most prominently represented in the teaching of the utopian socialist Claude-Henri de Saint-Simon (1760–1825), deeply influenced the group of writers which gathered in the 1830s and 1840s around Karl Gutzkow (1811–78), Heinrich Laube (1806–84), Ludwig Börne (1786–1837), Nikolaus Lenau (1802–1850), and the two most gifted writers among them, Heine and Büchner. In contrast to the German literary establishment of the imperial period, the poets of Young Germany believed in modernization, which they associated with a parliamentary constitution for free citizens, the emancipation of women and a united German nation state. Literature and the arts were an inherently political enterprise for them, and they agreed with the two liberal authors of the 'Encyclopedia of Liberalism', the *Staatslexikon*, Karl Rotteck (1775–1840) and Karl Theodor Welcker (1784–1868), who stressed the political character of the arts: 'the constitution is the highest expression of order, and the development of the arts must be closely interwoven with the development of the constitution and with legislation'.[9]

The critical journalists and writers who in the early decades of the nineteenth century gathered in the literary salons of Bettine von Arnim, Henriette Herz, Rahel Varnhagen and Fanny Lewald actively contributed to this politicization of German literature. Ingeborg Drewitz concluded that it was the achievement of these Berlin salons to 'preserve the ideas of the Enlightenment into the industrial era'.[10] Literary and political circles, such as masonic lodges and the pre-March *Burschenschaft* movement among students, always remained highly exclusive and isolated from the majority of the population. This did not differ, however, from developments in other European countries. It was only with the advent of the patriotic Gymnasts' Movement, founded in 1811 and revived in 1842 by Friedrich Ludwig Jahn (1778–1852), male choirs and other patriotic associations, that less educated and lower social groups from among the German *Bürgertum* took a more active role in forming public opinion.

The promotion of a popular cultural basis through these associations, however, did not guarantee the liberalization of German society. Ironically, the openly repressive nature of government policies targeting the rebels among the elite literary circles of the pre-March period triggered a greater literary and political interest from the

Bildungsbürgertum than after the nominal introduction of freedom of expression during the post-1850 Restoration era. Of great importance here is censorship. In reaction to the liberal demands of the Hambach festival of 1832, the Central Office of Political Observation regularly confiscated the publications of representatives of the Young German movement. Pre-censorship applied to newspapers, periodicals and any works with fewer than 20 printed sheets. Clever distribution policies and the persistent cooperation of author, publisher, printer and bookseller, however, assured that an eager and attentive – albeit small – readership regularly received works that were confiscated shortly after publication. The policies were draconian enough to force Heine, who refused to compromise on a less confrontational style, into permanent exile in France from 1833. Torn between his German patriotism and the disgust with which he watched from abroad the failure of the German liberals to overcome the repressive policies conducted from Berlin and Vienna, Heine wrote partly with bitterness, partly with compassion, about the 'great fool that calls himself the German people'.

After 1850, however, new laws made it even harder for writers, publishers and booksellers to hoodwink their censors. State licences, money deposits, spies, denunciation, incarceration, police investigations and the control of proofs before printing led to widespread self-censorship and a diminishing willingness of publishers to run risks with politically sensitive publications. Even so, the political division of Germany helped to some degree to alleviate the harshness of repression. A group of scientists and scholars at the University of Göttingen (the famous 'Göttingen Seven'), who in 1837 resigned in protest against the *coup d'état* of the new king of Hanover, Ernst August II (who had unlawfully annulled the kingdom's liberal constitution by refusing to swear an oath to it), eventually found employment again at other German universities. Among the 'Göttingen Seven' was the historian and literary scholar Georg Gottfried Gervinus (1805–71), whose *History of German Literature* called for an end to Romanticism and for a more realistic and critical sense among the intelligentsia in assessing Germany's political future. Young Germany was not strong enough a force, according to Gervinus, to overcome the country's intellectual and artistic stagnation:

> Our literature has had its day and, if German life is not going to stand still, then we must entice its talents . . . to turn toward the real world and the State, where the new spirit waits to be poured into the new material.[11]

Like Heine, Gervinus attacked the intellectual apathy which he thought was increasingly taking hold of Germany's political and cultural life, after the critical elite, silenced by censorship and emigration, had run out of steam and were superseded by the art of the Biedermeier era – mocked by the Young Germans and members of the *Bildungsbürgertum* as a 'culture of Philistines'. Like all ideal-types, the concept of the *Bildungsbürgertum* – a bourgeoisie with the academic qualification of the *Abitur* or a university degree, and regarded as distinct from the middle classes in industrial and commercial professions – is only of limited value, as dividing lines between various groups in the middle classes were constantly shifting and must not be drawn too strictly. 'Herr Biedermeier', a *petit bourgeois* simpleton, was first invented by literary satire in the 1850s, but soon became associated with the frugal lifestyle of a bourgeoisie that retired into the private, domestic sphere, which for many seemed the only answer to the defeat suffered by the rebellious cultural elites of the pre-1848 period.

Biedermeier was fed from many sources: the anti-modernism, anti-industrialism and anti-urbanism of the small-town, apparently well-ordered world of the *Bürgertum* lay as much at the root of Biedermeier as the demonic, anti-modern side of Romantic emotionality. Both were aptly expressed in the poems of Eduard Mörike (1804–75) and Lenau – himself once a member of the Young Germany movement – and the novellas of Adalbert Stifter (1805–68). Wilhelm Riehl (1823–97), the founder of German ethnology, similarly railed against the 'cosmopolitan' revolutionaries of 1848, who catered to the corrupting influence of the urban, proletarian masses, instead of defending the peasantry, the natural stronghold of the German nation. Catholic writers such as Görres, Jeremias Gotthelf (1797–1854) and Annette von Droste-Hülshoff (1797–1848) attacked the Young Germans for their worldly immorality, in particular their condemnation of conventional marriage and family values. Not all Biedermeier poets, however, withstood the tension between their desire to live in a 'wholesome old world' and the fundamental changes effected by the processes of urbanization and industrialization: Lenau went mad, Stifter killed himself, and Mörike died in embittered solitude.

In contrast to the literary products of the Young Germans whose reception always remained limited to a small circle, Biedermeier flourished, beyond literature, as a popular style of art. It provided furniture for the bourgeois German living room and paintings of harmonious families with pretty children. The mildly satirical pictures such as the 'Poor Poet', by the most famous Biedermeier artist, the Bavarian Carl Spitzweg (1808–85), enjoyed unbroken popularity among the German *Bürgertum* far into the imperial period. The style was often not without ambiguity. Using irony and satire, Wilhelm Busch (1822–1908) became the most celebrated Biedermeier caricaturist and writer through his work *Max and Moritz*, a moral tale about two badly behaved boys. The didactic focus of popular literature is also apparent in the most famous children's book of the period, Heinrich Hoffmann's *Struwelpeter*. Thus it was in the Biedermeier period that literature and the arts left the ivory tower of its classic and Romantic predecessors by adopting a more popular tone, while libraries, museums, concert halls, opera houses and theatres opened their doors to a wider public.

Royal operas and court theatres were either complemented or replaced by 'National Theatres', in Berlin (1807), Munich (1836) and the German Opera, built by Gottfried Semper 1841 in Dresden, where the middle classes gained access to the gallery and were no longer restricted to the stalls. In 1842, the French composer Hector Berlioz observed while travelling through Berlin that 'music is part of the air you breathe; you absorb it through the very pores of your skin. One meets it everywhere, in concert halls, church, theatre, in the streets, in the public gardens'.[12]

Ludwig van Beethoven's (1770–1827) idea of the new role music had to play in

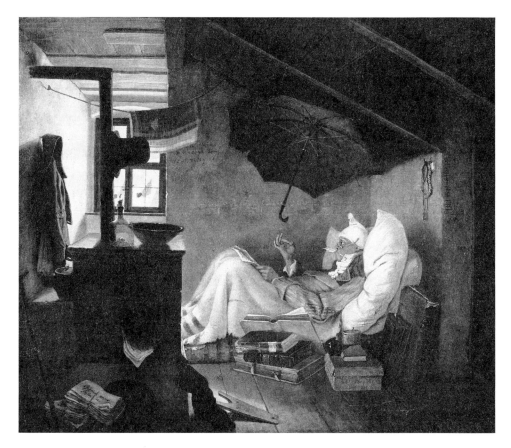

Illustration 5.2   *The Poor Poet* by Carl Spitzweg (1839)

German *bürgerlich* society sharply differed from the almost exclusive function of court music or *Tafelmusik* in the eighteenth century. His furious protest 'I shall not play in front of such swines', addressing an audience at the Vienna court which continued with small-talk during one of his concerts, reflects a change in the role and identity of the artist as an autonomous self-conscious individual, rather than as a hireling of princes. Art itself was taking on a more autonomous nature and the function of a substitute religion, to be worshipped together with the genius who produced it and the nation which gave birth to such greatness, the German *Kulturnation* (cultural nation).

Programmes therefore increasingly focused on German works, such as Beethoven's *Fidelio*, and Carl Maria von Weber's opera *Der Freischütz*, premiered in 1821 in the Berlin Schauspielhaus, built by Karl Friedrich Schinkel 1818–21. The increasingly national character of music and dramatic art expressed itself most prominently in Richard Wagner's operas *Rienzi* (1842) and *Tannhäuser* (1845), both premiered in

Dresden. National symbolism was also reflected in the transfer of Carl Maria von Weber's body from London to Dresden in 1844 to mark his significance for German culture.

Arnold Toynbee exaggerated when he wrote that in the nineteenth century 'when we say "music", we mean German music'. It is true, however, that music was not only the most abstract art and therefore closest to the emotional nature of the Romantic era, but it was at the same time the most universal and powerful art form. It transcended religious borders, social distinctions, dialects and mentalities within Germany and abroad. Apart from opera, the German *Lied* was a new musical genre which achieved international fame in the songs of Franz Schubert (1797–1828) and Robert Schumann (1810–1856), and which followed the Romantic ideal by blending two forms of art: poetry and music. As elsewhere in Europe the piano became a status symbol in the bourgeois salon, at which every daughter was expected to show her graceful musical skills. Interest among the *Bürgertum* in music associations, singing academies and public choir festivals, often with a patriotic and national sub-text that inspired the collection of large repertoires of folk songs, peaked in the revolutionary atmosphere of the 1840s. In the subsequent Restoration period, it was only the conscious retreat from political, anti-monarchical songs and theatre programmes that secured the survival of cultural associations.

The shift from a highly politicized cultural scene which enjoyed a short moment of almost unlimited freedom of expression in 1848, to the draconian restrictions during the Restoration period of the 1850s was sudden and extreme. If after the revolution, the gap between an elite and a mass audience narrowed, it happened at the cost of toning down radical political messages and liberal aspirations. It seemed after 1848 that German Realist writers such as Theodor Fontane (1819–98), Wilhelm Raabe (1831–1910) or Gustav Freytag (1816–95), could not live up to the great social and critical novels of their French and English counterparts, such as Charles Dickens, Honoré de Balzac and Gustave Flaubert. Nevertheless, a veritable reading revolution with a steady rise in literacy, a growing demand for local libraries from an increasingly sophisticated public, and an explosion in the number of periodicals, ranging from scientific and philosophical publications to satirical and fashion journals, accompanied the aftermath of the 1848 revolution.

As a typical product of the Restoration period, the magazine *Gartenlaube* introduced a new kind of journalism that was a far cry from the critical newspapers of the pre-March period and their constant battle against censorship and confiscation. Popularizing science, literature and art for the whole family, *Gartenlaube* reached an impressive weekly circulation of 100,000 in 1860; 15 years later, it sold 382,000 issues per week. In the years before unification, the production of cheaper paper, an improved postal service and the increase of leisure time as a result of shorter working hours created a new mass readership. Journals, encyclopedias and novels were the most popular reading materials consulted and borrowed from public libraries, whose numbers had already reached 2,000 by 1848. In 1867–8, in Berlin's 74 public libraries, almost 40 per cent of the regular users were craftsmen, 16 per cent *Gymnasium* pupils and students, 11 per cent workers, 9 per cent officials and clerks, 5 per cent teachers and 20 per cent women.[13] In the same year, the copyright laws were regulated, opening the way to allow the production of cheap editions of the German classics. Goethe's *Faust* sold 500,000 copies within a few days.

German rulers were aware of these trends and showed concern for a 'well-directed' popular education, in the words of King Ludwig I of Bavaria, the founder of Munich University, 'to ennoble the spirit and the habits of our people'. During the two decades before the political unification of Germany, one might therefore ask how successfully German art and literature asserted the claim of the German *Kulturnation* to intellectual and spiritual autonomy against the stifling control of the rulers and their governments.

IV   Towards a German national art and literature?

In the first half of the nineteenth century, the increasing importance of history as a scientific subject in its own right and the Romantics' rediscovery of the German past paved the way for the impact of historicism on all branches of German cultural and scientific life in the second half of the century. As John Breuilly points out in Chapter 27, below, nationalists discovered that not only history, whose supremacy Hegel had so firmly installed, but the history of German culture could be used to emphasize the superiority of a united German nation. Historicism supported the idea of the organic individuality of nations and cultures and the need to judge them according to their values and ideals. Figures of such universal appeal as Friedrich Schiller therefore became the exclusive embodiment of German national culture: the festivals of 1859 that celebrated Schiller's 100th birthday no longer revered the image of the revolutionary hero, as during the pre-March period, but of the national poet, worshipped in altar-like monuments as 'saviour' and unifier of the German people. Popular demand for his public veneration even made the Prussian authorities, who had banned Schiller's works from schools only five years earlier, announce a literary prize in the poet's honour.

This 'nationalization' of culture was confirmed by the developments in other branches of cultural life after 1850. The foundation of German ethnography, national economy, cultural history and sociology contributed to the intellectual growing together of a German nation. The most important bases of this nation, except for a common statehood, however, were language and law. Although the Grimm brothers' efforts to trace and reconstruct a German literary tradition from the Middle Ages to modernity founded their fame as Romantic collectors of folk and children's tales, their work also resulted in the creation of the first comprehensive dictionary of the German language. Jacob Grimm's (1785–1863) study of Scandinavian language and linguistics inspired his interest in the newly emerging academic subject of *Germanistik* (German language and literature) during the 1840s. In 1846, the first conference of German philologists gathered in Frankfurt am Main, and Jacob Grimm was elected president of the Congress of German Philology (*Germanistentag*). Heine's judgement of 1837 was shared by the German literary establishment after Wilhelm's and Jacob's deaths (in 1859 and 1863 respectively): 'Jacob Grimm's German grammar is a colossal work, a Gothic dome, where all German tribes raise their voices like a gigantic choir, each in its dialect'.[14]

At the same time, the rediscovery of Germanic legal traditions led to furious debates between the followers of Friedrich Karl von Savigny's (1779–1861) school of Roman law and those, like Karl Friedrich Eichhorn (1781–1854) and Georg Beseler (1809–88), who wanted to revive medieval customary law. Interest in the discovery of a medieval German heritage also guided the founders of the *Monumenta Germaniae Historica* (from 1819), the publication and annotated edition of historical sources which still continues today.

The invention of historical and national identity also dominated German architecture. In Munich, Leo von Klenze (1784–1864) was commissioned to build a Bavarian 'Hall of Fame', to honour Bavarian military heroes from the time of the Thirty Years War (1618–48). In Prussia, the king dedicated monuments to the soldiers who gave their blood in the Wars of Liberation against Napoleon. As Nipperdey emphasized, this gesture was understood and disliked by the people for what it was: an ill-chosen substitute for the promised but never granted liberal constitution. The tension between official, ruler-induced commemoration and a growing popular demand for national representation was never resolved, not even after unification.

More popular projects, which more genuinely expressed the idea of a German *Kulturnation* and which began to transcend the particularism of the German states, were the statues of 'great Germans' mushrooming in German cities and towns after the 1830s. In 1842, on the order of Ludwig I of Bavaria, the building of the Valhalla was accomplished. Situated on a hill overlooking the river Danube near Regensburg, the former imperial city which had housed the Diet of the Holy Roman Empire for centuries, the Valhalla was a temple erected in honour of the German heroes killed in the Napoleonic Wars. The whole nation was also represented in the monument of Arminius (17 BC–AD 21), the legendary hero who defeated the Roman legions of Quintilius Varus in the Teutoburg forest. Begun in 1841 and finished in the year of the declaration of the German Empire in 1871, it translated Arminius's victory over the Romans into a German victory over France. Similar popularity was achieved by the Luther monuments, which were financed by local Protestant communities and accompanied the festivals that transfigured the Saxon Reformer into a German hero who fought the dark forces of Rome and France, foreshadowing the *Kulturkampf.*

As an expression of secular, bourgeois culture, museums became sacred temples of the worship of the whole German nation and its achievements. Other public buildings also acquired an increasingly monumental character. The highest Bavarian court was built as a 'Palace of Justice', while post offices, town halls, schools and even public baths grew in size and ornament, sometimes much beyond their real importance. Political symbolism and splendour were no longer restricted to princely residences. Art and architecture were entering the public domain and public discussion.

Unlike many national monuments and festivals, German literature of the post-1850 period retained a predominantly provincial and inward-looking character. Before the works of Fontane, provincialism was the nature of the German literary scene: 'almost all [of Germany's] major writers in the period 1830–1890 were born and worked in the provinces'.[15] The reasons usually given for this situation are the same as for the thesis that Germany's liberal revolution failed in 1848: late industrialization and the lack of a national centre and capital such as Paris or London, due to the country's political fragmentation before 1871.

Recently, literary scholars and cultural historians outside Germany have generally started to acknowledge the great variety and spirit of experimentation, as well as the critical depth of German provincial literary and artistic production. The village novels of Berthold Auerbach (Moyses Baruch) deal with the problems of Jewish life in villages and small towns, while Paul Heyse (1830–1914), Friedrich Hebbel (1813–63) and Theodor Storm (1817–88) were masters of the novella with themes from their native environment – from the Bavarian mountains to the North Sea coast of Schleswig-Holstein. The discovery of tradition and the cult of the past did not exclusively focus on the nation as a whole, but regional culture also produced its version of cultural historicism. Germans were a nation of provincials – nowhere is this more obvious than in nineteenth-century German *Heimat*-literature.

Just as the German liberals in the 1860s became more moderate and recovered from the tempests of the 1848 revolution, the literary and artistic scene settled for a quieter and less provocative approach. The *Bildungsbürgertum* continued to push ideas of national and cultural unity, while more popular elements increasingly joined this German *Kulturnation*. As post-Romantic writers slowly reached beyond the horizon of their province, the moderately critical Realism of the 1860s did more for the popularization of art in Germany than the sharply critical, rebellious and highly abstract art of the pre-March period that preceded it, or the *fin-de-siècle* avant-garde that followed.

Notes:

1. Madame de Staël, 'Of the German universities', in *De l'Allemagne* (London: John Murray, 1813), pp. 171–2.
2. McClelland, C. E., *State, Society and University in Germany, 1700–1914* (Cambridge: Cambridge University Press, 1980), p. 157, and Thomas Nipperdey, *Deutsche Geschichte 1800–1866. Bürgerwelt und starker Staat* (Munich: Beck, 1983), p. 463.
3. Both quotes in Kenneth Barkin, 'Social Control and the Volksschule in Vormärz Prussia', *Central European History*, XVI (1983), pp. 47, 49.
4. Hahn, H.-J., *German Thought and Culture. From the Holy Roman Empire to the Present Day* (Manchester: Manchester University Press, 1995), p. 119.
5. Blochmann, Maria W., *'Laß dich gelüsten nach der Männer Weisheit und Bildung'. Frauenbildung als Emanzipationsgelüste 1800–1918* (Pfaffenweiler: Centaurus, 1990), pp. 31–2.
6. Riasanovsky, Nicholas, *The Emergence of Romanticism* (New York, Oxford: Oxford University Press, 1992), p. 73.

7. Voegelin, Eric, *Science, Politics and Gnosticism* (Chicago: Regnery, 1968), p. 77; Russell, Bertrand, *History of Western Philosophy* (London: Unwin, 1974), p. 705.

8. Craig, Gordon, quoted by Peter Russell in *The Divided Mind. A Portrait of Modern German Culture* (New Zealand, Essen: Die Blaue Eule, 1988), p. 74.

9. Rotteck, Karl, and Welcker, Karl Theodor, *Staatslexikon* (1840), vol. IX, p. 542.

10. Drewitz, Ingeborg, *Berliner Salons. Gesellschaft und Literatur zwischen Aufklärung und Industriezeitalter* (Berlin: Haude and Spener, 1965), p. 102.

11. Craig, Gordon A., *The Politics of the Unpolitical. German Writers and the Problem of Power, 1770–1871* (Oxford: Oxford Unversity Press, 1995), p. 147.

12. Ringer, Alexander, ed., *The Early Romantic Era. Between Revolutions: 1789 and 1848* (London: 'Music and Society', Macmillan, 1990), p. 109.

13. Glaser, Herrmann, *Deutsche Literatur–Eine Sozialgeschichte. Vom Nachmärz zur Gründerzeit: Realismus 1814–1880*, vol. vii (Hamburg: Rowohlt, 1982), p. 67.

14. Gerstner, Herrmann, *Brüder Grimm* (Hamburg: Rowohlt, 1973), p. 138.

15. Sagarra, Eda, *Tradition and Revolution. German Literature and Society 1830-1890* (London: Weidenfeld and Nicolson, 1971), p. 73.

Select bibliography

Barkin, K., 'Social Control and the Volksschule in Vormärz Prussia', *Central European History*, XVI (1983), pp. 31–52.

Craig, G. A., *The Politics of the Unpolitical. German Writers and the Problem of Power, 1770-1871* (Oxford: Oxford University Press, 1995).

Engelhardt, D. V., 'Romanticism in Germany', in Roy Porter and Mikulas Teich, eds., *Romanticism in National Context* (Cambridge: Cambridge University Press, 1988), pp. 109–33.

Heafford, M., 'The Early History of the *Abitur* as an Administrative Device', *German History*, XIII (1995), pp. 285–304.

LaVopa, A., *Prussian Schoolteachers: Profession and Office, 1763–1848* (Chapel Hill: University of North Carolina Press, 1980).

McClelland, C. E., *State, Society and University in Germany, 1700–1914* (Cambridge: Cambridge University Press, 1980).

Mosse, G. L., *The Nationalization of the Masses. Political Symbolism and Mass Movements in Germany from the Napoleonic Wars Through the Third Reich* (New York: Meridian, 1975).

Nipperdey, T., *German History from Napoleon to Bismarck, 1800–1866*, transl. D. Nolan (Dublin: Gill and Macmillan, 1996; German version, Munich: Beck, 1983).

Ringer, A., ed., *The Early Romantic Era, 1789–1848* (London: 'Music and Society', Macmillan, 1990).

Sagarra, E., *Tradition and Revolution: German Literature and Society, 1830–1890* (London: Weidenfeld and Nicolson, 1971).

Schleunes, K. A., *Schooling and Society. The Politics of Education in Prussia and Bavaria, 1750–1900* (Oxford: Berg, 1989).

Smith, W. D., *Politics and the Sciences of Culture in Germany, 1840–1920* (New York and Oxford: Oxford University Press, 1991).

Speitkamp, W., 'Educational Reform in Germany between Revolution and Restoration', *German History*, XIX (1992), pp. 1–23.

Turner, R. S., 'The Bildungsbürgertum and the Learned Professions in Prussia, 1770–1830', *Social History*, XIII (1980), pp. 105–35.

6

The revolutions of 1848–49 and the persistence of the old regime in Germany (1848–1850)

Wolfram Siemann

There is an anecdote about the Austrian Emperor Ferdinand I that penetrates right to the heart of Germany's problems in 1848: Ferdinand was not gifted with a brilliant mind, but at least Metternich had succeeded in instilling in him an immense revulsion towards any kind of representative body of the people. If it was only mentioned in conversation, Ferdinand felt threatened. This happened very frequently after the revolutionary unrest of 1848 had spread from France to Austria. His court physician was confronted with this sensitivity one day when the doctor told him innocently that he had an excellent constitution. The Emperor snapped, 'Why do you talk about constitution? Say nature, if you please!' This little story reflects a fundamental problem of the revolutionary era: the lack of readiness and maturity among the reigning elites to tolerate the achievements and changes the revolution brought in its wake.

At the beginning, the Prussian King Friedrich Wilhelm IV did not react as brusquely as his Austrian colleague: he promised, in March 1848, that Prussia would forthwith be one with the rest of Germany; he put on the black, red and gold national colours, ordered the troops to retreat from Berlin and seemed to accept national unification on a democratic basis. However, in November 1848 he confessed to the Bavarian ambassador, 'Now I can be honest again'; he had democratic newspapers and organizations banned and declared a state of siege in Berlin. A second question therefore arises: how far could monarchs, in so far as they were unwilling to bow to the revolution, still rely on the traditional pillars of their power: the police, the civil service and the army? This question addresses the issue of persistence of the old regime. It laid down the limits for a democratic development from the very beginning.

Another anecdote illustrates the contrasting level of action. The speeches of the members of the Frankfurt parliament, meeting in the Paulskirche, were taken down in shorthand and published in the local press as soon as possible. This enabled constituents to see whether their member was doing a good job in Frankfurt. One member was asked during a stay in his home town why, in contrast to most of the other members, he was never mentioned in the papers. He answered, 'My good fellows, this isn't true. How often do you read "general murmur"! I'm always part of that.'

To sum it up more precisely: politics became, for the first time in Germany, the subject of free public debate; but the question remains whether the populace was mature enough for practical democracy. There still exists the idea of the impractical 'professors' parliament' at Frankfurt, the idealist liberal dreamers of 1848 with no sense for *Realpolitik*.

However, the German problems of 1848 cannot be properly judged without taking into account the European context. Recent research on the revolution emphasizes this, as the revolutions of 1848–9 were pan-European phenomena. In trying to view the deeper motives of all those revolutionary movements, four basic conditions have everywhere to be taken into account.

First, there were similar kinds of constitutional demands and there were several models to which people could appeal. One was the French *chartre constitutionelle* of 1814, which became exemplary for several constitutions in the separate German states, and then the *Deutsche Bundesakte* of 1815, the constitutional charter of Germany, which laid down that all the member states of the Confederation should proclaim a constitution which included consultative assemblies organized on the principle of the social estates (nobles, burghers, peasants). This constitutional principle derived its impact from the unfulfilled demands of the middle classes for sufficient political participation in states that drew their legitimation from monarchy, following the Restoration of 1815. Political struggle everywhere developed into struggle for a new order based on a written constitutional charter. Revolutionary struggle expressed itself as a struggle for law and constitution all over Europe – as a struggle for civil and political rights. This was already the case in the July revolution of 1830; it was even more so, though, in the initial phase of the 1848 revolution, which drew its first impulse not from France at all, but from Switzerland and Italy. The revision or the institution of a new constitution was always the issue precipitating unrest: after the *Sonderbundskrieg* (War of the Conferation of Seven Catholic Cantons) in November 1847, Switzerland, formerly a loose federation of separate states, constituted itself as a federal state with central powers and a federal capital in Bern. A further victory for the revolution was gained on 16 February 1848, at Palermo, when King Ferdinand II of Naples and Sicily issued a constitution. The breakdown of the July monarchy in France started with demonstrations in favour of electoral reform on 22 February 1848, and ended with the abdication of the king and the proclamation of a republic. In Germany, the so-called *Märzforderungen* (March demands) that were circulating at the beginning of the revolution, centred on constitutional demands: (1) arming the people under elected officers; (2) civil rights, especially unconditional freedom of the press and of assembly; (3)

trial by jury, following the English (and French) examples; and (4) immediate institution of a national German parliament. In other words, a common denominator of all the European revolutions of 1848 was the fact that they were all constitutional movements at the same time. They ended with the proclamation of a constitution, first in the Swiss Confederation, Naples, Florence and Piedmont, later in Rome, Venice, Berlin and Vienna, and of course in Frankfurt.

The second basic condition was the European undercurrent of nationalism. The endeavour for national self-determination and independence was embodied in the German, Polish, Czech, Hungarian and Italian national movements. Among many nationalities the myth of the (unredeemed) nation grew and flourished during the first half of the nineteenth century, especially among the Greeks, Italians, Hungarians and Poles. Much of the oppositional propaganda in pre-1848 Germany included Germany as one of these nations. The roots of this nationalism could be found with the French Revolution of 1789, which constituted the primary example for a nation state with common national symbols. During the 'pre-March' period, the myth of the *Völkerfrühling* (spring of the peoples) developed under the Restoration systems. In the 1820s, it took the shape of philhellenism throughout Europe; in the 1830s, after the failure of the Warsaw uprising in November 1830, it manifested itself in a pro-Polish attitude.

These pre-revolutionary utopias gave considerable impact to the revolution in the spring of 1848; they soon faltered, however, when the possibility of integrating the nation into a common state began to manifest itself. The term 'eine Art Nationsanwärter' (a kind of aspirant nation) was appropriately applied by Hans Rothfels to characterize the nationalities of the nineteenth century: ethnic groups striving for more autonomy and struggling for political unity. Subsequently, whenever territorial sovereignty and the drawing of borders came into dispute, modern nationalism showed its destructive and belligerent power. The new nationality conflicts of 1848 and the following years were marked by the novel characteristic that both sides were convinced that they were in the right, trying to mobilize the entire nation: in Denmark for Holstein, in Poland for Posen, in Italy for Southern Tyrol. Revolution and war combined to form a dangerous compound, and the struggle for national unity grew into discord among the nations.

The third basic condition was the socioeconomic crisis of pre-industrial crafts; this stemmed from the effects of overpopulation and the beginnings of proletarianization in the cities and wide areas of the countryside (see Chapters 3 and 4, above). The common European factor was the final collapse of the old estate system, which had been the basis of the legal and social order governing everyday life. Pauperism, industrialization and the orientation of crafts and professions of all classes towards a market economy marked the long-term crisis of the traditional crafts. Importantly, with respect to these issues, the crisis of 1848–9 seemed to hark backwards: with Luddite unrest, anti-Semitism or the demand for guild protection of the craft, as opposed to the principle of freedom to practise a trade. This element especially reveals the ambiguous character of the 1848–9 movement, contradicting the interpretation of those events as an early stage of a history of progressive emancipation.

A fourth European dimension is manifested in the crop failures and subsequent famine and inflation of 1845 and 1846, culminating in 1847. Responses before the revolution grew to European dimensions: local unrest caused by famine spread in waves across countries on the one hand; on the other hand there was a growing tide of emigration in the second half of the 1840s, which have, after all, been called 'the hungry forties' (Theodore S. Hamerow). Suffering was worst in Ireland; but episodes of famine in many German regions – especially in Silesia – found much public resonance.

Demands for democracy, nationalist movements and the accumulated socioeconomic conflicts, combined to form a more general crisis, suddenly accelerating all political processes. Demands were speedily met that would have been punished as treason only a short time before. The escalating popular movement seemed so outrageous to some of its contemporary observers, 'crazy' even, that soon it was called 'the mad year' (*das tolle Jahr*).

The most recent research on the revolution has been following the manifold strivings and movements on a local, regional and broader level, and continues to do so. To guard against glib interpretations of the aims and driving forces in the revolution, its chances of success, and its reasons for final failure, historians have drawn attention to the 'complexity of 1848'. In hindsight, they find themselves faced with a revolution that failed because of the very diversity of the demands made of it.

To the contemporary observer, it might have appeared like this: the many-faceted combination of pent-up conflicts caused a gigantic surge of hope the moment it was unleashed. People believed that with fundamental reforms, new men and modern institutions, and a politics more sensitive to the popular mood, all the ills of the times could be cured at once. When hopes for the future are this high, disappointment will follow soon. Honeymoon and hangover were never far from each other. Questions about the 'complexity of 1848' cannot be answered by generalization. It is much more useful to get an overall view of the dynamics the revolution developed by distinguishing several levels of political action. What seemed like a single revolutionary process to contemporary observers can, by scientific analysis, be broken down to five separate levels. Thus it is much easier to explore the scope and the dynamics of democratic politics. Caricatures may help to illustrate these levels of action. It is the nature of caricatures to distort reality, so the pictures at hand are, at the same time, documents of the public dispute that started to evolve in Germany in the year of the revolution.

I Revolution at the grass-roots

This picture illuminates the first level of action: the revolution at the grass-roots. One can see its violent version in Illustration 6.1 showing the Vienna revolution in May 1848. The revolution at the grass-roots gave vent to spontaneous movements of the people. This happened on the barricades and at protest meetings in front of town halls

Illustration 6.1   Barricade-building in Vienna in May 1848: the revolution at the grass-roots

and royal seats. Whole villages marched to the castles of their princes in southwestern Germany. One could see all social strata of the population there; one could even hear social revolutionary voices; the lower classes let out their pent-up rage.

The population was fundamentally concerned with politics as never before. Even contemporary observers were astonished at this process, like the *Breslauer Zeitung* which reported on 23 March 1848 that it was 'quite common to hear men from the lowest classes, even women, uttering clear and sensible opinions about political and social questions; just as if they had studied them for years'.

The more recent German research on the revolution has discovered, following Edward P. Thompson and Georges Rudé, social protest as a special driving force of revolution; the importance of peasant uprisings and actions has become clear. Usually, the 1848–9 revolution is represented as a middle-class democratic revolution (*bürger-*

lich-demokratische Revolution) but in fact, in its early phases around one-third of uprisings were agrarian in character. However, the farmers seldom pursued the same goals as the middle classes. They aimed to be free of their landlords but recognized the authority of the princes. Some understood freedom of the press not as freedom of the printed word, but as freedom from oppression by their landlords.

Another third of those participating in the revolution from below consisted of members of the urban lower classes: labourers, apprentices, journeymen, impoverished tradesmen, railroad and factory workers took part in the events; in April 1848, the public was agitated by a series of strikes, especially in factories and railroad construction sites.

In conclusion, one can note that peasants, tradesmen and workers, some two-thirds of those involved in the popular movements of early 1848, had been directly affected by social and economic crisis. In other words: those who carried the revolution from below belonged mostly to the lower orders, and were sharply distinct from the nobility and the middle classes.

If we take a look at the victims of the street fighting in Berlin, Frankfurt and Vienna, at those injured and killed, we see that most of them were also small tradesmen, journeymen and apprentices. They were simple people, townspeople. The crisis of the traditional trades that had lasted for decades – a structural crisis – found its visible outlet on the barricades. This crisis had already become evident in the early summer of 1847, when several uprisings caused by hunger had broken out throughout Germany. At this time, a Württemberg newspaper article had called the people mainly concerned 'in all places not at all those who really suffered hunger . . . the people acting throughout Germany are on the contrary run-down tradesmen, journeymen, apprentices, women of the big cities [this because of the disturbances at the weekly markets] and so on'.

The role of women in revolution has been very much underestimated up till now. Illustration 6.1 even shows a woman building a barricade on the right-hand side. But one has to look further than the barricades to observe the role of women in the revolution. When asking about the space for political action for women which opened up with the revolution, we can be sure that working as an elected member of parliament in Frankfurt or in the state parliaments was most certainly not encompassed in it. However, women were very much present in the audience and actively tried to influence parliamentary decisions. They wrote press articles, letters to members of parliament or newspapers, took part in general assemblies, even spoke there in rare cases, and showed their political sympathies by wearing ribbons in the national colours, or even organizing petitions.

The most women could do within the institutional revolution was to organize themselves in their own associations. These women's societies, especially in the state of Württemberg and in the Rhine-Main area, in no way dealt exclusively with women's issues but were an active part of the political and national movement. Women donated jewellery and money for the German fleet, promoted 'ancient German' fashion in contrast to French fashion, which they now shunned, they organized lotteries to equip the citizens' militias, and organized help for the fleeing revolutionaries from Baden in the summer of 1849. Women did much of the work in German Catholic and Free Church communities, in which opposition to the orthodoxy of the two great denominations had brought together 150,000 people since 1845. These independent religious communities were an active part of political opposition, and women had equal rights here: they participated in their work at all levels, founded their own women's societies within the religious communities, and took part in educational and social work. Democratic and Free Church movements were closely connected in 1848–9.

So the people taking part in the revolution had many different goals, not only 'unity and freedom' like the liberal and democratic middle classes, as we read in general textbooks. The lower classes that carried the revolution reflected the decay of pre-industrial society; they aimed in many cases for the social conditions of the past: against free professions and freedom of movement, for the expulsion of strangers from town and state. A recently published book about social protest in the German states with the fitting title *Straße und Brot* ('Street and Bread') illustrates areas of life far removed from the parliaments. But in the second wave of the revolution in September 1848, and even more so in the revolution of May 1849, the former unity of the opposition was lost when the differences of interest within the grass-roots revolution came to light. This considerably weakened the revolutionary movement.

II The political revolution

The grass-roots revolution opened the way for the second level of action: for a free press and a public organized into political parties.

Everywhere the governments of the princes had to concede freedom of the press and the free formation of political societies, for the first time in German history. Rapidly, a non-parliamentary political public developed. Rightly, it has emerged from the shadows into the light of research in recent years.

Obviously, the artist of Illustration 6.2 has a problem in depicting a society on its way to becoming an argumentative democracy. The picture shows the 'Reich-sweeping-mill'. It symbolizes public opinion, as is written on the funnel (*öffentliche Meinung*). The handle is operated by the *Deutsche Michel* a as personification of the whole German people. The picture deals with the call for re-elections under the impact of the September revolution. Michel works the mill as a sweeper. Below, as election returns, liberal and constitutional members emerge in an orderly and civilized manner. Above, on the left, republicans and democrats fly away; on the right conservatives and royalists are blown out.

In 1848, we stand at the very beginning of organized political parties in Germany. What criteria characterized these parties? They were freely formed organizations; they made up their opinions internally by majority votes; they submitted to a common programme and were open to anybody of the same views. They aimed for votes in the coming elections, which they achieved quite effectively. It was not only the parliaments

Illustration 6.2   'Reich-sweeping-mill': the political revolution for free press and parties

which proved their political competence in 1848; large parts of the urban population showed their own political maturity. It is amazing how quickly people became used to dealing with party rules.

As a new and special trait these parties were no longer just appendages of parliamentary factions or the result of state protection. They developed their own life and the variety of this party life has so far not been adequately assessed. Roughly, five political lines of thought can be distinguished: the conservatives, the constitutional liberals, the democrats, the political Catholics (*Pius-Vereine*) and the *Arbeitervereine* (workers' societies), organized nationally in the *Arbeiterverbrüderung* (workers' brotherhood).

So there was by no means just one homogenous mass of the socially discontented. Political life in the larger cities – especially in the southwest – had already been structured before the revolution. At Mannheim, for example, a reading society named '*Harmonie*' was a focal point where the opposition gathered. Public life came to the revolution already prepared; and it is not surprising that the earliest publicly expressed 'March demands' (*Märzforderungen*) came from Mannheim at the end of February.

Carola Lipp described the life experience of the middle-class political elite in a typical profile of a citizen from Württemberg. This interested and active citizen would have a high social status, would be a member of the crafts society (*Handwerkerverein*) to represent his economic interests, would sing in the *Liederkranz* (song circle) to express his musical interests, would join a political society in 1848, maintain public order as a member of the militia, go to general assemblies and festivals, would be informed about the hopes and dangers of the time from newspapers, might perhaps serve as an honorary member of the *Feuer-Rettungs-Compagnie* (a kind of early fire brigade) while most probably not joining the failed march of the Gymnasts Associations, which sought to save the Reich constitution against the Prussian troops in Baden and the Palatinate. His wife would be a member of a society that educated neglected children, while his daughter would participate in embroidering the citizenship flag in the *Jungfrauenverein* (maidens' society), and he himself would join a society to support out-of-work labourers. In 1849, he would win a seat in the local council.

This is to say: the revolution was deeply rooted in regional life via these societies, and the city became the centre of the revolution wherever the historical traditions of local self-government persisted.

The political societies found their voices in their own newspapers. The hitherto moderate tone of the press, enforced by censorship, was replaced by forceful polemics. The local newspaper of every town, city or region was suddenly dealing with national politics and the work of the Frankfurt National Assembly. It is an extremely arduous task to explore the jungle of the provincial press, and so far nobody has carried out an exhaustive analysis. Yet it is necessary to do so. The change in the local papers shows especially well how deep political interest began to reach in the year of the revolution. The newspapers show how the nobility, the clergy and the magistrates reacted, how active the local voters were and the variety of political parties. In addition, there were leaflets, placards, caricatures, handouts, organized petitions: the printed media were ubiquitous and so reached down to the grass-roots level of the revolution.

For the first time in Germany, there was freedom to express one's opinion publicly in the press and in political parties. Of course this expression was controversial and in no way unanimous. It is possible to say that this practical freedom was detrimental to the impetus of the revolution, just like the split between the liberals and the democrats. But was not the articulation of different interests necessary and unavoidable? Especially with regard to Prussia we are now well informed about conservative societies and their press; they did indeed weaken the revolution. On the other hand, there existed a central coordinating body of the democratic parties, the *Zentrale Märzverein*. It channelled the countless activities of regional revolutionary societies into what was called the campaign for the Imperial Constitution towards the end of the revolution. For a while, it strengthened the revolution.

All movements of the popular revolution, the press and the parties aimed for political influence; and this was seen to be concentrated in the regional parliaments and the Frankfurt National Assembly.

III   The parliamentary revolution

So, we reach the third level of action: the elected bodies.

It is a fact frequently overlooked that in the year of the revolution there were elections not only in Frankfurt, Berlin and Vienna, but also in Munich, Stuttgart, Oldenburg, Bremen, Altenburg and so on – that is, everywhere where there were constitutions that had to be revised and made democratic. Much political energy was spent on this. It multiplied political activities and scattered them. At a local level, the old magistrates and mayors were sometimes driven out and a new local constitution was fought for, as well as a reduction of police power, and an extension of voting rights. Political energy was released and at the same time absorbed by German federalism.

This level – the elected bodies – was very much dominated by civil servants and the educated middle classes. Parliamentary parties developed, the members of which maintained close contact with their constituencies. The three levels of revolution at the grass-roots, press and societies, and the parliament were closely interconnected. A situation typical of new representative systems soon developed: the voters and those they had elected soon found themselves involved in an increasingly dangerous conflict. This conflict erupted in September when a revolutionary uproar threatened the continuation of the National Assembly. Not only later critics, but also some contemporary observers had a problem with the practices of the parliamentary system. Illustration 6.3 shows the members of the Frankfurt parliament on a see-saw. Heinrich von Gagern, president of the parliament, tries to hold his balance on top. To the left, the left-wing members are quarrelling; Arnold Ruge is already falling backwards over a precipice. On the right the right-wing members are fighting. The caricaturist's sympathies are with the moderate middle.

Nowadays the negative judgements about the reputedly impractical 'parliament of professors' have been revised. We have learned to take the proceedings of the parliament and its parties seriously, and are able to appreciate the enormous and unusual achievements of the Frankfurt National Assembly and the parliaments of the separate regions. They were faced with the task of finding a mode of parliamentary proceedings out of nothing. The 1848 parliaments, especially the Frankfurt Assembly, had to act in the face of immense outside threats and pressures, yet they arrived at results and compromises in the same way as any other parliament. It is easy to imagine the parliaments breaking down from external pressure and internal fragmentation, yet they did not. The members were not experienced in parliamentary proceedings, even if they had been members of former regional parliaments, yet they were able to work democratically even under the most extreme conditions. Past research has tended to criticize the conflicts and fragmentation; to acknowledge these as an innate part of a representative and democratic system is easier for us today than for the post-revolutionary observers used to an authoritarian system. Everything that shapes modern parliamentary life was in evidence even then: the influence of small but decisive minorities, politics working with changing majorities, with obstructive negative coalitions, tension between party

Illustration 6.3   The Frankfurt Parliament on a seesaw: the parliamentary revolution

discipline and the freedom of individual deputies, the influences from lobbies outside parliament and interest groups.

Even if nationalist feeling ran high in the German National Assembly, one could argue that a reasonable answer to the national question was proposed by the assembly. The aim of establishing a constitutional state within 'national' borders offered protection to national minorities and respected their languages and religions (Article 188 of the Imperial Constitution of 1849). A similar solution was proposed in the draft constitution drawn up by the Austrian parliament in Vienna for dealing with the problems of a multinational state. Neither of these constitutions were implemented but they suggested a way of achieving peaceful coexistence between several nationalities within a single state.

In 1848–9 the Frankfurt Assembly not only worked out a constitution for a unified Germany (which finally failed) but also engaged in concrete parliamentary politics. But how did democracy actually work in 1848? This question is asked more and more often nowadays. As the parliament achieved astonishing results there is no reason to deny its astonishing political maturity. But now the question arises as to why the constitution failed if all that was indeed so excellent. In this context we will have to consider the fact that the fate of the revolution as a whole was not exclusively, perhaps not even decisively, determined by voting in the Frankfurt Assembly.

IV   The governmental revolution

There were many more dimensions to the process. So we will now have to direct our attention to the fourth level of action: the ministries.

During the events of March the reigning monarchs were for a time disorientated and at a loss what to do. In Illustration 6.4 the caricaturist likens their actions to the random character of a game of roulette. The representatives of the European powers are shown waiting eagerly for the outcome. Where will the 'globe' come to rest – at progress, republic, equality, constitutional monarchy, anarchy, freedom or reform? On the left we see the Prussian King Friedrich Wilhelm IV, on the right Emperor

Mein Herr, machen Sie ihr Spiel fertig, während der Ball noch rollt!

Illustration 6.4   'Sir, finish your turn, while the ball is still rolling': the governmental revolution

Ferdinand I of Austria. In the background on the right the French King Louis Philippe is already leaving the game, having lost after the February revolution.

In fact the revolution almost everywhere stopped short of toppling the Princes. Parallel to the revolutionary events of March the reigning monarchs appointed commoners and liberal noblemen from opposition factions into their governments. These were the so-called March ministries, by means of which the monarchs seemingly gave power to the pre-March opposition. These reshuffles within governments seemed to provide evidence of the long-awaited breakthrough of the middle classes.

It is necessary to view the events not only in the light of their outcome but also from the perspective of contemporary expectations. For the majority of the middle classes the institution of those March ministries must have had a calming effect, as they interpreted it as a promise from the monarchs for future parliamentary politics. The achievements appeared to be so vast that it was time to 'close down the revolution', as people put it. In fact the new governments concentrated their executive powers on achieving 'law and order' in the face of the continuing revolutionary uprisings. With this, they played exactly the part the monarchs had cast them in: to make the revolution lose its force.

This was certainly evident in Baden after the failure of the Hecker revolution in April 1848. The government of Baden had Gustav Struve and Karl Blind tried by jury as leaders of the revolution. The Württemberg government accused the Württemberg revolutionaries of treason and tightened the criminal law concerning political offences. Even during the revolution, counter-revolutionary politics began in the separate states.

As they did against individuals, so governments also took measures against political societies. As early as the 12 July 1848, the Württemberg government had a democratic society in Stuttgart (the *Kreisverein*) banned. Bavaria prohibited democratic associations on 12 August 1848; the government of Hesse-Darmstadt suppressed local unrest by means of the army and the police. Even the provisional central government instituted by the Frankfurt National Assembly had the same aims. We hear again and again that this central authority was nothing but a powerless phantom. After the September uprisings, on 3 October 1848, this alleged phantom addressed a decree to all German states ordering the institution of a political police. The regional governments were ordered to investigate the existing political societies, their tendencies, programmes, major decisions, number of members and influence among the people. The provisional government also asked about their connections with societies in other German states.

This state security decree demanded no less than the general surveillance of all political societies by the police. The central power instituted by the revolution thus undermined its own roots. The March ministries of many separate states did likewise. Already in autumn 1848 Hanover, Bavaria and Prussia began their surveillance records on political activities. The persecuting authorities of counter-revolution later used them to eradicate the remnants of the political societies.

V   Monarchy and counter-revolution

The central government even used troops to achieve law and order. They had been given the central command of the former *Deutsche Bund*. This leads to the fifth level of action: the pillars of traditional monarchist power.

Illustration 6.5, taken from the *Düsseldorfer Monatshefte*, is entitled 'Panorama of Europe in August 1849'. One could call it a pictorial piece of reactionary politics. We see the map of Europe, on which three large figures are shown. Two of them hold brooms, symbolizing reaction. The figure on the left, pointing to the ships leaving full of refugees, is Napoleon III who has almost entirely finished cleaning his country. The one in the middle with the spiked helmet is the Prussian king still sweeping. His broom points to southwest Germany, from where the revolutionaries are being swept away. They are gathering under a big hat resembling a liberty cap inscribed 'Helvetia'. Just at the edge of that cap we can see a gallows with a hanged man, reminiscent of the court-martials in Baden. In Frankfurt, nothing is left but a scarecrow which may be interpreted as the remnants of Imperial Administrator (a rough translation of *Reichsverweser*) and parliament. Small figures scurry between the feet of the Prussian king; they are the reigning monarchs. Two of them stand a little apart from the teem-

Illustration 6.5   Panorama of Europe in August 1849: monarchy and counter-revolution

ing mass of the very small ones: one at Stuttgart with the Württemberg antlers, one near Munich dressed in a beer stein (mug). In the east, we see the Austrians still fighting the Hungarians. Near Warsaw only a burnt-out candle remains from the failure of the Polish revolution. In Denmark the Dane dances, obviously triumphant because of Schleswig and Holstein. If one looks one also discovers the German navy, but in letters only, on the water of the Baltic sea – there is no trace of ships. And on the other side of the English channel there is Queen Victoria in a carriage, looking without much interest through her glasses at the European spring cleaning.

The revolution had 'stopped before the thrones', as the contemporary saying put it. And that meant the executive power remained with the monarchs. The noble officers, the common soldiers of the professional armies and the civil servants in the administration and the police force stood ready in the hour of counter-revolution. The part local officials, magistrates and militias played in this context is a subject of its own, and as yet little researched.

The army, in particular, was used against the revolution; for the first time in April in Baden, then on a smaller scale in several places, again in September 1848 at Frankfurt, and again in the summer of 1849. The last phase of revolutionary uprisings, after Friedrich Wilhelm IV had declined the imperial crown, erupted in parts of Prussia, Saxony, the Palatinate and Baden, threatening to spread to Bavarian territory on the right bank of the Rhine and to Württemberg.

The example of Baden shows that the revolution was successful when it was taken up by the troops. This happened temporarily in Vienna, during the militia uprisings in the Rhineland and Westphalia, but completely and effectively only in Baden after the Grand Duke had been driven out. The Baden revolutionaries succeeded when they were able to institute a State Assembly to work out a constitution, and a provisional republican government. They had won the support of the population and at least some of the pillars of power: officers, state officials and judges.

The counter-revolution approached from beyond the borders. The Grand Duke asked from exile in Mainz for the help of Prussian and Reich troops. By order of the provisional central government at Frankfurt, its Minister of War directed contingents from Hessen, Württemberg and Nassau to Baden. Troops from Bavaria, Württemberg and Austria also stood ready to intervene from the east and the south.

We still know far too little about this campaign for a Reich constitution, this last wave of the revolution. It came to a sad end at Rastatt on 23 July 1849 when the 5600 revolutionary fighters encircled in the fortress signed the surrender. In contrast to events in Saxony and the Palatinate, in Baden Prussian court-martials bloodily liquidated the revolution. In addition, courts of war and civil judges sentenced another 1000 revolutionaries.

The decisive battle was not fought in Baden, but earlier and elsewhere; and the standing armies with their monarchs won. As yet very little is known about the role of the armies during the revolution. It was especially striking how seldom the professional armies took up the cause of the revolution. I tend to think they did not yet identify sufficiently with nationalist (in the positive sense) ideas. When Prussian soldiers shot Saxon guerrillas or Baden soldiers, they did not waste a thought on the fact that they were confronting Germans. During the revolution, soldiers only threatened to revolt when they were conscious of facing compatriots, but in 1848 that meant, in the eyes of the soldiers, Prussians, Saxons, Bavarians and so on, not Germans. The moment when the army started to side with the revolutionaries and protesters played an important part in the fact that there was virtually no bloodshed during the uprisings of 1989 in Dresden or in August 1991 in Moscow. Generals Windischgrätz and Radetzky, or Banus Jellacic, were successful in their fight for the Habsburg monarchy because they could use troops of different nationalities (Czechs and Croatians) against Germans in Prague or Vienna, against Hungarians in the east and against Italians in Upper Italy.

With all these factors we also have to consider the fact that the revolution of 1848–9 was part of a European movement that failed everywhere with the exception of Switzerland. The turning point in the European revolution was reached in other places much earlier than in Germany. In the summer and autumn of 1848 monarchist troops had suppressed the revolution in many European states: in Cracow, Posen, Prague, Paris and Upper Italy. In summer 1849 revolutionaries from other countries reached the German scene: the Russian officer Bakunin came in via Dresden; a Polish general led the forces in the Palatinate, supported by a Hungarian colonel; a Polish general commanded troops in Baden; legionaries came from France and Switzerland; Frenchmen, Swiss and Hungarians formed their own legions during the fight for the establishment of the Reich constitution. The traditional armies of the monarchies for the most part did not succumb to the challenge of the revolution, other than in Baden, in Vienna, or among the Prussian militia in the Rhineland and Westphalia. The regular troops were not ready to take up the cause of the revolution. In battles they always showed their superiority, supported by modern equipment. To put it more drastically: Prussian guns destroyed the national myth of the barricades.

The caricature above (Illustration 6.5) already interprets the revolution as only one part of the events which were happening throughout Europe. So the question as to what might have happened if Friedrich Wilhelm IV had accepted the imperial crown is completely futile. He would not have done it, as he was not a romanticist, but a coolly calculating monarch very much conscious of his power, and to whom military force meant more than any constitution.

VI   Conclusion

In the light of the demise of East German socialism there is nowadays much emphasis on the fact that it was only a minority that effected the revolution (see further, Chapters 19 and 22, below). The same question may be asked concerning the events of 1848, pointing to a problem that could, on all five levels, be termed the locations of non-action, the calm zones of the revolution. We still know far too little about them. At the turning point towards counter-revolution those calm zones suddenly gained importance; those zones of political lull that had remained quiet during the revolution or that had become estranged from it in the early months: for example, the rural population. Strengthening loyalty to the monarchs, a feeling of tiredness towards the revolution and a passive 'protest against protest'; in a way the 'silent majority' gave strength to the old powers-that-be even before the impetus of the revolution faltered on the other levels of action. For example, when in October 1848 there were open uprisings on the streets of Vienna, Franz Joseph took flight and found a warm welcome at Innsbruck. In general, the most recent research on the revolution has shown that from the summer of 1848 onwards, conservative and '*Kriegervereine*' (soldiers' societies) began to organize in order to fight the revolution; this was the case especially in Prussia and Austria, but also in Bavaria.

All in all, no single simple interpretation of the 1848–9 revolutions in Germany can be offered. Three central facts support this claim most emphatically:

- Those active in the revolution of 1848 were on all five levels unable to grasp the dynamics of the revolution as a whole. Their powers of judgement and decision were not up to it. There was no decisive centre of action.
- Those active in the events of 1848–9 did not have one single, clearly decided aim which they failed to achieve. The Reich constitution was one aim, but the revolution was about more than that.
- The roots of the revolution were ambiguous. On the one hand, it manifested a crisis of pre-industrial society, an answer to overpopulation, hunger, inflation, distress among the trades. It stimulated dreams of old times, of guilds, of a closed-in burgher mentality and work without machines. It awakened fear of class conflict which had hitherto been concealed through the restrictions on movement from one occuption to another. The revolution revealed that opposition to change lay deep within society; indeed, the revolution actually aroused such opposition to active resistance.

  On the other hand, the revolution was a crisis of political emancipation, which meant that new forms matured within society that were suitable for solving the problems of the future. Political parties, the press, the parliaments and the political societies were the new media of political emancipation. Under the domination of the pre-revolutionary elites they could only partially develop their possibilities. The bureaucratic-military bodies of the state and the old loyalties turned out to be stronger in the end. We should term the process a tentative and broken attempt at emancipation. The monarchist elites among the nobility did not see – in contrast to much earlier events in England – the chance that change within society offered them. Not one among the ruling monarchs of the larger German states was amenable to a constitutional compromise on the basis of 1848. This was amply proved during the bitter decade of reactionary politics that followed. The monarchs had been successful in deceiving their March ministers. They used them in the hour of their need; they dismissed them in the hour of reaction.

Only during the 1860s did the realization dawn among the reigning court elites that controversies in the sphere of public opinion and political parties did not endanger the state; on the contrary, press and parties could be seen and used as welcome allies of one's own politics. This, at least, was the approach taken by Bismarck. When he came to power in 1862, the memory of 1848–9 was still very much alive, much more so than is generally appreciated today. From this point of view, the revolution had not (yet) failed. The Prussian constitutional conflict, when an attempt to implant the parliamentary system into the largest German monarchy failed, can be seen as its late heritage.

The more we contemplate all those dimensions which are revealed when we view the different levels of action, the less able we are simply to state that the revolution failed utterly. The revolution gave the impetus to a long-term wave of modernization. National unity remained a real prospect, both experienced and recalled. The peasants remained victorious in any case: they were finally and irrevocably freed from their dependence on their landlords. The legal system had changed fundamentally at all levels. Political participation was established despite the subsequent reactionary Restoration. Prussia had become a constitutional state. The Frankfurt constitution remained exemplary for a hundred years, up to the times of the Parliamentary Council in 1948–9. The national revolution also had the effect of altering relations between the various German states in ways which are important for a study of Germany as a federal political system, although much more research is needed on this. To see the revolution simply as a failure would mean understating its meaning and importance in German history.

Select bibliography

Barclay, David E. *Frederick William IV and the Prussian Monarchy* (Oxford: Clarendon Press, 1995).

Langewiesche, D., 'Die deutsche Revolution von 1848/49 und die vorrevolutionäre Gesellschaft. Forschungsstand und Forschungsperspektiven'. Part II, *Archiv für Sozialgeschichte*, 31 (1991), pp. 331–443 (a critical general overview of research on the revolution carried out in the last decade, also excellent on specific points of specialism).

Sheehan, J., *German History, 1770–1866* (Oxford: Oxford University Press, 1989).

Siemann, W., *Die deutsche Revolution von 1848–9* (Frankfurt: Suhrkamp Verlag, 1985, 5th edn, 1993) (English translation, Macmillan, 1998).

Siemann, W., *Vom Staatenbund zum Nationalstaat. Deutschland 1806–1871* (Munich: Beck Verlag, 1995).

Sperber, J., *Rhineland Radicals. The Democratic Movement and the Revolution of 1848* (Princeton, NJ: Princeton University Press, 1991).

Sperber, J., *The European Revolutions, 1848–1851* (Cambridge: Cambridge University Press, 1994).

7

Revolution to unification

John Breuilly

The story of German unification has usually been told from the perspective of Bismarck and Prussia.[1] Other views were marginalized or dismissed as impractical. Subsequent historical emphases, for example in economic history, have often strengthened rather than challenged the accompanying sense of inevitability. For example, when John Maynard Keynes wrote that Germany was unified by 'coal and iron' rather than 'blood and iron', this made Prussia's rise to power appear even more irreversible than in older, politically oriented historical writing. Yet there have always been alternative views as well as views of alternatives, even if often ignored. Historians realized that in 1945 nation states can be unmade; in 1989–90 that they can be re-made. We have not yet lost our sense of surprise at that second unification. This sense needs to be projected into our understanding of the first unification.

I will argue that Bismarck was an 'outsider' and that the views on Prussia and the national question he propounded in the 1850s were unrealistic. However, the world rather than Bismarck's view of it changed rapidly between then and the mid-1860s. Now his realism became one of substance as well as tone. Under these changed conditions Bismarck's methods and objectives could be successfully put into practice, although the risk of failure remained high. This essay presents an argument; not all historians would agree with it; and it focuses on explaining unification rather than surveying the years between 1850 and 1871.

I Bismarck the outsider

Bismarck came to political prominence in 1847 when Frederick William IV summoned a United Diet. There was conflict over whether the crown should concede a written constitution. This was related to the previous king's promise of a constitution during the war against Napoleon. Royalists insisted Prussians had been animated by monarchical and religious loyalties; the liberal majority stressed the prospect of a constitution. Bismarck shocked both sides by declaring that Prussians did not care about such things but were preoccupied with material issues. His cynicism about political principles was already clear.

However, he was a monarchist, indeed in 1848 an outspoken reactionary. For him the revolution was the work of urban mobs and intellectuals, enjoying some success only because of the failure of nerve on the part of the king and his advisers. The rural population had no interest in the revolution. A recovery of nerve, a whiff of grapeshot and mobilizing the conservative majority would suffice to restore order.

The revolution was swiftly defeated, if not quite as Bismarck advocated. His reward for vigorous royalism was appointment as Prussian ambassador to the restored Diet of the German Confederation in 1851. This was a remarkable decision. Bismarck had attended university with a view to a career in the civil service but had soon abandoned that and retired to the life of a provincial squire. The constitutional and revolutionary politics of 1847–50 plucked him from obscurity. He became an ambassador without working his passage as bureaucrat or courtier and without training in the arts of diplomacy. He was an outsider and remained suspicious of court and bureaucracy all his life.

In the Diet Bismarck confronted Habsburg supremacy. In 1850 Austria had compelled Prussia to abandon a forward policy in northern and central Germany, in turn relinquishing her ambition of integrating non-German territories with the Confederation. The Confederation was restored and Austria intended to dominate it. Bismarck wanted to end Austrian primacy and regarded the Confederation as an absurdity. The other states had no independence and survived only by balancing Prussia against Austria. The most sensible arrangement would be two territorial spheres of influence dominated by Prussia and Austria. Quite where the boundary would be drawn, how Austria was to be persuaded to accept this 'solution', how the accompanying international complications were to be handled: these were matters to be settled according to circumstances. Bismarck's fixity of purpose was accompanied by flexibility of method. Some of his ideas dismayed principled conservatives, like agreements with Louis Napoleon and with nationalists opposed to the Habsburg dynasty.

II The improbability of Prussian success, 1851–1862

No matter how flexible Bismarck's methods, they had no chance of success through the 1850s.

II.1 Population

The population of Prussia in 1850 was 16 million, that of the German part of the Habsburg Empire 17 million, with another 16 million in non-German parts. Prussia's population was increasing more quickly than Austria's but remained inferior. She lagged far behind Russia (70 million) and France (35 million), although in the latter case this was an improvement upon the 3:1 ratio of 1820. Population is not a direct indication of state power but it is the base on which that power rests.

II.2 Economy

Prussian economic growth was rapid in the 1850s and 1860s, involving the emergence of new industries associated with coal, and iron and steel production. Prussia's growth outstripped that of Austria, France and Russia but this should not be exaggerated. An attempt at calculating shares of world manufacturing output in 1860 yields the following percentages: Britain – 20, France – 8, Russia – 7, Prussia – 5, Austria – 4. These are very rough but if anything exaggerate Prussia's share by equating her with the subsequent Second Empire. (This is a constant irritation with pre-1871 'German' statistics.) Prussia in 1860 had about the same proportion of her labour force (20 per cent) in manufacturing industry as France. Austria and France were not economically stagnant; rather they were not as dynamic as Prussia.

This dynamism enabled Prussia to dominate the German customs union (*Zollverein*). After 1848 the *Zollverein* was used in conflicts between Prussia and Austria, with struggles over the entry of Hanover and the terms of a renewal of the Zollverein treaty for another 12 years. Prussia used her predominance to prevent Austria joining. Struggle over control of the *Zollverein* flared up again in the early 1860s. This demonstrated Prussian economic influence over other states. However, it is not clear how this might be translated into political domination, especially as most of those states supported Austria to counterbalance economic subordination.

A second advantage lay in qualitative features of Prussian growth. By 1860 Prussia produced more steel than France, Russia or Austria. Prussia in 1850 had a more extensive railway network than France, Russia or Austria and by 1860 this had increased in relation to Austria. Given the importance of new methods of transportation and weaponry in the wars of unification, these indicators of Prussian superiority were vital. Prussian military leadership proved better able to harness these achievements than their opponents.

Yet such advantages had not translated themselves into political and military power by 1860. Government expenditure was a lower proportion of GNP than Britain or Austria and about the same as France. In 1860 Prussian expenditure on her army (36 per cent) was a lower proportion of state expenditure than in France (39 per cent) or Austria (51 per cent). That is reflected in army sizes: Austria – 306,000; France – 608,000; Prussia – 201,000.

II.3 Diplomacy and war

One must also consider how states related to one another. After 1848–9 it appeared that the settlement of 1814–15 had been restored. Russia had played her part as 'policeman' of Europe, helping Austria repress the Hungarian rebellion. Britain pursued a policy of maintaining a peaceful status quo in Europe, though not prepared to intervene directly. The German Confederation was restored under Austrian leadership. The one significant difference was that France was now ruled by a Bonaparte who did not accept the 1814–15 settlement.

The Crimean War (1853–6) destroyed the old alliance against France. She fought with Britain against Russia. The result was to push Russia out of European affairs and cause a breakdown in Austro-Russian relations. Austria had adopted a policy of armed neutrality, but one biased against Russia because of concerns about southeast Europe. The war revealed the importance of steam-powered transport. In 1813–15 Russia marched troops across Europe as quickly as any other state. In the mid-1850s she could not send soldiers or equipment to the Crimea as quickly as Britain and France with their steamships.

A consequence of the weakening of Austria was the war of 1859–60 against France and Piedmont. France now pursued a forward policy in Europe, presenting herself as the champion of national movements against the dynastic status quo. Austria was left isolated. The rapid transport of soldiers to northern Italy and deployment of new weapons produced devastating results on the battlefield. Austria sued rapidly for peace at the cost of Lombardy, sparking off a process that led to an Italian kingdom by the end of 1860.

Bismarck urged Berlin to exploit these Austrian setbacks. The Prussian government, for conservative and pragmatic reasons, declined to act as he suggested. Neutrality was adopted during the Crimean War as Prussia had no wish to alienate the other powers. In 1859 it was considered impossible to ally with Bonapartist France against a fellow German dynasty. As the war took on a national character in Italy it inspired thoughts of something similar in Germany, but not direct action against Austria. Instead Prussia demanded parity with Austria as the price of support, in particular command of the army on the border with France. Austria refused such demands and Prussia remained neutral. Objectively Austria's position was weakened but she remained more populous and powerful than Prussia in 1860. Bismarck had been transferred to Russia by a government anxious to take him away from the sensitive post in Frankfurt.

II.4 Culture

The failure of the German National Assembly in 1848–9 demonstrated support for national unity but also how limited and divided that was and how formidable were the obstacles.[2] People were more concerned with other issues and did not see the relevance of a nation state to these. Catholics looked to Austria; Protestants to Prussia. Inhabitants of smaller states feared domination from either Vienna or Berlin. Democrats opposed an authoritarian nation state. Liberals wanted to preserve state powers but to harmonize arrangements so that people could enjoy common rights throughout Germany. Each viewpoint commanded minority support but was regarded with indifference or hostility by many more. Those who wanted unity were compelled by failure to be more realistic. Given the lack of popular support and the hostility of the Habsburg dynasty to strengthening national institutions, they looked to Prussia.

There was little scope for a national movement during the 1850s. Counter-revolution made open politics impossible. Governments restricted the scope for cultural activity which might have promoted a sense of national identity. Economic growth brought increased migration, urban growth and better communications which could have promoted national identity. But most migration was short-distance and within state boundaries. The emigration of many political activists to the USA depleted the ranks of a national movement. Amongst elites people were more drawn together at state than national level, for example through the operation of a Prussian constitution from December 1848.

Towards the end of the 1850s a relaxation of controls allowed more communication across state boundaries. State restrictions had not prevented the emergence of a national press dominated by liberals. Associations with a national commitment such as choral societies, sharp-shooting clubs, gymnastic and workers' educational associations had a larger membership and geographical spread than ever before. The extent of national feeling was vividly expressed at the centenary of Schiller's birth in November 1859. Many people participated throughout Germany and in German settlements in Europe and overseas to celebrate someone who, both in his life and art, was taken to embody the idea of cultural nationality as something transcendent, even religious. Yet this involved at most a few hundred thousand people. It is difficult to know how many were inspired by the message propagated by the educated nationalists who organized the celebrations. In any case, these nationalists had little idea of how to turn their ideas to political account. Nevertheless, the centre of gravity of this movement was in Protestant regions, concentrated in northern and central Germany, which could be regarded as favourable to Prussia.

So there was no massive national sentiment in favour of a Prussian forward policy in German in 1860. The war in Italy and the liberalization of domestic politics in Prussia with the accession of William to power (Regent 1858; King 1861) encouraged a national movement which looked to Prussia for leadership, expressed in the formation of the National Association (*Nationalverein*) in 1859. But the *Nationalverein* never exceeded 25,000 members and was politically divided. Admittedly it could appeal to the expanding cluster of cultural associations and operate through a network of elite organizations and liberal parties in various states. Nevertheless, this does not suggest huge support. Outside Prussia even nationalists who looked to Prussia for leadership wanted to see a liberalization of Prussian institutions first.

II.5   Crisis in Prussia

The optimism associated with the 'New Era' soon faded. William was acutely aware of military weakness which precluded any ambitious foreign policy. He had been alarmed by the decrepit nature of the army revealed by partial mobilization in 1859. He was determined to increase the size of the army and length of service. Prussia's army was, uniquely amongst the major powers, a conscript army based on short-term service (two and a half years), followed by two years in the line reserves and fourteen in the reserve army (Landwehr). Prussia did not call up all those liable to service. William wanted to increase the call-up rate; extend line service to three years, line reserve service to five years, followed by eleven years in the Landwehr which would be reduced to garrison and rear-line duties. The reforms would more than double the size of the regular army, greatly increase that of the reserves, involve a massive expansion in the number of officers, the formation of many new infantry and cavalry regiments and vastly increased expenditure.

The liberal majority of the Prussian lower house (the Landtag) could not accept this. Liberals recognized the need for a stronger army but objected to the thrust of the reforms, for example, marginalizing the Landwehr, especially if the army remained firmly under royal control without parliamentary influence.

William refused to compromise. Parliament refused to approve budgets. A series of elections produced ever-larger and more determined liberal majorities. By the autumn of 1862 William was contemplating abdication. Bismarck had recently been transferred from St Petersburg to Paris where he remained in close contact with conservative circles in Berlin concerned that the king ride out the storm. The Minister of War, Albert von Roon, advised William that one man had the nerve and ability to do this for him, a man who had vigorously, even recklessly, defended royal prerogatives against parliamentary presumption. Bismarck was called to Berlin and appointed Minister-President in September.

The odds against success, either in the domestic crisis or the realization of his expansionist dreams, were huge. Public and parliamentary opinion, much of it shaped by wealthy groups with access to major newspapers and periodicals, opposed his appointment. Without military reform Prussia remained the weakest of the major powers. National sentiment, itself weak and divided, rebuffed overtures from a man known only for his defence of Prussian dynasticism. Austria, after setbacks in 1859–60, had embarked on constitutional reform and was proposing changes in the German Confederation designed to enlist national support.

III   The process of unification

Bismarck was appointed to solve the domestic crisis. He withdrew the pending budget but collected revenues, arguing that in the event of a stand-off between crown and parliament the executive must continue to run the country on the basis of laws already passed. Parliament rejected this novel theory ('the constitutional gap') but, as it also rejected extra-parliamentary resistance such as a tax boycott, Bismarck overrode that opposition. He tried to interfere with parliamentary immunity and to bribe or bully journalists to undermine liberal opponents. Bismarck probably wanted some compromise to end the crisis but the king and many conservatives would not countenance this.

The domestic crisis overshadowed all else. When Bismarck, addressing a parliamentary committee, made the speech containing the famous assertion that an effective German policy would have to be based on 'iron and blood' rather than parliamentary resolutions, he saw himself offering the liberals a realistic solution to the national question. However, liberals saw it as a threat to them and, given Bismarck's weak position, an empty one. His one major foreign policy move, support for Russian suppression of a Polish uprising in 1863, alienated liberal opinion. In 1863 Bismarck was confronted by an assertive German policy on Austria's part and had great difficulty persuading William not to attend a congress of German princes. Only the Schleswig-Holstein issue enabled Bismarck to escape from this unpromising situation.

III.1   The war against Denmark

Schleswig and Holstein were two duchies ruled in personal union by the Danish crown. Holstein was German-speaking and a member of the Confederation. Schleswig had German and Danish speakers and was not in the Confederation. Danish nationalists claimed Schleswig; German nationalists insisted on the indivisibility of the duchies. The succession of Christian IX to the Danish throne on the death of Frederick VII on 15 November 1863 did not automatically confer his succession to rule over the duchies as well. Christian IX signed a charter incorporating Schleswig into Denmark. German nationalists responded by demanding the title of Duke of Schleswig-Holstein be granted to Frederick, Duke of Augustenburg, who would bring both duchies into the Confederation.

The matter had been subject to international treaty since 1850. The major powers wanted the Treaty of London observed and were relieved when Austria and Prussia signalled this as their aim. The Danish government, under nationalist pressure, refused to comply with the treaty and in late 1863 the Confederation sent troops into Holstein. Denmark hoped for international support, if only because of concern about sea routes. British policy was undecided and unprepared for unilateral action. Napoleon was happy to let a crisis brew which he might exploit. Russia, though broadly pro-Danish, was unhappy with her nationalist intransigence and concerned to maintain good relations with Austria and Prussia as she suppressed the Polish insurrection.

Consequently there was no concerted international resistance when Prussian and Austrian troops invaded Schleswig at the end of January 1864, especially as their avowed aim was to enforce the terms of the Treaty of London, and they did not dispute Danish rights in Schleswig and Holstein or support the Augustenburg claim. No diplomatic advances were made during an armistice between April and June, the war was resumed and Denmark compelled to hand over the duchies to Austria and Prussia in October.

German national sentiment was marginalized once Austria and Prussia took control in January 1864. German nationalists were appalled at how Berlin and Vienna disavowed Augustenburg and treated the issue as a matter of treaties rather than national interest. Occasionally Austria or Prussia appealed to nationalism but in a cynical and self-serving way. For Austria the main advantage of sacrificing the good opinion of the national movement was that Prussia did so too. Vienna was happiest to pursue a policy of 'dualism' with Prussia which fitted with Confederal traditions and ensured dynastic control.

Unfortunately for Austria, Schleswig-Holstein was geographically remote and of no direct interest. Once the area was under joint Austro-Prussian control it was impossible for Austria to shape events. Austria sought support from Prussia on issues such as entry into the *Zollverein* and in Italy in exchange for giving Prussia a freer hand in Schleswig-Holstein. When that failed the leader of the dualist policy in Vienna, Rechberg, resigned in October 1864. Austria became more assertive and bid for nationalist support by taking up the Augustenburg cause. Opposition from Prussia made war appear likely but this was posponed by the Gastein Convention of August 1865 establishing separate military governments: Austria in Holstein, Prussia in Schleswig. Austria abandoned her constitutional experiment and the government made concessions to Hungarian demands for greater autonomy. Austria was clearing the decks for action in Germany.

It is doubtful whether Bismarck had any clear objective in November 1863. He could not afford to alienate the major powers and could only take an active position in defence of international treaty obligations in alliance with Austria. However, following military success Bismarck could contemplate annexation of the duchies. War removed treaty obligations. By keeping conditions for settlement vague or unacceptable to Denmark he ensured the continuation of military occupation. When forced to go along with the Augustenburg option once it was clear Danish authority would not be restored, he hedged it about with conditions which made it impossible for Frederick to accept. The result was *de facto* military occupation. The principal issue now was whether Bismarck was prepared to confront Austria and take direct control in the duchies. This appeared to be the case in early 1865 as Austria took up the Augustenburg cause. However, there was a powerful peace party in Berlin, including the Crown Prince. The King was proving difficult to persuade into war against a fellow German prince. There were problems raising war finance, especially given the constitutional crisis. Above all, it was not clear that the diplomatic and military balance of power favoured war. Prussia had secured no allies against Austria. The war against Denmark had proved a useful testing-ground for the military reforms and brought the Chief of the General Staff, Moltke, to the top. But many observers had been impressed with Austrian military effort. Moltke, though desirous of war with Austria, was realistic about the risks involved. In 1860 he had assumed a good chance of Habsburg success, the destruction of the defeated dynasty and major concessions to France and Russia by the victor.

Nevertheless, for Bismarck, a confrontation with Austria to settle issues in Germany was inevitable. The war against Denmark, the first military success since 1815, stimulated Prussian rather than German patriotism. Even some liberal nationalists began to see in a greater-Prussia policy a way forward. Bismarck had learnt that Britain and Russia were unlikely to interfere in crises in central Europe. He now had to ensure Austria's diplomatic isolation, secure alliances for Prussia and make the necessary financial and military preparations.

III.2   The war of 1866

The diplomatic key was France. After success in Europe in the 1850s Louis Napoleon had suffered setbacks in Mexico in the 1860s and his health was failing. The renewal of domestic opposition made success abroad important. His German policy was shaped by ideology and interest. He supported national movements, especially if he could tie them to France. This made it difficult to cooperate with the Habsburg Empire. His interests would be served by a breakdown of Austro-Prussian dualism which should provide opportunities for diplomatic and territorial profit.

Bismarck met with Napoleon at Biarritz in October 1865. Napoleon was difficult to pin down. He favoured some extension of Prussian influence in northern Germany. A weakening of Austria might help bring his Italian policy to completion. However, he had no wish to see Prussia become too powerful and pursued ideas of balancing this by the enlargement of some of the medium states. He was not averse to territorial gains; Belgium and the Rhinelands were vaguely mentioned. The policy was Bismarckian: no fixed plan but a determination to create and exploit favourable opportunities. It took little genius on Bismarck's part to secure Napoleon's good wishes.

Napoleon could help matters forward. Italian unification would only be complete with the removal of Papal authority in Rome and the recovery of Venetia. France backed the Papacy with soldiers and Catholic opinion in France made it impossible to abandon that policy. Venetia therefore became the principal objective. Prussia wanted Italian leverage against Austria and Italy had the same use for Prussia. In March 1866, with tensions mounting in Schleswig-Holstein, General Govone came to Berlin to secure an alliance against Austria. Both sides were suspicious that each would use the other to obtain concessions from Austria at their own expense. With Napoleon's support an agreement limited to three months stipulated that Italy would go to war with Austria if Prussia did. Prussia did not make the same commitment but agreed that, in the event of war, neither side would make peace until both had made territorial gains. This was to be Venetia for Italy and some unspecified equivalent for Prussia. Napoleon's calculation was made clear by a remark he made at the time:

> In this way [by means of the Prussian-Italian agreement] Italy will get Venice, and France will benefit by the conflict of the two powers whose alliance hems her in. Once the struggle has begun France can throw her weight into the balance and must obviously become the arbitrator and master of the situation.[3]

Napoleon also engaged in discussions with Austria and vaguely indicated the support he could offer in the event of war with Prussia. Ideas of enlarging states like Bavaria or Württemberg or even creating an independent Rhenish state attracted Napoleon. This should not offend national sentiments (indeed it was more in line with federalist views than Hohenzollern or Habsburg domination) and would secure client states for France. Austria agreed that Venetia would be ceded to Italy. Italy was in the fortunate position that both Prussia and Austria had promised her Venetia, but only after a war.

This commitment made it clear that Austria regarded maintenance of her position in Germany as the first priority. She was not prepared to negotiate division into territorial spheres of influence. Her preferred policy was dualism with Prussia. Although she flirted with more radical policies – support for Confederal reform, a direct imposition of Habsburg hegemony – this is best understood as departures from normal policy or ways of pressurizing Prussia into returning to dualism. Accordingly Austrian war aims in 1866 were less clear-cut than those of Prussia. Indeed, some in Austria regarded war as the most extreme method of compelling Prussia to return to dualism rather than as providing an alternative solution. This helps explain why all the medium German states (with the exception of Baden which abstained) voted in the Federal Diet in support of Austria in June 1866. Meanwhile the national movement was paralysed as German civil war approached.

Most contemporaries assumed an Austrian victory. The shift of power towards Prussia was taking place rapidly and was hardly appreciated. While Prussian military expenditure had doubled since 1860, Austria's had halved. The Italian alliance compelled Austria to divide her armies, sending 100,000 to the south, leaving 175,000 Austrian soldiers and 32,000 Saxons facing 250,000 Prussians in the north. The rapid collapse of the Hanoverian and Bavarian armies removed them from the equation.

The new capacities of mass mobilization were realized. Nearly half a million soldiers were transported to the battlefields of northern Bohemia, more than were present at the greatest of the Napoleonic battles fought at Leipzig in October 1813. The speed with which this was done was unprecedented. Prussia did best. One single-track railway ran north from Vienna into Bohemia; by contrast, Prussia used five lines to bring her troops southwards. Moltke adopted the novel and risky strategy of keeping his forces separate for faster movement, only concentrating them on the eve of battle. Consequently the Austrian commander, Benedek, was always on the defensive, reacting to situations created by Prussia. Even if there were moments when he could have counter-attacked to devastating effect, this defensive posture made it improbable that he would. Although Austrian artillery and cavalry matched that of Prussia, the new breech-loading rifle gave the infantry a decisive advantage against the Austrian doctrine of 'cold steel'. It was only possible to make and supply such a weapon with the new manufacturing technology now available and only Prussia with her well-educated and short-term conscript army could contemplate handling the problems of retraining and discipline involved.

III.3   Germany after Königgrätz

The Habsburg dynasty had no stomach for prolonged war after the first heavy defeat. Bismarck was anxious to accommodate this preference although he had to persuade William and Moltke not to continue the war, forcing the Habsburgs into renewed resistance and opening up possibilities of international interference. Austria suffered no territorial loss in Germany.

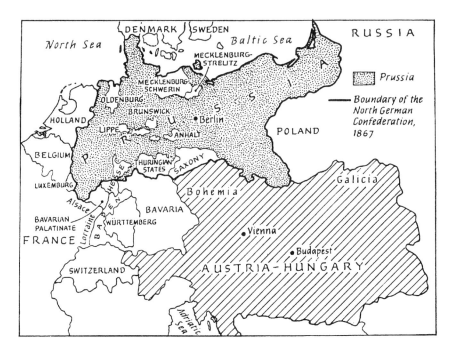

Map 7.1 Germany and Austria–Hungary, 1867

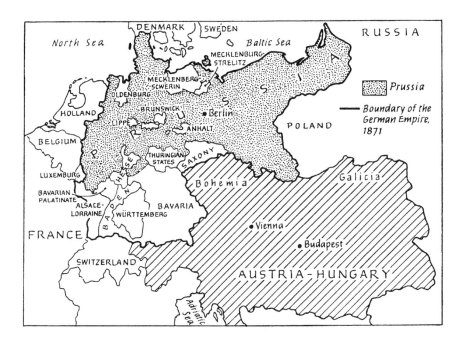

Map 7.2 Germany and Austria–Hungary, 1871

Hanover, the Electorate of Hesse and the Duchy of Nassau were less fortunate; they were annexed to Prussia, their princes deposed and, along with Schleswig and Holstein, transformed into Prussian provinces. The Free and Imperial City of Frankfurt am Main was also seized. A more extended territorial sphere of influence was established in the form of the North German Confederation comprising all the other German states north of the river Main. Bismarck brought the south German states into a secret military alliance. These states were also members of the *Zollverein*.

Bismarck recognized there was a limit to how much Prussia could absorb, even without diplomatic obstacles. In a memorandum written during the crisis of 1859 he had declared that Prussia should: 'march southwards with our entire army carrying frontier posts in our big packs. We can plant them either on the Bodensee or as far south as Protestantism is the dominant faith.'[4] The sense that Catholic populations would be difficult to absorb, whatever the common nationality, is clear. He even argued against taking part of Protestant Franconia from Bavaria because of the state loyalty that had been developed. This sensitivity to opinion expressed itself in two striking innovations in relation to Prussia and the North German Confederation.

In Prussia on the same day as the battle of Königgrätz (3 July), whose outcome was yet unknown, new Landtag elections were held. The liberal opposition was defeated by a surge of Prussian patriotism. Bismarck, basking in military triumph, returned to Berlin and a more compliant parliament. Surely royal prerogative would be asserted and parliament put in its place. Instead Bismarck introduced an Indemnity Bill. The government would put its measures to parliament for approval in the normal way; and parliament would not seek retribution for its treatment since 1862. It remained open to the government to resume non-parliamentary rule under the terms of the 'constitutional gap' doctrine. Nevertheless this was a symbolic concession to liberalism which angered conservatives. Bismarck believed that strong, stable government rested on the support of major social forces. These were never precisely defined but bourgeois liberals were clearly included. Bismarck's anti-liberal measures were not attempts to destroy liberalism but to force it into cooperation with him. Most liberal deputies accepted the olive branch, forming the National Liberal Party and leaving the oppositional minority in the Progressive Party.

Bismarck regarded this constitutionalism as the best way of integrating the new provinces. Hanoverians were not asked to exchange a Guelph for a Hohenzollern but subjection to a feeble and antiquated kingdom for citizenship in a poweful and modern constitutional monarchy. Although some (e.g., Hanover's Catholic minority) rejected the offer, the new provinces developed into powerful strongholds of National Liberalism.

Similar considerations informed Bismarck's policy in the North German Confederation. With war approaching in 1866 Bismarck declared that Prussia supported reform of the Confederation, including a popularly elected parliament. This seemed unlikely from a man ruling in defiance of his own parliament. Bismarck was, however, perfectly serious and the constitution drawn up for the North German

Confederation included this provision. His intentions are not clear. Analysis of elections to the Landtag had suggested that liberals were not genuinely popular. Bismarck had long argued that the monarchy could be popular. The new parliament, the Reichstag, could be used as a counterbalance to the Prussian Landtag. Anyway, Bismarck did not appear to be risking much. The Reichstag had limited powers. The legislative initiative was in the hands of the Bundesrat whose president was the King of Prussia and which consisted of state delegations with sufficient Prussian votes to veto unwelcome measures. The military component of the budget – over 90 per cent of Confederal expenditure – was exempt from parliamentary control. Nevertheless this was a bold move and laid the basis for the development of legitimate mass politics in Germany.

III.4   From North German Confederation to war with France

Bismarck had to integrate new Prussia into old Prussia, consolidate the North German Confederation and bring the south German states into his orbit. He also had to block revanchism in Austria and deal with French reactions to the unexpected outcome of 1866.

Agreement with the National Liberals was the key to the first two tasks. This party emerged as the largest in the Reichstag. An ambitious legislative programme was carried through including unifying measures in such matters as currency, weights and measures, commercial and labour relations law and common citizenship rights. Many constraints on a market economy were removed.

This was part of a burgeoning national movement which was Protestant, progressive and optimistic. The National Liberals believed history was on their side and that Bismarck was helping construct the modern state and society which would eventually sweep aside his kind of rule and values. Bismarck also emphasized the national and constitutional character of the Confederation to appeal to opinion in southern Germany and resist French claims to 'German' territory.

The bid for south German support included the formation of a customs parliament in which members of the Reichstag would be joined by popularly elected deputies from the south. The plan backfired. The elections provided Catholics, state loyalists and democrats with the opportunity to mobilize anti-Prussian sentiment. This unlikely alliance won a majority of seats. Strong anti-Prussian feeling continued to be expressed in south Germany up to 1870.

In Austria a new Chancellor, formerly Prime Minister of Saxony, Count Beust, aimed to regain influence in Germany. Under a new constitution of 1867 the Hungarian half of the empire was granted a large measure of autonomy on terms which benefited the Magyar majority. The Magyars opposed any ambitious German policy. This, plus financial crisis, the growing influence of Czechs in the western half of the Empire and a renewed concern with affairs in southeastern Europe, constrained Beust. He encouraged France in anti-Prussian policies but could offer little in return, especially if this might appear anti-German. While Prussian relations with Russia remained good, there was no help to be had there.

This left France isolated, especially as Britain regarded France as the major threat to European stability, a view strengthened by Napoleon's pursuit of profit from the new German arrangements. His government was unpopular at home and there was concern about the creation of a new power whose territories extended to the left bank of the Rhine. Ambitions about Belgium and the Rhinelands were set aside. By 1867 Napoleon was concentrating on Luxemburg which was bound in personal union with the Netherlands. The King of the Netherlands was prepared to sell Luxemburg to France but only with Prussian agreement. Once the matter became public, Bismarck used the storm of protest in Germany to insist that he could not give way.

Napoleon liberalized at home. The new, popular ministers who came into government in 1869–70 were more anti-Prussian than their predecessors. Military reforms expanded and improved the army. By 1870 France felt confident. Even if she began war alone she envisaged that other powers like Austria and Denmark could be drawn in.

Preparedness for war and sensitivity to further national affronts from Prussia were sparked off by news on 2 July 1870 that Prince Leopold, a member of the House of Hohenzollern, had been offered the Spanish crown. The French were sure this was another Prussian plot and demanded not only withdrawal of the candidacy but a clear undertaking that Prussia would never again engage in such a policy. The former was secured; the latter was used by Bismarck to justify a war in which France appeared the aggressor.

Did Bismarck plan for war with France? One cannot give definite answers about motives but can simply note various points. Bismarck's national policy in southern Germany was in disarray by early 1870. The idea of reviving the imperial title had foundered, partly on objections from the kings of Bavaria and Württemberg. Those governments faced crises over the issue of introducing Prussian-style military reforms. Moltke advised that the military balance of power would worsen. Prussia had further modernized her army after 1867. The extension of Prussia, the creation of the North German Confederation and the military alliance with the south German states meant Bismarck could call upon demographic resources roughly equal to those of France and the backing of a stronger economy. But the French were making military progress, had popular support for war against Prussia and might in the future secure alliances. There were good reasons, therefore, for settling issues through war with France. The Hohenzollern candidacy must be seen in this context. Bismarck denied knowing of the candidacy until just before it was made public. For many years historians were denied access to relevant documents. Once these were seen, after 1945, it was clear that Bismarck had lied. He had known of the matter from the outset and advised support for the candidacy.

It is going too far to say he did this to bring about war. As Bismarck pointed out, the French overreacted both in their judgement of the significance of a Hohenzollern on the Spanish throne and in demanding Prussian undertakings for the future. More likely is that Bismarck wanted another iron in the fire to be used if expedient and dropped if necessary. In July 1870 he decided to use it. Concern about continued French pressure, reversing slippage in the south German states and cutting the ground from under Austrian revanchism all led Bismarck to this policy.

The response of public opinion in Germany to the outbreak of war was gratifying. Strong anti-French sentiments were expressed. South German and Catholic soldiers fought as bravely as Protestants from the north. Yet we should not exaggerate. We know little about popular opinion which should not be confused with public opinion, in a press dominated by National Liberals. Common anti-French sentiment which led many hostile to Prussia and Bismarck to rally behind the national cause masked conflicting views about how Germany should be organized after the war.

The war began as in 1866, though on a more massive scale. German mobilisation was more rapid than that of France. In under three weeks over one million soldiers had reported for duty and nearly half a million had been moved to the French frontier, whereas the French had fewer than 250,000 soldiers in the army on the Rhine. France never recovered and was always on the back-foot, reacting to German moves. There were moments when action against divided German forces might have turned the tide but in the confusion of war it was expecting too much for such high-risk decisions to be taken. By early September the French had lost decisive battles and many soldiers. Although France continued to raise armies, they lacked the weapons, officers and experienced cadres lost in that first phase. War was no longer a matter of improvization, with chances of recovering from early setbacks, as in the revolutionary and Napoleonic period. War was about the capacity to send huge numbers of men with highly destructive fire-power quickly into the territory of the enemy and to smash that enemy before he was ready.

Where the war diverged from 1866 was in length and bitterness. This was a national, not a civil war. Bismarck was not concerned to save the Bonapartist state as he had been the Habsburg crown. He mistrusted French undertakings and thought only superior power would prevent a reversal of German triumph. Achieving that superiority included annexing Alsace-Lorraine and imposing a large indemnity. These objectives could be pursued at leisure as no other power was prepared to intervene. Nevertheless, Bismarck did not seek the total military destruction of France as advocated by Moltke.

V The new German state

Once victory was secured Bismarck could turn his attention to the entry of the south German states into a national state. There was no question of annexation as in 1867. The constitution was founded upon treaties made separately with each of the states. State rights and differences were respected.[5]

The imperial title was assumed by the King of Prussia. The dynastic emphasis was expressed in the foundation ceremony at Versailles. The Emperor was surrounded by

Illustration 7.1 *The Proclamation of the Empire in the Hall of Mirrors at Versailles* (18 January 1871) by Anton von Werner (1885)

fellow German princes, army officers and high state officials. The nation, including its parliamentary representatives, watched from outside as the dynasties constructed a nation state which forcibly excluded Austrian Germans and included Danish, Polish and French speakers. The imperial state was a thin layer of government superimposed on the states and heavily dependent on Prussia. The new state was reluctant to adopt national symbols. Manipulating the various conflicting institutions to secure his own power was Bismarck, the loner, the outsider, but surrounded with a nimbus of genius which raised him above the level of any other figure in Europe between 1815 and 1917.

This state has to be understood in terms of its sudden and violent creation. It was not the product of a steady convergence between power and culture, state institutions and national sentiments. As late as 1860 Prussia was in no position to challenge for dominance in Germany. Rapid changes in international relations, economic and technological performance, and the nature of war, opened up a brief window of opportunity for Prussia in the mid-1860s. It seems likely that Prussia would have soon lost these advantages, especially as other states came to appreciate their significance. The sentiment of nationality would have continued to grow in importance as this was a pan-European phenomenon and a central feature of modern society. However, there was no dominant political expression of that sentiment, neither territorial nor institutional. National feelings were ignored rather than exploited up to 1867 as a political genius, brought to leadership in Prussia through a domestic crisis, pursued with great flexibility objectives he had fixed upon a decade earlier. What had been impracticable then, now had become possible. Once the possible is made actual, the temptation is to make it appear inevitable. But there were always other possibilities. Germany was becoming more national but there was nothing preordained about how it became a national state.

Notes:

1. See below, Chapter 23 by Stefan Berger, on this kind of historical writing.
2. See Chapter 6 by Siemann, above, as well as my Chapter 27, below, on the national idea.
3. Quoted in Heinrich Friedjung, *The Struggle for Supremacy in Germany 1859–1866* (1935; re-issued 1966), pp. 113–14.
4. Bismarck, *Gesammelte Werke* (1924–35), vol XIV, document 724, Bismarck to Gustav von Alvensleben, 23 April/5 May 1859.
5. For further details see the next chapter.

Select bibliography

Hobsbawn, E., *The Age of Capital* (1975) for European background. T. Hamerow, *The Social Foundations of German Unification 1858–1871*, 2 vols (1969, 1972) is compendious. J. Sheehan, *German History 1770–1866* (1989) is superb. G. Craig, *Germany 1866–1945* (1978) is strong on political and military history.

For European diplomacy, W. E. Mosse, *The European Great Powers and the German Question 1848–1871* (1958) is still useful. On war and diplomacy, see W. Carr, *The Wars of German Unification* (1991). For Austria, see F. R. Bridge, *The Habsburg Monarchy among the Great Powers 1815–1918* (1990). For France, see R. Magraw, *France 1815–1914: The Bourgeois Century* (1983).

On nationalism, see the survey by H. Schulze, *The Course of German Nationalism: From Frederick the Great to Bismarck 1763–1867* (1991). D. Düding, 'The Nineteenth-Century German Nationalist Movement as a Movement of Societies', in H. Schulze, ed, *Nation-building in Central Europe* (1987), pp.19–49 is useful.

For the wars, see G. Craig, *The Battle of Königgrätz* (1965) and M. Howard, *The Franco-Prussian War: The German invasion of France, 1870–1871* (1961). For a broader approach, see D. Showalter, *Railroads and Rifles: Soldiers, Technology and the Unification of Germany* (1986).

For Prussia and Bismarck, see: L. Gall, *Bismarck: The White Revolutionary*, vol. I (1986); and O. Pflanze, *Bismarck and the Development of Germany*:vol. I: *The Period of Unification 1815–1871* (1990).

Kennedy, P., *The Rise and Fall of the Great Powers: Economic Change and Military Conflict from 1500 to 2000* (1988) and M. Mann, *The Sources of Social Power* vol. II: *The Rise of Classes and Nation-States, 1760–1914* (1993) place German unification into general and theoretical, if different, contexts.

I consider the subject at greater length in J. Breuilly, *The Formation of the First German Nation-State, 1800–1870* (1996).

Part II

1871–1918

Introduction to Part II: 1871–1918

John Breuilly

The German Second Empire was proclaimed in the palace of Versailles in January 1871. The site is significant – stressing the dynastic nature of the new state and that it was the product of success in war. That same date ended its life in November 1918 with admission of defeat in war and a revolution in favour of a republic. Not surprisingly, the centrality of war and monarchy in both the foundation and destruction of the first German nation state have shaped much of the historical writing on the Second Empire. This similarity of beginning and end has in turn to be related to the tremendous changes which took place in Germany over this half century. There is also the problem of setting the history of Germany into a broader context, asking how much that history resembled the history of other societies and states, as well as considering the significance of interactions between Germany and other countries.

There are four chapters primarily devoted to this period. (Some of the chapters on the period of the Weimar Republic also have something to say about the origins of certain political, economic or cultural features in the years before 1918.) As with Part I there is a rough division between political, social and economic, and cultural and intellectual history.

Political history is the main concern of the two chapters by Lerman. In Chapter 8, on Bismarckian Germany, the focus is on the constitutional arrangements of the new state, the dominant position of Bismarck within those arrangements and the evolution of politics between 1871 and 1890. In Chapter 11, on Wilhelmine Germany, the concern is with the changing character of politics, especially the emergence of mass politics, the particular position Wilhelm II occupied within the political system, and the debate over German foreign policy, in particular in relation to the origins and conduct of the First World War. In his chapter on social and economic history, Berghahn concentrates on the dynamic and changing character of Germany, in particular the rapid growth of population, urbanization and industry. Clearly this economic development and social change had important bearings on the emergence of mass politics and the capacity of the German state to bid for much greater influence in both Europe and the wider world. Finally, in his chapter on Wilhelmine culture, Jefferies draws attention to the great variety of styles and schools in art, architecture and other cultural fields, offering amongst other things an important corrective to one-dimensional representations of Wilhelmine culture as reflecting authoritarian traditionalism or cultural pessimism and as having little in common with other countries.

It is not possible to cover every aspect of the history of Germany in this period, a period which is second only to that of the Third Reich in the amount of research and volume of publications it has attracted in recent decades. 'Germany' now comes to mean the territory of the Second Empire. Habsburg Germany tends to disappear from view, figuring only as the hapless ally of 1914 or cultural hothouse of Vienna. Yet, given the increasing dominance of the national in politics, society and international relations, it is difficult to see how one could proceed otherwise. Popular culture is briefly addressed by Jefferies who considers the commercialization of culture, and by Berghahn who alludes to the rising expectations of ordinary Germans who experienced material improvement and could exercise more choice in such matters as where they lived and what job they did. However, there was no opportunity to look systematically at the subject of popular culture. The same point applies to the increased interpenetration of state and society, for example in terms of the development of welfare and public health policies, although these are touched upon by Berghahn. There is the very difficult problem of how to integrate the First World War into the period as a whole. Historians frequently sidestep this problem by stopping in 1914 and starting again in 1918, leaving the war years to special histories. That has not been the strategy adopted here. Instead, the war years have been placed within wider contexts which vary with the particular focus of different essays. Lerman relates war aims after August 1914 to pre-1914 foreign policy. Berghahn looks at how the war years reversed the growth in prosperity of the period up to 1914 and how this provided some of the popular basis for turning against the monarchy in 1917–18. Bessel, in his chapter in Part III, warns against exaggerating the extent to which a strong national consensus had been formed in August 1914. However, for a sustained military study of Germany at war one needs to go elsewhere.

Interpretations of the Second Empire have been greatly influenced by the manner of its demise and the question of its connection or lack of connection to the Third Reich. At one extreme there is the view that 1871 had seen the creation of a very peculiar kind of state with a distinct authoritarian and nationalist character which, combined with increased political centralization, rapid industrial growth and military innovation, represented a threat to peace and progress, a threat that manifested itself in war in 1914 and again in 1939. At the other extreme there is the view that Germany was but one national state and industrializing society amongst others and that the path towards war in 1914 was the product of the multiple and conflicting policies of the European powers. Neither extreme is sustainable. Good, detailed historical study rather grapples with complexities that undermine such extreme positions. However, that has by no means led to consensus, as will become clear to the reader of these essays. The history of the first German nation state remains a lively and contested one.

8

Bismarckian Germany and the structure of the German Empire

Katharine A. Lerman

The nature of the German Empire, founded by Bismarck in 1871 after three victorious Prussian wars, is central to all debates on the continuities and peculiarities in modern German history. Most obviously the impact of the First World War and defeat, the fragility of parliamentary democracy in the Weimar Republic, and the origins of the Nazi dictatorship can scarcely be assessed without an understanding of German society and political culture in the decades before 1914. Indeed, it was largely a preoccupation with Germany's responsibility for the two world wars which stimulated a revival of interest from the late 1960s in the history of the Empire. Yet the extent to which Germany followed a special or peculiar course of development which differed in key aspects from the experience of her (essentially western) European neighbours also focuses attention on the kind of state which Bismarck created. For while Germany's dynamic economic and social growth in the second half of the nineteenth century appears to locate her securely in the mainstream of western European industrializing nations, liberal historians have generally not been so sanguine about the political legacy of Bismarckian Germany.

Historical debate on the nature of the *Kaiserreich* has inevitably been overshadowed by the violent circumstances surrounding its birth in 1871 and demise in 1918, as well as by a consciousness of Germany's catastrophic impact on the international state system in the first half of the twentieth century. Once celebrated as the triumphant culmination of nearly two centuries of Prussian history, the embodiment of human progress and the vindication of the Germans' previously disappointed aspirations for nationhood, after 1945 Bismarck's creation came to be assessed primarily in negative terms. The 'unification' of Germany was a revolution, imposed from above, which defied rather than fulfilled the aspirations of the revolutionaries of 1848. Bismarck's wars signified the partition of the German nation, allowing a state to emerge which was not liberal, national or united. The Germany of 1871 was artificial and unnatural, an 'exotic plant' (Röhl) which could only be sustained in a hothouse of patriotism and war. Prussia's conquest of Germany imposed an authoritarian and illiberal vision of German national identity which could not tolerate alternative conceptions of German nationhood and permanently excluded the religious and ethnic minorities within the Empire.

For all the refinements to our picture of the Empire brought about in recent years by social historians and others intent on showing that there was 'another Germany' before 1914, most historical writing on the subject has tended to share this teleological perspective. Despite occasional pleas that Germans should not be ashamed of Imperial Germany or its history (Mommsen), the need to explain, if not the origins of the Third Reich then at least Germany's role in precipitating the First World War, dominates the historiography of the period.

Structural interpretations have proliferated in history textbooks which recite a whole litany of political, social and economic problems afflicting Germany before 1914. These are mainly rooted in socioeconomic analyses but draw on a liberal critique of the Empire which is as old as the Empire itself. In the 1970s Hans-Ulrich Wehler achieved widespread acclaim for an interpretative synthesis which drew attention to the unevenness of German industrial development, the proliferation of social tensions and antagonisms, and the growth of an interventionist state intent on preserving the political and social status quo. He argued that Bismarck's Germany was a semi-absolutist, pseudo-constitutional military monarchy, underpinned from 1879 by a powerful coalition of conservative economic interests (above all the agrarian Junkers) which determined the parameters of political change in Germany until 1918 and beyond.

Wehler's rigidly systematized and bleak representation of the Empire was soon subjected to increasing scholarly criticism. Yet attempts to 'normalize' the history of the Empire and no longer see it as a 'site of pathology' (Eley) also encountered problems. In the 1980s Geoff Eley questioned the causal relationship often drawn between politics and economics in the Empire and drew attention to the dangers inherent in an all too simplistic economic and social reductionism. But, while he successfully challenged assumptions about what constituted a 'healthy' or 'normal' development for a state and broadened the discussion of the political realm to include previously discounted social groups, his argument that Bismarck's unification, in removing the obstacles to the development of industrial capitalism in Germany, signified a German variant of a 'bourgeois revolution', ultimately only led back to the political peculiarities which distinguished Germany's history from that of her neighbours. A recent new survey of Imperial Germany by Volker Berghahn has highlighted the methodological and thematic diversity of current historical writing on the Empire and richly confirms the more general shift of interest away from political and diplomatic history. Yet although its stated aim is to write 'a history of German society in all its aspects', the central question it poses is the familiar political one of why Germany went to war in 1914.

The Empire Bismarck created survived for 47 years, slightly longer than Germany was divided after the Second World War. For all the mutations that the idea and reality of 'Germany' have undergone since 1871 and despite the existence of substantial disaffected minorities in Imperial Germany, Bismarck's 'lesser German' unification was successful in achieving a national legitimacy which it was beyond the capacity of two world wars and 40 years of division to extinguish. Clearly, as the Third Reich recedes further into history and a new, reunited Germany is consolidated, a Germany which is smaller, more democratic and less threatening within the European state system than its predecessors, historians will ask new questions and find different avenues of investigation into the nature and development of the Bismarckian Reich.

I The Imperial German political system

The political system of the Empire tends to defy classification, so much so that some historians have disputed whether it can be described as a 'system' at all. Bismarck himself adopted this approach, emphasizing that the strength of its constitutional arrangements would lie in their distance from 'principle, system and dogmatism' and preferring to leave much unclarified, to await resolution over time and in practice. The system was certainly complicated and unique (for only Meiji Japan adopted elements of the Bismarckian constitution) and it is possible to elevate different features of quite a delicate balance as being characteristic of the whole. This has encouraged historians to describe Imperial Germany variously as a military monarchy, a pseudo-constitutional state, a semi-constitutional state with parliamentary or plebiscitary additions, a Prusso-German semi-autocracy, and a pseudo-parliamentary regime. They have also invented a whole range of epithets to convey the senses in which the constitutional arrangements of 1871 were incomplete and unfinished (Schieder), represented a compromise (Nipperdey) or signified the deferment of hard political choices (Mommsen).

Historians have scarcely found it much easier to evaluate the functioning of the political system in practice. Notwithstanding the fact that all too often assumptions have crept into the debate, for example the expectation that Germany 'should' have developed into a parliamentary monarchy on the British model, its sheer originality as well as its rather improvised development from 1871 have led to conflicting interpretations of its progressive potential. For Wehler, it mattered little whether Germany was ruled by a 'Bonapartist semi-dictatorship' under Bismarck or subject to the 'polycratic chaos' which he saw as characterizing successive governments under Kaiser Wilhelm II; the essential framework remained the military monarchy with its sham constitutionalism and its entrenched 'pre-industrial' social supporters who successfully resisted political modernization before 1918. For others, the conflict between monarchical power and parliamentary pretensions in the Empire ensured that its political history would be more dynamic than Wehler's rigid construct, with its emasculated political parties and manipulative government strategies, could encompass – although even then opinions have diverged over whether Germany became a more monarchical or more parliamentary state after Bismarck's dismissal. Perhaps inevitably the very complexity, some might say fragmentation, of the political system has facilitated a great diversity of historical approaches and interpretations. Without an eye for the whole, the respective roles of the Kaiser and his court, the army, the Reich administration, the Prussian ministerial bureaucracy, the federal states and the political parties may be deemed more or less important solely according to the perspective of the viewer.

The constitution of 1871 essentially incorporated the main provisions of the constitution of the North German Confederation which was thrashed out between Bismarck and the National Liberals in the constituent Reichstag in 1867 and had always envisaged the eventual accession of the four southern states. It was certainly not a sham, grafted on to more traditional authoritarian structures with little more than a decorative function; and nor was it dreamed up by Bismarck without advice or consultation during a couple of days on holiday (as legend has it), although it unmistakably bore the imprint of his personality and aims. The constitution contained appeals to tradition and it aimed to accommodate the diversity of German experience, preserving Germany's federal structure and leaving the constitutions of the individual member states, most crucially that of Prussia – now enlarged by the annexation of Schleswig, Holstein, Hanover, northern Hesse, Wiesbaden and Frankfurt – untouched. But it also sought to provide a framework for the consolidation of a new nation state under Prussian leadership and it created an entirely new political structure, with national institutions, which was subject to considerable unitary pressure. In this respect it differed quite markedly from the much looser German Confederation which had preceded it.

The letter of the constitution can be briefly summarized, although a problem faced by both contemporaries and historians is that the political system never functioned as the original document intended. Sovereignty was theoretically vested in a federal council or Bundesrat which was composed of delegates from the various state governments and represented the apparently voluntary alliance of the German princes. A national parliament, the Reichstag, was established which was elected by universal and equal male suffrage, a very radical and democratic suffrage by the standards of the time. Legislation had to be passed by both the Reichstag and the Bundesrat, which combined some of the functions of a legislative upper house with its executive role. The Prussian king became the German Kaiser or Emperor, an imperial monarch who headed the political executive and the military apparatus, controlled all personnel appointments and enjoyed specific prerogatives such as the right to declare war or martial law in an emergency (though these needed subsequent Bundesrat approval). According to Article 17 of the constitution, it was the duty of the Kaiser 'to prepare and publish the laws of the Empire and to supervise their execution', but his decrees and ordinances, issued in the name of the Empire, had to be countersigned by the Reich chancellor before they became constitutionally valid. The Reich Chancellor was the sole Reich minister mentioned in the constitution and was appointed by the monarch. He presided over the Bundesrat and, on countersigning imperial orders, assumed 'responsibility' for them, a formulation which left much room for conflicting interpretations with respect to the chancellor's relationship with the Reichstag.

While the Bundesrat was a bulwark of federalism in the new Empire, the existence of a powerful national figurehead and a national, representative parliament was intended to counterbalance centrifugal forces and limit the self-assertion or 'particularism' of the states. The constitutional provisions can be seen as creating a delicate equilibrium, with the key institutions keeping each other in check and the Reich chancellorship, an office which Bismarck occupied continuously from 1871 to 1890, located at the fulcrum of the political system. However, Bismarck had not originally conceived of the chancellorship as a very significant post and he had not planned to assume the office himself. It was parliamentary pressure which secured the chancellor's right of countersignature and his, albeit limited, legal responsibility before the Reichstag. These combined powers placed the chancellor at the centre of the decision-making process and ensured that he would carry the main burden of coordinating the complex machinery of government.

Historians have tended to focus on the liberals' failure to achieve important concessions in 1867–71 such as a centralized Reich government with ministerial responsibility to parliament or effective parliamentary control over the military budget (which accounted for over 90 per cent of central government expenditure before 1890). Nevertheless it is questionable whether most liberals wanted the introduction of parliamentary government at this juncture (if at all) and they were very doubtful about the implications of universal male suffrage. Moreover, many of the most controversial decisions were of limited duration and there was every expectation that there would be further opportunities to revise them. The liberals were successful in modifying aspects of the original draft (for example the strengthening of the position of the Reich chancellor and the Reichstag's increased budgetary powers) but Bismarck basically determined the parameters of what could be achieved in the wake of the Prussian military victories. Yet Bismarck, too, had an interest in securing the future collaboration of the more moderate liberals and he was pushed further than he originally wanted to go. No individual or party was entirely satisfied with the constitutional arrangements which were passed by big majorities in the Reichstag and Prussian Landtag, but most accepted them as a basis for future development. For liberals especially, the achievement of a united Germany with a central executive and representative institutions was a major advance and in theory at least there was scope for Reich legislation to amend the constitution and extend the competence of imperial institutions.

The features of the constitutional structure which have aroused the most controversy are those which impeded a further liberalization or the progressive 'parliamentarization' of the Empire. Some of these, such as the lack of parliamentary control over the composition of the executive or the extraordinary status of the military (at its core the Prussian army) outside the new constitution, were evident from the outset. Others, such as the enormous potential power of the Kaiser, only emerged later with the accession of Wilhelm II or, as in the case of the ultimately tortuous arrangements for financing the Empire, were compounded by subsequent political decisions which shifted the balance in favour of the states.

The peculiar position of the Bundesrat, which by virtue of its composition and procedure could never fulfil the role of an imperial government or even play a central role in the decision-making process, was correctly calculated by Bismarck to present a formidable barrier to the expansion of parliamentary power. With delegates bound to vote according to the instructions of the state governments they represented, the theoretical sovereignty of the 'allied governments' was purely fictional and, when it came to the details of legislation, all the advantages rested with the administration in Berlin. Yet its mere existence was a fundamental obstacle to the development of a Reich cabinet responsible to parliament and its secret sessions contributed to the frustration of Reichstag deputies who repeatedly found that they had no means of calling the real decision-makers in Prussia to account.

Prussia's role as the dominant state within the Empire is generally cited as the most important impediment to the progressive evolution of the political system after 1871. Even after unification, Prussia continued to be ruled on the basis of the very limited constitution of 1850, which had placed few restrictions on the king's autocratic power. The Prussian military victories and the resolution of the constitutional conflict may have revolutionized the party system to the government's advantage but there had been no significant change in the power relationships within Prussia. In the event of a renewed clash between the king and the Prussian Landtag, there was no guarantee that the government would not once again exploit the alleged 'gap' in the constitution and resort to arbitrary rule. In fact, with liberalism's decline from the late 1870s, the plutocratic three-class suffrage, which allowed the richest 15 per cent of the electorate to choose two-thirds of the seats, began to produce conservative parliamentary majorities in the Prussian House of Deputies, which further undermined the political pressure within Prussia for reform. The composition of the House of Deputies, as well as the even more reactionary, hereditary House of Lords, came to impose legislative constraints upon Prussian governments which were in practice sometimes more willing to countenance reform.

There was no sense in which the Empire could have existed independently of Prussia, yet the Empire's federal structure effectively shielded and protected Prussia's hegemony. The German Kaiser was always the Prussian king; his power of command (*Kommandogewalt*) over the army ensured that those who aspired to change the constitutional status quo always had to reckon with the possibility that the monarchy might sanction violence to defend its power. The chancellor, too, was always the Prussian foreign minister and – with the exception of two brief interludes – Prussian minister-president; it was by virtue of the former position that he instructed Prussian votes in the Bundesrat. (When the incumbent briefly surrendered the premiership in 1872–3 and 1892–4 he found his power and the confidence of the states in his leadership severely curtailed.) Especially in the early years of the Empire, imperial legislation was drafted in the Prussian ministries and no laws were passed which had not been extensively discussed in the Prussian state ministry. As the Reich administration developed, too, it became inextricably interlocked with the Prussian ministerial bureaucracy; in terms of personnel and function their offices overlapped.

All the above features of the imperial German political system represented powerful barriers to constitutional change after 1871, and it is perhaps not surprising if most historians tend to be gloomy about the Empire's prospects for peaceful political reform and adaptation. Nevertheless, there is ample evidence that the Empire's political institutions were capable of evolution and development, even if the direction this took may not have conformed to existing political models and the overall effects were ambiguous.

The unitary pressures which were manifestly at work within the Empire are generally regarded as positive in their effects. Especially during the first decade of the Empire's existence, imperial institutions developed very rapidly and, facilitated by the dignified restraint of Wilhelm I as well as by the emotional appeal of 'Kaiser and Reich', the imperial monarchy gained popularity and respect. The urgent need for legislation to establish the economic and legal framework of the Empire ensured a significant role for the German Reichstag, despite its constitutional limitations, within the new polity. Its representative character, the relatively high election turnouts (especially in the nationalist elections of 1878 and 1887) and its public debates all helped it become a focus of German political life. The central Reich executive (or 'Reich leadership' as it came to be called) expanded dramatically under the authority of the chancellor. By the late 1870s a series of Reich offices had been created, each under a state secretary who could deputize for the chancellor.

It can even be argued that the relationship between Prussia and the Reich became far less clear-cut in the context of the growing momentum of imperial institutions. For all the complaints about a Prussification of Germany, it became increasingly apparent (especially to conservatives) that the identity of 'old Prussia' had been significantly 'diluted' by its integration into the new Empire. Prussia could no longer be governed without consideration of the wider interests of the Reich and, as Bismarck increasingly adopted the practice of making his state secretaries Prussian ministers without portfolio, the Prussian government could no longer retain an exclusively Prussian character. By the 1890s it was not merely the case that non-Prussians sat in the ministry of state, but that a Bavarian chancellor simultaneously became Prussian minister-president.

Yet immediately, of course, one must balance this perspective, for imperial institutions also evolved in ways which did little to further the cause of constitutional government. For example, the twin problems of defective civil–military coordination in the Empire and inadequate political control over the army grew steadily worse rather than better, even under Bismarck's chancellorship. The army effectively evaded political and parliamentary controls, and Bismarck himself was prepared to connive in this process by permitting the progressive emasculation of the office of Prussian war minister. (He preferred to see the minister's responsibilities carved up between several military agencies rather than bolster the authority of a potential rival.) Similarly the highly imperfect and provisional compromises which were struck in the attempt to ensure the Empire's financial solvency signified a growing entanglement between financial and constitutional issues to the detriment of both. Not only the federal governments but also state parliaments, elected according to indirect and very unequal suffrages, resisted efforts to transfer important powers of the purse to a democratically elected Reichstag with fewer scruples about taxing wealth and property. Finally, as the issue of the monarchical succession loomed ever larger, so did the growing significance of the Kaiser's court as a locus of political intrigue beyond the chancellor's control. The political vitality of the army and the court attests to the continuing importance of the 'extra-constitutional' realm in the decision-making process.

Altogether it must be stated that the Bismarckian government system never functioned very smoothly, although it would doubtless be wrong to conflate the problems of the Bismarckian and Wilhelmine eras and assume its future was fixed by 1890. The constitutional and political structure of the Empire, in which not only Prussia but some 20 other states retained their monarchies, courts, governments, diplomats, parliaments (with upper and lower houses) and – in some cases – their own armies in peacetime, was bound to be highly complicated and unwieldy. As will be seen, Bismarck himself was never very happy with the new structures which were superimposed on the old. Moreover, the latent incompatibility between rival monarchical and parliamentary claims to power conditioned German political life throughout the Empire's existence.

II   The role of Bismarck

Bismarck has remained the most controversial figure in modern German political history, with widely divergent assessments of his role and significance. Recent scholarly biographies of Bismarck have largely succeeded in demythologizing the 'great man' but have found it much more difficult to separate the man from his achievement. In so far as historians have tried to place the wars of 1864–71 and the Empire which emerged from them within a wider context of largely autonomous pressures for unification, they still run up against a series of problems pertaining to Bismarck's individuality and his responsibility for the political development of the Empire. For if the Empire was an artificial and anachronistic construction, this only attests further to Bismarck's successful manipulation of the national and liberal forces of his day, as well as to his ability to stem the tide of change after 1871. Whether German unification amounted to a limited 'revolution from above' or a 'bourgeois revolution' which signified the breakthrough of industrial capitalism in Germany, Bismarck emerges as the brilliant and shrewd tactician who succeeded in postponing the problem of political modernization for 60 years. Even Wehler was forced to concede that the traditional or pre-industrial forces in German society possessed in Bismarck a 'political potential *sui generis*'.[1] Once applauded as the architect of German unification, Bismarck is now much more likely to be judged critically as a man whose aims and methods imposed a massive burden on Germany's social and political development. Yet his exceptional status is not in doubt. Whether his legacy was positive or negative, historians cannot escape his dominating presence in the history of Germany and Europe from 1862 to 1890 (and beyond).

Bismarck's role within the imperial German political system after 1871 was so fundamental and decisive that he is widely seen as having instituted a 'chancellor dicta-torship'. For some, this dictatorship is defined chiefly in terms of his personal power and authority within the executive and his largely unchallenged role in determining policy. Others have argued that this interpretation is too 'personalistic', preferring to shift the focus from Bismarck's style of rule within the executive to the social functions of his 'Bonapartist dictatorship', a concept they see as combining the more traditional and authoritarian features of his government with more charismatic or plebiscitary ele-ments.

Bismarck's role in German unification undoubtedly ensured him a pre-eminent position in Prussia and the Empire after 1871. It also furthered a process, already underway during the constitutional conflict of the 1860s, whereby government and decision-making became increasingly associated with one man (especially in the eyes of his critics) and the main political division during the subsequent years he remained in office was between his supporters and opponents, those who affirmed the creation of the Bismarckian national state and those who rejected it. Yet if Bismarck appeared to place the monarchy in the political shade, enjoying many of the prerogatives of auto-cratic power within the executive and becoming, in the words of Wilhelm I, 'more nec-essary than I am',[2] there continued to be important practical and theoretical limitations to his position. Bismarck himself was all too aware of the potential scope at the Kaiser's court and within the army for independent decision-making and, of course, he needed a parliamentary majority for the passage of legislation and approval of the budget. Ultimately the monarch's power of appointment rendered the imperial chancellor as much a royal servant as a Reich minister. By 1890, when it was clear that Bismarck had no alternative basis of political support, Kaiser Wilhelm II felt free simply to dismiss him.

Between 1871 and 1890 Bismarck came to exert a tight grip over all aspects of pol-icy in the Empire and Prussia. Buoyed up by his outstanding achievement in restruc-turing the map of central Europe in 1866–71, it was inevitable that, as Reich Chancellor and Prussian Foreign Minister, he enjoyed a virtual autonomy in the sphere of foreign policy. He could be confident that, provided he could assert his will over the Kaiser and discipline the diplomatic service into complete subordination, there would be no questioning of his diplomatic wisdom and skill. Only at the very end of his chancellorship was there mounting disquiet within ruling circles over his conduct of foreign policy and, in particular, his efforts to maintain Russia's friendship. With respect to domestic affairs Bismarck's authority was, initially at least, subject to more significant constraints. His position was limited not only by the collegial structure of the Prussian government (which he deliberately avoided in the Reich) and the theoret-ical sovereignty of the states rather than the imperial executive, but also by more prac-tical considerations such as the availability of personnel, the nature of the party constellation and a degree of uncertainty about how the new constitutional system would function in practice. Yet Bismarck's interest in consolidating imperial institu-tions after 1871 never deflected him from the goal of consolidating his personal power.

His frequent improvisation and experimentation with the political arrangements within the Empire – resigning and reassuming offices, creating new institutions or resurrecting old ones, adjusting the balance between Reich and Prussian institutions first one way and then the other – was motivated as much by self-interest as by a desire to ensure smooth and stable government.

Bismarck's frequent tinkering with the political machinery of his new creation suggests a dissatisfaction with the system and his place within it which is hard to reconcile with the concept of dictatorship. Indeed, even confining the perspective to the executive, it is clear that power relationships in the first two decades of the Empire's existence were more fluid than is often suggested. The basis of Bismarck's power underwent perceptible shifts between 1871 and 1890 for, although the confidence of the Kaiser underpinned his position, his dependence on the monarchy waxed and waned according to the degree to which he could command the political support of parliaments, colleagues and states. For example, faced with a hostile Reichstag majority between 1881 and 1886, he found that he was more dependent on Wilhelm I's support than at any time since the constitutional conflict of the 1860s – a realization which cannot have enhanced his sense of security, as his predicament coincided with growing fears about the succession and suspicions of proliferating intrigues at court. Similarly, though his authority over the Prussian ministerial bureaucracy was undisputed by the 1880s, the task of achieving a consensus among the federal states became more difficult after the political changes of 1878–9 when they no longer felt threatened by the unitary implications of his collaboration with the liberals in the Reichstag. Bismarck increasingly had to resort to bullying tactics to preserve a superficial harmony and unanimity in the Bundesrat; from 1888, with Wilhelm II beginning to play a more active role in decision-making, the lesser states found again that they had more freedom to espouse alternative policy proposals.

Bismarck rapidly established his undisputed leadership over the imperial executive. He soon dismantled the single, centralized Reich chancellor's office which, under Rudolf Delbrück, had accumulated extensive power over imperial domestic affairs, and he preferred to institute a more decentralized imperial executive which, however, remained firmly under his personal control. While the state secretary of the foreign office enjoyed direct access to the chancellor, the state secretaries of the five main departments responsible for domestic affairs from 1878 communicated with him through a small personal secretariat, the Reich Chancellery, which was located in his residence in Berlin's Wilhelmstrasse. There was no form of collective government in the Reich and nothing which resembled an imperial cabinet. The new system ensured there would be a minimum of political discussion and consultation between the chancellor's subordinates and that all final decisions would rest with Bismarck.

In Prussia, Bismarck's position from 1871 was secure but not unassailable. Despite the parliamentary collaboration with the liberals for much of the decade, Bismarck had to work with Prussian ministers who had had no qualms in fighting the constitutional conflict alongside him and opposed, for example, the reform of Prussian local govern-

Illustration 8.1 *Bismarck with Emperor Wilhelm I in the Royal Palace* by Konrad Siemenroth (1887)

ment and abolition of Junker police powers in 1872. At the same time he came to resent a loss of freedom of manoeuvre which resulted not only from the need to work with a liberal parliamentary majority but also from what he perceived to be the stranglehold which liberal ministers had over the Prussian Ministry of State. Recent work has shown how Bismarck's ideas, even in the early 1870s, to institute extensive social welfare reforms ran aground when ministers with key portfolios such as trade resisted any kind of state intervention in the economy. The desire to subordinate the Prussian Ministry to his leadership was an important motive in Bismarck's anti-socialist offensive and break with the National Liberal Party in 1878. Only after the ministerial changes of the summer of 1879 (which, incidentally, paid little heed to the apparent change of political direction) did Bismarck finally establish his undisputed authority over the Ministry of State. From 1880 he also personally headed the Prussian Ministry of Trade, which meant that he was well placed to spearhead the new social insurance legislation.

Bismarck's success in taming and disciplining Prussian ministers reduced them to a status comparable with the state secretaries in the imperial executive. Bismarck had never found it easy to work with other people and he had always been intolerant of criticism and dissent. These traits were magnified once his political ascendancy was secured so that any kind of opposition or constructive questioning was effectively eliminated. Bismarck was frequently contemptuous of colleagues whom he variously criticized, even in the Reichstag, for being too independent, lacking in creativity or spineless. The task of finding men of calibre who had the personal and political skills to work with the Minister-President became increasingly difficult as time went on. In 1878 nine men refused the Ministry of Finance before one was persuaded to take over the post. Bismarck's hold over an ageing Wilhelm I meant that he could remove inconvenient colleagues in the 1880s, particularly those, like Botho Eulenburg, the Minister of the Interior, whom he suspected in 1881 of 'wanting to govern'.[3] His reluctance to initiate subordinates into his thought processes, his mistrust of potential rivals, and his conviction that naming a successor was the political equivalent of being dead, encouraged him to rely more and more on his son, Herbert, who was State Secretary of the Foreign Office from 1886.

Bismarck achieved a dictatorial position within the Reich and Prussian executives, but he was persistently thwarted in his efforts to control the course of Germany's political development. The heterogeneity of German society, Germany's dynamic economic and demographic growth, and the unwieldiness of the new constitutional arrangements all precluded the possibility that he could shape the peacetime domestic development of the Empire in the same way as he had forged its international status. As early as 1872 there were complaints within government circles that the 'Iron Chancellor', denied the conditions of conflict and war, lacked the requisite qualities and skills to promote the constructive evolution of imperial domestic politics. By the end of the decade Bismarck was widely perceived to be no longer the man he was, all too willing to set himself ambitious political and social goals which could never be achieved in the short time and with the limited means he now had at his disposal.

III Political developments during Bismarck's chancellorship

It has become customary to divide Bismarckian domestic politics into two quite distinct liberal and conservative eras, punctuated by Bismarck's break with the National Liberal Party in 1878 and his adoption of economic protectionism in 1879. Between 1867 and 1878 Bismarck continued the collaboration with the moderate liberal movement which had begun with the passage of the Indemnity Bill in 1866. During this period many important laws were passed which established the administrative and legal framework of the new Empire, and facilitated the creation of a national economy. At the same time the so-called *Kulturkampf* or 'struggle for civilization' against the substantial Catholic minority and its political representative, the Centre Party, was prosecuted with particular vigour by the Prussian government and its liberal allies, although it affected the lesser German states and impacted upon Reich legislation too.

In 1878, however, Bismarck deliberately sought a confrontation with his erstwhile political friends, introducing an unacceptable anti-socialist bill into the Reichstag and precipitating new elections. The new Reichstag subsequently approved a revised anti-socialist bill and, in 1879, a conservative–Centre majority passed a tariff law which signified the abandonment of economic liberalism. Thereafter, it is argued, government policies shifted markedly to the right in the 1880s, while Bismarck effectively consolidated his authoritarian or 'Bonapartist' dictatorship. The tariff levels were raised in 1885 so that German agriculture was afforded a similar degree of protection to that of industry, and the grain tariffs were increased again in 1887. The government continued to repress social democracy and pursued much more overtly nationalistic policies against the ethnic minorities within the Empire, above all the three million or so Prussian Poles. At the same time the state intervened more and more directly in economic and social life, not least instituting a comprehensive system of state social insurance provision which was a forerunner of its kind.

There is no doubt that the economic and political climate was very different in the 1880s from what it had been in the years immediately following political unification. The economic crash and subsequent slowdown in economic growth from 1873 helped to produce a crisis of confidence in economic liberalism by the late 1870s which manifested itself in heightened fears and insecurities among all social groups. Traditional practice as well as current anxiety ensured that many of those who felt most threatened by the vagaries of the market or the ferocity of foreign competition looked to the government to protect their interests and alleviate their distress. The growth of new social and economic problems inevitably cut across traditional political alignments, producing tensions and conflicts within political parties which were still in the main only loosely organized on the basis of ideological affinities, for example a shared view about dynastic, clerical or constitutional issues, and did not necessarily represent similar eco-

nomic interests. Inevitably, too, new political and social conflicts offered fresh opportunities for manoeuvre to a government which had no organic relationship with the
political parties in the Reichstag and which, in claiming to stand above party or sec-
tional interests, naturally favoured authoritarian solutions to the nation's problems.

Nevertheless there are several reasons for questioning whether dividing Bismarck's
chancellorship into two separate eras, each characterized with reference to conventional political categories of liberalism and conservatism, facilitates an understanding
of political developments between 1871 and 1890. The dichotomy tends to arise from
a focus on parliamentary politics, the relationships within and between the political
parties, and the shifting basis of the government's parliamentary support, although, as
we have seen, the parliaments and the political parties played a very specific and subordinate role in the political system as a whole. Moreover, even with respect to party
politics, the situation in the 1870s and 1880s can be better understood with reference
to the events of the previous decade than in conventional political terms. For German
unification did not immediately create political unity, and confessional, regional and
ethnic loyalties often remained more important in determining political alignments in
the first decades of the Empire than day-to-day political, economic and social issues.

Most obviously, the passions aroused by the *Kulturkampf* can scarcely be appreciated if viewed solely in the context of a liberal campaign against clerical obscurantism
or the progress of the secularizing state. Rather, in targeting Catholics and minorities
within the Empire, the *Kulturkampf* was widely understood by contemporaries to be a
war against the internal opponents of the lesser German unification, those whose territories had been defeated or annexed in 1866–71 and who regretted the exclusion of
Catholic Austria. In this sense German political life after 1871 essentially represented
the continuing struggle to achieve the national state. This struggle was admittedly
waged by different means from the military campaigns of 1864–71 but it appeared no
less urgent to supporters of the national idea in the light of the centrifugal pressures
within the new Empire and widespread fears that what had been achieved so dramatically could just as easily be undone. Even 20 years after unification ruling circles in
Berlin still harboured an almost paranoid anxiety that the Empire might yet dissolve
into its constituent parts. Party political alignments in the Bismarckian era inevitably
reflected the fundamental division between those who affirmed what Bismarck had
achieved and those who rejected it. Arguably, so long as Bismarck remained at the
helm, there was no way in which it could be otherwise. Events of the 1860s, as well as
the personality and style of the Chancellor, conspired to make one of the central issues
of Bismarckian politics the question whether one was for or against Bismarck.

The apparent discontinuities between the more liberal and progressive 1870s and
the more conservative and authoritarian 1880s have tended to focus the historiographical debate over the past 20 years on the scope and significance of the 'great change' or
Wende in 1878–9. Some historians such as Helmut Böhme have argued that the change
of course in imperial domestic politics at the end of the 1870s was so fundamental and
extensive that it amounted to a 'refounding' of the Empire on a conservative basis.

Bismarck, they maintain, exploited the spectre of socialist revolution and the popular clamour for economic protectionism in the late 1870s to forge a new coalition of government support based on the most powerful economic interest groups in Imperial Germany, the so-called alliance of 'iron and rye'. This coalition between heavy industry and large-scale agriculture then underpinned the Empire's domestic development until 1918, thwarting the gradual evolution of parliamentary democracy and ensuring a rigid adherence to the social and political status quo.

From 1879, it is widely claimed, Bismarckian politics are best understood as a form of *Sammlungspolitik* or the 'rallying' of all conservative and national forces which supported the state. Anti-liberal in origin (though this animus against liberalism was later superseded by the fear of revolutionary socialism) *Sammlungspolitik* was reinforced by manipulative strategies to stabilize the existing order. These included the targeting of political enemies and minorities as a means of 'secondary integration', as well as 'social imperialist' strategies to divert popular attention away from the need for political reform. While Bismarck's 'social imperialism' did not extend beyond a sudden interest in colonial acquisitions in the mid-1880s and the exploitation of war scares for election purposes, his successors were ultimately prepared to embrace naval armaments and world war to shore up the monarchy and prevent social and political modernization.

The idea that the Empire was 'refounded' in 1878–9 and that the decisions taken during these years somehow determined the domestic development of Germany for several decades to come has been subject to growing scholarly criticism on a number of counts. It has been argued that the thesis (which largely derived from the study of economic policy) exaggerated the importance of economic issues generally and the tariff legislation in particular. It oversimplified the relationship between politics and economics in the Empire and obscured the diversity and complexity of the economic interest groups which stood to gain or lose from government policies. Historians of both the Bismarckian and Wilhelmine eras have questioned the applicability of the *Sammlungspolitik* model to the specific years or policies they have studied, doubting whether the alliance of 'iron and rye' was as solid or durable as has been suggested and whether government was any more stable as a result. Too much emphasis has been placed on government manipulation and design, too little on more pragmatic considerations or autonomous developments which influenced imperial German decision-making. More generally, the assumption of a fundamental incompatibility between economic protectionism and the development of liberal or democratic politics has been contested, especially in the light of contemporary experience.

Recent research has confirmed that the turning point of 1878–9 was not as sudden, dramatic or consequential as is often supposed. Otto Pflanze, for example, has painstakingly shown how the decisions of 1878–9, far from signifying the existence of a Bismarckian 'grand strategy' to shift German politics to the right, arose out of a number of related but uncoordinated issues which preoccupied Bismarck from quite early in the 1870s. Among Bismarck's prime domestic concerns were: the need to solve the Empire's financial constitution in a way which made it more independent of both the states and the Reichstag; his wish to reform the tax system in Prussia and the Reich in a way which would lift the burden of direct taxation from the lower classes and place more emphasis on indirect taxation; and his desire to take steps to alleviate the 'social question', above all by instituting a comprehensive system of social insurance. With respect to these issues Bismarck's motives were never purely or even predominantly manipulative (even his social insurance schemes were motivated as much by his peculiar brand of Christian pietism as by the need to ensure the loyalty of the working man to the state). But they were broadly conservative, shaped as much by his social background and his essentially limited personal experience as by a genuine understanding of society's problems.

The preoccupation with the great *Wende* and the government's manipulation has distorted the longer-term origins of the change of course and led to an underestimation of the significance of forces which were largely evolutionary or beyond the government's control. The effect has been to turn Bismarck, not for the first time, into an all-powerful tiger who was forever willing to change his political stripes if it suited his Machiavellian purposes. The extent to which Bismarck pursued similar goals throughout his chancellorship has also been obscured by a tendency to focus exclusively on the parliamentary arena and judge his policies solely on the basis of what eventually reached the statute books. Significant elements of Bismarck's wider political plans never got further than the Prussian Ministry of State or the Bundesrat before they encountered opposition or were demonstrated to be impractical.

Seen in its proper context, the tariff, for example, was scarcely central to Bismarck's plans in 1879. Never committed to economic liberalism, Bismarck adopted protectionism rather belatedly and opportunistically in 1879 in the belief that it would bring economic and political advantages. But he was far more interested in other measures, such as the nationalization of the railways or the creation of a lucrative government monopoly on brandy or tobacco, as a means of raising revenue. Nor should the tariff's role in cementing the alleged *Sammlung* be overstressed. Although agriculture was always favoured by Bismarck's policies, the preferential treatment of heavy industry in 1879 has to be offset against the effects of some of his other proposals, for example his plans to regulate the private insurance market or tax stock market transactions, which would have imposed new financial burdens on German industry. Employers were concerned about many aspects of the government's social and fiscal policies in the 1880s, and customs tariff policy was arguably the one significant area in which agrarian and industrial interests could cooperate effectively. In 1884, Bismarck terrified industrialists when he controversially referred in a Reichstag speech to the 'right to work'. Bismarck frequently equated agrarian interests with the national interest, but he was never as considerate of the needs of industry and business as is often suggested.

From the perspective of parliamentary politics, too, there was a high degree of consistency, both in terms of Bismarck's parliamentary aims and the political aspirations of the parties, which is often overlooked. Throughout his chancellorship Bismarck was determined to prevent any extension of parliamentary power, a stance which soon led to tensions with the more left-wing National Liberals who remained committed to further constitutional change. The confrontation of 1878 was long in the making, as by the middle of the decade Bismarck sought a means of severing the left-wing from the party and facilitating the party's drift to the right. This never meant that he expected to be able to govern without the liberals or the middle classes they represented. Bismarck may have perceived even in the 1870s that, having lost their monopoly on the national idea and compromised their liberal ideals in the *Kulturkampf*, liberals could no longer claim to represent the majority of those classes whose support he deemed essential for the monarchy. But he remained convinced that the National Liberals represented the most dynamic and (outside Prussia) the most national forces in German society. He never seriously entertained the possibility that liberal parliamentary support could be permanently replaced by a coalition of conservative, clerical and particularist forces. Indeed, far from wishing to replace the National Liberals by the Centre as a party of government (as is sometimes suggested) Bismarck seems to have hoped that the easing of the *Kulturkampf* would weaken political Catholicism and hasten the progressive dissolution of the Centre Party. This in turn would have facilitated the integration or reintegration of Catholics into the mainstream liberal and conservative parties.

Bismarck's collaboration with the liberals in the 1870s was never very smooth, but the effects of his confrontation with them in 1878–9 on the party constellation scarcely suited his political purposes better in the longer term. After the party split in 1880, the National Liberals continued to support the government, albeit with a much greater degree of subservience than they had had to suffer previously. Yet the Chancellor scarcely had greater flexibility in terms of party coalitions. Having resented his parliamentary dependence on the liberals in the 1870s and regretted the loss of the freedom he had enjoyed in the years of the constitutional struggle, Bismarck wanted the possibility of an alternative parliamentary coalition, such as was presented to him by the conservative and Centre support for protectionism in 1879. Yet he had no illusions about governing with the Centre which was to remain on most matters implacably opposed to government policies throughout the 1880s. Nor did Reichstag elections (with the sole exception of the election in 1887) produce more conservative or compliant Reichstags. In the early 1880s it was the left liberals (and the Centre) who appeared to have gained most from the blow Bismarck dealt the National Liberals, and neither a conservative–Centre coalition nor a conservative–National Liberal coalition could command a parliamentary majority. Bismarck was never so isolated in terms of political support as he was between 1881 and 1886, and during these years he was literally forced to make a virtue out of 'government above the parties', scratching together *ad hoc* majorities according to the issue.

Inevitably, too, after a succession of defeats, he came to realize that there was little point introducing legislation into the Reichstag which had no chance of being accepted. In 1881 even the National Liberal leader, Bassermann, chided Bismarck for his (all too often half-baked and insufficiently considered) reform proposals and insisted that a breathing space was necessary after the legislative frenzy of the 1870s. The pace of legislative initiatives slackened and the Reichstag's role diminished in importance. Stagnation rather than conservative stability characterized the politics of the 1880s. In 1887 Bismarck achieved a notable electoral victory at a time of international crisis when the so-called Kartell (an electoral coalition of the two conservative parties and the National Liberals) defeated the opposition parties for the first time since 1878. Yet in practice even the Kartell could not provide a very stable or reliable basis of parliamentary support for the government, and Bismarck soon had reasons of his own to seek its destruction.

Above all, an examination of Bismarck's relations with the parliaments between 1871 and 1890 indicates the persistent, constant problem which arose from rival monarchical and parliamentary claims to power, compounded by the lack of any organic relationship between the executive and the legislature. Bismarck could rail against an electorate which did not understand his reform plans and reduce the number of occasions on which he appeared in the parliaments (he went five years without even speaking in the Prussian House of Deputies). But the government needed parliamentary support if it was to govern constitutionally. If the Reichstag denied it such support, the only recourse was to dissolve it and call new elections. Bismarck was prepared to use all the means at the government's disposal to swing the popular mood in elections or secure the passage of contentious legislation, above all army bills. He resorted to dramatic posturing and short-term expedients, such as the exploitation of the international crisis which was successful in the elections of 1887. But, faced with oppositional Reichstags between 1881 and 1887, he increasingly came to question the role of parliament itself. He harboured deep reservations about the consequences of universal suffrage; and he explored the possibility of bypassing the parliaments by such means as creating Prussian and Reich economic councils, organized on corporatist lines. He also threatened on many occasions to change the constitution by force, to impose a new franchise on the Reichstag or suppress it altogether, although ultimately a sense of realism prevailed until the last months of his chancellorship.

In exploring Bismarckian politics, historians have tended to focus on the exceptional situations, the government's apparent victories over the parties (in 1866–7, 1878–9, and 1887) as evidence of Bismarck's successful manipulation. The imperial German political parties have also attracted their share of the blame for political developments during Bismarck's chancellorship, having been variously accused of ideological rigidity, subversive materialism, negative campaigning, cringing conformity, an inability to transcend the representation of specific social milieux and an opportunistic willingness to change their political priorities under the impact of economic change and the rise of organized socialism. The parties, it seems, resigned themselves to political impotence and hindered the emergence of a progressive coalition dedicated to political reform. Nevertheless, despite the relative dearth of recent historical studies of Bismarckian high politics (excluding Bismarck biographies), especially in the 1880s, what is striking is how troublesome the party political situation was for Bismarck and how the routine

Illustration 8.2 Bismarck as a circus performer, keeping all the cabinet portfolios in the air (the Foreign Office on his nose) with a little help from the new Ministers of Interior and Finance. These three are 'the powerful ones'; 'actually no one else is needed' (Wilhelm Scholz in *Kladderadatsch*, 1881)

of parliamentary life gave him so little cause for satisfaction. The 'Iron Chancellor', who expected unquestioned authority within the executive and popular gratitude for the scale of his past achievements, could not accept the representative character of a German Reichstag which seemed perpetually intent on criticizing and thwarting his plans. Unable to implement the domestic reforms he believed were necessary, chiefly because of the hostility of the parties, the states or both, Bismarck's predicament was exacerbated because, as he was only too aware, he lacked a secure power base.

In the 1880s, if not earlier, the crucial context of Bismarckian high politics was the imminence of the monarchical succession. By 1881, when the left liberals gained the most seats in the Reichstag elections, Bismarck's chancellorship already appeared increasingly conditional. Despite Bismarck's efforts to bolster his personal authority and preserve his position, the growing likelihood of a change of Kaiser cast a huge question-mark over his political future. Wilhelm I, who had been born in 1797, clearly could not survive for much longer and change, whether under his reputedly liberal son, Friedrich, or his youthful grandson, Wilhelm, would have to come. In this situation the political parties could largely afford to bide their time, confident that sooner or later there had to be an era after Bismarck in which the decisive contest over the distribution of power in the new state could be fought on a much more level playing field.

No one in Prussia or the Empire could have anticipated that Bismarck would remain in power for nearly 30 years or come to enjoy such an unassailable position under Wilhelm I. As Lothar Gall has pointed out, at virtually every moment during his long career, his fall appeared imminent and likely. However, despite his indomitable personality, his spectacular successes between 1864 and 1871, and his formidable reputation, Bismarck never enjoyed political popularity or trust. He was always regarded as an exceptional individual whose chancellorship, too, represented a transitional phase before the establishment of new, more 'normal' conditions. In a sense, irrespective of the Empire's constitutional and political imperfections, Bismarck's confrontational style and his perennial threats to revise a constitution over which he claimed a monopoly, it was impossible for the new political system to stabilize as long as Bismarck remained at the helm. This was increasingly perceived by all those who came into contact with ruling circles in Berlin. It helps to explain the stagnation of imperial domestic politics by the middle of the 1880s and the dimensions of the protracted succession crisis from 1888. Above all, it accounts for the predominant mood of stunned relief which followed Bismarck's dismissal in March 1890.

Notes:

1. Wehler, Hans-Ulrich, *The German Empire 1871–1918* (1985) p. 27.
2. Pflanze, Otto, *Bismarck and the Development of Germany*, vol. 2, *The Period of Consolidation 1871–1880* (1990), p. 507.
3. Pflanze, Otto, *Bismarck and the Development of Germany*, vol. 3, *The Period of Fortification 1880–1898* (1990) p. 37.

Select bibliography

Berghahn, Volker, *Imperial Germany 1871–1914. Economy, Society, Culture and Politics* (1994).

Blackbourn, David, and Eley, Geoff, *The Peculiarities of German History* (1984).

Böhme, Helmut, *Deutschlands Weg zur Grossmacht. Studien zum Verhältnis von Wirtschaft und Staat während der Reichsgründungszeit 1848–1881* (1969).

Eley, Geoff, *From Unification to Nazism* (1986).

Engelberg, Ernst, *Bismarck*, 2 vols. (1985 and 1990).

Gall, Lothar, *Bismarck. The White Revolutionary*, 2 vols. (1986).

Mommsen, Wolfgang J., *Imperial Germany 1867–1918. Politics, Culture and Society in an Authoritarian State* (1995).

Pflanze, Otto, *Bismarck and the Development of Germany*, 3 vols. (1990).

Pflanze, Otto, ed., *Innenpolitische Probleme des Bismarck-Reiches* (1983).

Nipperdey, Thomas, *Deutsche Geschichte 1866-1918,* vol. 2: *Machtstaat vor der Demokratie* (1993).

Röhl, J. C. G., *Germany without Bismarck. The Crisis of Government in the Second Reich 1890–1900* (1967).

Schieder, Theodor, *Das deutsche Kaiserreich von 1871 als Nationalstaat* (1961).

Sheehan, James F., *German Liberalism in the Nineteenth Century* (1978).

Wehler, Hans-Ulrich, *Das Deutsche Kaiserreich 1871–1918* (1973); *The German Empire 1871–1918* (1985).

9

Demographic growth, industrialization and social change

Volker Berghahn

Population growth, urbanization and industrialization represented long-term processes that did not start with the founding of the German Empire in 1871 (see Chapter 4, above). What can be said at a most general level, however, is that all three developments experienced a further acceleration in the late nineteenth century.

This is true, to begin with, of demographic change. In 1864 some 39.4 million people lived in the area of central Europe that was to become united under Prussian leadership six years later, by which time the population had increased to just around 41 million. About 24.6 million of the inhabitants of the new German Empire were Prussians, followed by 4.8 million Bavarians, 2.5 million Saxons, 1.8 million Württembergians and 1.5 million Badeners, with the rest distributed among the smaller states. Some 1.6 million people lived in Alsace-Lorraine, annexed after the defeat of France. By 1913 no less than another 27 million people had been added to the 1871 figure, and the total would have reached over 30 million, if the around three million Germans were included who emigrated overseas between 1871 and 1911. In percentage terms the overall increase was more than 58 per cent.

In trying to explain this veritable population explosion, the baby boom of the optimistic years around the time of the founding of the Empire clearly constitutes a major factor, and birth rates continued to be relatively high in the decades thereafter. It was only in 1912 that lower-class parents, following the earlier middle-class lead, began to limit family size. An increase in life expectancy and a decline in mortality rates were the other major factors in the demographic equation. In 1870 life expectancy from birth averaged no more than 35.6 years for men and 38.5 years for women. After the turn of the century another ten years had been added (44.8 years for men and 48.3 years for women).

For a long time infant mortality remained almost level (and hence contributed relatively little to the demographic explosion). Between 1870 and 1880 no less than 211 of every 1,000 legitimately born babies in towns and cities died within the first year; the figure for the rural areas was somewhat lower at 183. Infant mortality reached a shocking 403 per 1,000 for children born out of wedlock (312 per 1,000 births in the countryside). All these figures barely improved until the turn of the century, after which survival rates for infants rose markedly. By 1914 the number of infant deaths among city-dwellers had dropped to 147 per 1,000 births (159 per 1,000 in rural areas). The picture for illegitimate children looked bleaker still: 261 deaths per 1,000 births in towns and cities and 287 per 1,000 in the countryside.

These additional millions who grew up in the new Empire were not evenly distributed throughout the land. Indeed, the demographic explosion is directly connected with the phenomenon of urbanization and *Landflucht* (flight from the rural areas). Again the processes that were at work here had set in before 1871, but the growth of towns and cities thereafter can only be described as staggering, as Table 9.1 demonstrates.

Put in percentage terms, cities like Dortmund, Essen and Kiel grew between 400 and 500 per cent between 1871 and 1910. Many others doubled and trebled in size. It was only to a certain extent that these growth rates were the result of high birth rates and rising life expectancies as well as declining infant mortality rates later on. Probably more significant were the additions as a result of internal migration. The set of global figures in Table 9.2 provides a first indication of the huge population movements from the rural to the urban areas that occurred during the imperial period.

Many of these men and women were long-distance migrants, especially from the eastern provinces of Prussia to the urban centres of central Germany and of the

Table 9.1   Growth of some major cities, 1850–1910 (000s)

City	1850	1871	1880	1900	1910
Berlin	412	826	1,122	1,889	2,071
Hamburg	175	290	490	706	931
Munich	107	169	230	500	596
Leipzig	63	107	149	456	679
Dresden	97	177	221	396	548
Cologne	97	129	145	373	517
Breslau	111	208	273	423	512
Frankfurt/Main	65	91	137	289	415
Düsseldorf	27	69	95	214	359
Nuremberg	54	83	100	261	333
Hanover	28	88	123	236	302
Essen	9	52	57	119	295
Chemnitz	34	68	95	207	288
Duisburg	9	31	41	93	229
Dortmund	11	44	67	143	214
Kiel	16	32	44	108	212
Mannheim	24	40	53	141	194

Table 9.2   Gains and losses through internal migration by region, 1907 (000s)

Region	Residents (total)	Natives/Staying	Natives/Left	Newcomers	Gains/Losses
Eastern Germany	12,066.2	11,708.1	2,326.7	358.1	−1,968.6
Berlin, Brandenburg	5,585.2	3,936.1	445.5	1,649.2	+1,203.7
Northwest Germany	6,881.9	6.106.8	495.7	775.1	+279.4
Central Germany	9,719.7	9,001.9	891.4	717.8	−173.6
Hesse	3,371.1	2,954.9	348.1	416.2	+68.1
Western Germany	10,171.1	9,080.6	449.4	1,090.5	+64.1
Southern Germany	12,580.5	12,200.0	431.4	380.5	−50.9

Rhine–Ruhr region. However, further research may well show that short-distance migrants were even more important – people who had grown up in the vicinity of the major urban centres. A good number of them retained their ties with their families back in the villages of the region, and some of them even lived the life of commuters on a daily or seasonal basis, especially at harvest time. These migrants are of considerable interest to the historian of popular culture, since it may be assumed that they did not immediately shed their earlier lifestyles and merely assimilated to city culture in the broad sense.

Here are some illuminating figures: at the time of the founding of the Empire, around 64 per cent of the population lived in small communities with under 2,000 inhabitants. By 1910 this figure had declined to 40 per cent. Meanwhile the share of towns with over 50,000 people had gone up from 8.9 per cent in 1870 to 26.7 per cent in 1910. Cities of over 100,000 inhabitants saw the most dramatic shift from 4.8 per cent in 1870 to 21.3 percent in 1910. Still, it would be wrong to suggest that pre-1914 Germany consisted mainly of big cities. In 1910 just over one quarter of the population continued to live in provincial towns of between 2,000 and 20,000 inhabitants, and in numerical terms the rural population added up to 21 million. However, in the meantime, so many millions had joined the stream of internal migrants, long- or short-distance, that over half of the population had left their place of birth and started a new life elsewhere, mostly in the urban parts of the Reich.

Finally, movements within cities must not be overlooked. Although precise statistics are difficult to come by, people frequently changed their abode within the same community, especially among the lower classes. Young unmarried migrants tended to live a particularly unsteady life, having to rely on lodgings with families in often incredibly cramped conditions. If there was a row, they would move out, often overnight. Nor is it too difficult to see that the huge demand for housing in the cities led to rapid rent increases, frequently putting the cost of an apartment beyond the reach of a low-income occupant family. So, something cheaper had to be found in a hurry. Frequent moves were also triggered by unemployment or job changes. Given the low wage levels, many workers would not hesitate, in times of prosperity, to switch to another factory up the road that offered more money. Indeed the search for improved material conditions and a 'better life' lay at the heart of most of the population movement. It is at this point that demographic change and urbanization intersect with industrialization.

There has been some debate as to whether the shift from an economy based on agriculture to one based on industrial production was as dramatic as had been assumed, and Hartmut Kaelble has offered comparisons with other countries like Denmark, which – he argues – experienced a more momentous industrial revolution. Whatever the relativities in international perspective may be, here it suffices to emphasize that the changeover was momentous enough to produce major social dislocations, but also to generate, at least from the 1890s onwards, a new prosperity and a general improvement in material and cultural conditions.

If we take the share of agriculture in the gross national product (GNP), this sector of the economy remained in the lead with 35–40 per cent until the 1880s. Industry's share then stood at 30–35 per cent. Just before the First World War, agriculture had fallen back to 25 per cent, with industry now in the lead (45 per cent), followed by the commercial and service sector at 30 per cent. This means that agriculture remained important in the national economy and, thanks to the population explosion, in fact witnessed an expansion of its production.

That there was still money to be made in agriculture is also reflected in the increased use of sophisticated machinery like tractors and steam threshers to achieve productivity gains. And yet these gains could not overcome a broader structural handicap that inexorably caused agriculture to fall behind the other sectors in the long run: industry as well as the tertiary sector were simply more productive. This was the part of the economy where new riches were accumulated. At the time of the founding of the Empire in 1870–1, the industrial sector achieved annual growth rates of 4.5 per cent. This rate declined to around 3 per cent during the 'great depression' between 1873 and 1896, before returning to averages of 4.5 per cent in the decades up to the First World War.

The production of coal and pig iron may serve as a more specific indicator of industrial expansion. In the 1880s, Germany produced some 47 million tons of coal per annum. By 1913 this figure had grown four-fold to 191 million tons. In 1870–4 pig iron production had reached an annual average of 1.6 million tons. Between 1910 and 1913 the average was 14.8 million tons. In the early years, much of Germany's iron and steel production was consumed by railway building and, even though the expansion of the network saw a marked slowdown thereafter, by 1910 the system had nonetheless grown to 61,000 kilometres from its 1870 starting point of about 19,000 kilometres.

Late nineteenth-century Germany greatly benefited from the rapid expansion of electrical engineering and chemicals. These were the new industries based on scientific breakthroughs and technological innovation that complemented the older industries of the first industrial revolution like coal, iron and textiles. In fact, it has been argued that the first and the second industrial revolutions occurred in Germany virtually at the same time, as the new industries experienced their most spectacular growth. In chemicals and pharmaceuticals in particular, Germany had by 1900 achieved a leading position in the world. By 1914 it had also outpaced Britain, the first industrial nation, in steel production.

That money was to be made in industry is also reflected in optimistic investment rates which hovered around the 43 per cent mark between 1905 and 1913, with agriculture's rate trailing well behind at about 11 per cent. Tax returns similarly tell of new riches that were being created. In 1895 the Prussian Inland Revenue counted 3,429 taxpayers with a declared wealth of 1–2 million marks. Another 1,827 even declared over 2 million marks. By 1907 these figures had nearly doubled to 5,916 and 3,425 respectively. The disposable incomes of these individuals, most of whom were in industry or finance, must be held against the national average of wages and salaries which then stood at 834 marks per annum. The fact that this average had risen from 506 marks per annum in 1870 and was to reach 1,163 marks per annum in 1913 indicates that, even if the material benefits of industrialization continued to be very unevenly distributed, there was at least some improvement in living standards also among the mass of the population who had virtually no assets and relied on their weekly wage packets. Thus miners, who had earned around 767 marks per annum in 1870, took home 1,496 marks per annum by 1913. Metal workers reached slightly higher wage levels from the mid-1890s onwards. Meanwhile white-collar employees, for example at the Maschinenfabrik Esslingen in southwest Germany, received 1,871 marks per annum in 1871 and 3,753 marks per annum in 1912. To be sure, these increases look less impressive when the inflation rate is factored in. Still, and with slight variations among authors, real wages grew by 30 per cent and more.

With agriculture clearly doing less well than industry, wage levels remained correspondingly lower here. On the large estates that were typical of the regions east of the river Elbe, the demand for land labourers remained high, but low returns, often exacerbated by inefficient management of the estates, made pay rises difficult, even if the lords had wanted to offer incentives to keep their labourers from wandering westward. Wage pressures could be relieved to some extent by the importation of cheap Polish migrant seasonal workers from the western parts of Russia, especially during harvest time. Unionization was prohibited. Given these conditions, many were no longer prepared to put up with often depressing living and housing conditions. They left for the city to find a job in better-paid industry. Another motive for leaving, especially among young land labourers and servants, was the patriarchal conditions on the large estates. The lords had been able to uphold their disciplinary and policing powers into the modern period and used them to curb freedom of movement. Leisure time was also strictly limited and regulated. Nor was there much to do after a long workday and city life became very alluring in this respect as well.

In other parts of the country, especially in the west, south and south-west the small family farm predominated. But fewer and fewer of them generated enough income to provide for all children. And so, like the land labourers in the east, the younger sons and daughters among them joined the trek to the cities in search of a better-paid job and a freer life. Some of them, as has been mentioned, continued to commute; most of them tried to establish a permanent base for themselves in the city, living as lodgers with other working-class families or, once married, looking for a small apartment in one of the large *Mietskasernen* ('rental garrisons') that mushroomed in the urban centres.

These were therefore the deeper causes of the massive internal migrations and the *Landflucht*: the hope for a better material life and the wish to escape from the traditionalist and restrictive conditions of the village or the estate. Even if factory discipline was very strict, at least one had a bit more money in one's pocket and disposal of leisure time was much freer. This story of socioeconomic change is also reflected in the age structure. By and large, the elderly stayed behind in agriculture; the young, men and women, moved to the cities where they had been told life was more exciting. What they discovered was that wages were barely above the poverty line. On the estates, meals and accommodation had often been free. Now a considerable percentage of the weekly income went into paying rent. To make ends meet, many families had to take in lodgers, and single beds were frequently shared between two or three people. Sanitary facilities were primitive, and illness, whenever it happened, was a disaster for the whole family. Ups and downs in the economy occasionally triggered higher unemployment rates. It was in such times that parents had to make further cuts in an already tight food budget. In the long run, to be sure, nutritional standards improved, but the main effect of this was that working-class families were able to put enough food on the table and no-one went hungry. Once or twice a week they might even be able to afford meat, with pork consumption, including sausage, quadrupling between 1850 and 1910.

It could be argued that a land labourer who moved to one of the new industrial centres, whatever the continued hardships he or she experienced (including a 10–12 hour daily work schedule six days week) was achieving some upward mobility by becoming an unskilled or semi-skilled industrial worker. Over time he might even rise to the position of skilled worker with better pay. Women, though, hardly ever got that far, while men, trying to move further upwards, soon hit a glass ceiling that the middle classes had erected. Nor, by and large, was it possible in Imperial Germany to gain upward mobility through marriage. Most workers married women of working-class or peasant background. Given the elitism of the educational system, intergenerational mobility also remained low, no matter how strongly working-class parents encouraged their children to improve their socioeconomic status by acquiring better qualifications.

In short, most blue-collar workers found that a clear line existed between them and the middle classes higher up the social scale. If urban societies had been highly differentiated and stratified even before the industrial revolution, the advent of the factory and the expansion of public administration produced new *Mittelstand* groups alongside the old *Mittelstand* of craftsmen, shopkeepers, teachers, petty civil servants and others. The number of university-trained professionals also increased, with people in tradi-

Illustration 9.1   'Someone's gone and swapped our little Joes again!' (Heinrich Zille, 1908). A reflection of the expansion of women's work in factories

tional urban occupations like lawyers and doctors being complemented by technicians, lab scientists and financial and marketing experts. Most of the upward (and downward) mobility in Imperial Germany occurred within this broad middle stratum, though often over two generations. The son of a primary schoolteacher might become a 'professor' in a *Gymnasium*; the son of a small craftsman might expand his father's workshop into a prosperous factory.

Those who were hoping to become part of the upper middle class found that the hurdles of social acceptance became higher. The craftsman's son who had become a successful entrepreneur did not necessarily gain access to the more exclusive circles in which private bankers, tycoons or higher civil servants would move, even if his accumulated wealth put him into the same income bracket. Though an individual's position in the marketplace provided a rough gauge for the system of social stratification, less tangible factors than income have to be added when we try to understand interactions among the middle classes. This is also true of relationships between the upper middle class and the nobility. Urbanization and industrialization had eroded, but had not been able to destroy the latter's position as the First Estate. The survival of the monarchical principle and of so many princely courts in central Europe after 1871 perpetuated its position. As a result historians had long assumed that the aristocracy provided the social and cultural model that the upper middle class tried to emulate. More recent research indicates that this 'feudalisation' process was much more limited than had been postulated. Most wealthy entrepreneurs or professionals, it appears, developed their own identity and pride in what they represented. A few, but by no means all, craved to be given a noble title or to be accepted into the social world of the landowning aristocracy. The dominant pattern was one of social separateness rather than merger or intermarriage, although this did not prevent cooperation at the level of politics whenever there was a coincidence of interests.

Before we deal with the question of whether the social differentiations and inequalities discussed so far amount to a society that was stratified by social class, we must ask if there were other categories that divided or united people in larger collectives. Clearly gender is one such category and its importance is discussed in Chapter 26, below. Religious denomination would appear to be another to be considered in this chapter.

With a few vacillations, the denominational balance remained roughly the same in Imperial Germany: Over 62 per cent of the population were Protestants, some 36 per cent were Catholics. The percentage of Jews actually declined, though this group experienced a numerical increase from 512,000 to 615,000 between 1871 and 1910. Jews shared the fate of other ethnic minorities of finding themselves in an ambiguous position. On the one hand, the removal of all legal discrimination opened up unprecedented opportunities to achieve social and economic success. Jews were disproportionately successful in the professions, in business, in the arts and in intellectual life more generally. On the other hand, their achievements fanned old prejudices against them among the Christian population. Anti-Semitism proliferated from the 1880s onwards and resulted in renewed, more selective discrimination. Thus it became virtually impossible to rise to higher positions in the civil service, the judiciary and the armed forces. Jewish scholars, however gifted and prolific, found it difficult to obtain professorships. Jews were also excluded from social clubs and associations. Many of them fought the drawing of such lines, some by joining the Central Association for German Citizens of the Jewish Faith whose name gave its aims away. Others became members of the Zionist movement which believed that equality without having to abandon their cultural identity was possible only in a Jewish national state.

Jewish protestations did little to undermine Christian prejudice. Catholics rejected their Jewish fellow citizens for religious reasons as the alleged 'murderers of Christ'.

Economic anti-Semitism charged Jews with usury and greed. And socially they continued to run up against the hauteur of the upper middle classes and the nobility which refused to socialise with 'those upstarts'. All this is meant to say that anti-Semitism cut across the above-mentioned lines of social stratification. It erected barriers of cultural and religious prejudice that were not directly related to economic status.

The same point applies in principle to the treatment of Catholics by the Protestant majority. Again, on the one hand, Catholics benefited from the expanding opportunities in education and business; on the other, they were held back in their advance. To some extent this 'backwardness' was self-imposed and due to the fact that Catholics, unlike many Protestants (and in this respect also Jews), remained more firmly rooted in their traditional provincial milieux in which the church continued to wield a powerful ideological influence. Thus Catholicism remained suspicious of the many manifestations of modernity, of urbanization and industrialization, of liberalism and the emergence of a more secular society. Even before the founding of the Reich this had led many Protestant liberals to view Catholicism as an obscurantist faith, under the thumb of the 'ultramontane' Vatican, that impeded socioeconomic and constitutional progress.

It is out of this sense that the Protestant majority joined forces with Reich Chancellor Bismarck after 1871 to launch the *Kulturkampf* against the Catholics. The latter were turned into 'enemies of the Reich', their institutions, above all the religious orders, were subjected to open persecution. Although Bismarck had his own reasons for unleashing this struggle (and for abandoning it a few years later), it deepened the denominational divide. Faced with ostracism, Catholics ventured even more cautiously outside the traditional milieu and fell behind Protestants. To be a Catholic remained a serious handicap when it came to promotion in the civil service, and not just in predominantly Protestant Prussia. Even in Bavaria, where the majority of the population was Catholic, the higher civil service was run by Protestants. The problem of denominationalism is most strikingly reflected in higher education where the share of Catholic students was disproportionately smaller. The contrast was less marked in the business world, especially in the Rhineland. Nevertheless, the crucial point to be remembered here is that it made a difference in society and the economy whether a person was Protestant, Catholic or Jewish, just as gender differences counted and women were disadvantaged *vis-à-vis* men with respect to jobs, social rights and legal position.

However, in the long run neither denomination nor gender proved as powerful a category of social inequality and stratification as that of social class. Certainly if being Catholic still counted for much in the 1870s, by 1913 it had become overlaid by criteria of class and status. One of the most telling indicators of the notion that Imperial Germany turned increasingly into a class society is to be found in the realm of political behaviour. Partly under the impact of the *Kulturkampf*, the Centre Party had become the party of Catholics, providing a political and ideological home to Catholic workers from the Ruhr industrial region, to Rhenish Catholic bankers, to Bavarian Catholic peasants and to Catholic landowners from Silesia. By 1912, however, this tie had loosened somewhat and Catholic workers now increasingly voted for social democracy which explicitly presented itself as a working-class party and explained the world in terms of class and rising class conflict.

Clearly, not merely millions of Protestant industrial workers, but also Catholic ones saw their daily experience more closely reflected in the interpretations of society that the socialists provided than what they were told by their anti-socialist priests. With political behaviour, social consciousness also shifted towards the importance of class as the determining feature of society. In their quest for a better life, for greater equality and upward mobility, industrial workers and their families had time and again come up against a strict divide. Conversely the middle classes, feeling threatened by the 'masses below', united to confine them permanently to a ghetto – physically, in terms of residential patterns and socially, by denying them access to channels of upward mobility. In doing so they enlisted the help of the state, first by having the government proscribe the working-class movement and later, from 1890, after the anti-socialist laws had lapsed, by police harrassment and vigorous prosecution in the courts.

Perceptions and misperceptions of reality can be as powerful in shaping historical developments as reality itself. The point is that for millions of German industrial workers perceptions came to coincide with their actual daily experiences and the realities of their lives. Consequently they began to raise their voices against the discriminations and blatant injustices, and in the age of universal suffrage gave expression to their grievances at the polls by voting in growing numbers for the Social Democrats who excoriated the monarchical class state with its rigid hierarchies and its immobilism. By 1912 the SPD had become the largest party in the Reichstag, attracting some 4.2 million votes (34.8 per cent) and gaining 110 seats.

From the perspective of the 1990s it is not easy to appreciate the full extent to which the repressive organs of the state were used to contain the perceived threat from the working-class movement. However, police surveillance, outrageous court decisions and army orders to be prepared for a violent coup against the socialists and the trade unions were not the only ways in which the state intervened in the lives of the 'dangerous classes'. Its approach amounted rather to a more or less judicious use of carrot and stick *vis-à-vis* industrial workers and of subsidies for the rest. Thus, while the government gave massive help to the 'ailing' agrarians, left behind economically by industry, by erecting protectionist tariffs against foreign competitors, as well as to industry and commerce at home (for example, through support of research) and abroad (for example, through diplomatic and naval protection), Bismarck began to use the powers of the state to introduce social welfare programmes.

The creation of a universal workers' accident insurance was so obviously advantageous to the employers as well, removing the imponderabilities of suits for negligence by injured workers, that it enjoyed broad support. Bismarck's old age pension and health insurance schemes were more controversial, and not just because of their costs. However, in the end the Reich Chancellor's argument prevailed that if workers were given a pension they would stay away from radical parties. In the long run the intro-duction of welfare state policies may not have worked as intended. The organization of the working class did not decline. Instead it witnessed a seemingly unstoppable rise. What these policies may have done was to strengthen the hands of the moderates within the working-class movement who advocated a gradual transformation of exist-ing socioeconomic and constitutional conditions against the radicals who talked of a violent overthrow. At the same time, state welfarism could not prevent the progressive polarization of national politics prior to 1914.

This applied, to begin with, to industrial relations. Although there were a few branches of industry that slowly moved towards a recognition of trade unions and wage bargaining, most employers' associations continued to pursue a hard line *vis-à-vis* the organized working class. Denied what they believed to be fair material demands, work-ers increasingly went on strike, to which the employers routinely responded with lock-outs. There were some very bitter labour conflicts in which the police and army promptly sided with the employers and the 'scabs' who were brought in. Overall, 1906 was the first really bad year, with 3,480 strikes and lock-outs. The last years of peace before 1914 saw a fresh wave of labour conflicts involving even larger numbers of workers. In the meantime the willingness of the majority parties and the Reich as well as Federal state authorities to make power-political concessions to the 'masses' also diminished. Indeed, in the eyes of the monarchical government as well as the middle classes and conservative agrarians the idea of constitutional reform in the direction of parliamentarism was so unacceptable that they used every means at their disposal to block a change in the status quo.

It was only in 1917, when the war was going badly, that the Reichstag gained a few additional powers of decision-making and that a promise of constitutional reform was held out, to be realized once victory had been won. Just making this promise for the future cost Chancellor Theobald von Bethmann Hollweg his job, because it was rejected by the powerful military leadership under Hindenburg and Ludendorff and the political forces backing them. The Kaiser was forced to renege on his famous Easter Message. A little more than a year later, Ludendorff went to see the monarch to tell him that the war had been lost militarily. State Secretary Hintze now came up with a cunning scheme. He proposed what amounted to a constitutional revolution: a new Reich government was to be appointed with the approval of the majority in the Reichstag. Germany, for all practical purposes, had become a constitutional monarchy with the Kaiser divested of his many supreme executive powers. The Social Democrats in parliament were among those who supported this solution that had been so persis-tently denied in previous years. Nor was it difficult to recognize the purpose of Hintze's move: in the hour of defeat the blame was to be shifted away from those who were in fact responsible both for unleashing the First World War and for prolonging it.

However, the 'revolution from above' of October 1918 could not stop the 'revolu-tion from below' that brought the collapse of the Bismarckian Empire from breaking out a month later. At the same time, the political and constitutional revolution that occurred in November 1918 cannot be understood without appreciating the socioeconomic changes of the previous years. If the war had been over by Christmas 1914, as so many confidently expected when it broke out in the summer, the Wilhelmine class state would probably have been stabilized. Yet, as the war turned total and required the mobilization of all resources, the masses began to bear not only the brunt of the sacrifices in lives at the front, but also of the decline in living standards at home. Whereas the scarcity of food due to the Allied blockade benefited agriculture handsomely, and armaments-related industries were profitably producing goods for military victory round the clock, the working classes saw their economic position deteriorate. After 1916 the middle classes also began to feel the pinch. Still, at least they had valuables and savings that they could deploy on the black market to barter food for their families. What in the long run would hit them worse was that they had bought government bonds in support of the war effort, redeemable with attractive additional interest earnings after victory. It was only after the defeat that nemesis hit them: their bond certificates quickly became worthless scraps of paper. They had been virtually expropriated.

For the majority of the population the advent of total war therefore meant socioeconomic change for the worse, not to mention the demographic and psychological impact of the unprecedented blood-letting in the trenches. Social tension rose. By 1917 the government had to cope with food riots and massive strikes. The earlier consciousness of living in a class society and the increased tensions now escalated into open class conflict. Even if the October Revolution of 1918 had succeeded, there is little doubt that German society and its once prosperous industrial economy would have emerged completely changed from the experience of war and defeat. As Part III on the history of the Weimar Republic will show, the collapse of the monarchy and the consequences of the November Revolution merely highlighted the extent of this change.

Select bibliography

Demography, urbanization and economic change

Bade, K.-J., *Population, Labour and Migration in 19th- and 20th-Century Germany* (1987).
Bry, G., *Wages in Germany, 1871–1914* (1960).
Desai, A. V., *Real Wages in Germany, 1971-1914* (1968).
Henderson, W. O., *The Rise of German Industrial Power, 1834–1914* (1975).
Lee, W. R., ed., *Industrialisation and Industrial Growth in Germany* (1986).
Stolper, G., *The German Economy from 1870 to the Present* (1967).
Witt, P.-Chr., ed., *Wealth and Taxation in Central Europe* (1987).

Society and political mobilization

Augustine, D., *Patricians and Parvenus* (1994).
Bigler, R. M., *The Politics of German Protestantism* (1972).
Dahrendorf, R., *Democracy and Society in Germany* (1968).
Evans, R. J., and Lee, W. R., eds., *The German Family* (1980).

Gay, R., *The Jews of Germany* (1992).
Gispen, K., *New Professions, Old Order* (1990).
Iggers, G. G., ed., *The Social History of Politics* (1986).
Knodel, J., *The Decline of Fertility in Germany, 1871–1939* (1974).
Kocka, J., *Facing Total War* (1987).
Lidtke, V., *The Alternative Culture* (1985).
Moses, J. A., *Trade Unionism in Germany*, 2 vols. (1982).
Ritter, G. A., *Social Welfare in Germany and Britain* (1983).
Sagarra, E., *A Social History of Germany* (1977).
Schofer, L., *The Formation of a Modern Labor Force* (1975).
Spencer, E. G., *Management and Labor in Imperial Germany* (1984).
Sperber, J., *Popular Catholicism in 19th-Century Germany* (1984).
Spree, R., *Health and Social Class in Imperial Germany* (1987).
Stern, F., *Gold and Iron* (1977).

IO

Imperial Germany: cultural and intellectual trends

Matthew Jefferies

In the opening chapter of his classic essay *Weimar Culture. The Outsider as Insider*, Peter Gay makes a startling admission: 'the Republic created little', he writes, 'it liberated what was already there'.[1] In other words, much that is celebrated as 'Weimar culture' was not the fruit of liberal democracy at all, but first began to blossom in the very different climate of the Second Empire. Whether one regards Gay's claim as exaggerated or not, it is certainly true that the imperial era saw a growing pluralism, dissent and diversity in German cultural life, and ultimately demonstrated a dynamism and zest for innovation which was hardly apparent at the Empire's birth. In the light of this, it is perhaps surprising that the cultural and intellectual developments of the imperial era have not received more attention from historians.

Whilst there are many monographs on particular aspects of pre-First World War German culture, and a growing number of valuable essay collections too, the sort of general studies which have helped to raise the profile of Weimar culture are conspicuous only by their absence for the Bismarckian and Wilhelmine periods. It is understandable that historians should be wary of searching for some elusive, all-embracing *Zeitgeist*, especially for a time of increasing complexity and contradictions. Yet however incomplete and impressionistic it must be, an overview is still required, not least to complement the wide range of new perspectives cast on the political and social history of Imperial Germany in recent years.

It is unfortunate that some of the most widely read attempts to analyse the cultural and intellectual life of the *Kaiserreich* have been written by historians primarily concerned with the roots of National Socialism. The result has been, on the one hand, an exaggerated and misleading emphasis on 'cultural pessimism', anti-rationalism and *völkisch* mysticism; and, on the other, a preoccupation with the 'unpolitical German' and the 'feudalized' bourgeoisie. No one would deny that these are dimensions to Imperial German culture worthy of discussion, but the wider picture has sometimes been lost by historians whose approach has seemed dangerously teleological. It is important, therefore, to stress right at the outset that many of the themes and trends in German cultural and intellectual life were common, to a greater or lesser degree, to Europe as a whole.

The decades either side of 1900 witnessed a far-reaching revolution in painting, architecture, music, literature, and indeed in almost every other art form: an upheaval which did not stop at national borders and which coincided with – and was nourished by – a similarly radical questioning of previous assumptions in scientific and philosophical life. This dual revolution in the realm of culture and ideas, usually subsumed under the convenient if problematic term 'modernism', helped to transform a Europe already undergoing dramatic economic, social and technological change.

Modernism in the arts revolted against the limitations of established representational codes and historical convention. It took very different forms – including a revived interest in 'primitive' cultures and folk myths as well as the shock of the new – and led to a rapid turnover in stylistic approaches – impressionism, symbolism, naturalism, cubism, futurism, expressionism – as the classical canon splintered and the international art trade developed into an increasingly sophisticated commodity market. Changes in the nature of arts patronage were accompanied by a breaking down of barriers between 'high' and 'popular' culture, and between the various art forms themselves.

Both modernization in general (industrialization, urbanization, the growth of mass politics and the mass media), and modernism in particular, provoked hostility wherever they appeared, and not only from enemies of progress and reactionary philistines. The costs of modernity – such as the alienation and anonymity of the big city, the loss of traditional lifestyles and the many threats faced by the natural world – were very real; whilst the arrogance of many modernists, who claimed to have triumphed over history, was always likely to arouse a hostile response. Indeed, the attitude of *épater les bourgeois* was an integral part of most modernist movements.

By the 1890s, intellectual disdain for the emerging mass society and its culture was widespread throughout Europe amongst thinkers on both the left and right of the political spectrum. Almost all the values associated with nineteenth-century civilization – liberalism, materialism, positivism, rationality – were called into question, giving rise to a profound scepticism about the benefits of 'progress' and the mood of malaise popularly associated with the *fin de siècle*. 'Modernists' were themselves hostile to many aspects of the modern society which had spawned them, but by no means all were pessimists. Indeed, many expressed a youthful optimism for the future and became engaged in efforts to reform society through art, whilst others preferred to retreat into a cultish aestheticism or hedonistic decadence.

However, for all that was essentially pan-European in character, there was clearly something particularly remarkable about a German culture which in these years not only played a decisive role in the development of abstract art, atonal music and modern architecture, but also produced Nietzsche, Einstein and Freud. It was as if the trends and themes which shaped European culture as a whole affected Germany in a particularly heightened and acute form. Most historians suggest it was the unusually rapid and intense experience of modernization which made pre-First World War Germany, in Modris Eksteins's phrase, the 'modernist nation *par excellence*'.

The relationship between economic and social modernization and cultural modernism is far from straightforward, but in searching for the cultural and intellectual trends which shaped Imperial Germany one has to put responses to modernization at the top of the list. There were, however, other pervasive themes which were important in the German case, and one deserves particular mention: the national question. The fact that culture *Kultur* had served as an important focal point of national consciousness in the century or so before unification ensured that the writer or artist had a more central role in German life than in many other countries. This did not subside after 1871, and cultural issues continued to be debated with an intensity and vigour untypical of other national contexts: attempts to define what was distinctively German, and how it differed from other national traditions, remained a major preoccupation of cultural critics and producers. At the same time, however, the manner in which Germany had been unified reduced rather than increased the chances of Germany developing genuinely national cultural institutions. The smaller German states, fearful of Prussian domination, saw cultural policy as an important area of autonomy, and as a counterweight to Berlin's hegemony. Cultural affairs therefore remained largely under their own jurisdiction – the only major exceptions were press and copyright laws – and any attempt to increase the imperial role met with fierce opposition, from Bavaria in particular.

The polycentric nature of German cultural and intellectual life – rightly highlighted as a positive consequence of German particularism – therefore continued, despite the rise of Berlin as a capital city of increasing importance. Germany's other cultural centres fell into three main categories: the many *Residenzstädte*, the seats of royal courts, where rulers had provided theatres, museums and academies; the old university towns, such as Leipzig and Jena; and towns with thriving art markets. The most important of the latter were Munich, Düsseldorf, Dresden and – beyond the borders of the Reich – Vienna. Until the 1890s, however, this apparent abundance was not reflected in diversity.

I *Gründerzeit* culture

At the time of unification, and in the economically turbulent years which followed (the so-called *Gründerzeit*), the arts in Germany had a deserved reputation for being conservative and unadventurous. The Academies of Fine Art, whose annual exhibitions or 'salons' were the crucial marketplace for most artists (the turnover of the 1888 salon in Munich was over one million marks), were bastions of tradition, unwilling to accept innovation or deviation from established conventions. As anyone familiar with the trials and tribulations of the French impressionists will be aware, this was by no means unique to Germany, but even so, the insularity and conventionality of the German academies were frequently recognized by contemporaries. At a time when paintings were expected to tell a story, to inspire, and to reflect lofty ideals, the predilection was for historical, mythological and biblical subjects, packed with detail and highly composed, yet executed in a style that was intended to given an illusion of reality, so that any evidence of artifice – the strokes of the paintbrush, for instance – had to be hidden from view.

The most successful German painters of the day were men like Franz von Lenbach (1836–1904), who dominated the artistic life of Munich until the 1890s and was best known for his many portraits of Bismarck, and Anton von Werner (1843–1915), who held a similarly dominant position in the Berlin art world. Werner produced many large and pompous paintings for the Prussian state, depicting scenes from the Franco-Prussian War and most famously the proclamation of Kaiser Wilhelm I at Versailles, first painted in 1877. These 'princely painters' (*Malerfürsten*), who mixed with kings, chancellors and great industrialists, lived in a truly palatial style and were probably respected more for their wealth than their creativity. Certainly Hans Makart, a Viennese artist, is remembered for his imposing studio – piled high with artistic treasures, and open to the public for an hour each afternoon – rather than his paintings.

German painters of the mid- to late nineteenth century did not, on the whole, belong to movements or even loose associations. They were highly conscious of their individual reputations and were often scornful of their 'competitors', particularly if they felt their place in posterity was under threat. With the exception of Adolph Menzel (1815–1905), who was always something of a maverick, the leading German painters consciously emulated the styles and themes of the old masters, in large and opulent canvases full of theatricality and pathos. The German historians Richard Hamann and Jost Hermand have drawn parallels between the heroic postures of *Gründerzeit* art and the cult of genius which pervaded other areas of early imperial culture: academic work, for instance, often concentrated on the biographies of great men, and Friedrich Nietzsche attempted to embody the whole of his philosophy in a single individual, Zarathustra.

Of course, the work of the 'heroic' *Gründerzeit* artists was out of reach of all but the wealthiest individuals and institutions, but many of the leading painters also produced smaller genre scenes for more modest budgets and surroundings. Middle-class Germans could also obtain original works by joining one of the many *Kunstvereine* – by 1900 there were over 80 of these 'art clubs' – which were established in major towns during the nineteenth century and which usually allocated paintings to members by lottery. For the vast majority of people, however, art came in the form of reproductions, which were often of high quality. The demand for reproductions, the success of the *Kunstvereine*, the popularity of art history as an academic discipline and the high attendance figures at exhibitions all testify to a great hunger for art in late nineteenth-century Germany: indeed, historians such as Thomas Nipperdey have made much of art's role as a surrogate religion in an increasingly secular society.

The popularity of painting in the manner of the old masters was complemented by a vogue for heavy, highly ornamental furniture – antique or reproduction – and dark, wood-panelled rooms. This was due in no small measure to the proselytizing of the writer and publisher Georg Hirth (1841–1916), who vigorously promoted the German Renaissance as the most suitable historical tradition on which to base a national style for the new Empire. The long-running debate on what should be the German national style in design and architecture was complex, since the aesthetic arguments were clouded by political symbolism. For instance, Hirth, and other liberal enthusiasts of the German Renaissance, were principally attracted to the *Dürerzeit* by its image as a golden age of civic responsibility, in which the sturdy burghers of towns like Nuremberg had maintained a proud record of self-government. Architecture was similarly an issue of political identity for the Catholic politician and art critic August Reichensperger (1808–95), a founder of the Centre Party and the most vociferous champion of the Gothic style. He celebrated the completion of Cologne cathedral in the 1880s as a fitting symbol for the new Empire, but fought in vain for the new Reichstag building also to be designed in what he termed the 'German style'. For others, however, it was essentially an economic issue: with the growing internationalization of trade, they argued, Germany would need to develop some sort of distinctive style of its own, if it was to compete with the established identities of British or French goods.

It was largely in response to the poor impression made by German applied art in the shop window of the great world fairs that a major exhibition was held in Munich's Crystal Palace in 1876. Visitors had to pass through a display of 3,000 pieces of historic German furniture and *objets d'art* under the banner of 'Our Fathers' Works', before they could reach the contemporary exhibits, most of which were in historical styles. The message of the exhibition was that German designers should study the work of their forefathers and continue in their traditions, even if machines had largely replaced the craftsman's hands.

However, with manufacturers always eager to outshine their rivals' products, and with designers anxious to show off their mastery of a range of historic styles, gained at a growing number of colleges of applied art (*Kunstgewerbeschulen*) or technical colleges, no uniform national style emerged. Whilst each historical style had its own rules and conventions, these became increasingly blurred in the later nineteenth century, with particular problems caused by objects and buildings with no historical prototype, such as telephones and cookers, railway stations and department stores. More often than not, the result was the sort of eclectic historicism which was by no means unique to Germany, but which became a prime target for German cultural critics at the turn of the century.

Taking their cue from these early modernist critiques, contemporary historians have tended to portray the *Gründerzeit* as a period of cultural and moral decline: as a time of nouveau riche speculators and their tasteless attempts at upward mobility (the sort of characters portrayed in Sternheim's *The Snob*, Fontane's *The Adulteress* or Heinrich

Mann's *Man of Straw*); of paintings made by and for vulgar upstarts; of pygmies posing as giants; of a superficial architecture and design, which hid shoddy workmanship behind a veneer of surrogate sophistication. There is a good deal of truth in all this, but such generalizations can be overplayed and it would be wrong to dismiss all the cultural products of the post-unification period as pompous and overblown *kitsch*. It is perhaps instructive to note that houses and apartment blocks from this era are highly sought after in contemporary Germany, and even reproduction German Renaissance furniture can now demand high prices at auction.

It is more doubtful whether the official art and architecture of the Empire will ever be regarded with much affection. The major imperial building projects – Paul Wallot's Reichstag building, completed in 1894; the Imperial High Court in Leipzig, designed by Ludwig Hoffmann and completed in 1895; or Raschdorff's new Berlin cathedral, built between 1894 and 1904 – were impressive only in their monumental scale. Similarly, the numerous statues and memorials erected in the name of Germania or (more frequently) Borussia were imposing rather than imaginative, and few would dispute Gordon Craig's assertion that 'the victory over France and the unification of the German states inspired no great work of literature or music or painting'.[2] Several of the largest monuments to unification, such as the Victory Column in Berlin (started in 1865 as a memorial to the war against Denmark, and finally unveiled in revised form on Sedan Day in 1873) or the Hermann Monument near Detmold (started in 1838 but not finished until 1875) were completed only with the financial assistance of the Emperor but, in general, neither Wilhelm I nor Bismarck showed much interest in culture.

This all changed with the accession of Wilhelm II in 1888. Wilhelm had dabbled in art since childhood, and went on to design trophies, uniforms, furniture and statues and to paint numerous pictures, under the tutelage of Anton von Werner. Although it is difficult to gauge the true extent of his influence, it is clear that – as in other areas of policy – Wilhelm tried to pursue a much more 'hands-on' approach to cultural affairs than his predecessors. As King of Prussia he was able to wield considerable influence through his powers of patronage and appointment in Berlin's cultural institutions. Several episodes are well known: in 1898 he denied the recommended award of a gold medal to Käthe Kollwitz because he disliked both the style and content of her work; in 1904 he interfered with the selection of paintings to be shown in the German pavilion at the St Louis World Fair, prompting a parliamentary outcry; and in 1909 the director of the National Gallery in Berlin, Hugo von Tschudi, was forced to resign after the Kaiser vetoed the purchase of some paintings by the French artists Courbet and Daumier, though the benefits of German particularism were once again demonstrated when von Tschudi was immediately invited to take up a similar position in Munich.

Wilhelm was also able to use his wealth and influence to pursue grandiose projects, including a wave of equestrian monuments to mark the hundredth anniversary of his grandfather's birth (contributing to a total of some 400 memorials to Wilhelm I and a staggering 700 to Bismarck erected during the Wilhelmine period), and an 'avenue of victory' (*Siegesallee*) in Berlin. The *Siegesallee* was an ambitious double row of 32 marble statues, designed to venerate the history of the Hohenzollerns, but which quickly became a target of satire and abuse (the writer Alfred Döblin condemned its 'byzantine emptiness and falseness of spectacle'). After its completion in 1901, Wilhelm invited the sculptors and artists who had worked on the project to court, where he addressed them with a speech on the role of art in society. In it he described art as a body of unchanging, eternal values, which could be used to uplift and educate the German nation, and especially the working class, to appreciate truth and beauty.

II Cultural critics and reformers

By the time Wilhelm made this speech, however, it was clear that he was already swimming against the tide. The idea that cultural values were somehow permanent and unchanging, that the rules of art had been laid down centuries before and would only be challenged by fools and charlatans, was increasingly difficult to uphold at a time when a broadly based movement for cultural renewal was advancing on many fronts. The groundwork for the reformers was laid by a multitude of cultural critics, whose attacks on *Gründerzeit* values came from very different angles, but often ended up hitting the same targets.

The most biting and brilliant of the critics was undoubtedly Friedrich Nietzsche (1844–1900), a master of German prose and a philosopher whose aphoristic style was unusually brutal and direct ('philosophizing with the hammer'), but unsystematic and frequently contradictory: his most enduring ideas, the 'Death of God', the 'Superman' and the 'Will to Power', continue to arouse controversy today. Nietzsche once described himself as the great 'seducer and pied piper', and he has certainly been cited as an influence by numerous very different movements and individuals. However, since he viewed creative people as the vanguard of humanity – he wrote that the world was only justified as an aesthetic phenomenon and that only art could make life bearable – it is not surprising that artists, writers and composers were amongst his most devout followers. Nietzsche was a fierce critic of almost every aspect of Imperial Germany and its culture, and anyone who sought change could draw inspiration from his highly emotive language.

Another inspirational figure with a problematic legacy was Nietzsche's one-time friend, and later sworn enemy, Richard Wagner (1813–83). Wagner's influence on late nineteenth-century Europe has been described by Norman Stone as 'immense', and not just because of his music – which was far more innovative than the Germanic mythology of his librettos might suggest – or his works of theory and criticism, which were full of anger and spite. A year before the composer's death, the Wagner festival theatre at Bayreuth was opened with a performance of *Parsifal*; less an opera than an initiation ceremony to consecrate the theatre, which was itself more temple than playhouse. The huge and fanatical audiences which flocked to Bayreuth in a spirit of holy communion every year thereafter were drawn by the prospect of seeing a total work of art, the *Gesamtkunstwerk*: a concept which was to hold a particular fascination for succeeding generations of German artists.

Amongst the many other cultural critics to emerge in the later nineteenth-century the writings of the *völkisch* 'cultural pessimists' (principally Paul de Lagarde and Julius Langbehn, although both Nietzsche and Wagner were also pulled into this sphere by their relatives and acolytes) have attracted particular attention from historians. Their work was first highlighted by a series of studies in the early 1960s by historians such as George Mosse and Fritz Stern, who argued that a distinctive 'Germanic ideology' developed in the second half of the nineteenth century, which was hostile to most aspects of the modern world, and which offered in its place a rag-bag of romantic, irrational and racist impulses, possessing a revolutionary dynamic, every bit as hostile to orthodox conservative thinking as it was to liberalism and socialism. It was suggested that these writers had a lasting and damaging influence on German society, and in particular on the educated middle class, the *Bildungsbürgertum*.

Ultimately, of course, the influence of particular writers and thinkers is extemely difficult to measure. The 'cultural pessimists' certainly had more readers than disaffected intellectuals on the fringes of academic life could usually expect, but the proponents of the 'Germanic ideology' thesis have been convincingly challenged on a number of levels. The intricacies of the debate cannot be entered into here, but it is significant for our narrative to note the way in which de Lagarde (1827–91), Langbehn (1851–1907) and others were savagely critical of historicism in the arts, and urged the development of new forms of cultural expression, based not on the pattern books of history, but derived from the soul and soil of the German *Volk*.

Langbehn, in particular, was an important figure for many German artists and architects. Not only did he reject the unthinking adaption of historical forms, but he also urged the reconciliation of utility and beauty in a way that echoed early twentieth-century functionalism; and although he was not in the same league as Nietzsche, he came up with some memorable aphorisms of his own, such as: 'the professor is the German national disease'; or 'the true artist can never be local enough'.

Langbehn's best-known work, *Rembrandt as Educator* (1890), helped to clear the way for a succession of widely read art pedagogues, who each in their own way tried to communicate to the general public the value of simplicity and spontaneity in artistic creativity, and to elevate the standing of folk art and vernacular traditions against the prevailing pomposity of imperial culture. These included Alfred Lichtwark (1852–1914), the long-serving director of Hamburg's *Kunsthalle*; Ferdinand Avenarius (1856–1923), the publisher of the popular cultural journal, *Der Kunstwart*; and Paul Schultze-Naumburg (1869–1949), whose writings on architecture and the landscape helped to sensitize many middle-class Germans to issues of town planning and conservation. The founding of artists' colonies in rural locations, such as one established in the 1890s on the windswept North German Plain at Worpswede, were a direct response to such pedagogic efforts.

The revolt against historicism inspired by this disparate group of cultural critics and pedagogues took a different guise in each of the arts, and nowhere was it clear-cut. The voices of renewal fell into two main camps: those who sought to re-establish continuity with folk values ('primitive' or naive art, vernacular architecture, folk tales, simple peasant clothing and so on); and those who looked for radically new approaches. Later, in the 1920s, these contradictions would become all too apparent, but for the time being, such distinctions were blurred by a shared contempt for the excesses of the *Gründerzeit* and a common vocabulary which placed emphasis on 'honesty' and 'sobriety'.

Chronologically, the first of the arts to experience the spark of revolt was literature. At the time of unification, in literature as in painting, it was believed that the ideal task of the creative artist was to depict what was uplifting, good and true. Thus, apart from Theodor Fontane's novels, which dealt in a rather subtle and subdued way with the stresses and strains beneath the surface of bourgeois life, German writers of the early imperial era showed little interest in social or political themes. This began to change in the 1880s when, inspired by Zola, Ibsen and others, a German variant of naturalism emerged in both Munich, where it was led by Michael Georg Conrad and revolved around the journal *Die Gesellschaft* and Berlin, where its leaders were the Hart brothers and Otto Brahm (1856–1912). Brahm was a co-founder and director of the so-called 'Free Stage' (*Freie Bühne*), where 'members only' performances allowed controversial plays to escape the censor. Naturalist writers brought contemporary social problems – such as the plight of the poor or the position of women in society – to the German stage for the first time, though the depth of their social engagement has often been questioned. The best known of the German naturalists was Gerhart Hauptmann (1862–1946), whose play *The Weavers* (1892) was condemned by Wilhelm II as 'gutter art' and initially banned in Prussia, but performed elsewhere in Germany.

Naturalism was also a trend in painting: Max Liebermann (1847–1935) painted artisans, peasants and housewives in an unsentimental, naturalistic style – his painting *Plucking the Geese* led to him being dubbed an 'apostle of ugliness' – before developing a lighter palette and falling under the influence of French impressionism. With another naturalist painter, Fritz von Uhde (1848–1911), Liebermann played a prominent role in the Secessions of the 1890s; a series of rebellions by German artists, who 'seceded' or withdrew from the art establishment in their state by refusing to show their work at the annual salon and establishing their own gallery space instead.

The Secessions, which effectively broke the stranglehold of the academies, and enabled modern art to establish a foothold in central Europe, began in Munich in 1892, and continued in Vienna (1897) and Berlin (1898). The exact combination of motives varied in each case: the conservative selection of works by salon juries; the hostility of juries to innovative foreign art; the cramped and insensitive ways in which pictures were hung; generational and organizational conflict, and so on. By no means all the Secessionists were modernists, and many were moved by economic rather than aesthetic motives, but this did not lessen the significance of their actions. The traditional importance of state patronage to artists in the German lands ensured that their rebellion against the art establishment also assumed a political character. This was especially the case in Berlin, where the Kaiser – who had nothing but baffled contempt for modern tendencies in art – became involved. As with many subsequent confrontations between modernism and the establishment, however, it was the latter which claimed to represent popular taste, and the Secessionists who were caricatured as 'elitist' and 'undemocratic'.

A number of the Munich Secessionists moved away from painting in the mid-1890s and turned to applied art and architecture. Thanks to former Secessionists like Peter Behrens (1868–1940) and Richard Riemerschmid (1868–1957), Munich for a time became a leading centre of the new style in design and architecture, known generally as *art nouveau*, but in Germany dubbed *Jugendstil*, after the graphic style of the journal *Jugend* (founded in 1896 by Georg Hirth, who embraced the new style every bit as enthusiastically as he had the German Renaissance). The close links between the Secessions and *art nouveau* were emphasized by the fact that in Vienna, where the architect J. M. Olbrich designed a purpose-built exhibition hall for the Secession, the new architecture and design was known as *Sezessionsstil*.

Jugendstil, like other manifestations of *art nouveau*, is regarded by design historians as a crucial transitional phase between historicism and modernism. The desire of its practitioners to find a fresh style, untainted by historical associations, led many to seek inspiration in the forms of the natural world: the result was the free-flowing, curvillinear style, which made an impact in most European states in the last years of the century. Many of the young designers who identified with the style had not enjoyed a formal academic training, and some like Henry van de Velde (1863–1957) expressed a social concern inspired by the British Arts and Crafts movement. If the new style was to integrate art and society, they argued, no object should be too small to be worthy of aesthetic concern, and wherever possible it should be made in workshops, where the artist had control over the whole production process and the worker was more than an alienated automaton. The workshop thus became the focal point of *Jugendstil* design, and the *Werkstätten* in Munich, Vienna and Dresden became large and profitable enterprises for a time, although their handcrafted furniture was invariably too expensive for the working-class families which featured so prominently in the designers' rhetoric.

Jugendstil was quickly taken up by mass manufacturers and provincial builders, and it very soon became just another style in the pattern books; the artists' colony established at Darmstadt by the progressive Grand Duke Ernst Ludwig of Hesse as a 'document of German art', represented its swansong. However, although it blossomed only briefly, the new style brought forth a host of young talent, including individuals who were to remain at the forefront of German architecture and design for the next 30 years or more.

Gordon Craig has written that 'before 1914 it was only on rare occasions that German artists were interested, let alone stirred by political and social events and issues'.[3] As the example of the *Jugendstil* designers suggests, this view is easily

Illustration 10.1 *The Springtime*, etching by Vogeler (1896). Spring, symbolising the fresh start offered by a new century, was a favourite subject of Heinrich Vogeler (1872–1942), a founder member of the 'back to nature' artists' colony at Worpswede

Illustration 10.2 The entrance court to the German pavilion at the 1900 Paris Exposition by Karl Hoffacker. World fairs such as this offered Germany a chance to challenge the leading nations in trade (Great Britain) and good taste (France). Hoffacker's bombastic architecture may have failed on the latter count, but many young and innovative German designers experienced an international breakthrough at this event

challenged. Of course, aesthetic narcissism and the idea of 'art for art's sake' did exist; and some like the writer Stefan George (1868–1933) retreated into a rather precious private universe, but the stereotype of the unpolitical German artist, seeking *Innerlichkeit* ('inwardness') instead of social engagement, is unhelpful and inaccurate. On the contrary, artists and aesthetes often played a prominent role in the multitude of social and cultural reform movements to emerge in turn-of-the-century Germany.

The best known of these is probably the youth movement, with its numerous hiking associations (*Wandervögel*), but many others existed under the broad umbrella of the *Lebensreformbewegung* (literally, 'movement for the reform of life'). This term was first used in print around 1896, to denote a host of autonomous organizations active in a wide range of fields, but all aiming for a fundamental reform of lifestyles. Some of the groups targeted the individual (abstinence, naturism, vegetarianism, homeopathic medicine), while others focused on society at large (housing reform, land reform, clothing reform, conservation and environmental protection).

Typical of the latter group was the German Garden City Association (founded in 1902). Germany's first garden city, at Hellerau near Dresden, never developed much beyond a village, but still became a focal point for the Wilhelmine reformers and a place of pilgrimage for many individuals, including George Bernard Shaw, who recognized kindred spirits at work. The settlement was built to a plan by Richard Riemerschmid around the factory of Karl Schmidt's *Deutsche Werkstätten* – one of the leading furniture 'workshops' – and also featured workers' housing by progressive architects, and a centre for rhythmic gymnastics, where pioneers of dance such as Mary Wigman and Gret Palucca were amongst the students.

The Garden City Association was, like most of the *Lebensreform* organizations, overwhelmingly middle-class in character, but attracted a bizarre mixture of reformist socialists, progressive liberals, anarcho-libertarians and *völkisch* nationalists. It has already been stated that the Wilhelmine reform movements embraced people with very different aesthetic approaches; much the same could be said of their political character. For instance, the principal theorist of the garden city idea in Germany was the notorious anti-Semite and arch-reactionary Theodor Fritsch, but the association's leaders, the Kampffmeyer brothers, were supporters of the SPD. Just as the 1920s were to bring an aesthetic polarization, so the political climate of the Weimar Republic was to turn erstwhile colleagues into bitter enemies.

Nowhere was this more apparent than in architecture: the well-known and highly politicized arguments of the 1920s, between 'modernists' and 'traditionalists', were fought out largely by former friends and associates from the same Wilhelmine organization, the German *Werkbund*. Founded in 1907, the *Werkbund* sought to resolve the dilemma on which the *Jugendstil* designers had foundered: namely, the proper role of artists, craftsmen and designers in an age of machine mass production. The reconciliation between art and industry, which the organization proposed, was to be on the latter's terms. Its membership thus included major industrial firms as well as individual businessmen, politicians and designers, all hoping that an 'ennobling' of the modern industrial world would not only boost German exports, but would also increase the self-respect of industrial workers, and thereby help to restore social harmony to the German people. Peter Behrens' work with the electrical engineering giant AEG is the best-known example of the organization's ethos in action, and the man once dubbed 'Mr Werkbund' further secured his place in the history books by employing all three of the future giants of European modern architecture – Walter Gropius, Mies van der Rohe and Le Corbusier – in his studio near Potsdam before 1914. Gropius's own project, the 'Fagus' factory at Alfeld (1911–13) became an icon of modernism in its own right, and introduced many of the design principles he was to pursue as director of the 'Bauhaus' in the 1920s.

Not all the products of *Werkbund* design were so unashamedly modern, but even so, *Werkbund* architecture is well summed up by Nipperdey's phrase 'modern buildings for modern people, proud of their modernity'.[4] The organization's work found relatively widespread acceptance amongst the general population – its 1914 Cologne exhibition attracted over one million visitors – and it even had some support in governing circles, as the choice of Peter Behrens to design the new German embassy in St Petersburg (1912) indicates. New ideas in music, which evolved in a way curiously parallel to the development of architecture – from 'late nineteenth century bombast to disquieting severity' as Norman Stone has put it[5] – may have been more difficult for the public to accept, but one should not take the whistles and cat-calls that accompanied Schoenberg's moves towards atonality as necessarily representative of the concert-going public as a whole.

III Technological and intellectual change

Of course, many Germans had neither the time nor the inclination to involve themselves in cultural issues, and no doubt the more zealous *Lebensreformer* and outspoken modernists appeared rather crankish to the proverbial man or woman in the street, but whether they knew it or not, all Germans at the turn of the century were participating in a cultural revolution of unprecedented proportions. The rapid development of a commercial popular culture was made possible by technological change – the first telephones (from the 1870s), typewriters (late 1870s), Kodak cameras (1880s), Emil Berliner's gramophone (1887), radio broadcasts (1900s) – but predicated on changes in the organization of capitalism (mass production and consumption) and mass education.

New printing techniques and almost universal literacy facilitated an explosion of printed matter. Between 1885 and 1913, daily newspaper circulation in Germany doubled and the range of popular fiction (such as Karl May's adventure stories), illustrated magazines and satirical journals (like *Simplicissimus*, launched in 1896 and with a circulation of 85,000 by 1904) all expanded dramatically. The development of electric lighting helped a proliferation of cabaret, revue and nightclub shows, providing not only a venue for the music of the tango, the bunny-hug and the turkey trot, but opportunities for writers of the quality of Frank Wedekind (1864–1918), who was described as 'a genius of smut', but whose 'Lulu' plays (*Spring Awakening* (1891); *Pandora's Box* (1894); and *Earth Spirit* (1895)) broke through the conventions of naturalist theatre and paved the way for expressionist drama.

Such subversive entertainment posed an obvious challenge to the censors. Laws on blasphemy, obscenity, incitement and 'gross mischief' were all used against the theatre and the press in Wilhelmine Germany – Wedekind himself spent some time in jail for 'insulting the monarch' – but efforts to introduce a new censorship law (the infamous 'Lex Heinze') met with impressive and largely effective opposition. In fact, as Robin Lenman has pointed out, the principal regulator of cultural production was now the market rather than the censor. In other words, avant-garde artists and writers were more worried about not finding buyers for their work than about police interference or stern lectures from the likes of Wilhelm II.

Rising levels of disposable incomes, and a gradual reduction in working hours, led to a growth in organized sport and increasing leisure opportunities. The institution which best represented this trend was the cinema. Gary Stark has claimed that a 'bioscope' performance at Berlin's Wintergarten in November 1895 was the world's first example of a film being shown to a paying audience; 10 years later there was still only a handful of permanent cinemas in Germany (the first films were shown in touring circus tents); but by 1914 there were some 300 cinemas in Berlin alone, and up to 3,000 in Germany as a whole. Of course, the movie was not yet regarded as an art form, but it was already an established and important leisure pursuit for millions of predominantly working-class Germans. In time, it would – along with other commercial entertainments – reduce the appeal of the vast mosaic of clubs and associations built up in the sociocultural milieu of the socialist labour movement. For the time being, however, workers' choral, theatre and reading societies continued to represent an important, if not exactly innovative, slice of German cultural life.

If the growth of a commercial mass culture was regarded with fear and suspicion by Germany's labour leaders, it was a similar story in the country's great seats of learning. German academics, struggling to cope with a four-fold increase in students between 1871 and 1914, felt that their authority, status and economic well-being were all under threat. Countless gloomy tracts were written to contrast the values of German *Kultur* with those of Anglo-Saxon *Zivilisation*, by which they meant the British 'shopkeeper mentality' or the cold commercialism of American life. However, despite the generally conservative outlook of most of their number – Craig describes professors at this time as the 'intellectual bodyguard of the Hohenzollerns'[6] – intellectual life did not stagnate in the Wilhelmine era. On the contrary, many German academics became preoccupied with trying to make sense of the atomization of modern life and its effects, which could be felt all around them. Thus it was in these years that sociology began to emerge as an academic discipline, with valuable contributions from Simmel, Tönnies, Troeltsch, and above all Max Weber (1864–1920), whose classic work on *The Protestant Ethic and the Spirit of Capitalism* (1904–5) explored the relationship between ideas and social development. Weber shunned both cultural pessimism and vulgar optimism, to produce a body of work noted for its subtlety, conceptual originality and methodological rigour. He perceived more clearly than most that whilst the modern world brought great benefits, it also posed new dangers of its own.

The most important intellectual milestones passed in these years, however, were in the natural sciences. After the discovery of X-rays (1895), radioactivity (1896) and the electron (1897), the physicist Max Planck (1858–1947) outlined what became known as quantum theory in 1900, and five years later, another future German Nobel prize winner, Albert Einstein (1880–1952), proposed his special theory of 'relativity'. Perhaps the most important aspect of Einstein's work was that it amounted to a denial of any absolute frame of reference, and thus called into question the very nature of scientific laws or, as Michael Biddiss has put it, 'opened up vast vistas of uncertainty'.[7]

Much the same could be said of the work of Sigmund Freud (1856–1939), the Viennese specialist in nervous ailments, who invented 'psychoanalysis' in the 1890s and whose publications *The Interpretation of Dreams* (1899) and *Three Essays on Sexuality* (1905), revealed the power of the subconscious. His work was epoch-making – even if *The Interpretation of Dreams* took eight years to sell its first 600 copies – because it called into question the entire conventional terminology of sanity, morality and rationality.

Freud's work on the subconscious mind was to have a great influence on the last major movement in Imperial German culture, expressionism. Much has been written on German expressionism in recent years, not least because an expressionist tendency – characterized by emotion, exaggeration and violent distortion – became manifest in every field of the arts at some point between 1905 and 1925. The principal expressionist groupings in German fine art, *Die Brücke* (founded in Dresden in 1905) and *Der Blaue Reiter* (founded in Munich six years later), produced some of the greatest paintings of the twentieth century, and two members of the latter group – Wassily Kandinsky (1866–1944) and Franz Marc (1880–1916) – were instrumental in the evolution of abstract art after 1910. In this, the relationship between expressionist art and music was very close: the first abstract artists cited music's lack of a 'subject' as justification for their move away from representational art, whilst the composer Schoenberg was also a noted portrait painter. The pursuit of the *Gesamtkunstwerk* led artists to use every available medium of expression.

German expressionists embodied many of the qualities and contradictions of modernism as a whole: proclaiming a new vision, yet turning to primitive folk art for inspiration; fiercely critical of bourgeois materialism, yet smart enough to secure the best prices for their work; anti-urban, yet fascinated by the city and unwilling ever to move far away from metropolitan life. The expressionists demonstrated that criticisms of rationality and materialism could be just as much an expression of modernity as of conservatism; and whilst much has rightly been made of the movement's apocalyptic strain, it is important not to lose sight of the more prosaic aspects of the expressionist phenomenon. As Thomas Nipperdey has pointed out, this revolution in art went hand in hand with a fundamental change in middle-class consciousness: modern art established itself in Germany not in spite of the middle classes, but because of them. New private art dealers – like the Cassirer brothers in Berlin – and many new patrons – like the bankers Karl Ernst Osthaus and August von der Heydt, in the industrial towns of Hagen and Wuppertal respectively – were vital for the breakthrough of expressionism, just as other bourgeois patrons commissioned buildings from *Werkbund* architects, and attended concerts by Schoenberg.

If nothing else, therefore, study of the cultural life of Imperial Germany can help to revise the still-popular cliché of the 'feudalized' German bourgeoisie, aspiring to nothing more than reserve officer status and an attractive duelling scar.

Notes:

1. Gay, P., *Weimar Culture* (London: Penguin, 1974), p. 6.
2. Craig, G., *Germany 1866–1945* (Oxford: Oxford University Press, 1978), p. 215.
3. *Ibid.*
4. Nipperdey, T., *The Rise of the Arts in Modern Society* (London: German Historical Institute, 1990), p. 20.
5. Stone, N., *Europe Transformed, 1878–1919* (London: Fontana, 1983), p. 400.
6. Craig, G., *Germany 1866–1945*, p. 205.
7. Biddiss, M., in P. Hayes, ed., *Themes in Modern European History 1890–1945* (London: Routledge, 1992), p. 88.

Select bibliography

Essay collections

Behr, S., Fanning, D., and Jarman, D., eds., *Expressionism Reassessed* (Manchester: Manchester University Press, 1993).

Chapple, G., and Schulte, H., eds., *The Turn of the Century. German Literature and Art* (Bonn: Bouvier Verlag, 1981).

Rogoff, I., ed., *The Divided Heritage, Themes and Problems in German Modernism* (Cambridge: Cambridge University Press, 1991).

Stark, G., and Lackner, B. K., eds., *Essays on Culture and Society in Modern Germany* (Arlington: University of Texas Press, 1982).

Teich, M., and Porter, R., eds., *Fin-de-Siècle and its Legacy* (Cambridge: Cambridge University Press, 1990).

Essays and monographs

Campbell, J., *The German Werkbund. The Politics of Reform in the Applied Arts* (Princeton: Princeton University Press, 1978).

Craig, G., 'Religion, Education and the Arts', in *Germany 1866–1945* (Oxford: Oxford University Press, 1978).

Dube, W.-D., *The Expressionists* (London: Thames and Hudson, 1972).

Eksteins, M., *The Rites of Spring, The First World War and the Birth of the Modern Age* (London: Black Swan, 1990).

Heskett, J., *Design in Germany, 1870–1918* (London: Trefoil Books, 1986).

Jefferies, M., *Politics and Culture in Wilhelmine Germany. The Case of Industrial Architecture* (Oxford: Berg, 1995).

Lenman, R., 'Painters, Patronage and the Art Market in Germany 1880–1914', *Past and Present* (May 1989).

Makela, M., *The Munich Secession. Art and Artists in Turn-of-the-Century Munich* (Princeton: Princeton University Press, 1990).

Nipperdey, T., *The Rise of the Arts in Modern Society* (London: German Historical Institute, 1990).

Pascal, R., *From Naturalism to Expressionism: German Literature and Society, 1880–1918* (New York: Basic Books, 1973).

Paret, P., *The Berlin Secession. Modernism and its Enemies in Imperial Germany* (Cambridge, MA: Harvard University Press, 1980).

Schorske, C., *Fin-de-Siècle Vienna: Politics and Culture* (Cambridge: Cambridge Unversity Press, 1981).

Stern, F., *The Politics of Cultural Despair* (Berkeley: University of California Press, 1961).

11

Wilhelmine Germany

Katharine A. Lerman

The transition from the 'Bismarckian' era, dominated by the consequences of political unification and the need to consolidate a national state, to the 'Wilhelmine' era, where the political agenda was shaped by the rise of a new kind of popular politics and the desire to secure Germany's place as a world power, represented a significant caesura in the lives of most subjects of the *Kaiserreich*. The changes in the political landscape from the late 1880s obviously reflected the rapid transformation of Germany's economy and society, as well as a shifting cultural climate under the impact of new intellectual currents (or the popularization of older ones) and ideological challenges. Many of these changes were not unique to Germany but had a wider European resonance. Yet for contemporaries the departure of the conservative 'founder of the Reich' in 1890 and the advent of the brashly self-assertive young Kaiser, Wilhelm II, appeared to symbolize the changed mood. From 1890 German politics reflected not only the fears and insecurities which accompanied unprecedented social change, but also the inflated expectations, overweening self-confidence and optimism about the future which were engendered by a growing consciousness of Germany's military and economic dynamism. This juxtaposition of anxiety with hubris and ambition is often remarked upon with respect to Wilhelmine Germany. But it makes the task of interpreting the direction of German policy before the First World War and, in particular, Germany's responsibility for that war particularly difficult for historians.

I The rise of mass politics

The decade of the 1890s has been seen by some historians as the crucial period when the masses made their dramatic and explosive entry into German politics. Geoff Eley has written of the 'decomposition' of the Bismarckian system of politics after 1890, linking this not so much to the political consequences of Bismarck's dismissal as to the growth of new political and social forces, and the fragmentation and decline of German liberalism. As the electorate expanded and became more politicized, it is argued that

Illustration 11.1 Wilhelm II in the uniform of the *Garde du Corps*, 1901

the older pattern of politics, which had pertained during the Bismarck era and depended on a significant proportion of the German population remaining outside the political process, was replaced by a new form of popular politics which was better adapted to the needs of a modern industrial society. Political parties, which had formerly functioned successfully as loose associations of prestigious notables who came together mainly to win elections, were now challenged by demands from new social groups for mass representation and participation. To survive in the political environment of the 1890s political parties had to become better organized, campaign more intensively during elections, and develop new strategies for mobilizing mass support.

Obviously the rise of mass politics was not a phenomenon confined to Germany. Across Europe, politics reflected the impact of industrialization and urbanization, improvements in education and literacy, the rise of the popular press, and the growing strength of civil society, as witnessed, for example, in the proliferation of voluntary associations and other organizations which sought to shape the contours of public life independently from the state. In most European countries, too, the growth of state intervention was bound to trigger some kind of popular response, especially from those who perceived that their interests were ignored or disadvantaged by state initiatives. Nevertheless, despite wider European trends, the breakthrough of the masses may be seen as particularly significant and consequential in the German context. The rapid pace of German industrialization, the authoritarian features of the Bismarckian political system, and the early introduction of universal male suffrage in 1867 were all peculiar to the German situation, serving to make the process of adjustment to the new political conditions particularly painful and traumatic for the established political parties. The rise of new political issues after Bismarck's departure in 1890, from commercial and fiscal policies to armaments and imperialism, as well as the severity of the structural crisis which affected German agriculture in the 1890s, contributed to the process of political mobilization, encouraging new forms of organization and popular protest among those who had previously lacked a political voice. Finally, the large number of nationalist associations and economic interest groups, which came into being after 1890 to address these issues, helped to develop new techniques of political agitation and a more demagogic political style, even if they never achieved the status of mass movements.

The most visible evidence for the impact of new social forces on German politics in the 1890s is undoubtedly furnished by the history of the German Social Democratic Party or SPD, whose membership and electoral support increased in leaps and bounds after the lapse of Bismarck's anti-socialist legislation in 1890 and whose strong presence on the left made itself felt across the entire political spectrum in Germany. Radicalized by 12 years of persecution and committed to defend the interests of the industrial proletariat, the party gained 19.7 per cent of the vote (35 out of 397 seats) in the Reichstag elections of February 1890 and attracted more votes than any other party. By 1912 over a third of the German electorate was prepared to vote for a party which had resisted all internal challenges and adhered rigorously to orthodox Marxism as its official ideology from 1891. Despite the electoral system's in-built bias against the party's urban voters (because constituency boundaries were never redrawn to reflect patterns of internal migration), the party gained 110 seats in the elections of 1912 and was the biggest party in the Reichstag on the eve of the First World War. In Prussia, however, the three-class suffrage ensured that it did not gain representation in the Landtag until 1908 (when it achieved 23 per cent of the vote but only eight out of

Illustration 11.2 *The Sozialdemokrat*, the mouthpiece of the German social democrats, announces the electoral successes in the Reichstag elections of 1890

a total of 433 seats). States such as Saxony and the city of Hamburg even adopted more restrictive franchises in order to thwart SPD majorities.

The SPD was the first German political party to develop into a highly organized, centralized, democratically structured and increasingly bureaucratic mass party. Its electoral success at national level (it only lost seats – but not votes – in the 'Hottentot elections' of 1907 which led it to rethink its strategy) was matched by a steady growth in its membership during the Wilhelmine era, so that by 1914 it had over one million members. The party offered its members a wide range of social and cultural activities from choral societies to cycling excursions, and has been seen as creating an entire 'sub-culture' in Wilhelmine Germany. Perhaps most importantly the party's supporters were sustained by an optimistic and all-inclusive ideology of progress which guaranteed that the future would belong to them.

The growth of the socialist movement was mirrored by the increasing strength of trade unionism in Germany before the First World War. Although the majority of German workers were not members of a trade union by 1914, socialist, liberal and Christian trade union organizations vied with each other to attract working-class support. The Free Trade Unions, affiliated to the SPD, were by far the most successful, developing from quite small and elitist organizations of activists in the 1890s to a formidable movement with nearly three million members by 1913. The General Commission under Karl Legien which directed the Free Trade Unions was able to exert considerable pressure on the political leadership of the SPD, for example opposing the use of the mass strike as a political weapon (which was urged by Rosa Luxemburg and the extreme left of the party under the impact of the Russian revolution of 1905) since it might provoke the authorities into military repression.

The political impact of the growth of the industrial working class has received much attention within the context of an historiography which is not only interested in understanding the role of the SPD in Wilhelmine politics but also in charting the early history of a movement which assumed major political importance in the later stages of the First World War and during the 'German revolution' of 1918–19. Nevertheless, while the growth of mass politics in the 1890s and early 1900s undeniably benefited the SPD, the debate among Wilhelmine historians concerning the politicization of the masses and the significance of the 1890s has tended to focus more on the role of popular forces in reshaping German conservatism and the right than on the incontrovertible evidence of mass mobilization by the left.

A marked feature of the Wilhelmine political landscape was the proliferation of nationalist associations such as the Pan-German League (1891), the Society for the Eastern Marches (1894), the Navy League (1898), the Imperial League against Social Democracy (1904) and the Army League (1912). While the membership of the Pan-German League never exceeded 23,000, the Navy League, bolstered by government support and the social prestige of prominent supporters, attracted 331,000 members on the eve of the First World War. These associations used to be seen as signifying an anti-democratic pluralism which served to bypass parliament and ultimately benefited the government. But detailed studies have shown that they were not pliant instruments of government policy, even if their goals sometimes overlapped. Their direct political influence has also often been exaggerated, although the Imperial League Against Social Democracy played a significant role in the Reichstag elections of 1907 and the high-profile propaganda of the Navy and Army Leagues helped to create the political climate in which successive navy bills and the army bills of 1912–13 were passed. The nationalist associations were quite prepared to criticize the government if it suited their political purposes (as during the Second Moroccan Crisis of 1911 when they expected substantial colonial gains in Africa after the despatch of the German gunboat *Panther* to Agadir) and they certainly were significant in generating a more radical and demagogic style of politics. But how far their mobilization of popular support extended beyond specific issues and created a new kind of populist politics which challenged the hegemony of traditional elites is debatable. Middle-aged bureaucrats, military men, professionals and businessmen figured prominently in the associations which, as a recent study of the Army League by Marilyn Coetzee has confirmed, were not ideologically committed to demolishing traditional patterns of political behaviour and whose membership often declined rapidly once the immediate objectives were achieved. The claim that they served to mobilize a new social constituency among the *Mittelstand* or petty bourgeoisie is at best unproven.

Probably more important in mobilizing large numbers of people who had previously remained outside the political process was the Agrarian League. The formation of the Agrarian League in 1893, largely in response to the commercial policies of the 'New Course' under Chancellor Leo von Caprivi, played a significant role in mobilizing rural interests behind the campaign for agricultural protectionism and became particularly influential in Prussia east of the Elbe. The mainly Catholic farmers' and peasants' associations fulfilled a similar role in the south and west of Germany. Recent research by David Blackbourn, Ian Farr and others has emphasized how the new agrarian radicalism in the 1890s was neither manufactured nor manipulated by the prominent Junkers in the Agrarian League for their own exclusive purposes (see the articles by Ian Farr and Hans Jürgen Puhle in *Peasants and Lords* edited by Robert G. Moeller; and the articles by Ian Farr, David Blackbourn and Geoff Eley in *Society and Politics in Wilhelmine Germany* edited by Richard J. Evans). Rather, it represented a genuine rural populism whose origins lay in local peasant grievances and the increasing economic insecurity of independent producers and craftsmen. If all the political parties, including the SPD in southern Germany, attempted to garner support from this new rural constituency in the 1890s, the outcome – the eventual realignment of the right – was by no means certain. The revolt of the *Mittelstand* initially played into the hands of the anti-Semitic splinter parties. Anti-Semitic deputies commanded 16 seats in the Reichstag in 1893 and their disappearance after 1900 is generally attributed to the incorporation of their anti-Semitic ideology into mainstream political conservatism. Ultimately those parties which succeeded in gaining or regaining the support of a disaffected peasantry were forced to change and adapt their programmes as a consequence. The Conservative

Party emerged from its trials in the 1890s unswervingly committed to protectionism, anti-Semitism and anti-socialism. The Centre, too, despite support from Catholic workers in urban areas, found itself having to cater increasingly to the needs of its predominantly peasant and *Mittelstand* constituency, a development which helps to explain its political shift to the right, at least until 1912–13.

The argument that the German masses became politicized in the 1890s is in many respects a compelling one but needs considerable qualification. Local and regional studies have highlighted the extreme volatility of rural politics in the 1890s and indicated that all the Bismarckian parties had difficulties adjusting to the new conditions. Nevertheless, if the established political parties found they had to become better organized and develop new means of mobilizing popular support, this appears to have been a response to a *decline* in popular participation in national elections rather than to the sudden entry of the masses into German politics. It has been pointed out that the turnout in the three Reichstag elections during the 1890s was lower than in the previous election of 1887 or the subsequent election of 1903. Turnout increased markedly over the whole period of the *Kaiserreich* from 51 per cent in 1871 to a remarkable 85 per cent in 1912, but there is no evidence that the decade of the 1890s was a particular watershed in this respect. Indeed, it is clear that the *Kulturkampf* of the 1870s was far more important in mobilizing the Catholic electorate (approximately one-third of the German population) than any of the 'modern' techniques developed by the parties or pressure groups after 1890. Not only the liberal parties but also the Conservatives and Centre were losing support in the 1890s; the activities of the Agrarian League and the Catholic peasant associations were attempts to counter this trend rather than mobilize new sources of support. The elections of 1898, which took place at the end of these allegedly crucial years of politicization, were also apparently the dullest on record, notwithstanding the calls of the Prussian Finance Minister, Miquel, for a *Sammlung* (rallying) of those parties which supported the state. Undoubtedly the masses were becoming progressively more politicized and involved in the political process, but the growth of mass politics, in Germany and elsewhere, appears to have been a longer, slower process rather than the notion of a sudden explosive 'entry' suggests.

Conclusions about the significance of the 1890s have often been too sweeping or based on partial and incomplete evidence. The Conservatives did develop a more modern party structure, but there were inevitable tensions within a political party which was hostile to democracy. If they ultimately capitalized on agrarian discontent, this was not self-evident in the 1890s. The Conservatives' share of the vote actually declined from 15.2 per cent in 1887 to 9.2 per cent in 1912, virtually halving the number of their seats in the Reichstag from 80 to 43. The Centre managed to regain its wavering peasant support but it never developed into a modern political party with membership contributions (like the SPD) or a clearly defined structure; rather, it remained a party reliant on committees of notables and Catholic associations, as well as priests and the church hierarchy during elections. Finally, too much emphasis has been placed on the decline of German liberalism during the 1890s, apparently squeezed between the rise of organized labour and the new agrarian radicalism which benefited the Centre and the right. Yet, taking the two wings of liberalism together, their share of the national vote remained quite constant throughout the Wilhelmine period, and the left-liberals clearly succeeded in picking up support among new, expanding social groups such as teachers and white collar workers. If the National Liberals lost Reichstag seats, this often reflected the distribution of its electorate across constituencies and its shortage of 'safe seats'; by 1912 both the National Liberals and the newly reunited left-liberal Progressive People's Party had to win most of their seats in the 'run-off' elections held between the two main contenders in constituencies where no one party had achieved an overall majority. It is true that the liberals developed an organized party structure later than the Conservatives (from 1904–5), that they could not rely on economic or Catholic organizations to mobilize popular support for them, and that they remained much more committed to the kind of elitist, notable politics which continued to bring them such success in municipal elections where the democratic franchise did not apply. Yet it would be a mistake to write off their national electoral support because they, like their main competitors, lost ground in the 1890s. The problems of the liberals had a longer gestation (they can be traced back at least to the introduction of universal suffrage in 1867 and the impact of the depression from 1873) and were not primarily attributable to an alleged failure to adapt to new conditions in the 1890s.

Altogether there has been a tendency to classify the Wilhelmine political parties too rigidly in terms of sociocultural milieu, for example Catholic, agrarian–conservative, Protestant–bourgeois and Protestant-working class, and to make assumptions about the popular support of parties on the basis of their membership, the concerns of their activists or the political strategies of their representatives in parliament. Jonathan Sperber's research on voting behaviour in the *Kaiserreich* indicates that the boundaries between such milieux were far more fluid than generally assumed and that voters could shift their allegiance between parties – not least the Conservatives and the SPD – which were previously considered completely antithetical. Men who were mobilized to vote conservative or liberal on a nationalist issue, for example in the elections of 1887 or 1907, might vote differently in an election, such as that of 1903, which revolved chiefly around the issue of the price of bread in the wake of the new tariff law. If a party's share of the popular vote remained fairly constant over the imperial era, this did not necessarily mean that its social constituency remained stable or unchanged.

Perhaps the most interesting conclusion of Sperber's forthcoming work on electoral behaviour concerns the popular support of the apparently proletarian SPD. Sperber challenges traditional assumptions by suggesting that only about 51 per cent of the party's voters in 1912 can be categorized as emanating from the (mainly Protestant) working class; the remaining 49 per cent appear to have been from the middle classes, again chiefly Protestant bourgeois but also secularized Catholics. Again, this may not be so surprising if it is remembered that one in three voters opted for the SPD in 1912 and that it gained over 75 per cent of the vote in a city like Berlin. If the SPD can claim credentials as a 'people's party' before 1914, gloomy assessments that it must have reached 'saturation point' in terms of its potential vote by 1912 appear wide of the mark. Its broader social appeal is also confirmed by the success of its mass peace rallies in 1911–12 which clearly attracted middle-class support. The electoral pact between the SPD and the Progressive People's Party for the run-off elections in 1912 may also not have been so unpopular with the supporters of both parties as some historians have assumed.

Altogether much has been written about the nature of the Wilhelmine political parties, but there clearly remains more to be learnt about their relations with each other in the contemporary context. It is understandable that historians have looked to the parties and nationalist associations of the Wilhelmine period to illuminate such issues as the social constituency of Nazism or the origins of *Lebensraum* (living space) ideology. It is undeniably important, too, to understand why it was that the SPD split during the First World War and how the later 'Weimar coalition' of Centre, left liberals and moderate socialists came into being. Nevertheless the danger of an overly teleological perpective can be that countervailing tendencies are all too often overlooked or ignored. In terms of its popular support, the SPD was not the same party in 1912 that it was in 1890; nor were the liberals (who also attracted working-class and Catholic support) so doomed as often supposed. Similarly, local studies can be invaluable in pointing to the shifting nature of political identities, the difficulties in forging internal party compromises and the variable factors which accounted for a party's support. To be a National Liberal voter in Hanover did not mean the same thing as being a National Liberal supporter in Württemberg or the Rhineland. But there is also a danger in extrapolating too much from local studies about national trends.

Finally, it must be stated that all the interest in the Wilhelmine political parties and nationalist associations cannot overcome one vital qualification concerning their political importance before 1914. Within the imperial German political system they could play only a very specific and prescribed role. However significant for the future, the development of the parties and the politicization of the masses could exert no more than an influence on the course of imperial domestic and foreign policy before 1914. To understand Wilhelmine high politics it is thus necessary to shift attention away from the trappings of democracy and the nascent populism at local level to the corridors of the bureaucracy in Berlin and the machinations at the Kaiser's court. However, at this level, too, there is lively controversy about the responsibility for German policy and considerable disagreement about how the political system was evolving.

II Wilhelmine government and the role of Kaiser Wilhelm II

Discussion of imperial domestic politics between 1890 and 1914 is inevitably overshadowed by the outbreak of the First World War and the issue of political responsibility. Bismarck's departure in 1890 and the embarkation of Germany's rulers on a new course which eventually embraced military and naval expansion, imperialism and war, focus attention on the nature of German decision-making processes. Yet the gulf between the written and real constitutions, the interplay between different power factors and the rapid growth of new political and social forces to challenge the established authorities all leave much scope for conflicting interpretations of Germany's political development between 1890 and 1914. The more extreme assertions of 20 years ago – that government policy after Bismarck was determined by the anonymous forces of an authoritarian polycracy (Wehler), that the real ruler in Berlin from 1897 was Kaiser Wilhelm II (Röhl) or that the Reich by the early 1890s was a virtually ungovernable entity (Mommsen) – may now have been abandoned or heavily qualified, but important differences of perspective and methodology remain. The assumption is now quite widespread in the historiography that the German political system was in a state of crisis before 1914, whether that crisis is defined as 'permanent' from 1890 (Wehler), 'latent' (Mommsen) or 'stable' (Nipperdey). But not all historians accept that such a crisis existed, let alone that the decisions of July 1914 were a response to the domestic impasse.

The debate about Kaiser Wilhelm II's 'personal rule' highlights some of the difficulties in interpreting German policy and decision-making before 1914, and points to the shortcomings of the political system as a whole. Kaiser Wilhelm II provided an essential element of continuity in German high politics from 1888 to 1918, yet there is little consensus among historians about the significance of his role. To a certain extent the debate rehearses some of the arguments which assume greater urgency later with respect to Hitler's position in the Third Reich. It reflects different kinds of historical explanation and familiar disputes about the importance of individual motivations and decisions within wider historical structures and processes. Yet it also reflects different frames of reference and different ambitions. The historian whose main interest is in high politics and the oligarchy at the top will obviously reach different conclusions from a historian who defines the regime more broadly, and is interested in the exercise of *Herrschaft* (power and authority) throughout society or the impact of Reich laws across a range of economic and social, public and private spheres. Similarly a chosen methodology may brilliantly expose the inadequacy of Germany's decision-making structures or the inferior quality of its government before 1914, but be quite inadequate if the aim is more ambitious and directed towards understanding the political, economic and social structures which supported German aggression in the first half of the twentieth century.

Neither contemporaries nor historians have doubted Wilhelm II's desire to rule personally. Encouraged as a young man to uphold Prussian autocratic traditions as a counterweight to the liberal tendencies of his parents, Wilhelm was convinced of his divine right to rule and wholly unwilling to play the modest role within the political system which his grandfather, Wilhelm I, had accepted. Within less than two years of his accession to the throne in June 1888, he had accumulated sufficient authority and prestige to force Bismarck's resignation. Convinced that he alone made German policy, that the task of ministers was to execute his orders and that his country 'must follow me wherever I go', Wilhelm was an irascible and unpredictable man who rarely tolerated contradiction. Among those who came into contact with the young monarch in the early 1890s, admirers praised his 'splendid qualities' and 'individuality' while his detractors lamented his 'immaturity', 'eccentricity' and 'psychic imbalance'.

Bismarck's departure plunged Germany into a protracted period of constitutional crisis which eventually clarified the extent to which the political settlement of 1867–71 had vested extensive powers in the imperial and Prussian monarchy. As King of Prussia, Wilhelm enjoyed prerogatives which had scarcely changed since the era of Friedrich Wilhelm IV, and in the 1890s he reinforced his position as 'the *de facto* minister-president' of Prussia by frequently presiding over meetings of the Prussian Ministry of State as 'crown councils'. In the Reich the constitution explicitly granted the Kaiser sovereignty in matters of foreign policy, the right to declare war and conclude peace, control of all personnel appointments in the administration (including the Reich chancellor), the right to dissolve the Reichstag, and personal command over the army and navy. It was above all Wilhelm's power of appointment which prevented the evolution of a more collective system of government after Bismarck's resignation, a development which was particularly fateful given that none of Bismarck's successors as chancellor could expect to enjoy comparable power and prestige within the executive. The Kaiser was able to remove ministers who proved too independent-minded or recalcitrant one by one, replacing them with men who knew that they owed their positions and allegiance exclusively to the crown.

In the 1890s Bismarck's successors struggled to maintain their authority in the face of a concerted drive by the Kaiser and his close friends to establish his 'personal rule'. But neither General Leo von Caprivi (1890–94) nor the ageing Prince Chlodwig zu Hohenlohe-Schillingsfürst (1894–1900) were able to prevent the progressive emasculation of the 'responsible government' which was simultaneously subjected to remorseless monarchical pressure, humiliating parliamentary defeats and damaging attacks by the bitterly critical 'Bismarck *fronde*'. From 1897 Hohenlohe was scarcely more than a 'straw chancellor' and was effectively excluded from key areas of decision-making. New ministers such as Bülow and Tirpitz, the State Secretaries at the Foreign and Navy Offices, enjoyed Wilhelm II's confidence and wielded more influence than the chancellor. While the Kaiser intervened more and more directly in political affairs, the 'responsible government' lacked all cohesion and departments went their own way.

This 'departmental anarchy' only ceased in October 1900 when Bernhard von Bülow became Reich Chancellor. A diplomat whose rapid promotion in the 1890s owed most to the influence of the Kaiser's best friend, Count Philipp zu Eulenburg, Bülow had promised in 1896 to institute 'personal rule in the good sense'[1] and he made his confidential relationship with the Kaiser the pivot of his government. By identifying himself closely with the Kaiser's will and making the retention of Wilhelm's trust his highest priority, Bülow effectively silenced ministerial opposition and restored the authority of the chancellor. But the new stability after 1900 was achieved at a high price. First, Bülow had no interest in strengthening collegiate government, promoting a sense of collective responsibility or even encouraging the circulation of information throughout the executive. Preferring more secretive methods and relying on a few close advisers, he alienated his colleagues and subordinates by presenting them with *faits accomplis* and he remained indifferent to the work of the ministerial bureaucracy unless it threatened to give rise to political complications. Departments and individuals thus continued to enjoy considerable administrative autonomy and their work was neither coordinated nor subjected to rigorous political control. Second, although, for example, Bülow's self-chosen role as the 'king's minister' was successful in the short term in discouraging Wilhelm II's direct interventions in political matters, it did nothing to dispel the monarch's conviction of his 'personal rule'. Once difficulties began to accumulate in foreign and domestic policy from 1905–6, Bülow found he had few reserves on which he could draw when the Kaiser concluded he needed to intervene more directly himself. For example, at a critical juncture in the First Moroccan Crisis of 1905-6 (when Wilhelm II's landing at Tangiers and treatment of the Sultan of Morocco as an independent sovereign provoked a major crisis in Franco-German relations and much talk of war before an international conference was convened at Algeciras in early 1906) the Kaiser insisted on appointing a new favourite, Heinrich von Tschirschky, as State Secretary of the Foreign Office. While Bülow was obliged to preserve a semblance of harmony with Tschirschky, there were soon rumours of a 'Tschirschky circle' and a 'Bülow camp', with Tschirschky privately criticizing the Chancellor's laziness and his lack of a single 'productive, positive idea' in foreign policy, and Bülow seeking to undermine Tschirschky's position with the Kaiser by spreading press reports of the State Secretary's close association with the Bismarcks.[2]

It was above all the *Daily Telegraph* affair of November 1908 which focused public attention on the consequences of the Kaiser's 'personal rule' (a contemporary term). The storm over the publication of Wilhelm's naive and ill-considered remarks in the British newspaper (the Kaiser claimed, for example, that he had helped draw up the British plan of campaign in the Boer War) constituted the most serious domestic crisis in his reign before 1914, for a time precipitating united and unprecedented condemnation from the Chancellor, the Prussian Ministry of State, the Bundesrat, the Reichstag and the press, and calling the future of the monarchy itself into question. Nevertheless, the opportunity was lost to extract constitutional guarantees from the Kaiser against a repetition of such events. Despite accumulating an impressive array of support, Bülow was content merely to secure verbal assurances from Wilhelm, effectively transforming the political crisis into a personal one between Kaiser and Chancellor and ensuring that its only lasting consequence would be Wilhelm's determination to dismiss him as soon as politically possible.

The debate on the Kaiser's 'personal rule' exercised contemporaries and has produced little consensus among historians since. The Kaiser himself felt utterly betrayed by his Chancellor in 1908, convinced that in cooperating closely with Bülow he had fulfilled the role of a constitutional monarch since 1900 and that there had been no question of 'an autocratic regime which circumnavigated the Reich chancellor'.[3] Historians, too, have been reluctant to interpret the interventions of 'Wilhelm the sudden' as constituting evidence of monarchical rule in Germany before the First World War. For many, 'personalistic explanations' of German decision-making before 1914 smack too much of the 'great man' theory of history and leave no scope for the evolution of more modern and anonymous processes of negotiation between different coalitions of interests. For others, the thesis of 'personal rule' ignores the significance of bureaucratic power in Wilhelmine Germany and in particular the extent to which the imperial bureaucracy succeeded, irrespective of the Kaiser's will, in playing an obstructive, preventive or ameliorative role in the decision-making process. Finally, historians have pointed to the defects in Wilhelm II's personality which made him an ineffectual and incompetent ruler. The Kaiser, it seems, was too weak, erratic, unpredictable, superficial, restless and peripatetic, to exert much of an influence on Berlin politics. His life was an endless whirl of state occasions, social events, military manoeuvres, court ceremonies, parades, cruises, foreign visits and hunting trips. Not bureaucratic by nature (but then neither was Bismarck or Hitler), he disliked routine work and never commanded the details of government policy.

Ironically it has often been those historians most critical of the thesis of the Kaiser's 'personal rule' (such as Mommsen and Wehler) who have been inclined to adopt virtually impossible criteria as a measure of the role of human agency in history, seeking to isolate Wilhelm from the wider institutional structure and ignore all the given constraints on the exercise of monarchical power. In searching for evidence of mature thought and a clarity of aims on Wilhelm's part, for consistency of purpose and a determined will to pursue matters to their conclusion, for concrete and unambiguous results of Wilhelm's actions, they have too often adopted the language and methodology of human intention and consequence which they purport to disdain. Clearly there is evidence of the Kaiser's direct involvement in decision-making from his decisive support for naval armaments, through his interest in specific areas of domestic legislation, such as social policy or the measures against the Poles in Prussia's eastern provinces, to his very frequent interventions in diplomacy and foreign policy. Moreover, if personal convictions are widely seen to have played a role in explaining the policies of Tirpitz, Miquel or Posadowsky (the conscientious State Secretary of the Reich Office of Interior responsible for much of the social legislation of the Wilhelmine era), it is quite ridiculous to deny the political importance of Wilhelm II's personality.

The tendency to define 'personal rule' as Wilhelm II's 'unconstitutional interference' (Mommsen) has proved particularly unhelpful. Much more fruitful has been new research into monarchical structures or 'the kingship mechanism' (Elias) in Wilhelmine Germany, so that even Wehler, who once dismissed the Kaiser as 'a weak figure atop a clay pedestal'[4] has revised his earlier assessment. There is now widespread agreement about the political significance of Wilhelm's powers of appointment and patronage, the effects of which reverberated throughout the entire bureaucracy as ministers, state secretaries and officials found that their influence waxed and waned in accordance with the favour and goodwill bestowed on them by the Kaiser. One state secretary later remarked that 'given the nature of the ruler, it was completely insignificant who was minister at any one time', for men who had no support in the parliaments or among the people had few means of opposing the monarch if they were determined to keep their privileges.[5]

The ultimate dependence of the entire internal administration on the Kaiser for their careers must be seen as an important qualification to any suggestions that real power resided with the 'independent bureaucratic government' (Mommsen) in Imperial Germany. Despite the growing professionalization, *esprit de corps* and self-interest of the bureaucracy and irrespective of its increasing impact on everyday life, the bureaucrats who staffed the Prussian ministries and Reich offices were essentially lawyers by training and (as was frequently lamented before 1914) many lacked even elementary political skills. A recent study of the 'social policy' of Berlepsch, the Prussian Minister of Trade in the early 1890s, concluded that it could not meet expectations because he took a bureaucratic rather than a political route to reform, simply trying to implement the Kaiser's February Decrees of 1890. Most of the men in the bureaucratic elite could not provide political leadership, a problem which was exacerbated because the Prussian Ministry of State was a very heterogeneous body, variously composed of bureaucrats, diplomats, generals, admirals and even ex-parliamentarians, who had all been appointed at different times for different reasons and shared none of the similarity of outlook characteristic of a modern party cabinet. On the two isolated occasions when the Chancellor and Prussian Ministry of State collectively confronted the Kaiser and insisted on the removal of a 'king's minister', namely the Köller crisis of 1895 and the Podbielski crisis of 1906, their victory soon proved a pyrrhic one since the Kaiser never forgave those who manoeuvered him into a position of constraint. In the Reich, unlike in Prussia, there was not even the semblance of a collective body before June 1914 when the very first conference of the heads of the Reich departments was held on the initiative of the State Secretary of Interior, Clemens von Delbrück.

Recent work on the Kaiser's court and entourage by John Röhl and Isabel Hull has ensured that Wilhelm can no longer be seen as an isolated individual but as operating within his own elevated and distinct power sphere. The Kaiser's court not only constituted the pinnacle of an elaborate social hierarchy in which the members of the civilian government generally occupied a very inferior position, but it was also fundamental to the real constitution of Wilhelmine Germany, linked to the state apparatus and military command posts through the influence of the Kaiser's civil, military and naval cabinets and serving also as an important communications network within the ruling elite. The size of the Kaiser's court expanded dramatically under Wilhelm II. It employed some 3,500 people at the turn of the century and also proved very costly to maintain, receiving 22.2 million marks from state resources in 1910. The precedence given according to birth, status and military rank, the pomp and ceremony, the invitations to balls and festivities, the honours, titles, orders and decorations bestowed by the monarch were all overt and visible symbols of the existence of a flourishing 'court culture' in Wilhelmine Germany. The position of the ruling elite cannot be understood without reference to its political and social dependence on the monarchy as an institution; nor can the mentality of those in high office be appreciated without reference to traditions of deference and the influence of monarchism as an ideology. Germany's monarchical structures may have had a much wider, deeper and more lasting impact on German society than is generally assumed. It is surely not without significance, for example, that both Franz von Papen and Kurt von Schleicher (the two Chancellors in 1932–3 who helped pave the way for Hitler) began their careers as royal pages at the Kaiser's court.

As well as the political and social hierarchies, the Kaiser stood at the apex of a third, quite separate hierarchy which was undeniably important in the *Kaiserreich*, namely the military. However incompetent Wilhelm may have been as the 'supreme war lord' and coordinator of Germany's armed forces, there was constitutionally no scope for any political interference in his 'power of command'. Indeed, effective political control over the army could only be exercised through the monarch, aided by his military cabinet. The army swore loyalty and obedience exclusively to the Kaiser, and the political significance of this relationship can scarcely be exaggerated. Invariably appearing in military uniform and surrounded by military men, Wilhelm often chose generals in preference to bureaucrats to head offices of state and, unlike ministers, generals had the right of direct access to the monarch whenever they wished. The German Foreign Office always suspected the influence of the Kaiser's military and naval attachés who had the potential to run a kind of parallel diplomatic service, circumventing the official diplomatic channels. Moreover, after the homosexuality scandals of 1906–9 ensured that Wilhelm's closest civilian friends in the so-called 'Liebenberg circle' were banned from court, the influence of the Kaiser's military entourage was unrivalled. Repeatedly, when it came to a clash between civilian and military authority, the Kaiser took the army's side. The plight of the 'responsible government' in 1913 during the Zabern affair, when Wilhelm insisted that the Chancellor, Bethmann Hollweg (1909–17) defend army transgressions in the Alsatian town and the Reichstag impotently passed a vote of no confidence, is a salutary reminder of the extent to which Wilhelmine Germany remained a military monarchy rather than a constitutional state.

The hereditary Prussian monarch thus continued to enjoy political, military and social power in Wilhelmine Germany and the significance of his prerogatives should not be underestimated. Transposing modern political categories and concepts on to pre-1914 Germany leads to distortions unless it is remembered that national state structures were relatively undeveloped, that the 'government' consisted exclusively of crown appointees and that, unlike the Kaiser, neither the political parties nor the bureaucrats warranted a mention in the imperial constitution. Moreover, despite occasional objections from modern historians to the term 'Wilhelminism' as a description of the era between 1890 and 1918), there can be little doubt that Wilhelm II's personality impressed itself on German politics and society, whether to inspire enthusiastic dreams of a new kind of 'imperial monarchy' or prompt intensely gloomy forebodings about the burden his reign placed on Germany's political development.

Finally, in Europe before 1914 monarchies still outnumbered republics as systems of state organization, and dynastic ties continued to exert an influence both on German foreign policy and on relations between the German federal states, most of which continued to be headed by monarchs and princes. A strong monarchy was seen as the single, proven, viable alternative to parliamentarism and (as Dominic Lieven has pointed out with respect to the Russian autocracy) it was the rational choice of government for all those, often highly intelligent people who resisted the latter. Before 1914 there was little real pressure, even from the people's elected representatives, for a full parliamentarization of the German political system. Even in October 1918, after four years of unsuccessful war, the evident nervous collapse of Wilhelm II and the establishment of a virtual dictatorship by the military, only a tiny minority within the left of centre political parties were republicans who wished to see the abolition of the monarchy altogether. After the establishment of the Weimar Republic, officials, judges and military officers continued to talk and behave 'in the old style', disaffected royalists were actively disloyal and the post-war crisis encouraged many to look back nostalgically on the 'good old days' before 1914. To understand fully the role of the monarchy before 1918, we must also research more thoroughly into the effects of its collapse.

III Armaments, foreign policy and war

The controversy over Germany's role in unleashing the First World War has largely been laid to rest by German historians. However much blame may be apportioned to the other protagonists in the July crisis of 1914 and whatever the significance of longer-term diplomatic, political, social, economic and intellectual forces in propelling Europe towards war in 1914, the direction of German policy in these crucial weeks is clear. The decision-makers in Berlin undoubtedly escalated the crisis after the assassination of the heir to the Austrian throne, the Archduke Franz Ferdinand, and his wife in June 1914. Their so-called 'blank cheque', assuring Austria of German support if she chose to deal energetically with Serbia (whom they immediately suspected was implicated in the murder), their pressure on Vienna to act speedily and decisively, their quashing of mediation attempts by other powers, and their secret preparations for war, all bear out the view, widely expressed within the imperial ruling elite, that Germany believed the moment had arrived to break out of her perceived encirclement by a hostile coalition of Entente powers. Kaiser Wilhelm II declared that it was 'now or never' for Austria to deal with the Serbs;[6] the Chancellor, Bethmann Hollweg, believed his hardest duty was to take this 'leap in the dark';[7] and the military began preparations for the two-front war which, in accordance with the dictates of the Schlieffen plan, would begin with the invasion of Belgium. After the Austrians began shelling Belgrade across the Danube on 29 July, Germany still insisted officially that the developing conflict should remain localized, yet she sacrificed the interests and security of her ally unashamedly. Austria was allowed neither the time nor the opportunity to achieve her objectives against Serbia before Berlin's declaration of war, and strategic planning ensured that she was called upon to relieve pressure on Germany by opening the Galician front. Only five days after Germany, and under pressure from her ally, Austria reluctantly declared war on Russia on 6 August.

There is also overwhelming evidence that Germany's rulers were fully conscious of the implications of their actions for the peace of Europe in 1914. Since the Balkan Wars of 1912–13, they had been preoccupied with the possibility of a general European war resulting from a crisis in the Balkans, a war which (as the Kaiser made clear to his military and naval advisers in December 1912) would almost certainly number Britain among Germany's enemies. Yet they were obviously prepared to risk such a war in 1914 not least because, given the scale of the arms race over the previous decade, they were convinced that their chances of victory would diminish if they procrastinated. Having secured Reichstag acceptance of two army bills in 1912 and 1913, the second of which constituted an unprecedented increase of military strength in peacetime, Germany was presented with a 'window of opportunity' before the effects of changes to the French and Russian military programmes made themselves felt by about 1917. Convinced that Germany was still a match for her enemies in 1914, the Chief of the German General Staff, Moltke, proposed to the German Foreign Secretary a few weeks before the Sarajevo assassinations that he 'should conduct a policy with the aim of provoking a war in the near future.'[8] On hearing the news of Russian mobilization at the end of July 1914, the Bavarian military plenipotentiary rushed to the Prussian War Ministry and recorded: 'Beaming faces everywhere. Everyone is shaking hands in the corridors: people congratulate one another for being over the hurdle.'[9]

If the material evidence of Germany's role as the pacemaker in the July crisis of 1914 is irrefutable, the twin issues of Germany's motivations in pressing for war and how best to interpret the general thrust of German diplomacy in the previous decades remain highly controversial. Germany's actions in 1914 have variously been seen as the logical consequence of a planned policy of aggression to achieve territory and world power (Fischer, Röhl), as the product of much more inchoate and ill-defined strivings for equality of status with the other imperial powers in Europe (Nippperdey), and as an extreme 'social imperialist' response to the Reich's domestic predicament by 1914 (Wehler, Berghahn). Similarly, assessments of German foreign policy between 1890 and 1914 shift uneasily between condemnation of her naval programme and diplomatic bullying, acknowledgement of a large measure of confusion and drift behind the aggressive posturing, and a preoccupation with the domestic determinants of foreign policy, sometimes to the extent that international relations are denied any significant degree of autonomy or inherent dynamism.

Germany's role in the origins of the First World War must be set within the wider context of the impact of German unification on the European state system from 1871. Prussia's spectacular military victories in the period 1864–71 not only presented the established European powers with a *fait accompli* which few had foreseen, but also signified the consolidation of a powerful new Reich in a part of central Europe which had traditionally served as a kind of defensive 'shock-absorber' within the state system. Moreover, Germany's military superiority from 1871, her burgeoning population and her growing industrial strength were all likely to be construed as potentially threatening by her neighbours, irrespective of the foreign policies her leadership pursued. The 'War in Sight' crisis of 1875, when the renewal of Franco-German tension prompted British and Russian warnings to Berlin that they could not tolerate another subjugation of France, is often seen as the first collective attempt by the European powers to contain Germany. The development of Bismarck's famous 'alliance system' which isolated France is also usually interpreted as his attempt to stave off the consequences of German unification, motivated by the need to prevent the formation of a hostile coalition and preserve his new creation.

Recent work by Lothar Gall and others has tended to downplay the longer-term significance of Bismarck's treaties and alliances and to question the extent to which even the Dual and Triple Alliances were integral parts of a wider 'system' which was meant to endure. Yet, if anything, this has rather heightened the impression that Bismarck's foreign policy was largely an exercise in crisis management. Despite his emphasis on the preservation of peace, his insistence that Germany was a 'satiated state' after 1871 and his effort to maintain the status quo in the Balkans through the creation of a balance of power, Bismarck's policies were subjected to new diplomatic, economic and domestic pressures from the late 1880s which called into question his conservative assumptions. In 1890 Germany may have 'lost control of the system' (Schroeder) when Bismarck's successors failed to renew the secret Reinsurance Treaty of 1887 with Russia (an omission which foreshadowed the formation of the Franco-Russian alliance of 1894). However, given the changed conditions in which foreign policy had to be conducted in the 1890s, with the rise of mass politics, the growth of nationalism and the renewed focus on imperial rivalries, some kind of realignment within the European state system was probably inevitable.

The Reich (which encompassed not only the territory of the reunited Germany of today but also territories which are now part of Poland, Lithuania, Denmark, Belgium and France) enjoyed a 'latent hegemony' in Europe between 1871 and 1890, and there were some optimistic, self-confident voices in the Wilhelmine era (such as the industrialist, Hugo Stinnes) prepared to predict that sooner or later Germany would come to dominate the continent of Europe even without a war. Yet Imperial Germany, like its Nazi successor, ultimately represented a threat to the peace and stability of Europe, not merely because of its size, strength or geographical location, but because of the foreign policy it pursued and its very nature as a state. How far German foreign policy before (and after) 1914 was conditioned by the way in which Germany was unified, how far the values of militarism and nationalism were integral to the self-identity of the new German state, and how far the Reich's status as a 'belated nation' ultimately served to propel her on to an aggressive course are ambitious and difficult questions to which there can probably be no satisfactory or conclusive answers. Yet, without adopt-

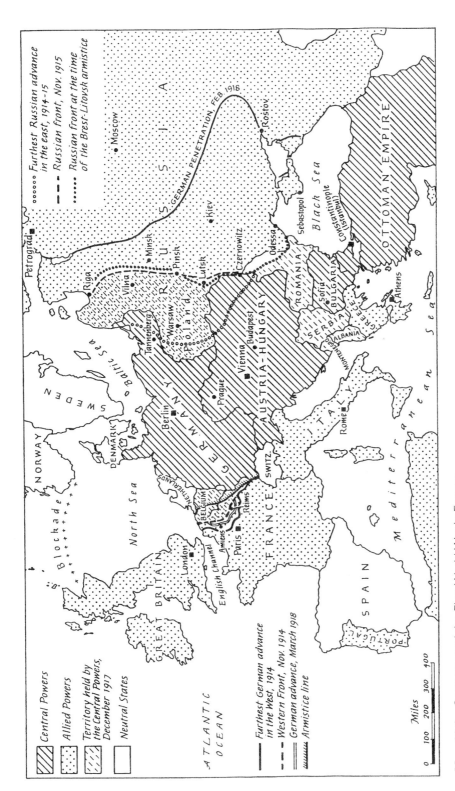

Map 11.1 Germany and the First World War in Europe

ing an overly fatalistic or determinist view about the Reich's development from 1871, there seems little doubt that the notion of a short, successful war as a panacea for all domestic and foreign ills penetrated deeply into the psyche of at least some of those who, having experienced the Prussian constitutional conflict and wars of unification as adolescents and young men, went on to assume high office in the Wilhelmine era. Long before he became State Secretary of the Foreign Office, Bülow (who had volunteered to fight in the Franco-Prussian War) extolled the virtues of the 'national idea' as an integrative device, insisted that Germany's fate depended above all on 'the sharpness of the Prussian sword' and called for the harnessing of all the nation's military and moral forces in preparation for the decisive great struggle which would probably come at the turn of the century.[10] The memoirs of men like Tirpitz, the State Secretary of the Navy Office (1897–1917), and Einem, the Prussian War Minister (1903–9), uniformly begin with accounts of their formative experiences during the wars against Austria or France and approvingly note the beneficial effects of the military victories on Prussian prestige. In July 1911 the Chancellor, Bethmann Hollweg, surveyed the national mood during the Second Moroccan Crisis and concluded, 'The people need a war.'[11]

The willingness of the 'men of 1914' to embark on a policy of war can be seen as the most extreme manifestation of a defensive, 'social imperialist' strategy to stabilize and legitimize the position of the ruling elite at a time when its power was increasingly threatened by democratic and socialist forces. 'I am putting the main emphasis on foreign policy', the new Foreign Secretary, Bülow, wrote rather self-evidently in December 1897, adding the much-cited words, 'Only a successful foreign policy can help to reconcile, pacify, rally, unite.'[12] The social imperialist interpretation of German foreign policy effectively circumnavigates the problem of defining the concrete objectives of German imperialism before 1914, seeing the pursuit of *Weltpolitik* (world policy) and naval armaments from 1897 as primarily serving an integrative function. Moreover, it usefully focuses attention on some of the more fearful and pessimistic assumptions within the ruling elite in July 1914 which seem to belie the dominance of a warmongering mentality. In this context, however, it should be noted that one important source which was used to draw a more sympathetic portrait of the *Angst*-ridden Chancellor in 1914, the published diaries of his private secretary, Kurt Riezler, can no longer be regarded as wholly reliable. In 1983 it was revealed that significant portions of the original Riezler diaries had been destroyed prior to publication and that the entries for July 1914 were significantly different in form from the rest of the diary.

Recent work (notably by Blackbourn and Eley) has tended to undermine the socio-economic basis of the social imperialist thesis and challenge the dichotomy drawn between the forces of progress and reaction in the *Kaiserreich*. For example, it is now difficult to argue that the policies of the ruling elite were supported by the powerful coalition of conservative economic interests which had first emerged in 1878–9. The alleged deal which was brokered between the agrarians and big industrialists in 1897–8, whereby an ambitious programme of *Weltpolitik* and naval armaments (to bring material benefits to the workers and divert attention away from the need for domestic reform) was coupled with the promise of a highly protectionist tariff, barely survived the 1898 elections and could not form the basis of a lasting anti-socialist *Sammlung* (rallying) of forces which supported the state. In addition, especially between 1898 and 1902, the government came into sharp conflict with the agrarians who played a major role in thwarting the Prussian canal bills of 1899 and 1901. The government felt under no obligation to pander to their interests when steering the tariff legislation through the Reichstag in 1902. Bülow was even prepared if necessary to negotiate new commercial treaties without a new tariff law.

It is also difficult to see the navy as serving the interests of a domestic *Sammlung* or primarily as an instrument of domestic policy. While the fleet did prove unexpectedly popular, the financial cost of building a huge navy of battleships ultimately put enormous strain on the Reich's constitutional, fiscal and social fabric and eventually encouraged dissension within the ruling elite. The anti-parliamentary implications of the navy laws of 1898 and 1900, which provided for a fixed number of ships to be built each year and their automatic replacement at the end of their lifetime, were more than outweighed by the effects of the growing Reich deficit. The significance of the Reichstag's power of the purse was even more apparent after the decision in 1906 to build dreadnoughts and enter into an openly hostile arms race with Britain. The huge profits expected to be made by German industries involved in the naval programme also never materialized. The government maintained its political control over both the planning and the implementation of the programme, never allowing the initiative to pass to economic interest groups. It successfully squeezed the profit margins of the armaments industry through encouraging an uneconomic expansion of private shipyards and competition for government contracts.

The political and strategic assumptions of the 'Tirpitz plan' clearly indicate that the State Secretary of the Navy Office was intent on building a fleet of huge battleships, ships which were unsuitable for colonial or commercial purposes but could present an effective challenge to the British Royal Navy. Historians may dispute the extent to which Tirpitz's aims were known and appreciated by the Reichstag, the wider German public and even within the ruling elite itself. In 1907, after the formation of the Bülow Bloc parliamentary coalition of liberals and conservatives, Tirpitz himself lamented to Bülow that 'the most knowledgeable and hence most dangerous experts on the true significance of the Navy Law, which at the moment is still not completely understood by most politicians . . . sit in the Centre Party',[13] a party which was now opposed to the government. Yet the drive to build the second strongest navy in the world cannot be dismissed as irrational by the standards of the time nor as a mere means to maintaining the domestic status quo. Rather, the 'Tirpitz plan' was the core of Germany's bid for 'world power' before 1914 and it involved subordinating the interests of German foreign and domestic policy to the needs of naval armaments. Supported by the Kaiser, Tirpitz refused to be deflected from his aims even after his strategic assumptions had been overtaken by the formation of the Triple Entente in 1907 (which suggested that the Royal Navy could no longer be viewed in isolation). Both Bülow and Bethmann Hollweg as Chancellor came to question the rationale of the naval programme, and in 1912, for the first time since the adoption of the Tirpitz plan, the army was given priority with respect to resources. But significantly the naval programme was never abandoned despite all the difficulties and Germany was only prepared to limit her battleship building before 1914 if Britain agreed unconditionally to remain neutral in a continental war.

Arguments that the ruling elite 'fled forwards' (Wehler) to escape its domestic problems in 1914 are also undermined by the manifest lack of a revolutionary situation or even an acute domestic crisis on the eve of 1914. Notwithstanding the SPD's gains in the 1912 elections, its agitation for Prussian suffrage reform and the rash of strike activity in 1912, there is also evidence of its commitment to radical reformism, a new willingness to cooperate with the government and, indeed, its integration into the state (although it must be stated that all of these developments were anathema to conservatives). The SPD voted for Bülow's failed financial reform in 1909 and the new constitution for Alsace and Lorraine (which included universal suffrage) in 1910. Moreover, however unwelcome the development was to members of the ruling elite, its support, along with that of the left liberals, was vital in securing the tax reform (including a capital gains tax on property) which financed the Army Bill of 1913. In July 1914 Bethmann Hollweg correctly calculated that if Russia, the autocratic *bête noire* of Europe's left, was made to appear the aggressor, then the SPD would rally patriotically behind a war of national defence. SPD deputies unanimously voted for the war credits on 4 August and the overwhelming majority welcomed the Kaiser's proclamation of a 'civil truce'.

Nor can it be said that the Reichstag posed a particularly serious democratic challenge to the ruling elite in the last years of peace. In the 1890s the clashes between monarchy and parliament had precipitated much talk of a *Staatsstreich* within the ruling elite, but after 1900 relations between executive and legislature became far more routine and cooperative. The Reichstag augmented its power before 1914 and achieved significant concessions such as measures to ensure the secret ballot in elections, remuneration for parliamentary deputies, and procedural changes to allow votes of no confidence. Yet there is little evidence to suggest that the Reichstag wished to use its legislative power to institute parliamentary government in Germany before 1914 or that parliamentary considerations appreciably entered into the calculations of Germany's leaders in the July crisis. The fact that the arms bills of 1912–13 were passed by a conservative-centre majority and the financial cover by a centre-left majority also undermines assertions that there was a complete domestic stalemate by 1914.

If there was a crisis in Germany on the eve of the First World War it was a perceived crisis rather than one based on an objective evaluation of prevailing conditions, having more to do with the fears of an increasingly fragmented right than the reality of the 'progressive challenge'. Moreover the complex of anxieties, hopes and expectations prevalent within the different groupings on the right needs to be analysed precisely. Fears about Russia's future military strength, the prospects for the next Reichstag elections due in 1917, the democratizing effects of further military expansion, the continuing vitality of state particularism, the implications of industrial capitalism, the odds for a renewal of the tariff law in 1917, the progressive collapse of the patriarchal order, all might combine with an enormous confidence in German military power, belief in the infallibility of the General Staff and expectations of a decisive Teutonic victory in the future battle against the Slavs. Evidence that individual conservatives within the bureaucratic elite felt 'besieged' in 1914 may be better explained with reference to the radical nationalist challenge, their declining influence within their profession or, indeed, their sense of isolation within an increasingly imperialist culture, rather than to the threat posed by socialism and democracy.

German foreign policy from 1890 remains notoriously difficult to interpret, not least because the Bismarckian consensus that the chancellor controlled this sphere of the state's activities came under challenge and there were no effective constitutional means for resolving conflicts over Germany's aims or interests. Thus it is possible to detect the broad outlines of German policy at different junctures – the hopes of the New Course to replace the 'wire to St Petersburg' with a *rapprochement* with Britain, the misplaced confidence of Holstein, a leading official in the Foreign Office, in Germany's ability to pursue a 'free hand' policy between Britain and the Franco-Russian combination from the mid-1890s, the desire of Bülow to exploit Russia's difficulties in 1904–5 to bully her into concluding a continental alliance against Britain. But such policies often overlapped and were contradictory, or they were never pursued consistently and unequivocally. Moreover, it is always possible to discern divergent tendencies, whether within the Foreign Office or between the Kaiser, chancellor and foreign secretary, to highlight the failure of coordination at the highest level and illuminate what appears to be a zig-zag course after Bismarck's departure. Hence even the personnel and policy changes of 1897 and Bülow's highly publicized call in the Reichstag that Germany, too, should have 'a place in the sun' have left many unconvinced about the extent of Germany's aggressive ambitions before 1914.

At a time when most of the earth's territories were already accounted for, the aims of German *Weltpolitik* were bound to be left vague and unspecified. Moreover, from 1898 the need to bring the navy safely through the 'danger zone' when it was particularly vulnerable to a British attack, ensured that German foreign policy, far from actively pursuing overseas possessions, had to be practised with restraint. To a considerable extent German foreign policy was reactive in the decade after 1900, whether seeking to test the Anglo-French entente, exploit the Russo-Japanese war or support the Austrian annexation of Bosnia-Herzegovina in 1908–9. In 1905 Germany had a good case in seeking to maintain the 'open door' policy in Morocco and in an era of prestige politics could legitimately assert her equal right to be consulted about the future of the North African state. But the execution of her policy during the First Moroccan Crisis was clumsy, heavy-handed and inconsistent. Her determination to test the Anglo-French entente resulted in her isolation and humiliation at the Algeciras conference of 1906, giving rise to the first complaints that she was encircled.

In the decade before 1914 Germany's interests undoubtedly grew in areas of the world such as the Balkans, the Middle East and Africa where it had been possible for Bismarck (notwithstanding his brief foray into colonialism in the mid-1880s) to profess with some justification that Germany was disinterested. Yet how far the desire to extend those interests underscored German policy in 1914 remains in dispute, as does the very nature and significance of German imperialism before the First World War. One recent study by Woodruff D. Smith has explored the origins of *Weltpolitik* as an imperialist ideology of modernity, with broad support within the bureaucracy and business community, and has argued that it aimed to promote German commerce and industry rather than to acquire colonies (although there was a colonial element). But it is maintained that *Weltpolitik* came into conflict before 1914 with a rival ideology of *Lebensraum*, which also had its proponents within the ruling elite (and notably within the radical nationalist associations) and aimed rather at the defence of traditional society against the effects of industrialization, for example through a migrationist colonialism in eastern Europe. Consequently those who supported *Weltpolitik* within the Foreign Office proved unable to assert their priorities from 1912, failing to persuade Wilhelm II and the conservative imperialists to agree to naval limitations with Britain in exchange for imperial agreements in Africa. But Smith does not directly consider the role of German imperialism in precipitating the First World War, primarily being interested in the ideological origins of Nazi imperialism.

In the 1960s the famous 'Fischer controversy', prompted by the publication of Fritz Fischer's books, *Germany's Aims in the First World War* and *War of Illusions*, not only focused attention on Germany's role in the July crisis but also prompted questions about the nature and status of Germany's extensive war aims after the outbreak of the hostilities. In asserting that the First World War was an aggressive war which was deliberately provoked by Germany, Fischer maintained that, unlike the war aims of the other belligerents, Germany's aims were formulated too quickly to be interpreted as the product of wartime exigencies. Five weeks after the outbreak of war and before the French 'miracle of the Marne' scuppered German hopes of a quick victory, Bethmann Hollweg drew up his 'September programme' which envisaged achieving 'security for the Reich in west and east for all imaginable time'[14] by such means as the military and economic subjugation of France and Belgium, the annexation of Luxemburg, the creation of a central European customs union (or *Mitteleuropa*) under German leadership, and the eventual fulfilment of Germany's war aims in colonial Africa and against Russia (these last being achieved when the punitive Treaty of Brest Litovsk was inflicted on the Bolsheviks in March 1918). However, while not denying that Germany developed concrete war aims during the First World War, proponents of the social imperialism thesis such as Wehler have preferred to see the numerous, megalomaniacal and boundless schemes of expansion, hatched not only by the imperial government and army but also by the leaders of the federal states, as yet another means of diverting attention from the issue of internal reform, an issue which inevitably became more pressing as the war continued. Only in 1918 did the opportunity arise for the 'unrestrained rhetoric' to become a reality. The establishment of a German Reich in the east in March 1918 was thus, in Wehler's view, 'the qualitative leap' which linked the foreign policy of Imperial Germany to that of Hitler, beginning 'the pre-history of the Second World War'.[15]

Important evidence which supports the thesis that the First World War was a premeditated war of aggression also relates to the so-called 'war council', which was summoned by the Kaiser to the Berlin Schloss on 8 December 1912. Historians now have several versions of this meeting at which the Kaiser discussed with his top military and naval advisers the possibility and desirability of a general European war arising over the Balkans. Moreover recent research by John Röhl has confirmed that the Chancellor was informed of the meeting within 24 hours (some historians such as Wolfgang Mommsen had concluded from his absence that the council was devoid of political significance) and that measures agreed on 8 December, such as the need to prepare the German public through the press for a war against Russia, were put into effect. At the war council the military urged an immediate war, but Tirpitz argued for 'a postponement of the great fight for one-and-a-half years' (until June 1914) when the Kiel Canal would be widened to allow the passage of dreadnoughts and the navy would be better prepared for a war against Britain. At the very least the council indicates why a general European war did not develop out of the Balkan wars of 1912–13. Germany proved willing to cooperate with the other powers to ensure the crisis remained localized.

Some historians, however, such as the Swiss historian, Adolf Gasser, have gone further and argued that the First World War was deliberately planned from December 1912. John Röhl has uncovered retrospective references over the ensuing weeks to the decisions taken at the council and also new evidence of Germany's economic and financial preparations for war between 1912 and 1914. The whole debate about this extraordinary event tends to lead back to the nature of decision-making processes in Germany on the eve of the First World War and historians' inability to agree on the answer to the famous question, posed by the Austrian Foreign Minister, Berchthold, in 1914, 'Who rules in Berlin: Bethmann or Moltke?'[16] Paradoxically, Mommsen, who has blamed the outbreak of the First World War on the 'weakness and confusion' within the ruling elite and Bethmann Hollweg's ultimate powerlessness to enforce his strategy against the military and the Kaiser's court, is most inclined to dismiss the war council because the Chancellor was not present. Others, however, emphasize the strength of the Chancellor's position in July 1914, deny there was a division between the military and civilian leadership, and see the war originating in a consensus which lasted until the military defeats of August and September 1918.

Ultimately the direction of German policy in the last months of peace, the extent to which it was supported by a domestic consensus or arose, rather, from military pressure or the isolation of the ruling elite, can only be clarified by further research. In Imperial Germany, as elsewhere in Europe, foreign policy remained an arcane sphere where decisions were taken by a handful of men. Few were privy to the assumptions of those men and it was a brave Reichstag deputy who used the occasion of the budget debate to criticize the conduct of foreign policy publicly. Yet the actions of the 'men of

1914' were not merely guided by their individual and collective concerns but also conditioned by their positions within the wider institutional and political structure. Only close examination of that structure can determine why it was, for example, that the Kaiser's 'now or never' response to the assassinations at the beginning of July served to pull the bureaucratic, diplomatic and military elements within the elite into line, while his recognition that 'every cause for war has vanished' and readiness to mediate for peace on 28 July could effectively be disregarded.[17]

For all the ambiguities in interpretations of German foreign policy before 1914, the impression it created in the chancelleries of Europe was disastrous. The aggressive rhetoric of Germany's rulers, the succession of misconceived and bullying policies, the persistent attempts to extract maximum advantage from international crises, the sheer inconsistency and unpredictability of German diplomacy in many areas, as well as the refusal to enter into any kind of naval arms limitation agreement, all created apprehension among Germany's neighbours and confirmed her role as the main disturber of the peace before 1914. In Britain, Foreign Office officials became convinced as early as 1907 that Germany was seeking to dominate the continent of Europe, and Churchill, as First Lord of the Admiralty in 1911, voiced his disquiet over the combined naval and military strength now at the disposal of a government which was not accountable to parliament. In Russia, five months before the outbreak of the First World War, a leading newspaper maintained that 'The foreign policy of Germany for forty years has consisted in a systematic frightening of her opponents with the prospect of war', and urged the government to stand firm in a subsequent crisis.[18] In France, too, the decision for war in 1914 was widely understood as a refusal to submit to German domination and the Balkan issue scarcely merited any public discussion.

The Entente powers thus had few doubts about the offensive nature of German diplomacy before 1914, just as they were of one mind in blaming Germany for starting the war. In 1919 they also had no qualms about including the 'war guilt' clause in the Treaty of Versailles. Drawing no distinction between the old *Kaiserreich* and the new republic, they made Germany and her allies accept responsibility for all the damage and destruction wrought by the war. Furthermore, they expected her to pay.

Notes:

1. Röhl, J. C. G., *Germany Without Bismarck. The Crisis of Government in the Second Reich, 1890–1900* (1967), p. 194.
2. Lerman, K. A., *The Chancellor as Courtier. Bernhard von Bülow and the Governance of Germany 1900–1909* (1990), pp. 139–40, 187–9.
3. *Ibid.*, p. 246.
4. Wehler, H.-U., *The German Empire 1871–1918* (1985), p. 64; cf. *Deutsche Gesellschaftsgeschichte, 3 vols, vol. 3 1849–1914* (1995), pp. 854–7.
5. Lerman, *Chancellor as Courtier*, p. 328.
6. Kaiser's marginalia on report from Tschirschky to Bethmann Hollweg, 30 June 1914, in I. Geiss, ed., *July 1914. Selected Documents* (1967), p. 64.

7. Erdmann, K. D., ed., *Kurt Riezler. Tagebücher, Aufsätze, Dokumente* (1972), 14 July 1914, p. 185.
8. Rohl, J. C. G., ed., *From Bismarck to Hitler* (1970), p. 70; F. Fischer, *War of Illusions. German Policies from 1911 to 1914* (1975), p. 402.
9. Pogge von Strandmann, H., 'Germany and the Coming of War' in R. J. W. Evans and H. Pogge von Strandmann, eds., *The Coming of the First World War* (1990), p. 120.
10. Bülow to Eulenburg, 23 December 1889, in J. C. G. Röhl, ed., *Philipp Eulenburgs Politische Korrespondenz* vol.1: *Von der Reichsgründung bis zum neuen Kurs 1866–1891* (1976), pp. 388–90.
11. Wehler, *Deutsche Gesellschaftsgeschichte*, vol. 3, p. 1151.
12. Röhl, *Germany Without Bismarck*, p. 252.
13. Lerman, *Chancellor as Courtier*, p. 185.
14. Fischer, F., *Germany's Aims in the First World War* (1967), p. 103.
15. Wehler, *German Empire*, p. 211.
16. See Taylor, A. J. P., 'The Ruler in Berlin', in *Europe: Grandeur and Decline* (1967), p. 159.
17. See Geiss, *July 1914*, pp. 64 and 256.
18. Spring, D. W., 'Russia and the Coming of War', in Evans and Pogge von Strandmann, *Coming of the First World War*, p. 76.

Select bibliography

Berghahn, Volker R., *Germany and the Approach of War in 1914* (1993).

Berghahn, Volker R., *Imperial Germany 1871–1914* (1994).

Berlepsch, Hans-Jorg von, *'Neuer Kurs' im Kaiserreich? Die Arbeiterpolitik des Freiherrn von Berlepsch 1890 bis 1896* (1987).

Blackbourn, David, *Class, Religion and Local Politics in Wilhelmine Germany. The Centre Party in Württemberg before 1914* (1980).

Coetzee, Marilyn S., *The German Army League. Popular Nationalism in Wilhelmine Germany* (1990).

Eley, Geoff, *Reshaping the German Right. Radical Nationalism and Political Change after Bismarck* (1980).

Eley, Geoff, *From Unification to Nazism. Reinterpreting the German Past* (1986).

Elias, Norbert, *Über den Prozess der Zivilisation. Soziogenetische und psychogenetische Untersuchungen*, 2 vols. (1969). See also, J.C.G. Röhl, The 'kingship mechanism' in the Kaiserreich in *The Kaiser and his Court. Wilhelm II and the Government of Germany* (1994).

Epkenhans, Michael, *Die wilhelminische Flottenrüstung 1908–1914* (1991).

Evans, Richard J., ed., *Society and Politics in Wilhelmine Germany* (1978).

Fischer, Fritz, *Germany's Aims in the First World War* (1967).

Fischer, Fritz, *War of Illusions. German Policies from 1911 to 1914* (1975).

Gall, Lothar, *Bismarck. The White Revolutionary* 2 vols. (1986).

Gasser, Adolf, *Preussischer Militärgeist und Kriegsentfesselung 1914. Drei Studien zum Ausbruch des Ersten Weltkrieges* (1985).

Geiss, Immanuel, ed., *July 1914. The Outbreak of the First World War: Selected Documents* (1967).

Geiss, Immanuel, *German Foreign Policy 1871–1914* (1976).

Hull, Isabel V., *The Entourage of Kaiser Wilhelm II, 1888–1918* (1982).

Lerman, Katharine A., *The Chancellor as Courtier. Bernhard von Bülow and the Governance of Germany 1900–1909* (1990).

Lowe, John, *The Great Powers, Imperialism and the German Problem, 1865–1925* (1994).

Moeller, Robert G. (ed.), *Peasants and Lords in Modern Germany* (1986).

Mommsen, Wolfgang J., *Imperial Germany 1867–1918. Politics, Culture and Society in an Authoritarian State* (1995).

Nipperdey, Thomas, *Deutsche Geschichte 1866-1918, vol. 2: Machtstaat vor der Demokratie* (1993).

Retallack, James, *Notables of the Right. The Conservative Party and Political Mobilization in Germany 1876–1918* (1988).

Röhl, John C. G., *Germany Without Bismarck. The Crisis of Government in the Second Reich 1890–1900* (1967).

Röhl, John C. G., *The Kaiser and his Court. Wilhelm II and the Government of Germany* (1994).

Röhl, John C. G., and Sombart, Nicolaus, eds., *Kaiser Wilhelm II. New Interpretations* (1982).

Schoenbaum, David, *Zabern 1913* (1982).

Schroeder, Paul, 'World War One as Galloping Gertie: A Reply to Joachim Remak', *Journal of Modern History*, XLIV, 3 (1972).

Smith, Woodruff D., *The Ideological Origins of Nazi Imperialism* (1986).

Sperber, Jonathan, *The Kaiser's Voters. Electors and Elections in Imperial Germany* (forthcoming).

Stargardt, Nicholas, *The German Idea of Militarism. Radical and Socialist Critics 1866–1914* (1994).

Wehler, Hans-Ulrich, *The German Empire 1871–1918* (1985).

Wehler, Hans-Ulrich, *Deutsche Gesellschaftsgeschichte, vol. 3: Von der 'Deutschen Doppelrevolution' bis zum Beginn des Ersten Weltkrieges, 1849–1914* (1995).

Some basic statistics for Germany, 1815–1918

Statistics for 'Germany' before 1871 are confusing. Some figures are for the area which was to become the territory of the German Second Empire in 1871. Such statistics are only of limited use for long-run comparisons because that geographical unit made no sense whatsoever before 1871. Some statistics are for the territory of the German Confederation. However, that territory excluded part of the population of Prussia (the provinces of East and West Prussia and the Grand Duchy of Posen) and the eastern half of the Habsburg Empire as well as its Italian possessions. Furthermore, some collections still exclude the Austrian part of the Confederation, although there is no possible excuse for so doing. Some statistics are for the area covered by the German Customs Union (*Zollverein*). Even statistics for individual states are a problem. Figures for the Napoleonic period have not been included because the territories of individual states changed with bewildering rapidity, so much so that some cartographers largely gave up compiling political maps and turned their attention to such things as 'natural frontiers'. Even in the stable period after 1814–15 there are some difficulties. Prussia was greatly expanded by annexation in 1867 while Austria lost Lombardy in 1867 and Venetia in 1871. Statistics were not always gathered by the same methods. This point should particularly be borne in mind when comparing labour force statistics before and after 1871 and one should also note that the different states before 1871 would not have used precisely the same methods or applied them with the same degree of accuracy. Prussia was always noted for her superiority in this regard. Finally, one should note that statistics are generally more reliable the later they are compiled. The pre-1871 statistics in particular provide little more than orders of magnitude, sometimes involve estimates, and frequently do not add up.

1   Population before unification

The German Confederation

Total population (in millions)

1822	39.6
1843	49.4
1864	53.7

Individual states in 1841: population in the German Confederation (in millions)

Austria	16.6
Bavaria	4.4
Hanover	1.7
Saxony	1.7
Württemberg	1.7
Baden	1.3

None of the other states had a population of over 1 million; their total population amounted in 1841 to about 5.5 million, ranging from about 734,000 inhabitants in Kurhesse to some 28,000 in Schaumburg-Lippe.

The table does not include Prussia, figures for which are given below for its whole territory, both within and outside the Confederation. It is, however, worth providing the population of the Habsburg territories within the Confederation as this was always regarded as the 'German' part of the empire.

Prussia

1820	10.3
1840	14.9
1870	19.4*

*This excludes the additional 4.5 million subjects gained by annexation in 1867.

Austria–Hungary

1820	25.5
1870	34.8

2. The German Second Empire

Population (in millions)

1870	40.8
1880	45.0
1890	49.2
1900	56.0
1910	64.6

Composition of the labour force for the territory of the subsequent German Second Empire

Date	Primary sector	Secondary sector	Tertiary sector
1800	62	21	17
1825	59	22	19
1846	57	23	20
1861	52	27	21
1871	49	29	22

Composition of the labour force for the German Second Empire

Date	Primary sector	Secondary sector	Tertiary sector*
1882	41.6	34.8	23.7
1895	35.0	38.5	26.5
1907	28.4	42.2	29.4

*This includes the unemployed and those on unearned incomes.

Part III

1918–1945

Introduction to Part III: 1918–1945

Mary Fulbrook

The period from defeat in the First World War to defeat in the Second World War saw Germany experience two political extremes: its first attempt at democracy, with the abdication of the Kaiser and the proclamation of a republic on 9 November 1918, and one of the most reprehensible dictatorships of the modern age, following the appointment of Hitler as Chancellor on 30 January 1933. With the unleashing of a second World War, and the purposeful mass murder of around six million human beings in unprecedented industrial genocide, the collapse from democracy into dictatorship has understandably aroused the most virulent historical controversies. Was the collapse of Weimar democracy inevitable, rooted in fatal compromises at its inception, or could the rise of the NSDAP have been avoided, particularly if other economic policies had been pursued in the late Weimar years? What were the structures of power in the Third Reich and how should the role of Hitler be interpreted? How, in particular, can that almost inconceivable crime, the Holocaust, be represented and explained?

The essays in this section tackle some of these questions, on which there is by now an almost insurmountable literature. Again, not everything could be covered in equal depth; as in earlier sections, the foreign policy and military history of the period is taken largely as given, and the focus is primarily on domestic social, economic, cultural and political patterns. Richard Bessel first provides a panoptic overview of the development of Weimar democracy as it emerged in the turmoils of the aftermath of the First World War, and characterizes some of the deep tensions and compromises which marked it from its birth. Niall Ferguson takes up the central question of the inter-war economy, addressing the arguments about degrees of leeway open to politicians at this time. For all the 'doom and gloom' flavour of its political history, Weimar was also a time of extraordinary cultural creativity. Elizabeth Harvey examines some of the fascinating and complex ways in which modern culture was expressed and refracted in what was still a fragmented and diverse society. Jill Stephenson then takes up the question – which, although intrinsically connected with the collapse of Weimar democracy, can be treated as analytically distinct – of the rise of the NSDAP and the ways in which it was able to capitalize on the chaotic economic and political conditions of the closing Weimar years. Ian Kershaw provides a broad view of the structure of the Nazi dictatorship and Hitler's role within it, in the context of current theoretical controversies, while Nicholas Stargardt explores conflicting accounts and interpretations of the Holocaust.

12

Germany from war to dictatorship

Richard Bessel

There are times in which conditions that were thought to be unshakeable and eternal
all are called into question. The feeling spreads that the ground is being pulled out
from under people's feet. Such a time descended upon Germany after 1918.
Germany's great-power status was gone; the social strata which had identified themselves with it found that there was no longer any air for them to breathe. One lived from
hand to mouth and saw oneself time and again on the edge of the abyss and
catastrophe.[1]

'The population is beginning to go crazy.' ('*Die Einwohnerschaft fängt an, verrückt zu
werden.*') Thus the police director in Stuttgart began a directive to the city's police in
early August 1914, a few days after war had been declared.[2] He was referring to the
panic about suspected spies and alleged acts of sabotage which had accompanied the
excitement with which the German public greeted the outbreak of war. The wild,
unfounded rumours circulating around the city, the Stuttgart Police Director wrote,
gave one the impression of being 'in a lunatic asylum', and he observed, more prophet-
ically than he possibly could have imagined: 'There is no telling what will happen if
times really become more difficult'.

As we know, times did become more difficult. August 1914 was a turning point even
more profound than could have been predicted at the time, shattering the apparent
certainties of the pre-1914 world and marking the beginning of a period 'in which conditions that were thought to be unshakeable and eternal all are called into question'
and in which the feeling spread 'that the ground is being pulled out from under
people's feet'. Few nation states have tumbled more precipitously into catastrophe
than did Germany between 1914 and 1933. A prosperous, apparently stable and self-
confident nation plunged into a world war and lost it, experienced the collapse of
monarchic and then of democratic government, saw its economy ravaged by the worst
inflation and then the worst depression the world had ever seen, and succumbed to a
vicious racist political movement which led the country down the path to dictatorship,
world war and mass murder. The tragic history of Germany in the two decades which

followed the outbreak of the First World War is a history of political, economic and social instability, and of a profoundly misplaced search for a return to stability and security.

For many years it has been a commonplace to describe the events of 1914 as an out-pouring of popular enthusiasm for war, with cheering crowds confidently wishing the nation's young men a glorious and speedy march to Paris, as the declaration of war 'released a heady excitement that swept the whole country'.[3] As we have come to appreciate more recently, however, what occurred in the summer of 1914 was rather more complex and the emotions stirred up by the outbreak of war rather more ambiva-lent than often has been assumed. Alongside demonstrations of patriotic enthusiasm there were manifestations of anxiety and fear. In late July 1914 hundreds of thousands of Germans took part in peace demonstrations; while many Germans rushed to the colours once war was declared, many others desperately sought to have their sons exempted from military service; many rushed to remove their savings from banks and hoarded food; and many more found themselves thrown out of work as unemployment reached unprecedented levels with the economic dislocation which followed the mili-tary mobilization. Already at the outbreak of war tensions were present which would grow to tear German society and the German polity apart in the next few years. While the nervous hopes for a quick and glorious victory initially overwhelmed the less posi-tive reactions to the outbreak of war, once the quick and glorious victory failed to mate-rialise the public mood turned progressively darker. As Gerhard A. Ritter and Klaus Tenfelde have observed in their mammoth account of the condition of German work-ers in the Empire, 'seldom do social-historical caesura allow themselves to be fixed so clearly as for the year 1914'.[4] To which may be added (and perhaps even more impor-tantly), psychological-historical caesura as well.

With the outbreak of world war, the pursuit of which required the mobilization of the whole of society, the mass of the German people no longer could be excluded from or marginalized in political life; the old order, in which government remained largely insulated from popular representation, was not going to emerge from the war intact. The problem of how to integrate the German people into German political life sur-faced in wartime discussion about reforming the (Prussian three-class) franchise, the participation of the trade-union leadership in drafting and operating the Auxiliary Service Law of 1916, the Peace Resolution passed by a majority of the Reichstag in July 1917, the mobilization of popular annexationist opinion with the Vaterlandspartei in 1917, and the mounting social and industrial unrest of 1917 and 1918. The old order proved woefully inadequate to deal with the new challenge. The Kaiser was marginal-ized from government and military planning, and by late 1918 had become so loathed that abdication and flight formed his only remaining option; the civil administration had abdicated responsibility to the military, which with the declaration of war had taken over domestic administration in accordance with the Prussian Law of Siege of 4 June 1851 and which tried and failed to subordinate the German economy completely to military needs with the 'Hindenburg programme' of 1916. Failure to manage the wartime economy in a manner regarded as either efficient or fair, while millions of men were being slaughtered on the battlefield, brought the political system into disrepute. The basic political question put on the table by wartime mobilization and its failure was: what would take its place?

The course and conduct of Germany's First World War made it difficult, and finally impossible, to come up with an answer which might have preserved political stability and social cohesion. Germany's pursuit of war exacerbated existing social, economic and political divisions, and thus undermined chances for achieving political stability in the aftermath of the conflict. Obviously, losing the war did not help, but given the unrealistic expectations which had been aroused and the wartime sacrifices which had been demanded, it is difficult to imagine *any* post-war settlement which the German people generally would have regarded as satisfactory. (The case of Italy, which achieved first its 'mutilated victory' and then Fascism, certainly suggests that victory would not necessarily have led to stable democracy.) The *leitmotiv* of Germany's war was not political or spiritual unity in the sense of some 'spirit of 1914' or 'front community'; it was division. The conduct of the war exacerbated conflicts between government and people, between the civil authorities and the military, between front and home front, between rich and poor, between producers and consumers, between employers and employees, between town and country. Failure to achieve quick victory and mounting casualties and suffering made the issue of war aims all the more difficult and divisive, leading on the one hand to the formation and rapid expansion of the radically annexationist Vaterlandspartei and on the other to the split of the Social Democratic Party, and provoked mounting social and industrial unrest, a 'covert military strike' involving soldiers who shirked dangerous military service in their hundreds of thousands from the spring of 1918, and, finally, revolution.

Parliamentary government – the great goal of the revolutionaries of 1848 – was inaugurated in Germany on 28 October 1918, when the Reichstag passed a law stipulating that henceforth the Reich government was dependent upon the confidence of the parliament. By the time the Kaiser abdicated and fled to Holland, Germany already had had effective parliamentary government for over a month – in the form of the government of Prince Max von Baden, which rested on majority support in the Reichstag rather than the confidence of the Emperor. Yet the depth of the social and political divisions which had grown since 1914 was such that when Germany's military rulers Paul von Hindenburg and Erich Ludendorff – realizing that the war was lost and that Germany needed a parliamentary government in order to negotiate with the Allies – opened the door to a genuine parliamentary system, the change was almost superfluous. Indeed, on the same day that Germany finally formally achieved parliamentary government, 28 October 1918, the first naval mutiny began in Wilhelmshaven. Political reform very quickly gave way to political revolution.

The divisions exacerbated by the war not only undermined the imperial political system; they also constituted an extraordinarily difficult and damaging legacy for the democratic system put into place following defeat in 1918. Four aspects of the emergence of democracy from the 'German revolution' proved particularly important for its subsequent development and demise:

- The precipitate collapse of the old regime meant that political power essentially fell into the laps of the Majority Social Democrats around Friedrich Ebert, who were far from being enthusiastic revolutionaries and who found themselves having to take responsibility for the mess left behind by their predecessors. This, of course, was essentially what Ludendorff had had in mind when, on 29 September, he admitted the game was up, demanded that Germany seek an armistice on the basis of Wilson's 14 Points, and urged the formation of a government with majority support in the Reichstag. Instead of those who had led Germany into war and left her defeated and bankrupt being blamed for the unrest which followed the end of the war, it was the unwilling revolutionaries of November 1918 who became identified with the disorder which accompanied the birth of democracy.
- The collapse of the old regime in the autumn of 1918 and the revolution which gave birth to the Weimar Republic were in large measure a consequence of war weariness and military collapse. As the great mass of Germany's soldiers knew well, once it became clear that victory was not on the cards, the only way to get out alive was to jettison the Kaiser and capitulate to the Allies. And this is what they did: when the final military collapse came, the navy mutinied and the army disintegrated, and the one thing of which the old army remained capable in November and December 1918 was carrying out its own demobilization. This was the military reality behind the famous 'Ebert-Groener Pact' – initiated on 10 November 1918, when General Wilhelm Groener, who had been named Ludendorff's successor as Chief Quartermaster General on 29 October, telephoned the new Chancellor Friedrich Ebert and promised the army's support for the new government provided the new government oppose left-wing radicalism. Thus, at the moment of its birth, the new democratic political system did not have a reliable armed force at its disposal.
- The financial and economic problems left behind by the war were colossal, yet their dimensions were not fully appreciated by a war-weary, impoverished, fed-up population which looked to peace and to a new democratic government for rapid improvements. The German people did not understand that the task of Germany's post-war government, whatever its composition or constitution, would be less to distribute the material benefits of peace than to distribute poverty. In the event this was done by taking the oft-trodden economic path of least resistance chosen by weak governments: inflation. Whether or not the choice of such a path was avoidable (and Niall Ferguson, in the following chapter, asserts that it was), it was a response to an extraordinarily difficult political predicament. One of main burdens which the new democratic system faced was the accumulation of unrealistic popular expectations – hardly a sound basis for successful democratic government.
- From the outset the new governmental system lacked the support of a large proportion of the German population, many of whom had been shocked by defeat and rev-

olution, still felt loyalty to the Kaiser, regretted the crumbling of the rigid social and political lines of authority embodied in the imperial system, and refused to accept the legitimacy of the new regime. Thus, from the moment of its birth, the first successful attempt to establish a governmental system in Germany on the basis of popular sovereignty was burdened by the fact that a large proportion of the German people did not recognize its legitimacy.

Against such an unpromising background, Germany's new political masters generally opted for continuity rather than change, and in the crucial months after the November Revolution (and before the Weimar constitution was drafted), key decisions were reached which shaped the Weimar Republic for the whole of its short life. The first was the decision in effect to maintain the existing state administrative structure. The assumption of power by the 'Council of People's Representatives' in November 1918 notwithstanding, and despite the radical changes instituted with regard to labour relations (including the abolition of the restrictive *Gesindeordnungen* governing agricultural workers), the predominant tendency in German government during 1918–19 was continuity. The November Revolution was a revolution in which senior civil servants continued to run their departments with the agreement of the provisional government and in which, although the police momentarily disappeared from view, local government officials remained at their posts (and, in the months which followed easily marginalized the 'council movement').

The second key decision was to postpone, which essentially meant to reject, a radical restructuring of the economy. After state controls had provoked such hostility during wartime, it was unlikely that extending state direction of the economy would win widespread support. Furthermore, the economic demobilization, combined with the frightening shortages of food and fuel and the continuing blockade pursued by the victorious Allies, undercut the case for structural change; the needs of the moment appeared too pressing to allow for experiments whose outcome was uncertain. On 15 November 1918, a few days after the Kaiser's abdication, a key decision was reached when leaders of industry and the socialist trade unions signed the Stinnes-Legien Agreement: the employers conceded trade-union recognition and the eight-hour day while the trade unions implicitly abandoned demands for wholesale nationalization and a socialist transformation of the economy. This presaged the main outlines of Weimar economic policy: preservation of the capitalist system, with grudging acceptance of the interests of labour when necessary. Agreement by employers and unions and the opting for pragmatic emergency measures rather than a fundamental restructuring effectively postponed any possible socialization until after the National Assembly elections of 19 January 1919. These elections resulted in a majority for democratic parliamentary government, not for socialism: the Majority Social Democrats received 37.9 per cent of the vote, and the Independent Social Democrats 7.6 per cent. Henceforth if Germany was going to be governed democratically, it was not going to be socialist.

The third area of decision concerned the constitutional framework. This too was largely fixed before the Weimar constitution was ratified, or even written. Just two days after the National Assembly convened in Weimar at the beginning of February – Berlin was considered too dangerous a venue following the Spartacist uprising in the capital during January – the Reich government submitted a bill 'Concerning the Provisional Exercise of Political Power'. Two days later, on 10 February 1919, the National Assembly passed it, and thus confirmed the essential constitutional outlines of the Weimar Republic: the National Assembly was empowered to adopt both a new constitution and 'other urgent national laws' (i.e. it could act as a legislature); the individual states were represented in an upper house; and a Reich president, who was responsible for conducting government business, was to be elected by the National Assembly and in turn was to appoint a cabinet which needed to possess the confidence of the Assembly. As Eberhard Kolb has pointed out, 'while all these arrangements were designated "provisional", in practice the basic structure of the constitution – with the Reichstag, president and cabinet – was thus predetermined before formal discussion about the constitution had begun.'[5]

In parallel with the political arrangements which emerged in the months following the November Revolution, the Weimar constitution was far from being the constitution of a socialist republic. It was essentially a liberal document, written largely by Hugo Preuß, a leading left-liberal jurist whom Ebert named as state secretary in the Department of the Interior in November 1918 and who became Reich Minister of the Interior from January 1919. However, it did not reflect a single, consistent picture of how a society was or should be governed and structured. Rather, it was, at once, a stirring declaration of democratic principles and a contradictory collection of compromises which reflected the divisions which characterized German politics. The main areas of compromise were:

- Centralism/federalism. Originally the framers of the Weimar constitution had hoped to make a radical break with the Prussian-dominated federal structure of the Empire and to construct a more strongly centralized, unitary state. This would have meant the break-up of Prussia and the creation of a very different set of administrative subdivisions of the Reich. However, the various state governments were able to mobilize effectively against this change. Many of their old prerogatives indeed were abolished: Bavaria and Württemberg no longer could maintain their own postal and railway administrations and, most importantly, the military became a central government (as opposed to essentially Prussian) institution. (The Reichswehr thus became the first *German* – as opposed to Prussian or Bavarian – army in modern German history.) But the *Länder* retained considerable executive powers with regard to the courts, education and the police.
- Parliamentary/presidential government. The Weimar constitution essentially combined parliamentary and presidential democracy. On the one hand, the Reichstag was to be the central institution of government, the expression of the sovereign

people's will and the organ responsible for legislation. On the other hand, and partly to offset fears that a parliament with a socialist majority (which never materialized) might become dominant, the Reich president was given considerable powers: supreme command of the armed forces, the power to appoint and dismiss governments as well as to dissolve the Reichstag, and (in accordance with Article 48 of the constitution) the power to rule by decree, bypassing the Reichstag, in the event of a national emergency.

- Public/private ownership. The Weimar constitution effectively looked both ways on the question of property ownership. In the articles on basic rights (Articles 109–64) the constitution guaranteed the economic status quo and the right to private property. At the same time, however, it provided for the possibility of taking private concerns into public ownership.
- Church/state. Here too the Weimar constitution looked in two directions at once. On the one hand, it reflected long-standing liberal and social-democratic desires by stating that there was to be 'no state church'. On the other hand, however, the hopes of radical anti-clerics – such as the Independent Social Democrat Adolf Hoffmann, who as head of the Prussian Culture Ministry in late November 1918 banned religious education from schools and provoked vociferous protest – were rejected, and important points about church privileges and religious instruction in the schools were conceded.

The constitutional system put into place in 1918 and 1919 was thus a compromise, which reflected the social and ideological divisions of the country and which itself was compromised in the years which followed.[6] The same may be said for the first parliamentary government, which was formed after the National Assembly elections: a coalition of the Majority Social Democrats (with seven members in the new cabinet, including Chancellor Philipp Scheidemann and Reichswehr Minister Gustav Noske), the left liberals of the DDP (with three cabinet members, including Interior Minister Hugo Preuß) and the Catholic Centre (the Christian People's Party, with three cabinet members, including Matthias Erzberger, Minister without Portfolio, who was responsible for the Armistice negotiations). (The new Foreign Minister, Count Ulrich von Brockdorff-Rantzau, had no party affiliation.) The three parties which comprised the 'Weimar coalition' each entered government with different motives: the Social Democrats wanted to defend the gains, as they saw them, of the revolution, and to ensure a strong position for organized labour; the Liberals wanted to support parliamentary democracy and act as a brake on socialist initiatives; and the Centre was concerned to protect private property and to prevent nationalization, to protect the position of the Catholic Church, and to preserve the federal structure of the Reich. What united all three parties was concern to prevent further radicalization.

It may be easy, with the benefit of hindsight, to criticize the compromises which created the shaky foundations of the Weimar state. However, the challenges facing Germany's new rulers were considerable: the sudden, and largely unplanned demobi-

Illustration 12.1 *The Pillars of Society* by Georg Grosz (1926): biting satire illustrative of the way in which the fledgling Republic was attacked from both left and right, for different reasons

lization of roughly six million soldiers who flooded into Germany between November 1918 and January 1919; the abrupt termination of wartime production; the huge over-hang of war-related debt; catastrophic shortages of coal and food during a period of continued Allied naval blockade; precipitous declines in labour productivity; Polish insurrections which led to most of the provinces of Posen and West Prussia becoming part of the new Polish state; the loss of Alsace-Lorraine and concern that the Allies might dismember Germany; a serious refugee problem as Germans flooded into the Reich from territories lost to France and Poland; and, in early 1919, an upsurge of industrial unrest and radical protest which erupted in serious outbreaks of violence in Berlin, the Ruhr, Munich and a number of other places. Against such a background, it is hardly surprising that the 'Council of People's Representatives', which had assumed provisional responsibility for the Reich government in November 1918, was desperate to keep the wheels of state administration turning, marshal some armed force behind itself and to re-establish order – even if this meant keeping the bureaucracy inherited from the old regime at their desks, vastly overestimating the revolutionary threat and sending in right-wing *Freikorps* units against militant workers. When Gustav Noske took on the role of 'bloodhound' of the revolution and hired the *Freikorps* to suppress real and imagined revolutionary threats to the new government, it was an expression of a deep, at once both understandable and paranoid, concern to re-establish order at a time of extreme uncertainty.

Given the acute difficulties which Germany faced after the First World War, it is hardly surprising that the compromises which framed the establishment of the Weimar Republic soon began to unravel. The German people's search for security and stability was profoundly disappointed.

On the domestic political front, Germany experienced mounting instability. While the collapse of the old regime in November 1918 had been largely free of violence, the same could not be said of the events which followed. On 28 December the three USPD members of the six-man 'Council of People's Representatives' left the provisional government in protest at the suppression of unrest in Berlin by the military. (USPD members left the Prussian government on 3 January 1919.) This was followed by the 'January Uprising' of the revolutionary shop stewards and the newly formed Communist Party (Spartacus League) in Berlin, which was easily and brutally suppressed (and the two leaders of the Spartacists, Rosa Luxemburg and Karl Liebknecht, were murdered). A wave of unrest spread across the country during the first half of 1919, with strikes, open challenges to government authority and, in Bremen and Munich for example, short-lived attempts to set up radical 'council republics'. In March 1920, the military *putsch* engineered by Wolfgang Kapp, the former chairman of the Vaterlandspartei, and General Walther Freiherr von Lüttwitz was defeated by a general strike, but not before armed conflict had broken out in a number of cities and after which tens of thousands of militant workers in the Ruhr formed a ramshackle 'Red Army'. In March 1921 a communist uprising in the central German industrial region around Merseburg was suppressed by police acting effectively as a military

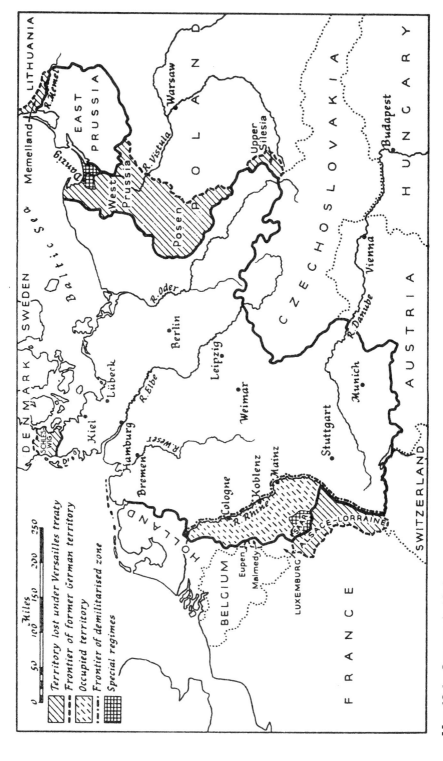

Map 12.1 Germany in 1919

LITHUANIA

EAST
PRUSSIA

R. Memel

Memelland

Danzig

West Prussia

Posen

R. Vistula

Warsaw

Upper
Silesia

POLAND

CZECHOSLOVAKIA

Budapest

HUNGARY

Baltic Sea

SWEDEN

DENMARK

R. Oder

Berlin

Leipzig

Weimar

Vienna

R. Danube

AUSTRIA

Munich

Stuttgart

Kiel

Lübeck

Hamburg

Bremen

R. Weser

R. Elbe

SCHLES-
WIG

HOLLAND

Cologne

Koblenz

R. Rhine

Mainz

SAAR

ALSACE-LORRAINE

Eupen

Malmedy

LUXEMBURG

BELGIUM

SWITZERLAND

FRANCE

Miles

0   50   100   150   200   250

Territory lost under Versailles treaty

Frontier of former German territory

Occupied territory

Frontier of demilitarised zone

Special regimes

force. Three armed uprisings of Polish insurgents, in 1919, 1920 and 1921, punctuated the history of post-war Upper Silesia. Political demonstrations frequently ended in violent confrontations. Crime reached epidemic proportions during the post-war and inflationary years. And political life in the early Weimar years was characterized by a large number of political murders: in addition to Luxemburg and Liebknecht in January 1919, among those who fell victim to political assassins was Hugo Haase, the Independent Social Democratic leader who joined Ebert in the 'Council of People's Representatives' in November 1918 and who was shot in front of the Reichstag on 8 October 1919 (and died of his wounds a month later); in August 1921 Matthias Erzberger, the Centre Party politician who had been the driving force behind the Peace Resolution of 1917, who had signed the Versailles Treaty on behalf of the German government in 1919, and who as Finance Minister (from June 1919 to March 1920) had initiated a fundamental reform of Germany's taxation system, was murdered by two members of the right-wing terrorist Organization Consul; and on 24 June 1922 Germany's Foreign Minister, Walther Rathenau, the Jewish industrialist who had organized Germany's war economy, was shot dead as he left his home in Grunewald for the Foreign Office. Altogether, German political life experienced a marked decline in peaceful civilized behaviour in the aftermath of war and revolution.

On the party political front, the apparently broad support for democratic politics indicated in the 1919 National Assembly elections soon faded. Already in the Reichstag elections of June 1920 there emerged a pattern which became a defining characteristic of Weimar politics: parties which accepted governmental responsibility, and thus responsibility for necessarily unpopular decisions, subsequently lost massively at the polls. The SPD lost nearly half its 11.5 million votes (37.9 per cent) in 1919, falling to barely six million (21.7 per cent) in 1920 while the Independent Social Democrats (who had left government) saw their vote mushroom; the DDP lost more than half its 5.6 million votes (18.5 per cent), falling to just over 2.3 million (8.3 per cent); and the Centre Party captured 3.8 million (13.6 per cent), as opposed to the nearly six million (19.7 per cent) which the 'Christian People's Party' had attracted in 1919. With that, the 'Weimar Coalition', which had captured roughly three-quarters of the popular vote at the outset of the Weimar Republic, no longer commanded a majority in parliament. It was never to do so again.

On the economic front, the surprising success of the demobilization was undermined by inflation. In the short term, the post-war German economy appeared to perform rather well, with a rapid decline in unemployment (which virtually disappeared in 1921 and 1922) and a sharp recovery in economic activity. However, these apparent successes had their price. For one thing, sooner or later the government's massive deficit spending had to come to an end, and when it did so, and the inevitable bill had to be paid, the suffering created by a necessarily harsh currency stabilization was considerable. For another, the inflation provoked tension and conflict, not only in economic affairs but also political and social life. Rising prices were a constant source of friction, while price controls also often caused anger. The ramshackle continuation of wartime price controls for agricultural produce, for example, ensured the ongoing hostility of the farming community; rent controls ensured the continuation of a desperate housing shortage; and rapidly rising prices provided a constant stimulus to labour militancy and anger at the marketplace. Two particularly telling indications of the degree to which the inflation undermined Germany's political and social stability are the 'first (and last) major civil servant strike in Germany history' (Andreas Kunz), which occurred in February 1922 (and which the employees lost), and the upsurge in anti-Semitic attacks on businesses, which had its most ugly manifestation in the mob violence against Jewish shops in Breslau on 20 July 1923. The inflation damaged not only the German economy but also the civilized fabric of social and political life.

On the foreign political front, the unrealistic hopes which had accompanied the Armistice – that the Allies would deal generously with a democratic Germany which had jettisoned the Kaiser – were dashed when the draft of the Versailles Treaty was presented to the Germans on 7 May 1919. For once, Germany's political divisions were overcome: all parties were united in rejecting the treaty, and Chancellor Scheidemann dramatically declared that the treaty was unacceptable to the Reich government. However, German protests left the Allies unmoved, and on 16 June the final treaty terms were presented in the form of an ultimatum. The army leadership admitted its inability to prevent an Allied military advance, and, after Scheidemann's government resigned on 20 July rather than sign the treaty, a new SPD-led government (with Gustav Bauer as Chancellor but without DDP members) declared itself willing to accept the Versailles *Diktat*, as it became known in Germany. The treaty did not aim to create a Wilsonian 'peace without victors or vanquished' but rather to ensure that Germany no longer could be a military aggressor and that French security interests would be safeguarded. This meant imposing territorial losses (many of which had already occurred) – Alsace-Lorraine to France, Eupen-Malmedy to Belgium, much of Upper Silesia and most of Posen and West Prussia to Poland, and North Schleswig to Denmark; Germany lost her colonies; the size of the armed forces was limited to 100,000 men, and the manufacture or possession of offensive weapons was prohibited; the Allies occupied strategic bridgeheads across the Rhine, and the Rhineland was demilitarized; and Germany was saddled with (as yet unspecified) reparations. In order to provide a basis for these terms, Germany was compelled, with Article 231 (the notorious 'war-guilt clause'), to admit responsibility for launching the war. Among Germans there was near universal agreement that such treatment was unjust and intolerable – making the Versailles Treaty perhaps the only political issue around which there was widespread agreement in Weimar Germany.

Finally, on the military front, the Reichswehr came to occupy a peculiar position of domestic military dominance and foreign military impotence, which turned old conceptions of the role of the military upside down. Although the German military had disintegrated almost completely in 1918, it was reconstituted remarkably quickly thereafter, only to be sharply reduced in size by the terms of the Versailles Treaty. The reduction in the size of the army, and the concomitant growth of *Freikorps* units which

were called upon to suppress domestic unrest and fight Polish insurrection in the eastern Prussian provinces, meant that, for a crucial period, the German army did not possess a monopoly of armed force in the country. The army response to this situation was
ambivalent. This ambivalence was demonstrated painfully with the Kapp-Lüttwitz
putsch in March 1920, when *Freikorps* commanders attempted to seize power in Berlin
and Defence Minister Noske discovered that there were no army units at his disposal
prepared to suppress the rebellion; the head of the *Truppenamt* (Troop Office – the disguised General Staff), General Hans von Seeckt, announced that it was impossible to
commit troops to the government's defence; and army commanders throughout the
country were prepared to support the right-wing insurgents. Despite its compromised
behaviour in 1920, the Reichswehr was not subsequently harnessed to strict civilian
control, however. Instead, power was consolidated in the hands of von Seeckt, who
emerged during the crisis year of 1923 as the effective arbiter of German domestic politics.

In 1923 the compromises on which the republic initially had been based crumbled,
and behind republican government loomed the spectre of military rule. It was the
Reichswehr which was sent into Saxony and Thuringia in October and November
1923 to subdue their left-wing governments; and when Hitler staged his aborted coup
attempt in Munich on 8/9 November, Ebert proclaimed a state of emergency and
placed executive powers in the hands of von Seeckt, who quickly liquidated the
Munich *putsch* and established central control over the maverick Bavarian Reichswehr.
Yet paradoxically, the moment at which Germany came closest to military rule was
also the moment when its military was at its weakest, for the impotence of the
Reichswehr as a military force had been exposed with brutal clarity when, on 11
January 1923, French and Belgian troops marched unopposed into the Ruhr in order
to secure overdue reparations. The response of the German government to the Ruhr
occupation, passive resistance (subsidized by recourse to the printing press and accompanying the complete destruction of the German currency), was perhaps necessary
given popular opinion, but it offered no way out of the political, economic, diplomatic
and military cul-de-sac into which Germany had marched.

In the autumn of 1923, the Weimar Republic faced a crisis which called its survival
into question and which, as Gerald Feldman has observed, 'threatened the very existence of civil society itself as well as the political order and the integrity of the German
state'.[7] The currency had become completely worthless; the unwillingness of rebellious
German farmers to sell their produce for paper marks threatened the urban population
with starvation; employer–employee relations in industry had broken down; the
French had occupied Germany's most important industrial area, and passive resistance to that occupation was bankrupting the country; economic activity was declining
rapidly, and unemployment was rising; criminality was increasing; social and political
unrest reached a post-war peak; the desperate need of the Reich government for armed
force at its disposal brought Germany close to military dictatorship; and effective government had become possible only through repeated recourse to emergency legislation

which effectively marginalized the Reichstag. Stresemann's Vice-Chancellor, the Socialist Robert Schmidt, was quite candid about this, when he admitted that a 'measure of dictatorship would have to be exercised by the government in order to gain control of the situation'.[8] By the autumn of 1923 there seemed very little of Weimar democracy left.

Yet the republic survived. Why? In part, one might explain the survival by the fact that there was little real alternative. With French troops in Essen, the idea of the Reichswehr openly assuming control of government was not really an option; nor was the installation of a revanchist right-wing regime openly committed to breaking the 'chains' of the Versailles *Diktat*. With the mark totally debauched and complete economic collapse staring Germany's rulers in the face, there was no real alternative but to take the hard decisions about government finance and seek an accommodation with the French which would allow the establishment of a stable currency. The depth of the crises of late 1923 made the politics of the 'republicans of reason' (*Vernunftrepublikaner*) the only viable option. This is not to deny that overcoming the 1923 crisis and the political and economic stabilization of 1923–4 formed a considerable achievement, however. And credit for this achievement is owed first and foremost to Gustav Stresemann, during whose 'hundred days' as Reich Chancellor, from 13 August to 23 November 1923, the difficult and indeed heroic task of stabilization was achieved in the face of unprecedented chaos and without Germany yet slipping into dictatorship.

Stresemann's service to the Weimar Republic during his lengthy tenure as Foreign Minister (beginning in August 1923, when he was also Chancellor, and lasting until his death on 3 October 1929) was no less important than his brief tenure in the Reich Chancellery. In both the short and the medium term, the emergence from crises of 1923 and the subsequent stabilization rested on a settlement of Germany's foreign political position no less than it did on a domestic–political settlement. (Post-war Germany's first great diplomatic coup, the Rapallo Treaty signed with Soviet Russia in April 1922, may have been successful in upsetting the western Allies and in providing a foundation for cooperation between the Reichswehr and the Red Army, but it was no substitute for re-integration with her neighbours to the west.) The two were closely interrelated. An end to the inflation and the restoration of Germany's financial position rested on settling the reparations issue, which in turn rested on coming to terms with the French – in effect recognizing French security interests and coming to terms with the fact that Germany had lost the war. By demonstrating the bankruptcy of a policy of intransigence and unwillingness to face the consequences of wartime defeat, the hyperinflation and the Ruhr occupation in effect paved the way for a provisional settlement of the reparations issue. The repayment plan drawn up by the commission under the chairmanship of the American banker Charles Dawes opened the door to massive foreign, largely American, investment which helped fuel Germany's economic upturn in the mid-1920s; to the Locarno Treaty of 1925, which provided a framework for the peaceful settlement of disputes between Germany and her western neighbours and ended Germany's foreign political isolation; to the Allied military evacuation of the Ruhr; and to Germany's entry into the League of Nations in September 1926 as a permanent council member.

Notwithstanding the advantages which reaching agreement with France brought to Germany, Stresemann attracted criticism from the right for in effect accepting the conditions of the hated Versailles Treaty. The fragility of the foreign political *rapprochement* achieved during the mid-1920s became apparent when, in 1929, the ratification of what was to be a permanent settlement to the reparations issue, prepared under the chairmanship of Owen D. Young (chairman of the board of the American General Electric Company), provoked a storm of protest in Germany and provided a focus around which the radical right could coalesce in a vicious plebiscite campaign against the 'enslavement of the German people' allegedly brought about by the Young plan. Although ratification of the Young plan made possible the final evacuation by the French military of the Rhineland on 30 June 1930, and even if, as Steven Schuker has claimed, once all payments and defaults on debts are tallied the Americans in effect paid 'reparations' to Germany, the benefits of the settlement were far from apparent to many Germans.

From 1924 until the end of the decade, the Weimar Republic enjoyed a measure of domestic social and political stability. These were the republic's 'golden years' of relative stabilization. The unrest and violence which had characterized public life in Germany between 1919 and 1923 ebbed. The political extremes of left and right were the big losers in the Reichstag elections of December 1924, while the parties which supported the republic – the SPD, DDP, DVP and the Centre – saw their representation in the Reichstag increase; the SPD-led Weimar coalition continued to offer Prussia, which comprised roughly two-thirds of the Reich, stable democratic government firmly committed to the republic; the conservative right, initially resolutely hostile to the republic, appeared to have become reconciled, as the conservative DNVP joined a Reich government coalition for the first time in January 1925 and began to play by the rules of the republican game; and Friedrich Ebert's successor as (and first popularly elected) Reich president, Field Marshal Paul von Hindenburg – while bringing a conservative, military-minded approach to the office of head of state – acted within the constitution and by his presence appeared to reconcile many conservative Germans to a republic which had been born in defeat and revolution. Thus supporters of Weimar democracy appeared to have had some good reasons to take heart when, in the Reichstag elections of May 1928, the Nazis were able to gather a mere 2.6 per cent of the popular vote and the SPD emerged as the party with by far the largest vote and was able, in June, to form a Reich government under the leadership of Hermann Müller. To some extent, the stability and security which had been blown apart after July 1914 appeared to have been reconstituted or replaced.

Nevertheless, all was not well even during the Weimar Republic's brief sunny spell. The German electorate had not entirely been converted to the republican cause. The extreme racialist right, although subdued after its support declined in the second

Reichstag elections of 1924, had not gone away; the Communists continued to attract the support of millions of voters; the conservative DNVP, although participating in Reich government coalitions from the beginning of 1925, had not completely jettisoned its anti-republican disposition (which would re-surface with a vengeance after 1928); and the inflation and stabilization had left a residue of bitterness among hundreds of thousands of people who had lost out and blamed the Weimar 'system' for their plight. Once the clouds of economic crisis began again to gather over Weimar Germany, the cracks in the democratic polity would widen dangerously.

The economic and political stabilization realized in the mid-1920s gave scope for the development of what has become known as the Weimar 'welfare state'. The achievements of the Weimar Republic during the period of 'relative prosperity' (1924–28) were impressive, especially after the turbulence of the republic's early years. Living standards, which had plummeted during the final stages of the hyperinflation, rose considerably. Housing construction, which had virtually come to a halt during the war and had not fully recovered during the inflation (when rent controls acted as a great disincentive to building new dwellings), rose substantially (with considerable state financial involvement) (see Table 12.1). Municipal governments undertook impressive public works schemes, which gave their cities new airports, exhibition centres, housing estates and swimming pools. On 16 July 1927 the crowning achievement of the Weimar 'welfare state', the 'Act on Labour Exchanges and Unemployment Insurance' was enacted, to cover the major area left uncovered by Bismarck's social insurance programmes of the 1880s: by extending statutory unemployment insurance to roughly 17.25 million employees, this scheme embraced more people than did such insurance in any other country.

However, as Werner Abelshauser has pointed out, 'the Weimar Republic was an overstrained welfare state',[9] and the achievements of the years of 'relative stability' became damaging liabilities once the depression arrived. The 1927 unemployment insurance legislation had been enacted at a time when unemployment was quite low, and the envisaged level of employee and employer contributions allowed for the support of about 800,000 unemployed; a further 600,000 could have been supported from

Table 12.1 Housing construction in Germany, 1919–33 (showing net increase in dwellings)

1919	56,714	1924	106,502	1929	317,682
1920	103,092	1925	178,930	1930	310,971
1921	134,223	1926	205,793	1931	233,648
1922	146,615	1927	288,635	1932	141,265
1923	118,333	1928	309,762	1933	178,039

Source: Statistisches Jahrbuch für das Deutsche Reich 1924/25 (1925), pp. 101–2; *Statistisches Jahrbuch für das Deutsche Reich 1926 (1926),* p. 89; *Statistisches Jahrbuch für das Deutsche Reich 1934 (1934),* p. 155.

Illustration 12.2 A school class in the farming village of Bonfeld (in Württemburg, in south-western Germany), in about 1928. Note the size of the class, which was typical in Weimar Germany, and that a number of children were attending school without any shoes. Most of the boys in the picture were killed in the Second World War

a need fund of the Reich Office for Unemployment Benefits and Unemployment Insurance. However, as we know, unemployment soon far surpassed these levels. Within a year the unemployment insurance scheme was up against its financial limits, and by 1930 the critical financial position of the Reich Unemployment Office meant that a rise in contributions was urgently required – the issue which precipitated the split between the SPD and DVP which destroyed the last truly parliamentary Weimar government.

The unhappy history of unemployment insurance points to a fundamental problem which plagued the Weimar Republic: the changed relationship of the German people to the German state which had emerged from the First World War. Popular expectations of what the state could and should provide for its citizens outstripped what the Weimar system was able to deliver. The resulting bitterness, and its political ramifications, may be illustrated well by the case of the war dependants. The war had left behind hundreds of thousands of widows, orphans and invalids, who looked to the state for support. Not only did this cast a shadow over the lives of many people; the resulting pensions burden also put enormous demands on government finances. In Germany, for example, Robert Whalen has claimed that 40 per cent of national (i.e. Reich) government expenditure went towards paying war-related pensions. Yet, despite all the money paid to war widows and invalids, almost everyone involved was left dissatisfied: on the one hand, war victims who felt that they were being inadequately compensated; on the other, officials who saw government expenditure spinning out of control. Not surprisingly, attempts to limit such expenditure provoked angry protest, particularly in the early 1930s when the economic crisis reduced government revenues and added to pressure to cut expenditure. Between 1928 and 1933 the budget for war victims' pensions was cut by one-third, leaving hundreds of thousands of people – who had been promised during the war that 'You can be sure of the thanks of the Fatherland' – deeply angry. Yet there was no democratic way to square the circle. Neither the funds nor the parliamentary majorities existed on which to base taxation and spending policies which might have satisfied war victims. Expectations of what the German state could and should provide had been raised to such an extent that they could not be met.

This suggests that even during the years of 'relative stabilization' all was not well with the Weimar Republic. The profound social, economic, political and psychological destabilization which had set in with the First World War had not really been overcome; underlying economic problems remained, and the relative political stability of Weimar's 'golden years' rested on shaky foundations. This was particularly apparent in the German countryside, where a combination of high farm indebtedness, low prices for agricultural produce and high taxes was driving farm producers into bankruptcy and political radicalism – a disturbing sign of which was the terror campaign of rural radicals in Schleswig-Holstein in 1928. No less damaging was the fact that participation in government did not cement German conservatism into republican politics. As the two liberal parties – the DDP and the DVP – had found in the early years of the republic, the conservative DNVP discovered that its reward for accepting the responsibilities of government was a sharp decline in popular support: compared with the result in December 1924, the DNVP lost nearly a third of its vote in May 1928. Consequently the party returned to radical opposition to the republic. Under the intransigent leadership of media magnate Alfred Hugenberg, who became chairman of the DNVP in October 1928, Germany's conservatives set out on a path which led to the formation of a common front with the Nazis in the campaign against the Young plan in 1929 and in the Harzburg Front in 1931, and to the formation of a coalition government with Adolf Hitler in 1933. And while the two liberal parties saw their popular support dwindle and the conservatives lost roughly a third of their supporters, many voters turned to special-interest parties – betraying a lack of faith in a democratic politics which focused on the common good.

These developments, and the rapid growth of the Nazi Party from 1929 onwards (discussed by Jill Stephenson in Chapter 15 below), reflected a decomposition of popular support for traditional elite politics. This was accompanied by a crisis of state and government of unparalleled proportions in the early 1930s. On 27 March 1930, with the collapse of the coalition government led by Hermann Müller, the Weimar parliamentary system effectively ceased to function. Its successor, put together on 30 March by the Centre Party politician Heinrich Brüning, rested not on a coalition in the Reichstag but instead depended ultimately on the confidence of the Reich president and his willingness to sign emergency legislation as sanctioned under Article 48 of the constitution. Following the elections of 14 September 1930, when the NSDAP captured over six million votes to become the second largest party in the Reichstag, forming any government based on a stable parliamentary coalition became almost impossible. Brüning faced a rapidly deteriorating economic situation and mounting political unrest; the Social Democrats found there was little they could do but to tolerate Brüning's attempts to deal with the mounting financial difficulties with deeper and deeper expenditure cuts, for fear of opening the door to a government even further to the right and in order to protect its own 'Weimar' coalition (with the Centre Party) in Prussia; and the conviction was growing that the mounting problems facing Germany could not be tackled within a strictly democratic framework.

There has been much debate about Brüning's intentions – whether he was in effect a 'heroic' figure desperately struggling against economic catastrophe and political radicalism, or whether he was concerned to use the crisis to reshape government in a more authoritarian direction and pursued policies which made a bad situation even worse. Much of this debate revolves around the economic policies of the Brüning government, which are discussed in the following chapter by Niall Ferguson. However, two points are worth stressing here.

First, whatever his motives and however limited his room for manoeuvre, Brüning's was an essentially authoritarian project. Effectively removing the Reichstag from the business of government and undercutting the autonomy of local government, which was overwhelmed by the effects of the economic slump, were not accidental or unfortunate side effects of an idealistic attempt to preserve Weimar democracy. After the collapse of the Müller government, it was fairly clear that there would be no going back to the political system created through the compromises of 1918–19 or the settlements of 1923–24.

Second, during his period as Chancellor, Brüning's focus remained very largely upon foreign policy, in particular the goal of freeing Germany from reparations. For Brüning, harsh emergency measures were not only a (perhaps unavoidable) means by which to cope with an economic and fiscal crisis of unprecedented proportions, nor were his policies only an attempt to instrumentalize the crisis in order to achieve constitutional reform of a more authoritarian mould. (In his memoirs, published in 1970, Brüning revealed that if he had had his way constitutional reform would have ended with a monarchist restoration).[10] They also were designed to demonstrate to the Allies that the reparations burden was intolerable, and thereby to get the burden of reparations lifted entirely – that is, to achieve a major foreign–policy success, to take a decisive step towards undoing the Versailles Treaty, to win a major economic victory, and thus to gain popularity at a single stroke.

That is not quite how things turned out. The reparations burden was indeed lifted: in July 1931, with the Hoover Moratorium, international debt payments were suspended for one year; and a year later, at the Lausanne Conference of June–July 1932, Germany's reparations were cancelled. However, Brüning – who had gambled his own and his country's future to achieve this victory – did not survive in office long enough to reap the benefits of this success. Instead, that fell to his successor, Franz von Papen. However, von Papen's right-wing 'cabinet of barons' faced problems of such magnitude – mass unemployment, a rising tide of political extremism and violence, and an almost complete breakdown of parliamentary business once the Nazi Party had emerged from the elections of July 1932 with 230 Reichstag deputies – that the victory in Lausanne was hardly sufficient to tip the scales. Von Papen, whose power rested solely on his ability to gain approval for emergency legislation from the aged Reich President and who suspended the SPD-led government of Prussia on 20 July, aimed for authoritarian government in the place of the discredited democratic system. However, his authoritarian project had negligible popular support, and his short, turbulent period in the Reich Chancellery demonstrated the impossibility of establishing stable government without support of – or against – the mass of the German people. Similar lessons could be drawn from the unhappy history of von Papen's successor, Reichswehr General Kurt von Schleicher, whose attempts to gather support across the political spectrum – from the NSDAP's organizational leader Gregor Strasser to the Christian and socialist trade unions – came to nothing and who lasted in office less than two months before making way for the coalition headed by Adolf Hitler.

The attempts during the early 1930s to use the crisis to replace Weimar democracy with a more authoritarian state structure misfired, for a number of reasons. First, they aroused little popular support, and, short of a staging a successful military coup, it was probably impossible to impose a system of rule against the wishes of virtually the entire population. Second, the Reichswehr was ultimately unwilling to intervene actively to impose authoritarian rule. That is to say, the army wanted to develop its armaments programmes and lay the ground for future expansion, not get involved in a domestic civil war. Third, the problems facing German governments in 1931 and 1932 probably were beyond the ability of *any* government to master. Not until the economic cycle had begun to turn (as we now know it did towards the end of 1932), Germans' expectations had been reduced, and foreign–political limitations to Germany's room for manoeuvre had been removed, could a government hope to put a new political settlement into place. Thus, the achievement of Brüning, von Papen and von Schleicher essentially was to remove important obstacles to the establishment of a Nazi dictatorship bent on repression at home and expansion abroad. By eliminating reparations from the foreign-policy agenda, they helped to remove an important constraint on the foreign policy of their successor; by demonstrating the bankruptcy of authoritarian elite politics without substantial popular support, they paved the way for an extraordinarily dangerous authoritarian populism; by failing to impose their own solutions they put themselves in a weak position to prevent Hitler from imposing his – with substantial popular support – in 1933.

It is a remarkable feature of the collapse of the Weimar Republic that the left played so marginal a role. As German democracy withered, neither the Social Democrats nor the Communists really offered a practicable alternative. For the Communists, who drew on the jobless and the inhabitants of urban slums for support and whose electoral support grew as the economic crisis deepened, apparent strength was in fact testimony to the political weakness of a German working class stricken by mass unemployment. The real function of the KPD consisted of (1) providing a spectre of unrest and red revolution which frightened respectable Germans, and (2) splitting the left. The division of the left did not so much serve to prevent successful resistance to German fascism; for such resistance to have overcome the combined forces of the Nazi Party and the German state even the combined SPD and KPD probably would have been too weak. Rather the division effectively prevented the SPD from making the overtures to a middle-class electorate which might have permitted its successful transformation into a 'people's party' (as finally occurred in the Federal Republic), for fear of losing working-class support to the Communists. For the Social Democrats, who drew support from among the 'respectable' working class, the economic crisis undercut what was left of their once powerful position in Weimar politics. As the main pillar of the original Weimar coalition, the dominant coalition partner in Prussia, and allied with Germany's largest trade-union movement, the SPD had been a serious contender for political power. But it was precisely this which made the established elites so determined to keep the Social Democrats out of government in the early 1930s. Clinging to their faith in legality as the republic disintegrated, watching their electoral support dwindle while mass unemployment cut the ground from under the trade unions, the SPD became a helpless onlooker as the crisis deepened.

With the party system in disarray, the economy spiralling downward, the left crippled, governments in Berlin lacking parliamentary or popular support, and the social and political culture corroded by a breakdown in civilized behaviour, the grave of the Weimar Republic had already been dug by the time Adolf Hitler was handed the keys to the Reich Chancellery on 30 January 1933. The Nazis did not so much destroy the Weimar Republic as take advantage of its prior decomposition. The failure to achieve a solid democratic stabilization during the 1920s had left an opening for a radical, anti-democratic political movement which could appeal across the class, confessional and regional divides which hitherto had characterized German politics. Once the depression struck with full force, the ground had been well prepared for the NSDAP to become the largest political party that Germany had ever seen.

What the Nazis promised was an end to the divisions which characterized German society and politics – a 'folk community' (*Volksgemeinschaft*) in the place of a divided class society, an end to paralysis of government and to disorder (which was provoked in no small measure by the Nazis themselves). That is to say, the Nazis appeared to offer an end to the 'times in which conditions that were thought to be unshakeable and eternal all are called into question', when 'the feeling spreads that the ground is being pulled out from under people's feet', when Germans saw themselves 'time and again on the edge of the abyss and catastrophe'. The tragedy, of course, is that in fact the Nazis offered no such thing. Instead they pulled the ground from under people's feet more effectively than any political movement has done before or since, and drove Germany – and eventually the entire European continent – headlong into catastrophe.

Notes:

1. Niekisch, Ernst, *Gewagtes Leben* (1958), pp. 173–4.
2. The directive was published subsequently in the Berlin press: *B.Z. am Mittag*, Nr. 186, 9 August 1914: 'Ein schwäbischer Dienstbefehl'. Reproduced in Bernd Ulrich and Benjamin Ziemann, eds., *Frontalltag im Ersten Weltkrieg. Wahn und Wirklichkeit* (1994), p. 29.
3. Thus Gordon A. Craig in his *Germany 1866–1945* (1978), p. 339.
4. Ritter, Gerhard A. and Tenfelde, Klaus, *Arbeiter im Deutschen Kaiserreich 1871 bis 1914* (1992), p. 3.
5. Kolb, Eberhard, *The Weimar Republic* (1988), p. 17.
6. This formulation, 'the compromised compromise', comes from Lutz Niethammer, *Bürgerliche Gesellschaft in Deutschland, Historische Einblicke, Fragen, Perspektiven* (1990).
7. Feldman, Gerald D., *The Great Disorder, Politics, Economics and Society in the German Inflation 1914–1924* (1933), p. 699.
8. Quoted in Feldman, *The Great Disorder*, p. 700.
9. Abelshauser, Werner, 'Die Weimarer Republik – Ein Wohlfahrtsstaat?', in Werner Abelshauser, ed., *Die Weimarer Republik als Wohlfahrtsstaat. Zum Verhältnis von Wirtschafts- und Sozialpolitik in der Industriegesellschaft* (1987), p. 31.
10. Brüning, Heinrich, *Memoiren 1918–1934* (1970), p. 194.

Select bibliography

Bessel, Richard, *Germany after the First World War* (1993).

Bessel, Richard, and Feuchtwanger, E. J., eds., *Social Change and Political Development in Weimar Germany* (1981).

Carsten, F. L., *The Reichswehr and Politics, 1918–1933* (1966).

Childers, Thomas, ed., *The Formation of the Nazi Constituency, 1918–1933* (1986).

Evans, Richard J., and Geary, Dick, eds., *The German Unemployed. Experiences and Consequences of Mass Unemployment from the Weimar Republic to the Third Reich* (1987).

Feldman, Gerald D., *Army, Industry, and Labor in Germany 1914–1918* (1966).

Feldman, Gerald D., *The Great Disorder. Politics, Economics and Society in the German Inflation 1914–1924* (1993).

Feuchtwanger, E. J., *From Weimar to Hitler: Germany, 1918–33* (1993).

Fowkes, Ben, *Communism in Germany under the Weimar Republic* (1984).

Fritzsche, Peter, *Rehearsals for Fascism. Populism and Political Mobilization in Weimar Germany* (1990).

Harsch, Donna, *German Social Democracy and the Rise of Nazism* (1993).

Heiber, Helmut, *The Weimar Republic* (1993).

Kolb, Eberhard, *The Weimar Republic* (1988).

Kershaw, Ian, ed., *Weimar: Why Did German Democracy Fail?* (1990).

Kocka, Jürgen, *Facing Total War: German Society 1914–1918* (1984).

Kunz, Andreas, *Civil Servants and the Politics of Inflation in Germany 1914–1924* (1986).

James, Harold, *The German Slump. Politics and Economics 1924–1936* (1986).

Jones, Larry Eugene, *German Liberalism and the Dissolution of the Weimar Party System 1918–1933* (1988).

Lee, Marshall, and Michalka, Wolfgang, *German Foreign Policy 1917–1933: Continuity or Break?* (1987).

Lee, W. R., and Rosenhaft, Eve, eds., *The State and Social Change in Germany, 1880–1980* (1990).

Moeller, Robert G., *German Peasants and Agrarian Politics, 1914–1924. The Rhineland and Westphalia* (1986).

Mommsen, Hans, *The Rise and Fall of Weimar Democracy* (1996).

Mommsen, Hans, *From Weimar to Auschwitz: Essays in German History* (1991).

Mommsen, W. J., ed., *The Emergence of the Welfare State in Britain and Germany* (1981).

Nicholls, A. J., *Weimar and the Rise of Hitler* (3rd edn, 1991).

Peukert, Detlev J. K., *The Weimar Republic. The Crisis of Classical Modernity* (1991).

Schuker, Stephen A., *American 'Reparations' to Germany 1919–33: Implications for the Third-World Debt Crisis* (1988).

Stachura, Peter D., ed., *Unemployment and the Great Depression in Weimar Germany* (1986).

Stargardt, Nicholas, *The German Idea of Militarism. Radical and Socialist Critics 1866–1914* (1994).

Whalen, Robert Weldon, *Bitter Wounds. German Victims of the Great War, 1914–1939* (1984).

13

The German inter-war economy: political choice versus economic determinism

Niall Ferguson

Berthold Brecht and Kurt Weill's musical *The Rise and Fall of the City of Mahagonny* received its premier in Leipzig on 9 March 1930. Unemployment in Germany at that date, according to the contemporary figures based on trade union members, stood at 20 per cent. The annual inflation rate was negative: the cost of living had fallen by around 4 per cent in the previous 12 months. Output in most sectors of the economy had been falling for around a year and a half. The German economy was in the grip of a deep recession, with no sign of recovery in view. Yet only seven months before, the German government had been obliged to accept the recommendation of the Young committee that it should continue to pay annual reparations to the victors of the First World War until 1988. The sum transferred as reparations in 1930 alone was equivalent to around 2.4 per cent of national income, rather more than the entire German trade surplus for the year. It is in this context of deepening economic gloom that Mahagonny's nihilistic 'Alabama Song' is perhaps best seen:

> Oh, show us the way to the next little dollar,
> Oh, don't ask why, oh, don't ask why,
> For if we do not find the next little dollar,
> I tell you we must die, I tell you we must die.

With its jarring rhythms and discordant melody, the 'Alabama Song' is, of course, one of the 'classic' products of Weimar culture, and deserves its place in cultural histories of inter-war Germany. But the song is of interest to economic historians too, for there is an influential line of argument which maintains that the rise and fall not only of the city of Mahagonny, but also of the Weimar Republic itself, was a function of an increasingly desperate hunt for 'the next little dollar' to service the country's external debts.

Even if they do not accept this particular diagnosis, most historians would at least accept that economic factors were at the root of the violent political fluctuations which characterized German history in the period between 1918 and 1933. Indeed, many writers have drawn a direct causal link from Weimar's dismal economic performance to the failure of parliamentary democracy. According to this view, the twin crises of inflation and depression – separated by a few, less-than-golden years of 'relative stagnation' – alienated so many voters from the parliamentary system that its collapse was inevitable.

At first sight, such hypotheses have much to recommend them. After all, it was in the same month that 'Mahagonny' received its premiere that the last properly parliamentary government of the inter-war period – that of Hermann Müller – resigned because of unbridgeable differences between the coalition partners on the subject of unemployment insurance. However, the direction of causation often assumed – from the economic to the political – is open to question. It can just as persuasively be argued that the direction was, in fact, the other way around, with political factors causing the violent economic fluctuations of the period. Indeed, historians of the period can roughly be divided into two groups: those who maintain that politicians and other decision-makers had 'room for manoeuvre' – that politics, in short, was paramount – and those for whom essentially uncontrollable economic or 'structural' factors were decisive. To a large degree, the historiography of the inter-war German economy has been dominated by this basic dichotomy between belief in political 'free will' and economic determinism. Was the hyperinflation of 1923 inevitable, or was it the result of errors of fiscal and monetary policy? Was the deflationary crisis of 1930–2 inevitable, or was it deliberately exacerbated by Müller's successor as Chancellor, Heinrich Brüning, for political reasons?

Another (closely linked) division of historiographical opinion is between those who see Germany's position as externally determined – by the Versailles Peace Treaty of 1919 and other foreign impositions – and those who see internal factors as being of greater importance. For most Germans during the 1920s, it was an article of faith that Germany's problems were primarily a function of the 'shameful peace'. Above all, the reparations demanded by the victorious Allies were seen as a crushing burden on the economy.

There are some historians who still take the view that reparations – that search for 'the next little dollar' – doomed the republic. However, there has been a growing tendency since the war to question this view, and to seek the causes of Weimar's failure within Germany itself. Within the literature which concentrates on internal politics, the clearest sub-division of opinion is between those historians who see the excessive power of labour as a source of economic and political weakness, and those who see the excessive power of big business as the real problem. Although other social divisions have been studied by historians (for example, religious, gender and generational divisions), class conflicts, or at least the distributional conflicts between interest groups, remain of primary concern to historians of the interwar economy.

Illustration 13.1 'The Loan' (*Simplicissimus*, 28 June 1922)

I The problem: twin crises

That inter-war Germany suffered severe economic instability can be easily illustrated. Between 1890 and 1914, the German Reich had experienced a period of relatively good economic performance. The economy as a whole had grown at an average annual rate of around 2.8 per cent. Inflation had been negligibly low – a little more than 1 per cent per annum – and there had been relatively little unemployment. To be sure, the fruits of this economic expansion had been distributed quite unequally by modern standards. There had also been considerable cyclical fluctuation. But wages had certainly kept pace with inflation and in some sectors actually grew faster. Moreover – a point often overlooked – the period saw a significant shift towards more progressive taxation at the state and local levels.

These 'golden years' ended abruptly with the First World War, and Germany did not experience anything comparable until after the Second. It is important to emphasize this, if only to point out that economic crisis preceded the creation of the Weimar Republic by nearly five years. For the period 1914–18, the best available index suggests that, in real terms (i.e., allowing for inflation) net national product fell at an average annual rate of around 4 per cent during the war, with both agricultural and industrial production declining steeply. At the same time, a serious inflationary problem developed: the official cost-of-living index rose at annual rates of 32 per cent during the war, twice the comparable figure for Britain. Prices on the large black market rose even more rapidly. The crisis period of 1918–19 saw a still worse deterioration.

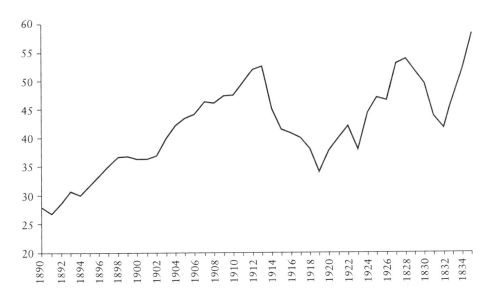

Figure 13.1 German net national product at market prices, adjusted for inflation and territorial changes, 1890–1935 (billion marks)

There were, it is true, some positive developments after 1919. The economy grew rapidly between 1920 and 1922. Moreover, unemployment was relatively low in Germany in the immediate post-war years, especially compared with Britain and the United States. However, these years also saw accelerating inflation, the annual rate exceeding 100 per cent for most of 1920 (though it did drop sharply in the first half of 1921). Thereafter, prices rose rapidly again and in July 1922 the monthly rate of inflation for the first time passed 50 per cent – the technical threshhold of hyperinflation. For nearly two years thereafter, there was economic chaos. Output once again fell and unemployment soared to more than 25 per cent (with more than 45 per cent of trade union members on short-time).

The years between 1924 and 1928 were once thought of as Weimar's 'golden years'; but on closer inspection the most that can be said is that things were not quite as bad as they were in the periods immediately before and after. The economy grew rapidly in 1924, 1925 and 1927, but there was virtually no growth in 1926 and 1928. Unemployment in 1926 reached a peak of more than 20 per cent. It was only a meagre consolation that inflation was low – indeed, had fallen below zero in 1926.

From March 1929 onwards, however, this downward trend became unstoppable as the economy plunged into a severe deflationary crisis. At its lowest point in June 1932,

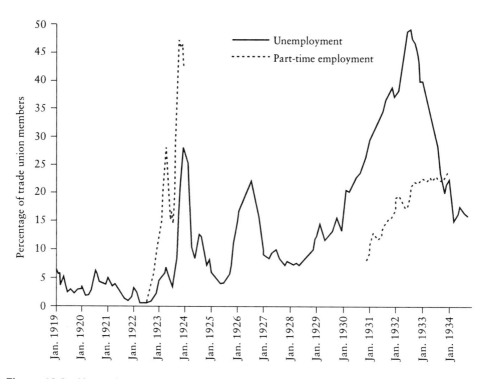

Figure 13.2   Unemployment among trade union members, 1919–1934

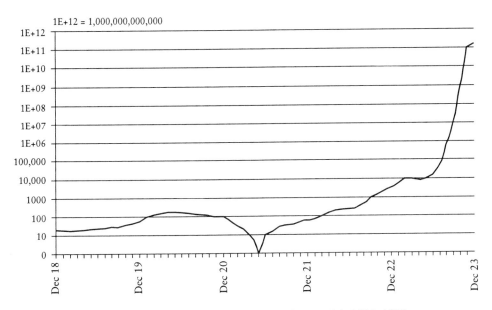

1E+12 = 1,000,000,000,000

Figure 13.3   Annual inflation rate (cost of living index, log. scale), 1919–1923

the annual rate of deflation reached minus 12 per cent. This was just one symptom of a second great economic collapse. Overall in the period of the slump, prices fell by more than one-fifth and output by about the same amount. At its worst in the summer of 1932, more than 45 per cent of trade union members were recorded as being out of work. No other major economy suffered such a severe downturn. Unemployment rates were calculated in different ways from country to country, but appropriately adjusted figures suggest that the German unemployment rate was two-thirds higher than the British in 1932.

In short, compared not only with its past and later performance but also with the contemporary performance of other economies, the German economy was extremely unstable in this period. In this light, it is not surprising that so many historians have seen the political collapse of Weimar as essentially economically determined. The only real debate about the consequences of economic instability concerns the relative importance of inflation and unemployment. It is a popular misconception that because high unemployment coincided with rising Nazi support, the unemployed must have voted for Hitler. Although some did, unemployed workers were more likely to turn to Communism than to Nazism, whereas middle-class voters were relatively more important to National Socialist electoral success; and in their case, the memory of inflation was at least as traumatic as the immediate experience of the slump. The social burdens of the slump were, after all, to a significant degree concentrated on those – predominantly workers – who lost their jobs. The effects of the inflation, by contrast, had been universally felt, but with a disproportionate impact on people living on savings or higher salaries. Certainly, middle-class observers often seem to have been more shocked by the earlier crisis – even those businessmen who managed to avoid the worst effects of inflation were appalled by the wiping out of savings, the sudden levelling of income and wealth distribution, the increased criminality. The Hamburg banker Max Warburg described Germany in 1922 as 'a society divided into three classes of society: one that suffers and goes under in decency; another that profiteers cynically and spends recklessly; and another that writhes in desperation, and wishes to destroy in blind fury whatever is left of a government and society that permits such conditions'. At around the same time – as if to illustrate his point – a still obscure South German demagogue named Adolf Hitler was blaming 'the distress of the small rentier, pensioner and war cripple' squarely on 'this weak republic [which] throws its pieces of worthless paper about wildly in order to enable its party functionaries and like-minded good-for-nothings to feed at the trough'. Simply because it took until 1930 for the losers of the inflation to be effectively mobilized by the Nazis does not mean that the economist Lionel Robbins was wrong when he called Hitler 'the foster-child of the inflation'.

II External pressures: can't pay versus won't pay

How are we to account for Weimar's twin economic crises? For most Germans, ranging right across the political spectrum, it was an article of faith that Weimar's principal economic problem was the Treaty of Versailles, and the reparations imposed on Germany by the victorious powers in 1919. Some historians continue to share that view, which found its most influential expression in the English economist John Maynard Keynes's book, *The Economic Consequences of the Peace*.

There is much to be said for the 'can't pay' thesis. From 1914 onwards, there were severe external pressures on the German economy and these did not cease until 1932. Even before the armistice had been signed, the Reich debt had risen to 150 billion marks – 85 billions in 'gold marks' (or 1913 marks, adjusting for wartime depreciation), compared with less than 5 billion before the war. In addition, state and local debts amounted to around 22 billion gold marks. Moreover, the state was already committed to paying pensions to more than 800,000 war wounded, 530,000 war widows and 1.2 million war orphans, as well as compensation to the owners of certain kinds of property lost during the war.

The peace simply added to these existing burdens; but it added much more than most Germans had anticipated. This was because most Germans did not fully grasp that the war had been lost, whereas from the moment Ludendorff demanded his 'immediate armistice to avoid a catastrophe' – arguably 'the stab in the front' which caused the hitherto relatively firm home front to collapse – the western powers acted as if Germany had surrendered unconditionally. For nearly a month, the American President Woodrow Wilson chose to ignore the parliamentary legitimacy of the new government of Max of Baden, as good as demanding a political revolution against the monarchy as a precondition of peace. And even after such a revolution broke out in early November, the British navy continued its blockade of German ports, ensuring that conditions in German cities worsened rather than improved during the first half of 1919. The Versailles peace – itself a muddled compromise between the victors – was thus imposed on a thoroughly destabilized country.

In economic terms, the peace was not all bad: the loss of Germany's colonies and most of her army and navy implied a considerable financial saving as well as strategic setback. But in other respects the burdens were heavy indeed. The loss of around 11 peripheral chunks of territory, the equivalent of 13 per cent of the Reich's area, mattered economically because that territory included important industrial regions. Germany also lost virtually all that remained of its merchant marine and a substantial number (5,000) of locomotives. These losses in themselves appalled the German delegation, but there was worse to follow. On the legalistic rather than historical premise that Germany had started the war, the treaty required indemnification not only for damage to occupied territory, but also (at the insistence of the Australian government) for the costs of Allied war pensions. So astronomical was the total implied – a figure of 480 billion gold marks was mentioned, which would have made the Reich's total liabilities equivalent to over 1,700 per cent of national income – that it was decided to leave the bill blank pending further discussion. Until then, the Germans were supposed to pay the costs of any occupying forces and 20 billion gold marks by way of a down payment. Keynes – echoing the German delegates at Versailles – denounced all of this, arguing on the basis of detailed calculations about the German balance of payments that the most Germany could pay was some 41 billion gold marks spread over 30 years. If more was asked, he warned:

> vengeance . . . will not limp. Nothing can then delay . . . that final civil war between the forces of Reaction and the despairing convulsions of Revolution . . . which will destroy . . . civilisation and progress.

When a total of 132 billion marks was finally agreed in 1921 he naturally dismissed it – as did most Germans – as far too high.

Keynes's dire prophecy after Versailles was extremely influential at the time in Britain; and subsequent events appeared, at least superficially, to vindicate him. Yet there was always a good deal of suspicion (especially in France) that German protestations of insolvency were fraudulent, or at least exaggerated. In recent years, this charge has been reiterated by a number of writers, including Sally Marks and Stephen Schuker. The 'can't pay? won't pay!' school makes two telling points. Firstly, the 1921 total was in fact closer than Keynes admitted to the sum he had considered realistic two years before. According to Marks, 82 of the 132 billions were purely 'notional', in that so-called 'C bonds' to that value would only be issued at some unspecified future date when German economic recovery was sufficiently advanced. Thus Germany's immediate obligations in 1921 were less than 50 billion marks – as little, in fact, as 41 billion (taking account of what had been paid after 1919). That had been Keynes's idea of a viable total in *The Economic Consequences*. Moreover, inflation had substantially reduced the real value of Germany's internal debt by mid-1921 to around 24 billion gold marks. So as a percentage of national income, total public sector liabilities including reparations were around 160 per cent.

The second point (made by Schuker) is that the Germans received at least as much in the form of loans from abroad which were never repaid as they themselves paid in reparations. Altogether, between 1919 and 1932, Germany paid around 19.1 billion gold marks in reparations (the Germans insisted it was much more, but tended to overvalue assets they handed over). But in the same period, net capital inflows to Germany totalled around 27 billion gold marks. Of this money, much was never repaid, because it took the form of investments denominated in paper marks which were reduced to worthlessness by hyperinflation in 1923; or deposits in German banks which were effectively frozen after the 1931 banking crisis.

There is no question that reparations need to be put in perspective. Germany was not alone in emerging from the war weighed down with debts and shorn of valuable assets and territories. Indeed, Germany was in some respects better off than its former allies, the Ottoman and Habsburg Empires, and better off than the Russian Empire too. Indeed, even France and Britain had total debt burdens – including substantial sums owed to a foreign power – of a similar order to that of Germany. As a proportion of national income, the British national debt in 1921 was in fact almost exactly the same as total German liabilities as calculated above. On the other hand, the German balance of payments was much weaker than the British because of the loss of overseas investments and the merchant marine, all of which had been important sources of foreign currency before the war. Although foreign lending allowed the Germans to run trade deficits and pay reparations for much longer than he had expected, Keynes was right that at some point the system was bound to break down. Even in the absence of the depression, there would have been a German debt crisis eventually. For even if German exports had picked up sufficiently to exceed imports for a sustained period – unlikely in the absence of global free trade – the 'C bonds' would then have ceased to be notional. In the sense that foreign investors could not ignore this *potential* 82 billion gold marks of debt when assessing Germany's future creditworthiness, the C bonds were always a more onerous burden than Marks claims.

At the same time, the fact that France and Britain were also heavily burdened with debts meant that, from the outset, there were limits to what they could afford to do to impose their peace terms on Germany. Full-scale occupation of Germany was never seriously contemplated: the most the French were able to do was to occupy the Rhine ports and later the Ruhr area when the Germans defaulted on reparation payments, and these sanctions in no way facilitated the collection of the indemnity; quite the reverse. Thus the Allies expected the Germans to execute the punitive terms of the treaty on their behalf – a novelty, since the reparations imposed on France in 1815 and 1870–1 had been combined with military occupation. Reparations after

1919 were treated as part of the Reich budget, and, not surprisingly, democratically elected politicians were extremely reluctant to approve taxes for this purpose. The fact that the sums actually transferred in the 1920s were less as a proportion of national income than (for example) the sums transferred by France to Germany between 1940 and 1944 or the sums transferred from East Germany to the Soviet Union after 1945 is thus beside the point; in both these cases the collecting power was far more coercive. The short answer to the 'can't pay? won't pay!' argument is 'won't pay? can't collect!'

This brings us back to the question of determinism versus free will. Historians like Marks and Schuker are quite right that the Germans sought to avoid paying reparations. Between 1919 and 1923, there seems little doubt that at least some politicians saw currency depreciation as a way of undermining the Versailles system, believing that a weak mark would boost German exports so much that the western powers would be forced to revise the treaty, if only to defend their own economies from German 'dumping'. In the mid-1920s, the liberal Foreign Minister Gustav Stresemann saw the conclusion of trade treaties in a not dissimilar light, aiming to 'conduct foreign policy by economic means, as this is the only respect in which we are still a great power'. And, after 1930, Brüning sought (as he later put it) 'to make use of the world crisis to put pressure on all the other powers', in the belief that deflation would, once again, boost German exports and thereby force revision. In short, no Weimar government seriously wanted to 'fulfil' the terms of the London Ultimatum, the Dawes plan or the Young plan. But two points must be made. First, all these efforts to get rid of reparations had only very limited success. Only after inflation, stagnation, deflation and complete economic collapse were reparations finally suspended in 1932. If nothing else, this suggests that avoiding payment was less easy than historians have sometimes made it sound: a case of 'won't pay? can't not pay!', perhaps. Second, to argue that the Germans could have paid even more than they did begs the question: what constitutes a tolerable level of unrequited transfer? For a democratic state, the majority of whose population refused to recognize that Germany had lost the war, much less surrendered unconditionally, it might be said that *any* reparations were intolerable. The so-called 'Chancellor of fulfilment' Joseph Wirth expressly ruled out a new tax on property because it would 'declare the [London] Ultimatum [of 1921] to be 80 per cent possible'. Such views, more than anything else, determined the maximum sum which German governments were able to transfer as reparations. It is to the domestic politics of Weimar that we must therefore turn – and to the other, less well-known reparations which the Germans wished to pay to themselves.

III Internal factors: politics versus economics

If external factors are ultimately inseparable from internal factors, then much the same can be said about the dichotomy between economics and politics within Germany itself. The reality of the inter-war period was that the two became entangled as never before. In many ways, this politicization of economic life – and economization of political life – was a legacy of the First World War. It was the war which caused the role of government to expand, so that the state not only became the economy's biggest customer for labour, goods and services, but also vastly extended its powers of legal regulation to cover trade, capital exports, the internal distribution of raw materials, prices, rents and, to some extent, wages. In 1914, public spending had accounted for 18 per cent of net national product. In 1917, it reached a peak of 76 per cent. The tide of state economic power receded substantially after the collapse of Germany's military position, but it never returned to its pre-war level. Between 1919 and 1932, total public spending was equivalent to, on average, 34 per cent of NNP, nearly twice its pre-war level. Nor did the state wholly relinquish its new powers of regulation.

At the same time, increasing power was wielded after 1914 by organized economic interest groups. The strength of cartells and associations was a distinctive feature of German industry even before the war, when they had mainly been concerned with (relatively modest) price-fixing and (relatively unsuccessful) resistance to the demands of organized labour. When the war came, however, it seemed sensible to delegate considerable amounts of regulatory power to them, rather than create entirely new state organs. Some economic associations thus acquired a public, statutory character – allocating raw materials in a particular sector, for example, or controlling prices and exports. As Gerald Feldman has shown, such tendencies were especially pronounced in the iron and steel sector. This system of 'self-regulation' was partly but not entirely wound up after the war and there remained a number of areas in which private and public sector responsibilities continued to overlap – notably in the process of wage negotiation. The assumption remained pervasive that business interests should be given special consideration in all matters relating to the economy. The very fact that the words *die Wirtschaft* signified both 'big business' and 'the economy' in Weimar politics was indicative of this.

However, it was not only heavy industry which was able to influence the making of economic policy. The traditional influence of Prussian landowners did not end with the revolution. Indeed, the acute plight of the agricultural sector – constantly sinking into debt as commodity prices plummeted – in some ways served to increase agrarian influence in politics. At the same time, the various social groups which Germans lump together as the *Mittelstand* – small businessmen, white-collar employees and so on – were also able to exert at least as much political pressure as they had been able to do in the Wihelmine period – though the fissiparous tendency which characterized all middle-class politics in the 1920s was especially evident here. Finally, there is no question that the organizations of manual labour, whose influence had been much circumscribed before 1914, came to exercise an influence over policy-making every bit as important as that played by big business.

This was a consequence of the war and the revolution of November 1918. Although the likelihood of a Bolshevik-style revolution in Germany now tends to be played down by historians, fear of such a descent into civil war was strong enough to persuade

German business leaders (as well as some senior military officers and civil servants) of the expediency of a post-war understanding with the socialist trade unions, whose leaders generally shared their aversion to the radical left. The agreement of 15 November 1918 between the industrial magnate Hugo Stinnes and the trade union leader Carl Legien was one of four vital compromises which the majority Social Democrat leaders made in the first days after the proclamation of the republic. (The others were with the army, the federal states and the constitutional liberals.) Formally, it meant the concession to workers of the eight-hour day and large nominal wage increases; in practice it meant that business and the new government would do everything possible to avoid high post-war unemployment and serious falls in working-class living standards, which it was widely feared would lead to a second revolution. As far as men like Legien were concerned, ambitious plans for 'socialization' (meaning everything from nationalization to the institutionalization of workers' power within works' councils) were of less importance than these basic commitments to reduce working hours, maintain full employment and raise wages. These, in conjunction with redistributive taxation and increased public spending on housing, health and education, were the reforms they had always hoped to achieve in Germany without the upheaval of revolution. For their part, Stinnes and other businessmen certainly did not relish concessions on such issues, but saw them as preferable to the sort of wholesale expropriation taking place in Russia. In the short run, they also opened up the possibility of continuing state subsidies, loans at low real interest rates, liberalized exports and tax breaks – so long as these could be justified as being necessary to maintain employment.

The institutional arrangements which developed out of this hastily concluded compact between big business and organized labour were exceedingly complex. National organs like the Central Community of Labour and the Reich Economic Council jostled for influence over economic policy with new Reich ministries for Labour, the Economy and Reconstruction, traditional organs of economic management like the Reichsbank, wartime relics like the price control boards and new bureaucratic excrescences like the foreign trade control bureaux. At the local level, firms had to deal with a multiplicity of institutions and, especially in the early 1920s, a torrent of regulations. Often, decision-making was simply stalemated by the application of the principle of 'parity', whereby employers' and employees' interests had to be equally represented wherever economic matters were being debated. In short, Weimar's political economy was a tangle to which no simple label – 'corporatism', 'organized capitalism' 'welfare state' – can do justice. Even to sub-divide industry into rival light and heavy industrial blocs, following David Abraham, is to do a violence to the convoluted and fragmented reality.

Perhaps the most obvious focus for distributional conflicts was the Reich budget, for it was the budget which determined tax rates and social security contributions, pensions and benefits, subsidies to industry and certain kinds of social expenditure. As we have seen, reparations accounted for a significant proportion of total Reich spending each year between 1920 and 1932, and they actually exceeded the deficits for the period 1924–31. But they do not explain the full extent of government deficits in the inflation period: if one simply deducts reparations from total expenditures (adjusting domestic spending for inflation), large deficits remain for the years 1919, 1920 and 1923.

True, as Eichengreen and Webb have pointed out, inflation would have been lower in the absence of reparations and thus revenue would have been higher in real terms (the reverse of the 'Tanzi effect' whereby higher inflation reduces the real value of tax receipts). The temptation is strong to conclude, as they do, that reparations were therefore the key to Weimar's financial problem. Yet the implication that without reparations there would have been no deficits is open to question. For Weimar's political economy was as much riven by internal as by external distributional conflicts. Even if there had been no reparations, it is easy to imagine the various competing interest groups simply bidding up total expenditure to take up the slack.

The trouble was that German politics in the 1920s was not just a zero-sum game; in fiscal terms, it was a negative-sum game. As the debates on Matthias Erzberger's tax reforms of 1919–20 showed, there was no real willingness to balance the budget, even before the publication of the London Ultimatum and even at a time when inflation was levelling off. Radical – perhaps too radical – increases in direct taxation were accompanied or followed by even larger increases in expenditure on the railways or on the reconstruction of the merchant marine, the main objective of which was to create jobs. In short, the republic existed to pay not only reparations to the victorious Allies but

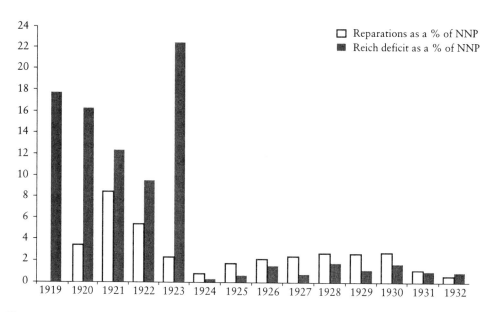

Figure 13.4 Reparations and Reich deficits as a percentage of NNP, 1919–1932

also reparations to the Germans themselves. Had the former been reduced, it is probable that the latter would simply have been increased.

Between 1919 and 1923, reparations to the working classes not only meant that post-war unemployment was postponed. Because it led to inflation, it also meant that the distribution of income and wealth in Germany was considerably equalized, even allowing for the fact that an elite of enterpreneurs protected their wealth from erosion by investing in 'real values' and foreign currency. For, if foreign lenders ended up paying for foreign reparations, it was domestic lenders who ended up paying for much of the cost of domestic reparations. By the end of 1923, people who had invested in pre-war bonds and shares or war loans – any financial asset, in fact, which was denominated in paper marks – found the value of their investments reduced to virtually nothing. The revaluation legislation which was subsequently enacted did something to make good these losses; but ultimately it could not possibly alter the fact that a massive transfer – in the form of an inflationary tax on savings – had been effected.

After 1924, 'domestic reparations' continued to be paid, though in a less spectacular fashion. The reforms to the tax system introduced by Luther in 1924 made the overall impact of the Reich budget slightly less progressive than it would have been had Erzberger's reforms worked. But they had not: in the later inflation years, tax deducted at source from employees' wages had been about the only direct tax efficiently collected. If anything, then, the end of inflation probably reduced the share of the tax burden which fell on workers. Inasmuch as 'social expenditures' by the Reich, states and local government tended to rise during the mid-1920s, there was a further redistributive effect.

However, transfers to workers were not only effected through taxation and expenditure, but also through wages which, if unions and employers could not agree, were often imposed by the Labour Ministry's system of binding arbitration. One of the most important debates in modern economic history was precipitated by the publication in 1979 of an article by Knut Borchardt, which argued that this system made the economy inherently 'sick' in the mid-1920s because arbitration led to excessive real wages, which squeezed company profits and thus reduced investment. In saying this, Borchardt appeared to endorse the contemporary argument advanced by the Reich Association of German Industry that nothing short of a dismantling of the post-revolutionary arrangements governing industrial relations could have restored the economy to health.

The evidence that labour costs were excessive in the 1920s seems, at first sight, quite convincing. For example, the share of wages as a proportion of national income (as compared with income from capital) rose sharply between 1914 and 1932. However, it is one thing to say that Weimar Germany was a more equal society than Wilhelmine Germany and another to say that this was why investment tailed off in the 1920s (especially as the share of wages in national income was not so very different in the years of the 'economic miracle' after 1947). Recent research on this point by Theo Balderston has arrived at rather different conclusions.

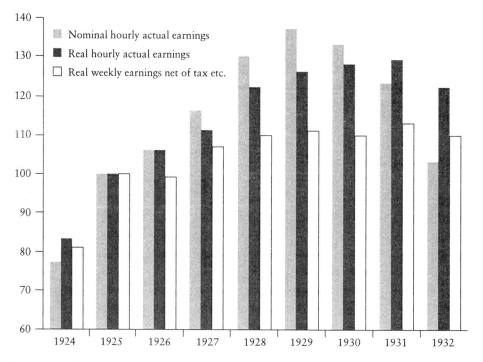

Figure 13.5 Collectively contracted earnings, 1924–1932 (1925=100)

Balderston acknowledges that real wages were rising relative to productivity and export prices, though the rise was less than spectacular when shorter hours, tax and insurance deductions are taken into account. But he denies that this was what caused profits to stagnate and investment to fall. He maintains that rising real wages were needed to increase the 'participation ratio' – i.e., to attract additional men and women into the workforce – at a time when world demand for German exports was rising.

So if the 'real wage position' was not the problem, how are we to explain the undoubted decline in investment and the relatively greater severity of the slump in Germany? Balderston finds the most plausible culprit not in the labour market but in the capital market. Of course, for some historians of the left – such as Dick Geary – there has always been a strong preference for any explanation for the slump which blames capital rather than labour for it. He and others have attached considerable significance to decisions taken in 1928 by industrial employers to adopt a tougher line with labour which culminated in the Ruhr lock-out of that year, arguing that this marked the breakdown of that corporatist partnership between capital and labour on which Weimar rested. This may be true in a political sense, but it is not a satisfactory economic explanation of the fall in investment and general business pessimism of which the Ruhr lock-out was a consequence, rather than a cause. Balderston's argument is more sophisticated. He stresses the damage done to the German capital market by the inflation. Savers and investors who lost out in the crisis of 1923–4 were wary of making the same mistake twice – especially those who had bought public sector bonds, which had been exceptionally bad investments. When the Reich, states or local authorities wished to borrow money after 1924, they thus found the market for new bonds extremely weak even when high yields were offered. This (combined with the low liquidity of the banking sector) obliged governments at all levels to reduce their deficits and attempt to balance their budgets. And the first items of expenditure to be reduced were local authorities' budgets for housing and other infrastructure investment – precisely the sector which fuelled British recovery in the 1930s.

IV   Real and imaginary alternatives

Whether the labour market or the capital market was to blame for reducing investment will doubtless continue to be debated. There still remains, however, the further question of whether governments could possibly have done anything to stop the downward economic spiral which ensued. And here we return once again to the debate between economic determinism and political room for manoeuvre.

There is little doubt that fiscal and monetary policy made the slump worse between 1930 and 1932. Attempts to balance the budget and to preserve the convertibility of the Reichsmark clearly had the effect of exacerbating deflation. According to critics of the Chancellor at the time, Brüning, there was no economic need for this; his motives were primarily political (to get rid of reparations and alter the constitution). Economic historians such as Holtfrerich claim that the government could instead have increased borrowing, rather than trying to balance the budget, giving a proto-Keynesian stimulus to demand through public works schemes; or it could have devalued the Reichsmark, allowing a reduction in interest rates and boosting exports. It is certainly pleasant, if tantalizing, to imagine such Keynesian policies being adopted five years before the publication of Keynes's *General Theory*. But to these suggestions Borchardt and James have given three answers. First, contemporary alternative policies came too late in the day and did not envisage a big enough counter-cyclical boost; even if they had been tried, therefore, they would not have had much success. Second, they could not have been tried: the government was not free to act as it wished, because of restrictions on the Reichsbank's reserve law imposed by the Allies after the inflation. And third, the memory of the inflation meant that there would have been public panic at the news of increased Reich deficits, leading, self-defeatingly, to cash withdrawals from banks and further deflation. These arguments are largely endorsed by Balderston.

The determinist view thus seems to have prevailed, at least for Weimar's last years. However, simply because there was no *effective* alternative to a policy of deflation, does not mean that Weimar's economic collapse was inevitable from the outset. For, as both Balderston and Borchardt show, what really constrained both investors and politicians in the slump was the fear of a second great inflation. A question which needs urgently to be addressed is therefore whether there were alternatives to the inflation. As with all counterfactual hypotheses, the suggestion that there might have been can only be tentative. Nevertheless, it seems a more plausible scenario than the alternatives to deflation discussed above.

As we have seen, the key to the inflation was monetary expansion caused principally by uncontrolled short-term government borrowing. Was this avoidable? Conceivably. In early 1920, prices stopped rising and actually began to fall, mainly as a result of speculative capital in-flows, but also because price increases had largely absorbed the wartime monetary overhang. This presented a real opportunity to stabilize the currency – not, as happened in Britain, to deflate to the pre-war exchange rate, but merely to stabilize at the existing rate, which was around 10 per cent of the pre-war rate. (This was roughly what happened in France.) Such a formal devaluation, in conjunction with cuts in spending and increases in indirect taxes, could have effectively avoided the descent into hyperinflation, particularly if combined with the deregulation of trade and the labour market. Although such a policy would have meant a cut in living standards and an increase in unemployment, it would have been a significantly 'softer landing' than actually happened in 1923. Although it would have disappointed foreign investors, the experience of 1924 – when they returned to the German market despite far greater losses – suggests that the disappointment would soon have been forgotten.

It is not difficult to see why this was not done. Economically, it might have been possible, even preferable. Politically, it was impossible. First, the fear of unemployment was too great. Second, the belief that financial stabilization would make the collection of reparations easier was too widespread. This might seem to consign any counterfactual hypothesis to the realm of idle speculation. Yet with hindsight, there are good reasons for questioning the rationality of such contemporary assumptions. It seems unlikely that a rise in unemployment in 1920 would have led to anything as serious as the disorder and violence unleashed in 1923. Moreover, the evidence suggests that the strategy of trying to get rid of reparations by means of inflation was misconceived. Allowing the mark to depreciate may have boosted German exports, but it boosted Allied exports to Germany even more (hence the huge trade deficit of 1922). This was hardly an inducement to treat Germany more generously. Thus we are bound to conclude that hyperinflation happened not just because it was the line of least political resistance, but also because its benefits were exaggerated and its costs understated. Tragically, its legacy seems to have compelled Brüning to take the line of greatest economic resistance.

There is of course an easier way of answering the question: was there an alternative to the extremes of inflation and deflation which characterized the Weimar period? The answer is that there was, and it was called National Socialism. The nature of the economic recovery which took place in Germany after 1933 illustrates not so much what ought to have been done by a democratic regime, but why a democratic regime could not have done it. Although there is some evidence of an increase in industrial output in the second half of 1932, there is little reason to believe that Germany would have recovered any more successfully than France without the massive programme of state investment undertaken by Hitler. Between 1933 and 1938, the public sector accounted for between 44 and 49 per cent of gross investment. The lion's share of this had a military purpose, as the increase of military spending from just 1.5 per cent of gross national product in 1933 to 20 per cent in 1938 suggests – though even this understates the importance of rearmament, since many apparently non-military investments in transport and infrastructure (most famously, the *Autobahnen*) had strategic objectives.

The results were, at least by comparison with what had gone before, impressive. Between 1928 and 1932, gross national product had fallen by about a fifth in real terms. Between 1932 and 1938 it rose by three-quarters. Industrial output in the same periods had fallen by 42 per cent, then rose by 110 per cent. Unemployment fell from its appalling peak in 1932 to a negligible level in 1938: just 400,000. Yet there was only the most moderate inflation, in itself not unwelcome after the deflation of the slump. How was this possible? Public spending rose by more than 120 per cent. Although taxes and social insurance were increased, total public debt went up from 14 billion Reichsmarks to 42 billion Reichsmarks, and 60 per cent of new debt was short-term. The money supply expanded by more than 70 per cent. Yet wholesale prices rose by no more than 16 per cent between 1933 and 1937; and although the trade deficit widened, the consequences were in fact far less dire than pessimists like the Reichsbank President Hjalmar Schacht feared. Moreover, actual weekly wages rose by around 18 per cent. Although that figure reflects longer working hours rather than higher real hourly rates, it demonstrates the limits of Schacht's warning that 'the standard of living and the extent of armament production are in inverse ratio'. If aggregate output increased enough, both could go up without drastically compromising the rearmament programme.

The explanation for the relative success of Nazi economic policy lies in the fact that private consumption was restrained in a way which had been more or less impossible under Weimar. The bulk of industrial output was accounted for by producer goods, not consumer goods. As investment rose, so private consumption as a percentage of national income fell from 83 per cent to 59 per cent. To give a striking example: in 1937, beer consumption per capita was 60 per cent lower than it had been ten years before. The Germans were never so sober as they were under Hitler. In other words, the Nazi recovery was not 'Keynesian': the state was not engaged in 'kick-starting' a stalled market economy by boosting demand. On the contrary, private consumption was actually reined in to allow rearmament to proceed with minimal inflationary consequences. (The restoration of price controls and the extension of exchange controls served the same purpose.) In addition, considerable ingenuity was expended on disguising the extent of the fiscal stimulus: government borrowing was concealed behind the bogus Metallurgical Research Office, which effectively took over from the Reichsbank the discounting of treasury bills.

Although many of the economic controls used by the Nazis had in fact been developed in the Weimar period, none of this would have been possible without a radical transformation of the German political system, to eradicate that institutional pluralism which had ultimately been responsible for the extreme 'go-stop' swings of Weimar economic policy. Hitler's earliest political statements show that he understood the need for political centralization. As early as 1920, he and his associates in the German Workers' Party had called for 'the creation of a strong central power for the Reich; the unconditional authority of the political central parliament over the entire Reich and its organizations; and the formation of corporations based on estate and occupation for the purpose of carrying out the general legislation passed by the Reich in the various ... states'. Of course, by 1933 he had replaced any notion of parliamentary centralization with the 'leader principle'; and in practice, as is well known, political centralization in the Third Reich was always to some extent compromised by the uneasy dualism of party and state and the 'polycratic' tendencies which Hitler's style of leadership encouraged. The deficiencies of Nazi organization were laid bare by war. Nevertheless, there is an important sense in which the Nazi state was less polycratic than its predecessor. The destruction of the trade unions and the creation in their stead of the Labour Front and the subordination of the employers' associations to the Reich Estate of German Industry marked the end of 'corporatism' as it had evolved in the 1920s. It is important to emphasize that these changes marked the end of autonomy for both organized labour and business, though the freedom of the latter was more gradually eroded. In particular, restrictions on private sector access to the capital market and on the distribution of profits meant that even before the promulgation of the Four Year Plan, most firms' economic freedom of action was severely limited. Hitler's famous declaration in the Four Year Plan memorandum – 'the job of the Reich Economics Ministry is simply to set out the national economic tasks; private industry has to fulfil them' – perfectly encapsulated the subordination of economics to politics which had been achieved.

Between 1918 and 1939, the German economy was capable of one of three things: it could pay reparations to the victors; it could pay 'reparations' to its own working class; or it could rearm for 'a war of revenge'. It could not do all three; nor could it do just two of these. Weimar failed because it attempted to do the second while pretending to do the first (as well as secretly beginning the third). This confusion was less the product of conscious political decision-making than the spontaneous outcome of an overcomplex political process in which economic interests were given too much weight. By contrast, Hitler saw what Weimar politicians had failed to see: that economics should come second to politics. True, he had one obvious advantage: the changed international situation after 1932 meant that he did not need to pay reparations or even conceal rearmament. But he still needed to make a choice between rearmament and working-class living standards. It can be argued that he sought to avoid such a choice – that was certainly the view of Tim Mason. But the evidence for a successful restriction of living standards to allow a non-inflationary programme of rearmament – and rearmament sufficient to bring Germany a decisive victory in Europe – is overwhelming. German workers in the 1930s were no longer being paid domestic reparations, as they had been in the 1920s; they were getting a slowly diminishing share of a quite rapidly growing cake. And although Hitler's Third Reich ultimately lasted even less time than Weimar's 'city of Mahagonny', it was not its internal economic weakness which determined that – reassuring though the notion of Nazi self-destruction might be. In the final analysis, it was the superior organizational efficiency of its enemies which was decisive.

Select bibliography

Abraham, David, *The Collapse of the Weimar Republic. Political Economy and Crisis* (1981).

Balderston, Theo, 'War Finance and Inflation in Britain and Germany', *Economic History Review*, 42 (1989).

Balderston, Theo, *The German Economic Crisis, 1923–1932* (1993).

Borchardt, Knut, 'Constraints and Room for Manoeuvre in the Great Depression of the Early Thirties: Towards a Revision of the Received Historical Picture', in Balderston, Theo, *Perspectives on Modern German Economic History and Policy* (1991).

Eichengreen, Barry, *Golden Fetters. The Gold Standard and the Great Depression, 1919–1939* (1992).

Feldman, Gerald D., *Iron and Steel in the German Inflation, 1916–1923* (1977).

Feldman, Gerald D., *The Great Disorder. Politics, Economics and Society in the German Inflation* (1993).

Ferguson, Niall, *Paper and Iron. Hamburg Business and German Politics in the Era of Inflation, 1897–1927* (1995).

Geary, Dick, 'Employers, Workers and the Collapse of the Weimar Republic', in Ian Kershaw, ed., *Weimar: Why did German Democracy Fail?* (1990).

Holtfrerich, Carl-Ludwig, *The German Inflation, 1914–1923* (1986).

James, Harold, *The German Slump. Politics and Economics 1924–1936* (1986).

Kaiser, David E., Tim W. Mason and Richard J. Overy, 'Debate: Germany, "Domestic Crisis" and War in 1939', *Past and Present* 12 (1989).

Kershaw, Ian, ed., *Weimar: Why did German Democracy Fail?* (1990).

Keynes, John Maynard, *The Economic Consequences of the Peace* (1919).

Kruedener, J. Baron von, ed., *Economic Crisis and Political Collapse. The Weimar Republic, 1924–1933* (1990).

Maier, Charles S., *Recasting Bourgeois Europe. Stabilisation in France, Germany and Italy in the Decade after World War I* (1975).

Marks, Sally, 'The Myths of Reparations', *Central European History* 11 (1978).

Mason, Tim W., 'The Primacy of Politics: Politics and Economics in National Socialist Germany', in S. Woolf, ed., *The Nature of Fascism* (1968).

Noakes, Jeremy and Geoffrey Pridham, eds., *Nazism, 1919–1945*, vol. II: *State, Economy and Society, 1933–1939* (1984).

Overy, Richard J., *The Nazi Economic Recovery, 1932–1938* (2nd edition, 1996).

Overy, Richard J., 'Germany, Domestic Crisis and War in 1939', *Past and Present* 116 (1987).

Schuker, Steven, 'American Reparations to Germany, 1919–1933', in Gerald D. Feldman and

Elisabeth Müller-Luckner, eds., *Die Nachwirkungen der Inflation auf die deutsche Geschichte, 1924–1933* (1985).

Webb, Stephen B., *Hyperinflation and Stabilisation in Weimar Germany* (1989).

Witt, Peter-Christian, 'Tax Policies, Tax Assessment and Inflation: Towards a Sociology of Public Finances in the German Inflation, 1914 to 1923', in Witt, ed., *Wealth and Taxation in Central Europe. The History and Sociology of Public Finance* (1987).

14

Culture and society in Weimar Germany: the impact of modernism and mass culture

Elizabeth Harvey

The history of cultural life in Weimar Germany is usually, and rightly, associated with upheaval and transformation. Accounts of Weimar culture have emphasized the way in which forces for change – the upsurge in the aftermath of the First World War of the reformist and revolutionary left, the establishment of democracy, and longer-term economic and technological modernization – interacted with each other to foster modernism in the arts and to promote the development of a new 'mass culture'. The new mass culture, for contemporaries a crucial sign of the arrival of 'modernity', transformed the context of artistic production and consumption, shaking the dominance of the educated bourgeoisie as arbiters and consumers of culture. Germany in the 1920s, torn by political and economic crises but outstanding for its pluralist and cosmopolitan cultural climate and its cultural innovation, became the object of fascination for foreign observers and visitors.

It also became the object of intense self-analysis by its own critics and cultural commentators. Contemporaries were highly sensitive to the cultural changes they were witnessing. An outpouring of comment and criticism greeted the various manifestations of cultural modernity and documented the fascination, ambivalence and often fierce hostility aroused by phenomena as diverse as jazz, twelve-tone music, plays about abortion, anti-war paintings, film palaces and pulp fiction. In the eyes of their enemies, these types of cultural output, which were in different ways products of economic and social modernization, became the scapegoat for those changes: cultural conservatives accused them of contributing to a comprehensive national crisis, and of undermining social stability, moral values and cultural standards. At the same time, right-wing attacks on modernism in the arts and mass culture became attacks on the republic itself, which because it provided a framework for cultural innovation became identified with it. Through such attacks, cultural debates in Weimar Germany became polarized to an extreme and politically destabilizing degree.

In recent years much effort has gone into refining our understanding of the cultural transformations of the Weimar period and of the positions adopted by the participants in contemporary debates on cultural issues. There is, however, a risk of allowing the polarized contemporary debate to distort our perceptions of German cultural life in the Weimar years. It is possible to focus exclusively on discourses about modern art, the new media and mass entertainments without examining assumptions about their social impact and their distribution beyond the big cities, in particular beyond Berlin. This essay therefore places particular emphasis on the issue of cultural transmission and reception. It focuses for the most part on the arts and entertainments which were publicly shown or performed, though it also considers the new medium of radio; for reasons of space, it leaves aside the novels and poetry of the period. It emphasizes the significance of innovations in cultural life, and of Berlin as a focus of cultural experiment, but it also considers how far developments in artistic modernism shaped cultural life in the provinces, and considers how social class and regional differences affected the reception of the new media and mass entertainments. When looking at cultural conservatism, it draws attention not only to the ideas of individual conservative theorists and the arguments of conservative parties or organizations at national level, but also to the practice of cultural conservatism at the grass-roots, particularly in provincial Germany. Looking at the social history of Weimar culture from these angles may, it is hoped, enhance our understanding of it as a history of uneven development.

I Cultural innovation and experiment

To draw attention to the limits and unevenness of the breakthrough of 'cultural modernity' is not to deny the momentum of innovation which so impressed or alarmed contemporary observers. Artistic conventions and established assumptions about the function of art had already been widely challenged in Wilhelmine Germany, as Matthew Jefferies' contribution to this volume shows (see Chapter 10, above). However, the republic provided a context in which aesthetic experiment and committed left-wing art flourished as never before. The revolutionary upheavals of 1918–19 and the advent of democracy inspired artists and politicians to draw up programmes of cultural revolution and cultural reform. Expressionist poets, painters and architects greeted the revolution with enthusiasm, believing a new age had dawned. When a certain disillusion with its consequences set in, artists sympathetic to the left, together with journalists and critics, continued to provoke the bourgeoisie and the new republican establishment with work which was frequently satirical and deliberately shocking or shrill. Some looked to the newly founded KPD as the source of a class-conscious proletarian counter-culture and to the Soviet Union as an alternative model of modernity to western capitalism. Meanwhile, the republican state itself fostered a degree of political and artistic pluralism. The Weimar constitution declared, albeit with some qualifications, that censorship 'does not take place' and proclaimed the freedom of the arts and scholarship. Censorship did in fact continue, but the boundaries of what was tolerable to the state authorities were extended. The newly democratized municipal and regional governments became a source of patronage, in a number of cases favouring the performance or display of avant-garde works as a badge of their progressiveness. Despite the strain on public finances in the early years of the Weimar Republic, reaching a crisis at the height of the inflation, politicians at local and *Land* level continued to channel substantial public funding into the arts. As Gerald Feldman has commented, it was remarkable that an impoverished Germany in the wake of the First World War continued to maintain so many theatres and more than 30 opera houses.

The impact of the avant-garde was felt most in the world of 'high' culture, which remained a sphere dominated by an educated bourgeois public. Changes in the cultural sphere which had a greater impact on the mass of the population were those taking place in the entertainments industry through technological advances and new investment. Home entertainment began from 1923–4 onwards to include radio. Cheap entertainment outside the home could be found at variety theatres, at the new sports stadia, in bars and dance halls, and above all at the cinema, the commercial mass entertainment *par excellence*. By the end of the 1920s there were more than 5,000 cinemas in Germany; in 1928, the peak year for cinema-going, around 353 million cinema tickets were sold. By comparison, attendance figures for the performances staged by municipal theatres in 87 towns and cities in 1926–7 were just under 12 million.[1]

The new cinemas and sports stadia were part of the changing urban landscapes of the 1920s. Local government efforts to improve the urban environment focused on the construction of new public parks, libraries, transport and housing schemes. Such reforms, often advocated and implemented by Social Democrats in cooperation with bourgeois politicians, were fuelled by an optimistic vision of the hygienic management of cities and their populations. But at the same time department stores and advertising hoardings were shaping cities in a different way as sites of consumerism, stimulating aspirations – even though the dream of American-style mass consumption was still far from being realized in Weimar Germany – towards a fast-moving urban consumer lifestyle. In this process, women – as wage-earners and as housewives, as salesgirls and shoppers – played key roles.

The salesgirl and the woman shopper represented facets of the potent composite myth of the Weimar 'new woman'. The myth was widely propagated in the media: illustrated magazines revelled in images of cigarette-smoking, motorbike-riding, silk-stockinged or tennis-skirted young women out on the streets, in bars or on the sports field. To an extent there was a social reality underlying the image: women had gained formally equal rights under the Weimar constitution, a growing number of middle-class as well as working-class women in the 1920s were working outside the home in jobs in the professions and in the service sector; a growing number of (particularly young and single) women spent their leisure at sports clubs and cinemas. Women thus constituted a more visible presence in the public sphere and in the economy than they had done before 1914 or 1918. But the myth as concocted by and debated in the media overlaid this reality with a mixture of fantasies and fears about women's increasing sexual independence (or voraciousness) and sexual knowledge, and about their presence on the street or in the cinema, dance-hall or lecture room. In the end, any and every facet of 'modern womanhood' became incorporated into the 'new woman': 'she' was both a devouring *femme fatale* and a cross-dressing lesbian, a sportswoman and an efficient housewife, a movie-going typist and a bluestocking student. But incoherent as it was, the 'new woman' myth expressed perceptions of cultural change and represented to Germans of both sexes many of the intoxicating and threatening dimensions of modernity.

If the 'new woman' was one powerful symbol of cultural change, Berlin came to embody it in terms of a geographical location. The capital of the republic became the site on which competing and conflicting visions of its modernity were – at least partially – realized. One strand of this perceived modernity was the cultivation of iconoclasm and experiment in the arts. Much of the artistic avant-garde gravitated to Berlin, and as the new 'insiders' of Weimar culture (to borrow Peter Gay's image) they found institutional footholds and receptive audiences there. Thus Schoenberg began teaching master classes in composition at the Prussian Academy of Arts in 1925, while Hindemith taught composition at the Staatliche Musikhochschule from 1927 onwards. Meanwhile at the Staatsoper major milestones of the new music were premiered, for instance Berg's *Wozzeck* in 1925. The Nationalgalerie promoted the work of contemporary German painters, while powerful private gallery directors vied with each other to sell 'difficult' contemporary art to public galleries and private collectors and to market their 'star' artists. Beyond the world of the arts establishment, fringe art forms flourished in clubs, bars and cabarets. Such venues provided outlets for lesser-known and experimental performers and pieces, and a place where a sub-culture such as that of Berlin's homosexual community could thrive.

At the same time, Berlin was developing as a centre of mass cultural production – in journalism, film and fashion – and as a showcase for the latest cultural imports from abroad. Of the big publishing houses, Ullstein stood out: it produced from its new printing house in Tempelhof newspapers and periodicals which ranged from the quality *Vossische Zeitung* to the popular *BZ am Mittag*, and included the most successful Ullstein publication of all, the *Berliner Illustrirte Zeitung*, whose circulation peaked at over 1.8 million in July 1929. As a city of cinema, Berlin had the giant studio complex of UFA at Neubabelsberg as the major German centre of film production; and a plethora of cinemas, ranging from the pseudo-rococo palaces of the Kurfürstendamm seating a thousand or more apiece to the smaller cinemas in working-class neighbourhoods. Fashion design and production was concentrated around the Hausvogteiplatz, where small firms – many of them Jewish – competed fiercely with each other to turn the latest Paris lines into wearable women's fashions – 'Berliner Chic' – for the elite and for the mass market. The different branches of cultural production in Berlin fed off each other: stars of stage and cinema had their images reproduced and amplified by the illustrated press, women could study the designs of Berlin fashion houses as worn by an actress in a Pabst film, by a revue singer or a model in the *Berliner Illustrirte* – even if their budget only ran to buying cheaper imitations in the nearest department store.

American cultural influence on Germany in the Weimar period was by no means restricted to Berlin. However, cultural imports from the USA found particularly enthusiastic audiences in the capital. The Tiller Girls and Josephine Baker drew Berlin audiences and evoked images of America and Americans as capable of technical brilliance as well as energy, expressiveness and daring. Jazz was one of the most popular, but also one of the most controversial, cultural imports from the United States: jazz-playing dance bands could be found all over Berlin in hotels, cafés and bars. And American films seemed to go down better in Berlin than in Germany as a whole. Remarking on the disappointing box-office figures in Germany for the films made by Ernst Lubitsch in America after 1923, one contemporary observer remarked in 1926 that 'The Kurfürstendamm and Germany are two very different things'.[2] In its embracing of American culture, Berlin seemed to some observers more American than America.

In contrast both to the image of Berlin as centre of revolutionary art and bohemian lifestyles, and the view of the city as the capital of commercialized mass entertainment, the public authorities promoted a different vision of the city as a progressive polity providing an efficient urban infrastructure, combating social evils through appropriate welfare intervention and encouraging a democratic culture based on a rational lifestyle balancing work, domesticity and healthy leisure pursuits. Modern architects associated with the Bauhaus believed such a culture would be fostered by functionally designed mass housing projects, and they began from the mid-1920s onwards to gain major contracts in Berlin: building societies and the electrical engineering company Siemens commissioned housing projects, and under Martin Wagner as director of the municipal central building administration from 1927 onwards police stations and public swimming baths came to be designed in the new style as well. Even if these projects comprised only a fraction of new building in the city, they were striking symbols of the 'New Berlin'.

To contemporaries, developments in Berlin clearly embodied important shifts in culture and society which were affecting Germany generally. Accepted norms governing the form, content and exclusivity of 'high culture' were being challenged by the avant-garde. 'Mass culture' was becoming more pervasive, and its spread was seen as contributing to social homogenization: the rise of entertainments such as the cinema and the radio appeared to be loosening people's ties to traditional cultural milieux. In hindsight, however, these processes appear less straightforward. Recent studies which have focused on cultural life in the provinces, and on questions of class and cultural consumption, have been helpful in adding to and modifying the picture of cultural change.

II   Keeping pace with the capital? The avant-garde in provincial Germany

It is generally agreed that the various competing styles and versions of modernism, though flourishing spectacularly in the Weimar years, never actually dominated German cultural output in quantitative terms or in terms of public performances, exhibitions or bestseller lists. As far as the production and reception of modernist work in different parts of Germany are concerned, local and regional studies have contributed to a history of Weimar modernism which takes into account the different cultural conditions in different parts of Germany, while avoiding an oversimplified view of the provinces as constantly lagging behind the pace-setter, Berlin. At the same time, they acknowledge the extent to which some provincial contexts really did prove less receptive than the capital to aspects of avant-garde artistic production.

There were in the Weimar period, as had been the case in Wilhelmine Germany, important centres of avant-garde creativity outside Berlin. The Bauhaus, for instance, was set up in Weimar and moved to Dessau in 1925, only leaving Dessau after a Nazi motion passed by the city authorities in August 1932 forced the school to relocate to Berlin. The emergence in the mid-1920s of the 'New Objectivity' movement (*Neue Sachlichkeit*) in the visual arts – which can be seen in part as a reaction against the intensity, rage and emotionalism of Expressionism – was by no means centred on Berlin, though important *Neue Sachlichkeit* painters such as Georg Grosz, Rudolf Schlichter and Christian Schad were based there. It flourished rather in a number of provincial centres, notably Karlsruhe, Dresden, Munich, Hanover, Cologne and Düsseldorf, as Sergiusz Michalski emphasizes in his recent study.

Artistic modernism was promoted by some (though certainly not all) provincial city politicians who sought to overcome the stigma of provincialism and wanted to 'catch up with the metropolis' not only in the quality of their town's cultural facilities but in the content of its publicly subsidized arts programme. Thus, for instance, the Wiesbaden city authorities appointed the progressive theatre directors Carl Hagemann and subsequently Paul Bekker, the latter overseeing productions of Křenek's jazz-inspired opera *Jonny spielt auf* and the German premiere of Schoenberg's *Erwartung*. In the Ruhr, as Matthias Uecker has shown, the city councils of Bochum and Essen backed the conductor Rudolf Schulz-Dornburg in his campaign to convert local audiences and music critics to the work of Schoenberg, Webern, Honegger, Stravinsky and Bartok. However, few involved in the arts world of the Ruhrgebiet shared Schulz-Dornburg's commitment to the vision of a gigantic Ruhr metropolis which would dwarf London and New York in size and be united by the 'new art': as an out-and-out advocate of modernism, the conductor remained an exception in the generally more conservative cultural climate of the region.

On the whole, theatre directors and conductors in provincial towns and cities tempered their enthusiasm for new work with consideration for the preferences of subscription-buying audiences. Despite the growth of the Social Democratic *Freie*

Illustration 14.1 *The Cologne Swimmer* by Karl Hubbuch (1923)

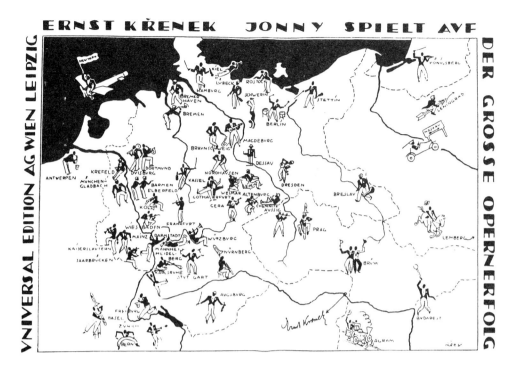

Illustration 14.2   A map showing all the places where Křenek's *Jonny spielt auf* was performed. A drawing by Rudolf Smirzits issued by Universal Edition on the occasion of the opera's first Vienna performance (1927)

Volksbühne, which supplied cut-price theatre tickets to its largely working-class membership, concert and theatre audiences were still predominantly middle-class and tended to be middle of the road in taste. The institutions of provincial cultural life remained – despite the buffeting taken by the middle classes during the inflation – what they had been in the *Kaiserreich*, a focus of middle-class sociability, bound by middle-class conventions. (Whether audiences which were more socially mixed would have been more adventurous in their tastes is another question.) Theatre schedules and concert programmes including more advanced contemporary works tended to be cushioned, just as they are today, by more familiar and reassuring items to keep audiences happy. Thus it was reported that in Wiesbaden in 1927 the subscription audience reacted to Darius Milhaud's experimental three-part miniature opera (*opéra minute*) with bewilderment, but was 'compensated and cheered' by the next item on the programme, a 'very graceful' performance of a piece by Pergolesi.[3] Studies of the theatre schedules in Heidelberg and Bochum show a predominance of light contemporary comedies and farces, operettas (increasing as a proportion of productions during the depression as public subsidies were cut and the pressure grew to maximize ticket sales), and classic plays and operas from the eighteenth and nineteenth centuries: serious contemporary drama comprised a minority of productions. At the Heidelberg city theatre, only one work by Brecht was performed during the whole of the Weimar era.

The need for caution in programme planning was underlined by cases where the scheduling of consciously progressive and avant-garde work provoked outright hostility. One such case was the world premiere of Bartok's 'musical pantomime' *The Miraculous Mandarin* at the Cologne Opera House in November 1926. Bartok had wanted the work premiered in Germany as he had expected its reception there to be particularly favourable; however, he had hoped for a premiere in Berlin or Munich, and took up the offer from Cologne only with some trepidation as, according to one biographer, Bartok 'did not trust the Cologne audience'.[4] The premiere ended in uproar, with the audience yelling and booing in the auditorium. Konrad Adenauer, the then mayor of Cologne (and later first Chancellor of the Federal Republic of Germany), then intervened personally to ban further performances. The work was never performed in Germany again during the composer's lifetime.

Sometimes rejection of new work was coupled with a quite explicit hostility to Berlin and a sense of provincial self-assertion against the decadence of the centre. In 1929, for example, the Heidelberg city theatre organized a one-off performance of the new play by Peter Martin Lampel, *Revolte im Erziehungshaus*, a work inspired by scandals concerning the maltreatment of inmates in reformatories. Reaction in the Catholic local daily *Pfälzer Bote* was withering: 'And if one result of this performance in the "provinces" is clear, then it is that it arouses horror at the moral nihilism of a certain Berlin.'[5]

Generally, therefore, the influence of artistic modernism extended well beyond the avant-garde mecca of Berlin, making its mark on publicly subsidized and publicly consumed art in smaller provincial towns as well as in larger cities. This process was aided by consciously progressive municipal and *Land* authorities, public and private galleries and art societies, and by theatre and orchestra directors committed to promoting the work of the avant-garde alongside the traditional repertoire. Public reaction to the works of the modernists was predictably diverse, ranging from enthusiasm (*Jonny spielt auf*, for instance, was an enormous popular hit), through respectful curiosity to suspicion, bewilderment or straightforward hostility.

III   Mass culture: a force for social and regional homogenization?

The extent to which the emergence of a mass culture in Weimar Germany lessened social and regional differences in cultural consumption, taste and expectations is a question that has aroused debate. Assessing the notion that new forms of entertainment acted as a force for regional and social homogenization involves looking both at the pattern of take-up and availability of these entertainments, and at the question of how far the shared experience of the same entertainment might have had a socially 'unifying' effect.

One strand of the discussion of the social impact of mass culture revolves around the extent to which it eroded class differences. 'High' culture, as already mentioned, continued to be a predominantly middle-class pursuit. But contemporaries were also struck by the revolutionary sight of cinema audiences where the wives of bank managers sat alongside sales assistants, or of the crowd at the Berlin six-day cycle races where high society and low life alike watched, cheered and got drunk. However, historians have argued that even within the working class, social differences continued to determine patterns of cultural choice: unskilled workers, for instance, were more likely than skilled workers to be attracted by the new commercial entertainments, while skilled workers were more inclined to devote leisure time to activities offered by the flourishing labour movement organizations.

Nor is the notion of a specifically female type of 'classless' consumer without its problems. Weimar's 'new woman' was constructed in such a way as to embody, among other things, the 'classless' consumer of fashion and of modern entertainments, particularly cinema; conversely, recent research (for instance by Patrice Petro) has emphasized the way in which the cinema in Weimar Germany targeted female audiences. But the powerful images dating from the period of women as consumers of modern entertainments should not obscure the financial and time constraints on working-class women's leisure. Admittedly, girls and young single women from the working class, even when they lived with their parents and were expected to do housework, had opportunities for cultural consumption in terms of time, if not in terms of spending power. However, contemporary surveys indicated that for working-class mothers real leisure time, as opposed to the time spent outside the place of paid employment, was minimal.

The extent to which audiences for the new entertainments spanned social classes and the degree to which working-class women had access to them have therefore to be assessed carefully. Even the experience of seeing the same film could be class-specific: workers might see it poorly projected in the local fleapit while the middle classes would be more likely to see it in a film palace, perhaps accompanied by a full orchestra. Moreover, if working-class and middle-class cinema-goers were mingling in the same cinema or sports stadium the classes were still likely to have been segregated on the basis of ticket prices.

Some scepticism may also be appropriate with regard to any subjective sense of cross-class unity which might have been gained from a common experience of the same entertainment – say the latest Charlie Chaplin film or a sporting event. It is plausible that any feeling of community transcending class in the auditorium or on the stands was likely to be fleeting in the face of the acute social and political divisions in Weimar society. A popular Berlin journalist reported, for example, that when at the six-day cycle races the band played *Deutschland, Deutschland über alles*, the public in the best seats applauded and the crowd on the stands whistled and booed.[6]

Looking at cultural life in smaller provincial towns and cities provides another useful perspective on the availability, take-up and social impact of mass culture. Modern forms of entertainment were certainly extending the range of leisure activities available to small-town populations. However, access to the new entertainments varied greatly depending on the region and the size of the locality. Rural Pomerania, to take an extreme example, was hardly touched by modern leisure customs or facilities. Dime novels, village taverns and sports competitions – as 'modern' as leisure pursuits got in Pomerania – were in evidence to the extent that the Pomeranian clergy felt called upon to complain about them, but church holidays, in particular the harvest festival, were the prime source of popular entertainment. Radio, that supposed force for cultural homogenization across classes and regions, was scarcely known.

Radio is a particularly striking case in which assumptions about the impact of new mass media across different classes and across the country as a whole become qualified when the evidence is looked at closely. Superficially, the story of the rise of radio in the Weimar Republic is one of the triumphs of the new medium. The first public radio programme began broadcasting in October 1923 from Berlin; other regional stations also started up in 1923–4, while the nationwide Deutsche Welle was established in 1926. The number of registered radio listeners increased steadily and by 1932 there were 4.2 million registered radio sets. However, as Karl Christian Führer has demonstrated, these figures showing an impressive overall growth in radio use concealed both high drop-out rates during the 1920s by (presumably disappointed) listeners abandoning their radio licences, and significant disparities across the Reich in the distribution of listeners. For most of the 1920s, the regional transmitters emitted such weak signals that to pick them up outside a certain radius (in 1926 around 50–70 kilometres) would-be listeners needed an elaborate and expensive radio set: the cost of such a set would in the late 1920s have swallowed half of the average monthly income for the average working-class urban household. In 1927 only 31 per cent of the German population lived in areas within which the cheaper 'detector' sets could be used.

The difficulties with reception and the resulting costs of buying adequate radio sets, together with the often stodgy and highbrow programmes offered, made radio a medium which was used disproportionately by the middle classes: only about a quarter of the radio audience by the end of the Weimar Republic was working-class. Radio can therefore hardly be seen as a major force bridging the class divide. In regional terms, the difficulties with reception made radio a medium of urban-dwellers. Of the Berliner Funkstunde's registered listeners, 83 per cent lived in Berlin and Stettin, the cities where the company's two transmitters were located. In April 1932, radio ownership in big cities of more than half a million inhabitants had reached 46 per cent of households; in villages of fewer than 2,500 inhabitants, only 10 per cent of households had a radio. The sluggish take-up of radio in rural areas was in spite of the efforts of 'radio vans' (*Werbewagen*) equipped with demonstration sets which travelled round rural areas trying to drum up interest in the medium. It confounded the hopes of radio companies and politicians that radio above all was the medium with the potential to bring the wider world to rural Germany and perhaps even counteract the flight from the land by making rural life less monotonous.

Illustration 14.3   Radio propaganda vehicle in a small town in the Mark, 1927

When considering the impact of new media and entertainments on German cultural life it is also important to stress the local context in which they were consumed. A case study by Konrad Dussel and Matthias Frese of leisure in the town of Weinheim in Baden (population *c.* 16,000) shows for the Weimar years the impressive variety of leisure activities and facilities available to such a small town. These included cinema, though only from 1925: in that year Weinheim's first cinema was opened by a café owner who built an extension onto his café, and by early 1930 three cinemas were in operation. Their typical offerings at this time included detective films and, with sound film a relative novelty, operetta films such as *Der Zarewitsch*, shown in Weinheim in March 1930 with a musical prelude on gramophone record. 'Educational' films, dealing discreetly but suggestively with themes of 'forbidden love' and venereal disease, featured at late showings on Saturday nights. The jazz craze, too, hit Weinheim in the 1920s: revellers going out on Whit Monday 1926 could find a 'Jazzband Concert' either at the tavern 'Zum Goldenen Bock' or at the Café Vogel.

However, even with the novelty of films at the local 'Alhambra' and jazz in the local tavern, leisure in Weinheim in the 1920s and early 1930s continued, as was the case before the war, to revolve around pubs and clubs, with men constituting the majority of regular pub-goers and club members. Once women got married, it seems, they stayed at home while their husbands went out in the evenings. With 'bourgeois' and 'proletarian', Catholic and Protestant clubs, Weinheim's associational life reflected the political, social and confessional divisions of the town. Commercial entertainments, even if consumed by a socially heterogeneous audience, did not substantially erode these divisions. This could be seen as confirmation of the continuing strength in the small-town context of cultural milieux based on class and political allegiance.

While the role of Weinheim's clubs and associations in structuring its members' leisure time and providing public entertainments did decline in the 1930s, this appears to have been due not so much to the rise of 'mass entertainments' as the destructive impact of Nazi rule on associational life after 1933. The effects of the regime having wiped out much of Weinheim's locally organized cultural life, the organization *Kraft durch Freude* ('Strength through Joy') could come in and fill the vacuum.

IV   The reaction against modernism and mass culture

Partial though it was, the impact of artistic modernism and mass culture in the Weimar period was sufficient to provoke a powerful backlash, especially among a section of the middle classes: only a section, it must be emphasized, since after all the enthusiastic audiences for avant-garde art and the new music, such as they were, were drawn largely from the educated bourgeoisie. Nevertheless, it has been remarked that while in other countries similar changes were occurring in cultural life, in Weimar Germany a particularly sharp middle-class reaction against them could be observed. This, Detlev Peukert has suggested, could have been because the idea of the nation being degraded by foreigners took root so strongly in post-First World War Germany; because domestic developments in the republic threatened the security of the middle classes politically and economically as well as culturally; and because middle-class Germans were accustomed to an idea of Germany as an outstanding 'cultural nation' (*Kulturnation*) with a heritage particularly meriting protection.

Admittedly, a sense of alienation from and alarm about the new cultural forces was not restricted socially to the middle classes nor politically to the parties of the right. There were also mixed reactions on the left to the works of the avant-garde. Although left-wing intellectuals such as those associated with the periodical *Weltbühne* – many of them, as their enemies noted, Jewish – were committed advocates of artistic modernism, Social Democratic cultural experts were more inclined to promote to workers the tried and tested products of the bourgeois cultural canon rather than the works of the avant-garde, while Communist cultural organizations pursued their own goals of creating a proletarian counter-culture. The left was also dubious about aspects of commercial mass culture. Social Democrats were as concerned as bourgeois organizations about the impact of pulp fiction on youthful minds, even if they did end up in 1926 opposing the law restricting the sale of pulp fiction. Both Social Democratic and

Communist organizations regarded the rise of the cinema with concern, fearing that the labour movement would never be able to offer a socialist alternative to match the sophisticated products of the international film industry. Nor was anti-urbanism, though particularly associated with *völkisch* blood and soil myths and the idea of youth taking to the land as the route to national rebirth, a monopoly of the right. While municipal SPD politicians praised the social achievements of modern, progressively run cities, on the radical fringes of the left there were anarchists and socialists who denounced modern cities as irredeemably steeped in the evils of capitalism and who saw rural communes as the road to a classless and peaceful society: a number of such communes were founded as a consequence in the immediate post-war years and again in the depression. Left-wing responses to the cultural innovations of the Weimar years were thus complex and ambivalent. Nevertheless, there was on the whole more openness and curiosity on the political left than on the right regarding both avant-garde art and the new forms of mass communication: this can be seen for instance, in the efforts of the SPD and KPD to distribute films they regarded as progressive, and to use films as promotional material for members.

The harshest attacks on modernism and the greatest anxieties about the impact of modernization on cultural life emanated from bourgeois organizations and from the right. Much of the research on the cultural conservatism of the right has focused on its intellectual history, and in particular on that strand of cultural conservatism which labelled itself 'young conservatism', 'neo-conservatism' or 'conservative revolution'. Neo-conservatism was far from homogeneous, and was certainly not even wholeheartedly 'anti-modern'. Some theorists did indeed preach ruralism and racial mysticism, but others, as Jeffrey Herf in particular has shown, emphasized the need to harness technological progress to an authoritarian political framework. However, neo-conservative thinking had a number of common themes: that the stale and stiflingly bourgeois culture of Imperial Germany was better dead; that the republic had crushed and wasted the positive national energies unleashed by the war; that Weimar's cultural life was irredeemably debased by foreign and Jewish influence and 'shallow materialism'; and that a new order was needed, a 'Third Reich' in which elite rule would bring about class harmony, a restoration of gender differences, a synthesis of the 'best elements' in nationalism and socialism, and the victory of German *Kultur* over 'civilization'.

Politically, the neo-conservatives were a failure. Their interventions in Weimar politics were a shambles, and the futility of their attempts to influence Nazi policies after 1933 was brutally demonstrated when one of their main spokesmen, Edgar J. Jung, was shot dead as part of the regime's score-settling at the time of the Röhm purge in June 1934. However, as networkers and self-publicists they were highly effective. One particularly fertile 'ideas factory' of neo-conservatism was Motzstraße 22 in Berlin (just down the street from the bars and revue theatres of the Nollendorfplatz), where a number of right-wing clubs, circles and periodicals had their headquarters. Thanks to publishing houses such as Eugen Diederichs and J. F. Lehmanns, as Gary Stark has shown, neo-conservative ideology gained a clearer profile and reached an extensive readership, particularly among the ranks of the bourgeois youth movement (*bündische Jugend*).

Neo-conservatism was just one particularly vociferous strand of conservative cultural critique in the Weimar period. There were other interest groups and lobbies who took a gloomy view of contemporary cultural life. One group with an obvious axe to grind were those who continued to write tonal music, paint figuratively and design buildings in a more traditional style (trademark: the pitched roof): feeling sidelined and resentful of the avant-garde, conservative composers, artists and architects talked of 'fads', decried the quality of modernist work, and predicted that their time would come again.

Another grouping in the broad camp of cultural conservatism consisted of the churches and organizations such as the 'Working Party for the Restoration of the Health of the Nation' (*Arbeitsgemeinschaft für Volksgesundung*). These organizations campaigned against 'immorality' in modern life, whether this took the form of atheism, blasphemy, nudism, pornography, prostitution, homosexuality, birth control, abortion or companionate marriage. Cultural experts from the Zentrum and the DNVP railed against the 'tides of filth' engulfing Germany and Berlin in particular, and called for tougher censorship as a matter of cultural hygiene. One step in this direction was the passing by the Reichstag of a bill to 'protect youth from pulp fiction and pornography', the *Gesetz zur Bewahrung der Jugend vor Schund- und Schmutzschriften* of 18 December 1926. On the basis of this law, an index was set up of publications which were not to be sold to young people under 18: 'true crime' publications, erotic magazines and sex education books were among the 103 publications on the index by 1930.

As well as examining conservative theories and arguments, however, an analysis of the politics of cultural defence in the Weimar Republic also needs to take into account how conservative cultural attitudes at local level were reinforced by and articulated through associational life and local politics. Such a perspective can also raise the question of how the organized middle classes in Weimar Germany reacted to and sought to contain the process of cultural change, and how successfully they were able to do so.

Heimatvereine and the *Verein für das Deutschtum im Ausland* are two examples of middle-class 'cultural defence' organizations. Provincial *Heimatvereine*, as studies by Celia Applegate and Karl Ditt have shown, were typically run by schoolteachers and local history enthusiasts and often supported by local and regional governments. They offered the public-spirited middle classes a forum where they combined sociability with the 'idealistic' task of discovering and preserving (and, if necessary, inventing) local identities and traditions. Such associations put on folk evenings with dialect plays and folk dancing, set up *Heimat* museums featuring obscure 'bygones', agitated for nature conservation, and ran campaigns against the proliferation of advertizing hoardings.

The idea of defending culture, though here culture was defined more in national than local terms, was also central to the work of the *Verein für das Deutschtum im Ausland* or VDA (Society for the Protection of Germandom Abroad) which set out to protect German culture against erosion by foreign influences, particularly in Germany's borderlands and beyond its borders: its 1,500 local groups, including local women's sections and youth groups run by schools, were, like the *Heimatvereine*, a presence in middle-class associational life dating back to the *Kaiserreich*. VDA events spanned the divide between the tradition of German classicism and contemporary German nationalism: lectures on 'Goethe in Bohemia' were juxtaposed with musical entertainment by the local Stahlhelm band.

All these activities can be seen as attempts to shore up middle-class cultural hegemony as well as the notion that authentic German culture was best preserved in locations remote from the big cities and above all Berlin. The VDA praised German communities abroad who seemed to be preserving cultural traditions (folk-dancing, church-going, family prayers) which were being increasingly challenged at home; *Heimatvereine* celebrated regional folk traditions as a bulwark against the homogenizing and centralizing influences of modern urban culture. The dilemma for these organizations, however, was how to reconcile a firm stance against the evils of modern culture without lapsing into nostalgia and escapism.

From 1929–30 onwards, the depression and the shift to the right in Weimar politics assisted the cause of cultural conservatism in a number of ways. With the country gripped by full-blown economic and political crisis, the vague but apocalyptic calls by the neo-conservatives for a 'new Reich' or a 'Third Reich' became more insistent. Such positions as had been won by the avant-garde were meanwhile being undermined both financially and politically. Although surprisingly few theatres and concert halls closed down altogether, cuts in local government spending forced theatres and orchestras to modify their programmes so as to ensure greater commercial viability, much as they had also done during the period of hyperinflation. Theatres increasingly substituted operettas for opera, concert organizers became more reluctant to programme contemporary works. Politically, the tide was running strongly against committed left-wing cultural efforts and against the avant-garde. In 1932 restrictions on the Communist press proliferated, and Communist freethinkers' organizations were banned by emergency decree. Even before the appointment of Hitler as Chancellor, a purge of those identified with the cultural avant-garde was beginning: thus, for instance, after the Reich government's coup against the *Land* government in Prussia in July 1932, two prominent advocates of the new music, Leo Kestenberg and Franz Schreker, were dismissed from their posts as music adviser in the Prussian Ministry of Education and director of the Staatliche Musikhochschule respectively.

The National Socialists, who emerged onto the battleground of cultural politics from around 1929 onwards, joined the bandwagon of cultural conservatism while giving it additional momentum. Laying claim to the leadership of the movement against mass culture, modernism, Americanism, Bolshevism, and female emancipation, the Nazis used their cultural activism – focused on the *Kampfbund für deutsche Kultur* – to try to enhance their standing among the propertied and educated middle classes. The self-styled Nazi cultural expert Alfred Rosenberg launched violent and scurrilous attacks, such as those in his 1930 polemic *Der Sumpf: Querschnitte durch das 'Geistes'-leben der November-Demokratie* ('The morass: a cross-section of "intellectual" life in the November-democracy') on all that was 'Jewish', 'nigger', 'Bolshevik', and 'perverse' in German cultural life. A foretaste of what would be in store if the National Socialists were to gain power in the Reich was provided in Thüringen in 1930–1. As Minister of the Interior and Education in the Thüringen *Land* government from January 1930 until April 1931, the National Socialist Wilhelm Frick presided over a campaign to remove modern art from museums and public buildings and impose restrictions on the performance of jazz music.

Thus before 1933 the contours of the National Socialists' cultural policy were visible, even if much of the detail emerged fully only after their takeover of government in the Reich. It was becoming evident that the footholds gained by the avant-garde in Weimar's cultural life would be destroyed, that the cultural organizations of the left would be smashed, and that both 'high culture' and mass entertainment would be made to serve Nazi purposes. But cultural conservatism would have to be brought under control and oriented towards Nazi ends as well. The 'struggle for German culture' had to be forward-looking, blending the traditional and the modern, and be based not merely on the celebration of folk culture and the diversity of *Heimat* traditions, but on the application of 'scientific' racism and the incorporation of all classes and all parts of Germany into a close-knit national whole. Where mass culture under the conditions of Weimar democracy might have partially eroded but certainly not eliminated class divisions and regional diversity in German cultural life, National Socialism set out to impose cultural homogeneity through coercion.

Acknowledgement

I would like to thank Karl Christian Führer for his extremely helpful comments and suggestions on an earlier draft of this essay.

Notes:

1. *Statistisches Jahrbuch deutscher Städte* vol. 24 (= Neue Folge vol. 3) (1929), pp. 329–30.
2. 'Debatten über den deutschen Film', *Film-Kurier* 9 (1927), no. 76 (unpaginated). I am indebted to Karl Christian Führer for this reference.
3. Haddenhorst, Gerda, 'Das Wiesbadener Theater in der Zeit der Weimarer Republik', *Nassauische Annalen*, 100 (1989), pp. 243–64, here p. 246.
4. Zielinski, Tadeusz, *Bartok* (Zurich: Atlantis Verlag, 1973), p. 259.
5. Dussel, Konrad, 'Von Bert Brecht zu Hanns Johst? Deutsches Provinztheater 1918–1944 im Spiegel seiner Spielpläne', *Universitas* 9 (1988), pp. 976–89, here p. 985.
6. 'Sechstagerennen', in *Sling: Die Nase der Sphinx oder Wie wir Berliner so sind* (Berlin: Buchverlag Der Morgen, 1987), p. 172.

Select bibliography

Abrams, Lynn, 'From Control to Commercialization: The Triumph of Mass Entertainment in Germany, 1900–25?', *German History* 8 (1990), pp. 278–93.

Alter, Peter, ed., *Im Banne der Metropolen: Berlin und London in den zwanziger Jahren* (Göttingen: Vandenhoeck and Ruprecht, 1993).

Applegate, Celia, *A Nation of Provincials: The German Idea of Heimat* (Berkeley, Los Angeles and Oxford: University of California Press, 1990).

Ditt, Karl, *Raum und Volkstum: Die Kulturpolitik des Provinzialverbandes Westfalen 1923–1945* (Münster: Aschendorff, 1988).

Dussel, Konrad, 'Von Bert Brecht zu Hanns Johst? Deutsches Provinztheater 1918–1944 im Spiegel seiner Spielpläne', *Universitas* 9 (1988), pp. 976–89.

Dussel, Konrad, and Frese, Matthias, *Freizeit in Weinheim. Studien zur Geschichte der Freizeit 1919–1939* (*Weinheimer Geschichtsblatt*: Herausgegeben im Auftrag der Stadt Weinheim an der Bergstrasse, Heft 35, 1989).

Feldman, Gerald D., *The Great Disorder: Politics, Economics and Society in the German Inflation, 1914–1924* (New York and Oxford: Oxford University Press, 1993).

Führer, Karl Christian, 'Auf dem Weg zur "Massenkultur"? Kino und Rundfunk in der Weimarer Republik', *Historische Zeitschrift* 262 (1996), pp. 739–81.

Führer, Karl Christian, *Wirtschaftsgeschichte der deutschen Rundfunkgesellschaften 1923 bis 1932* (Berlin: Verlag für Berlin-Brandenburg, 1996).

Gay, Peter, *Weimar Culture: The Outsider as Insider* (London: Penguin, 1974).

Haxthausen, Charles W., and Suhr, Heidrun, eds., *Berlin: Culture and Metropolis* (Minneapolis and Oxford: University of Minnesota Press, 1990).

Herf, Jeffrey, *Reactionary Modernism: Technology, Culture and Politics in Weimar and the Third Reich* (Cambridge: CUP, 1984).

Hermand, Jost, and Trommler, Frank, *Die Kultur der Weimarer Republik* (Frankfurt am Main: Fischer, 1988).

Jones, Larry Eugene, 'Culture and Politics in the Weimar Republic', in Gordon Martel, ed., *Modern Germany Reconsidered 1870–1945* (London: Routledge, 1992).

Kater, Michael, 'The Revenge of the Fathers: the Demise of Modern Music at the End of the Weimer Republic', *German Studies Review* 15 (1992), pp. 295–315.

Kniesche, Thomas W., and Brockmann, Stephen, eds., *Dancing on the Volcano: Essays on the Culture of the Weimar Republic* (Columbia, SC: Camden House, 1994).

Lane, Barbara Miller, *Architecture and Politics in Germany 1918–1945*, 2nd edition (Cambridge, MA: Harvard University Press, 1985.

Laqueur, Walter, *Weimar: A Cultural History 1918–1933* (London: Weidenfeld and Nicolson, 1974).

Meskimmon, Marsha, and West, Shearer, eds., *Visions of the Neue Frau. Women and the Visual Arts in Weimar Germany* (Aldershot: Scolar Press, 1995).

Michalski, Sergiusz, *New Objectivity: Painting, Graphic Art and Photography in Weimar Germany 1919–1933* (Cologne: Benedikt Taschen Verlag, 1994).

Nolan, Mary, *Visions of Modernity: American Business and the Modernization of Germany* (New York and Oxford: Oxford University Press, 1994).

Petersen, Klaus, *Zensur in der Weimarer Republik* (Stuttgart and Weimar: Metzler, 1995).

Petro, Patrice, *Joyless Streets. Women and Melodramatic Representation in Weimar Germany* (Princeton, NJ: Princeton University Press, 1989).

Peukert, Detlev J. K., *The Weimar Republic: The Crisis of Classical Modernity* (London: Allen Lane, 1991).

Plummer, Thomas G., *et al.*, eds., *Film and Politics in the Weimar Republic* (New York: Holmes and Meier, 1982).

Rosenhaft, Eve, 'Brecht's Germany, 1898–1933', in Peter Thomson and Glendyr Sacks, eds., *The Cambridge Companion to Brecht* (Cambridge: Cambridge University Press, 1994).

von Saldern, Adelheid, 'Der Wochenend-Mensch: Zur Geschichte der Freizeit in den Zwanziger Jahren', *Mitteilungen aus der kulturwissenschaftlichen Forschung* 15, Heft 30, March 1992.

Stark, Gary, *Entrepreneurs of Ideology: Neoconservative Publishers in Weimar Germany* (Chapel Hill, NC.: University of North Carolina Press, 1981).

Steinweis, Alan E., 'Weimar Culture and the Rise of National Socialism. The Kampfbund für deutsche Kultur', *Central European History* 24 (1991), no. 4, pp. 402–23.

Uecker, Matthias, *Zwischen Industrieprovinz und Großstadthoffnung. Kulturpolitik im Ruhrgebiet der zwanziger Jahre* (Wiesbaden: Deutscher Universitäts-Verlag, 1994).

Wernecke, Klaus, 'Kinobesuch als Freizeitvergnügen. Der Spielfilm als klassenübergreifendes Medium in der Weimarer Republik', *Mitteilungen aus der kulturwissenschaftlichen Forschung* 15, Heft 30, March 1992.

Westphal, Uwe, *Berliner Konfektion und Mode 1836–1939. Die Zerstörung einer Tradition*, 2nd edition (Berlin: Edition Hentrich, 1992).

15

The rise of the Nazis: *Sonderweg* or spanner in the works?

Jill Stephenson

I Contours of the debate

> It is a party without history which suddenly emerges in German political life, just as an island suddenly emerges in the middle of the sea owing to volcanic forces.[1]

Thus the Comintern agent Karl Radek characterized the effect on the German political scene of the electoral success enjoyed by the National Socialist German Workers' Party (NSDAP) in September 1930, when, from a tiny political base, it achieved 6.4 million votes (18.3 per cent of the total) and 107 seats in the Reichstag, as the second strongest party after the Social Democrats (SPD). For Radek, normally an acute observer of the German scene, the NSDAP suddenly came from nowhere. By contrast, for some commentators in the 1950s and 1960s, most notoriously the American William Shirer, it was all too clear where National Socialism had come from: German history from Martin Luther to Frederick the Great and the Kaiser – via Fichte, Hegel and Nietzsche, among others – formed a logical continuum of subservience to authority, rampant nationalism and inherent anti-Semitism. Between these two simplistic extremes, it is possible to tease out both continuities from previous German history and a peculiar combination of early twentieth-century circumstances which, together, created the conditions in which National Socialism could take root and thrive. Both the continuities and the peculiarities have their counterparts in the history of other countries. In particular, anti-Semitism had deep roots in many European societies. Further, the dislocation effected by industrialization, and, more immediately around 1930, the catastrophic effects of the great depression, produced extreme political responses across the continent. In addition, the survival of Bolshevism in Russia was seen by many Europeans as a threat, contributing to a conservative reaction and the emergence of fascist movements on the political fringe in most countries in the inter-war years.

But the German reaction to the problems of the early twentieth century was so much more virulent than that anywhere else that there has, ever since, been a quest to discover why Germany was different, or even 'peculiar'. Some have read the history of Germany in the entire modern period as a prelude to the Third Reich, with the French historian, Edmond Vermeil, giving an extreme example of this view:

> If, in addition to the influence of territorial Lutheranism, we take into account the influences of Counter-Reformation Catholicism and Romantic idealism, from which the twentieth-century national ideology stems, we can understand the German social *mystique*. To Germans this meant the organic State, the new Reich conceived as a planned community . . . . Here was the *Volkstum*, the popular totality of Germany.[2]

Others made intellectually disreputable assertions about the flawed nature of the German 'national character', with A. J. P. Taylor claiming that, even if its methods were widely disliked, the Third Reich 'was also a system which represented the deepest wishes of the German people. . . . It was a tyranny imposed upon the German people by themselves',[3] because only thus could they achieve the domination of their neighbours which they desired.

So, did modern Germany follow a 'special path' (*Sonderweg*) of development which led logically to dictatorship, war and genocide? This determinist and pessimistic view was challenged by historians like Gerhard Ritter who argued, by contrast, that:

> It is a very great mistake to believe that the modern function of leader of the people is in any way the heritage and continuation of the old, monarchic power of the princes. Neither Frederick the Great, Bismarck, nor Wilhelm II were the historical precursors of Adolf Hitler. His precursors were the demagogues and Caesars of modern history, from Danton to Lenin and Mussolini.[4]

It followed that the National Socialists were able to come to power because of a strange coincidence of crises amounting almost to an 'industrial accident' – like dropping a spanner in the works. Yet to the new generation, writing in the 1960s and 1970s in the wake of the Fischer controversy about the First World War's origins, there seemed to be too much of a coincidence about Germany's central role in precipitating two major wars in 25 years. While rejecting crude prejudices about a German 'national character', some argued that Germany had taken a 'wrong' turning in the later eighteenth century. According to Wolfgang Mommsen, after 1945 'the Germans gradually rejoined the common stream of Western political culture from which they had gradually dissociated themselves since the Enlightenment'.[5] Karl Dietrich Bracher identified 'the deep schism between German and Western political thought, and the emergence of a special German sense of destiny with anti-Western overtones'.[6] Earlier, Werner Conze had argued that 'in the nineteenth century, elements were already recognizable in the early national movement which later emerged, grossly distorted, within National Socialism'.[7] Others found their explanation in what Volker Berghahn has described as 'the structural peculiarities'[8] of German society in the later nineteenth and earlier twentieth centuries. Germany's road to modernity combined the mutually contradictory forces of rapid, thoroughgoing industrialization and a political and social system inherited from *ancien régime* Prussia. According to Hans-Ulrich Wehler, the traditional elites devised cunning strategies for containing the new social forces, which merely delayed domestic confrontation until after 1918.

Whatever its precise origins, this *Sonderweg* allegedly diverted Germans from 'normal' western development, which is characterized as progress towards a democratic, parliamentary and humanitarian polity and society, embodying values and standards deriving from the Enlightenment. Whether there was a common western model is doubtful, given the marked differences in development of France, Britain and the USA, for example. But here the question is: was there something peculiar about Germany's development as a modern society which predisposed its citizens to embrace National Socialism and its inhuman values? Or, conversely, was the fledgling democratic republic deprived of the chance to make a healthy start because of a combination of crises, from attempted revolution in 1918–19, through the Versailles Treaty and the great inflation of 1923, to the economic depression at the end of the 1920s?

The problems to which the singularity of the German experience have been attributed are, broadly, modernization, militarism and immaturity. While these features can be identified in other countries, it was their extreme form and their idiosyncratic inter-relationships in Germany which seemed to create the preconditions for cataclysm. Certainly, modernization in the German Empire of 1871–1918 meant rapid, intensive and highly successful economic, industrial, technological and scientific development, which created new, assertive (urban) social classes and put some of the traditional (often rural) sections of society on the defensive. At the same time, political life was dominated by the pre-industrial elites, with an authoritarian monarchy reinforced by a powerful army and an influential landowning social class. This system allegedly deprived genuine democrats of political experience which, after 1918, was evident in their political 'immaturity' once a democratic system was established. The wider background for this development was the 'immaturity' of the German nation state, whose 'late development' in a *Mittellage* – in a central, encircled position in Europe – pushed the country's leadership into a defensive mentality which was manifested in an increasingly offensive foreign policy, with the accent on military superiority and preparation for war.

More recently, however, it has been argued – particularly by British historians of Imperial Germany – that a Prusso-centred approach does not reflect the diversity of experience throughout the Empire, that the picture of a co-opted industrial and professional middle class underestimates their self-confidence and autonomy, and that the variety of political and associational activities at local level gave many Germans experience of public life before the advent of parliamentary democracy at national level. The imperial government and its allies had to accommodate the aspirations of the new social forces in both the middle and the urban working classes, even if ultimate authority continued to rest with the Kaiser and his circle (see the chapters in Part II, above). It can further be argued that Germany was not a 'western' country but a central

European country, sharing some characteristics with its western neighbours and also some with those in neighbouring areas of *eastern* Europe. While the 'modern' aspects of German development mirror those of some western countries, the continuing power and status of a traditional landed elite and the authoritarian system itself are recognizable as part of the eastern European pattern. The search for overseas colonies and the creation of an ocean-going navy show Germany in 'western' mode, while the desire for a contiguous land empire, as famously manifested in the 'September Programme' of Chancellor Bethmann Hollweg in 1914, matches the pattern of expansion of countries like Russia and Austria-Hungary. With its 'western' landholding small farmers and 'eastern' latifundia with tenant farmers or wage labourers, Germany straddled Europe as a hybrid nation. On the whole, these contrasting elements coexisted in uneasy tandem, but where their paths intersected there might be confrontation, or even collision, between urban Germany's industrial economy and society – the most modern in Europe – and the traditional 'backward' sections of society which felt increasingly threatened by new classes, institutions and practices.

II Changes in the party-political landscape

Under the Empire, these differing regional and social patterns were represented in sociocultural structures which broadly reflected political allegiances. In the 1960s, Rainer Lepsius adopted the term 'milieu'[9] to describe these structures which, he argued, promoted remarkable party-political stability, from 1871 to 1928. For example, urban factory workers might belong to the Social Democratic milieu. Beyond merely voting for or even joining the SPD, this implied an entire lifestyle, with these workers and their families using local Social Democratic leisure and welfare facilities, reading the party's press and generally insulating themselves from the institutions and values of the Imperial German establishment. German Catholics comprised another major milieu, with their own sub-culture parallel to that of the Socialists. Liberals and Conservatives formed, for Lepsius, the two other major milieux, and while there were 'dissidents' who belonged instead to peasants' associations or regional parties, they were relatively small in number. But this did not indicate political coherence across the country: for example, 'conservatism' meant very different things to landowners in East Prussia, industrialists in the Ruhr and peasants in southern and western Germany. Thus party loyalty was often mediated through the milieu; that is, the milieu was the immediate focus of loyalty, with the political party a more distant construct.

While the First World War and its aftermath, including economic and social crises, disoriented many Germans in the 1920s, the political geography of the later Weimar Republic provided a hospitable environment for the growth of National Socialism. After 1918, the fault-lines in the existing milieus became ever more apparent, with substantial numbers deserting them for what Rudy Koshar has called 'apolitical'[10] social or single-issue associations which were not attached to a particular party but were, nevertheless, in many cases, highly political. The chief contribution of these special interest groups was to undermine the existing parties. With the fall of the monarchy, traditional Protestant conservatives, now assembled in the DNVP (German National People's Party), had lost the initiative, and their electoral fortunes in the 1920s (see Table 15.1) revealed that they had been reduced to a disaffected rump, leaving those who regarded themselves as Germany's rightful leaders without a secure powerbase. The DNVP's core of support in the East Elbian landowning class was both consistent in its opposition to the democratic republic and unable to comprehend the concept of a 'loyal opposition'. This was not critical while the DNVP languished on the margins of Weimar politics, but when it began to ally tactically with the growing battalions of the NSDAP, from 1929, it would prove fateful. Further, while young conservative intellectuals rejected the DNVP's old-fashioned nationalism, they aimed for a 'conservative revolution' and were susceptible to the appeal of what Kurt Sontheimer characterized as 'anti-democratic thought',[11] which bred attitudes which fatally undermined Weimar democracy. These young conservatives lacked the political organization to campaign effectively, and, again, some gravitated towards the NSDAP.

At the same time, as myriad tiny, single-issue splinter parties fragmented an already fissiparous landscape, support for the parties of the political centre haemorrhaged. Shifting coalitions of several parties became customary by the later 1920s, with the virtual eclipse of the republic's two liberal parties, the Democrats (DDP) and the People's Party (DVP). Admittedly, two of the three partners in the original 'Weimar coalition' of 1919, the SPD and the Roman Catholic Centre Party, remained substantial forces, with the Centre (in Bavaria, the BVP – Bavarian People's Party), especially, the establishment party in strongly Catholic areas, where it could sometimes command between a third and half of the vote (see Table 15.2). But coalitions between the

Table 15.1   Reichstag election results, 1928–33 (votes in millions with rounded percentages)

	1928	1930	1932 (July)	1932 (Nov.)	1933
SPD	9.15 (29.8%)	8.58 (24.5%)	7.96 (21.6%)	7.25 (20.4%)	7.18 (18.3%)
KPD	3.26 (10.6%)	4.59 (13.1%)	5.28 (14.3%)	5.98 (16.9%)	4.85 (12.3%)
DDP*	1.51 (4.9%)	1.32 (3.8%)	0.37 (1.0%)	0.34 (1.0%)	0.33 (0.8%)
DVP	2.68 (8.7%)	1.58 (4.5%)	0.44 (1.2%)	0.66 (1.9%)	0.43 (1.1%)
Centre/BVP	4.66 (15.2%)	5.19 (14.8%)	5.78 (15.7%)	5.32 (15.0%)	5.50 (14.0%)
DNVP	4.38 (14.2%)	2.46 (7.0%)	2.18 (5.9%)	2.96 (8.4%)	3.14 (8.0%)
NSDAP	0.81 (2.6%)	6.41 (18.3%)	13.75 (37.3%)	11.74 (33.1%)	17.28 (43.9%)
Others	2.30 (7.5%)	4.84 (13.8%)	1.20 (3.3%)	1.22 (3.4%)	0.63 (1.6%)
Total**	**30.75**	**34.97**	**36.88**	**35.47**	**39.34**
Percentage poll***	75.60%	82.00%	84.02%	80.57%	88.73%

Notes:
* In 1930, the DDP changed its name to 'Deutsche Staatspartei'.
** This is the total of *valid* votes cast, excluding spoilt papers.
*** This is the turnout – the percentage of those entitled to vote who did vote, including those who spoilt their ballot papers.
Source: Statistisches Jahrbuch für das Deutsche Reich (1933), p. 539.

Table 15.2 The Centre Party in the Reichstag
elections of July 1932 and March 1933 (electoral
districts providing the strongest support for the
Centre Party/BVP, in percentages of the total
number of votes cast)

	July 1932	March 1933
Düsseldorf East	20.6	19.6
Württemberg	21.8	17.7
Westphalia South	23.6	22.5
Palatinate	23.8	22.7
Franconia	24.7	22.4
Baden	29.1	25.4
Westphalia North	32.9	28.7
Düsseldorf West	34.0	30.4
Oppeln	34.6	32.3
Upper Bavaria/Swabia	36.6	29.0
Cologne/Aachen	40.5	35.9
Koblenz/Trier	46.2	40.9
Lower Bavaria	48.0	37.6
National average	15.7	14.0

Source: Statistisches Jahrbuch für das Deutsche Reich: (1932),
p. 542; (1933), pp. 540–1.

Centre and the SPD were always a marriage of convenience, and the depression's stresses rendered irretrievable the breakdown which had become increasingly likely by the later 1920s. Further, the rightward shift in the Centre's national leadership in the later 1920s repelled some supporters, including industrial workers in the central/southern Black Forest region in southwest Germany. At the same time, claims Oded Heilbronner, 'Catholic social life steadily disintegrated throughout the Weimar period'.[12] The result was that, in the 1920s, the Centre Party could attract barely half of the Catholic vote.

The Socialist milieu alone had traditionally enjoyed class homogeneity, but by the 1920s the SPD was not the only party claiming to represent proletarians. Although it had seemed the strongest party in the early Weimar years, the SPD was out of government during the years of relative stability in the mid to later 1920s, returning in 1928 to face the economic crisis (see Chapter 12, above). Its weakness lay partly in the increasing reluctance of other major parties to work with it, because it was associated with the 'social state', especially with the social welfare reforms which were resented by employers and many in the middle classes. By the later 1920s, the SPD could not attract even half of the working-class vote. According to Tim Mason, the SPD and the Communist Party (KPD) together – not that they ever actually worked together – could attract only about one half of the total working-class vote. Nevertheless, some middle-class Germans were alarmed that several million of their compatriots voted either for the Communists or for the other party with a Marxist programme, the SPD. There was widespread dismay at the success of the revolutionary left in Russia in 1917, and at the establishment in Germany of a party, the KPD, whose first loyalty was to international revolution.

It is clear that during the 1920s many non-proletarian Germans became less rather than more confident in the new democratic political system which gave the mass of the people a voice, through elections to responsible authorities at local, *Land* (state) and Reich (national) levels. Their insecurity was enhanced by the massive economic and financial crises which struck twice in a decade and disposed many to seek stability in 'strong government'. While runaway inflation in the early 1920s had ruined some middle-class Germans and terrified many others, the great depression around 1930 was a crisis of modern economies which damaged Germany – the leading European industrial economy – particularly severely, creating acute hardship among industrial workers especially. At the same time, agricultural recession had bred poverty and insecurity, particularly in Germany's many small rural communities. Many blamed the republican system itself for their problems, and became susceptible to the siren call of the new radical right. As William Sheridan Allen has said 'they had no effective organization to express their often inchoate and even contradictory antipathies. More precisely, they had too many organizations – none of them effective – as radical Rightist grouplets sprang up all over the country'.[13]

Starting as just one of these 'grouplets', the NSDAP developed a formidable organizational structure which enabled it, in only a few years, to absorb other fringe political groupings as well as some of the 'apolitical' organizations – including peasants' leagues – which were the beneficiaries of both the breaking down of traditional milieux and discontent with the status quo. A party which could exploit popular fears, prejudices and aspirations, which could utilize modern technology to impart its message, and which campaigned with the zeal of a religious movement, could make a powerful impact in times that were, certainly in the view of contemporaries, abnormal. These tactics of harnessing modern methods to exploit often atavistic grievances proved successful in winning widespread electoral support for the NSDAP in the years 1930–2.

The question must be posed: why was it the Nazis who prevailed? Why, for example, did the KPD not reap the major political benefits of the 'crisis of capitalism' around 1930 in a country with a large and sophisticated urban working class? In a sense it did, with its vote increasing noticeably from the later 1920s through 1932 (see Table 15.1). But the KPD's modest success was overshadowed by the explosion of the Nazi vote, whose size was undoubtedly enhanced by those who were alarmed by the very fact of the Communists' gains. For the most part, the KPD could appeal to only a limited section of German society: proletarians who were disaffected with the SPD. It enjoyed success in the depression as the party of the unemployed, but its anti-capitalist rhetoric terrified almost anyone with a vested interest in the capitalist system – businessmen, shopkeepers, peasants and pensioners, among others. Its role in the attempted revolutions of 1918–19 was vividly remembered a decade or so later. Much is made of the enmity between the SPD and the KPD, with long memories of conflict between revolutionaries and 'revisionists' within the pre-1914 SPD, even before the wartime split and post-war recriminations. Certainly, *after* January 1933 some activists in the two socialist camps made common cause against Nazism even before the Comintern adopted 'Popular Front' policy in 1935. But before 1933 Communists and Social Democrats were sufficiently mutually hostile to rule out cooperation between them before the Nazi government's savage attacks on both. The mirage of two social-ist parties, together commanding between 35 per cent and 40 per cent of the national vote, combining to thwart Hitler, remained just that. The most significant effect of this consistently strong show of support for the parties of the left was the fear it generated, in the minds of the God-fearing, property-owning, law-abiding classes, of a proletarian revolt of the kind that had (apparently) occurred in Russia.

III   The rise of the Nazis

Fear of the left was manipulated most successfully by the NSDAP, with its paramili-tary wing, the SA (storm troopers), ostentatiously in the front line combating 'the reds' in the streets of Germany's towns in the early 1930s. The violence perpetrated by the SA alarmed some, but many others were relieved that someone was taking action against 'Bolshevism'; as Richard Bessel has said, the SA's very presence on the streets was propaganda for the Nazi cause. Nazi propaganda was a powerful weapon, partic-ularly when it was deployed utterly unscrupulously, with mutually irreconcilable promises made to different social or regional groups at the same time but in different locations. But what enabled the NSDAP to disseminate its propaganda was the grow-ing strength of its organization. The NSDAP was founded, as the German Workers' Party, in 1919. Even after changing its name in 1920 and Hitler's assumption of the leadership in 1921, it remained just another radical *völkisch* (racist-nationalist) fringe party among many in the early 1920s. The notoriety gained following its attempted seizure of power in Munich in November 1923 and Hitler's subsequent trial and imprisonment was short-lived, but, with the refounding of the party in February 1925 and Hitler's assertion of supremacy as Führer (leader), the NSDAP embarked on a period of increasingly energetic recruitment, organization and electoral canvassing. Elections became vitally important to the party's strategy in this period because Hitler had decided, while in Landsberg prison in 1924, that: 'we shall have to hold our noses and enter the Reichstag against the Catholic and marxist deputies. If outvoting them takes longer than outshooting them, at least the results will be guaranteed by their own Constitution!'[14]

That is, after the failure to seize power unconstitutionally, the NSDAP would work within the parliamentary system to try to achieve enough electoral support to enable it to claim power as its democratic right.

Particularly after the appointment in 1928 of Gregor Strasser as head of the party's organization office in the Brown House in Munich, a developing network of regional and local party organizations flourished across the country. But the NSDAP did not merely organize vertically, from the centre down through *Gaue* (regions), districts and local branches; it also created horizontal organizations to try to cater for the interests of virtually every social and occupational group. In the later 1920s, Nazi organizations for doctors, lawyers, teachers, students, war veterans, motor car drivers . . . and many more were created. There were Nazi organizations for both women and young people, and a Nazi Factory Cell organization aimed to bring industrial workers into the party. Strasser's aim was to create within the party a microcosm of society which would expand as more recruits joined, and which would eventually assume the organization of German society as a whole, once political power had been won. And these organizations did expand, particularly during the depression, as committed local activists spread the word that Adolf Hitler could and would bring a solution to Germany's problems. In the vertical organizations, although party discipline was strictly enforced, the *Gauleiter* (regional leader) had considerable scope for initiative, tailoring his activities and propaganda to local conditions. Thus the NSDAP could compete effectively with the SPD and KPD for working-class support in some industrial areas of the Ruhr and in Saxony, for example, even if there remained parts of Germany, like some Rhineland villages, where lack of support made it impossible to create more than a rudimentary network.

The party's work at local level was carried out by a skeleton staff of full-time officials reinforced by an army of volunteers of both genders who were unpaid enthusiasts. They canvassed and proselytized for the Nazi cause, making collections of money and goods to sustain party activities, including the provision of welfare assistance to needy fellow citizens who were casualties of the depression. But only speakers accredited by the leadership in Munich were permitted to make speeches publicizing the party's policies. The NSDAP excelled at other forms of propaganda, like posters, leaflets, parades, rallies. Its central office exploited modern technology, making slides and films which could be hired by local branches for use in recruiting drives. New local branches were established by activists from neighbouring localities, and leading Nazis toured the country to draw audiences to meetings in villages as well as cities. None was more indefatigable in this than Hitler himself, whose public appearances were carefully stage-managed to achieve the greatest effect. Over the years, Hitler developed a highly effective style of both public oratory and individual charm which won him a vast personal following. His stature within the party was elevated by the adoption of the *Führerprinzip* (leadership principle) which ensured that authority was imposed from the top, with obedience unconditionally required and indiscipline a cardinal sin. In the country at large, his image was enhanced by the opportunistic relationship which he entered with the DNVP, initially in 1929 when they both campaigned against the new reparations settlement in the Young plan. Sharing a platform with the DNVP's leader, Alfred Hugenberg, at the meeting held at Bad Harzburg in October 1931 to attack the Weimar democratic system, and addressing industrialists at their club in Düsseldorf in January 1932, helped to raise Hitler's, and therefore the NSDAP's, acceptable public profile.

Illustration 15.1 Hitler during his speech to the meeting at Bad Harzburg on 11 October 1931, when the Nationalists and the Nazis together demonstrated against the Weimar democratic system. Hugenberg (DNVP President) is to the right of Hitler and Duesterberg (leader of the *Stahlhelm* Nationalist paramilitary organization) is on the extreme right

Looking back at the 1920s and 1930s through the filter of the Second World War and the Holocaust, it is perhaps hard to comprehend how a party with such repellent attitudes came to win massive electoral support. But in its election campaigns the NSDAP was not offering the German people war and genocide. Anti-semitism and xenophobia were certainly explicit in much of its propaganda, but, in addition, the party projected a variety of views with simple and attractive slogans and some messages that were, often deliberately, confusing. The pledge that Hitler would provide every German woman with a husband, for example, was manifestly specious in a population with some two million more women than men, but it sounded a note of optimism for some. Promising to overturn the Versailles Treaty of 1919 appealed to a much wider range of opinion than merely that of unreconstructed nationalists. Promising to reassert Christian moral standards, and to eradicate the decadence and immorality which, many believed, characterized Weimar (urban) society and culture appealed to many in both rural areas and the urban middle classes. Promising to combat the 'threat' of Bolshevism appealed to much the same constituency. Above all, promising to create jobs, with priority for fathers of families, suggested the possibility of escape from the worst effects of the depression. Particularly once the electoral breakthrough had been achieved in September 1930, the Nazi leadership abandoned its early anti-capitalist and anti-Christian radicalism and constructed a new image for the party as the protector of all that was German, decent and stable, explicitly contrasting itself with both the internationalism and the alleged licentiousness of radicals and socialists on cultural and moral issues. The party whose ideology Hugh Trevor-Roper dismissed as 'this vast system of bestial Nordic nonsense'[15] courted the Christian churches and their congregations, with conspicuous success among Protestants, especially.

The archetypal Nazi voter has been described as a young middle-class male Protestant from a small town in northern or eastern Germany. Certainly, it has long been customary to blame the middle classes, in particular the *petite bourgeoisie*, for the rise to power of the National Socialists. Small shopkeepers, white-collar workers, peasant farmers and rootless ex-servicemen were deemed particularly susceptible to the Nazi message and some in these categories were among the party's earliest supporters, before the depression destabilized political life and made the NSDAP an attractive option for other groups. In addition, it has been argued, particularly by Richard F. Hamilton, that many in the upper bourgeoisie – substantial business, managerial and professional people – turned to Nazism from 1930, even if it is now doubted, following the massive findings of Henry A. Turner, that 'big business' made significant corporate donations to the NSDAP, in spite of Nazi attempts to solicit them. The mainstream Marxist view of Hitler as the lackey of big capital perhaps found support from one major businessman, Thyssen, who entitled his memoirs *I Paid Hitler*, but it is not a view that has recently been seriously entertained by more than the occasional scholar outside the former Soviet bloc.

By contrast, the work of a distinguished British Marxist historian, Tim Mason, showed in the 1970s that a significant number of 'proletarians' – perhaps 3.5 million, in July 1932 – actually voted for the NSDAP, constituting perhaps about 25 per cent of their support. Building on this, from about 1980 it has been increasingly argued that, in terms of both its membership and its electoral support, the NSDAP was a genuine *Volkspartei* (people's party), attracting both members and voters in significant proportions from all sections of society, including the manual working classes. While most historians now accept that some blue-collar workers voted Nazi, they tend to argue that these were non-unionized workers in smaller concerns, and that the KPD enjoyed better success in attracting unemployed former factory workers, while the SPD retained a strong base of support among the manual working class. Others, however, notably Jürgen Falter, have claimed, on the basis of sophisticated statistical studies, that the NSDAP received virtually *proportionate* support from manual workers – that workers, as about 45 per cent of the German population, by the early 1930s constituted between 40 per cent and 45 per cent of the Nazi electorate. If many historians remain sceptical about this, there is nevertheless now broad agreement that the traditional lower middle-class interpretation was too narrow. People from all social classes voted for the NSDAP, but it seems likely that proletarians were somewhat underrepresented and non-proletarians rather overrepresented.

This distribution affects the extent to which Nazism was a 'small town' phenomenon because most proletarians lived in or around large towns and cities, and formed a significant proportion of their populations. Yet there were strong Nazi organizations in large cities like Berlin and Hamburg, as well as in the 'cradle' of the movement, Munich. In the depths of the depression the NSDAP could attract desperate voters in industrial centres like Chemnitz (Saxony) and the Ruhr towns. In these places, however, the parties of the left remained strong and dominant, whereas in small towns with a rural hinterland and widespread hostility to the left the Nazis could prosper. In rural villages the position was more complex. In some, the influence of the Catholic Church remained strong, and with it came adherence to the Centre Party, or, in Bavaria, the BVP. In others, like Heilbronner's Black Forest region, previous support for a peasant league transferred to the NSDAP as a national party which might have a better chance of representing their distress than a narrow local group. This was a pattern discernible in both north and south Germany, in both Protestant and Catholic villages.

As for the other 'archetypal' characteristics, there is little dispute that Protestants were more attracted to National Socialism than Catholics, at least until 1932–3.

Illustration 15.2   National Socialist election propaganda in Berlin, 1932

Hostility to the NSDAP on the part of the influential Catholic hierarchy, into the spring of 1933 at least, contributed to this, keeping rural Catholics relatively loyal to the Centre/BVP while urban Catholics proved particularly susceptible to National Socialism. Again, while contemporaries accused women of bringing Hitler to power, it became customary from the 1970s to deny that women had voted as strongly as men for the NSDAP. More recently, however, Helen Boak has shown that 'because of the preponderance of women in the electorate, the NSDAP received more votes from women than from men in some areas before 1932 and throughout the Reich in 1932'[16] (see Table 15.3). Further, while the NSDAP was explicitly an activist party of the young, some of its staunchest supporters were to be found in the oldest age-groups, among pensioners, or those living on rents or savings, who were over 65, although the next most loyal group was the under-25s, those who had grown up in the Weimar years. The young unemployed were more likely to vote for the KPD than for the NSDAP. Finally, in terms of region, the most enthusiastic support for the NSDAP was mainly to be found in northern areas like Schleswig-Holstein and in eastern areas which had a border with Poland, the region where the territorial effects of the Versailles Treaty were particularly keenly felt. Some parts of both southern and western Germany lagged behind, but even in Württemberg, hardly a stronghold of Nazism, electoral support trebled between 1930 and July 1932 (see Table 15.4 and Map 15.1).

Table 15.3   The shares of the total vote (in %) cast by men (m) and women (w) for the NSDAP in selected areas in Reichstag elections, 1928, 1930, July 1932([1]), November 1932([2]) and 1933

	1930		1932[1]		1932[2]		1933	
	m	w	m	w	m	w	m	w
Bremen	12.9	11.1	29.9	30.9	20.8	20.9	30.8	34.4
Magdeburg	19.8	18.7	36.3	38.9	31.1	34.0	38.1	43.3
Leipzig	14.6	13.1					34.1	38.8
Wiesbaden	29.1	26.0	43.0	43.7	36.1	36.8	44.9	47.3
Bavaria	18.9	14.2	29.2	25.6	27.4	24.7	36.2	34.4
Augsburg	14.9	10.4	25.2	21.1	24.5	21.6	33.4	31.4
Regensburg	19.7	13.1	23.3	17.3	20.0	14.9	33.1	28.9
Ansbach	34.6	33.3			47.6	50.0	51.2	55.6
Dinkelsbühl	33.2	31.9			54.4	56.1	58.6	61.5
Ludwigshafen	17.4	14.0			28.6	27.7	34.5	34.9
Cologne	19.8	15.5	26.4	22.8	21.8	19.2	33.9	32.9
Konstanz			32.0	26.0	26.1	21.8	35.9	32.8

Source: Helen L. Boak, '"Our Last Hope": Women's Votes for Hitler – A Reappraisal', *German Studies Review*, XII, 2 (May 1989), Table III, p. 297. Figures are missing for some areas in individual elections.

Table 15.4   Percentage of votes cast in favour of the NSDAP (Reichstag elections of 1928, 1930, July(^{1}) and November (^{2}) 1932 and 1933)

	1928	1930	1932^1	1932^2	1933
1 East Prussia	0.8	22.5	47.1	39.7	56.5
2 Berlin	1.4	12.8	24.6	22.5	31.3
3 Potsdam II	1.8	16.7	33.0	29.1	38.2
4 Potsdam I	1.6	18.8	38.2	34.1	44.4
5 Frankfurt a.d. Oder	1.0	22.7	48.1	42.6	55.2
6 Pomerania	1.5	24.3	48.0	43.1	56.3
7 Breslau	1.0	24.2	43.5	40.4	50.2
8 Liegnitz	1.2	20.9	48.0	42.1	54.0
9 Oppeln	1.0	9.5	29.2	26.8	43.2
10 Magdeburg	1.7	19.5	43.8	39.0	47.3
11 Merseburg	2.7	20.5	42.6	34.5	46.4
12 Thuringia	3.7	19.3	43.4	37.1	47.2
13 Schleswig-Holstein	4.0	27.0	51.0	45.7	53.2
14 Weser-Ems	5.2	20.5	38.4	31.9	41.4
15 East Hanover	2.6	20.6	49.5	42.9	54.3
16 South Hanover-Brunswick	4.4	24.3	46.1	40.6	48.7
17 Westphalia North	1.0	12.2	25.7	22.3	34.9
18 Westphalia South	1.6	13.9	27.2	24.8	33.8
19 Hesse-Nassau	3.6	20.8	43.6	41.2	49.4
20 Cologne-Aachen	1.1	14.5	20.2	17.4	30.1
21 Koblenz-Trier	2.1	14.9	28.8	26.1	38.4
22 Düsseldorf East	1.8	17.0	31.6	27.0	37.4
23 Düsseldorf West	1.2	16.8	27.0	24.2	35.2
24 Upper Bavaria-Swabia	6.2	16.3	27.1	24.6	40.9
25 Lower Bavaria	3.5	12.0	20.4	18.5	39.2
26 Franconia	8.1	20.5	39.9	36.4	45.7
27 Palatinate	5.6	22.8	43.7	42.6	46.5
28 Dresden-Bautzen	1.8	16.1	39.3	34.0	43.6
29 Leipzig	1.9	14.0	36.1	31.0	40.0
30 Chemnitz-Zwickau	4.3	23.8	47.0	43.4	50.0
31 Württemberg	1.9	9.4	30.3	26.2	42.0
32 Baden	2.9	19.2	36.9	34.1	45.4
33 Hesse-Darmstadt	1.9	18.5	43.1	40.2	47.4
34 Hamburg	2.6	19.2	33.7	27.2	38.9
35 Mecklenburg	2.0	20.1	44.8	37.0	48.0

Source: J. Noakes and G. Pridham, eds, *Nazism 1919–1945* (Exeter: Exeter University Press, 1983), vol. 1, p. 83.

IV   The destruction of democracy

The National Socialists were able to triumph partly because of their opportunism and their industry, and partly because of the failings of others: for one thing, no other party, including the Communist Party, campaigned as effectively. On 30 January 1933, Adolf Hitler, the leader of the largest parliamentary party, was appointed Chancellor in the proper constitutional manner by President Hindenburg, although he had on 13 August

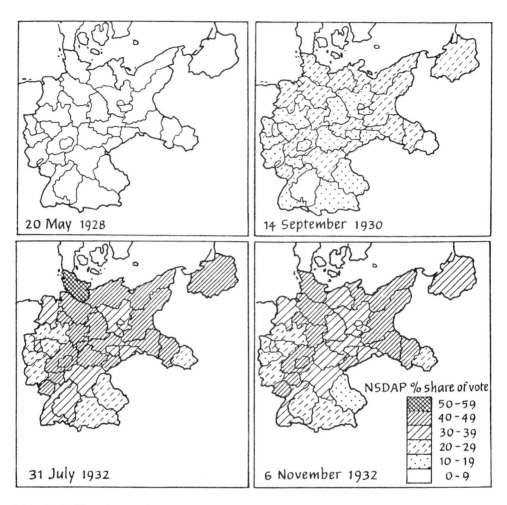

Map 15.1   The electoral fortunes of the Nazi Party, 1928–32

1932 declined to offer Hitler this post on the grounds that 'he could not justify . . . the transfer of the whole authority of government . . . to a party that was biased against people who had different views from their own'.[17] That understated refusal was made after the Nazis' spectacular performance in the July 1932 national elections, when they attracted 13.75 million votes, their highest total in a genuinely free election, making them by far the largest parliamentary party. In another Reichstag election in November 1932, their vote fell by two million, on a lower turnout (see Tables 15.1 and 15.4). While the NSDAP remained the largest parliamentary party, there were further signs, in local elections in November and December 1932, that their vote had peaked in July

1932 and was on a downward slide (see Table 15.5). Perceiving this, Gregor Strasser urged Hitler to accept the proffered vice-chancellorship before the party's position was further eroded. Hitler's insistence on holding out for the chancellorship and nothing less contributed to Strasser's resignation on 8 December 1932. Given the party's declining fortunes, Strasser should have been proved right: the time *should* have passed when it seemed necessary to offer Hitler the chancellorship. Yet seven weeks after Strasser's resignation, Hitler got what he wanted.

There was nothing 'inevitable' about Hitler's appointment as Chancellor, even if, as leader of the largest single party in the German parliament, it was perhaps his democratic right. Rather, the essential preconditions of Hitler's success were widespread disillusionment with the parliamentary system and the machinations of the clique of right-wing politicians and advisers around the aged President. It is now clear that the democratic parliamentary system established in 1919 was destroyed before Hitler came to power. Larry Jones believes that it never recovered from the economic and social crises of the immediate post-war years, while Detlev Peukert holds that, after the fall of the last SPD chancellor in March 1930, 'the real question . . . was no longer

Table 15.5   Local elections in Saxony and Thuringia, November/December 1932 – the number of votes cast for the NSDAP

	Nov. 6	Nov. 14	Dec. 3
Urban areas			
Dresden	134,330	104,107	
Leipzig	128,558	101,690	
Plauen	33,720	26,840	
Chemnitz	79,766	69,538	
Weimar	11,003		7,122
Gera	16,577		13,809
Jena	8,420		6,459
Gotha	10,046		7,565
Eisenach	8,002		5,980
Apolda	6,389		4,430
Rural districts			
Weimar	20,570		15,778
Meinigen	22,180		16,193
Hildburghausen	16,616		12,839
Schleiz	22,835		8,941
Greiz	14,322		10,997
Gera	17,735		12,769
Saalfeldt	14,739		10,645
Rudolfstadt	11,381		8,102
Armstadt	18,821		15,693
Sondershausen	16,313		11,352

Source: Dietrich Orlow, *The History of the Nazi Party, 1919–1933* (Newton Abbott: David and Charles, 1971), pp. 288–9.

whether the republican constitutional system could be saved or restored: it was what would come in its stead'.[18] Genuine parliamentary government came to an end in March 1930, when Brüning accepted the chancellorship without a parliamentary majority. Thereafter, presidential power was used to justify and enforce the decisions of a minority government – including, under Papen, the utterly illegal dismissal of the SPD-led caretaker government of Prussia on 20 July 1932. Some remnants of the Weimar system lingered on beyond January 1933: a parliamentary election was held, but in an atmosphere of intimidation, on 5 March 1933; the constitutionally necessary two-thirds Reichstag majority for the 'Enabling Law' on 23 March 1933 was engineered; and, finally, the President remained in office. Hindenburg's death, and the merging of the offices of chancellor and president in the person of the 'Führer', Hitler, on 2 August 1934, removed the last vestige of the democratic system of the Weimar Republic.

By 1931–2, then, Weimar democracy had been effectively destroyed, although the outward forms remained until Hitler liquidated them in the first half of 1933. It was already clear by then that an authoritarian government, without genuine parliamentary control, would be established – and indeed, was in the process of being established. But the old right, with more or less grudging acquiescence from the liberal parties and the Centre, faced a major problem, especially in the highly politicized atmosphere of the depression, with a high turnout (consistently over 80 per cent) at national elections. Could it, in a new authoritarian regime, force its will on the country, especially on a country where lawlessness was commonplace, with street battles being fought daily in Germany's towns and cities by rival paramilitary gangs? Certainly, the old right could, and did, destroy the Weimar Republic. But because of its own low level of popular support, evidenced in the poor showing of the DNVP, it could not construct a plausible and stable authoritarian system, although both Brüning and Papen used general elections to try to win support that would enable them to do so. That is why the conservatives turned to the NSDAP, with its still massive electoral support, in December 1932/January 1933. And that is why parliamentary democracy was replaced, not by a traditional right-wing authoritarian dictatorship (as happened in most of central and eastern Europe, and in the Iberian Peninsula), nor by Communism, as in the USSR, but by Nazism.

V Conclusion

Where does all this leave the argument between *Sonderweg* and 'spanner in the works'? The NSDAP did not suddenly emerge from nowhere. There were countless small, radical right, fringe groups in existence during the 1920s, many of which came into the Nazis' orbit, often delivered by a leader – like Julius Streicher in Nuremberg – who was attracted by the idea of belonging to a larger and potentially more effective grouping, under dynamic leadership. It was the Nazis' singlemindedness and their skill that welded countless protest groups into a disciplined yet messianic political party. But they did not create the sense of grievance that motivated people to join these groups in the first place, and to desert traditional allegiances deriving from a particular milieu but only tenuously related to a genuine political party. Many Germans nursed a sense of both personal and national grievance long before the depression of the early 1930s, deriving from the lost war and the penalties that that loss incurred in terms of national humiliation and personal impoverishment, particularly through a worthless currency.

But, in the end, the idea of a 'special path' is also flawed because it implies that this was the path which Germany naturally followed because of its recent history and development. It suggests that the Weimar Republic could not have proved workable under any conditions because of ideas formulated in the early nineteenth century, or because of structures maintained, against the odds, under the Empire. Counterfactual propositions are rarely satisfactory, but had Germany been pursued to unmistakable defeat in 1918–19, as the American military leadership wished, then there might have been no room for the 'stab-in-the-back' myth which obsessed Hitler and served for many others as an excuse. Had early Weimar governments shown more responsibility, by not resigning in protest at the peace treaty or the reparations settlement, or by introducing deflationary policies before the currency lost its value altogether, then politics might have seemed more stable and a whole swathe of middle-class voters might not have been traumatized, making them highly susceptible to the Nazi appeal. Yet there was a weakness in the German system, deriving from its hybrid nature as it straddled central Europe. The most advanced industrial economy coexisted with backward agriculture, both in the large East Elbian estates and in the small peasant farms of the west and south. There was not a single agrarian interest but rather both a politically reactionary landlord class and a potentially radical small peasant class. There were well-organized skilled workers, whose institutions offered little to unorganized workers in small concerns. There was a burgeoning professional class with too many well-educated recruits – including women and Jews – swelling the ranks of medicine, teaching and law. There were Protestants and Catholics, with memories of the *Kulturkampf* in the 1870s, and, in some cases, even longer memories of the Reformation and the Thirty Years War. Liberals were a dwindling group, yet still insisted on being divided into two political parties. Bavarians and Prussians had hardly a good word for each other. This, then, was Germany's special problem: that there were too many particularisms and too few grounds for consensus. Thus it was possible in Germany for a wrecking element to succeed: the democratic system of Weimar was sabotaged by those who had never believed in it and who were supported by a greater number who became disillusioned with it as democratic institutions like parliaments and trades unions failed to provide solutions to immediate economic, social and political problems. As Peukert has said, the democratic system was damaged before the depression struck. But it was the depression which gave the NSDAP its chance, with what Tom Childers has called its 'volatile constituency' attracted by its 'catch-all strategy' as a protest movement.[19] To that extent, perhaps the judgment of Karl Radek, quoted at the start of this essay, was sound enough after all.

Notes:

1. Quoted in Schulz, G., *Faschismus. National-Sozialismus. Versionen und theoretische Kontroversen 1922–1972* (Frankfurt am Main: 1974), p. 61.
2. Vermeil, E., *The German Scene* (London: Harrap, 1956), p. 15.
3. Taylor, A. J. P., *The Course of German History* (London: Methuen, 1961), p. 248.
4. Ritter, G. (1955), quoted in J. C. G. Röhl, *From Bismarck to Hitler. The Problem of Continuity in German History* (London: Longman, 1970), p. 9.
5. Mommsen, W. J., 'The Return to the Western Tradition: German Historiography since 1945', in Hartmut Lehmann, ed., *Occasional Paper No. 4* (Washington: German Historical Institute, 1991), p. 7.
6. Bracher, K. D., *The German Dictatorship* (London: Penguin, 1971), p. 38.
7. Conze, W., *The Shaping of the German Nation* (London: George Prior, 1979), pp. 98–9.
8. Berghahn, V. R., *Modern Germany. Society, Economy and Politics in the Twentieth Century* (Cambridge: Cambridge University Press, 1982), p. viii.
9. Lepsius, M. R., 'Parteiensystem und Sozialstruktur. Zum Problem der Demokratisierung der deutschen Gesellschaft' (1966), republished in M. R. Lepsius, *Demokratie in Deutschland* (Göttingen: Vandenhoeck and Ruprecht, 1993), pp. 32–50.
10. Koshar, Rudy, *Social Life, Local Politics, and Nazism. Marburg, 1880–1935* (Chapel Hill: University of North Carolina Press, 1986), pp. 85–90, 126–66, 179–208.
11. Sontheimer, K., *Antidemokratisches Denken in der Weimarer Republik* (Munich: Nymphenburger Verlagshandlung, 1962).
12. Heilbronner, Oded, 'Catholic Plight in a Rural Area of Germany and the Rise of the Nazi Party', *Social History*, 20, 2 (May 1995), p. 233.
13. Allen, W. S., *The Nazi Seizure of Power. The Experience of a Single German Town 1922–1945* (1st ed, 1965; here, London: Penguin, 1989), p. 25.
14. Noakes, J., and Pridham, G., eds., *Nazism 1919–1945*, vol. 1 (Exeter: Exeter University Press, 1983), p. 37.
15. Trevor-Roper, Hugh, *The Last Days of Hitler* (revised edn, London: Pan, 1962), p. 55.
16. Boak, Helen L., '"Our Last Hope"; Women's Votes for Hitler – A Reappraisal', *German Studies Review*, XII, 2 (May 1989), p. 303.
17. Noakes and Pridham, *Nazism*, vol. 1, p. 104.
18. Peukert, Detlev J. K., *The Weimar Republic. The Crisis of Classical Modernity* (London: Allen Lane, 1991), p. 249.
19. Childers, Thomas, 'The Limits of National Socialist Mobilisation: the Elections of 6 November 1932 and the Fragmentation of the Nazi Constituency', in Thomas Childers, ed., *The Formation of the Nazi Constituency* (London: Croom Helm, 1986), pp. 238, 240, 242, 244, 252, 254.

Select bibliography

In addition to the books cited in the notes:
Broszat, Martin, *Hitler and the Collapse of Weimar Germany* (Leamington Spa: Berg, 1987).
Childers, Thomas, *The Nazi Voter* (Chapel Hill: University of North Carolina Press, 1983).
Eschenburg, Theodor, *et al.*, *The Road to Dictatorship. Germany 1918–1933* (London: Oswald Wolff, 1970).
Falter, Jürgen W., *Hitlers Wähler* (Munich: 1991).
Fischer, Conan, *The Rise of the Nazis* (Manchester: Manchester University Press, 1995).
Hamilton, Richard F., *Who Voted for Hitler?* (Princeton: Princeton University Press, 1982).

Kater, Michael H., *The Nazi Party. A Social Profile of Members and Leaders, 1919–1945* (Cambridge, MA: Harvard University Press, 1983).

Kolb, Eberhard, *The Weimar Republic*, trans. P.S. Falla (London: Unwin Hyman, 1988).

Maier, Charles S., *The Unmasterable Past. History, Holocaust, and German National Identity* (Cambridge, MA and London: Harvard University Press, 1988).

Manstein, Peter, *Die Mitglieder und Wähler der NSDAP 1919–1933* (Frankfurt am Main: Peter Lang, 1989).

Mason, Tim, *Social Policy in the Third Reich. The Working Class and the 'National Community'* (Oxford: Berg, 1993), chs 1 and 2.

Mühlberger, Detlef, *Hitler's Followers* (London: Routledge, 1991).

Nicholls, A. J., *Weimar and the Rise of Hitler* (London: Macmillan, 3rd edn, 1991).

Nicholls, Anthony and Matthias, Erich, eds., *German Democracy and the Triumph of Hitler* (London: Allen and Unwin, 1971).

Noakes, Jeremy, *The Nazi Party in Lower Saxony, 1921–1933* (Oxford: Oxford University Press, 1971).

Orlow, Dietrich, *The History of the Nazi Party, 1919–1933* (Newton Abbott: David and Charles, 1971).

Pridham, Geoffrey, *Hitler's Rise to Power. The Nazi Movement in Bavaria 1923–1933* (London: Hart-Davis MacGibbon, 1973).

Schnabel, Thomas, ed., *Die Machtergreifung in Südwestdeutschland. Das Ende der Weimarer Republik in Baden und Württemberg 1928–1933* (Stuttgart: Kohlhammer, 1982).

Stachura, Peter D., ed., *The Nazi Machtergreifung* (London: Allen and Unwin, 1983).

Turner, Henry Ashby, *Big Business and the Rise of Hitler* (Oxford: Oxford University Press, 1985).

16

Hitler and the Nazi dictatorship

Ian Kershaw

Despite libraries of books on the Third Reich, the questions posed by the rapid descent, within a few years, of a modern, civilized, economically advanced country into barbarism, war and systematic genocide still demand answers, and will continue to do so.

As research on the mechanisms of Nazi rule intensified during the 1960s and 1970s, and was followed by far-reaching analysis of the behaviour and attitudes of different social groups in the Third Reich, attempts were made to look afresh at the collapse of civilization in Germany. The focus shifted from a heavy concentration on the personality, ideology and actions of Hitler himself – which had sometimes been used to shore up exculpatory or apologetic interpretations of a nation driven to war and catastrophe by 'the will of an individual, of a madman'[1] – to analysis of the functioning of the 'system' of Nazi rule as a whole. Arising from this shift, a concept which has gained increasing recognition as a fruitful way of looking at the development of the Third Reich is that of 'cumulative radicalization', initially devised by Hans Mommsen.[2] It is suggestive of how forces unleashed by the National Socialist takeover of power and the often competing interests and policies of different powerful groups within the regime created a spiral of increasingly radical measures – a dynamic of racist persecution and expansionism culminating in war, genocide and unprecedented destruction. It implies, in addition, the unstoppable process of a regime careering more and more out of control, resorting to ever wilder urges to destroy and plunder, dependent increasingly on raw force as coherent structures of government and administration disintegrated and boats were recklessly burnt in an all-out genocidal war. Since that process ruled out any possibility of a compromise peace, 'cumulative radicalization' meant ultimately, therefore, self-destruction, as well as destruction on a monumental scale.

If the term offers a useful descriptive piece of shorthand for the process leading to the climacteric 'running amok' (as Mommsen calls it) of the Nazi regime,[3] it remains less than self-evident just why, exactly, the highly developed and sophisticated German state should have 'imploded' and capitulated to the irrational drive of 'cumulative radicalization'. Such a tendency does not appear to have been a feature of fascist (or quasi-fascist) states in general. Neither Mussolini's Italy nor Franco's Spain could be said to have offered similar cases of 'cumulative radicalization'. In a differently structured state, but one frequently compared with the National Socialist regime, that of the Soviet Union, there was certainly a dramatic escalation of terror and repression under Stalin. But that escalation ceased with the dictator's death. It was 'despotic radicalization' related to Stalin's form of dictatorship, rather than 'cumulative radicalization' inherent in the system itself.

The process of 'cumulative radicalization' appears, then, to be peculiar to the Third Reich. How should it be explained? A full answer would have to incorporate at least some of the following: expectations lodged in the vision of national renewal represented by Hitler; the drive of the Nazi movement's followers to implement the diffuse Party Programme; the pressure emanating from the security police to find new ideologically determined victims; the readiness of non-Nazi national-conservative elite groups to participate in the undermining of legality through the growing cancer of the police state, and to find wide areas of affinity with the regime's unfolding racial and expansionist goals; the willingness of much of society to collaborate in discrimination against minorities; the successful propagation among, especially, the younger generation of racist, militarist and extreme chauvinist ideas, all founded in beliefs in cultural superiority; and the self-reinforcing barbarism of the war itself and of complicity in genocidal actions.

Beyond these elements of an answer, it would also be important to consider the impact on government of the highly personalized, 'charismatic' rule of Hitler. Not least, it would also be vital to take account of the personal ideological 'vision' and the actions of Hitler himself. Historiographically, historians who have concentrated on the personal role of Hitler have seldom deployed the concept of 'cumulative radicalization'. Those 'structuralist' (or 'functionalist') historians, on the other hand, who have found the concept useful, have tended, on the whole, to downplay Hitler's personal role and to look instead to the functioning (or dysfunctioning) of the 'system' as a whole. Hans Mommsen, for instance, explicitly excludes Hitler as a causative force of 'cumulative radicalization' with the comment that 'it is a serious mistake to concentrate study of the Nazi tyranny on an analysis of the role which Hitler occupied in it'.[4] It would indeed be hard to argue convincingly that the will, whims, dictates or personality disorder of Hitler were all that mattered in pushing on the 'cumulative radicalization'. But to ignore or underrate the personal contribution of Hitler would surely be equally mistaken. Hitler needs to be fully incorporated in, rather than omitted from, an analysis of 'cumulative radicalization'.

A premiss of what follows is that 'cumulative radicalization' indeed provides a fruitful concept in analysis of the Third Reich. A further starting point is that the Nazi regime was a peculiar type of modern state, and that this peculiarity is closely and specifically related to the impact of Hitler's personal exercise of power upon existing channels of authority. This can be conceptualized – using Max Weber's terminology – as the superimposition of 'charismatic' upon 'bureaucratic' (or 'legal-rational') authority. ('Charismatic authority' is used here as a technical term, implying a sense of 'mission' associated by the 'following' with the perceived extraordinary qualities of the leader, and a highly personalized form of rule which, because of its dependence upon avoidance of failure or 'routinization', remains acutely unstable.) A further premiss, then, is that Hitler's power was real and immense, that he was neither a 'weak dictator' – a misleading implication[5] – nor a sort of front-man for other forces. The exercise of that level of power and autonomy – extraordinary even among modern dictatorships – had, so my argument runs, a direct and crucial bearing on the process of 'cumulative radicalization'. But – a final premiss – it is taken for granted that Hitler's power was not static, but expanded in consequence of the weakness, miscalculation, tolerance and collaboration of others, both inside and outside Germany.

It is important, therefore, to ask how Hitler came to be in a position to take or shape momentous decisions. This question has to be answered by looking to forces outside Hitler himself, since it is certainly true that dictators, including Hitler, 'are as dependent on the political circumstances which bring them to power as they in turn influence these'.[6] Hitler's role, in other words, has to be seen not simply in personal terms, but also as itself a 'structure' – and the most vital one – in the system of rule subject to the process of 'cumulative radicalization'.

Without the comprehensiveness of the crisis of the Weimar state, the speed and radicality of the collapse of civilization after 1933 would have been unthinkable. From the outset, the Weimar Republic had faced serious problems of legitimacy, both among wide sections of the population and within the very power elites on whom the state was dependent. Under the impact of the crippling depression beginning in late 1929, economic, social and governmental crises blended into an acute and unsustainable multi-dimensional legitimacy crisis of the state system itself. An authoritarian solution became increasingly inevitable. But the traditional national-conservative power elites were too weak to provide it.

An attack on civil liberties also became more and more likely, whatever the eventual outcome of the crisis. Liberal principles were under strong attack long before Hitler's takeover. One sign was growing paranoia about law and order at a time when, in fact, despite a sharp rise in political violence, actual criminality was far lower than it had been in the early 1920s. Another indicator was the growing pressure in the medical profession, strongly influenced by ideas of eugenics and 'racial hygiene', for legislation for the voluntary sterilization of those suffering from hereditary illnesses. A third example of the changing climate was the increasingly shrill clamour against 'double earners', aiming to hound women out of jobs if their husbands were also employed.

As each profession and social group increasingly felt itself disadvantaged and alienated by Weimar's failure, the attractiveness of a radical new start spread. Again, the links with an assault on human rights, including menacing signs of widening hostility towards Jews, were evident. Owners of shops and small businesses, threatened by consumer cooperatives and big department stores, found it easy to swallow the Nazi line of blaming Jewish ownership of such stores for their troubles. In the countryside, too, economic misery in the impoverished farming community readily translated itself into anger directed at 'inner enemies' and scapegoats – for the most part seen as Marxists and Jews. Many young Germans were swept into the path of the Nazis not only through misplaced idealism, but also because of poor job prospects. Once subjected to the prevailing ethos in the Hitler Youth or the SA (*Sturmabteilung* or stormtroopers), they could soon find themselves marching through the streets attacking the 'Reds' or singing 'When Jewish blood spurts from the knife'. Students, their career expectations often vanishing before their eyes, were frequently among the most radicalized of the younger generation. Many of those who came to run the Reich Security Head Office during the war, and were most closely implicated in genocidal policies and action, had imbibed *völkisch* ideals in universities during the early years of the Weimar Republic. In the early 1930s, during the depression, the progress made by the Nazis in universities was alarming. A climate hostile to Jews, Marxists, and 'the un-German spirit' in intellectual life increasingly took hold among students, and also among many of their professors who had seen their own careers blighted. Overlaying the interests of different social groups, the polarization of left and right in Weimar's 14-year 'latent civil war',[7] the explosion of political violence in the early 1930s, and the whipped-up anti-Marxist hysteria of a right now in the ascendancy, pointed in the direction of a potential bloodbath if the Nazis were to win power.

The expectations, in other words, of differing sections of society in a national rebirth were massively heightened by Weimar's terminal, comprehensive crisis. And frequently built into such expectations was an assault on liberal values and human rights. The radicalization that burst through after 1933 was, therefore, waiting to happen if a government could be found which was prepared to sanction it and release the pent-up forces.

Such a government, it was increasingly felt outside the ranks of Social Democrats and Communists, had to be a strong, authoritarian force on the right, capable of crushing Germany's internal 'enemies', establishing national unity, and restoring law and order. The more the pluralistic party system of Weimar was seen to have failed, the greater the feeling became that the party system should be done away with altogether and replaced by leadership that put the nation above party interest. The prospect of a restoration of the monarchy which, at least nominally, had represented the whole nation was not universally welcomed. But the two Reich Presidents during the Weimar Republic – the Social Democrat Friedrich Ebert and the monarchist war hero Paul von Hindenburg – had both been, in different ways, divisive figures. A new form of national leader capable of embodying the disparate social and political expectations and transcending – at first, it was widely recognized, by force against internal 'enemies' – the divisions, would, given some initial success, have a good chance of building an impressive platform of popular acclaim. That would be even more forthcoming following any success in overcoming the almost universally detested terms of the Versailles Treaty. Since revisionist hopes (of different kinds) were entertained in almost all sections of German society, success in the arena of foreign policy was guaranteed to win not only massive popular acclaim, but also the fervent backing of the national-conservative power elites – not least, in the army leadership. And during the terminal crisis of Weimar, the ending of reparations had opened up the possibility of rebuilding and modernizing the army and the return – at least gradually – to a more assertive foreign policy. This was all the more possible and likely in the event of a strong German nationalist government, given the self-evident fragility of the post-war settlement. In this, too, the Weimar crisis offered the preconditions for the subsequent rapid radicalization under Hitler.

During the terminal crisis of Weimar, of course, Hitler had increasingly appeared to many to offer the greatest hopes of national redemption. By 1932, over 13 million Germans – well over a third of the electorate, a substantial achievement in the Weimar electoral system – wanted a Hitler government. The radical demands for change – including a ruthless showdown with the Marxists and harsh discrimination against Jews – which formed central elements of the Nazi platform, were thereby assured of extensive, though far from universal, support. An army of activists in the huge National Socialist Movement – party membership numbered 850,000 by January 1933; the SA had by then around 425,000 members – ensured that there would never be any shortage of fanatics pressing for the implementation in government policy of the amalgam of phobias and prejudice that served as the Party Programme.

As a movement drawn from the most disparate social groups, with a catch-all appeal and utopian goals of national unity and resurgence, belief in a supreme leader who embodied the 'idea' and 'mission' of National Socialism was vital. Hitler himself, experiencing the fragmentation of the *völkisch* movement during his imprisonment in 1924, had recognized the need for the NSDAP, when it was refounded in 1925, to be built on principles of absolute obedience to the leader. Despite a constant tendency to factionalism and a number of internal crises, the growing prospect of attaining power had kept the movement intact in the following years. After the most serious of such crises, that surrounding the resignation from his party offices of Gregor Strasser in December 1932, Hitler had deliberately dismantled the organizational framework of the party that Strasser had created and once more put the emphasis solely on propaganda objectives focused, beyond the immediate task of getting to power, on vague and visionary goals of national resurgence. The party therefore entered the Third Reich not with a rationally devised organizational structure set to penetrate and take over the state, but purely as a vehicle for Hitler's 'charismatic leadership', incorporating diffuse and often contradictory social expectations of its vast following and demanding outlets for these in actionism directed at target groups for retaliation and discrimination.

Meanwhile, the deliberately and purposefully manufactured Führer cult had been embraced in differing degrees by over a third of the population. Many more, still hesitant at this stage, would be won after 1933 as Hitler's image was converted by saturation propaganda from that of party leader to 'great' national leader. And, at the centre of indescribable adulation and sycophancy, his already outsized ego swelling as success followed success – all attributed by propaganda to his own 'achievements' – not the least of the believers in the cult constructed around him was Hitler himself.

. . .

It is hard to exaggerate the significance of the Führer cult for the working of the regime. The traditional power elites had entered into their 'entente' with Hitler in

Illustration 16.1 Hitler as mass politician. He worked hard on producing the appropriate body language to accompany his speeches: an unusual concern amongst politicians of the pre-television era

January 1933 because he alone controlled the masses on the nationalist right. They had thought they could pen him in. But in reality, his position had been strong from the beginning. Though the conservatives outnumbered the Nazis in the coalition cabinet, Hitler, as Reich Chancellor, Goering, in charge of the Prussian police, and to a lesser extent Frick, as Reich Minister of the Interior, held the key positions. The anti-Communist hysteria – as prevalent among conservatives as among Nazis – played into Hitler's hands following the Reichstag fire in late February 1933, when draconian emergency decrees were promulgated, effectively abolishing civil liberties and setting aside the Weimar constitution. The takeover of power from below in the provinces after the election on 5 March, and, later that month, the passing of the Enabling Act, which empowered the cabinet to introduce legislation and removed thereby the dependence upon the Reichstag and the Reich President's willingness to grant emergency decrees, further bolstered Hitler's position from the outset. Already, the efflorescence of the Führer cult was remarkable. The naming of innumerable town squares and main streets after 'the people's Chancellor' was only one outward sign that no conventional change of government had taken place. The vicious onslaught on the left, bringing the internment of tens of thousands in prisons and makeshift new 'concentration camps' (the first set up at Dachau, outside Munich in March 1933), destroyed within weeks the seemingly powerful Socialist and Communist parties. Within six months of Hitler's appointment as Chancellor, the remaining parties had been suppressed or had dissolved themselves, leaving a one-party state. At the same time, institutions, organizations, clubs and associations throughout the country had been going through a process – for the most part voluntary rather than forced – of *Gleichschaltung* (or nazification). By the summer, Hitler's position *vis-à-vis* his conservative partners had already been strengthened inordinately.

Following his initial foreign policy coup – the withdrawal of Germany from the League of Nations in October 1933 – Hitler was for the first time to play the card of plebiscitary acclamation – seeking acclaim by plebiscite for an action already completed and known to be massively popular. Further plebiscites following the death of Reich President Hindenburg in 1934, the remilitarization of the Rhineland in 1936, and the Anschluß of Austria in 1938 brought, whatever the absurdity of the actual results, further demonstration inside and outside Germany of Hitler's unassailable popularity. This plebiscitary acclamation, which he could call upon almost at will, was a crucial basis of Hitler's power – demoralizing opposition, underlining his strength to the conservative elites, and showing the outside world that he had the overwhelming majority of the people behind him. It provided Hitler with a platform that enabled him to gain increasing autonomy from the traditional elites. Within a remarkably short time, their hopes of containing him and using him as a vehicle for the restoration of their own power had been shown to be vain ones.

Still, as long as Reich President Hindenburg, the hero of the First World War, lived, Hitler's power was relatively constrained. Hindenburg represented an alternative source of loyalty; the army owed its allegiance to the Reich President as head of state and supreme commander; and Hitler's position as head of government was dependent on the President's prerogative. The massacre of the SA leadership, an increasingly disruptive element threatening the consolidation of Nazi rule, at the end of June 1934 – carried out with the backing of the army – and the rapid assumption of the powers of head of state by Hitler at Hindenburg's death on 2 August amounted to a second 'seizure of power'. The position of Führer was now institutionalized, as Hitler's new title of 'Führer and Reich Chancellor' indicated. (The title became simply 'Führer' in 1939.) The army and civil servants swore an oath of loyalty not to an abstract constitution, but to Hitler personally. The Führer state was fully established.

Hitler's power now knew no formal bounds. Prominent constitutional theorists did their best to give legal meaning to his personalized authority. According to one of the foremost experts on constitutional law, Ernst Rudolf Huber, 'the power of the Führer' was 'comprehensive and total, . . . free and independent, exclusive and unlimited'.[8] Hans Frank, the leading Nazi lawyer, claimed that the Führer's will, resting on 'outstanding achievements', had replaced impersonal and abstract precepts as the basis of law.[9]

Forms and structures of collective cabinet government could scarcely remain intact in the face of such claims. Meetings of the cabinet became more and more infrequent following Hindenburg's death. That of 5 February 1938 turned out to be the last during the entire Third Reich. Government increasingly fragmented into separate offices of state, with no central coordination of policy, and with Hans-Heinrich Lammers, head of the Reich Chancellery, serving as the sole link between Hitler and individual government ministers. Legislation followed a laborious and inefficient process of circulation of written drafts to ministers until there was general agreement. Access to Hitler, apart from favoured ministers such as Goebbels, was often difficult, and made even more so because of the dictator's frequent absences from Berlin and his highly unbureaucratic and idiosyncratic style of working.

Usually, Hitler would get up late in the morning, read the press cuttings prepared for him, have a lengthy lunch (normally attended by regulars like Goebbels and Goering, other favoured party big-wigs, adjutants and other members of his immediate entourage, and some invited guests), see diplomats or other important visitors during the afternoon, spend the evening in a less formal meal, followed by a film, and then launch forth into a monologue until the small hours to those stifling their yawns and able to hold out. He seldom read documents and memoranda prepared by the state bureaucracy or submitted by ministers. These were usually summarized verbally by Lammers in his periodic audiences. Some ministers – Agriculture Minister Walther Darré is an example – were effectively barred from seeing Hitler for years. Nor did Hitler send out a regular stream of written missives and directives. 'He took the view that many things sorted themselves out on their own if one did not interfere', remarked one of his former adjutants after the war.[10] He dictated his own speeches, and signed formal laws, but apart from that wrote remarkably little. A less bureaucratic style of leadership from the head of a modern industrialized country would be hard to imagine. Orders were for the most part verbal, and transmitted – in so far as they concerned government ministers – through Lammers. The scope for misunderstanding and confusion was extensive. Significant policy decisions needed Hitler's approval. But for prestige reasons the

Führer could not be dragged into factional in-fighting. The image of infallibility had to be preserved. Alongside his personal temperament, disdain for bureaucracy, and social Darwinist instinct of siding with the stronger in a conflict, this enhanced his detachment from the daily business of government. For the practice of government and administration this meant frequent delay, postponement or sometimes abandonment of proposed legislation which had been the subject of lengthy preparation.

Relations between the apparatus of state government – central, provincial and local – and the party at the differing levels were left unclarified and undefined. This provided a recipe for unending conflict. Headed by the weak and ineffectual Rudolf Hess, the Party's Political Organization interfered – with varying degrees of success – in policy formation in many areas. It was incapable of providing a coherent influence on rational policy choices. But in certain key areas central to the 'idea' of National Socialism, especially race policy and the persecution of the churches, the party subjected the state bureaucracy to relentless pressure through agitation aimed at putting the 'vision' of the Führer into practice. The concessions made by the government ministries to give legislative voice to such pressures, only to be followed by further agitation demanding new legislation, ensured the continued upward ratcheting of radicalization.

This process was further advanced by entrusting vital areas of policy, directly associated with the ideological goals of the regime, to special organizations outside the normal state administration, and directly subordinate to Hitler. The Office of the Four-Year Plan, for example, established in 1936, was meant to be a small and unbureaucratic unit to overcome the impasse in the economy which had built up. Goering's empire-building ensured that it developed into a huge, sprawling organization functioning alongside (and in practice dominating) the state Economics Ministry. The creation, also in 1936, of a centralized German police, headed by the fanatical and ambitious Heinrich Himmler and his right-hand man, the ruthless, ice-cold Reinhard Heydrich, and merged with the Nazi movement's most committed ideological elite, the SS, also spawned an enormous power-block – the most dynamic and ideologically driven sector of the regime.

The SS police empire stood outside the control of any government ministry. It was dependent solely upon Hitler, and justified itself as an executive agency of the 'will of the Führer'. This enabled it to develop its own agenda, legitimated by recourse to the Führer's 'mission', and to expand its target groups largely as it wished, thereby justifying the demand for still further expansion of its own activities and personnel. Hence, following Hitler's attacks on the homosexual activities of Röhm and other SA leaders in 1934 – actually a device to cover up the power-political reasons behind the liquidation of the SA leadership – the police could expand their persecution of homosexuals. In the wake of the 'church struggle', surveillance was extended even to minute Christian sects which were enthusiastic in their support of the regime. And in the crucial sphere of anti-Jewish policy, Eichmann was able to make his career, starting in an insignificant position (but in a vital policy area) in the SD's (*Sicherheitsdienst* or Security Service) Jewish Department, and ending as the manager of the 'final solution'.

The pressure from the police (in which, in a significant move in 1936, the criminal police had been blended in with the security police) to widen the net of surveillance and repression, and extend the target groups, was central to the process of 'cumulative radicalization', and took place with little or no direction from Hitler. The plans – already in 1937 when the number of internees had declined to its lowest point since 1933 and the reason for their existence was starting to become questionable – to expand the concentration camps provide a pointer to ways in which the self-feeding radicalization within the police organization operated. The expansion into Austria and Czechoslovakia in 1938–9 then brought new groups of victims and enlarged activities for the police. War and conquest from 1939 onwards gave the SS-police apparatus under Himmler and Heydrich unimaginable opportunities for unfolding the wildest, most megalomaniac schemes, resting on a continent-wide network of repression and terror.

The structures – perhaps 'structurelessness' would be a better description – of the Third Reich already briefly outlined provided the framework within which the 'idea' of National Socialism, located in the person of the Führer, became gradually translated from utopian 'vision' into realizable policy objectives. Territorial expansion and 'removal of the Jews', both central features of Hitler's ideology, had by 1938–9 come into the foreground as feasible policy options. In the following years they would escalate into genocidal war.

Illustration 16.2 Propaganda from *Der Stürmer*. 'The Jews are our Misfortune'. Pervasive stereotypes of the Jews were designed to exacerbate anti-Semitism in German society

Anti-Jewish policy provides a telling illustration of the way 'cumulative radicalization' operated. There was no central coordination before 1939. But the aim of 'getting rid of the Jews', precisely because of its lack of precise definition, infused every aspect of the activity of the regime. The potential existed, therefore, for the unfolding of ever new discriminatory initiatives from the most diverse directions aimed broadly at the exclusion of Jews from German society and their forced emigration abroad. Hence, boycotts, legislation, 'aryanization' of the economy, physical violence, police measures, and party agitation guaranteed an escalation of the persecution of the Jews. Hitler needed to do little other than indicate his approval (or lack of disapproval) for such actions to gather momentum.

He was involved in 1935, for example, in the promulgation of the notorious Nuremberg Laws only following a summer of violence and agitation stirred up by party organizations. When, chiefly for economic reasons, the party's actions were seen to have become counterproductive, and he was under pressure on the one hand to introduce radical measures against the Jews and on the other to quell the disturbances which had punctuated the spring and summer, Hitler decided at the last minute to introduce legislation during the Nuremberg party rally. Some radicals wanted more draconian measures. But the legislation calmed down the agitation for the time being, while opening up countless further avenues for discrimination and persecution. It had, in other words, an immediate practical function in defusing dysfunctional activism while serving nevertheless as a step on the ladder of 'cumulative radicalisation' in the 'Jewish question'.

The subsequent wave of agitation unleashed from below in 1938, and accompanying the foreign-policy tension in the summer of that year, then had its own culmination in the nationwide pogrom of 9–10 November 1938, instigated by Goebbels but explicitly approved in its most radical form by Hitler. The consequence was not only draconian legislation excluding Jews from the economy, but also the placing of anti-Jewish policy henceforth under the control of the SS.

In foreign policy, Hitler played a much more direct and overt role. But here, too, the process of 'cumulative radicalization' cannot solely be attributed to his intentions and actions. The 'coups' that he pulled off between 1933 and 1936 were wholly in accord with the interests of the traditional power elites. Certainly, Hitler determined the timing and maximized the propaganda effect. But the withdrawal from the League of Nations, the reintroduction of military service and expansion of the army, the bilateral naval treaty with Britain, and the remilitarization of the Rhineland were scarcely moves 'against the grain'. In the most spectacular demonstration of the weakness of the western powers – the remilitarization of the Rhineland – the army leaders certainly evoked Hitler's contempt through their anxiety over the possibility of French and British intervention. But they had nothing but approval for the aim of the Hitler's action. And the danger was in reality minimal – at any rate far lower than Hitler later claimed in order to play up the boldness of his move. As late as November 1937, when Hitler alarmed his top military leaders with his indications of early expansion into Austria and Czechoslovakia, there was no disagreement about the need to attain German hegemony in central Europe. The

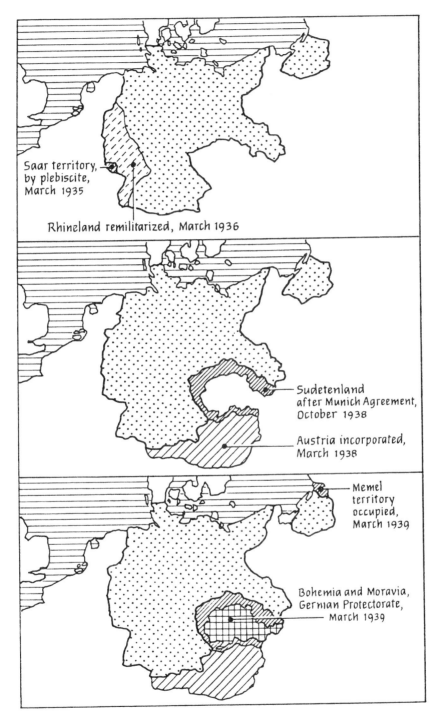

Map 16.1 Pre-war expansion

worry was solely about the risk of war with the great powers. Pressure, mainly on economic grounds, for the subsumption of Austria within the German orbit had up to then largely come from Goering, rather than Hitler. No section of the German elite differed with Hitler on the need to incorporate Austria in one form or another within the Reich. The Anschluß, when Schuschnigg forced matters to a head by his attempt to stage a plebiscite on Austrian autonomy, was as good as universally welcomed.

The Czechoslovakia crisis of summer 1938 was another matter. But by then Hitler's power had been substantially strengthened in relation to the army by the Blomberg–Fritsch affair, followed by his major triumph in Austria. As regards the prospect of military action against the Czechs, Ribbentrop, the new Foreign Minister, was outrightly hawkish. Himmler and Goebbels also backed Hitler's aggressive course. But otherwise, the worries about an unnecessary risk of war against the western powers prevailed. During the summer, General Beck, the chief of staff of the army, voiced his opposition in increasingly forthright memoranda, even advocating facing Hitler with a 'general strike' in the most literal sense – the collective refusal of the generals to obey an order to invade Czechoslovakia. But Beck was not supported by the commander-in-chief of the army, the weak and servile von Brauchitsch. In truth, the army leadership was divided. It had also been weakened by the Blomberg–Fritsch crisis at the beginning of the year. The resolution of this crisis – in which the War Minister Blomberg had been ousted because of his marriage to a woman with a shady past, and commander-in-chief of the army, Fritsch, had been forced out through trumped up charges (subsequently proved to have been based on mistaken identity) of homosexual practice – had effectively transformed the Wehrmacht leadership, the only powerful force left in the state capable of challenging Hitler, into no more than a functional elite, an executive agency of the Führer. When Beck resigned, no one followed him.

However, his replacement, Halder, found himself, together with the head of the Abwehr, Admiral Canaris, at the centre of the nascent conspiracy to have Hitler deposed in the event of an attack on Czechoslovakia that autumn. Whether the conspiracy would have come to anything is an open question. But it indicated the beginnings of a break with Hitler of a number of individuals who served, or had served, the regime in responsible positions in the Wehrmacht, the Foreign Ministry and elsewhere. In the event, of course, the appeasement policy of the western powers, desperate to avoid war, and the intervention by Mussolini (prompted by Goering – as anxious as any to rule out the prospect of war with Britain) forced Hitler to be content for the time being with a negotiated settlement to give him the Sudetenland rather than the war he wanted with the Czechs to gain the whole of Czechoslovakia at one fell swoop. But the West had shown it was unwilling to fight. Hitler had been correct in what he had claimed throughout the summer. Those who had opposed his line were, as a result of the readiness of the western powers to buy Hitler off, seriously weakened. The following summer, during the crisis over Poland, there was no opposition from the generals. Among ordinary people, too, who had been panic-stricken at the thought of war in summer 1938, the mood was far calmer. The Führer had pulled it off on every occasion before. He would do so again. The western powers had given in over the Sudetenland. They were hardly likely to go to war over Danzig. Hitler had, so he said, seen the western leaders at Munich, and they were no more than 'little worms'.[11] When asked by Goering on the eve of the war why it was necessary to gamble everything, Hitler replied: 'Goering, all my life I have gone for broke.'[12]

The war was, indeed, a gigantic gamble. But from Hitler's point of view, the risk had to be taken. Any delay – a characteristic argument – would merely strengthen the enemy. Time, he asserted, was not on Germany's side. The 'cumulative radicalization' of foreign policy over the previous years, and especially the triumphs of 1938, had gravely weakened those forces, above all in the Wehrmacht, which had pushed so strongly for expansion only to find themselves in the end inextricably bound up with a high-risk policy they had been instrumental in creating.

. . .

During the war, the 'structurelessness' of the regime – reflecting the impact of Hitler's 'charismatic authority' on the governmental system – became hugely magnified. Central government splintered. Lammers was less able to play a coordinating role as his own access to Hitler (now constantly shielded by Bormann) declined. Party interference in government under Bormann as head of the re-named Party Chancellery from 1941 onwards, following Hess's flight to Scotland, intensified. Hitler himself became an increasingly remote figure, spending most of his time in his field headquarters in East Prussia, physically detached from the centre of civil government in Berlin. The greatest chances of influencing him fell, apart from the ubiquitous Bormann, to those few who could always rely upon gaining access, such as Goebbels, Goering, Himmler, Ley and Speer. Not surprisingly, therefore, Hitler's interventions in policy-making, though frequent, were usually sporadic and arbitrary, based on one-sided and piecemeal information. Under the strains of total war from the end of 1942 onwards, the regime ran increasingly out of control. Hitler often seemed detached and out of touch, unable to or uninterested in resolving the overwhelming problems that were building up. It was little wonder that by early 1943 even Goebbels could hint not just at a 'leadership', but at a 'leader crisis'.[13]

During the first years of the war it had been different. The victories over Poland, then, especially, over France drove Hitler's power, standing and popularity to its zenith in the summer of 1940. But the triumphs (and the brutality that followed them) concealed for the time being the fragility of Germany's hold over much of Europe. The reality, acknowledged by Hitler and the German leadership, was that Britain was still undefeated; that intervention at some point by the USA with all its might and resources could not be ruled out; that the USSR – desperately preparing for the invasion it expected around 1942 – was bound to Germany only by the cynical opportunist pact of August 1939; and that the Reich's economic base, unless there were further expansion, was precarious indeed.

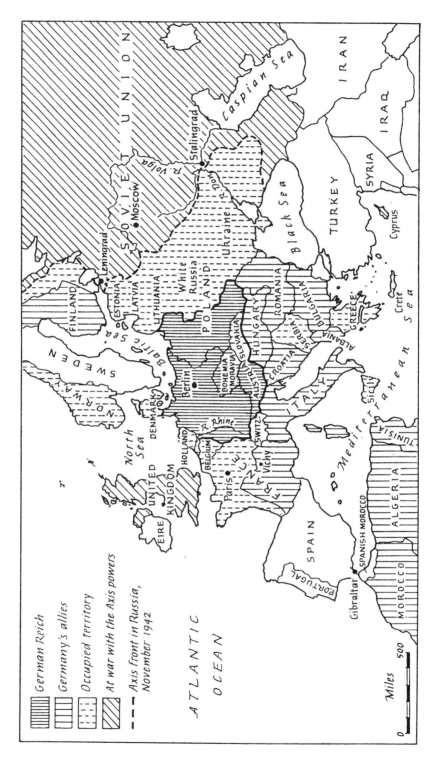

Map 16.2 Nazi Germany at its zenith 1942

Without waiting for victory over Britain, Hitler had already, following the conquest of France, given orders to begin preparations for an attack on the Soviet Union – the ideological arch-enemy. In spring 1941, these preparations took concrete shape. This would be a different war to that in the west, a 'war of annihilation', as Hitler told his generals.[14] The army was complicitous in the orders for the shooting of Soviet commissars, who were not to be treated as comrades but were to be liquidated on capture. The army, brutalized by its experiences of the ruthless inhumanity in occupied Poland, its ranks infected by propaganda about the 'Jewish-Bolshevik world enemy', was also ready to collaborate in the operations of the SD's 'task forces' (*Einsatzgruppen*) to wipe out political enemies and Jews behind the front lines. With the orders to the *Einsatzgruppen*, given in the weeks before the invasion of the USSR, the 'quantum jump' into genocide was taken.[15] Once this jump had been made, the killing could only escalate.

'Operation Barbarossa' – the invasion of the Soviet Union – was meant to be over long before the end of the year. Despite the extraordinary advances initially made after it was launched on 22 June 1941, this was already looking unlikely before the German troops found themselves bogged down in the ice and the mud, condemned to exposure in a Russian winter without adequate clothing or provisions. With the entry of the USA into the war in December 1941, and the certainty of the conflict dragging on into the indefinite future with the balance of resources tipped heavily against Germany, Hitler's gamble was already effectively lost, even if the Wehrmacht continued to fight tooth and nail over every yard of ground and total defeat was still over three years away.

The 'cumulative radicalization' of anti-Jewish policy had meanwhile escalated into all-out systematic genocide. The power-crazed plans of the police and SS under Heydrich and Himmler for the mass removal of Jews in Poland to make way for the resettlement of ethnic Germans from the Baltic and other parts of eastern Europe had proved unrealizable. Ghettos – some, like Lodz and Warsaw, huge in size – had been hastily set up, initially meant as temporary measures, prior to further deportation eastwards to a huge Jewish reservation. The continuation of the war vitiated such schemes (which would doubtless in practice have resulted in a form of genocide, though not necessarily the form which actually emerged). Already in mid-1941 there were suggestions that the Jews in the ghettos should be liquidated rather than fed during the coming winter. By that time, the *Einsatzgruppen* were shooting thousands of Jews in the USSR. And pressure was building up meanwhile from police and party leaders within Germany to have Jews from the Reich deported eastwards – to ghettos already bursting at the seams. By late summer or early autumn 1941, it had been decided that mass extermination was the solution, and that killing by poison gas offered potential 'efficiency' in the plan to annihilate all the Jews in Nazi-occupied Europe. The first of the extermination camps in the General-Gouvernement was commissioned in September, at Belzec. Its personnel were drawn from those who had acquired expertise in killing by poison gas during the so-called 'euthanasia action' within Germany – the liquidation of around 100,000 mentally ill and incurably sick patients of asylums – which had been 'officially' ended (after doctors had nominated even more victims than the Nazis had imagined there to be) in August 1941. By December 1941, the first killing installations were in operation at Chelmno in the Warthegau, a part of western Poland annexed to the Reich. The following month, the orchestration of the 'final solution' was worked out at the Wannsee Conference. By spring 1942, the mass killing of Poland's big Jewish population in the extermination camps of what came to be called '*Aktion Reinhard*' – Belzec, Sobibor, and Treblinka – was underway. By then, too, the enormous extermination camp at Auschwitz-Birkenau, with its huge capacity for production-line murder, was also in operation.

It is not credible to imagine that the 'final solution' as it emerged in the latter half of 1941 – the attempt to exterminate the entire Jewish population of Europe – was implemented without the approval, let alone without the knowledge, of Hitler. The barbarous guidelines for the occupation of Poland, then for the invasion of the USSR, had been laid down by Hitler. Pressed for affirmation of his written authorization, in autumn 1939 he had explicitly, on his own headed notepaper, empowered his doctor, Karl Brandt, and the Philipp Bouhler head of the Chancellery of the Führer of the NSDAP, Viktor Brack, to carry out the killing of the mentally sick. Goebbels referred to Hitler in early 1942, as the death camps moved into full operation, as 'the undismayed champion of a radical solution' to the so-called 'Jewish question'.[16] Probably not least because of the difficulties which had arisen from the killing of the mentally sick and incurable, Hitler would have shied away from a written authorization in the case of the extermination of the Jews. But his verbal approval for initiatives in all probability emanating from Heydrich's office in the Reich Security Headquarters would have been necessary and was, as Eichmann later claimed, most likely given a couple of months after the invasion of the Soviet Union.

As military defeats mounted during the second half of the war, and as the bombs rained down ever more heavily on German cities, the popularity of the now distant figure of the Führer, who, without triumphs to announce, no longer wanted to face his once adoring public, went into steep decline. The 'successes' which had been essential to sustaining 'charismatic leadership' were by now a distant memory, the Führer cult a residual and ritualized propaganda product largely devoid of the spontaneous effusions of support which had been so vividly present during the early years of the regime.

Even so, strong reserves of popular support for Hitler remained. More important still: since all the power groups in the now crumbling regime had earlier committed themselves to Hitler, had become implicated in the criminal actions of the regime, and had burnt their boats with the Führer, they now felt no option other than to stick with him. This included most of the generals in the Wehrmacht – the one body capable of deposing Hitler. The minority of courageous officers, and of civilians from different backgrounds and positions, who at great peril joined the conspiracy to assassinate Hitler, did so in the recognition that they had to act without the backing of most of their colleagues, and without popular support. The chance of ending the regime from within collapsed with the failure of the attempted coup of 20 July 1944. In the gathering chaos as the war drew towards its finale, the complete fragmentation of authority below Hitler ruled out any alternative to following the dictator to the bitter end. Only in the last days were other leading Nazis prepared to challenge Hitler's authority. But even in these last days, in the unreal world of the bunker, generals awaited Hitler's orders to pass on to no longer existent army divisions.

. . .

A key to explaining the process of 'cumulative radicalization' in the Third Reich, I have suggested, can be found in the workings of the type of 'charismatic authority' embodied in Hitler's dictatorship. As Führer, Hitler was the linchpin of the entire 'system' – which, in reality, was fragmenting ever more under the impact of his leadership. He was the only link with its various, usually competing, parts. But, outside the realm of foreign and military policy, his direct intervention was seldom needed in order to drive forward the escalating radicalization of the regime. All that was required was for him to set the tone, give the green light, provide the broad guidelines for action, and sanction initiatives of others.

Such initiatives usually fell within the process which one leading Nazi described as 'working towards the Führer'.[17] This meant anticipating what Hitler wanted, second-guessing his intentions, doing everything possible to push forward his loosely defined long-term goals, not waiting for instructions before using one's own initiative. Hitler's presumed aims and intentions served, therefore, to activate the activists and to legitimate their actions. At the grass-roots of the party, this could mean, for example, agitation to hound out Jews from the economy and turn them into social pariahs. In the state bureaucracy, it justified ever more radical attempts to turn vicious but open-ended ideological imperatives into specific and concrete discriminatory legislation. Not least, in the ever-expanding SS and police organization, the tasks associated with the Führer's 'mission' offered endless scope for the unfolding of new, inhumane 'projects' (and accompanying power, status and enrichment), especially in the conquered eastern territories.

Among ordinary citizens, far removed from the centres of power, 'working towards the Führer' also had its meaning – if a more metaphorical one. Ideological motives were not necessarily dominant, or even present, when neighbours or workmates were denounced to the Gestapo. But the screw of repression was nonetheless tightened by countless such acts. Doctors looking for more 'modern' ways of creating a 'healthier' society could take a lead in pressing for measures on sterilization and recommend their patients for the 'euthanasia' programme. Or businessmen, anxious to rid themselves of competition, could use anti-Jewish legislation to close down a rival concern. These few examples illustrate how 'working towards the Führer' – unforced collaboration, using the broad ideological aims embodied in Hitler as a legitimation – could contribute to driving on an unstoppable radicalization which saw the gradual conversion of an ideological 'mission' into concrete policy objectives.

The 'idea' personified in the quasi-deified figure of the Führer held together the antagonistic forces within the Nazi movement itself. It also incorporated the distinct but related aims of the national-conservative elites in the economy, state administration, and – not least – army. The lack of definition of the 'idea' was itself an advantage. Building a united, racially homogeneous 'national community', restoring national strength and pride, establishing a 'Greater Germany', bringing ethnic Germans 'home into the Reich': all these aims corresponded with the hopes of millions. War to attain 'living space' (*Lebensraum*) and racial extermination were by no means seen by the mass of Hitler admirers during the rise to power or at the height of his triumphs in the 1930s as implicit in them. But the boundaries were fluid. The 'idea', represented by Hitler, provided a plebiscitary base and underlying consensus for the regime, whose aggressive dynamic was increasingly spiralling out of control.

The 'charismatic' nature of Hitler's position as Führer – a quasi-messianic personalized form of rule that arose from the desire for national rebirth and unity in a country traumatized by national humiliation and paralysed by political collapse – could of its essence not settle into 'normality' or routine, or sag into mere conservative authoritarianism. Visionary goals of national redemption through European domination and racial purification were at the heart of the regime. These meant constant dynamism and self-perpetuating, intensifying radicalism. The longer the regime lasted, the more megalomaniac were its aims, the more boundless its destructiveness. Its gamble for world supremacy meant war against an alliance of extremely powerful allies. It was a gamble against the odds, in which the regime risked its own destruction and that of Germany itself. This was Nazism's essential irrationality. Hitler's 'charismatic' leadership implied, therefore, not just an unprecedented capacity for destruction, but also an inbuilt tendency towards self-destruction. In this sense, the suicide of the German dictator on 30 April 1945 was not merely a welcome, but also a logical, end to the Third Reich.

Notes:

1. Ritter, Gerhard, *Das deutsche Problem. Grundfragen deutschen Staatslebens gestern und heute* (1962) (extended edition of *Europa und die deutsche Frage*, 1948), p. 198.
2. Mommsen, Hans, 'Der Nationalsozialismus. Kumulative Radikalisierung und Selbstzerstörung des Regimes', in *Meyers Enzyklopädisches Lexikon*, vol. 16 (1976), pp. 785–90. And see now Hans Mommsen, 'Cumulative Radicalization and Progressive Self-Destruction as Structural Determinants of the Nazi Dictatorship', in Ian Kershaw and Moshe Lewin eds., *Stalinism and Nazism. Dictatorships in Comparison* (1997).
3. Mommsen, Hans, 'Hitlers Stellung im nationalsozialistischen Herrschaftssystem', in Gerhard Hirschfeld and Lothar Kettenacker, eds., *Der 'Führerstaat': Mythos und Realität* (1981), p. 70.
4. Mommsen, 'Hitlers Stellung', p.70; translated, Hans Mommsen, *From Weimar to Auschwitz* (1991), p. 187.
5. I explore the limitations of this concept at length in *The Nazi Dictatorship*, 3rd edn. (1993), ch. 4.

6. Mommsen, Hans, 'Hitlers Stellung', p. 70; *From Weimar to Auschwitz*, p. 187.
7. Bessel, Richard, *Germany after the First World War* (1993), p. 262.
8. Huber, Ernst Rudolf, *Verfassungsrecht des Großdeutschen Reiches* (1939), p. 230; translated in Jeremy Noakes and Geoffrey Pridham eds., *Nazism 1919–1945: A Documentary Reader*, 3 vols. (1983, 1985, 1988) (= N&P), vol. 2, p. 199.
9. Frank, Hans, *Im Angesicht des Galgens* (1953), pp. 466–7; trans. N&P, vol. 2, p. 200.
10. Wiedemann, Fritz, *Der Mann, der Feldherr werden wollte* (1964), p. 69; trans. N&P, vol. 2, p. 208.
11. International Military Tribunal, *Trial of the Major War Criminals*, 42 vols. (1949), vol. 26, p. 343; trans. N&P, vol. 3, p. 742.
12. Hill, Leonidas E., ed., *Die Weizsäcker-Papiere 1933–1950* (1974), p. 162.
13. Speer, Albert, *Erinnerungen* (1969), p. 271.
14. Halder, Franz, *Kriegstagebuch*, 3 vols. (1962–4), vol. 2, pp. 336–7.
15. The phrase is that of Christopher Browning, *The Final Solution and the German Foreign Office* (1978), p. 8.
16. Lochner, Louis, ed., *The Goebbels Diaries* (1948), p. 103; Elke Fröhlich, ed., *Die Tagebücher von Joseph Goebbels*, Part II: *Diktate 1941–1945*, vol. 3, p. 561.
17. Speech by Werner Willikens, State Secretary in the Ministry of Food, 21 Feb. 1934, Niedersächsisches Staatsarchiv, Oldenburg, Best. 131, Nr. 303, Fol. 131v; trans. N&P, vol. 2, p. 207.

Select bibliography

Balfour, Michael, *Withstanding Hitler*, (1988).
Bartov, Omer, *Hitler's Army: Soldiers, Nazis, and War in the Third Reich* (1991).
Bessel, Richard, ed., *Life in the Third Reich* (1987).
Bracher, Karl Dietrich, *The German Dictatorship* (1971).
Broszat, Martin, *Hitler's State* (1981).
Browning, Christopher, *Fateful Months* (1985).
Browning, Christopher, *The Path to Genocide* (1992).
Buchheim, Hans, *et al.*, *Anatomy of the SS State* (1968).
Bull, Hedley, ed., *The Challenge of the Third Reich* (1986).
Bullock, Alan, *Hitler. A Study in Tyranny* (1952).
Bullock, Alan, *Hitler and Stalin. Parallel Lives* (1991).
Burleigh, Michael, and Wippermann, Wolfgang, *The Racial State* (1991).
Burrin, Philippe, *Hitler and the Jews. The Genesis of the Holocaust* (1994).
Caplan, Jane, *Government without Administration* (1988).
Carr, William, *Hitler: A Study in Personality and Politics* (1972).
Dülffer, Jost, *Nazi Germany. Faith and Annihilation* (1996).
Fest, Joachim C., *The Face of the Third Reich* (1972).
Fest, Joachim C., *Hitler* (1974).
Fleming, Gerald, *Hitler and the Final Solution* (1986).
Frei, Norbert, *National Socialist Rule in Germany* (1993).
Geary, Dick, *Hitler and Nazism* (1993).
Gellately, Robert, *The Gestapo and German Society* (1990).
Graml, Hermann, *Antisemitism in the Third Reich* (1992).
Hildebrand, Klaus, *The Third Reich* (1984).
Hiden, John, and Farquharson, John, *Explaining Hitler's Germany*, 2nd edn. (1989).
Hirschfeld, Gerhard, ed., *The Policies of Genocide* (1986).

Hoffmann, Peter, *The German Resistance to Hitler* (1988).

Jäckel, Eberhard, *Hitler in History* (1984).

Jäckel, Eberhard, *Hitler's World View* (1981).

Kater, Michael, *The Nazi Party* (1983).

Kershaw, Ian, *Popular Opinion and Political Dissent in the Third Reich* (1983).

Kershaw, Ian, *The Hitler Myth* (1987).

Kershaw, Ian, *Hitler. A Profile in Power* (1991).

Kershaw, Ian, *The Nazi Dictatorship*, 3rd edn. (1993).

Kirk, Tim, ed., *Nazi Germany* (1995).

Large, David Clay, ed., *Contending with Hitler* (1991).

Mason, Tim, *Social Policy in the Third Reich* (1993).

Mommsen, Hans, *From Weimar to Auschwitz* (1991).

Müller, Klaus-Jürgen, *Army, Politics, and Society in Germany, 1933–1945* (1987).

Noakes, Jeremy, ed., *Government, Party, and People in Nazi Germany* (1980).

Noakes, Jeremy, and Pridham, Geoffrey, eds., *Nazism. A Documentary Study*, 3 vols. (1983–8).

Overy, Richard, *War and Economy in the Third Reich* (1994).

Overy, Richard, *Why the Allies Won* (1995).

Peterson, Edward, *The Limits of Hitler's Power* (1969).

Peukert, Detlev, *Inside Nazi Germany* (1987).

Stachura, Peter, ed., *The Shaping of the Nazi State* (1975).

Stephenson, Jill, *Women in Nazi Society* (1975).

Stephenson, Jill, *The Nazi Organisation of Women* (1981).

Stoakes, Geoffrey, *Hitler and the Quest for World Dominion* (1987).

Weinberg, Gerhard, *The Foreign Policy of Hitler's Germany*, 2 vols. (1970, 1980).

Welch, David, ed., *Nazi Propaganda* (1983).

Welch, David, *The Third Reich. Politics and Propaganda* (1993).

17

The Holocaust

Nicholas Stargardt

By the time the Nazi regime collapsed in the rubble of Berlin in 1945, six million Jews had been killed. This 'final solution of the Jewish question', to use the Nazi euphemism with its nineteenth-century ring, began with the German attack on the Soviet Union on 22 June 1941. In the wake of the advancing German army, specially selected SS units, or *Einsatzgruppen* began to carry out mass shootings. Initially, their victims were Jewish and non-Jewish men, women and children increasingly being included from August onwards. Shootings by relatively small mobile units continued even after the establishment of the death camps in 1942. Some 2.2 million Jews in total were shot, burned and beaten to death by such units made up of SS men, police reserve battalions and gendarmes as well as regular soldiers. By November 1941 at the latest, this continuously escalating, yet in many of its details improvised, campaign of mass murder was placed under the central control of the SS, directed by Heinrich Himmler and his deputy Reinhard Heydrich. Local initiatives continued apace. In the autumn, a gas van was tried out at Semlin in Serbia as an automated form of killing. At Chelmno in Poland, the commander of one *Einsatzgruppe*, Herbert Lange began to deploy mobile gas vans in December 1941, left over from the so-called 'euthanasia' action against asylum patients, this time in order to kill Jews and gypsies. His 'experiments' in gassing accounted for 145,000 deaths. Himmler authorized the extension of the use of gas. At Chelmno, Sobibor, Belzec, Majdanek and Treblinka the exhaust from static diesel engines was pumped into specially constructed chambers. At a camp for Soviet prisoners of war, Auschwitz, a cyanide compound used as a pesticide was tested on a group of inmates. This was 'Zyklon B'. The technique, in which pellets of the compound were tipped into a chamber from a vent in the ceiling, became the standard technique for a vast and rapidly assembled bureaucratic and industrial machinery of mass murder.

Across German-occupied Europe the Jewish population was being separated out, registered, stripped of their property, deported to ghettos and transit camps and on to the archipelago of labour and death camps. On arrival the deportees were divided

Illustration 17.1   Prisoners in a barracks in Buchenwald concentration camp. Second row from the bottom, seventh from the left, is the writer Elie Wiesel

between those to be gassed immediately (including all children and the women who accompanied them) and those who might be worked to death, some of whom were employed in disposing of the corpses. Gas chambers and the adjacent crematoria were usually disguised as delousing stations, victims deceived into undressing for the 'showers', in order to make burning of the naked corpses and recycling of their clothing easier. When the crematoria could not cope with the numbers, as in the summer of 1944, the corpses were burned in open trenches. After death, the victims' clothes, hair, spectacles and gold teeth were systematically collected by special squads of camp inmates, supervised by the SS and their local allies and tallies sent back to the Reich Economic Ministry. In addition to the Jews, over a quarter of a million gypsies were slaughtered in the mass shootings and the camps. A lesser but still unquantified number of male homosexuals, a smaller number of female homosexuals, and so-called 'asocials',

Illustration 17.2   Upon arrival in Auschwitz, Jews were divided into two groups: those who were to work and those who were to be exterminated immediately

including people who were supposedly poor, unemployed, vagrant, drunken or work-shy, were consigned often to their deaths within the camp system.

The death camps built upon a concentration camp system whereby small armed minorities were able to wield complete power over very large majorities. Much has been written about the mechanisms of terror and the mentality of inmates. The exponential increase in numbers from March 1942 on and the short period between most victims' arrival and their deaths cannot have left time for any kind of collective mentality to develop. About some camps we also know very little: two Jews survived Belzec, one of whom, Chaim Hirschmann, was killed by Poles in Lublin in 1946. Although Auschwitz-Birkenau accounted for the greatest single toll of Jewish lives, the hurried German retreat on that sector of the eastern front meant that a far greater number of inmates also survived it than from camps which the Order of the Death's Head closed according to its own plans. From 1943 onwards, special units of prisoners, usually composed of Jews and Soviet prisoners of war, disinterred the mass graves in order to burn the remains of those killed by the Einsatzgruppen and realize Himmler's objective of obliterating any trace of the slaughter for posterity. At the same time, however, both the private fascination of the executioners and of the SS as an organization precipitated the creation of extensive photographic documentation. This pattern of destroyed and retained evidence, of survivors' testimony and its absence leaves a complicated patchwork in which we know an enormous amount about many aspects of the Holocaust and very little about others. Because of the power of the visual record this also deeply affects what images of the Holocaust we have.

Primo Levi, reflecting with a dispassionate intensity on what it meant to survive, felt a need to note that: 'We who survived the camps are not true witnesses.' As he explained,

> We, the survivors, are not only a tiny but also an anomalous minority. We are those who, through prevarication, skill or luck, never touched bottom. Those who have, and who have seen the face of the Gorgon, did not return, or returned wordless.[1]

But the question of the 'typicality' of survivors' testimony is only one of the frustrations to communicating their experience. A considerable amount has been written about the guilt experienced by those who survived towards those who did not; rather less has been written about the guilt of those who have never experienced anything remotely approaching these conditions towards those who attempt to recount what they were. But as George Orwell was honest enough to note in a piece of self-critical journalism after the liberation of Bergen Belsen, for many Western observers the physical aspect of the SS perpetrators often seemed far less abnormal and by extension, at an instinctive level, less threatening than that of their surviving victims. Certainly, after an initial explosion of public information about the death camps, in western Europe and the United States as well as in censorship-ruled Eastern Europe a blanket of silence descended on the actual experience of persecution. Even psychoanalysts in the United States, many of them Jewish, did not begin to recognise that survivors had undergone what Henry Krystal came to call 'massive psychic trauma' until the term could be legitimated by quite other subjects, such as veterans of the Korean War. The Eichmann trial of 1960, with its spectacular publicity and symbolic power of being staged in Jerusalem, changed all this. Yet, serious historical investigation and debate only began in the mid-1960s with the publication of Raul Hilberg's *Destruction of the European Jews*. Whilst some survivor witnesses, like Levi, wrote about what they had seen soon after their liberation, many waited, protecting both themselves and their children from their experience. As a good number of the unpublished memoirs deposited in the Wiener Library, London, state, the authors often waited until their grandchildren were born before they decided that they must not allow the memory to be forgotten. Psychoanalysts, for their part, have begun to work on the trauma experienced by the second and third generation.

It is nonetheless only by engaging with the memories of those who survived that it is possible to reconstruct the particular states which the persecutors produced in their victims and themselves. Even now, there is an unfortunate division of labour among those historians who work with written and oral testimony: virtually no historian seems able to work on the testimony of both victims and perpetrators. Although many survivors report on aspects of the system of domination in which they found themselves as well as on the brutalized and self-destructive collusion it engendered in other inmates, few had the inner resources to watch this process take hold of themselves and explain it afterwards. Even fewer were able to enter, in such conditions, imaginatively into the mentality of their oppressors. Yet, there are some outstanding exceptions to this rule, whose insights into the mentality of both sides of the camp world suggest new questions for historians. A Viennese-trained psychoanalyst, Bruno Bettelheim, was fortunate enough to be released after 'only' a year in pre-war Dachau and Buchenwald. During his incarceration he set himself the task of observing and understanding his own and others' psychological transformation as his own personal survival strategy. In his explanation, guards and prisoners 'learned' to occupy the respective roles of brutal, punitive fathers and terrified, penitent and dependent children. Privacy and control over bodily functions like defecation were removed. Alongside the physiological damage caused by brutal punishment (again often anally directed), utterly inadequate nourishment (with a concomitant loss of drive), cold and overwork, this regression to the dependency of early childhood undid years of self-confidence in adult prisoners. The importance of Bettelheim's insight was to propose that neither guards nor prisoners had to fit any particular psychological profile at the outset, but that sadistic and collusive behaviour, inner withdrawal or psychic 'splitting' could all be learned under the intense pressures of a totalizing environment. Although Bettelheim himself never experienced the death camps, elements of his psychological explanation have been strongly endorsed both by former prisoners such as Elie Cohen and Eugen Kogon and by the sociologist Wolfgang Sofsky as a valuable way of understanding the mental worlds of those Jews who were spared immediate death in the camps. They are in no sense a complete explanation of the psychological dimensions of the Holocaust. Such constructions also run the risk of making the experience seem deceptively accessible, for they rely upon methods of psychoanalytic interpretation which were never expected to handle such events and whose abstract formulation may even serve to distance us from their reality.

Recent work on the units involved in mass shootings raises questions about the explanations of perpetrators' mentality taken from the death camps. Based on the memoirs of Hoess, the Commandant of Auschwitz, and others, the mentality conveyed often draws on the cliché of the 'efficient German', guarding against real emotional involvement in the killing through a variety of distancing mechanisms: the division of labour and responsibility within the 'machine'; euphemisms like 'special treatment' to refer to murder; the retention of a separate private life of home and family. In fact, a number of personnel brought their wives or lovers to visit the camps. Furthermore, the Wehrmacht, *Einsatzgruppen* and police battalion units involved in the mass shootings were small and mobile, underpinned by an *esprit de corps* with its own strong sense of belonging rather than by any implied alienation from a bureaucratic process. Moreover, their ways of killing were face to face – shooting, burning, hanging, beating – and involved the expenditure of personal will and fantasy, as well as a considerable amount of energy in which the object was in no doubt. Such behaviour requires a wider repertoire of psychological explanations which engage with the positive will to torture and kill.

In one of his last collections of essays, *The Periodic Table*, Primo Levi recounted a post-war correspondence he developed with one of the German chemists whom he had worked under as a prisoner in Auschwitz. What began as a business correspondence between two professionals in Germany and Italy developed into a personal effort on both sides to address the issues of the German's power over prisoners in the camp and involvement in the Holocaust. As Levi showed, at each point that his correspondent approached the reality of what he had done, he veered off into vague and abstract language, couching his feelings in high-flown clichés. This, Levi concluded, was not accidental. It also stands in sharp contrast, as Levi's own writing exemplifies, to the dry and matter-of-fact narratives of many survivors.

The horror lies in the simple detail. It does not need to be extracted from it. Dinora Pines, after working with survivors as a psychoanalyst, has suggested that such literalness may derive not just from a fear of not being believed, of encountering Holocaust denial. As Pines puts it in her foreword to Elie Cohen's *Human Behaviour in the Concentration Camp*:

> It is impressive to read his account, which he writes objectively, without anger. Yet the reader is inevitably moved to pain, depression and despair at man's inhumanity to man, as if he must express these powerful feelings for the writer. In this way Dr Cohen's writing reflects many survivors' difficulty in expressing powerful feelings for themselves. My clinical experience in working with survivors of the Holocaust leads me to believe that the survivor's anger is deeply repressed and expressed through others, such as the analyst in the analytical situation – since anger would have led to death in the camps.[2]

It is the emotional shorthand of the dispassionate detail which endows so many memoirs with exceptional power. It is fitting that it should be those victims who survived to bear witness who should provide so much of the symbolic language of its commemoration. The exceptional is invested also in our attachments as viewers to the everyday object. The last room in Yad Vashem displays a child's shoe.

The complicated process by which societies at large repress memory and recall experience is not unique to the Holocaust. In some version most twentieth-century societies which have been rent by mass violence, whether through war or civil war or mass persecution, seem to layer the experience with a generation of amnesia before beginning, if then, to discuss the experience itself. In the case of the holocaust, this layering has to be glimpsed behind the public acts of official commemoration and, in the case of post-war West Germany, official apology.

The very terms in which much public discussion of the Nazi period was couched in West Germany well into the 1980s, the 'overcoming of the past' (*Bewältigung der Vergangenheit*) suggested a 'past' whose details were too horrific to specify except in rather stilted and carefully policed abstractions, carefully removed from the cadences of everyday speech. This language has characterized the rituals of apology and restitution which West German governments have made part of their relations with the European Community, the USA and Israel. When, in a formal address to the

Bundestag on the fiftieth aniversary of *Kristallnacht*, Philipp Jenninger attempted to explain why he thought most Germans had come to support Hitler by 1938, he was universally criticized for committing a major international *faux pas*. In his flat-footed fashion he had departed from the established formulae, an inept yet nonetheless real enough attempt to engage. The 'overcoming of the past' also implies a nation whose emotions are still locked down despite attempts to break them open, an endeavour in which Alexander and Margarete Mitscherlich's *The Inability to Mourn* (1967) established a benchmark for discussions of this problem in Germany.

The last decade has seen a major shift in public perceptions with a heightened social and moral awareness, at least in western Europe and the US, of the significance of what is now virtually universally referred to as 'the Holocaust'. In Germany, a post-1968 generation felt neither immediately responsible nor any great need to deny responsibility. Hollywood feature films shown in Germany, first *The Holocaust* and more recently *Schindler's List*; documentaries such as Claude Lanzmann's *Shoa*, as well as local productions like *Das schreckliche Mädchen* and *Jakobs Gold*, have played their part in a growing international culture of commemoration, exemplified by Yad Vashem in Jerusalem and the Holocaust Museum in Washington. The very fact that the term 'Holocaust' has largely lost its original Zionist connotations of a 'blood sacrifice', with its questionable implication of posthumous redemption through the foundation of the state of Israel, suggests a growing willingness to think about the historical events themselves.

However much historians may strive to write about the 'final solution' as an impersonal set of events, they cannot help contributing to moral arguments in their own societies. The gulf which still persists between, on the one hand, the abstraction of much of the language of historical debate and the highly literal narratives of reminiscence, on the other, will come, I think, to be seen as symptomatic of a particular phase of learning how to write – and with it to think and feel – about one of the most shocking and horrific events of the still very recent past.

I The decision and the means

The last decade of scholarship has seen a major controversy between so-called 'Hitlerist' or 'intentionalist' explanations and so-called 'structuralist' or 'functionalist' ones. As we shall see, both of these approaches have their intellectual and moral points of reference in arguments made by Allied and exiled commentators during and immediately after the war. On the 'intentionalist' side, historians like Lucy Dawidowicz and Gerald Fleming have stressed Hitler's personal anti-Semitism, his reception of pseudo-scientific notions of biological racism in pre-war Vienna, his willingness to blame Germany's defeat in the First World War on the Jews and finally his ominous warning to the Reichstag on 30 January 1939, that

> If the international Jewish financiers outside Europe should succeed in plunging the nations once more into a world war, then the result will not be the bolshevization of the earth, and thus the victory of Jewry, but the annihilation of the Jewish race in Europe.[3]

For Dawidowicz and Fleming, the pre-war acts of the Nazi regime left no doubt as to the virulence of its anti-Semitism. There were random attacks, beatings and murders of Jews by the storm troopers immediately after Hitler came to power. On 1 April 1933, the party called for a boycott of Jewish shops and businesses. Within the year Jews were forced out of the civil service and the legal and medical professions. In 1935, the Reichstag was summoned to join the annual Nazi Party rally in Nuremberg to rubber-stamp new laws on German marriage and citizenship which reduced Jews to second-class citizens. Measures aimed at the expropriation of Jewish property and the forced emigration of Jews were introduced, which reached a peak after the annexation of Austria in 1938, culminating, in November, in the burning of synagogues and looting of Jewish shops as Josef Goebbels ordered the party activists into 'spontaneous action'. These major initiatives occurred against a backdrop of unremitting verbal and rhetorical violence in the Nazi press, in which the speeches of Hitler, Goebbels and Julius Streicher played a key part. For 'intentionalists', Hitler is the central actor who plotted the murder of the Jews from the outset.

So-called functionalist and structuralist-minded historians regard the decision to murder European Jews as more contingent. That Hitler's own views and Nazi policy were virulently anti-Semitic is not under question; rather, the issue is when did the decision to murder the Jews become the only 'final solution'? Each stage of persecution clearly prepared the way for more extreme measures and so formed a progression of sorts, but at what point were other alternatives discarded by the Nazi leadership? This has meant separating the general climate of rising anti-Semitism fostered by Hitler and other leading Nazis from the specific timing and character of the decision to murder European Jewry. For Karl Schleunes, the road to Auschwitz was a 'twisted' one, marked by abrupt halts when other concerns such as ameliorating public opinion in western Europe and the US during the Berlin Olympics took precedence. It was marked also, in Schleunes' view, by hesitancy on Hitler's part. For instance, when party 'radicals' and more 'moderate' Interior and Justice Ministry bureaucrats could not agree over how many grandparents were required in order to define someone as Jewish in 1935 or over the question of levying a collective punitive tax on German Jews in the wake of *Kristallnacht*, Hitler prevaricated and took the more moderate line. Finally, if the original goal from Hitler's entry into politics in 1919 was already focused on mass murder, why did the regime actively encourage Jews to emigrate until 1940?

Linked to the question of 'when' is the issue of how the 'final solution' was ordered. Did Hitler personally order the 'final solution'? Both Goering – in an order to Heydrich on 31 July 1941 – and Himmler – in his speeches to SS commanders – refer to fulfilling the 'Führer's wish'. Moreover, we have much evidence of Hitler's views from his circle of intimates, especially the diaries of Josef Goebbels. But no direct written evidence has been found, even after the opening of the former Soviet archives. Martin Broszat and Hans Mommsen have argued that it is unlikely that there ever was a formal order from Hitler. They lay great store by the different factions at work within the regime, vying with each other for Hitler's approval whilst he procrastinated. They also stress the extent to which decision-making was actually left to the initiative of local leaders. For them, the period of the mass shootings was symptomatic of a period of improvised, *ad hoc* exterminations, which were endorsed from above but planned from below. For them the Wannsee Conference, planned in November 1941 and finally staged by Heydrich in January 1942, marks the beginning of a full-scale programme of mass extermination with the coordinated deportation of western as well as eastern European Jews and the construction of the death camps.

It has become hard to hold to an extreme position on either side of the 'intentionalist' and 'structuralist' divide. As more and more circumstantial evidence has been introduced, the areas of consensus have gradually grown to a point, where – if the central questions under dispute still remain unresolved – at least the range of plausible answers has narrowed greatly. It is generally accepted that 1941 was the crucial year, although it is still unclear whether a formal decision in favour of extermination preceded the attack on the Soviet Union, as Helmut Krausnick has argued, accompanied it, as Christopher Browning believes, or followed in its wake, as Christian Streit and Philippe Burrin have contended. The evidence for a later date is based on two facts: first, although the killing units in eastern Europe far exceeded their formal brief of shooting 'Jewish commissars', they did not interpret these orders in a uniform manner, some murdering whole communities, some sparing the women and children; second, the deportation of western European Jewry did not begin until the winter of 1941–2. Finally, the SS and police battalion commanders in the field depended on the active cooperation of the Wehrmacht. Although the army command was generally prepared by May 1941 to fight the war against 'Bolshevism' as a 'war of annihilation' – an ideological elision of Jew and Communism, which, as Jürgen Förster and Christian Streit have argued, was important to winning over key non-Nazi constituencies in the army – the Berlin leadership could not know beforehand how agreements made between the army and the SS would be implemented in the field. This helps to make sense of the particular operation of command structures within the SS and the police battalion, giving units the task of murder with indefinite but competitive quotas to be achieved. The units, in their turn, surprised even Heydrich and Himmler by accelerating the rate of killing, so establishing a fateful dynamic between ruthless and ambitious subordinates anxious to over-fulfil their orders and superiors who set ever higher targets.

I am myself most persuaded by Burrin's argument that Hitler did eventually issue a verbal or possibly written instruction, but not until late September or the very beginning of October 1941. What Hitler really thought at any time is a deeply problematic issue, but Burrin's shrewd reading of the available evidence here is carefully contextualized and psychologically perceptive: he argues that Hitler believed the war against the Soviet Union was going badly by late August and early September, and that the worse Hitler thought the war was going, the more he returned to his 'prophecy' of January 1939 that the war would lead to the destruction of European Jewry. In any event, I would also have to agree with those sophisticated 'intentionalists' who argue that, however much mass extermination may have been a decision dependent on specific

Map legend:

- Refugees c. 280 000 Jews left Europe 1933-40
- 70 000 Jewish refugees to Russia, 1939-41

Camps and centres labelled on map:
Neuengamme 1940, Bergen-Belsen 1943, Ravensbrück 1942, Stutthof 1942, Vught 1940, Brandenburg, Sachsenhausen 1936, Treblinka 1942, Mettelbau-Dora 1943, Moseritz Obrawalde, Chelmno 1941, Warsaw Ghetto, Buchenwald 1937, Grossrosen, Sobibor 1942, Hadamar, Theresienstadt Ghetto, Auschwitz 1940, Majdanek 1943, Belzec 1942, Eichberg, Natzweiler, Dachau 1933, Hartheim, Mauthausen 1938

Key:
- ≈≈ Borders of the Greater German Reich
- ······ Under German rule
- ■ Concentration camps
- ▲ Euthanasia centres
- ★ Extermination camps
- ✪ Combined concentration and extermination camps
- 1942 Date camp/centre established

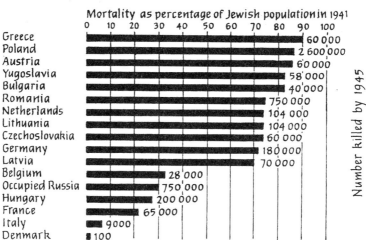

Mortality as percentage of Jewish population in 1941

Country	Number killed by 1945
Greece	60 000
Poland	2 600 000
Austria	60 000
Yugoslavia	58 000
Bulgaria	40 000
Romania	750 000
Netherlands	104 000
Lithuania	104 000
Czechoslovakia	60 000
Germany	180 000
Latvia	70 000
Belgium	28 000
Occupied Russia	750 000
Hungary	200 000
France	65 000
Italy	9000
Denmark	100

Map 17.1   The Holocaust

conditions, it was the Nazi regime in general and Hitler in particular that had created the atmosphere in which this was discussable at all, let alone a real policy option.

The particular international context of the war must be balanced against a continuity with pre-war domestic policy. There are a number of striking links between the pre-war sterilization and medical killing campaigns, the so-called 'euthanasia action' and the much greater number of Jews murdered between 1941 and 1945. First, Hitler personally authorized the 'euthanasia action' in writing. By the time the 'final solution' was launched, protests and rumours about the killing of asylum patients had forced the regime to retreat. So it is possible that Hitler chose not to commit himself to paper again. Second, Hitler himself mistakenly dated his own authorization of adult 'euthanasia' from October to 1 September 1939. He made the same mental slip subsequently when referring to his 30 January 1939 'prophecy' about the fate awaiting the Jews in the event of war, again citing it as 1 September 1939, the day war started. This suggests that he thought that the war legitimated mass murder of all those who had no place in his post-war order. Third, as in the summer of 1941, so in the autumn of 1939, centrally organized killing seems to have been preceded by local initiatives: SS squads killed some 4,000 mental patients in Poland from 29 September to 1 November 1939. Fourth, in both exterminations technical planners and medical personnel were actively involved in setting numerical targets and in implementing procedures to 'select' victims, a method usually reduced in the asylums to the filing of forms and in the camps to examination by a cursory glance. As the T-4 'euthanasia action' wound down, so many of its personnel were transferred to the *Einsatzgruppen* and to set up the death camps.

In the debate between intentionalists and structuralists, advocates of each interpretation have sought to claim moral ascendancy, intentionalists insisting on rejecting any ambiguity or conditionality to the link between Nazism and mass murder, structuralists refusing to excuse those non-Nazi German elites – military, business, administrative and professional – from complicity by heaping all the responsibility onto one figure. The first position makes sense of Allied charges against the Nazi leadership at the Nuremberg trials, the second of prosecuting all subordinates who claimed they were just following orders. In both cases, the use of evidence is highly complicated by the interest of alleged perpetrators in shifting the blame after 1945.

Behind historians' disputes over the close interpretation of circumstantial evidence about decision-making lie fundamental differences in their interpretations of the character of the Nazi state itself. Those who take a strongly 'intentionalist' line, such as Fleming, hold to a rather traditional notion of totalitarianism. In this totalitarian model the regime is held to be omnipotent in relation to society as well as internally monolithic and subordinated to the unbending will of the dictator. Neither individual initiative nor dissent have a place here. The 'structuralist' interpretation, on the other hand, holds that the state was inwardly fragmented into a plurality of competing institutions, and that relationships of power within the state and between the state and society did not flow only from the top down. If the totalitarian model takes its cue from the post-war writings of Hannah Arendt and C. J. Friedrich, the idea of the Nazi state as fragmented and polycratic goes back to Franz Neumann's *Behemoth*, an impressive and critical study of the regime while it was still in power. Historians such as Hans Mommsen, Jane Caplan and Martin Broszat were interested in exploring the internal contradictions within the dictatorship, the competing hierarchies of power and the chaotic as well as increasingly radical 'solutions' which these internal conflicts precipitated. From this point of view, Hitler has come to be seen as a leader who ruled not by initiating but by holding back and arbitrating between different factions. Thus what appear in the intentionalist account as stepping stones towards extermination appear in the structuralist reading as a series of *ad hoc* compromises, whose logical progression only becomes obvious in retrospect. The 1 April 1933 boycott and the so-called *Kristallnacht* of November 1938 come out as initiatives launched by Goebbels, in part to satisfy party radicals that the regime was in earnest, in part to win favour with Hitler. On the other hand, the framing of the Nuremberg Laws and the measures of economic expropriation show Hitler taking the more 'moderate' of the options presented to him. To a large extent, opinion among historians has swung towards this view of the Nazi state as polycratic rather than monolithic. What such close scrutiny obscures, however, is the question of how far these qualifications apply in some measure to the internal fault lines within all states. Chaotic, internally faction-ridden as the regime may have been, it still proved itself, in the midst of waging a war on several fronts, capable of planning, coordinating and executing a policy of mass extermination over an entire continent.

The theoretical models which historians draw upon in order to build their interpretations carry with them not only key concepts but particular conceptual languages. Much of the conceptual language of structuralist accounts of both the Nazi state and the 'final solution' derives from functionalist sociology, from American-inspired reworkings of the ideas of Max Weber. This is a language of impersonal 'processes' and bureaucratic rationality in which solutions 'evolve' without apparent exercise of agency or will, let alone fantasy. Despite the patent sincerity of historians such as Martin Broszat or Hans Mommsen in denouncing the crimes of Nazism, the language of their concepts carries a disturbingly distancing message. The very dehumanized abstraction of such formulations appears to shy away from the truly human dimensions of what was perpetrated. This application of concepts designed for 'normal' political sociology to the most extreme actions of the most extreme regime in twentieth-century Europe inadvertently conveys a 'normalizing' message, even though the historians themselves were intent on ensuring that those non-Nazi groups within society which played a vital part should be shown to be culpable as well.

The decision to build specially designated death camps was both a logical progression in the growth of the SS state and appears to have been taken by Himmler for purely logistical reasons. The Foreign Ministry's preferred solution of 1940, deporting the Jews to Madagascar, was envisaged, not as a type of colonial resettlement but as a place where they would die. Once Madagascar was ruled out because of the continuing war with Britain and because the attack on the Soviet Union opened the way to murder in Poland and the eastern front, Himmler – greatly concerned about the psychological stress which mass shootings placed on his men – also fantasized about the Pripet marshes, the swamps of Siberia and types of murder in which it was the environment which would do the killing. The significance of these alternatives is not that the 'final solution' itself would have been less murderous, but that the institutional arrangements actually implemented – what in the last half century has achieved enormous symbolic power as 'modernity' gone wrong, industrialized killing in the extermination camps – were arrived at almost incidentally. It was a bureaucrat's solution to the logistics of a problem in which neither man nor nature was to be fully trusted.

II The racial paradigm

The very use of the term 'structuralist' in this debate is something of a misnomer. Although the term implies a type of bureaucratic automatism, nobody has claimed that a particular structural situation made mass murder *inevitable*, the *only* possible outcome. Willy nilly we return to the question of human actors and their intentions. What the particular conditions of the war on the eastern front did patently do was to provide unprecedented scope to particular groups within the regime. The parallels already noted between the pre-war policy of 'euthanasia' and the 'final solution' have been pursued by historians as a way of tracing a wider set of continuities of intent leading to Auschwitz beyond the views of Hitler and the Nazi leadership. This has involved taking the biological metaphors of Nazi propaganda seriously and investigating the intellectual consensus that emerged among key professional groups during the 1920s and 1930s over establishing social policy on the basis of ideas about race and eugenics.

In Germany but also in France, Britain, the US and Scandinavia, the eugenics movement grew out of the enthusiasms of late nineteenth-century social Darwinists interested in medicalized models of social reform: the poor and indigent were seen not so much as victims of social conditions, but as 'poor breeding stock', incapable of creating a better social environment for themselves. The last decade has seen an upsurge of interest among historians in this area, leading to important studies by Ernst Klee, Gerhard Baader, Achim Thom, Klaus Dörner, Karl-Heinz Roth and Michael Burleigh on medicalized killing under the Nazis. Paul Weindling has traced the complex development of the various strands of the eugenicist movement and its shifting emphases. The work of Detlev Peukert and Liz Harvey raised disturbing questions about the prehistory of Nazi social policy in the imperial and Weimar periods. What has become clear is that, whilst real political decisions were taken within the secret inner spheres of the regime, both much of the initiative and the criteria for action came from key lobbying groups within the professional middle classes. Just as implementation of the 'final solution' depended on the active participation of non-Nazi business, administrative and military elites, so too the creation of what Michael Burleigh has aptly dubbed the 'racial state' depended on a wide measure of consensus among physicians, lawyers and bureaucrats.

On the basis of late Weimar legislative drafts as well as racial hygienists' interpretations of eugenics, measures for compulsory sterilization were introduced in July 1933 by the Interior and Justice Ministries and applied to an ever wider array of persons: the supposedly 'hereditarily ill', 'asocials' (including prostitutes, the 'feeble-minded', the 'work-shy' and vagrants), gypsies and homosexuals. Gisela Bock has shown how some of these ideas translated into Nazi policy in her pioneering study of the forced sterilization of women. How precisely – or more often how vaguely – these groups were defined and who was caught in the net became markedly more punitive after Himmler took over control of the police and Gestapo in 1936. Between 320,000 and 350,000 people were sterilized. Between the winter of 1938 and the summer of 1941, some 5,200 children and 70,000 adults with mental or physical disabilities were killed.

Götz Aly has been particularly influential in tracing the fateful nexus between the SS and such eugenicist intellectuals. The SS, after all, also contained a disproportionate number of graduates (including a high proportion of doctors and lawyers). In two studies, he has argued that Himmler was guided by a grand plan for the wholesale demographic reconstruction of central and eastern Europe. The extermination of the Jews was to be followed by the expulsion or extermination of up to 30 million 'Slavs'. Reconstruction was to take the form of 'repatriating' the German communities scattered beyond the – by now greatly expanded – borders of the Reich. A start was made in negotiations with Mussolini about the future of the German communities in Northern Italy, the former South Tyrol. In his second and more recent study of the role of these planners within the 'final solution', Aly has shown the way in which their 'Germanizing' projects were sometimes carried out at neighbouring desks to those planning the deportation and murder of Europe's Jews. Shocking and disturbing as such 'plans' are, they serve as a salutary reminder that the 'final solution' was not just an irrational application of bureaucratic rationality. For those who increasingly took charge of the bureaucratic machine there was an overarching racist rationale. As Aly notes, the plans themselves changed and always differed from the actual practice – the planned targets were always higher than those achieved.

Further light on the projects and strategy mapped out by leading SS organizers and intellectuals is provided by Ulrich Herbert's recent and beautifully crafted biography of the police and SS official Werner Best. Highly educated and mildly disdainful of the emotional anti-Semitism of Hitler or Streicher, Best wrote numerous articles advocating what he dubbed a 'rational anti-Semitism'. Hitler spoke of the need for 'ethnic cleansing in Poland [*völkische Flurbereinigung*]' on 7 September 1939. Best had already advocated this in 1936. The circumstances in which men like Best were given a free hand may have been generated during the war, but what Aly's and Herbert's studies show us is that these 'new men' already knew rather well what they would try to achieve once their moment came: complete realization of a hegemonic and ethnically homogeneous, or *völkisch*, nation state was the principle; mass murder or mass expulsion was a matter of expediency. Not only do such works remind us what a Nazi-dominated 'post-war settlement' might have entailed, they also show that the path to Auschwitz looks less 'twisted' and contingent when we look at the careers and ideas of those within the SS who would eventually implement the 'final solution'. The 'final solution' was more than an insane orgy of ultimately suicidal destruction, the grandiose last act of the regime's *Götterdämmerung*. It was part of an even more grandiose scheme of racial demography, which was only partially realized. These were plans which depended on the active engagement of many beyond the narrow circle of the Nazi leadership.

From this point of view, it is not accidental that the first carbon monoxide gas vans were borrowed from the so-called 'euthanasia' campaign; nor that the first test victims of Zyklon B were Soviet prisoners of war. Both were considered racially inferior, or, as the regime's eugenicists termed it, 'life unworthy of life'. Consideration of racial policy and ideas opens up a double perspective on the 'final solution'. First, it helps to locate notions of race and anti-Semitism within the specific expectations linked to the war against the Soviet Union. Second, racial policy evolved from pre-war domestic policy, in particular the application of so-called 'racial hygiene'. Historians like Stefan Kühl have extended this interest in the discourse on eugenics and race to bring in the comparative question of how far these ideas – including specific approval of Nazi sterilization laws – were shared by professional and elite groups in North America and western Europe. But this should, in turn, remind us that we need to be wary of attributing too much explanatory power to particular modes of thought, however morally obnoxious. The 'final solution' was not fashioned in all the places where even blatantly racist notions of eugenics enjoyed respectability. Instead, what investigation of 'racial hygiene' and eugenics opens for us is a window on one, but only one, of the allegedly 'modern' strands connecting a large number of German professionals to the regime and its genocidal policies.

III Knowledge and responsibility

Daniel Goldhagen has recently revived the notion of 'collective guilt', used by the Allies towards 'the Germans' in 1945. Goldhagen combines specific findings of virulent anti-Semitic attitudes among the executioners of the non-elite, non-SS units, in particular the members of the police reserve battalion 101 – much of this building on research materials also used by Christopher Browning – with a general 'framework for analysis'. Here the chief ingredient is the claim that a peculiarly virulent and socially deep-rooted anti-Semitism marked German culture from the medieval period onwards: the key scapegoat of medieval Christianity thus seamlessly becomes the key scapegoat of nineteenth- and twentieth-century German nationalism.

Goldhagen, like Browning and Omer Bartov and others before him, is undoubtedly right that many of these executioners were willing perpetrators. Where Goldhagen has been criticized, by Browning among others, is for reducing his explanation to a single factor: German anti-Semitism. Where Goldhagen permits the non-German guards and executioners – about whom we still know far too little – a multi-causal explanation for their participation, the Germans are reduced to a mono-causal model. This approach seems deeply flawed in a number of respects. A will to violence can occur within a single generation. Long-range explanations explain both too much and too little: why then and not before or indeed continuously?

The history of anti-Semitism is long but it is also a discontinuous history. The content as well as the social and political weight of anti-Semitism were not constant. German society did witness a revival of political anti-Semitism at the end of the nineteenth century, but the comparative perspective is lacking here. Germany was no more anti-Semitic than contemporary France, very much in the grip of the Dreyfus affair, and anti-Semitic views were also indulged at both popular and elite levels, though usually less noisily, in Britain and the United States. Even in the late Weimar years, anti-Semitism seems to have been of far more importance to the 'old fighters' of the SA than to Nazi voters. Anti-Semitism had also been contested and opposed throughout the period 1880-1933 by powerful voices on the left. In the years after the Nazi seizure of power, these voices were silenced or rendered innocuous through the terror apparatus of party and state, through exile and through 'inner emigration' as former anti-fascists abandoned politics and withdrew into private life. Finally, the intellectual content of anti-Semitism throughout western Europe and the US changed under the impact of social Darwinist ideas about race from the 1880s on. Anti-Semitism on its own can no more explain why the 'final solution' occurred in Germany and not elsewhere than can the prevalence of racial eugenicist ideas: on the one hand, many Germans did not subscribe to such notions; on the other, such discourses were widely diffused elsewhere.

Historians influenced by Benedict Anderson have tended to view 'national character' not as a permanent imprint but, rather, as a series of imaginative projections, often stimulated by political campaigns and social policy. This perspective builds on the critique of any simple notion of a single collective identity, whether purportedly based on nation, race, class or gender, which does not set out how these identities are constructed and sustained. To write in the 1990s of an essential and collective 'German' seems not only intellectually crude but bordering on the racist. It might be more useful to think of the Nazis' project as an attempt to remake national sentiment by all the means at their disposal – propaganda, terror and social policy – once they had come to power.

At a day-to-day level, non-Jews were discouraged by the Gestapo from having social contact with Jews and, as Robert Gellately has shown, many Germans willingly complied. Moreover, they spied on their neighbours and denounced those who refused to abandon old Jewish friends and acquaintances. In addition to the major moves to expel Jews from economy and society described at the beginning of this chapter there was a host of petty restrictions and local initiatives aimed at Jews. 'Jews' who were not religious and often did not think of themselves as Jews had to be artificially defined and identified. As Ian Kershaw has shown, in the 1930s a Hitler 'myth' permeated widely in German society, in which the 'Führer' was treated as a benign deity, supposedly ignorant of the failings of his underlings. In the increasingly Manichaean mind-set projected by Nazi propagandists the Jew was portrayed as the source of all ill. What was new about this ideological onslaught by the regime was its intensity and the lack of alternate voices in public. But there is also a difference between the projection of propaganda images and their absorption into the common sense of everyday life.

The historiography of the last two decades has tended not just to broaden our notion of complicity with the regime beyond the SS and the Nazi leadership, it has also tended towards a more nuanced and differentiated account of what consent and resistance, collusion and indifference meant. This was a regime which, whilst responding to – as well as attempting to manufacture – 'Aryan' German public opinion in various ways, also worked to achieve a passive and quiescent public. When did the change in public perceptions occur? Or did German working-class electors, for instance, most of whom had voted for non-fascist parties pre-1933, remain unaffected by the regime's racial policies? The work of Detlev Peukert and Lutz Niethammer suggests that many responded in the mid-1930s by withdrawing into essentially private worlds, though Hitler's foreign policy successes, from the remilitarization of the Rhineland in 1936 to the Anschluß in 1938, do seem to have impressed many former opponents.

There is a rising tide of evidence, however, emerging from the work of historians like Ulrich Herbert, Susanne zur Nieden and Frank Stern, that attitudes did change fundamentally after 1942, during the years of air raids and increased deployment of forced foreign labour. By the later stages of the war, the formerly separate functions of concentration camps, transit camps, labour camps and camps for Soviet prisoners of war were increasingly blurred as the system buckled under the increasing and contradictory pressures of acute labour shortages within Germany, the regime's own commitment to murder as many Jews as possible and its unwillingness to feed, house or clothe 'racially inferior' Russian forced labourers adequately. Increasingly too, the boundaries between the camps and the rest of German society were crossed. As current research is showing, many of the utilities and factories in German cities came to be manned by prisoners who were housed outside the main camp complex in hostels near their place of work.

By the end of the war, foreign workers in Germany in their various categories numbered over seven million, a section of the population far too large to remain socially invisible. As Herbert and others have argued, this racial hierarchy of forced labour gave an everyday meaning to the regime's racist propaganda: Jews and Russians were subject to the most brutal discipline and received the lowest rations; their conditions ensured that they also appeared visibly different. This tangible experience of racial politics in everyday life, even after most Jews had been deported, does seem often to have permeated the consciousness of even non-Nazi German workers. At best, it prevented the establishment of any widely held sense of common fate and humanity (despite such heroic exceptions as some of the 'Edelweiss pirates') and at worst gave a specific and casually everyday meaning to the notion of Germans as a 'master race'. Along this spectrum of thinking of Jews, Russians, Ukrainians and Poles as 'different', 'not us' or 'subhuman' there were obviously many gradations of emphasis between indifference, hostility and outright collaboration in murder.

When the 130,000 German Jews who remained in the 'old Reich' after the outbreak of war were rounded up and deported to the 'east', very few voices were raised even within private circles to object. The response seems to have been largely characterized by vaguely hostile indifference. This was not because opposition to the regime was impossible: in 1936, Bavarian Protestants organized mass protests against interference in the liturgy of their worship by the Reichbishop in Berlin and won; from 1938 on, Bavarian Catholics came into increasing conflict with the regime over the removal of crucifixes from schools, a conflict which persisted during the war years and the deportation of the Jews. But the scope of these protests, as Ian Kershaw has shown, was circumscribed. Although goodwill towards the regime dwindled in the countryside under the impact of taxation, requisitioning and labour shortages, these were protests against specific aspects of Nazi policy. The specificity of these grievances contrasts sharply with the evasions and circumlocutions which accompanied popular reference to the fate of the Jews, thereby further marking the gulf which had been established between Jews and other Germans.

Acts of philo-Semitic solidarity were the exception. In a quite dramatic episode, in late February and early March 1943, 150–200 non-Jewish wives of Jewish men demonstrated outside party and SS offices in Berlin until their husbands – destined for the death camps – were released. Such an act of opposition was wholly exceptional and may have owed its success not only to the women's strong emotional attachments but also to the Reich Security Main Office's fear of bad publicity concerning events in the centre of the capital.

But even widespread hostility did not mean a readiness to take action against Jews, nor after the relative embarrassment of *Kristallnacht* did the regime attempt to enlist such 'spontaneous' popular involvement. In both the 'euthanasia action' and the 'final solution', the regime combined large-scale propaganda about the issues in general with secrecy about the actual facts of killing. Yet, studies by David Bankier and Susanne zur Nieden have revealed the extent to which atrocities – if not the 'final solution' in its entirety – became an open secret in wartime Germany. Clandestine listening to the BBC, letters home from soldiers on the eastern front and conversations with those on leave contributed to a social undercurrent of news by rumour. These were also generally private communications, often vague and imprecise in their details.

Private conversation was also significant in the way in which news travelled within the regime itself. News of the mass shooting of 34,000 Jews at Babi Yar in the Ukraine on 29 September 1941 was brought to the German military authorities in Paris by a returning officer in December: this was how they learned what 'deportations to the east' entailed. There were relatively few occasions when the regime's leaders stated what their murderous activities were in front of a large audience. Even in Himmler's addresses to party and military leaders, in October 1943 and January 1944, in which he told them that the 'final solution' involved 'exterminating – meaning kill or order to have killed' all Jews without exception, he did not mention gassing or describe the methods involved. Himmler would have known that many in his audience already knew of the mass shootings in eastern Europe. What was new was that this was being officially confirmed to them in an assembly where they were simultaneously sworn to secrecy and by extension to collective complicity. Some sense of the moral and psychological issues involved in acknowledging complicity at this level of the Nazi administration comes out of Albert Speer's repeated insistence that he had left the meeting in Poznan before Himmler spoke on 6 October 1943. Whether or not Speer was actually present, it is very hard to believe that he could have moved in Hitler's inner circle, let alone organized the war economy with its increasing dependency on forced labour, without knowing of the conditions and fate of many of the workers. Here Gitta Sereny's subtle account of her conversations with Speer discloses his psychological need, at least after 1945 but possibly even at the time, to avoid directly acknowledging his conscious participation in the 'final solution'. Some such element of 'knowing without knowing' may also have been present in many of those who heard rumours in everyday life.

IV Conclusion

In April 1988, Tim Mason reflected in one of his last essays on the question of 'whatever happened to "fascism"'. By this he meant the decline of any theoretical concept of a generic fascism, a construct which could be used for serious comparative analysis, of the kind which had animated his own studies of Mussolini's Italy and Hitler's Germany, and which had so influenced a whole generation of historians writing during the 1960s and 1970s. In Mason's view this gradual move away from writing about fascism as a general topos had less to do with the heated debates about the concept's theoretical underpinnings than with a silent shift in intellectual consensus. As he put it, 'the most extreme peculiarities of German Nazism have thus slowly and silently come to dominate our moral, political and professional concerns'[4]. The older class-based models of fascism had been deployed to considerable effect to analyse the social composition of the mass movements on their rise to power and the attitudes and interests of social, economic and political elites towards them both before and after the seizure of power. But the increasing attention to eugenics and biological racism over the last decade has effectively broken with this comparative perspective and produced a new racial paradigm specifically applicable to Nazi Germany. This shift has depended on asking new questions. It has also accompanied a wider shift in social and cultural history away from explanations based on general structural models and towards a concern for the inner meaning of social actors' attitudes and beliefs. Such shifts are significant. They are also not the last word. It remains to be seen, however, whether another generation of historians will yet be able to restore some elements of Mason's comparative agenda, albeit influenced by different categories of analysis and in search of answers to different questions. Beneath the fashioning of a new historical consensus, what remains striking is how specialized research on the Holocaust has continued to be: those who study the perpetrators rarely study the victims and vice versa, and those who work in this field rarely write about other periods of German history. With the tearing down of the 'Iron Curtain' there is a real need also to research and track the links between the Holocaust and the other social histories of eastern Europe, to move beyond the duality of Jews and Germans. It may be that new questions can only be formulated by crossing the various sub-disciplines which have sprung up.

The 'final solution' was uniquely terrible. This does not require that it must have a single, unique cause. Pinning down the specific set of wartime conditions in which that decision was actually reached still left the choice open. As historians have shifted their focus from the intentionalist–functionalist debate towards the racial programmes shaped within the regime and professional lobbying groups, so this has led to a rethinking of what Nazism and fascism represented. The intentionalists relied on a model of a totalitarian state with an unambiguous chain of command and the functionalists operated with the notion of an internally fragmented and polycratic dictatorship. But, in the process of the debate, the terms of how state and society connected to one another have gradually come to be rethought. As historians have come to accept that the regime was more inwardly chaotic than could fit the theory of totalitarianism, so they have also had to take the contending programmes and ideas of different factions within the regime seriously. This has coincided with serious research on eugenicist issues. Finding the links with the views and practices of professionals concerned with reproduction, sexual orientation, criminology and clinical psychiatry has recovered a different set of cultural attitudes and taken us back into debates about 'degeneration' and medical ethics, which were never a Nazi monopoly and, disturbingly, did not disappear with the Nazis either. In the process, what it meant to be a Nazi can no longer be defined restrictively in terms of party or SS membership. Knowledge and complicity were both wider and more complex than that. As the links between the 'final solution' and areas of Nazi social policy have been explored, so in turn mass murder has come increasingly to be regarded as the ultimate, rather than the exceptional, sphere of Nazi policy-making.

Notes:

1. Levi, Pirmo, *The Drowned and the Saved*, pp. 63–4.
2. Dinora Pines in Cohen, Elie, *Human Behaviour in the Concentration Camp* (London: Free Association Books, 1988), p. xiii.
3. *Dokumente der deutschen Politik* (Berlin: Junker and Dünnhaupt, 1940), vol. 7, pp. 476–9.
4. Mason, Tim, *Nazism, Fascism and the Working Class* (Cambridge: Cambridge University Press, 1995), p. 324.

Select bibliography

The 'final solution' has generated a huge and extremely diverse historical literature, with numerous sub-disciplines within it and is currently the subject of a very interesting study being prepared by Dan Stone of New College, Oxford. The following bibliography is only intended to offer an English-language guide to further reading on some of the issues and historians mentioned in this chapter.

Aly, Götz, 'Endlösung' (Frankfurt am Main: Fischer, 1995; English translation forthcoming, London: Arnold, 1998).

Browning, Christopher, *Ordinary Men: Reserve Police Battalion 101 and the Final Solution in Poland* (London/New York: HarperCollins, 1992).

Hilberg, Raul, *The Destruction of the European Jews*, 3 vols. (New York: Holmes and Meier, 1985).

Marrus, Michael, *The Holocaust in History* (London: Weidenfeld and Nicolson, 1988).

Four important collections of essays with contributions from a number of scholars discussed here at different points are:

Cesarani, David, ed., *The Final Solution: Origins and Implementation* (London: Routledge, 1994).

Crew, David, ed., *Nazism and German Society, 1933–1945* (London: Routledge, 1994).

Hirschfeld, Gerhard, ed., *The Policies of Genocide: Jews and Soviet Prisoners of War in Nazi Germany* (London: Allen and Unwin, 1986).

Pehle, Walter, ed., *November 1938: From Reichskristallnacht to Genocide* (New York: Berg, 1991).

Key intentionalist readings are:

Dawidowicz, Lucy, *The War against the Jews, 1933–1945* (London: Weidenfeld and Nicolson, 1977).

Fleming, Gerald, *Hitler and the Final Solution* (London: Hamish Hamilton, 1984).

For a new synthesis, see Burrin, Philippe, *Hitler and the Jews: The Genesis of the Holocaust* (London: Arnold, 1994).

For an overview of the intentionalist-functionalist debate, see also Kershaw, Ian, *The Nazi Dictatorship* (London: Arnold, 1989).

On pre-exterminationist policy, see Barkai, Avraham, *From Boycott to Annihilation: The Economic Stuggle of German Jews, 1933–1943* (Hanover, NH: Brandeis, 1990).

On non-Jewish victims see:

Grau, Günther, ed., *Hidden Holocaust? Gay and Lesbian Persecution in Germany, 1933–1945* (London: Cassell, 1995).

Kenrick, Donald and Puxon, Gratton, *The Destiny of European Gypsies* (London: Chatto, 1972).

On the links between the different elements of Nazi race policy, see:

Burleigh, Michael, *Death and Deliverance: 'Euthanasia' in Germany c. 1900–1945* (Cambridge: Cambridge University Press, 1994).

Burleigh, Michael and Wippermann, Wolfgang, *The Racial State: Germany, 1933–1945* (Cambridge: Cambridge University Press, 1991).

Müller-Hill, B., *Murderous Science: Elimination by Scientific Selection of Jews, Gypsies and Others, Germany, 1933–1945* (Oxford: Oxford University Press, 1988).

Weindling, Paul, *Health, Race and German Politics between National Unification and Nazism, 1870–1945* (Cambridge: Cambridge University Press, 1989).

On the issue of social complicity, see:

Bankier, David, *The Germans and the Final Solution: Public Opinion under Nazism* (Oxford: Oxford University Press, 1992).

Gellately, Robert, *The Gestapo and German Society: Enforcing Racial Policy, 1933–1945* (Oxford: Oxford University Press, 1990).

Goldhagen, Daniel, *Hitler's Willing Executioners: Ordinary Germans and the Holocaust* (London: Little, Brown and Co., 1996).

Herbert, Ulrich, *A History of Foreign Labour in Germany, 1880-1980* (Ann Arbor: University of Michigan Press: 1990).

Kershaw, Ian, *Popular Opinion and Political Dissent in the Third Reich: Bavaria, 1933–1945* (Oxford: Oxford University Press, 1983).

Peukert, Detlev, *Inside Nazi Germany: Conformity, Opposition and Racism in Everyday Life* (Harmondsworth: Penguin, 1993).

Sereny, Gitta: *Albert Speer: His Struggle with Truth* (London: Macmillan, 1995).

Stern, Frank: 'Antagonistic Memories: the Post-war Survival and Alienation of Jews and Germans', in Luisa Passerini, ed., *Memory and Totalitarianism: International Yearbook of Oral Histories*, vol. 1 (Oxford: Oxford University Press, 1992).

On occupation policy, see:

Bartov, Omer, *The Eastern Front, 1941–1945: German Troops and the Barbarisation of Warfare* (London: Macmillan, 1986).

Hirschfeld, G. and Marsh, Peter, *Collaboration in France: Politics and Culture during the Nazi Occupation, 1940–44* (Oxford: Berg, 1989).

Schulte, Theo, *The German Army and Nazi Policies in Occupied Russia* (Oxford: Berg, 1989).

For survivors' testimony, see:

Kogon, Eugen, *The Theory and Practice of Hell: The German Concentration Camps and the System Behind Them* (London: Secker & Warburg, 1950).

Levi, Primo, *If This is Man* (Harmondsworth: Penguin, 1979).

For psychological approaches to the experience of camp inmates, see:

Bettelheim, Bruno, *The Informed Heart* (Harmondsworth: Penguin, 1986).

Cohen, Elie, *Human Behaviour in the Concentration Camp* (London: Free Association Books, 1988).

Pines, Dinora, 'Working with Women Survivors of the Holocaust', in Pines, *A Woman's Unconscious Use of Her Body: A Psychoanalytical Perspective* (London, Virago, 1993).

On memorials, see Young, James (ed.), *Holocaust The Art of Memory: Memorials in History* (Munich and New York: Prestel, 1994).

Part IV

Germany since 1945

Introduction to Part IV:
Germany since 1945

Mary Fulbrook

Defeat in the First World War was never completely accepted by the elites of Imperial Germany, who withdrew into the wings and allowed democratic forces to carry the opprobrium associated with the hated Versailles Treaty. The political and social tensions which had characterized Imperial Germany had been exacerbated rather than exorcized by the First World War; it was to take the excesses of the Nazi dictatorship and subsequent total defeat and military occupation after the Second World War for new solutions to be sought to the apparently vicious spiral of militarist nationalism and domestic instability in Germany.

In the period after 1945, the Cold War increasingly took precedence. Germany was divided less because of any coherent Allied plans for dealing with the Germans than because of the rapidly deteriorating relations between the superpowers. Within each of the rump states which were created in 1949, willing German elites cooperated with their respective occupying powers to develop radically new and opposing political forms. In the west, a stable and increasingly prosperous capitalist democracy was created; in the east, a communist state which radically revolutionized the social and economic structure of its area.

The chapters in Part IV analyse these quite startling transformations. Mark Roseman queries the bases of and explanations for West German stabilization and measures the extent of real change and deep-rooted democratization of West German political culture over 40 years. Mark Allinson provides a differentiated view of the establishment and development of the East German dictatorship, which cannot be simply equated with the preceding Third Reich. The divergences between the social structures of the two states, and the differences in social classes and groups are the subject of Chapter 20, while the complex debates on and cultural constructions of national identity in the shadow of Auschwitz are analysed by Erica Carter in Chapter 21. Whether or not the GDR was – to adopt a debate more generally applied to Weimar – 'doomed from the start', its ultimate collapse after 40 years of at least outward stability was intimately related to changes in its external parameters of existence, as Jonathan Osmond shows in his examination of the interplay of domestic and international factors in the collapse of the communist dictatorship and German unification.

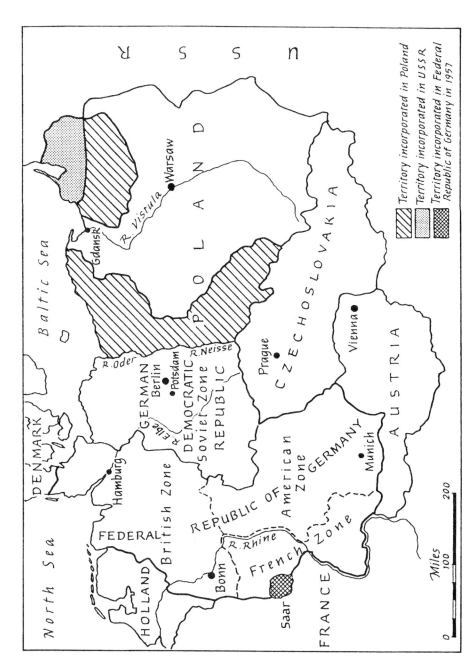

Map IV Germany divided post 1945

18

Division and stability: The Federal Republic of Germany, 1949–1989

Mark Roseman

Unlike the historiography of the Wilhelmine, Weimar or Nazi periods, the literature on West German history offers no prevailing orthodoxy or defining controversies. There is no equivalent to a *Sonderweg* theory, no central debate like that between functionalists and intentionalists for the Third Reich. This may be because West Germany's history ended too recently for scholars yet to have gained a clear perspective. Indeed, we are not even sure whether the unification of 1990 really was the end of an era: after all, though *West* Germany as a separate state has ceased to exist, the Federal Republic as a set of institutions continues. Alternatively, the key point may be that the (happy) absence in this period of a catastrophe akin to the outbreak of the First World War or the rise of Nazism means that there is no single overriding issue to which all other questions can be subordinated. Whatever the reason, the outcome is that we have to approach a survey of West German history without that convenient armoury of theories and interpretations available to the historian of earlier epochs.

However, even if we lack the grand debates, we can at least identify two sets of questions which in one shape or another inform a great deal of the writing about the post-1945 period. What interested many scholars was the question of how it was possible that such a well-functioning and stable democracy could be created on the same soil that had allowed Weimar to wither and die, had proved so receptive to the ideas of National Socialism and had committed so much energy and so many resources to the demonic projects of *Lebensraum* and the Holocaust. Was the FRG's success perhaps thanks to the constraints and support provided by the new external environment – by the Allied presence, the Cold War and the division of Germany? Or were institutional innovations within West Germany itself responsible? How central was the 'economic miracle' and what put the dynamism into the Deutschmark? These questions were often asked in wonder or admiration, but also tinged with anxiety. At each stage of West Germany's development fears were expressed that some prescriptive German flaw might re-emerge and bring the whole edifice crashing down. In the 1960s many observers thought the end of the economic boom would be the FRG's downfall; in the 1970s, others believed terrorism and the political disaffection of the young could spell the end of democracy. Those particular anxieties were rapidly confounded by the republic's continuing solidity, but today observers are asking whether the end of the division – of Germany and of Europe – has at last undermined the special post-war framework for stability.

Alongside the issue of stability, the other recurrent question has been about restoration, continuity or new beginnings. During the 1970s and 1980s, a great deal of historical research was carried out into the FRG's formative years. Historians wanted to know whether the emerging institutions, social structures, elite composition and value systems were essentially Weimar revivals or even continuations from the Third Reich or whether they constituted something genuinely new. More recently, historians have cast their gaze beyond the occupation period and asked whether the 1950s, in turn, were characterized by conservatism and restoration, or instead constituted a period of dramatic social change.

The following survey of West Germany's history thus focuses on these two themes of the balance between restoration and change, and the origins and nature of West German stability. Because the historiography is so diffuse, it is not possible to identify every point where the survey draws on or differs from established interpretations. However, in one respect the present essay does take a clear-cut position in relation to the existing literature, in that it argues that recent research on early West German history has produced something of a paradox. On the one hand, West German historians of the post-1968 era have indisputably shown the enormous amount of institutional, social and personnel continuity or restoration that initially characterized the FRG. Yet at the same time, because many of these historians have been critical of the existing political order, they have been less willing to acknowledge that this was a republic which almost from the start was dramatically more successful and stable than its hapless Weimar predecessor. The paradox is, therefore, that we are left with a story where remarkably limited innovation seems nevertheless to have generated an enormously different outcome.

To solve this puzzle, the present survey begins by arguing that (important geopolitical changes apart) there were indeed few decisive structural, personnel or cultural differences between Weimar and Bonn. What initially favoured the Bonn republic was instead that its peculiar and protracted birth under Allied occupation, and in the aftermath of Holocaust and total war, meant that it emerged without the antagonisms, instabilities and fears which so burdened Weimar from the beginning. Thus 'restoration or new beginning' when applied to the republics themselves, rather misses the point. It was the different kind of baptisms by fire from which Weimar and Bonn emerged, rather than any niceties of their internal structures, that was initially crucial. Second, it will be argued here that, whilst Bonn in many respects returned to Weimar habits, it also witnessed subtle but vital changes in the discourse and outlook of the population. The experience of war and defeat led to the construction of different historical and political narratives, pushing some political alternatives (nationalism and revanchism, for example) off the agenda. However, really radical social and economic change came only in the late 1950s and 1960s, in the wake of economic growth and the expansion of mass consumerism. Against the background of these changes, and the student revolts which they helped to bring about, a genuinely new and liberal political culture emerged in the 1960s and 1970s.

I   The emergence of the new political order, 1945–1949

I.1   The zero hour and new beginnings

For most Germans who lived through it, the 1945–9 years were the most traumatic period of their lives. Defeat had been total and overwhelming, destroying the last vestiges of illusions about the Third Reich's invincibility. The enormous psychological impact of total defeat was reinforced and exacerbated by the almost total disruption of social life. By the end of the war, many German towns were just piles of rubble occupied by a tiny remnant of their former inhabitants. Population mobility was staggeringly high – perhaps as many as half the population was on the move in 1945. Expellees, refugees, prisoners of war, displaced persons, evacuees and many others thronged the roads and packed the few operating trains. In contrast to the wartime experience, food supplies collapsed and in spring 1946 and 1947 rations levels in industrial areas fell to starvation levels. Food shortages, Allied restrictions and other problems kept the economy in a near vegetative state.

Most Germans were preoccupied with their survival, and merely passive recipients of what was decided on the political stage. For a small but crucial minority of Germans, however, including many returning exiles, the early post-war years saw new ideas and the revival of hopes for reform. The reformed Social Democrats (SPD) aspired to the creation of a new more humane society, coupling the old dreams of responsible public control over the economy with a more explicit emphasis than their Weimar forebears on the importance of parliament and the rule of law. Even more significant was the decision by bourgeois politicians to form a non-denominational Christian Democratic Party (CDU), bridging that division between Catholics and Protestants which had undermined the centre-right of German politics since the nineteenth century. For leaders of both political parties, many of whom had already played important roles in the Weimar Republic, the Allies were an important source of hope – and this impulse towards co-operation was to be a crucial foundation of the eventual settlement.

I.2   The Cold War and its impact

The period 1946–7 saw the Cold War lay its glacial hand on Europe. From the summer of 1947, the USA and Britain moved over to a policy of rapidly reconstructing western Germany as a prelude to any future agreement with the Soviet Union. Icy stand-off metamorphosed to high drama in 1948 when the Soviet Union blockaded Berlin (which although under Four-Power control was located within the Soviet zone of occupation) in response to the introduction of a new currency, the Deutschmark, in the Western zones. The Cold War increasingly dominated Allied behaviour towards western Germany and the perceptions and behaviour of West Germany's own statesmen and population. For many Germans, the Cold War's powerful psychological impact derived not just from the objective threat posed by the presence of Soviet troops just across the zonal border but also from the resonances of past experiences, including class conflict in the Weimar period, Nazi anti-Bolshevik propaganda and the expellees' direct experiences of Soviet brutality (few reflected on how Russia had been treated under Nazi tyranny). At the same time as being a time of fear, the Cold War also represented a psychological and political opportunity for Germany to be counted among the free world against the communist threat.

Between 1947 and 1949, the international order began to take on a radically different cast to the inter-war period. In geoeconomic terms, a world of more open trade and closer European integration was just beginning to emerge. The creation of the International Monetary Fund and the first General Agreement on Tariffs and Trade signalled the US desire to create a functioning multilateral world economy. On the European level, the Marshall plan – and the creation of the Organization of European Economic Cooperation to administer it – was encouraging greater trade between the western European powers. On the political and military side, these new economic structures were paralleled by the formation of ever closer military cooperation. In April 1949 the NATO agreement was signed, holding out the promise to Europe of being protected under the American nuclear umbrella. Though by 1949, when the FRG came into being, many of these new structures or trends were still very far from being firmly established, they were nevertheless to form a crucial ingredient in the FRG's success.

I.3   Institutions and structures in the new West German state

Whilst it was encouraging the development of new institutional forms on the international stage, the Cold War was in many ways narrowing the options within Germany itself. The American urgency for creating an economically viable and politically self-contained western German entity led them to drop many of their earlier reform and denazification measures. The British were similarly dissuaded from engaging in social experiments. Those military government reform initiatives that remained often met with opposition from entrenched German groups, and had to be dropped in the interest of the rapid creation of a West German state. The result was that the new constitution was remarkably similar to that of Weimar. Both were federal capitalist systems, based upon a proportional representation system in the lower house, and a regionally based upper house. In almost every branch of law, the Weimar precedent represented the orientation point. In civil service and judiciary there was a remarkable degree of institutional and personnel continuity.

However, the new state did incorporate a number of important changes, some of them the result of lessons drawn from the Nazi era, some the logical consequence of the German division. First, there was the simple fact that this was conceived explicitly as a provisional state, created in anticipation of the emergence of a reunited Germany. In recognition of this provisionality, the constitution was called simply the Basic Law and never put to popular vote. Whilst not necessarily encouraging strong identification with the new state, this provisional status did at least make it easier for the parties involved in drawing up the constitution to bury their differences; it also made it easier to exclude the public and thus deracinate much of the constitutional debate.

On the political front, the most crucial innovation was that the destruction of Prussia and the reorganization of the other states within the western zones created the basis for a far more balanced federal system. A second important set of reforms concerned the way in which the popular will was expressed. As far as the electoral system was concerned, the list voting of Weimar was replaced with a mixed two-vote system. An electoral hurdle denied representation to parties with less than 5 per cent of the vote. The plebiscitary elements of Weimar's constitution were scaled down. There were also changes concerning the way parliament itself operated, most importantly the introduction of the constructive vote of no confidence. Finally there was the major institutional discontinuity: the German army was initially not re-established, re-emerging only after an extended period of absence and explicitly subordinated to NATO.

Some important modifications were introduced to the economic and financial system as well. The creation of a central bank independent of political control ensured public confidence in the stability of the currency. Following the introduction of the DM in June 1948, Ludwig Erhard, soon to become the FRG's first Economics Minister, not only rapidly dismantled much of the control apparatus which had hitherto administered the post-war economy, but also went further in the direction of a market economy than the framework of the inter-war period: cartels were now outlawed and the protectionist trend of the inter-war years was replaced by a consistently free trade approach.

Another, less obviously propitious, contrast between the new republic and that of Weimar was that the Allies exercised and retained so many powers. The Federal Republic of Germany could not conduct its own foreign policy, indeed had no Foreign Minister, relating to the outside world almost exclusively through the medium of the Allied High Commission. The output of the Ruhr, the FRG's industrial heartland, was controlled by the International Ruhr Commission, a body created in 1949 to meet French anxieties that Germany's economic weight might be deployed against it. West Germany was not allowed its own armed forces. In short the new republic was at best semi-sovereign.

I.4   The radicalization that did not take place

For all the lessons learned from the past, the republic was thus born in circumstances that were at least as constrained and ignominious as those faced by Weimar. In addition to the limits on its sovereignty noted above, the economy had been consolidated by a currency reform and deflation every bit as harsh as that which had ended the hyperinflation of 1923; the Cold War phase had led to a disappointing of the left's hopes for reform just as far-reaching as the failure of socialization initiatives in 1918–20; the losses of territory in the east and the presence of millions of expellees and refugees on German soil created a potential for revanchism far greater than had the Versailles Treaty. And yet, by dint of the shock effect of war and defeat, the role and function of the Allies, and the pro-western élites who had managed to position themselves as makers of public opinion, neither public behaviour or attitudes, nor the results of the first federal elections in September 1949 pointed to the public alienation, disaffection or radicalization which had been such a feature of the Weimar period. The radical right had been so discredited (and, it has to be said, discriminated against by Allied electoral practices) and the Communists marginalized that the politicians of the centre ground had emerged at least as strong as they had ever been. True, there were no simple majorities – the proliferation of parties (12 were represented in the first federal parliament) showed that the new constitutional provisions had not succeeded in ending the problem of political fragmentation. But Germany in 1949 seemed to be a far less openly embittered or divided society than it had been at the end of its post-WW1 stabilization in 1924. The real question, though, was whether this was merely an artificial product of the shock, exhaustion and Allied control of the occupation years. How would the system develop as Germany gradually regained its independence?

II   The stabilizing of the political order, 1949–1957

II.1   Germany becomes part of a western order

German history had shown that stability at home was unlikely to be achieved without a set of secure external relationships. Yet, although the Cold War had undoubtedly created a psychological and strategic climate facilitating West Germany's acceptance among the western powers, key obstacles remained. How could German politicians join the western club without selling out the goal of German reunification? How could the West German desire for a speedy return to sovereignty be reconciled with European, particularly French desires to exercise continuing political and economic control? How could the American insistence that the FRG make a major contribution to the defence of Europe be squared with opposition to German rearmament both within Germany and in the rest of Europe?

Despite these challenges, West Germany rapidly attained a secure place within the western club. The formation of the European Coal and Steel Commission by the Paris

Illustration 18.1 French President Charles de Gaulle with Federal Chancellor Konrad Adenauer, 4–5 September 1963, in Bonn. The new amicable Franco-German relationship was a conspicuous feature of the post-1945 world

Treaty of 1951 ended the inequality of the Ruhr control, and reassured Germany's neighbours that German resources would not be used against them. It also started the ball rolling towards closer European integration, culminating in the formation of the European Economic Community in 1957. On the military front, after a failed attempt to form a joint European army, Germany was invited into NATO in 1955, and with its membership came the return to near full sovereignty – though the Allies retained rights over Berlin, the stationing of troops on German soil, and considerable emergency powers. Finally, the London Claims Conference and the agreements with Israel produced an acceptable debt settlement, even if it fell far short of the true cost of German crimes.

The relative ease of the process had, of course, much to do with the common fear of the Soviet Union. The security guarantees provided by the large number of US troops stationed on German soil were another factor. The continental powers were helped by past negative experience and American encouragement to see the virtues of economic integration as a source of both stability and prosperity. The absence of nationalism within Germany was another vital ingredient. Even so, the rearmament issue proved particularly contentious for the FRG, and the SPD's concerted campaign against it enjoyed support both from those who opposed any new military commitment and those who feared that it would seal the division between East and West Germany. Here Konrad Adenauer played a crucial role in 'selling' the FRG's involvement to the West German public – a point to which we will return below.

II.2 Legitimating the social order

Another lesson of history was that a republic which failed to solve the 'social question' had little chance of success. Here the opening situation was paradoxially more auspicious than that of Weimar, despite the enormously greater challenges of reconstruction faced by Bonn. For one thing, there was a recognition on all sides that the constitution should not make Weimar's mistake of promising what could not be delivered. The Cold War, and the fact that the hardships of the immediate post-war period had dampened popular expectations, all reduced the pressure labour was able to bear or willing to apply for more radical reforms. Moreover, again unlike Weimar, war veterans or their widows did not enjoy the political or moral status to allow them to form a vociferous claimant community.

Yet, there remained a large gulf between the emphasis of the government parties and their allies on a fairly unfettered market economy and the labour movement's determination to introduce at least some of its dreams for the creation of a more socially responsive socioeconomic system. Labour's demands came to a head in 1950 with the call for formal representation of labour within management of industrial enterprises, or 'codetermination'. In the end, a variety of circumstances, not least the fact that the government was dependent on trade union cooperation in the Schuman plan negotiations, produced a compromise which all sides could live with. Labour's success in getting equal representation on the supervisory boards of the iron and steel industry in the 1951 Act, and a weaker right to speak in other industries in 1952, was enough of a symbolic achievement to prevent the alienation of the left from the new system.

The other major social problem needing resolution was the position of millions of refugees and expellees on West German territory. Here, the problem was solved by effective law-making and above all by economic growth. The Law for the Equalization of Burdens made large transfers of resources to the expellees but because the levies could be paid over an extended period and thus were in effect a tax on growth they were at little cost to the established population. Fairly rapidly, government-assisted expellee businesses were to be an important source of innovation and growth in the relatively underdeveloped rural areas of Bavaria, Lower Saxony and Schleswig-Holstein.

These measures were important in legitimating the new order, particularly as they were passed at a time when prosperity had not reached the majority of the population and unemployment remained high. But in the course of the 1950s there was little doubting what was the main cement of the Federal Republic's social fabric – extraordinary and sustained economic growth. Factors contributing to the growth included a propitious international environment, the considerable scope for catching up on innovation opportunities wasted in the inter-war and immediate post-war years, the fact that despite the heavy bombing much of German capacity had remained intact, the steady stream of highly qualified labour in the form of expellees and migrants from the GDR and the favourable fiscal and monetary framework. At first, growth was accompanied by high unemployment and some price increases, giving rise to considerable unease. But the slowly but steadily rising wage levels of the 1950s created perhaps the new republic's biggest claim to popular support and gradually dispelled the deepseated suspicion held by many Germans that democracies were incapable of running society effectively. Though the 'social' in Erhard's 'social market economy' was initially more claim than substance, in 1957 the welfare state was able to make a quantum leap forward in the form of the new pensions law, which created dynamic pensions linked to the general growth rate of the economy.

II.3 Emergence of the *Kanzlerdemokratie*

A striking fact of the Federal Republic's life was that despite the many limits to Germany's sovereignty and freedom of action the government was able from a very early stage to speak and act with an authority denied to any German government or leader since Bismarck, with the exception of Hitler. In part this was because the Nazis had crushed the centrifugal tendencies within German society – the ability of army leaders, civil service, businessmen, labour, Prussian aristocrats and other groups to defy the government. In part it was because the Allied presence and the dissolution of the German army had protected the nascent German administration in the immediate post-war period from having to do the sort of deals with other power groups which had so undermined Weimar leaders. The destruction of Prussia also eliminated the confusions and resistances built into the uneven federal structure of pre-Nazi Germany. Finally, of course, the distribution of power within parliament itself, and above all the very substantial position enjoyed by the CDU even in the first electoral period was a crucial prerequisite of decisive action.

But on top of these factors there was Konrad Adenauer's personal authority. Despite taking office well after retirement age, Adenauer exuded a mixture of patriarchal but determinedly civilian authority and a canny, on-the-level and unbombastic rhetorical style. His control over cabinet and parliament was so marked that it was said he had invented a new political system: the 'Chancellor-Democracy'. His most important contribution was in the area of foreign policy. Adenauer's commitment to close western integration, his belief that it was only through such western ties that Germany could restyle itself into a stable democracy, coupled with his personal authority, allowed him to 'deliver' the western strategy at home, despite the fact that it was clearly pushing the prospects of unification with East Germany ever further into the distance.

II.4   Values and attitudes in the new republic

How far had attitudes and values changed within the new republic? Many critical observers felt that few Germans had learned much from the past. Opinion polls for much of the 1950s suggested that the population was not much more influenced by democratic ideas than it had been a generation earlier.

It was understandable that left-wing critics should talk of a 'restoration'. And yet the political and ideological climate in Bonn was very far from being a replication of Weimar. The biggest break was, of course, in the marginalization of nationalism and the emergence of new attitudes towards Germany's place in the wider world. The sense of the new realities of world power penetrated to every aspect of German life. When it came to attitudes on more domestic matters, it is true, there were many continuities – in middle-class anti-communism, for example, and a strong desire for order. Yet, whereas in Weimar the bourgeoisie had shown itself willing to embrace a culture of violence in order to crush the left, restore order and re-establish Germany's place in the world, after 1949 there was a very conscious effort to return to old niceties. Guides to etiquette and good behaviour, to *guten Ton*, sold in hundreds of thousands. Whilst for left-wing critics this emphasis on decency and order was both stifling and hypocritical and was often not particularly democratic (aiming to produce the decent, loyal state citizen rather than the active democrat), it gave the old civic virtues of the bourgeoisie a place they had not enjoyed in Weimar.

In Weimar, many on the right had sought to unify society by crushing the organized left. In post-'49 Germany, a strong, anti-pluralistic yearning for unity remained. But instead of aspiring to create unity by force there was an almost wilful desire to believe that German society was *already* unified. The popular sociologists of the time – Geiger, Schelsky and others – reflected and reinforced the desire to believe that here was a society where class divisions were a thing of the past. As a result, even when the rhetoric of political leaders still had a strident Weimar tone, contemporaries often experienced this rhetoric as being out of keeping with the times, a 'ghost-like' reminder of social divisions that no longer existed.

Overstating the case, one could argue that it was precisely the restorativeness, the return to bourgeois values of decency and civility, that marked Bonn out from Weimar. What was new, too, was that conservatism was so successful. In 1957 the CDU managed to get an absolute majority of the votes, achieving something that Hitler had been unable to do even in the unfree elections of March 1933. Stifling as the Cold War climate may have been, by the second half of the 1950s, German society was probably more united in ideology and values than at any time in its history.

II.5   Germany in denial

There is no doubt that there was considerable obfuscation of the past, denial of involvement, indeed a conspiracy not to mention it. Most German people were unwilling to confront their role in Germany's crimes. But the hegemonic myths of the post-'45 era were far more constructive than those which had held sway in the inter-war period. After all, the twists and turns that allowed a whole generation of civil servants and businessmen to emerge with careers intact from the denazification panels, nevertheless at the same time did involve each individual distancing themselves from their pasts. This was very different from the glorification of tradition or the stab in the back legend which had so undermined Weimar. The kinds of narratives that Germans privately and publicly constructed after 1945 to make sense of what had happened revolved round the lessons that had been learned from the defeat – lessons such as the ability to put your shoulders to the wheel and build a better society, or the ability of European nations to work together. They did not involve denying the defeat or plotting ways to overturn the terms of the post-war settlement.

And yet there was a brittle, exaggerated quality to life in the 1950s which could not be healthy in the longer term. You could see it in the intensity with which an entire generation threw itself into work and personal enrichment; you could see it in the strained silences of family life. Indeed, families in this period suffered in many respects from a double burden. On the one hand, the very different experiences of home front and battle front had created communication gaps and distances between husbands and wives. Cramped housing conditions and long working hours added to the strain. On the other hand, there was the communication gap between the generations about the politics of the past. Youngsters growing up in the 1950s often felt they were living a double lie – the lie of happy families, and the lie of a society that would not face up to its past – both of which led them in the 1960s to denounce what they saw as bourgeois hypocrisy.

III   Challenge and reform, 1957–1974

III.1   Into the 1960s: the surface of stability

At the end of the 1950s the FRG presented a picture of stability and success. Continued economic growth now began to bring truly unparalleled prosperity to the whole population. The implications for the patterns and rhythms of everyday life were probably more far-reaching than in any phase of economic growth since industrialization. Consumerism entered with a vengeance. The self-service shop rapidly replaced across-the-counter service; the German public began to travel abroad in their millions, the car became the dominant form of transport, television took over in the living room, the laid-back culture of rock and roll invaded the youth scene and so on.

Against this background, the political scene converged on the middle. The SPD responded to the CDU's success with the famous Bad Godesberg party programme of 1959, in which it formally jettisoned much of the Marxist ideology which in any case had long ceased to influence party policy. As well as now embracing the market economy (though still calling for more state intervention) the party also endorsed Adenauer's broad pro-western international framework. Since a number of influential figures within the CDU began to accept the need for somewhat greater state intervention in economic and social policy, the ideological gap between the two major parties was now very small indeed. In 1966, when the combination of a very minor recession and a more serious crisis in the mining industry led temporarily to great anxiety about Germany's economic development, the CDU and SPD joined together to form the Grand Coalition – a government which lasted for three years.

Yet in the course of the 1960s it became apparent that this stable surface was in some ways rather misleading. For one thing, the massive overreaction to the 1966 recession indicated that Germany's political stability might still be very dependent on the economy's capacity to deliver. The Weimar-style reflex of the Grand Coalition suggested that the economic difficulties were being stylized as a national emergency. Brief successes for the far-right Nationaldemokratische Partei Deutschlands (NPD) in regional elections were another worry. However, more significant than the immediate impact of recession were a series of broader changes at home and abroad that were beginning to challenge the consensus.

III.2   Losing faith in Cold War logic

The clear logic which Adenauer had drawn, and persuaded his fellow countrymen to draw from the international scene began to lose its plausibility. In the first place, the erection of the Berlin Wall in August 1961 discredited the magnet theory that West Germany could undermine East Germany by its own attractiveness. It began a tortuous and conflict-ridden process within West Germany's political establishment towards finding some sort of modus vivendi with the GDR. For Konrad Adenauer, still in office when the Wall was created (he was replaced by Ludwig Erhard as Chancellor in 1963), the Berlin crises also reinforced a growing disillusionment with American leadership, which the Germans felt had been ineffectual. There was a growing sense that America no longer had West German security needs at the heart of its strategic objectives. This view was to intersect over the following decades with a different strand of criticism which emerged in the wake of the Vietnam War, namely, that American imperialism was in fact a greater threat to peace than Soviet expansionism. In the second half of the 1960s, bitter public conflicts over foreign policy broke out for the first time since the struggle over rearmament in the 1950s.

III.3   The birth of a protest movement.

The explosion of protest that took place above all among university students towards the end of the 1960s was, however, motivated only partially by the Vietnam War. As

Illustration 18.2   A couple of months after the erection of the Berlin Wall on 13 August 1961, West Berliners greet their relatives and friends in the East, separated by the notorious death strip

elsewhere in the western world, the rise of affluence began for the first time to reveal its slightly ambiguous implications for the stability of public order. Though it had helped to deal with the classical 'social question', it began to throw up new needs and discontents. 'Post-material' values began to emerge, not least exported from the USA via its new youth culture. In Germany, perhaps even more important was that protest culture interacted with a far more deep-seated sense of unease at the FRG's failure to confront its past. On top of all this, there was a problem of chronic underfunding in the university sector. In the period of the Grand Coalition there was no genuine opposition to articulate people's discontents; the result was the rapid growth of the APO or Extra-Parliamentary Opposition. In 1967, the student Benno Ohnesorg was shot dead by a policeman during a protest against the Shah of Iran and this triggered a wave of demonstrations, sit-ins and other actions. Every aspect of the Federal Republic became subject to question, its bland Cold-War self-assurance denounced as lies and deceit.

III.4   Revolts, reaction and reform

Youthful protest seldom enjoys much impact unless the adult generation has in some sense or another delegated to young people the task of shaking things up. This was certainly the case in the 1960s where, under the surface, a sense of the need for more openness and liberality had been steadily developing, particularly among the educated bourgeoisie. Perhaps a first indication of the changing intellectual climate had been the *Spiegel* affair in 1962, when the government had heavy-handedly infringed the rights of the press and had then deceived parliament in the process. Public reaction showed that the characteristic German middle-class reflex of approving any government action if it kept the peace was now being replaced by a commitment to constitutionality and civil liberty. Franz-Josef Strauss, the then Defence Minister, had to go, and Adenauer's own prestige never recovered – he was replaced the following year. Henceforth governments were to be increasingly constrained by the informal constitution of public opinion. More specifically, 1963 saw a number of leading thinkers calling for fundamental reform of Germany's education institutions – giving a clear signal to the student community that change was required. There was thus a kind of symbiosis between a slow liberalization of the thinking public and the growth of student protest.

It is true that the student movement itself was often illiberal and dogmatic. Even sympathizers such as Jürgen Habermas warned against a left-wing fascism. Moreover, the direct result of student protest and subsequently of terrorism was often to provoke the state to measures of greater illiberality. The joint decision of *Bund* and *Land* in January 1972 to tighten the existing controls on the political activities and attitudes of applicants for the civil service (*Radikalenerlass*), and the subsequent huge expansion of individual screening and checks, showed the state at its rigid worst. It is possible that even without the student movement liberalization would have accelerated and thus that the only direct results of protest were the negative ones of state control. To most observers then and since, however, the collision between protest movement and a Federal Republic still in many respects dominated by the Cold War is seen as a decisive step towards greater democracy and pluralism. In the new climate there was an explosion of reform at all levels, resulting not least in the emergence of a new Social-Liberal government coalition in 1969. The clarion call of the new Chancellor, Willy Brandt, for inner reform, more democracy and codetermination enjoyed a wide resonance.

III.5   *Ostpolitik* and *Vergangenheitsbewältigung*

It was both symptom and result of the greater openness and liberalism that emerged in the 1960s that the Federal Republic was able to kick aside two of the ideological props which had been essential to its stability in the 1950s. One was the total embargo on recognition of the GDR. After some early moves by the Freie demokratische Partei (FDP) during its period of opposition, the new Social Liberal Coalition of 1969 initiated a series of measures which saw talks in Moscow in 1969 and treaties with Moscow and Poland in the following year, brought the heads of government of the two German states together for the first time in 1970 and culminated in the new Basic Treaty of 1972. Following a series of improvements in transit arrangements between the states and a Four-Power agreement in 1971 which clarified (though did not resolve) the status of Berlin, in the Basic Treaty the two states recognized each other as separate states, although the Federal Republic did not renounce its aspirations to national unification or accept the GDR as a separate *nation*.

The other 'prop' or taboo of the 1950s to be broken was the silence about the past. The creation in 1958 of a new Central Office for Prosecution of National Socialist Crimes had been a first step in this direction. The 1960s saw a series of profound analyses from German scholars about the workings of the Third Reich and a growing willingness on the part of schools to tackle this difficult period. Willy Brandt's famous gesture, in December 1970, of falling to his knees before a monument to those who died in the Warsaw uprising, made such an impact because it publicly brought together these two strands: the new amity with the Warsaw Pact powers and the willingness publicly to acknowledge Germany's responsibilities in the past.

IV   Crisis and consolidation, 1975–1989

IV.1   The end of the miracle

Many observers have seen for Germany, as for France, the events of the late 1960s and their impact as marking 'the end of exceptionalism'. And in many respects such challenges as confronted the Federal Republic in the post-1973 period have been comparable to those facing other western states. Like most other states, the stormy growth of the post-war decades came to an end. In 1974–5, West Germany hit its first serious post-war recession. Henceforth, mass unemployment was a permanent feature, rising from the million mark in the post-1975 years to over two million after the second major recession in 1979–80. The economic slowdown was not a sign that West Germany had lost its earlier abilities; rather the oil crisis, the ending of a special post-war 'catch-up' period, and the emergence of a new set of geoeconomic conditions (the weakening of the dollar, the emergence of competition from Far East and newly developed countries) created a more unpredictable and challenging growth environment for all European countries.

Under these conditions the bubbling reform atmosphere of the late 1960s and early 1970s rapidly lost its fizz. After the fall of Willy Brandt (his private secretary turned out to be a GDR spy) in 1974, the new Chancellor Helmut Schmidt rapidly came to lay increasing emphasis on consolidation rather than reform. The hope that had emerged, after Erhard's fall, that demand management by the federal government could prevent recessions, proved illusory. Instead, the problem of stagflation reared its head in the 1970s. Particularly after 1979, all attention came to be devoted to controlling state spending, a struggle which continued when the CDU returned to government in 1982 and which lasted through the 1980s. Aside from the intensifying economic constraints, the checks and balances of a federal system in which the *Länder* were largely in the hands of the opposition, as they were in the 1970s, also set limits to reform. Under these conditions, the SPD increasingly lost its way. In gradually dropping any aspirations to control demand and unemployment levels, the SPD in many ways anticipated the so-called *Wende* – the return to CDU control which followed the FDP's defection in 1982.

Similarly, the student movement fragmented, its most radical advocates descending during the 1970s into the terror of the Red Army faction. A series of spectacular actions including the attack on the German embassy in Stockholm in 1975, the 1977 murders of the Attorney-General Siegfried Buback and Hanns Martin Schleyer, president of the German Employers' Association, and the abduction of a Lufthansa flight to Mogadishu, all confronted the West German state with difficult challenges but had little in common with the reformist enthusiasm of the earlier period. The only more positive expression of that spirit was the emergence in the 1980s of the Green Party as a major political movement, in many regions threatening or eclipsing the FDP as the third force between the major parties.

The 1980s, as elsewhere, saw considerable public disaffection with the political process. On top of the reduced freedom of manoeuvre imposed by the new financial and economic situation there were other reasons for the new much-commented-upon alienation from the established parties. In a global world, the centres of decision-making seemed to many people more and more remote. Political scandals came to light that might have remained under the carpet in more deferential times, and several senior German politicians had to resign in the wake of dirty tricks allegations or of accepting improper payments. The growth of television created a false openness, with politicians ostensibly answering questions, but in reality staking out bargaining positions in ongoing decision-making processes. The result of such exposure was that, as elsewhere, politicians became slicker and slicker and less and less credible.

And yet even if it shared in certain common western problems of attrition, in comparative terms the West German state proved its durability and strength. It remained one of the strongest economies in the world. It controlled the inflationary pressures of the post-oil-crisis period far better than most other developed economies. True, the economic difficulties in conjunction with the large number of foreign 'guest workers' now on German soil did give rise to some racist protest, but in general the political impact of deep recession, contrary to many fears, gave little comfort to the extremist parties of left and right. In short, in a changed world, West Germany remained a pillar of stability.

IV.2   Problems of national identity

In many ways, then, West Germany had by the mid-1970s completed the transition from maverick to model state. But in other respects its situation remained distinctive and troubled – and as always the criss-crossing of history and geopolitics was at the heart of the specific German problem.

First the difficult past would not go away. For a long time, one of the key demands of the CDU had been to combat the growing lack of any link to the notion of Germanness on the part of the younger generation with a renewed historical consciousness of the *Vaterland*. Helmut Kohl, Chancellor since 1982, wanted to realize this vision, as did a number of prominent conservative-minded historians such as Michael Stürmer. But the celebrated *Historikerstreit* of the mid-1980s revealed that, although the passing of time and the weakening of the Cold War meant that some things which had been left unsaid on the right were now sayable again, it was impossible to resurrect a 'wholesome' or 'usable' past for easy national identification.

Secondly, the FRG's geopolitical position remained highly individual and complex and a source of considerable contention and division. As a front-line power, the FRG continued to experience the special vulnerability of being the probable battleground of any future war, and the territory most likely to be subject to Soviet blackmail and pressure. In the post-Vietnam era this led many Germans, notably Helmut Schmidt, to be particularly sensitive to signs that the Americans were pulling back from their global commitments. President Carter's stance at the SALT talks of allowing the Soviets a clear conventional and tactical nuclear superiority in Europe for the sake of parity in strategic nuclear weapons at the global level, met with particular criticism. It was Schmidt whose proposals led to the NATO twin-track decision of 1979, which threatened to station tactical nuclear missiles on European soil if negotiations with the Soviet Union failed to reduce the number of SS20s aimed at Europe. On the other hand, again as a front-line power and as a power with developing relations with the GDR, the FRG saw itself as having a special interest in *détente*. The twin-track decision was thus notably divisive, since it ranged those who believed that NATO and the USA should be doing more for Europe against those, including very many young people, who believed the growth in nuclear armaments was itself the biggest danger to their security. The stationing of the first Pershing missiles on German soil in the early 1980s led to massive protest marches. It was not least on this issue that the SPD became deeply divided.

Nevertheless, one should not exaggerate the threat posed to West German stability by these issues. The CDU, despite its somewhat more national-minded rhetoric, in fact pursued the same *Ostpolitik* as the SPD. Like the SPD, too, the CDU sought closer ties with the FRG's western neighbours to reassure them about its *rapprochement* with the east. In the continuing West German foreign policy conception, German unification, if it were ever achieved, had to go hand in hand with closer European union. For most West Germans of the younger generations the national issue was of very secondary importance. The GDR was far more of a foreign territory than France, Britain or Italy. Whilst conservative thinkers worried that the lack of national awareness would ultimately deny the Federal Republic the kind of inner resources necessary to weather a serious crisis that were available to other classic nation states, West Germany in fact seemed to other observers in fact to benefit from the 'post-national' consciousness of many its citizens.

V   Division and stability

During the 1980s statesmen as varied in their views as Andreotti, Mitterand and Thatcher all directly or indirectly expressed a wish that West Germany should retain its separate existence and not aspire to recreating a single German nation. That showed how successful the FRG had been – but it also showed that there was a fear that reunification might undo all that had been achieved. Was this justified? Were the FRG's successes based on shaky foundations, likely to be undermined once unification took place?

There was little doubt that the divisions – of Europe and of Germany – had together simplified the task of creating a stable republic in the post-war period. For one thing, the proximity of a Soviet threat, whether real or perceived, had created a commonality of interest between West Germany and its neighbours. Most Germans eschewed nationalism in favour of the idea of a common western interest; similarly, Germany's neighbours had to subordinate their animosity towards the former enemy to a recognition of their mutual interdependence and vulnerability in the age of the superpowers. Second, the division of Germany had made for a more manageable state: the destruction of Prussia created the basis for a more balanced federal structure; the new more equal confessional balance facilitated the emergence of a non-denominational Christian Democratic Union.

Yet at least as important in creating and consolidating the new order were the changes Nazism, war and defeat had bequeathed to Germany. The combination of the exhaustion and disillusionment of the broad population, on the one hand, and the active political minority's awareness of the need for reform, on the other, provided the crucial prerequisite for the success of democratic rebirth in Germany.

In any case, West Germany rapidly outgrew dependence on the conditions of its birth, acquiring in the 1960s a pluralistic and democratic political culture, a post-nationalist liberalism that often put to shame the nations that had helped bring the new state into being. This was particularly apparent in the 1980s. In Britain and the USA, that decade saw entire regions and social classes simply cast on the scrap heap by the policies of Thatcher and Reagan. In France, it saw extreme racism become part of the political mainstream. In the Federal Republic of Germany, by contrast, the sensitivity to social harmony, the incorporation of regional interests, the pressure to compromise, all of which were built into its formal and informal political systems, made such developments unthinkable. It was and is not plausible that the end of the Cold War and the end to division would simply undo these changes.

Even if one ignores the quality and strength of the FRG's political culture, the argument that the new geopolitical situation of a post-Cold War world would inevitably revive the old temptation to look eastwards and perforce create instabilities in Germany is implausible. Even without the Cold War, the world is very different from the inter-war period. To take one very obvious example, in a world of nuclear weapons any thought of a 'Barbarossa' – waging the knockout blow against Russia to create a stable German empire in east Europe – is clearly a non-starter. But far more significant is the change in geoeconomics. The slogans of central European empire-building or *Lebensraum* made sense only in an imperialist and highly protectionist world, where each nation had to secure and control its own hinterland of markets and raw materials. The end of the Cold War has done nothing to revive this scenario – on the contrary, it has contributed to a further opening of world markets and trade.

In short, it is hard to accept the view that the Federal Republic's stability was dependent on its remaining a divided state. In one crucial sense, however, West Germany's very success did leave it ill-equipped to cope with the challenges of reunification. Precisely because it was so well able to win the support of its citizens and foster what was in many cases a clearly non-nationalist identity, it has lacked the broad public sympathy and legitimacy for the sacrifices required to complete the national unification process. There are dangers inherent in the resulting tensions and conflicts, but they are dangers with which the Federal Republic, with its durable political institutions, powerful economy, and ability to accommodate regional interests, is able to cope at least as well as any of the maturer democracies of Europe.

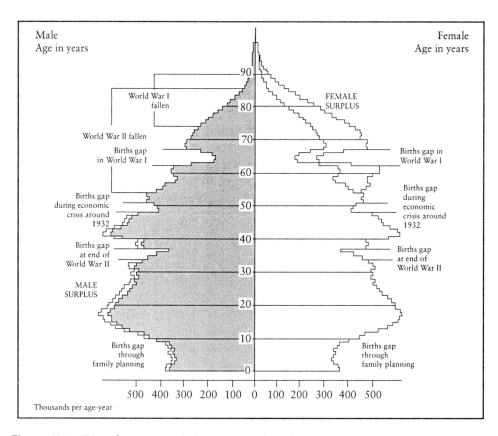

Figure 18.1 West German population structure in 1981

Table 18.1 Bundestag election results, 1949–1994 (000s)

In this table results are not given for insignificant party affiliations, which generally gained less than 1 per cent each, so that figures below do not add up to 100 per cent. The only exception was the election of 1949, where such other groups gained, taken together, 6.2 per cent.
a) Total votes gained in the whole country, b) percentage of total votes, c) number of seats, before 1990 excluding deputies of West Berlin, because Berlin was under an especial international status, d) disappeared later from the German system of political parties.

	14.8.1949			6.3.1953			15.9.1957			17.9.1961		
Eligible	31.2 mill.			33.1 mill.			35.4 mill.			37.4 mill.		
Turnout	24.5 mill.			28.5 mill.			31.1 mill.			32.8 mill.		
% voting	78.5			85.8			87.8			87.7		
	a	b	c	a	b	c	a	b	c	a	b	c
CDU/CSU	7,359	31.0	139	12,440	45.2	243	15,008	50.2	270	14,298	45.3	242
SPD	6,935	29.2	131	7,945	28.8	151	9,496	31.8	169	11,427	36.2	190
FDP	2,83	11.9	52	2,628	9.5	48	2,307	7.7	41	4,029	12.8	67
KPD/DKP (Kommunistische Partei Deutschlande)	1,362	5.7	15	0,607	2.2	—	—	—	—	—	—	—
DP[d] (Deutsche Partei)	0,94	4.0	17	0,898	3.3	15	1,007	3.4	17	GPD	2.8	—
BHE[d] (Bund der Heimatvertriebenen und Entrechteten)	—	—	—	1,614	5.9	27	1,374	4.6	0,871	—	—	—
Centre[d]	0,728	3.1	10	0,217	0.8	2	0,086	0.3	—	—	—	—
Bavaria Party[d]	0,986	4.2	17	0,466	1.7	—	0,168	0.5	—	—	—	—
WAV[d] (Wirtschaltliche Aufbau Vereinigung)	0,682	2.9	12	—	—	—	—	—	—	—	—	—
SRP/NPD (Sozialistische Ruchspartei)	0,429	1.8	5	0,296	1.1	—	0,309	1.0	—	0,263	0.8	—
DFU (Deutsche Friedens-Union)	—	—	—	—	—	—	—	—	—	0,61	1.9	—

Table 18.1 *continued*

In this table results are not given for insignificant party affiliations, which generally gained less than 1 per cent each, so that figures below do not add up to 100 per cent. The only exception was the election of 1949, where such other groups gained, taken together, 6.2 per cent.

a) Total votes gained in the whole country, b) percentage of total votes, c) number of seats, before 1990 excluding deputies of West Berlin, because Berlin was under an especial international status, d) disappeared later from the German system of political parties.

	19.9.1965 38.50 mill. 33.4 mill. 86.8			28.9.1969 38.7 mill. 33.0 mill. 86.7			19.11.1972 35.4 mill. 31.1 mill. 91.2			3.10.1976 42.0 mill. 38.1 mill. 90.7			5.10.1980 43.2 mill. 38.3 mill. 88.7		
Eligible Turnout % voting	a	b	c	a	b	c	a	b	c	a	b	c	a	b	c
CDU/CSU	15,524	47.6	245	15,195	46.1	242	16,794	44.8	225	18,397	48.6	244	16,900	44.5	226
SPD	12,813	39.3	202	14,066	42.7	224	17,167	45.9	230	16,099	42.6	213	16,262	42.9	218
FDP	3,097	9.5	49	1,903	5.8	30	3,129	8.4	41	2,995	7.9	39	4,030	10.6	53
KPD/DKP	—	—	—	0,197	0.6	—	0,114	0.3	—	0,141	0.4	—	0,080	0.2	—
GDP	—	—	—	—	—	—	—	—	—	—	—	—	—	—	—
Centre[d]	—	—	—	—	—	—	—	—	—	—	—	—	—	—	—
Bavaria Party[d]	—	—	—	—	—	—	—	—	—	—	—	—	—	—	—
WAV[d]	—	—	—	—	—	—	—	—	—	—	—	—	—	—	—
SRP/NPD	0,664	2.0	—	1,422	4.3	—	0,207	0.6	0,122	0.3	—	0,067	—	0.2	—
DFU[d]	0,434	1.3	—	—	—	—	—	—	—	—	—	—	—	—	—

	6.3.83 44.08 mill. 39.2 mill. 89.1			25.1.87 45.3 mill. 38.2 mill. 84.3			2.12.90 60.4 mill. 46.9 mill. 77.8			1994 60.4 mill. 47.0 mill. 79.1		
	a	b	c*	a	b	c*	a	b	c*	a	b	c*
CDU/CSU	18.9	48.8	244 (+11)	16.7	44.3	223 (+11)	20.3	43.8	319	19.5	41.5	294
SPD	14.8	39.2	193 (+5)	14.0	37.0	186 (+7)	15.5	33.5	239	17.1	36.4	252
FDP	2.7	7.0	34 (+1)	3.4	9.1	46 (+2)	5.1	11.0	79	3.1	6.9	47
Greens	2.1	5.6	27 (+1)	3.1	8.3	42 (+2)	1.7	3.8	—			
NPD	0.09	0.2	—	0.2	0.6	0.1	0.4	—				
DKP	0.06	0.2	0.2	—	—	—						
PDS (Parteides Demokratischen Sozialismus)	1.1	2.4 0.4	1.2	8**	—	3.4	7.3	49				
REP (Republikaner)	1.0	2.1	—	0.8	1.9	—						

* +11 Berliner MdB

** The parties got seats although they did not gain 5 per cent of the total votes because of special provisions for the former GDR where they got more than 5 per cent. In 1994 this will no longer be the case.

Source: C.C. Schweitzer, Detlev Kausten, et al. (eds) Politics and Government in Germany 1944–1994. Basic Documents (Oxford: Berghahn Books, 1995), p. 442.

Table 18.2 Real growth of the West German economy, 1951–1980 (%)

Year	%	Year	%
1951	10.4	1966	2.9
1952	8.9	1967	−0.2
1953	8.2	1968	7.3
1954	7.4	1969	8.2
1955	12.0	1970	5.8
1956	7.3	1971	3.0
1957	5.7	1972	3.4
1958	3.7	1973	5.1
1959	7.3	1974	0.4
1960	9.0	1975	−2.7
1961	5.4	1976	5.8
1962	4.0	1977	2.7
1963	3.4	1978	3.3
1964	6.7	1979	4.5
1965	5.6	1980	1.8

Source: V.R. Berghahn, *Modern Germany* (Cambridge: Cambridge University Press, 1982), p. 262.

Table 18.3 Structure of the labour force by sector, 1907–1972 (%)

Year	Agriculture	Industry and handicraft	Tertiary sector Total	Commerce/ Banking
1907	35.2	40.1	24.8	12.4
1925	30.5	42.1	27.4	16.4
1933	28.9	40.4	30.7	18.5
1939[a]	25.9	42.2	31.9	17.5
1950[b]	23.1 (26)	(45)	(29)	
1960	13.2 (19)[c]	(48)	(33)	
1962	12.5	46.0	41.2	17.5
1970	8.3			
1972	7.7	46.1	46.2	16.5
1975	(12)	(49)	(37)	

Notes: [a] Reich Territory of 31.12.1937.
[b] Fed. Rep.; figures for GDR in brackets.
[c] GDR figure for 1959.
Sources: V.R. Berghahn, *Modern Germany* (Cambridge: Cambridge University Press, 1982), p. 263.

Table 18.4 Exports of major industrial nations as a percentage of GDP from 1913 to 1987

Country	1913[1]	1928[1]	1938[1]	1950[1]	1958[2]	1960[2]	1970[2]	1980[2]	1987[2]
Germany	19.3	14.4	5.4	8.5	15.1	19.0	21.2	26.5	28.7
UK	23.4	17.2	9.2	16.9	23.0	20.0	22.5	27.2	26.3
Italy	9.7	8.8	6.3	7.9	11.6	14.6	15.4	21.8	19.7
US	6.6	6.0	3.7	3.8	4.3	4.9	5.6	10.2	7.6
Japan	14.3	14.5	14.9	8.4	11.8	11.1	11.3	14.9	13.2

Notes: [1] Goods only.
[2] Goods and services.

Source: Weidenfeld, H. and Zimmermann, H., eds., *Deutschland-Handbuch* (1989), p. 623.

Select bibliography

Balfour, Michael, *Germany, the Tides of Power* (London: Routledge, 1992).

Berghahn, V. R., *The Americanisation of West German Industry, 1945–1973* (Leamington Spa: Berg, 1986).

Berghahn, V. R., *Modern Germany: Society, Economy and Politics in the Twentieth Century* (Cambridge: Cambridge University Press, 1987).

Dahrendorf, Ralf, *Society and Democracy in Germany* (London: Weidenfeld & Nicolson, 1968).

Fulbrook, Mary, *The Divided Nation: A History of Germany 1918–1990* (London: Fontana Press, 1991).

Kramer, Alan, *The West German Economy* (Oxford: Berg, 1991).

Larres, Klaus and Panayi, Panikos, eds., *The Federal Republic of Germany since 1949: Politics, Society and Economy before and after Unification* (London: Longman, 1996).

Nicholls, A. J., *Freedom with Responsibility* (Oxford: Oxford University Press, 1995).

Pulzer, Peter, *German Politics, 1945–1995* (Oxford: Oxford University Press, 1995).

Smith, Gordon, *Democracy in Western Germany: Parties and Politics in the Federal Republic*, 3rd edn (Aldershot: Dartmouth, 1986).

Rogers, Daniel, *Politics after Hitler. The Western Allies and the German Party System* (London: Macmillan, 1995).

Schwarz, Hans Peter, *Adenauer. From the German Empire to the Federal Republic* (Oxford: Berghahn Publishers, 1995).

Smith, Eric Owen, *The German Economy* (London: Routledge, 1994).

Turner, Henry A., *The Two Germanies* (New Haven: Yale University Press, 1987).

Turner, Ian, ed., *Reconstruction in Post-War Germany: British Occupation Policy and the Western Zones, 1945–1955* (Oxford, New York and Munich: Berg, 1989).

19

The failed experiment: East German communism

Mark Allinson

The German Democratic Republic may eventually rate merely a historical footnote, having occupied little of Germany's geography and chronology. In the 1990s, however, the wealth of historical material suddenly available, and the personal and political need to exorcise the latest German dictatorship, have produced an outpouring of work on the GDR, and a variety of interpretations of its history and place in the wider context of German history.

Dispassionate assessments of GDR history are difficult, essentially for political reasons. During its lifetime (1949–90), the GDR's own accounts were almost exclusively one-sided and adulatory, while western reports, particularly in the earlier years, highlighted the GDR's repressive nature. Only from the later 1960s were these publications regularly balanced by more analytical works which accepted the GDR's existence, such as those by Hermann Weber and Dietrich Staritz.

After the collapse in 1989 of the Socialist Unity Party of Germany (SED), the GDR's ruling communist party, much historical work was based on the premiss that the GDR was an illegitimate dictatorship and morally an *Unrechtsstaat* ('a state based on injustice'). The legal legitimacy of SED rule and the GDR's existence is still sometimes questioned just as it was during the Cold War.

The first stated aim in the hitherto most extensive investigation, the *Bundestag* report commissioned after unification, illustrates well the spirit of such politicized history:

> By a precise analysis of the totalitarian power structures of the SED dictatorship, the Inquiry Commission should help to ensure that those forces which were decisive in organizing the repression of people in the GDR never again receive a political chance in united Germany.[1]

The commission also intended to highlight the SED's 'deformation' of individuals' lives and to allow the 'victims' at least 'historical justice'.[2] Much attention was devoted to establishing the relative 'political responsibility' of those involved in the GDR's political structures.[3] The dramatic language and the investigation's avowedly political aims suggested that the authors reached their conclusions in advance.

The commission's chairman, Rainer Eppelmann, a long-standing opponent of the SED, was a leader of the 1989 revolutionary movement. Was this history written by the 'victors'? Much GDR history has been written by active opponents of the SED, or by those with an interest, often based on political conviction, in stabilizing the expanded FRG's structures, and must be seen in this perspective. Since 1990 bitter rows have raged over who may write GDR history, with attempts made to discredit historians regarded as too close to the old regime.

Apart from heavy criticism of the GDR's systems and structures, much attention has centred on the Ministerium für Staatssicherheit (Ministry for State Security), the infamous Stasi, effectively the GDR's secret police. Here the boundary between history and current politics is most blurred, as the Stasi files, now administered by a government agency, have been used to discredit many linked to the ministry, particularly those still active in political life. However, the validity of the Stasi (or any other) files is uncertain: some individuals were unaware of their classification as Stasi 'informal informants', and whether prepared by the Stasi or another official source, reports of societal dissatisfaction may have been cleansed or exaggerated before being passed upwards. Interpreting the GDR's enormous paper legacy is highly problematic.

Those who identified with their former state have taken a different approach. The SED's successor party, the PDS (Party of Democratic Socialism) is a good example and has published (among much else) its response to the Bundestag report. These authors' aims were also clearly stated: 'to oppose *from left-wing standpoints* this attempt to claim the power of interpretation over a significant part of German history'.[4] Generally such work has not exclusively defended SED policies or denied power abuses, but has tried to analyse where the SED's interpretation of socialism failed. Typically, such authors have incorporated a critically comparative approach to the FRG.

However, not all historical writing on the GDR is avowedly politicized, though even the absence of a clear condemnation of the SED has sometimes been criticized. Much work has analysed the GDR's political and societal structures and scrutinized particular episodes from a more objective academic perspective. Equally clearly, GDR history-writing did not emerge from a void in 1989–90, but built on earlier foundations, augmented by newly available material. For instance, the SED's repressive nature was already well documented, notably by Karl Wilhelm Fricke. This tradition continues in work on the Stasi and the post-war Soviet internment camps. However, practically all historians distance themselves from the style of pre-1989 GDR publications, written as self-legitimation and for explicitly party political purposes.

Leaving aside the various motivations for GDR histories, what key issues are involved? Much disagreement centres on the comparison, implied or direct, between the GDR and the Third Reich as totalitarian dictatorships, and the claim that East Germans lived under unbroken dictatorship from 1933 to 1989. Left-wing writers sharply reject such comparisons as a falsification of GDR history and a relativization of Nazi atrocities which attempts to mask continuities between the Third Reich and the FRG, and to discredit socialism by association with Nazism. Totalitarianism has re-emerged as a concept in historical and political science. However, even the Bundestag report noted that to compare was not to equate, and that important differences, such as the Second World War and genocide, existed between the two states. Beyond such theoretical debates, more empirical approaches attempt to establish means of comparing and distinguishing the political and social structures of both periods. How was SED rule maintained – purely by a strong Soviet military presence, or by tacit popular acceptance of the party? Why did so many participate in the structures established by the communists who attained political ascendancy after 1945? Why did SED rule then collapse so quickly? How stable was SED rule, and how and why did this vary over time?

A further, associated argument centres on the GDR's long-term independent viability and, by extension, of communist political systems (particularly since the USSR's collapse). Could the GDR have survived, or was it doomed to fail? The view was advanced by Mitter and Wolle in *Untergang auf Raten* ('Downfall by Instalments') that the GDR was essentially doomed after the popular uprising of June 1953 was crushed: 'We are dealing with a state party which was already politically finished in June 1953 and nonetheless ruled for a further 36 years.'[5] Other writers, such as Thomas Neumann, see Stalinism and eventual collapse as the inevitable outcome of Marxist politics. Was the GDR's fate really sealed at any specific point before 1989? If so, why did stability last and arguably grow into the 1980s? Could any realistic alternatives have saved the country or speeded its demise? These debates are linked to economic history and the GDR's international situation. Did *Ostpolitik* precipitate collapse or delay it? Did the GDR ultimately exist merely at the Soviets' whim? The international dimensions are crucial to understanding the GDR's internal dynamics.

The periodization of GDR history remains essentially unchallenged, falling into five major periods: first, direct Soviet occupation from 1945 to 1949, while the basic political structures were created; second, from the GDR's creation in 1949 to the Berlin Wall's erection in 1961, during which period socialist political and economic structures were strengthened and developed under the SED's Walter Ulbricht (despite the June 1953 uprising and the emigration of over two million citizens). Third, between 1961 and 1971, with the population secured behind the Wall, the system consolidated and experienced a relatively golden age and limited economic liberalization. In 1971 there was another rupture when Erich Honecker assumed power. International economic crisis and growing internal dissent dashed initial hopes of a GDR which fulfilled citizens' needs. The final period, from mid-1989 to 1990, marks the disintegration of SED rule and the surrender of GDR sovereignty.

While this periodization accurately reflects political developments, it masks various ongoing structural trends. For instance, the internal organization of the SED and the other parties and mass organizations developed progressively until the late 1950s, after which a high degree of stability essentially endured until late 1989. Conversely, popular attitudes were already altering years before the GDR collapsed. We clearly need a more differentiated approach to GDR history.

Bearing in mind these interpretative problems, this chapter attempts to explain the GDR's structures and to explore the system's apparent stability against the background of the threats it regularly experienced throughout the 1945/49–1989 period.

I   Establishing the structures

Nobody imagined in 1945 that the Soviet zone of defeated Nazi Germany, heavily war-damaged and with a population long exposed to anti-Bolshevik propaganda, would become a stable communist state. The essential prerequisites were Germany's Cold War division, and occupation by the Soviet Military Administration in Germany (SMAD), which used its sovereign power to advantage the German communists, especially those returning from Moscow exile with plans to establish a powerbase.

Until 1989 the communists exploited not only their Soviet protection, but also the moral superiority of their anti-fascist past. Many Communist Party (KPD) members had suffered greatly while actively opposing Nazism. After 1945 this apparently unimpeachable record was used to legitimize socialism. The communists further argued that Nazism derived from capitalism, that returning to the Weimar Republic's political and economic system would threaten a fascist revival, and that the division of democratic forces during Weimar had facilitated the NSDAP's power seizure. Thus political unity should underpin Germany's future. Those who disagreed were branded Nazi sympathizers.

Believing Marxism–Leninism was scientifically proven, many communists sincerely hoped to avoid renewed catastrophe. However, to be a credible antidote to Nazism the party could not ignore democracy and impose a one-party system. Walter Ulbricht summarized KPD strategy in May 1945: 'It must look democratic, but the power must be in our hands.'[6]

This strategy constantly guided the communists. The first German officials appointed to head city and provincial governments were mainly bourgeois. However, the crucial posts (education, law and order) were usually assigned to reliable communists. The SMAD also permitted the re-establishment of 'democratic' political parties. Alongside the KPD, the SMAD licensed the SPD, a Christian Democratic Union (CDU) and a Liberal Democratic Party (LDPD). However, these parties' autonomy was limited as the overriding 'unity' principle required the parties to agree policies unanimously in a 'Democratic Bloc', effectively guaranteeing a KPD veto. When KPD proposals were rejected, the communists' anti-fascist credentials were used to accuse the other parties of endangering democratic reconstruction. By late 1945 many CDU and LDPD members reverted to more conservative policies. Consequently the SMAD regularly intimidated and removed politicians who opposed socialism too vociferously. While many politicians moved west, those who stayed usually remained silent to preserve their positions. For decades the CDU and LDPD officially proclaimed socialism while many grass-roots members remained unconvinced but could only attempt to influence politics by remaining within their parties.

While the CDU and LDPD were quite easily controlled, the SPD, as an alternative workers' party, posed greater difficulties. Many Germans feared communism and associated the KPD with the hated Soviets; unsurprisingly the SPD became more popular. Fearing defeat in free elections, the communists and the SMAD campaigned to unite the two parties to preserve communist influence, citing the anti-fascist imperative and the need to avoid the allegedly damaging division of the workers' parties during Weimar.

Though many social democrats feared communist domination, by Easter 1946 the campaign succeeded – at least in the Soviet zone where the SPD voices warning against a *Zwangsvereinigung* ('forced merger') were drowned out by emotive anti-fascism. The merger was approved not by ballot but by delegates who either genuinely backed the merger or were pressurized by the Soviets. Many socialists felt these machinations presaged an undemocratic system. The new Socialist Unity Party of Germany (SED), apparently a broad party, was initially constituted with total parity between commu-

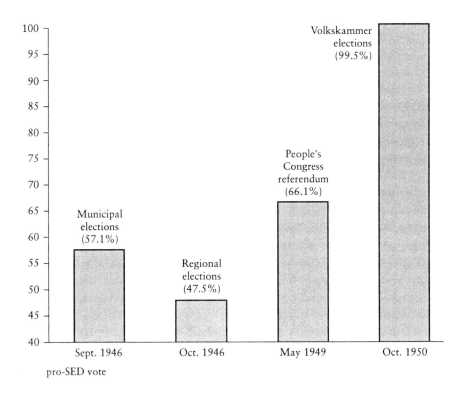

Figure 19.1 Stabilization of the voting system: how the pro-SED vote was ensured

nists and social democrats and inherited the KPD's privileged position in the Soviet zone's civil government. Yet by 1948 socialist unity was abandoned as, under Soviet protection and amid Germany's deepening division, the communist element transformed the SED into a Leninist 'party of a new type', and abandoned parity. The SED expelled the many committed social democrats and others who rejected the new Moscow-inspired line. This ideological overhaul was achieved with the agreement of senior former SPD leaders, notably Otto Grotewohl, whose motives ranged from self-preservation to conviction about communist policies. By 1948, with the zone's state apparatus and economic management mainly in SED hands, career considerations encouraged many social democrats to conform quietly. As the Soviets forbade an independent SPD, committed socialists had to choose between the SED or illegal opposition and probable punishment.

The SED's creation and subsequent communist domination still excites controversy. This development was arguably the first sign of renewed dictatorship, and that the SED's coercive, deceptive nature was predetermined. Clearly the merger resulted from pressure on individuals, while its SPD opponents were denied equivalent publicity. The SED's creation invited vitriolic attacks from the western SPD. Yet the notion of *Zwangsvereinigung* in 1946 is too broad: many social democrats (and communists) wanted and believed in workers' unity; even after the purges of the early 1950s, the SED still included ideologically committed members as well as careerists and opportunists.

The SED completed the party system in 1948 by creating two satellite parties. The Democratic Farmers' Party (DBD) reflected the SED's failure to unite workers and farmers, but attempted to integrate rural communities into political life on the SED's terms. Similarly, the National Democratic Party (NDPD) enabled reformed Nazis and conservative nationalists to participate in reconstruction within the SED's framework. The Soviet forces ensured no competing parties emerged. The DBD and NDPD therefore presented socialist policies to their target groups without challenging SED hegemony, and additionally attracted CDU and LDPD voters, enabling the SED to 'divide and rule' within the framework of political unity; both new parties joined the Democratic Bloc, strengthening SED control. As the bloc parties' political autonomy was weakened by moral blackmail and SED or Soviet coercion (particularly at the highest levels), so they acquired a role as 'transmission belts' to convey the SED's policies to the particular societal groupings they represented (Christians, farmers, etc.).

Alongside the parties, the SMAD also licensed various mass organizations, each firmly under KPD/SED control. On the unity principle, only one organization was permitted for each population sector. Through the Free German Trades Union Fedation (FDGB), the Free German Youth (FDJ), the Democratic Women's Association (DFD) and numerous similar organizations, the SED reached most of the population, including the many who otherwise distanced themselves from socialist politics, and prevented the development of independent movements which might challenge SED hegemony. Though membership of such organizations was never obligatory, their

Illustration 19.1   Erich Honecker, Chairman of the Central Council of the Free German Youth (later to become leader of the GDR, 1971–89), visits apprentices at a youth construction site, Berlin, 1952

officially unimpeachable democratic, anti-fascist principles made refusals to join politically suspect. For instance, failure or refusal to join the FDJ might jeopardize university entry.

Structurally, the theoretically pluralist party system differed from the Third Reich, while the mass organizations system was extremely similar. Despite being apparently democratic, the political system was firmly under SED control and supervised by the Soviets, the ultimate powerbrokers. No alternative avenues remained for potential opponents, whatever their anti-fascist credentials. By the early 1950s, every party and organization formally acknowledged SED supremacy. Functionaries who refused such loyalty were forced out in campaigns against 'reactionary, backward elements', or saw the impossibility of opposition and simply withdrew, sometimes to western Germany.

The GDR's establishment on 7 October 1949 further guaranteed SED power as the constitution outlawed attacks on 'democratic' institutions and politicians, creating a legal framework to neutralize opponents. Media control, underpinned by a licensing system, was also firmly in the 'democratic' hands of SED trustees.

The unity principle behind SED control also underpinned the electoral and government systems. Officially to prevent fascism's re-emergence, the Democratic Bloc parties and organizations presented a joint electoral ticket; the distribution of seats in the Volkskammer ('People's Chamber') was agreed beforehand. The population simply voted for or against the unity list. As those using the available, but usually inaccessible, booths were suspected of voting against the official candidates and therefore against democracy, even the first 'unity' elections of 1950 achieved a 'Yes' vote of 99.72 per cent on a 98.73 per cent turnout, a precedent which endured (largely without manipulating results) until 1989. Referenda in the 1950s merely underlined these structural parallels to the Third Reich.

Though the GDR's structures resembled a parliamentary democracy (People's

Table 19.1(a)   Distribution of seats in the Volkskammer, 1963–1989

Party	Seats	%
SED (Socialist Unity Party)	127	25.4
FDGB (trades union)	68	13.6
FDJ (youth organization)	40	8.0
DFD (women's organization)	35	7.0
Cultural League	22	4.4
CDU (Christian Democratic Union)	52	10.4
LDPD (Liberal Democratic Party)	52	10.4
NDPD (National Democratic Party)	52	10.4
DBD (Democratic Farmers' Party)	52	10.4

Source: DDR Handbuch, vol. 2 (Cologne: Verlag Wissenschaft und Politik, 1985), p. 1440.

Table 19.1(b)   How the SED actually enjoyed a majority in the Volkskammer: many members of the mass organizations were also SED members

Party	Seats	%
SED	271	54.2
CDU	54	10.8
LDPD	52	10.4
NDPD	54	10.8
DBD	52	10.4
Members of no party	17	3.4

Source: DDR Handbuch, vol. 2 (Cologne: Verlag Wissenschaft und Politik, 1985), p. 1440.

Chamber, prime minister, president/Council of State), in practice the state apparatus merely shadowed the SED's own organization, which included policy departments equivalent to every ministry. This apparatus developed policy initiatives which were formally proposed to the government and parliament. In line with party discipline, which bound every member to execute party policies, the SED's government officials then implemented party decisions. This system of party control was repeated at regional and district level and guaranteed by 'democratic centralism', which required every level of party and state to obey decisions taken higher up. Thus the GDR's power structures varied significantly from the Third Reich's comparatively shambolic organization (see Chapter 16, above). The close cooperation of state and party bodies, the frequent interchange of personnel between both hierarchies and the marriage of state and party functions in key officials at each level generally ensured party superiority over the state without conflict. The Third Reich's competing offices and unclear command lines were replaced with a plurality of strictly ordered vertical hierarchies (SED, state, mass organizations, bloc parties), within which the SED hierarchy was ultimately paramount. The system did not depend on a leadership personality: neither Ulbricht nor Honecker presented himself as a charismatic leader comparable to Hitler, though the trappings of status (e.g., portraits in public buildings and newspapers) continued a long tradition, not peculiar to Germany. By the Honecker era these structures had stabilized and stagnated. Administratively, the country was effectively on automatic pilot.

However, despite the SED's cleansing and the other parties' and organizations' avowals of loyalty, many still preferred different options. In the late 1940s and early 1950s, before the system stabilized, many spoke out in local meetings. Within the SED, however, the principle of 'party discipline' was so established that most critics nonetheless supported the national leadership. An atmosphere of intimidation based on internal party cleansings and the developing Stasi progressively neutralized most waverers, at least publicly. The SED leadership's control over its apparatus and its allies was, however, never total inasmuch as many instructions were never realized by often inefficient or apathetic local groups. Although this undermined SED attempts at totalitarian rule, before 1989 it never threatened the party's overall authority.

Two further factors enhanced the SED's early hegemony. First, many East Germans loyally supported socialism and were not yet disillusioned by later political and economic crises. Second, most Germans were initially too concerned with rebuilding their lives to take much interest in politics. When normality returned, the political structures were already so entrenched that most people could only act within them. This was, for many, the price of defeat and occupation.

II The road to socialism

As noted above, Marxism identified capitalism as the principal precursor of fascism; consequently capitalism must be eradicated. Over 20 years eastern Germany was transformed and divided from western Germany.

In 1945–46 a thorough land reform was enacted, and business owners with Nazi connections and wartime profiteers forfeited their firms, which were nationalized, along with banks and essential industries, or became 'Soviet limited companies'. Thus some 40 per cent of East Germany's industrial capacity came under state control. These economic changes heralded radical socialist development. The new SED-controlled economic ministries extended party influence beyond the purely political arena.

From July 1948 the zone's economy was coordinated in overly ambitious central plans, though the attempt was fraught with difficulties. As trade with the West faltered following the 1948 currency division, the GDR attempted greater autarky by establishing a new heavy industrial sector alongside huge projects to mine the inferior brown coal, its only abundant natural resource, and to replace wartime building losses. Such major investment in heavy industry and mechanical engineering left little capacity for consumer needs. Increasing demands were made on workers, who were encouraged to work extra shifts and to continually overfulfil production targets while food and other commodities remained in short supply and often expensive. Few workers identified with a workers' government which appeared to exploit them.

In July 1952 Ulbricht announced 'the building of socialism', predicting a 'class struggle' against opponents of socialism's historic mission. Various austerity policies were introduced and farmers who resisted the agricultural cooperatives (LPGs) paid tax penalties; food shortages worsened as some farmers fled before collectivization. The SED also introduced Marxist–Leninist school curricula, strengthened border security and undermined churches' influence over young people.

Most contentious was the unremunerated 10 per cent productivity increase with which the 'workers' government' incensed most workers. The SED stuck rigidly to this policy, despite eventually rescinding (at Soviet insistence) the other harsh measures introduced since July 1952. When a group of builders marched on the GDR's ministry building they were joined by thousands of disgruntled Berlin workers for whom the productivity demands were the final straw after years of toil for little reward. Though the government reluctantly recanted, these protests provoked widespread uprisings the following day, 17 June 1953. Though most rioting occurred in Berlin, many other areas were affected by strikes (though only a minority participated). Some SED offices were ransacked and members feared to display their party badges. The demonstrators were originally enraged by the 10 per cent quota increase and poor living standards, but many quickly demanded German unity and the SED leadership's removal, effectively questioning the GDR's socialist identity. However, no natural leaders emerged, reflecting the SED's successful monopolization of political structures and opportunities, and the police efficiently dealt with individual ringleaders. Finally Soviet tanks suppressed the uprising.

The 1953 uprising clearly demonstrated the importance of Soviet military presence in upholding SED power. Nonetheless, once the initial uprising was quashed normality quickly returned. Already many party and state careers depended on the GDR's continued existence, and many activists remained loyal to the state's anti-fascist credentials, though few believed the official explanation of the uprising as a Western-inspired counter-revolutionary *putsch* attempt. Within the party, and therefore state, leadership the uprising ironically strengthened Ulbricht's position against a grouping in the party hierarchy plotting his removal. As Moscow was unwilling to appear to be surrendering to the demonstrators, the SED's leader was secure. In any case, Ulbricht's SED opponents mainly did not wish to endanger the party's rule.

SED hegemony was never seriously challenged again before 1989. Both party and people learned from the events. Those who had hoped to contest the political system guaranteed by the USSR's occupation rights acknowledged the SED's strength and either left the country or, more commonly, resigned themselves to the situation. Disturbances elsewhere (Hungary and Poland in 1956, Czechoslovakia in 1968) caused significant ripples of dissent (particularly among intellectuals and the young, though mainly not workers) but no organized opposition, arguably because of the residual fear Soviet tanks had inculcated in 1953. Yet popular perceptions of SED rule were not exclusively and negatively shaped by 17 June 1953 until the autumn of 1989. The rebellion's crushing did not imply that most GDR citizens spent 36 more years awaiting, let alone plotting, the SED's downfall. While 17 June 1953 clearly established the boundaries of permissible political activity in the national consciousness, popular reactions and behaviour patterns were also shaped by later consolidative developments, notably improving living conditions, the emergence of a generally reliable

Figure 19.2 Numbers leaving the GDR, 1949–1961
*1961 value refers to January–August only

welfare state and better career prospects. As Niemann has pointed out, far fewer people left the GDR after 1953. Skilled workers were particularly underrepresented among those arriving in the West. The 1953 uprising effectively cleared the air.

Meanwhile the SED developed arguably less abrasive methods of achieving its social, political and economic aims after June 1953, though the essential structures remained. Although some economic progress was achieved and living standards rose, they lagged behind the FRG's (always the GDR population's reference point). Political motivations apart, this lack of relative prosperity still caused hundreds of thousands to emigrate every year. The GDR economy could not survive this manpower loss indefinitely. As most of those 'fleeing the republic' left via the open border to West Berlin (the borders to the FRG were closed in 1952) Ulbricht recommended to the Soviet leader, Khrushchev, that the border to West Berlin also be sealed. Thus the Berlin Wall was erected on 12–13 August 1961 and travel to the West was forbidden to most GDR citizens until 1989.

Although the Berlin Wall was viewed internationally as an admission of failure by the GDR and Soviet governments, some GDR citizens, alarmed by the open border's potential dangers, initially welcomed it. Few imagined the Wall's longevity. Though a radical measure against previous failures, it secured new successes. The economic progress of the late 1950s was consolidated by a more stable labour market, more reliable economic planning, and a growing popular acceptance that, with the borders closed, one might as well make the best of things.

Meanwhile, the building of socialism progressed apace. Destalinization after 1956 notwithstanding, Ulbricht succeeded in ousting the remaining threats to his power within the SED hierarchy by 1958. Following industrial socialization during the 1950s agriculture was almost totally collectivized in 1960, with farmers' widespread opposition overcome by a concerted campaign by party and state agitators and Stasi threats. Small traders, artisans and service industry businesses were also encouraged to join cooperatives. (The final wave of socialization overtook small businesses in 1972.) Economic socialization and collectivization gave the SED-controlled ministries more direct power, while stifling private initiative and potential economic pluralism. An attempt to allow groups of 'People's Own Companies' (*Volkseigene Betriebe*, VEBs) more autonomy in the 'New Economic System' of 1963 was abandoned in 1970 as the SED realized that it was undermining its political control.

Not content with socializing the economy, Ulbricht also attempted popular ideological conversion. Though his attempt to impose Ten Socialist Commandments in 1958 was mainly unsuccessful, the more dedicated shunned religious ceremonies to perform socialist naming ceremonies and socialist burials. More effective was the education system's overhaul. Within the obligatory ten-class 'polytechnical' system, all pupils studied Marxism–Leninism and visited workplaces to experience socialist economics and working methods. Marxism–Leninism also became obligatory in higher education. The introduction of national service in 1962 exposed all young men to socialist ideology for a further 18 months. The SED isolated the churches from young people by

Illustration 19.2   Walter Ulbricht during a visit to a pioneer camp on the International Day of
the Child, 1 June 1962

effectively banning religious education in state schools and introducing a secular com-
ing-of-age ceremony, the *Jugendweihe*, in which young people pledged themselves to
the socialist fatherland, its leading party and its (atheist) ideology. Practically all young
people participated in this ceremony by the late 1950s. Though the SED successfully
distanced much of the population from religion, commitment to socialism was only
superficially achieved, and began to disintegrate in the deteriorating economic situation of the mid-1980s.

In all areas of state and society, including the legal system, socialist measures were
introduced during the 1950s and 1960s. Finally a new constitution was promulgated
in 1968, defining the GDR as a 'socialist state' and legally enshrining the SED's leading role. The new constitution preceded the replacement in 1971 of the ageing
Ulbricht as SED First Secretary by Erich Honecker. His accession was greeted opti-
mistically, and coincided with the FRG's new *Ostpolitik*, enabling the GDR's increasing international recognition. The SED's failure, however, to implement the human
rights stipulations of the 1975 Helsinki Accord, designed to ensure freedom of movement between countries, was regarded with disappointment and bitterness by many, as

was the 1976 cultural crackdown, in marked contrast to Honecker's original protestation of 'no taboos' in cultural life.

Honecker aimed to maintain the SED's power monopoly, but attracted unfavourable comparisons with Gorbachov's reformist Soviet Communist Party after 1985. Under Honecker, political life became routine, punctuated every five years by SED congresses which simply re-elected the leadership. Political objectives and legitimations remained unchanged; the leadership grew older; life simply continued. Honecker did, however, embark on an ambitious programme to improve living standards. Subsidies for essential goods and social security benefits were increased. The highlight was a scheme to provide modern housing: by the late 1980s the SED claimed to have built or modernized three million flats.

These popular schemes with tangible results were, however, highly costly and exacerbated a financial crisis. The failure of economic reform in the late 1960s and the concentration of resources in a few new technologies left the GDR economically unstable. High social welfare costs, alongside draining commitments to defence and inflated bureaucracies, resulted in neglect of capital maintenance and investment. Rising fuel costs in the mid-1970s aggravated the GDR's indebtedness. The country was living beyond its means and even substantial foreign loans only temporarily alleviated the situation, while the long-term causes were not addressed. Though socialism was financially imperilled by the 1980s, the population hardly noticed the deepening crisis as Honecker maintained his social policies, ignoring the debt mountain. Meanwhile, popular opposition emerged, particularly directed at the environmental costs of the attempts to avert economic collapse; even within the party apparatus alternative economic policies were formulated in the late 1980s. The leadership, however, resisted calls for economic liberalization, fearing the ramifications for SED power. Worsening economic conditions and the GDR's indebtedness clearly helped provoke the 1989 uprisings and the state's eventual collapse.

III Winning hearts and minds

We have seen how the post-war situation and SED policies created a costly 'real existing socialism' within a political straitjacket. What of the millions within this system? The sudden collapse of 1989–90 suggests that GDR citizens shared the predominant Western evaluation of an illegitimate state imposing its ideology on an unwilling population. However, widespread GDR nostalgia subsequently emerged, not only amongst the recently disempowered carriers of the system. Initially, unification created bitterness amongst many East Germans who wished to contribute to a united Germany and felt their life's work was being ignored. Relatively strong support for the Party of Democratic Socialism (PDS) and the contrast with the clear support for radical change during 1989–90 suggest a more complex relationship of citizens to state and party than simple resentment.

It is perhaps often forgotten that Germany in 1945 was a defeated nation, expecting to pay for defeat. Furthermore, although many East Germans feared Soviet occupation and associated the KPD/SED with it, some still venerating Hitler, many others hated Nazism and welcomed the opportunity to start afresh. Most Germans therefore initially felt obliged to tolerate the new regime, while a significant proportion actively supported an anti-fascist and/or socialist future. Encouraged by land reform and nationalization, optimism gripped many East Germans. Most, detached from developments in the West, viewed their zone's early development as a logical progression; the extent of SED hegemony was not immediately apparent (though some quickly drew parallels with the NSDAP's power mechanisms).

Public opinion reports rarely mention the GDR's legitimacy directly, though the GDR's foundation was welcomed by many who erroneously hoped it would ease eventual German unification. However, in the 1950s there were frequent reports of individuals who regarded Adenauer as Germany's true leader or who revered their 'Führer, Adolf Hitler'. General optimism about German unity persisted into the 1960s, encouraged by the SED, though the population often complained that socialist policies deepened Germany's division. Those expelled from Germany's eastern territories long resisted emotional integration with the GDR. Thus, many citizens failed to identify closely with the state they accepted in practice. GDR identity and socialist commitment were closely linked, but the German question was never forgotten. In a 1968 survey 65 per cent of East Germans regarded the GDR as their fatherland, but 33 per cent still thought of 'Germany' first.[7] During the 1970s and 1980s only about 50 per cent of young people identified with the GDR, and during the 1980s, particularly post-Gorbachov, Marxist–Leninist commitment declined sharply.[8] Even SED functionaries recognized in 1989, as socialism was overthrown, that a non-socialist GDR had no legitimate role.

Some historians believe that East Germans learned how to behave under a dictatorship during the Third Reich and therefore accepted the GDR more readily. This thesis is supported by early opinion reports which reveal much popular cynicism. Agricultural collectivization was predicted, long before 1960, by landworkers suspicious of communism. Many felt they would gain little from protesting, as the ruling party was bound to win. Rumours predicting the worst regularly spread in the 1950s and 1960s. During international crises panic buying occurred alongside rumours that 'the war' had started. In the earliest years youngsters on work camps or outings were sometimes reported to have been deported to Siberia. That such erroneous reports were widely regarded as part of the natural order suggests both that many did not regard their country as a normal democracy and that they were resigned to their fate. The lesson of the Third Reich and the post-war imposition of socialism seemed to be that one must accept the prevailing political atmosphere while hoping for change; the Hungarian uprising produced little open protest in the GDR but much unwarranted optimism about impending reform.

Nevertheless, opposition also existed alongside resignation. The expulsions from the border areas in 1952–3 outraged many, while the *Jugendweihe*'s introduction was fiercely opposed by active church-goers. Anti-SED graffiti, swastikas and oppositional leaflets regularly appeared, particularly in the earlier years. However, open opposition was relatively rare and concentrated on specific grievances and everyday conditions rather than existential questions. Only once, in 1953, did this ill feeling develop into a general uprising. Otherwise the widespread resentment was experienced individually rather than collectively. The standard SED line that the economic difficulties were principally bequeathed by Hitler did not impress a population aware even after 1961, via Western television and other sources, of considerably better conditions in the FRG. Travel restrictions were themselves a long-standing irritant.

Despite the daily annoyances and restrictions on freedom of movement, most GDR citizens accepted their situation and lived within it. Like people everywhere, they built families and strove to further their careers and improve their surroundings. The population was encouraged to be active within the SED-dominated social and political framework, and involvement in the organizations and political parties was taken to indicate support for the SED and socialism. However, the genuinely popular mass organization activities generally involved sport, holidays or other material advantages and cannot imply ideological commitment to the SED; those desiring personal advancement could not exclude themselves from the FDJ or FDGB, nor refuse national service. The mass organizations' rapid collapse in 1989–90 demonstrated that most members lacked true devotion. The huge votes for the Westernized CDU and the long-derided social democracy in March 1990 suggested that 40 years of ideological education and propaganda had hardly affected most East Germans.

In the early years most non-socialists simply distanced themselves from the mass organizations which were run by a small, overburdened nucleus. As career opportunities became increasingly dependent on socialist commitment through 'social activity', most people began to participate, but once they had gone through the motions they withdrew into a world which neglected SED values. Before 1961 it was still possible to leave the GDR, but thereafter there remained only internal emigration, centred on family life and, increasingly, Western television. Under Honecker the SED tacitly accepted that complete control, the hallmark of true totalitarianism, was impossible, and the SED even came to accept the population's essentially apolitical nature. The pressure to display constant socialist commitment diminished; even Western television became less of a taboo. Thus was established the 'niche society' in which most people, and even many SED members, combined public conformity and private indifference. By the 1980s, over two million were party members, but despite ideological training many were principally motivated by career development and outward appearances. The sharp membership decline during 1989–90 demonstrated the opportunism: the PDS retained only 10 per cent of its members.

The SED achieved little more than socialization to particular behavioural norms. The population grew accustomed to comprehensive kindergarten provision, FDGB holidays, workplace collectives, and to flag parades on national holidays. The SED even succeeded in divorcing most people from active Christianity. Certainly the population grew accustomed to 'real socialism', but general acceptance of broad socialist principles did not imply support for the SED once alternatives became possible. Had the bulk of the population been truly committed to socialism, instead of paying lip service to it for want of other options, the collapse of 1989–90 could never have occurred.

Alongside the true believers, the opportunists and the apolitical majority were those who consistently opposed SED rule. Initially these were mainly groups who lost status from the economic reorganization, but also traditional conservatives and liberals, many moderate social democrats, and unrepentant Nazis. The SED presented its opponents as a threat to anti-fascist democracy and established vigorous police control and repression to counter opposition, however mild, by groups or individuals.

Alongside the Soviet troops, which were particularly active in the first years, the principal organ was the Stasi, which considered itself the 'shield and sword of the party'. The Stasi infiltrated practically every sphere of life with undercover officers or 'informal colleagues' who reported dissident comments or activities. Knowledge of the Stasi's potential omnipresence prevented the public expression of most negative opinion and stifled much opposition at birth. The Stasi also actively coerced individuals and groups to loyalty to the SED. Even the churches, the only permitted organizations outside direct SED control, were infiltrated by Stasi officers.

The Stasi was ultimately unable to prevent the emergence in the 1970s and 1980s of new, more politically dangerous opponents angered by the contradiction between the SED's avowed peace policy and the GDR's role in the arms race, and by ecologists concerned about cavalier environmental policies. Protest also focused on human rights issues. Most dangerously, these opponents often appropriated socialist terminology, challenging the SED's ideological monopoly. In the 1980s many pastors allowed opposition meetings in the sanctuary of church buildings and made the churches' internal communications systems available. Though the Stasi succeeded in infiltrating many groups, it could not prevent enthusiasm for nuclear disarmament and environmentalism spreading amongst younger people for whom the SED's original anti-fascist legitimations appeared increasingly irrelevant.

Though the peace and environmental groups became known in the GDR, thanks largely to the Western media, hindsight has often overestimated their importance. The groups' significance lay in their very existence as assembly points for the mass protests of late 1989. Public protests such as those in Leipzig in early 1988, though small-scale, demonstrated that not all opposition could be doused. However, the vast majority did not participate in such protests and remained unconcerned by the issues involved, reflecting the Stasi's enduring intimidatory strength and the abiding memory of June 1953. Despite widespread dissatisfaction among many of the inactive, for most citizens the causes remained linked to the increasing difficulties of everyday life and the continuing arbitrariness of bureaucratic decisions, particularly concerning visits to the West.

IV Conclusions

In hindsight, it seems indisputable that the GDR's existence was guaranteed only for as long as this coincided with the USSR's interests and the Berlin Wall protected the economy against a mass exodus to the West. The repressed dissatisfaction felt by many who never openly protested before 1989 is reflected not only in the many applications for exit visas despite the personal disadvantages of such applications, but also in the rush to emigrate via Hungary in 1989. Nonetheless, most of those already holidaying in Hungary when the borders opened returned home. Despite real socialism's difficulties, the GDR had become a home. While German unification or the end of SED rule seemed impossible, most people were prepared to live and work within the framework, and a significant proportion were dedicated to preserving it. Over 40 years a common identity developed; many citizens experienced pride in their country's achievements, without necessarily supporting the SED. The dichotomy between GDR identity and rejection of the SED found expression after 1989 in GDR nostalgia alongside the majority's clear desire to abandon 'real socialism'. This sense of community, fostered in adversity, must principally explain the GDR's enduring stability within the context of divided Europe, despite the distance between the SED and many of its subjects.

In explaining the GDR's relative long-term stability we must not neglect the many sincere adherents of socialism. The KPD/SED's claims to anti-fascist legitimacy achieved widespread acceptance both inside and outside the party, particularly immediately after 1945 when many saw salvation in a socialist future which would outlaw fascism; many felt the end was far more important than the means. Even in the early 1960s many remained optimistic that the SED could successfully build socialism and that the future belonged to the GDR, not the FRG. Only later, when the power structures and behaviour patterns were already established, was it apparent that socialism would not bring great material welfare. Many socialists nonetheless remained committed to the SED and almost unquestioningly accepted that a return to capitalism would mean less social welfare and raise the spectre of a fascist revival. This dedication to socialism was shared by many in the security services. Their role, alongside those who served the party and state apparatus for more opportunistic reasons, should not be overlooked. A stable GDR would not have survived for long if the majority of the population had continually and actively opposed it. This was a dictatorship in which many connived and with which most made their peace. So ingrained was the system after 40 years that even many who instigated the 1989 revolution envisaged reforming rather than overthrowing the GDR, which they hoped would retain a form of socialism. Against this background, questions of guilt and responsibility for the GDR as a political entity seem misplaced.

It is tempting to assume that the GDR was doomed to failure almost from the outset as a state founded and maintained against the will of its subjects. Certainly the GDR can be regarded as a dictatorship: the SED leadership and its many loyal and disciplined agents exerted fierce control over the rest of the population's lives, from frustrating careers to shooting would-be escapees at the border. However, historians who regard the June 1953 revolt as the root of eventual collapse neglect the fact that it was after 1953, if not 1961, that the GDR properly stabilized, at least in terms of individuals' outward conformity, if not of their inner commitment. The later economic collapse resulted from external pressures as well as the SED's economic mismanagement, which sacrificed much to ideological demands and the USSR's interests, even when these clashed with the GDR's. Meanwhile, social and political stability essentially remained until Gorbachov's accession in the USSR, his policies wilfully refuted, despite popular aspirations to a freer society, by Honecker, who correctly perceived in them the seeds of the system's destruction. Ultimately it was this external impetus which disrupted and ended SED rule in 1989, just as it had established it 43 years earlier.

Notes:

1. Deutscher Bundestag, 12. Wahlperiode 12/7820, 31.5.1994, 'Bericht der Enquete-Kommission, 'Aufarbeitung von Geschichte und Folgen der SED-Diktatur in Deutschland', p. 5.
2. *Ibid.*
3. See, for example, *ibid.* pp. 24–7, 33.
4. *Ansichten zur Geschichte der DDR* (1994), vol. 5, p. 7 (italics added).
5. Mitter, A., and Wolle, S., *Untergang auf Raten* (1993), p. 551.
6. Leonhard, W., *Die Revolution entläßt ihre Kinder* (1990), p. 440.
7. Niemann, Heinz, *Meinungsforschung in der DDR* (1993), p. 323.
8. Henderson, K., 'The Search for Ideological Conformity', *German History*, 10:3 (1992), pp. 321–2.

Select bibliography

Baring, A., *Uprising in East Germany* (New York: Cornell University Press, 1972).

Černý, J., Keller, D., and Neuhaus, M., *Ansichten zur Geschichte der DDR* (Eggersdorf: Verlag Matthias Kirchner, 1994).

Childs, D., ed., *Honecker's Germany* (London: Allen and Unwin, 1985).

Childs, D., *The GDR. Moscow's German Ally* (London: Unwin Hyman, second edition, 1988).

Dennis, M., *German Democratic Republic. Politics, Economics and Society* (London: Pinter Publishers, 1988).

Fulbrook, M., *The Divided Nation: Germany 1918–1990* (London: Fontana, 1991).

Fulbrook, M., *The Two Germanies 1945–1990. Problems of Interpretation* (Basingstoke: Macmillan, 1992).

Fulbrook, M., *Anatomy of a Dictatorship. Inside the GDR 1949–1989* (Oxford: Oxford University Press, 1995).

McCauley, M., *The GDR since 1945* (London: Macmillan, 1983).

Niemann, H. *Meinungs-forschung in der DDR: Die geheimen Berichte des Instituts für Meinungs forschung an das Politbüro der SED* (Cologne: Bund-Verlag, 1993).

Scharf, C.B., *Politics and Change in East Germany* (Boulder, CO: Westview Press, 1984).

Sontheimer, K., and Bleek, W., *The Government and Politics of East Germany* (London: Hutchinson, 1975).

Staritz, D., *Geschichte der DDR, 1949–1985* (Frankfurt am Main: Suhrkamp, 1985).

Thomanek, J.K.A., and Mellis, J., eds., *Politics, Society and Government in the German Democratic Republic: Basic Documents* (Oxford, New York, Munich: Berg, 1988).

Weber, H., *DDR: Dokumente, 1945–1985* (Munich: dtv, 1986).

Weber, H., *Die DDR 1945–1986* (Munich: Oldenbourg, 1988).

Woods, R., *Opposition in the GDR under Honecker, 1971–85* (London: Macmillan, 1986).

20

Ossis and *Wessis*: the creation of two German societies

Mary Fulbrook

German society after the war was in a state of crisis. The images of ruined sky-lines, jagged shells of hollow buildings etched against the sky, and women and children in rags pushing cartloads of possessions through the heaps of rubble, are perhaps the most compelling visual summaries of this moment. Demographically, it was utterly skewed by the loss of men in the war (see Figure 20.1). German society was also a society on the move. The shifting of the eastern border to the Oder–Neisse frontier, and the loss of territories further east to the Soviet Union and Poland, unleashed the greatest population migration in central Europe for several centuries – a migration which had already started in the closing months of the war, as Germans fled in front of the advancing Red Army. And while refugees and expellees trekked westwards, numerous displaced persons, former prisoners of war, foreign workers and forced labourers, sought to return to their homes. In the first decade after the end of the war, around 12 million people who had formerly lived elsewhere were accommodated on the soil of West Germany – around one-fifth of the population of the Federal Republic were essentially 'immigrants'.

Nearly half a century later, when the Berlin Wall, that infamous symbol of the Cold War, was finally breached on 9 November 1989, Germans celebrated a sense of national reunification. Yet, within days – even hours – of the opening of the Wall, it became clear that West and East Germans had effectively become strangers to one another. Affluent, fashion-conscious Westerners gazed at East Germans in jeans and cheap black leather jackets queueing eagerly for taken-for-granted Western goods such as bananas, oranges and stereo equipment. The differences were symbolized by the cars characteristic of each side: BMWs and Volkswagens versus Wartburgs and Trabants. Jokes about Trabis and bananas, about Deutschmark nationalism and the elbow society, proliferated as East and West Germans realised how little they appeared to have in common. The contrasts were not only with each other, but also with the

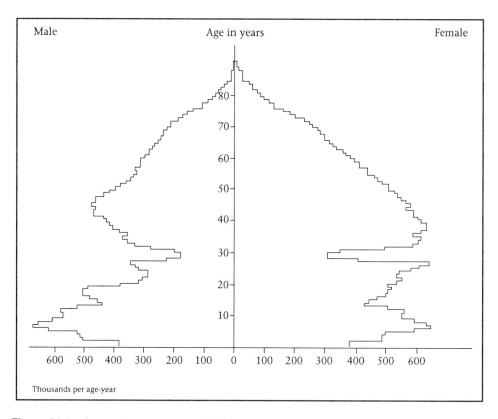

Figure 20.1   Age and sex structure, 1946

common past. Both German societies had changed a great deal since the early post-war days.

There is as yet no established set of controversies over the comparative social history of the two Germanies – indeed, there is as yet no synthesis of East German social history at all, as relevant research materials have only become available since unification. Both public and scholarly attention has tended to focus on the political structures of the dictatorship. Any new approach to East German social history must both take seriously the impact of this dictatorship on society – indeed, the very deep impregnation of society by the state – but at the same time examine the ways in which society was resistant to political intrusion, or changed in directions which were unintended by the regime. This chapter first sketches general changes in the overall shape of society in the two German states, and then looks at the impact of these societal changes on different groups within society.

Illustration 20.1 Refugees and expellees on treks from the eastern provinces into the western occupation zones, 1945

I Political division and societal history

Key societal differences were initially effected by the occupying powers. In the West, for all the problems with the term 'restoration', continuity rather than change was the rule. Although the major war criminals were brought to some kind of justice at the Nuremberg Trials, the more general denazification policies were of little long-term effect. By March 1946, denazification had been reduced to a matter of individual self-justification, and the process was essentially wound up with few long-term effects by the early 1950s. Similarly, by 1946 Britain and the USA had come to the view that it was in their interest to rebuild the West German economy. The announcement of the Marshall Plan in June 1947, and the introduction of the currency reform on 20 June 1948, consolidated this shift. There was only minimal restructuring of the capitalist system. Pressures for socialization of the mining industry were resisted and the measures proposed by the *Land* governments of Hesse and North-Rhine-Westphalia were vetoed. Despite an early determination to break up the highly cartelised German economy, there was effective resistance on the part of German entrepreneurs. The 'social market economy' associated with West Germany's first Economics Minister, Ludwig

Erhard, differed in many respects from the much more state-directed economy of Nazi Germany; nevertheless, general continuities in the capitalist industrial system as a whole are more striking than specific differences.

Meanwhile, far more radical measures for restructuring were effected in the Soviet zone. In September 1945, about 7,000 agricultural estates of over 100 hectares (around 250 acres) in size were expropriated from their previous owners, and the land was divided and redistributed as small peasant plots or taken into state-owned farms. This land reform laid the basis for later collectivization of East German agriculture, and abolished the economic base – and the very existence – of the historically significant Prussian Junker class. Similarly drastic measures were adopted with respect to industry and finance, starting with the centralization of banking and insurance in July 1945. Over the following two years, many major industrial enterprises were expropriated (partly legitimated by a plebiscite in Saxony in 1946). Some industrial enterprises were taken into Soviet ownership as joint-stock companies (SAGs) as a part of their reparations policy; others became, from April 1948, state-owned *Volkseigene Betriebe* (VEBs). The SAGs were phased into East German state ownership as VEBs from 1949 to 1954. At the same time, denazification policies were deployed as a means to achieve significant shifts in personnel, particularly in areas which were of strategic political importance.

With the creation of two separate German states in 1949, early divergences were consolidated. West Germany was – primarily for political reasons at the start – tied into Western European economic arrangements (starting with the European Coal and Steel Community) which were the precursors of the European Economic Community in 1957 (later the European Community and eventually the European Union). In the 1950s the Federal Republic enjoyed its renowned 'economic miracle', with average annual growth rates of around 8 per cent. The early, rapid economic growth began to stabilize, and even falter, in the mid-1960s, and the German economy was adversely affected by the oil crises of 1973 and 1979 and the more general recession of the 1980s. Nevertheless, the West German economy continued to perform strongly in comparative terms, with the Deutschmark – almost a national monument – providing a benchmark of currency stability in Europe.

Economic development was accompanied by significant shifts in West German social structure. The old, heavy industries of the Ruhr were displaced in significance by the rise of high-tech industries. The European Common Agricultural Policy was accompanied by a decline in the proportion of the population working on the land. Thus the traditional blue-collar and agricultural sectors of society shrank in proportion to the number of white-collar workers and those employed in the service sector. From the later 1950s, but particularly after the flow of refugees from the GDR was stemmed by the erection of the Berlin Wall in 1961, there was a significant influx of foreign labour from the Mediterranean countries. By the late 1980s, West German society was marked by a combination of widespread affluence with pockets of poverty, particularly among the 'guest worker' communities. It was a much more urbanized society, with a majority of the population living in cities or large towns. It was, too, an ageing society: a declining birth rate, and the rising life expectancies of an older generation, put in jeopardy the implicit social contract of the insurance schemes covering West German health and well-being from cradle to grave.

The East German regime, under the leadership of the Communist SED, energetically pursued policies designed to transform the structure of East German society in rather different directions. In the summer of 1952, the building of socialism was announced. This included the first wave of the collectivization of agriculture, followed in 1960 by a second wave. By the later 1960s, most of the agriculturally productive land in the GDR was in fully collectivized farms (LPGs), which became increasingly specialized in the course of the 1970s and 1980s. At the same time, industry was subjected to state ownership and central planning and control. While major industrial enterprises had already been expropriated during the occupation period, in the 1950s remaining private enterprises were subjected to adverse, discriminatory measures, such that they shrank to a relatively insignificant sector of the East German economy. In

Illustration 20.2   A new 'production collective' of turners and button-makers is founded on 25 June 1958 at the House of Artisans in Berlin. Collectives were awarded a high priority in East German life and outward conformity and enthusiastic assent were expected of individuals

1958, many small enterprises were transformed into a rather curious category of mixed enterprises 'with state participation'; in 1972 these mixed enterprises were finally taken into state ownership. Only a few artisanal occupations remained in private hands in the 1970s and 1980s. Centralized economic planning was reformed in the New Economic System (NES) introduced in 1963, which gave more leverage to intermediate management levels. The political backwash of 1968 led, however, to a recentralization of the East German economy from 1970, although with a higher degree of specialization and more importance attached to consumer goods than was evident in the 1950s. Attention was focused on adequate housing and social policies.

Honecker's proclaimed 'unity of economic and social policy' was, however, ill-equipped to face the international economic crises of the 1970s and 1980s. The GDR had a number of advantages due to its unique situation in the Soviet bloc as a kind of stowaway in the EEC and poor twin of the affluent West. The GDR's economic difficulties were nevertheless only massaged and camouflaged, not cured, by injections of Western help such as the Strauß credit of 1983; and Honecker was increasingly unwilling to face up to the real economic problems. From the early 1980s, evidence of economic decline and, indeed, impending national bankruptcy, was largely ignored, as Honecker pursued his own blinkered policies at the expense of sober proposals for achieving economic viability. From both above and below, recognition of growing economic and environmental damage played a role in the implosion of the GDR in late 1989.

Differences in economic organization and levels of material affluence were not the only important factors shaping societal divergence. Just as important were differences in state/society relations. While West Germans enjoyed a diversity of political parties, social institutions, leisure clubs and so on, in East Germany the ruling communist party, the SED, sought to dominate society through state-run organizations. There was no area of work, social life or leisure which was not in some way controlled by one of the official institutions of party and state. The only partial exceptions were the churches, which, after an early period of persecution and hostility, eventually enjoyed a unique status as officially tolerated (if politically constrained) 'autonomous social institutions in socialist society'. The deep penetration of East German society by the communist state was established with some difficulty in the 1950s, but was one of the keys to the apparent stability of East German society from the 1960s to the early 1980s.

Thus, over the 40 years from the foundation of the two states in 1949 to the collapse of communist domination in the GDR in 1989, major differences in political systems, regime policies, and roles in the international system had produced indelible marks on the two German societies. At the same time, secular trends – industrialization, mechanization, the shift away from heavy industry and from labour-intensive agricultural techniques, the expansion of the service sector, the growth of computer technologies – led to certain lines of development shared, although at different speeds and to different extents, by the two German societies (see Figures 20.2 and 20.3). What was the impact of these wider trends and broader contexts on the constitution of particular social groups?

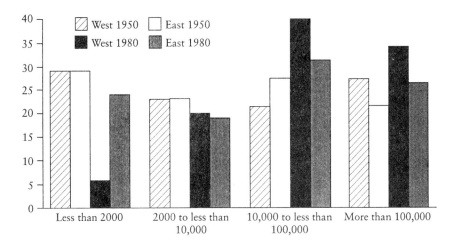

Figure 20.2 Percentage of the population living in communities of different sizes in East and West Germany, 1950 and 1980

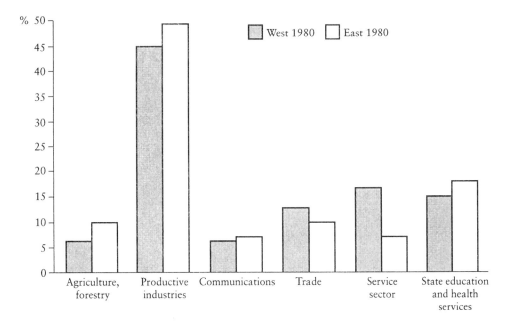

Figure 20.3 Employment by occupation type in East and West Germany (%)

II Elites and 'middle classes'

Striking differences in the social history of the two Germanies are evident among the more privileged and elite groups. Despite the theoretical 'dictatorship of the proletariat' and associated 'withering away of the state' predicted in Marx's theory of pure communism, the actually existing GDR found itself in the 'transitional stage' of a Marxist–Leninist dictatorship of the vanguard communist party. And despite the theoretical equality of citizens in a Western democracy, real power, wealth and privilege remained unequally distributed in the Federal Republic of Germany.

At the apex of GDR society were, undoubtedly, the political bigwigs. Top politicians enjoyed a lifestyle and privileges to which the majority of the population were denied access. Many lived in the exclusive compound of Wandlitz, a little way north of Berlin, where – within walls – they could enjoy a relatively luxurious lifestyle, with Western goods available in well-stocked supermarkets, and leisure and sports facilities denied to the rest of the population. This compound was popularly known as Volvograd, on account of the chauffeur-driven Volvos; top individuals also had a variety of other 'perks of the job', such as exclusive hunting lodges and private country retreats, which (although essentially modest and petty-bourgeois by Western standards) unleashed a good deal of fury among East Germans when revealed in late 1989.

Below the truly powerful elite were far larger numbers of political and organizational functionaries, or official carriers of the regime. Closely associated with and under the control of the ruling communist SED were the affiliated bloc parties and mass organizations, the various levels of state and government, and the organs of control and coercion (see Chapter 19, above). The officials of these organizations formed a broader, but still relatively closely defined, functional elite under central SED control. Promising young people might find themselves caught in a complex situation: upward mobility was inevitably tied to a high degree of political conformity. Promotion was determined by political commitment, subordination to the vicissitudes of party discipline, and the selection mechanisms of *Kaderpolitik* (cadre politics). In the late 1940s and 1950s, this was preferably combined with a previously *dis*advantaged social background. In the 1960s, in particular, rapid upward social mobility was possible; but from the 1970s, social mobility was much less marked, and the East German elite began to reproduce itself, combined with a degree of ageing and stagnation. By the 1980s, some scholars have suggested that middle-rank functionaries were experiencing considerable frustration at the blocking of their career prospects by the older generation.

What of the broader middle classes? Given the GDR's changed social structure, the term 'intelligentsia' is often used rather than 'bourgeoisie'. Many traditionally 'bourgeois' occupations obviously shrank to relative insignificance in the GDR: small, independent shopkeepers, private firms, and other elements of what used to be called the *Besitzbürgertum* (property-owning bourgeoisie) disappeared almost by definition (although a very small number of independent enterprises managed to cling on). But other 'bourgeois' occupations in the GDR – traditionally the preserve of the *Bildungsbürgertum*, the professional or educated bourgeoisie – showed interesting lines of continuity, with some groups affected more than others.

Those professions which were highly politically relevant experienced the greatest changes. There was, for example, considerable turnover in legal personnel in the GDR, in marked contrast to West Germany. Although crucial to the regime's socialization policies, it took somewhat longer to weed out the educational profession. Despite a quite extensive early turnover of teachers, with rapidly trained *Neulehrer* (new teachers), barely older than their pupils, installed in the early months of the occupation period, unwelcome vestiges of a previous era nevertheless lingered in the 1950s and 1960s. However, over time, changes became apparent. Political control of schools became ever more intense, with active FDJ groups within schools and the careful vetting and disciplining of staff. Similarly, in higher education increasing political surveillance and control ensured a growing conformity, as well as fostering a degree of provincialization among the professoriate. Apart from the so-called *Reisekader*, those conformists with permits to travel, most academic staff had only restricted access to international publications and international conferences.

Members of the East German technical intelligentsia found themselves in a complex position: the regime both needed, and also to some extent feared, them. Insofar as they were prepared to toe a minimalist line of conformity, they enjoyed a relatively privileged position. In the course of the 1950s, incentives – such as higher incomes – were offered to highly skilled people (such as medical doctors) who might otherwise have been tempted to join the flow of refugees through the still-open border of Berlin to the West. In the 1960s, following the building of the Wall, Ulbricht's policies of modernisation were predicated on a belief in the 'technological-scientific revolution', and again technical expertise was accorded a relatively high status. The records suggest that, on the whole, members of the intelligentsia – in the broad sense used by GDR officials in compiling their own opinion reports – retained a rather cautious political stance in the GDR, tending to remain quiet on matters of political contention.

As far as the cultural sphere is concerned, the picture is also differentiated. There were many who were prepared to work on behalf of the regime through newspaper and magazine journalism, and the production of propaganda. Equally, in the more rarified sphere of 'highbrow culture' a significant handful explicitly supported the regime (such as Anna Seghers or Hermann Kant), in addition to those few who maintained a critical distance, but were sufficiently supportive, or useful for the regime's image abroad, to retain a high profile and relatively privileged status within the GDR (Stefan Heym, Christa Wolf). Others maintained some sort of disaffected distance from the regime, but clung on in some form within the GDR, while a prominent but comparatively tiny minority were forced or chose to leave (Wolf Biermann, Monika Maron, and others). If one includes pastors and priests under the cultural intelligentsia, then a quite complex picture emerges: the churches were left to denazify themselves after the war, which meant in the event a startling continuity of clerical personnel after the end of the

Third Reich. But from the 1950s onwards, the SED adopted a highly proactive stance *vis-à-vis* the Protestant Churches in particular, seeking to infiltrate and influence their policies and personnel. By the 1980s, a highly ambiguous picture had emerged, in which state-sustaining as well as more dissident Christians could be found in prominent positions in the Protestant Churches (contrast Manfred Stolpe and Rainer Eppelmann, for example).

The price of any pursuit of professional interests – the prerequisite for which was appropriate higher education – was a degree of conformity. Those who refused to conform were excluded from straightforward career paths (often having to study theology and opt for a career in the church instead); outspoken critics suffered imprisonment or exile; but the majority chose to remain within defined parameters. It should also be remembered that an important and substantial minority of the GDR elite felt some enthusiasm for at least the ultimate goals, if not always the immediate means, of the Marxist–Leninist state. In any event, over time 'actually existing socialism' attained an air of permanence (accepted even in the West, with *Ostpolitik* and subsequent agreements) in which people made the best lives they could. By the 1980s, one in five of the adult population were members of the SED – a clear measure of outward conformity if not ideological commitment.

In the more open political conditions of West Germany, there was not the same degree of political constraint: nevertheless, despite multiple centres of power and social influence, this was far from being a completely egalitarian or genuinely pluralist society. Despite the explicit political break with Nazism in West Germany, there were marked continuities of personnel in the early post-war years. Many entrepreneurs and financiers who had known of, helped to finance, and benefited from the exploitation of slave labour in Nazi concentration camps, survived the momentary hiccups of denazification to continue their economic successes under democratic auspices in the 1950s. A striking continuity of personnel within the legal profession was also – or should have been – something of a moral blight for the new *Rechtsstaat* (state based on law). The restoration of jobs and pensions to civil servants who had served under Hitler was ensured under a controversial piece of legislation in 1951.

Quite apart from the question of continuities with the Nazi period, which inevitably faded in salience over time, there were powerful inbuilt tendencies towards the reproduction of social inequalities. Although the old Prussian/German aristocracy had lost its social basis as a landowning caste, its prestige and influence lingered on, bearing witness to the power of 'cultural capital': many historically resonant names (often prefaced by 'von') could be found among leading professional, economic and political circles of West Germany. Moreover, in a country where many *Länder* (regional states) retained a tripartite (rather than comprehensive) school system, educational qualifications often served as credentials legitimating the reproduction of social status: high school leaving qualifications (the *Abitur*), a university degree, and often also a doctorate, were strongly correlated with a privileged social background. West German employers, managers and politicians – and even trade unions – enjoyed a degree of structural and cultural closeness, often institutionalized (as in the preparation of policies for parliamentary legislation). The importance of political parties in making nominations for key posts (even including university chairs and directors of institutes) also tended to reproduce an establishment.

Generational and cultural changes, particularly after the eruptions of the later 1960s, began to erode these patterns, while the rise of new social movements and citizens' initiatives in the 1970s and 1980s challenged the inbuilt structures of power and decision-making. Moreover, creative writers, film-makers, visual artists and other culturally creative spirits adopted an explicitly and self-consciously critical role. Controversies over the character of West German society and identity were often played out in the highbrow media, with contributions from writers such as Günter Grass, the left-liberal philosopher Jürgen Habermas, and (as in the so-called historians' dispute of 1986–7) historians ranging from Ernst Nolte and Michael Stürmer on the right to scholars of a more left-liberal persuasion such as Hans-Ulrich Wehler, Jürgen Kocka and others.

At the same time, the more general socioeconomic changes described in the previous section led to changes in the character of the middle classes. Rapid economic growth in West Germany was accompanied, at the lower levels, by a significant expansion of the proportion of employees in white-collar work and the service sector compared to traditional blue-collar jobs. This led to a widespread perception of upward social mobility which was, in fact, a function of changes in the shape of the social structure as a whole, rather than increased mobility (both upwards and downwards) across dividing lines within a static social structure. Thus it was possible that by the late 1980s – particularly for those blind to the presence of a largely foreign underclass – West Germany appeared to be a predominantly affluent, urban and well-educated society.

III Workers and peasants

The GDR claimed to be a 'workers' and peasants' state'. The workers, in particular, were allotted a leading role – but only through their vanguard party, the Marxist–Leninist SED, whose task it was to try to transform the actually existing consciousness of the East German working class into what it ideally ought to be. Hence, in practice, the experience of most workers in the GDR was not quite along the idealistic lines originally envisaged by Karl Marx. The psychological experience of alienation was not removed at one stroke of the philosopher's pen as private enterprises were transformed into 'people's own enterprises' (VEBs). But, at the same time, the experience of blue-collar work in the GDR was more complex and multifaceted than might be thought when the only comparison is with the obviously more affluent and liberal West.

Wages and standards of living were much lower than in the West. But job security was assured: there was no official unemployment. Both the right and the duty to work were enshrined in the 1968 constitution. Sociological surveys of workers in the 1970s show that a sense of *Geborgenheit*, or security, was rated rather highly by workers who otherwise showed a quite realistic sense of adverse comparisons with the West on factors like wages and working conditions.

Having a job did not necessarily mean actually working at full capacity; there were many bottlenecks in supplies, for example, of raw materials or spare parts, which meant that production was often faltering and long periods of under-employment were experienced. Both wages and conditions of work varied quite widely with the sector of industry. In some areas, particularly highly sensitive fields such as uranium mining, appalling conditions of work and an almost wilful disregard for health and safety considerations were accompanied by high rates of pay and short-term benefits. In others, a long and tedious day in poor conditions was matched only by the pinched miseries of a low income and poor housing conditions, ameliorated only marginally by the high level of state subsidies for basic foodstuffs, transport and rent.

The representation of workers' interests in the workers' and peasants' state was also somewhat ambiguous. Many felt that the official trade union, the FDGB (which enjoyed a membership covering, according to the official statistics, slightly more than the total number of people officially in work) hardly represented their interests, and the FDGB's records are full of complaints about paying membership dues when there was no chance of affecting wages and conditions through union action as in the West. And, despite frequent unofficial work stoppages (most spectacularly on 17 June 1953), there was no right to strike in the GDR. On the other hand, some research suggests that workers' brigades performed useful functions as transmission belts for the representation of interests, and the FDGB records also reveal on occasion a real concern with ironing out problems in the workplace and listening to workers' complaints: there is no automatic conception of management always being right.

Many workers too seem to have continued a long-standing tradition in Germany of pride in their work, and enjoyment of the companionship of comrades: the workplace cannot be viewed as simply a location of oppression. Feelings of solidarity among workplace colleagues – who did not have to compete with one another for scarce jobs, or fear redundancy – were one element of the post-1989 'ostalgia', or nostalgia for at least partly 'good old days'. But some aspects were less welcome, such as the constant campaigns for increased productivity (which mostly meant enhanced exploitation of labour) in which an enforced collective competitive spirit was to take the place of market forces or real incentives. And ultimately – as 1989 showed – many workers were prepared to vote with their feet and head for higher wages and living conditions in the West if offered the opportunity.

In West Germany, a shrinking working class enjoyed increasing affluence and shorter working hours in a society where inequalities of wealth remained large. Implicitly, workers agreed that it was better to make a bigger cake than to argue over the way the cake was cut. Early post-war trade union radicalism was tamed under the influence of the Marshall Plan and the Americanization of industrial culture. The new, streamlined system of trade unions cooperated with management to ensure the smooth functioning of the capitalist economy. Although agreements in 1951, 1952 and 1976 relating to co-determination and works' councils were by no means uncontroversial – seen by some employers as too much of a concession, and by many workers as not enough – labour relations in the Federal Republic were comparatively smooth. In the 1950s, demands for wage increases were restrained, and over the following three decades the Federal Republic enjoyed a reputation as a relatively low-strike economy. Moreover, factors such as mechanization, computerization, and the shift away from heavy industry, as well as the fact that many of the lowest paid jobs were taken by *Gastarbeiter*, meant that ever fewer West Germans identified themselves as members of the blue-collar working class.

With the mechanization of agriculture and EC subsidies, flight from the land was the most marked feature of West German rural life, with a dramatic decline in the proportion of the population working on the land to little over 5 per cent in the 1980s. Many farmers found it more profitable to turn over at least some of their land and rooms in their farmhouses to a growing tourist industry – bed-and-breakfast accommodation and leisure pursuits took the place of tilling the fields. As the percentage of people living in small villages and hamlets shrank, from a little under a third (29 per cent) of the population in 1950 to only 6 per cent of West Germans in 1980, so too the character of these small communities changed. No longer relatively cut off from the outside world, they were increasingly linked up by improved communications: fast roads, television and the telephone combined with tourism to transform the character of rural life in West Germany.

The character of rural life was transformed in East Germany, too, but in rather different ways. For one thing, there was not the dramatic shrinking of the rural population experienced in the West: the percentage of the East German population living in communities of less than 2,000 declined only marginally, from 29 per cent in 1950 (the same as West Germany) to 24 per cent – still around a quarter of the population – in 1980. Nor did communications improve so dramatically: roads remained somewhat parlous and potholed in many areas, public transport was irregular and infrequent (if cheap), and although the possession of television sets increased in the 1970s and 1980s, only a small percentage of the population (9 per cent in 1988) had a telephone at home – and most of this 9 per cent was to be found among the political elite in towns. On the other hand, while to all outward appearances rural society in East Germany looked remarkably unchanged (the villages retaining a dusty, old-fashioned appearance, with cobbled, relatively traffic-free streets and little appearing to be happening), as far as the social organization of agriculture and the character of peasant life was concerned the changes were far-reaching. The expropriation of large estates, and later collectivization of agriculture, significantly affected the character of rural life. Agricultural workers were no longer tied to the estates of particular landowners, nor were they peasants in their own right, but rather they worked on collectivized farms which were essentially run as increasingly specialized enterprises. In comparison at least with the peasant agriculture of neighbouring Poland, the much more mechanized

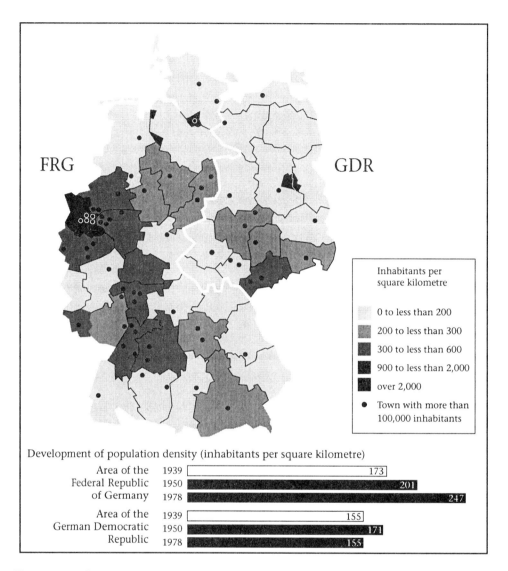

Figure 20.4   Population density and towns with more than 100,000 inhabitants

and large-scale agriculture of East Germany was relatively productive, although it could not compare with West German agriculture's sheltered and privileged position in the European Community.

IV   Cross-cutting patterns of social identity

Many social identities, such as gender, youth, generation, region, ethnicity and religion, cross-cut socioeconomic classes. While the Federal Republic introduced policies directly affecting some of these areas, more strenuous efforts were made by the GDR regime, often with unintended and even counterproductive consequences.

In West Germany, once the early post-war heyday of the *Trümmerfrauen* (women working in the rubble) was over, women's roles tended to revert to the traditional 'three Ks' of children, kitchen, church (*Kinder, Küche, Kirche*). Despite constitutional and legal commitments, and despite an increasingly vocal middle-class women's movement in the West, simple factors such as lack of sufficient affordable childcare worked against full equality in the workplace: women remained predominantly in part-time and lower-paid occupations, and often worked out of economic necessity rather than for self-realization or career fulfilment (although there were key changes over time, as in political participation and visibility: see further Chapter 25, below). In the GDR, economic priorities combined with ideological commitment to dictate the full participation of women in the paid labour force. A combination of factors including extensive child care facilities (crèche, kindergarten, after-school care, even boarding facilities), abortion on demand within the first 12 weeks of pregnancy (introduced in 1972), and – to reverse the declining birth rate – the subsequent introduction of generous maternity leave and benefits meant that, by the 1980s, fully half the workforce was female. However, despite rough numerical equality as far as participation in education, training and employment was concerned, women remained predominantly in lower status jobs, in lower positions within hierarchies, and (with one or two notable exceptions) never gained a serious foothold in the higher echelons of politics. Moreover, many East German women continued to bear the brunt of domestic responsibilities in the privacy of their own homes (where a traditional division of labour proved rather reluctant to wither away). For many women the lack of real personal choice, and the combination of a traditional domestic role with paid employment, were experienced less as 'emancipation' than as a 'double burden'.

As with gender, biological age may have very different meanings for different social classes, under different circumstances. Babies and toddlers in the GDR were more likely to experience institutional care and enforced conformity (even in such matters as being lined up in crèche like a work brigade for potty training) than to enjoy the more child-centred, individualized early socialization of West German youngsters who tended to stay at home until starting school at the age of six. While the West German young were exposed to a self-conscious and sometimes awkward attempt at active democratization, East German schoolchildren learned to repeat the official shibboleths and never step out of line. Heavy priority was given to seeking to capture the minds and hearts of the rising generation, through a wide variety of organizations (the Ernst Thälmann Youth Organization, Young Pioneers, Free German Youth) and indoctrination. As early as 1954, a secular state ceremony, the *Jugendweihe*, was introduced as an alternative to confirmation in church and, through very serious sanctions against those who refused, a means of pressurizing children to conform. But the SED's attempts at the enforced production of socialist personalities were not entirely successful. Youth non-conformity was a constant thorn in the flesh of the East German authorities. Fighting the cultural (and hence political) influence of the decadent West, from the Elvis Presley/rock 'n' roll crazes of the 1950s via beat music and jazz in the 1960s to the rock concerts of the 1980s, was a perpetual preoccupation of the East German regime, reflected in extensive records in the Central Party Archives. Youth disaffection and youth revolt were, in different ways, of political importance in West German social history, too, particularly in the 1960s, with the student revolts, youth demonstrations, and challenges to the *spießbürgerlich* amnesia of a repressed past, and – in very different vein – later with a rising concern about drug abuse among the young.

Generation in both Germanies proves to be an important and often overlooked category of analysis. In Germany after 1945, there are certain key generations which may be delineated, even if rather crudely and in inchoate terms. There is the generation of those who experienced the Third Reich as adults, which one might call the deeply divided KZ (concentration camp) generation, including as it did both those *Mitläufer* who sustained the Nazi regime, and those of their opponents who had survived incarceration or exile. This generation was crucial to the establishment of the two German states, and it was the bitter experiences of the latter, the anti-fascists, who stamped their mark on the legitimating credentials of the GDR, while it was the former who lent an aura of uneasy suspicion to the democratic virtues of the first years of the Federal Republic. The 'HJ-generation' consisted of those slightly younger Germans socialized under the Third Reich through such organizations as the Hitler Youth (hence 'HJ') or its sister organization, the League of German Girls (*Bund deutscher Mädel*, BdM). Some analysts have argued that it was this 'HJ generation' that proved to be particularly reliable and conformist 'carriers' of the two new German regimes. It is possible that many GDR functionaries of this generation, whose political conformity was rewarded with rapid promotion in the 1960s, proved particularly loyal in state service until, in middle age in the 1980s, they found their paths to the very top blocked by a generation of elderly politicians. There was, then, in the GDR, what might be called the FDJ generation, socialized through the East German Free German Youth organization, perhaps paralleled by the '68'ers of the Federal Republic; both were stamped by formative socialization experiences within (and often in reaction against) the opposing political systems; it was, interestingly, the FDJ generation that spearheaded the revolution of 1989. Of course, it should be added, not everyone born in certain years would necessarily identify with everything (or even anything) implied by these generational labels.

Germany has historically been characterized by great regional variations (see earlier chapters in this book). The federal structure of West Germany allowed many regional differences and identities to be preserved through the decentralized *Länder*. The geographically smaller, less densely populated and politically highly centralized East German state started to iron out regional differences, particularly after the *Länder* were replaced by the smaller *Bezirke* in 1952. Nevertheless, some regional cultures in the GDR proved resistant to change, particularly where rooted in socioeconomic differences (rural Mecklenburg versus the industrial south) or where fostered by the state

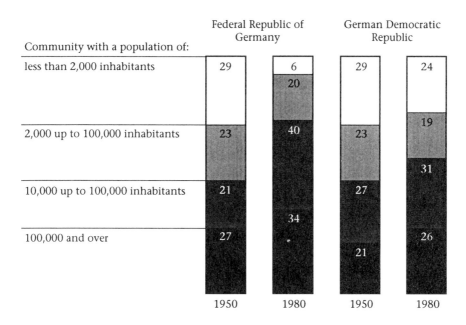

Figure 20.5 Distribution of population by percentage in communities of different sizes

(for reasons of tourism or international respectability). The Sorb community in the southeastern region of the GDR enjoyed a special status, with dual-language signs and the protection of local customs, although urbanization and assimilation into the industrial working class tended to dissolve the conditions for the survival of an essentially rural culture and language community. Regional identities can be (re-)created: it was relatively easy, after the fall of the Wall, for areas such as the Catholic Eichsfeld – previously severed by the Iron Curtain – to resurrect its distinctive Catholic identity, or for a re-established Thuringia to claim that it was the 'heart' of Germany.

As far as minority communities were concerned, the position in West Germany was one of ambiguity and mixed messages. West Germany's citizenship laws were based on the Law of 1913, and consolidated by the loss of territories in 1945: they embodied an essentially ethnic/cultural concept of 'German-ness', which bestowed rights of citizenship on those who had been citizens of Germany in the borders of 31 December 1937 (i.e. prior to Nazi expansion) and their descendants; qualifications for acquiring citizenship included tightly defined cultural and economic criteria. Although those excluded from citizenship on racial grounds in 1935 were given some priority in regaining their citizenship, officially ordained 'philo-Semitism' (being nice to Jews, while still stereotyping them as different) in the 1950s ran at odds with widespread popular anti-Semitism in a population where very few Jews remained in any event. And the rather restrictive rules on new applications for citizenship left even long-term

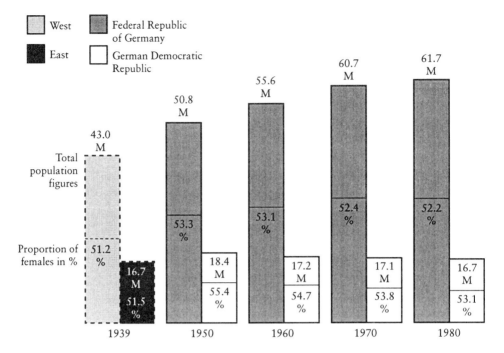

Figure 20.6 Population growth (in millions)

residents who had been born and bred in West Germany, such as second- and third-generation descendants of *Gastarbeiter* (euphemistically termed guest workers), without political representation, while 'ethnic Germans' from territories lost to Germany after 1945 were entitled to 'return' to the 'homeland', even if they and their ancestors had never set foot on the soil that became the Federal Republic. At the same time, West Germany's uniquely liberal asylum laws (a legacy of the guilt incurred by the Third Reich) led to rising numbers of people seeking political asylum in the Federal Republic. Despite the substantial numbers involved, West Germany's conservative political elites continued to maintain the stance that 'Germany is not a country of immigration'. In a sense, they were right: Germany had a long tradition of relying on migrant labour for economic reasons, while preserving a restrictive definition of citizenship. But it was at a considerable social, economic and political cost as far as the immigrant communities were concerned.

Despite its proclaimed internationalism, the numbers of foreign workers in the GDR were very much smaller and were largely kept apart from the local population. Workers from countries such as Mozambique and Cuba were kept in segregated hostels. Occasional workplace incidents involving foreigners which are reported in the FDGB files suggest a residual degree of racism among East German workers (which included rather traditional anti-Polish sentiments), but under the restrained political conditions obtaining in the GDR this never attained the degree of public impact experienced in West Germany. Nor did the GDR define citizenship in such restricted ethnic/cultural terms, particularly after its shift to a class definition of nation in the 1970s (see Chapter 27 below), although it has to be added that the GDR never enjoyed quite the same pressure from immigrants for citizenship as did its more affluent Western twin – rather the reverse.

Religion is, and has been for centuries, a key aspect of identity in Germany. Here too, political division determined a marked divergence in the social meaning of religion and the roles of the churches. In West Germany after the war, the massive influx of refugees diluted previously relatively homogenous and insulated Catholic and Protestant communities, which had in some areas virtually preserved the religious–political boundaries of 1648. Although the churches as institutions retained considerable importance in West German life, processes of secularization tended to make religious practice (if not belief) less widespread among the population over the following decades. In the GDR, which had a predominantly Protestant population in 1949 (around 15 million Protestants and one million Catholics in a total population of around 17 million), massive campaigns against Christianity in the 1950s were followed by a more muted, but no less insidious, attempt to co-opt the churches. This culminated in the separation of the East German Protestant churches from their all-German links in 1969, the development of the notion of a 'church within socialism', and the church-state agreement of 6 March 1978. The latter, however, backfired as far as the state was concerned, and gave religion a heightened political salience in the 1980s (countering earlier tendencies towards secularization as in the West), and in turn led to significant involvement of Protestant pastors and other Christians in the dissident movements of the 1980s and the revolution of 1989.

Finally, a word may be said about less tangible matters. Given the intrusion of the state into virtually every aspect of East German life, including the high politicization of leisure activities and sport (which was less a matter of individual enjoyment than national prestige), there was no area of life entirely free from a degree of collectivization and pressure. This inevitably had its effects on social psychology. Restraint and suspicion (at times based in fear of Stasi surveillance), along with feelings of solidarity rather than competition, were widely prevalent (though far from universal) and ambiguous modes of being among citizens of the GDR. These patterns of interpersonal relations were in some contrast to varying behavioural patterns evident in the very different political conditions in the West. The old definition that 'social history is history with the politics left out' could hardly be less apposite.

V   The fractured nation

This brief survey has sought to sketch some of the ways in which society in the two German states diverged over 40 years of separation. There were, of course, common

elements, relating not only to a common past, but also to general trends such as industrialization, revolutions in technology, a changing international culture, and the prevalence of the mass media (with television insidiously invading through a porous Iron
Curtain). Family links were maintained, with particular salience for those living on the
eastern side of the Wall. There were common interests in peace and *détente* in central
Europe. The remilitarization of both states in 1955–6 was accompanied on both sides
of the Iron Curtain by distinctive pacifist voices, if more muted and suppressed in the
GDR (where, following the introduction of conscription in 1962, the church was able
to win an alternative form of military service in 1964, not bearing weapons). The social
movements and identity politics in the West in the 1970s found parallels in the new
political activism of peace initiatives, environmentalist and human rights groups in the
far more difficult political conditions of the GDR in the 1980s.

But for all the refractions of similar trends through different political prisms, perhaps
the most striking feature of German social history after 1945 is the growing divergence
of the two German societies. Despite some limited but clear breaks with the Nazi past
in the West immediately after defeat (particularly with respect to political and military
elites), in its first two decades West German society was essentially marked by continuity, followed eventually by delayed processes of rupture and change from the later
1960s. East German society followed a different timescale: massive early structural
transformation was followed from the 1960s by social stabilization, even – by the 1980s
– stagnation. Ultimately, a common language, a common heritage, and a residual sense
of common national identity, were fractured by deep-rooted and extensive differences
in the very constitution of social classes, life chances, cultural attitudes and patterns of
behaviour. In short, the people had been constituted to become quite different social
beings in the two German states.

Select bibliography

With the opening of the East German archives, there is much new research on the social history of the GDR: however, the early fruits of this research are still largely available only in
German. This select bibliography therefore includes some slightly older English-language classics and textbooks which have not as yet been replaced by new syntheses, as well as a selection
of recent German publications including some excellent collections of essays and source
materials.

Baylis, T., *The Technical Intelligentsia and the East German Elite* (Berkeley: University of
    California Press, 1974).
Berghahn, V., *The Americanisation of West German Industry* (Leamington Spa: Berg, 1986).
Bessel, R. and Jessen, R., eds., *Die Grenzen der Diktatur* (Göttingen: Vandenhoek and Ruprecht,
    1996).
von Beyme, K. and Zimmermann, H., eds., *Policymaking in the German Democratic Republic*
    (Aldershot: Gower, 1984).
Childs, D., ed., *Honecker's Germany* (London: Allen and Unwin, 1985).
Dennis, M., *German Democratic Republic* (London: Pinter, 1988).
Edwards, G. E., *GDR Society and Social Institutions* (London: Macmillan, 1985).

Fulbrook, M., *Anatomy of a Dictatorship: Inside the GDR, 1949–1989* (Oxford: Oxford University Press, 1995).

Helwig, G., *Frau und Familie: Bundesrepublik Deutschland – DDR* (Cologne: Verlag Wissenschaft und Politik, 1987).

Kaelble, H., Kocka, J. and Zwahr, H. eds., *Sozialgeschichte der DDR* (Stuttgart: Klett-Cotta, 1994).

Kleßmann, C., *Die doppelte Staatsgründung* (Göttingen: Vandenhoeck and Ruprecht, 1982).

Kleßmann, C., *Zwei Staaten, eine Nation* (Göttingen: Vandenhoeck and Ruprecht, 1988).

Kleßmann, C. and Wagner, G. eds., *Das gespaltene Land: Leben in Deutschland 1945 bis 1990: Texte und Dokumente* (Munich: C. H. Beck, 1993).

Kocka, J., ed., *Historische DDR-Forschung* (Berlin: Akademie Verlag, 1993).

Kolinsky, E., *Women in West Germany* (Oxford: Berg, 1989).

Krejci, J., *Social Structure in Divided Germany* (London: Croom Helm, 1976).

Ludz, P. C., *The Changing Party Elite in East Germany* (Cambridge, MA: MIT Press, 1972).

Maaz, Hans-Joachim, *Behind the Wall: The Inner Life of Communist Germany* (New York and London: W. W. Norton, transl. 1995).

Mayer, G., *Die DDR-Machtelite in der Ära Honecker* (Tübingen: A. Francke Verlag, 1991).

Naimark, Norman, *The Russians in Germany* (Cambridge, MA: Harvard University Press, 1995).

Ostow, Robin, *Jews in Contemporary East Germany* (London: Macmillan, 1989).

Vollnhals, C., ed., *Entnazifizierung* (Munich: Deutscher Taschenbuch Verlag, 1991).

Wallraff, G., *Lowest of the Low* (London: Methuen, 1988).

21

Culture, history and national identity in the two Germanies since 1945

Erica Carter

It is late August 1992, and the attention of the international press fixes on the port town of Rostock on the Baltic coast. On 24 August, a group of youths begin a campaign of violence against asylum seekers housed in hostels in the Lichtenhagen suburb of the city. Over the next few days, the hostel and neighbouring buildings will be ransacked, cars will be torched, police and 'foreigners' physically assaulted – all to an accompanying chorus of 'Germany to the Germans: foreigners out!'

But what press reports will emphasize is not only the damage done in Rostock to buildings and material possessions, or even the physical aggression that has by 1992 become so much a part of life for immigrants and asylum seekers in post-unification Germany. Public anxiety will centre instead on the bizarre response to the riots from the ordinary citizens of Lichtenhagen. In anti-foreigner riots in the Saxon town of Hoyerswerda one year earlier, crowds of local residents had gathered to support the rioters with shouts of encouragement, applause, or other gestures of approbation. In Rostock, too, it is not until Thursday 29 August that 2,000 demonstrators will register a protest against the racist excesses of the riots. For now, the rioters are accompanied by a crowd of bystanders whose stance towards the events appears as one of staunch, if muted approval. The Austrian news magazine *Profil* sums up the outrage of commentators at home and abroad when it writes of the Rostock riots: 'not only have several hundred marauding skinheads and violent youths seen themselves as justified in taking the law into their own hands; their actions have been accepted, indeed welcomed by the people of Lichtenhagen.' This is, concludes the magazine, 'a caesura in postwar German history'.[1]

In both Germanies after the war, mainstream culture at least paid lip service to a prohibition on behaviour that recalled the anti-Semitic and racist excesses of National

Socialism. In the GDR, which claimed an identity as an anti-fascist state, popular xenophobia and anti-Semitism (of which there were certainly numerous instances) were officially suppressed. In the Federal Republic, the state's position was more contradictory. While on the one hand, far-right parties that publicly preached racism (the nationalist NPD or the new right Republikaner Party) were officially tolerated, as was widespread popular hostility to so-called guest workers, the 1949 constitution, on the other hand, outlawed discrimination on grounds of sex, descent, race, language, homeland, origin, faith, religion or political opinions.

When this constitutional promise of tolerance was flouted in Hoyerswerda, Rostock and elsewhere, many observers made connections with the nationalist fervour that had surrounded unification in 1990. The Federal Republic had demanded of its citizens a loyalty to the constitution and the rule of law. Events in the early 1990s suggested, however, a swing in popular allegiance to more archaic forms of national belonging. Many in Germany seemed now to identify most strongly, not with visions of Germany as a modern nation state founded on democratic government and the rule of law, but with primordial appeals to an ethnically pure *Volk* whose identity was sustained by the exclusion of alien or foreign elements: witness the Rostock slogan, 'Germany to the Germans – foreigners out!'

I National culture and identity in the two Germanies

It has been a regular contention of political history that nationalism was a spent force in post-war Germany. Certainly, political nationalism was actively suppressed in the GDR, and remained in the FRG the preserve of fringe parties on the far right. In the context of that analysis, however, something of a historical riddle is presented by the resurgence in the early 1990s of right-wing nationalism, in the guise not only of anti-foreigner violence in Rostock and elsewhere, but of increased popular and electoral support for the ultraright. The far right garners much of its support from groups at the socioeconomic margins: from disaffected youth, the unemployed, the socially disadvantaged. But what has given their politics of despair its nationalist inflection, if post-war nationalism was indeed so effectively suppressed as existing historiography would claim?

In the rest of this chapter, we will trace some of the ways in which a cultural history of post-war Germany might begin to answer that question. The hypothesis that frames the following account is that, while the ethnic nationalism that has recently made such a disturbing reappearance was for many decades suppressed, or at least marginalized from political life, both post-war Germanies experienced persistent difficulties in overcoming the problematic *cultural* legacy of authoritarian nationalism.

That argument is advanced in full cognizance of the pitfalls of ascribing to the two Germanies after 1945 a common national culture or shared national identity. Especially since unification in 1990, it has become clear that 40 years of separate development produced sharp cultural differences between so-called *Ossis* and *Wessis* (inhabitants of the GDR and FRG respectively – see Chapter 20 above). The distinctions begin at the level of language; thus studies in comparative linguistics have registered, not only lexical differences, but national (as opposed to regional and dialect-based) variations in grammar, spoken and written style and register. East–West divisions were further cemented by the emergence of distinct education systems: the one, in the FRG, based on a three-tier structure that tended to cement class-cultural hierarchies from secondary level; the other, in the GDR, structured according to strictly egalitarian principles (though these were not always realized in the often authoritarian classroom practice of GDR schools). Some of the divergent tendencies in the literature, arts and mass media of the GDR and FRG will be traced later in this chapter; and these will illustrate – as does, at greater length, Mary Fulbrook's chapter in this book – that there is good reason for caution about attributing to the former GDR and FRG a common national culture, or a shared national identity. The organization, not only of the political systems of the two German states, but also of cultural forms, practices and institutions around the opposing philosophies of socialist collectivism versus Western liberal individualism, produced an apparently ever-widening gulf between the cultural identities of the two Germanies East and West.

II Two Germanies: a common cultural heritage

Or did it? While German division produced a clear divergence between socialist and capitalist cultural forms, the FRG and the GDR continued to share a common – and highly problematic – cultural heritage. Cultural debates in both states returned repeatedly to German fascism, and focused on the extent to which the Nazi past had been 'overcome'. The issue of *Vergangenheitsbewältigung* (overcoming the past), moreover, was not only related in those debates to Nazism and the Third Reich. The Nazi vision of a racially pure culture embodying the spiritual essence of *Volk* and Reich was certainly the most repugnant version of cultural nationalism that German history had produced: but it was by no means without historical precedent. From the late eighteenth century, aspirations for a German nationhood achieved politically, through the formation of a democratic nation state, existed in tension with a cultural nationalist and Romantic vision of a German identity grounded in folk, blood and soil. That *völkisch* conception of national identity, though officially rejected by both post-war German states, continued even after 1945 to shape popular conceptions of national belonging and citizenship. In the GDR, which claimed for itself a supranational identity as a state rooted in international socialism, political nationalism was officially reviled; but a cultural nationalist structure of feeling survived in policies and practices that suppressed social difference in all its various forms. Homosexuality, for instance, was decriminalized in the GDR in the early 1970s – unlike the FRG, which retained Paragraph 174 of the Civil Code that rendered homosexuality a criminal offence. The everyday experience of lesbians and gay men in the GDR, by contrast, was one of official intolerance and public vilification. Similarly, the largest indigenous ethnic minority, the Sorbs, were officially feted for their contribution to national culture in the GDR; yet in reality, Sorb communities were uprooted and local cultures fragmented by large-scale resettlement through the 1970s and 1980s, when the regime identified Sorb territory in the southeast GDR as the main source of raw materials (lignite, or 'brown coal') to feed post-1971 industrial expansion. A further example: the tiny minority of foreign workers and students from socialist states in the developing world (Angola, Mozambique, Vietnam) was in theory more politically integrated in the GDR than in the West. Thus (for what this was worth under a totalitarian regime) they enjoyed a right to vote in local elections that was never granted to migrant workers in the West. In fact, however, since they lived largely in hostels or barracks, and since integration programmes in schools, universities or local communities were non-existent, migrant minorities remained on the social margins. As one post-1989 commentator on minority issues in the former GDR put it 'the exclusion of everything "alien," or more precisely, of everything defined as alien, is by no means a new phenomenon or a western import, but a reaction familiar from the old days of the SED – just one of the many means by which GDR society sought to sustain its own identity'.[2]

In the FRG, the same tension between official guarantees of minority equality, and actual sociocultural exclusion, has been visible throughout the post-war period. Here however, that contradiction is explicitly inscribed in two conflicting passages of the constitution. On the one hand, the opening articles of the Basic Law embrace liberal-democratic definitions of the citizenry as a political community enjoying equal rights and civil liberties. Yet this sociopolitical model of citizenship is undermined by later sections of the constitution which proffer instead an ethnically based and culturally exclusionary definition. The Federal Republic is unique among Western European states in basing access to citizen status, not on *ius soli* (citizenship by territory), but *ius sanguinis* (citizenship by blood). Thus Article 116 of the Basic Law defines as an FRG citizen 'everyone ... who, as a refugee or expellee of German ethnicity [*Volkszugehörigkeit*], or as a spouse or descendant of such a person, has been admitted to the territory of the German Reich as it existed on 31 December 1937.'

Even the Basic Law, then, fails to resolve the contradiction between classical liberal models of the nation state as a political community of equal citizens, and Romantic nationalist conceptions of an ethnically defined nation. The effects of that contradiction have been most keenly felt in the post-war Federal Republic by the large migrant minority that, by the mid-1990s, constituted over 8 per cent of the German population. This substantial minority has been lauded by successive post-war governments for its economic contribution to national life. As the CDU apologist for multiculturalism, Heiner Geißler, put it in 1991 'the German economy . . . needs foreigners as a labour force, as consumers and as taxpayers'.[3] And yet this public celebration of migrant minorities as participants in the national economy is rarely matched by the sociopolitical recognition of 'foreigners' as equal citizens. Unlike second- or third-generation ethnic Germans from eastern Europe – the so-called *Aussiedler* whose linguistic and cultural links to Germany are tenuous, but whose ethnic German origins grant them immediate access to FRG citizenship – 'foreigners' born and raised in Germany have no automatic right to naturalization. Thus, despite the temporary relaxation of naturalization procedures under the 1990 Aliens Law, the vast majority of non-ethnic German migrants remain non-citizens with no voting rights at either local or national level.

The situation of migrant minorities stands, in other words, as a pointed reminder of the continuing oscillation in definitions of German identity between liberal Enlightenment models of the nation as a pluralist collectivity (in which, amongst others, migrant workers who settled in Germany would be included as equal citizens), and Romantic visions of an internally homogeneous *Kulturnation* stripped of 'foreign' influence.

III The Allied response to fascism, 1945–9

In an effort to trace some of the historical shifts and tensions between these polarized conceptions of national culture and identity, let us turn first to the period after 1945: the brief interregnum under Allied control, before Germany was divided into two opposing states. On 7–8 May 1945, Germany submitted its unconditional surrender to the four Allied powers: France, Great Britain, the USA and the Soviet Union. Thus ended 12 years of National Socialist rule in Germany and six years of a world war that had left millions dead, and Germany itself physically decimated. A provisional government was set up in the first weeks of May 1945 under Admiral von Dönitz; but on 23 May, the Dönitz government was dissolved, and the Allies assumed supreme power in Germany.

The stated aim of Allied military government was three-fold: demilitarization, denazification and democratization of a country which, under fascist rule, had orchestrated a bloody war, and perpetrated unprecedented horrors in the concentration camps and gas chambers. Allied government began, then, with an apparent consensus on the general thrust of policies for reconstruction. The rather abstract formulation on which that consensus was based, however, produced an increasing divergence in denazification policy and practice amongst the four occupying powers. The sharpest distinctions were those produced by philosophical differences in understandings of the origins of German fascism. The Western Allies subscribed to a liberal individualist view of fascism as a manifestation (albeit a highly corrupted one) of political will. In this view, it was to the distortion of German collective and individual consciousness that National Socialism was most centrally to be attributed. The Law for Liberation from National Socialism (*Befreiungsgesetz*), which came into force in the Western zones in March 1946, shifted the emphasis of denazification definitively away from a Soviet-style structural purging of Nazis from public life, and towards an examination of the predispositions of individual Germans to fascism. Under the terms of the *Befreiungsgesetz*, German citizens were to submit to tribunals questionnaires on all aspects of their political activity under the Third Reich. That information was used as a basis for the categorization of individuals under one of five possible headings: major offenders, offenders, lesser offenders, followers or fellow-travellers, and the exonerated.

The denazification tribunals were accompanied by initiatives for democratic re-education, ranging from film screenings on such issues as wartime atrocities or the Holocaust, through academic exchange programmes, mobile libraries and school visits, to an extensive reform of the press and media system. It was in this latter area that Western cultural policy arguably made its greatest impact. Following the introduction of a licensing system that allowed cultural production by Germans to recommence, individuals were licensed to publish newspapers in the Western zones. Most of these were regionally based and politically independent; and such titles as the *Frankfurter Rundschau*, the *Süddeutsche Zeitung* and *Die Welt*, or the liberal weeklies *Die Zeit* and *Der Spiegel* – all of which emerged under Allied occupation – were stable enough to survive the rigours of political and economic change after 1949, and to become the leading 'quality' publications of post-war West Germany. In the words of two recent commentators: 'the period of Allied control of the press was decisive in shaping the longer-term pattern of the press up to the present day'.[4]

The same was true of the long-term development of broadcasting in West Germany. Here again (at least until the advent of new communications technologies and the broadcasting reforms of the 1980s), the medium remained regionally based in broadcasting stations initially established under Allied control. The denazification and re-education policies of the Western Allies, in other words, left their mark on post-1949 West Germany in the form of a diversified, decentralized and (at least theoretically) politically independent cultural sphere.

To the GDR, Soviet denazification delivered a very different cultural legacy. According to the economistic marxist analysis that underpinned denazification in the Soviet zone, fascism was the outcome, not centrally of the psychological dispositions of the German people, but of capitalist politico-economic development. The focus of denazification in the Soviet zone was thus not individual but structural; it centred on the dismantling of such sections of the military–industrial complex as were located in eastern Germany, as well as on the erasure of National Socialist influence from public life. Thus, along with land reform, the dismantling of large sections of East German industry and the transportation of plant and raw materials as reparations to the Soviet Union, the Soviet military command concentrated its energies on removing ex-Nazis from public office, and on promoting communism. In the political arena, the drive towards Soviet-style communism was most visible in the forced merger in April 1946 between the Social Democratic Party in the Eastern zone (SPD), and the communist KPD. The party that emerged from that union, the Socialist Unity Party (SED) moved quickly to the position as the Soviet Union's political mouthpiece that it was to sustain until the founding of the GDR in 1949, and indeed throughout the country's 40-year history.

IV German cultural intellectuals: humanism and its limits

Mary Fulbrook has described denazification in the four zones of occupation as polarized between a Western focus on rehabilitation, and a Soviet concern with structural transformation.[5] There was, however, a third prevailing tendency in this period that emanated, not from the occupying powers, but from indigenous cultural intellectuals. In the Soviet zone, a coalition of socialist writers and intellectuals came together as early as July 1945 to form the Cultural Association for the Democratic Renewal of Germany (*Kulturbund zur demokratischen Erneuerung Deutschlands*). Under the leadership of the writer Johannes R. Becher, who took up the presidency after returning from Soviet exile, the *Kulturbund* committed itself to a revival based on the 'true German cultural values' represented by Enlightenment humanism, and embodied in the writings of such figures as Goethe, Schiller or Lessing. In late 1940s Germany, that tradition was seen as having survived in the work of exiled writers – Anna Seghers, Arnold Zweig or Bertold Brecht (all of whom returned after 1945 to the Soviet zone) – or in

Illustration 21.1   Hildegard Knef and Wolfgang Borchert in *The Murderers Are Among Us* (1946)

such powerful post-war anti-fascist statements as Wolfgang Staudte's 1946 film *The Murderers Are Among Us (Die Mörder sind unter uns)*. That film – the first production of the Deutsche Film-Aktiengesellschaft (DEFA) under whose monopoly GDR film production was later organized – ends with a demand for the pursuit of war criminals in the context of a democratic restoration of the rule of law. 'We have no right to judge', says the protagonist Dr Mertens (Wolfgang Borchert), 'but we have a duty to accuse.'

Mertens is led to that insight by his lover Susanne (Hildegard Knef), whose love convinces him that human values can survive despite the immensity of Nazi crimes. The film evinces, in other words, a commitment to a new moral and political order grounded in the humanist tradition – a commitment typical of cultural responses to fascism from German intellectuals both East and West. The *Kulturbund*'s manifesto demanded, for instance, the 'rediscovery and promotion of the democratic humanist tradition that is the national heritage of our people'. In the West, the same call for a humanist revival echoed through the founding statements of key post-war cultural initiatives. In April 1946, the writers Hans Werner Richter and Alfred Andersch launched the periodical *Der Ruf (The Calling)* which aimed – as indicated by its sub-title, 'Independent Writings from the Young Generation' – to act as mouthpiece for a rising generation of democratic Germans. Like the founders of the *Kulturbund*, the editors of *Der Ruf* saw in Enlightenment humanism a specifically German source of post-war cultural transformation. In one important statement from *Der Ruf* in 1946, Alfred Andersch for instance called for 'a new socialist humanism' rooted in an alliance between 'young Germany' and the youth of Europe.[6]

From the beginning, *Der Ruf* opposed Allied re-education policies, which it saw as unjustly tainting the German majority with the stain of guilt for 'the crimes of a minority'.[7] This, coupled with the journal's support for democratic socialism, led quickly to Allied censure, and finally to the banning of *Der Ruf* in April 1947. Its successor in the literary sphere, the group of left-liberal writers brought together in September 1947 to form the *Gruppe 47*, reiterated in its founding principles *Der Ruf*'s demand for homegrown forms of cultural democratization. Indeed that demand was one that echoed across the field of cultural production in the West. The immediate post-war period saw, for example, a wave of so-called rubble films (*Trümmerfilme*): productions by German directors set amongst the ruins of a defeated Germany, and thematizing the nation's cultural destruction and future renewal. Titles like Helmut Käutner's *In Those Days (In jenen Tagen*, 1947), Harald Braun's *Between Yesterday and Tomorrow (Zwischen gestern und morgen*, 1947) or Rudolf Jugert's *Film Without a Title (Film ohne Titel*, 1948) used Germany's ruined cities as a visual metaphor for the demolition of German cultural tradition and identity. In life stories from the inhabitants of that ruined landscape, however, they found traces of a humanity that could provide the basis for moral reconstruction in a post-fascist Germany. *In Those Days*, for instance, is a retrospective of the Third Reich, told from the perspective of a car whose life-span exactly parallels the twelve years of National Socialism. The stories of the car's owners make up a patchwork tale of everyday resistance and petty heroism: a narrative which, as the voice-over (the car) tells us at the end, points the way to a rediscovery of human values and thus to a viable future for the post-war nation.

Equally indebted to the new humanism was the philosopher Karl Jaspers, who wrote in his seminal analysis of German guilt, *The Guilt Question* (*Die Schuldfrage*, 1946) that 'we know ourselves to be first and foremost part of humanity; we are in the first instance human beings, then Germans'.[8] But there is, finally, a contradiction in Jaspers' work – one that dogged post-war humanism in all its manifestations. Cultural renewal was seen by Jaspers and others to depend on the revival in Germany of such universal values as tolerance, respect for the dignity of human life, and free and open communication. Paradoxically, however, universal humanity was invoked in the context of an appeal to a very particular and limited community, the German nation. Witness for instance Jaspers' use of the first person plural in the opening paragraphs of *Die Schuldfrage*: 'We want to learn to talk together. . . . not simply to reiterate our own opinions, but to hear the thoughts of the other.'[9]

Jaspers' appeal here to 'we the Germans' as a national community of the guilty produces (as do arguably all cultural constructions of communal identity) a division between self and other, 'us' and 'them', that undermines his demand for universal free communication. His preoccupation with a specifically German form of national guilt threatens, in other words, to privilege a German perspective, and to marginalize that of the 'others' who were the victims of National Socialism. That this is the result, moreover, not just of failings in Jaspers' rhetoric, but of a broader philosophical weakness in post-war humanism, is evidenced by a similar ethnic exclusivity in other cultural representations. Despite the denunciation of anti-Semitism in most *Trümmerfilme*, for instance, the films only rarely feature Jewish characters. More telling still are the narrative conventions that developed around such Jewish representation as was present in post-war film. Though certainly shown as the victims of Nazi persecution, Jewish figures in the *Trümmerfilme* are without exception removed by their own hand from the narrative; invariably, they commit suicide, usually at a moment when capture and deportation to the death camps seem inevitable.

This cinematic stereotype of the suicidal Jew highlights the ultimate inadequacy, not only of the *Trümmerfilme*, but of post-war humanism in general, as a vehicle for the engagement with the other that such as Jaspers demanded. Philosophical critiques of humanism have regularly noted its incapacity to grasp what might be termed the other within the self; and certainly the *Trümmerfilme* seem unable to confront, either the racist pathologies of its German characters, or the brutalization that was the product of Nazi persecution of the Jews. These films not only falter on the threshold beyond which they must portray their German characters as the perpetrators of racist murder (the Jews kill themselves): they also never dare represent the torture and humiliation that would transform deported Jews from fully rounded characters loaded with melodramatic pathos, to dehumanized camp inmates.

It was, moreover, not only the ethnic other – the Jew – who was omitted or repressed from historical narrative. The post-war Enlightenment subject (Dr Mertens in *The*

Murderers Are Among Us, or such writers as Becher, Richter or Andersch) was in the majority of cases not only ethnically marked as German; he was also gendered, the male heir to a masculine tradition. Feminist historians of post-1945 Germany have shown how central was women's contribution to economic and cultural regeneration. The so-called rubble women (*Trümmerfrauen*) were put to work in their thousands after the war to clear the ruins of the bombed-out cities; they took on the heaviest of 'male' manual labour, working as crane drivers, coal miners or industrial labourers. Women were politically active, too, in local women's committees and peace groups; they denounced, amongst other things, their men's penchant for war, and demanded a woman-oriented transformation of culture and politics in Germany. Some of those calls were answered, by equality clauses in both 1949 constitutions for instance. And yet, in the philosophical texts, the films and literature of the period, it is men – from Goethe to Brecht, from Lessing to Böll – who figure as the bearers of Enlightenment, culture and history. As one recent history points out, there was widespread resistance in the West in particular to women's participation in cultural and intellectual life: there were almost no women film or theatre directors: women artists, though active, received little recognition: and even such well-known writers as Elisabeth Langgässer or Luise Rinser were largely shunned by the literary establishment and cultural critics.[10]

In terms of Germany's attempted rupture with fascism, the period from 1945 to 1949 presents, in sum, a contradictory picture. Denazification in the Soviet zone in the end only paved the way for a regenerated dictatorship masquerading as democratic centralism. In the West, denazification by questionnaire and tribunal proved overly bureaucratic and open to abuse. Many former Nazis escaped sanctions, and party members were in any case universally rehabilitated under the FRG's general amnesty in 1951. Cultural intellectuals in all four zones created their own, specifically German response to fascism; but that response seemed compromised, ultimately, by its intellectual rooting in a Germano-centric and gender-exclusive version of the humanist tradition.

V German history as other – its repression and its return

It is a reflection of the limitations of post-war denazification that in 1976, three decades after the end of World War II, the prominent GDR novelist Christa Wolf could still strike a chord when she wrote, 'What is past is not dead; it is not even past. We cut ourselves off from it; we pretend to be strangers'.[11] So began Wolf's monumental autobiography *Patterns of Childhood (Kindheitsmuster)*, first published by the GDR's most significant literary publisher, the *Aufbau-Verlag*, and released in West Germany one year later. Previous works of fiction, including *Divided Heaven (Der geteilte Himmel*, 1963) and *The Quest for Christa T. (Nachdenken über Christa T.*, 1968) had established Wolf, both as a committed socialist, and as a modernist whose practice was often at odds with the GDR's official socialist realist aesthetic. *Patterns of Childhood* extended Wolf's experimentation with modernist form; her autobiographical narrative of a childhood under National Socialism was continually fractured by a second story – the narrative of a two-day visit to Wolf's former home in what is now Poland – as well as by discursive passages debating the nature of autobiographical writing and historical memory.

The book, in other words, set out not only to recapture a lost past – the history of the often ambivalent relationship of post-war generations to German fascism (Wolf herself was born in 1929, four years before the Nazi seizure of power). *Patterns of Childhood* also impressed upon its readers the necessity of debate on the relationship between their own (often highly contradictory) memories, and official histories of the Third Reich. That the book was indeed hailed as stirring back into life 'a whole swathe of the past' is in part a testament to the special status of Wolf and other literary intellectuals in the GDR.[12] In what came to be known as the East German 'land of reading' (*Leserland DDR*), novelists and poets enjoyed a privileged cultural status. Officially celebrated as the socialist heirs to Germany's great literary tradition, writers were at the same time held in high regard by the GDR populace. In a situation in which the press and broadcasting were dominated by party dogma, and where the popular arts – popular music, television, fashion and so on – often offered little more than pale imitations of Western models, literature (as sales and readership figures amply testify) was valued for its capacity to lend authenticity to the representation of GDR experience.

But readers' enthusiasm for *Patterns of Childhood* cannot only be explained by the high profile of literary works *per se* in the GDR. In its concern with personal memory as the source of a new form of knowledge about the national past, the novel was symptomatic of a broader sea change in post-war cultural responses to German fascism. Post-war humanism, as we have seen, had called for a return to Enlightenment values as the source of a regenerated German identity. In Wolf's novel, by contrast, the writer delves into the recesses of her own (enlightened socialist) identity, and finds buried here the residues of other selves – the exile nostalgic for a lost Polish home, the child born under and formed by National Socialism. These figures from a barely suppressed past are at one and the same time alien to, but also embedded within the narrator's present-day identity; we 'cut ourselves off' from a past which, however, 'is not dead; it is not even past'.

VI The flight from the past: two paths to modernity

This perception that fascist history enjoyed a lively afterlife in the subjectivities of individual Germans, was, even by the mid-1970s, a recent one. For over a decade after German division in 1949, both Germanies had given every appearance of turning their faces from the past, and had focused instead on building futures beyond National Socialism. In the GDR of the 1950s, the SED continued structural transformations begun under Soviet military rule. The building of socialism after 1949 involved, amongst other things, the restructuring of the education system along Marxist–Leninist lines; the formation of a socialist mass culture, through the youth and women's organizations, for example (the Free German Youth, the Pioneers, the Democratic Women's League of Germany and others), or through the staging of mass rallies and other spectacles to celebrate occasions of historical note (May Day, the anniversary of the October revolution, and so on). A further plank in socialist cultural planning was the secularization of all areas of public life; thus religious instruction in schools was abolished, and in 1954 the state introduced the *Jugendweihe*, an adolescent initiation rite designed to replace religious confirmation. In literature and the arts, socialist realism was enshrined as the official state aesthetic; and a highly ramified system of state censorship was put in place with the creation in 1951 of the Bureau for Literature and Publishing (*Amt für Literatur und Verlagswesen*) and the State Commission for Artistic Affairs (*Staatliche Kommission für Kunstangelegenheiten*).

That the pathway to socialism was a rocky one is indisputable: witness, for instance, the June uprising of 1953, when demonstrations spread across the GDR in protest against increases in productivity targets ('work norms') for industrial workers. Witness too the considerable diversification of socialist cultural practices during the post-Stalinist 'thaw' of 1953–6: a period in which such prominent figures as Bertolt Brecht and Stefan Heym were able, despite the constraints of censorship, to voice at least some of the most urgent arguments for political reform.

And yet efforts to revisit and reassess the fascist past were obstructed throughout these early years by the GDR's (highly questionable) definition of itself as an anti-fascist state that, in the transition to socialism, had definitively severed links with the Third Reich. Not until 1990, during the interregnum between SED rule and unification with the West, did the then Prime Minister, Hans Modrow, publicly admit the GDR's equal historical responsibility with the FRG for German fascism. On the one hand, then, historical continuities between Nazism and East German state socialism were officially disavowed. This did not on the other hand produce a conception of the GDR as arising *ex nihilo* from the ruins of 1945. Against the 'zero hour' rhetoric of some West German intellectuals, the SED regime posed a Marxist vision of the GDR as heir to a hitherto suppressed tradition of progressive forces in history. Thus, while modernist high art, for instance, was officially rejected – for its formalism, its 'decadent' preoccupation with marginality, and most centrally, for its insistence on radical rupture with the historical past – the SED on the other hand embraced cultural forms expressive of a historically rooted socialist modernity. Hence, for example, the SED's early enthusiasm for architectural modernization on a grandiose scale; for, as stated, for example, in July 1950 in the government's Sixteen Principles of Town Planning, the modernized GDR city would stand as an emblem of 'the social order of the German Democratic Republic, the progressive traditions of our German people and the great aims which are set for the construction of Germany as a whole'.[13]

This self-identification of the GDR regime with progressive historical forces – foremost amongst these the revolutionary working class – had contradictory cultural effects. At times, it produced a clear cultural pluralization. There are still, for instance – despite the activities of the *Gruppe '61* and the *Werkkreis Literatur der Arbeitswelt* – few

Western equivalents of the workers' writing circles and industrial residencies for writers that began after the Bitterfeld writers' conference of 1959. The so-called *Bitterfelder Weg* embarked upon at that event produced some genuine cross-fertilizations between 'high' and 'low', bourgeois and working-class cultures. Christa Wolf's portrayal of factory life in *Divided Heaven* (1963), and Erwin Strittmatter's portrait of agricultural labour from the same year, *Ole Bienkopp*, are two examples.

If, however, the GDR's achievement after fascism was to reinstate subordinate class groupings as modernity's heirs, then one of its chief historical failings lay arguably in its inattention to those other identities that Nazism had so brutally excluded from the historical process. To be sure, cultural practitioners in the post-war GDR produced some compelling portraits of the fascist persecution of cultural difference: Bruno Apitz's Holocaust novel *Naked amongst wolves* (*Nackt unter Wölfen*, 1958) for instance, or Konrad Wolf's film of a German-Jewish love affair *Stars* (*Sterne*, 1959). Yet the range of forms in which engagement with the cultural other might occur, was strictly limited. According to official doctrine, one primary feature of the socialist realist work of art was its so-called solidarity with the people (*Volksverbundenheit*). Potentially, this commitment to the *Volk* might have produced an infinite cultural diversification. In reality, however, 'the people' were defined, not as a heterogeneous body with potentially diverse forms of cultural expression, but as a collectivity that should at least aspire to a unitary class identity. Literature, visual art, the mass media and other cultural forms were given a key role in fostering working-class identification; hence official calls for the socialist realist work of art to adopt a partisan (*parteilich*) perspective that would allow it to approach questions of social life from the standpoint of the working class.

This equation of 'progressive' culture with working-class identity produced some unfortunate blindspots in official cultural representations. The GDR was putatively a state from which social inequality was on the way to being expunged; but the privileging of class in GDR culture produced a blindness to equally persistent inequalities – of gender, sexuality or ethnicity for instance – which survived intact in the GDR despite that state's formal commitment to egalitarian principles. To take the example of gender: while women were granted formal equality at work – and by the late 1980s, over 90 per cent of GDR women were in full-time employment – cultural stereotypes of femininity and masculinity were pervasive, and women and men remained largely confined to conventional social roles. In the overwhelming majority of households, for instance, women continued, despite their commitment to waged work, to bear primary responsibility for childcare and domestic labour; and the GDR workplace too was marked by traditional hierarchies that confined women to the lower echelons (Margot Honecker, Education Minister and wife of the SED leader Erich Honecker, was a notable but rare exception).

The official myth that a class-identified GDR populace had become the bearers of a uniformly progressive socialist modernity had problematic consequences, too, for the GDR's relation to the recent past. Officially, fascism belonged to a past epoch which the GDR had overcome in the transition to socialist modernity. That this position was untenable was later demonstrated by writers, artists and intellectuals who, from the late 1960s, began more vigorously to explore the GDR's historical continuities with fascism. That it had seemed sustainable until that point was due in no small measure to the GDR's symbolic projection of what psychoanalysis would term the 'bad other' of Nazi history onto West Germany. If socialist modernization was seen by the SED regime to have produced in the GDR a radical break with Third Reich barbarism, the Federal Republic, by contrast, was vilified for its continued commitment to capitalist regeneration; for in the Marxist–Leninist view, it was precisely capitalist modernity that had been the wellspring of German fascism.

The Federal Republic, of course, countered with its own myth of progressive modernity versus barbaric tradition. On the one hand, the post-war Western state – unlike the GDR – did formally acknowledge its historical responsibility for German fascism. That acknowledgment took various forms, including compensation for (some of) the victims of Nazi terror, privileged access for Jewish immigrants to German citizenship, political and economic support for the state of Israel, and an open door policy on political asylum, the latter designed to repay West Germany's debt to an international community that had given refuge to Germans fleeing Nazi persecution. But these compensatory gestures in no sense implied a recognition of the FRG state's continuity with German fascism. On the contrary, post-war governments were as vociferous as their GDR counterparts in claiming that modernization had produced a definitive rupture with National Socialism.

Modernization began at the constitutional and political level with the institutionalization in 1949 of the structures of Western-style representative democracy: a two-tier parliament, an electoral system based on proportional representation, a strong constitution designed to safeguard basic rights, and a separation of powers between the Federal government in Bonn (*Bund*) and the federal states (*Länder*). Federalism in particular had important implications for cultural policy and practice in the post-war state. Unlike the GDR, where the Leninist interpretation of democracy as 'democratic centralism' had produced a centralization of culture under state and party control, the so-called cultural sovereignty (*Kulturhoheit*) of the *Länder* produced a refreshing regional pluralism. The distinctive identities of regional urban centres from Hamburg to Munich were nourished throughout the 40 years of German division by generous subsidies from *Länder* governments to theatre, film, music, the visual arts and literature. This regionalization of identities was further cemented by education policies which, though nationally coordinated through the Standing Conference of Ministers of Culture (*Ständige Konferenz der Kultusminister*), preserved important local structural and pedagogic distinctions. Thus, for instance, confessional schools in the Catholic and conservative-dominated states of Bavaria, the Rheinland Palatinate, North-Rhine Westphalia and elsewhere tended in the early post-war years to view the curriculum as a vehicle for the promotion of the Christian faith, while the Protestant-dominated and social democratic states of Baden-Württemberg, Hamburg and Schleswig-Holstein, by contrast, favoured a fully secularized primary and secondary education. Post-1960s experiments with secondary-level comprehensives were similarly more pervasive in the SPD states (most prominently in Hesse) than in conservative regions where the traditional and highly selective three-tier system remained the norm. That regional differences fostered at school level did, moreover, continue to structure individual and collective identities in the FRG is perhaps best illustrated by patterns of cultural consumption in adult life. Thus, for instance, in West German broadcasting, the regional audience remained a key target group – and this even after the advent of new technologies (satellite and cable) that might have seemed to privilege audiences constituted at national or indeed supranational level. A final instance is the West German press. There have been in the post-war period some successful national publications: the tabloid *Bild*, or the right-of-centre quality titles *Die Welt* and the *Frankfurter Allgemeine Zeitung* (*FAZ*). But it is a measure of the success of cultural decentralization that the daily newspaper found on breakfast tables across the Federal Republic is still statistically more likely to be a local or regional title – the *Süddeutsche Zeitung* in Munich, in Berlin the *Berliner Morgenpost* or *Der Tagesspiegel* – than a national publication.

Modernity in the form espoused in government policy had, then, a distinctly regionalist flavour. There was, however, a second thrust to modernization in the FRG whose cultural implications were rather different. Under Adenauer's Economics Minister, Ludwig Erhard, the Federal Republic in the 1950s pioneered the model of the so-called social market economy, which – as Mark Roseman's contribution to this volume shows in more detail – combined a 'hands-off' approach to state economic planning with an embracing of the free market as a route to democratization. Post-war observers were divided on the implications for culture of this embracing of enlightened capitalism as a route to post-fascist modernity. Conservative apologists for a free market system modelled on the 'American way' pushed hard for an Americanization of the economic system through the liberalization of markets, the academic and commercial development of the business disciplines – management, marketing and public relations – and a reorientation of economic policy towards consumer-led growth. These were, for instance, the ingredients of West Germany's so-called economic miracle as presented in Ludwig Erhard's self-congratulatory volume *Prosperity for All* (*Wohlstand für alle*, 1957). Erhard was, however, cautious about the cultural benefits of Americanization. In a climate of conservative hostility to mass culture American-style – a hostility exemplified by moral panics over the effects of popular film, youth culture and popular music (the first and most notorious film target was Willi Forst's apparently sympathetic portrait of prostitution in *The Sinful Woman/Die Sünderin*, 1951: in relation to music, jazz, swing and rock 'n' roll especially were denounced as offensive and un-German) – Erhard too urged restraint in the cultural realm. Thus his writings promoted a nationally specific mode of cultural commodification that, while certainly drawing on American mass market models, would preserve 'German' traditions of quality, good taste and technological excellence.

Left-wing observers were yet more sceptical of the cultural benefits of capitalist development. In 1962, the social philosopher Jürgen Habermas published what was to become a pivotal text in left-liberal cultural debates, *Structural Change in the Public Sphere (Strukturwandel der Öffentlichkeit)*. In Habermas's neo-Marxist analysis, the rise of capitalism and the concomitant emergence of the bourgeois class were linked with the development of an enlightened public culture whose key vehicles included the press, the bourgeois novel, and public discourse in the salons and coffee houses of the eighteenth-century intelligentsia. Marxist thinkers after 1949 were divided on the fate of the classical bourgeois public sphere. Habermas himself saw it as threatened by advancing commodification, but, especially in his later writings of the 1970s and 1980s, he sustained a belief in the possible survival of the Enlightenment tradition through a commitment to democratic values as embodied in the Basic Law (hence Habermas's famous defence of what he terms 'constitutional patriotism'). The older generation of Western Marxists were more sceptical. The Frankfurt School Marxists of the early post-war period (so-called because of their affiliations to the Frankfurt-based Institute of Social Research, closed by the Nazis after 1933) saw capitalist development as having produced a cultural order in which aesthetic, moral, cultural and spiritual values were subordinated to the demands of capitalist accumulation. Capitalist domination had reached its apotheosis in the collusion under Nazism between monopoly capital (Krupp, Thyssen, Siemens *et al.*) and the fascist state: a collusion that had produced the extraordinary excesses of slave labour in the munitions factories, and mechanized mass slaughter in the death camps at Auschwitz and elsewhere. Enlightenment traditions had finally died in the gas ovens at Auschwitz; thus, the Frankfurt School philosopher Adorno famously concluded, critical cultural activity survived at best in the realm of an autonomous art that radically distanced itself from the means-ends rationality of the market.

The commitment to highbrow modernism that was the logical conclusion of Adorno's arguments was not shared by less politically pessimistic figures on the liberal left: the writer Heinrich Böll for instance, whose work was notable for its combination of critical political engagement with a more accessible realist aesthetic. But what was common, not only to Adorno, Habermas and Böll, but to conservative theorists of modernization, was their perception of the nature of the forces underpinning historical development. Erhard's free market conception of the liberal individual (the entrepreneur unfettered by market regulation, the free-spending consumer) as the motor of historical progression was of course radically opposed to the Marxist championing of the (working-class) collectivity; but for both, it was the rationally constituted subject born in the age of Enlightenment that had been – and would in some accounts continue to be – the bearer of progressive developments in modern history.

VII 1968 and after: modernity's subject fragmented

On 2 June 1967, a demonstration was staged in West Berlin to protest against an official visit by the Shah of Persia. The protest culminated in confrontations between demonstrators and police, and with the shooting of a student, Benno Ohnesorg. Those events were to become a turning point in West German cultural–political development.

The left-liberal intelligentsia had for some time expressed unease over the failure of a putatively modernized Federal Republic to sever links with National Socialism. The Auschwitz trials of the early 1960s had shocked the country with their revelation of the numbers of war criminals who lived on unpunished as apparently ordinary citizens. The Grand Coalition of 1966 had installed ex-Nazis in high office: Kurt-Georg Kiesinger as Chancellor, with the somewhat compromised Heinrich Lübke continuing as President. All this, combined with the lack of effective opposition under the all-party Grand Coalition, and a series of scandals exposing ex-Nazis in public life, had by the late 1960s fuelled a spirit of hostility to the status quo. This disaffection, most keenly felt by a rising generation too young to have experienced fascism, crystallized in the student unrest of the late 1960s and early 1970s. Ohnesorg's death especially gave new impetus to leftist student groups such as the Socialist League of German Students (Sozialistischer Deutscher Studentenbund – SDS); it confirmed their Marxist analysis of post-war West Germany as a state dominated – as was the Third Reich – by the dehumanizing forces of capitalist accumulation and state control.

The response of the student left was an energetic commitment to the Marxist utopia of working-class revolution. But the grass-roots unrest fomented in the so-called extra-parliamentary opposition after 1967 involved much more than a class-based challenge to post-war cultural–political consensus. The emergence through the 1970s and 1980s of new social movements across the political spectrum – the women's movement, the ecology and peace movements, single-issue citizens' initiatives (*Bürgerinitiativen*), squatters' groups – revealed a West German polity fractured, not only along lines of class, but of gender, sexuality, region and generation.

The identity politics of the period posed two kinds of challenge to the Enlightenment mythology on which the FRG was founded. The ecology and peace movements in particular, with their warnings of nuclear catastrophe and ecological collapse, raised key doubts over the vision of historical progress that had underpinned socioeconomic development in both post-war German states. That challenge to rationalist conceptions of a progressive history was reinforced by a new scepticism over Enlightenment rationalism's capacity to represent the multiple identities in and through which history was made. From feminism, for instance, came insights into the gender blindness of existing histories: witness the efforts of feminist historians, writers, artists or film-makers to recapture the lost narratives of women 'hidden from history'. The fracturing of the subject of German history which those feminist efforts entailed was echoed across the spectrum of cultural production in the period. The renaissance of West German film under a new generation of *auteurs* – Rainer Werner Fassbinder, Wim Wenders and Werner Herzog were the most enduring – was characterized by a new concern with the complexities of subjective encounters with German history, in Fassbinder's historical melodrama *The Marriage of Maria Braun* (*Die Ehe der Maria Braun*, 1979), for instance, in Helma Sanders-Brahms' autobiographical portrait of her mother, *Germany, Pale Mother* (*Deutschland, bleiche Mutter*, 1980), or in Alexander Kluge's idiosyncratic *The Patriot* (*Die Patriotin*, 1979).

Illustration 21.2   Kluge's *The Patriot* (1979): a schoolteacher (Hannelore Hoger) digs for traces of a different national history

The emphasis in films from the so-called New German Cinema on recent history as a post-modern patchwork of competing narratives and identities was paralleled in contemporary historiography by a turn to local and oral history, which produced a similarly pluralized picture of German historical experience. It was, moreover, not only the *collective* identity of 'Germany' that began now to fragment. We saw in Wolf's *Patterns of Childhood* one example of how literature of the period used conceptions of the fractured self to explore a new *subjective* relation to German identity and history. The pervasiveness of this historical subjectivism was evidenced, too, by the engagement amongst younger intellectuals with the post-modern philosophies of Lyotard, Baudrillard and Foucault, or with psychoanalysis as a tool for understanding psychic attachments to political formations. Klaus Theweleit's 1977 study of the psychology of the fascist male, *Male Fantasies (Männerphantasien)* was a key text in this regard; more significant still was Alexander and Margarethe Mitscherlich's *The Inability to Mourn (Die Unfähigkeit zu Trauern*, 1967), now part of the recognized canon of historical writing on the post-war period. The Mitscherlichs' social-psychological account of the FRG as a nation incapable of overcoming its psychic investment in fascism was warmly received in a West Germany whose younger intellectuals seemed obsessed with the same search to unearth the residues of fascist history in contemporary German identity.

Post-1968 interiority, moreover, was not confined to the West. Ulbricht's replacement in 1971 by Erich Honecker as First Secretary of the SED ushered in a period of unprecedented cultural openness in the GDR. The new liberalism was evidenced by official toleration of previously vilified popular cultural forms (rock music, Western dress, discotheques, etc.), as well as of literary works exploring individual conflicts with state socialism, from Ulrich Plenzdorf's youth cultural lament *The New Sorrows of Young W.* (*Die neuen Leiden des jungen W.*, 1972), through Irmtraud Morgner's picaresque fantasy of a woman's life, *Troubadora Beatriz* (1974), to Monika Maron's bleak account of environmental pollution and state censorship, *Flight of Ashes* (*Flugasche*, 1981). *Flight of Ashes* appeared after the 1976 expatriation of the dissident singer-songwriter Wolf Biermann, an affair that marked the beginning of a renewed clampdown on cultural opposition. Maron's novel, accordingly, was banned in the GDR; but the centring of the narrative on the psychological torment of a woman journalist caught in the conflict between the political demands of socialism and a more personal ethical and emotional agenda made the novel nonetheless typical of a decade or more of GDR literary subjectivism.

VIII 1983–1996: the return to nation?

The legacy of the cultural movements of 1968 and after was, then, a newly diverse, 'post-modern' conception of German identity. The German 'nation', it had now to be acknowledged, was an unstable and internally heterogeneous construction, an entity fractured by differences of class, gender, sexuality, region, ethnicity, etc., and (in the perception of GDR intellectuals especially) marked by contradictions between subjective desires and collective ethico-political demands.

In the face of such cultural instability, there has been since the early 1980s something of a retrenchment to apparently more comfortable conceptions of unitary nationhood. The conservative *Wende* (turning point) that followed Helmut Kohl's election as West German Chancellor in 1983 involved what many saw as a problematic reassertion of national values. One notorious example was Kohl's comment early on in his term of office on the 'grace of belated birth' that supposedly distanced post-war generations from responsibility for National Socialism, and allowed them to look towards a more positive future for late twentieth-century Germany. Parallel controversies raged through the 1980s in the cultural realm: witness, for instance, the heated debates sparked by Edgar Reitz's 1984 epic *Heimat* over the new patriotism in contemporary West German film; witness too the historians' debate (*Historikerstreit*) of 1986–7, which featured such prominent figures as Ernst Nolte and Jürgen Habermas in conflict over the legitimacy of reclaiming patriotic values from some corners of the history of National Socialism.

The GDR, too, witnessed from the early 1980s a re-engagement with hitherto denigrated national traditions, in the reinstatement of the Prussian legacy in official history, for instance, or in the exploration within dissident movements of points of convergence East and West (the networking activities of the women's and peace movements are one example). But it was the 'quiet revolution' of 1989 that most forcefully reasserted the centrality to German identity of concepts of *Volk* and nation. When the crowds on the streets of Leipzig, Dresden and Berlin changed their slogan from 'we are *the* people' to 'we are *one* people' (*Wir sind ein Volk*), and when, in the elections of spring 1990, they chose the Conservative Christian Democrat (CDU) and Christian Social (CSU) coalition as the political force that promised the most rapid route to unification, commentators abroad and at home (the writer Günter Grass was amongst the most persistent) feared that Germany was set to abandon the liberal dream of pluralist democracy in a Germany ruled by and for the people, in favour of an all-too-familiar authoritarian and monolithic vision of nation.

The truth, at the time of writing, is that Germany remains as ever balanced between these competing national models. On the one hand, as the 1992 Rostock atrocities amply demonstrate, unification has indeed provoked a resurgence of right-wing nationalism and racist violence. On the other hand, the German model of federal democracy remains amongst the most successful in Europe in guaranteeing civil rights and social justice to its citizens. More than this, cultural trends are inexorably towards a pluralization of cultural forms and identities. Grass-roots pluralism is perhaps most strikingly evident in the cultural productions of Germany's most politically and economically marginal group, the migrant workforce. Some of the most vibrant literary works of the 1990s were penned by first- and second-generation migrant writers: Emine Sevgi Özdamar, whose novel *Life Is a Caravanserai* (*Das Leben ist eine Karawanserai*, 1992) received the Walter Hasenclever literary prize in 1992; or the poet and essayist Zafer Senoçak, whose essay collection *Atlas of Tropical Germany* (*Atlas des tropischen Deutschland*, 1993) offers an especially eloquent plea for a multiethnic and multicultural Germany. Turkish-German hip-hop – surely amongst the most startling of contemporary cultural creolizations – has blossomed in the inner cities of a Germany that may refuse to recognize Turkish migrants politically as citizens, but which has long since acceded to their cultural influence. As ever, then, the question of what is 'German' remains open, and German identity a site of contestation over competing constructions of nation.

Notes:

1. Misik, Robert, 'Die Dämonen ziehen ein', *Profil* 36 (31 August 1992), p. 43.
2. Krüger-Potratz, Marianne, *Anderssein gab es nicht. Ausländer und Minderheiten in der DDR* (Münster, New York: Waxmann Verlag, 1991), p. 2.

3. Geißler, Heiner, 'Kein Grund zur Angst. Ein Plädoyer für eine multikulturelle Gesellschaft', *Der Spiegel* 41 (1991), p. 2.

4. Bullivant, Keith, and Rice, C. Jane, 'Reconstruction and Integration: the Culture of West German Stabilization 1945 to 1968', in Rob Burns, ed., *German Cultural Studies. An Introduction* (Oxford: Oxford University Press, 1995), p. 219.

5. Fulbrook, Mary, *The Fontana History of Germany 1918–1990. The Divided Nation* (London: Fontana, 1991), 141–50.

6. Andersch, Alfred, 'Das junge Europa formt sein Gesicht', *Der Ruf*, 15 August 1946. Reproduced in Klaus Wagenbach *et al.*, eds., *Vaterland, Muttersprache. Deutsche Schriftsteller und ihr Staat seit 1945* (Berlin: Verlag Klaus Wagenbach, 1994), p. 55.

7. *Ibid.*, p. 57.

8. Jaspers, Karl, *Die Schuldfrage. Von der politischen Haftung Deutschlands* (Munich: Piper, 1965), p. 16 (first edn., 1946).

9. *Ibid.*, p. 7.

10. Bullivant and Rice, 'Reconstruction', pp. 224f.

11. Wolf, Christa, *A Model Childhood*, transl. Ursule Molinaro and Hedwig Rappolt (London: Virago, 1983), p. 3. The translation 'Patterns of Childhood' is preferred by many critics, since it avoids the didactic connotations of the term 'model': connotations that the author herself resisted, since the identity she portrays herself as having assumed as a child under National Socialism is presented as deeply problematic.

12. Anonymous participant in a public debate on *Patterns of Childhood* following a reading by Wolf at the GDR Academy of Arts, 8 October and 3 December 1975. Reproduced in Karin McPherson, *The Fourth Dimension. Interviews with Christa Wolf* (London: Verso, 1988), p. 62.

13. The sixteen principles of town planning are reproduced in Ian Latham and Jane Brierley, eds., *Architectural design profile* (New York: St. Martin's Press, 1982), p. 3.

Select bibliography

Burns, Rob, ed., *German Cultural Studies. An Introduction* (Oxford: Oxford University Press, 1995).

Carter, Erica, *How German is She? Postwar West German Reconstruction and the Consuming Woman* (Ann Arbor: University of Michigan Press, 1997).

Clyne, Michael, *Language and Society in the German-speaking Countries* (Cambridge: Cambridge University Press, 1984).

Eley, Geoff, 'Modernity at the Limit: Rethinking German Exceptionalism before 1914', *New Formations* 28 (spring 1996), pp. 21–45.

Elsaesser, Thomas, *New German Cinema: A History* (London: BFI/Macmillan, 1989).

Fulbrook, Mary, *The Fontana History of Germany. 1918–1990, The Divided Nation* (London: Fontana, 1991).

Fulbrook, Mary, *The Two Germanies 1945–1990. Problems of Interpretation* (Basingstoke: Macmillan, 1992).

Goodbody, Axel, and Tate, Dennis, eds., *Geist und Macht. Writers and the State in the GDR* (Amsterdam: Rodopi, 1992).

Humphreys, Peter J., *Media and Media Policy in Germany: The Press and Broadcasting since 1945* (Oxford: Berg, 1994).

Kaes, Anton, *From Hitler to Heimat. The Return of History as Film* (Cambridge, MA and London: Harvard University Press, 1989).

Kolinsky, Eva, *Women in West Germany: Life, Work and Politics* (Oxford: Berg, 1989).

O'Brien, Peter, 'Identity Crisis in the New Germany,' *Debatte* 2(1) (1994), pp. 64–81.

Pommerin, Reiner, ed., *The American Impact on Postwar Germany* (Providence and New York: Berghahn, 1995).

Suhr, Heidrun, 'Ausländerliteratur: Minority Literature in the Federal Republic of Germany'. *New German Critique* 46 (1989), pp. 71–103.

22

The end of the GDR: revolution and voluntary annexation

Jonathan Osmond

I The German question and the legitimacy of the GDR

Writing in 1844 in *Germany: A Winter's Tale*, Heinrich Heine characterized the smell of Germany's future as 'old cabbage and Russian leather'. Add to these the fumes of burning lignite and the exhausts of Trabant two-stroke engines, and one might in a sour-tempered moment claim to have captured the scent of the German Democratic Republic. Heine was writing a while before the first unification of Germany. The GDR existed only in division until its unification with the Federal Republic of Germany on 3 October 1990. Since that date the smells, sounds and sights of eastern Germany have altered in numerous ways, drawing the land closer to its mighty western neighbour, but there remain elements of unease, discontent and even anger on both sides of what had been the most fortified border in Europe. The revolution in the GDR – for revolution it surely was – brought immediate joy to many East Germans but it did not succeed in bringing lasting reform to the state. Instead it paved the way for the absorption of the GDR into an enlarged Federal Republic, a course which certainly meant for many people enhanced freedoms, opportunities and living standards, but also levels of insecurity unfamiliar from GDR days.

The ambiguities of these events have been reflected in their treatment by politicians, intellectuals, journalists, political scientists and historians. Portrayals have ranged from the exultant and self-satisfied to the angry and complaining, usually – but by no means always – observing a west–east demarcation. Along this line are the political memoirs of Wolfgang Schäuble, proud to have negotiated the unification treaty for Chancellor Helmut Kohl but crippled by a would-be assassin nine days after German unity; the plangent self-justifications of GDR leaders Erich Honecker, Egon Krenz, Günter Mittag and Hans Modrow; the uncompromising warnings against unification by novelist Günter Grass; and the depiction of psychological devastation by East German psychotherapist Hans-Joachim Maaz.

Illustration 22.1 A parade celebrating the thirtieth anniversary of the German Democratic Republic, 1979

The panoply of issues in current debates includes: the nature of the revolution and its appropriation; the legitimacy of retribution against those in authority in the GDR; the balance between economic freedom and social justice; the extent of popular collusion in the communist system and the ways of confronting it now; the respective contributions to union of the old and new federal states; and the ownership and interpretation of the GDR's history. Put in these general terms, the disputes may appear anodyne and remote. In practice, they involve real people in bad and in good situations: a woman being refused an abortion on religiously defined grounds she does not share; members of a farming family losing their house and employment to a West German claimant; a border-guard being imprisoned for disobeying orders to shoot escapees; a wife learning that for years she has been spied upon by her husband for the security service; a worker in the Saarland on the French border facing a tax increase to finance the unification of Germany up to a Polish border he has never seen; the reuniting of a family; the opening of a profitable new business; the renovation of a street; a first Mediterranean holiday; and the opportunity to read and discuss critically. All these experiences are laden with the meanings of unification, and it will be a long time before they can be analysed dispassionately, especially in Germany itself. From a racist attack on the street to an academic discussion of the continuities of German history, the revolution in the GDR and German unification have opened up the German question once more, but added to it new clauses.

In the autumn of 1989 hundreds of thousands of GDR citizens took to the streets of the major cities, demanding the political and social changes of which others, fleeing to the Federal Republic via third countries, had despaired. This two-fold popular pressure played its part in bringing about change in the party and state leadership and the opening of the GDR's borders. Thereupon the very nature of the GDR came into question, democratic elections were held, and a swift process of economic, social, and then political unification with the Federal Republic was set in train. To understand these events, however, one must first look back further: to the very status of the GDR and to the tensions building within it by the 1980s.

From its foundation, the GDR was subject to the criticism that it was an 'artificial' state, defined only by the original Soviet occupation and by the political purposes of the German communists. Such a viewpoint was not restricted to those in the Federal Republic who disputed the legitimacy of the state. In the GDR in August 1989 Otto Reinhold, the rector of the Academy of Social Sciences of the party Central Committee, was writing of the GDR: 'It can be conceived only as an anti-fascist, socialist state, a socialist alternative to the FRG. What right would a capitalist GDR have to exist beside a capitalist Federal Republic? None, of course.' This equation of the state with its political system was to prove a liability in 1989–90, despite the fact that all states are in a sense 'artificial', in that they are created out of particular historical circumstances. The shape of Poland since 1945 or the creation and re-creation of the Austrian Republic in the twentieth century are both related instances of states defined in territory and political system by warfare and power politics, but their integrity has not been challenged in the way that the GDR was challenged and annulled. The fact that the GDR was based almost entirely upon a political project meant that the state itself was vulnerable when the political system collapsed, but primarily because there was an alternative resolution to the crisis, namely unification with the hugely successful Federal Republic next door.

This is not to deny that the GDR had over 40 years established an identity of its own and a degree of loyalty amongst large numbers of its citizens. In part this identity was based upon regional particularities; the role of the Saxons, Thuringians,

Mecklenburgers, Brandenburgers and Berliners should not be underestimated. In part it rested on pride in the achievements of the GDR after the calamity of world war and in the face of Western hostility. In part it was due to the high degree of social protection afforded to the working population. The political authorities themselves made great play of the distinctive nature and contribution of the GDR, and by the 1980s had distanced themselves from expectations of German unity, while at the same time linking the GDR to the wider German past, both 'progressive' and – in the cases of Martin Luther, Frederick the Great, Otto von Bismarck, and the Prussian conspirators of July 1944 – the less obviously 'progressive'. If a separate GDR identity was being fostered, it was, of course, reinforced by the isolation of the GDR from the West after the building of the Berlin Wall in 1961.

In 1989–90 these elements of 'artificiality' and vulnerability of the state on the one hand and distinct identity and citizen loyalty on the other combined to produce the volatile mixture of pressure for reform from within, population haemorrhage and a rising clamour of demands for German unity. That they did so was dependent, however, on events outside Germany.

II The GDR and the wider world

The limited scope for political change in the states of the Warsaw Treaty Organization had been demonstrated most pointedly in 1953 in the GDR, in 1956 in Hungary, and in 1968 in Czechoslovakia. On all three occasions Soviet troops had been instrumental in crushing popular revolt and/or communist reformers. The Poles had a more varied experience, but General Jaruzelski's declaration of a State of War in 1981 to combat the independent trade union Solidarity was intended in part to prevent Soviet military intervention. In Rumania Nicolae Ceauşescu managed to detach himself somewhat from Soviet tutelage, but only by being more ghastly than the party leaders elsewhere. The famous crisis points were matched by numerous other instances when Soviet pressure was brought to bear on domestic politics. In the GDR, Walter Ulbricht's ejection from the party leadership in 1971 was due in large measure to Moscow's displeasure with his reluctance to develop ties with the Federal Republic, and conversely in 1984 his successor Erich Honecker's proposed visit to that other Germany was scotched by a cautious Kremlin. It was shortly thereafter, however, that the reliance of the East Berlin leadership upon Soviet military might began to be thrown in doubt. The selection of Mikhail Gorbachev as General Secretary of the Communist Party of the Soviet Union in March 1985 ushered in a period of attempted openness and restructuring in the USSR which was to culminate in a clear message from Gorbachev that his forces would not intervene in the affairs of fellow Warsaw Treaty Organization members and his encouragement of those in the GDR Politbüro who wished to push out Honecker and save communist rule through reform, albeit of an ultra-cautious type.

The talk of reform in Moscow, the worldwide acceptability of Gorbachev, and the withdrawal of ultimate Soviet military support were accompanied by other, often contradictory messages from fellow communist states. Polish striving for change and the resultant political and economic instability of the 1980s were not generally admired in the GDR, either by the party leadership or the population at large. Unsavoury prejudices played a large part in this. Greater economic leeway in Hungary, on the other hand, was viewed positively by the many East German holiday-makers to that country, if not by the East Berlin regime. Much further afield the Chinese communists' savage treatment of the student protesters on Tiananmen Square in June 1989 outraged reformers and moderates in the GDR, especially when the party leadership went out of its way to congratulate its Beijing counterpart. Within the Politbüro, however, there were also those who hoped to avoid recourse to such tactics within the GDR. The implicit threats from Honecker, State Security (Stasi) head Erich Mielke and others were real enough, but they served to generate anger, instability and a search for other solutions, even within the Socialist Unity Party of Germany (SED).

The GDR looked westward as well as eastward, and if anything the Federal German contribution in the 1980s appeared to be one of bolstering the GDR. Massive bank loans, brokered in part by the Catholic conservative Prime Minister of Bavaria, Franz Josef Strauss, pulled the GDR out of the worst of its economic difficulties at the beginning of the decade and allowed the regime to continue its social policy of heavily subsidizing necessities. Then in 1987 Honecker's rescheduled visit to Bonn was permitted by Gorbachev, and he revelled in this assertion of the separate identity and political parity of the GDR. Meanwhile the Federal Republic over the years performed another useful function for the GDR leadership by buying out substantial numbers of GDR *émigrés*. From the perspective of East Berlin these were malcontents whose departure could only strengthen socialist rule.

III   Origins of domestic grievance

There were indeed causes for discontent at home, although most of them were not new and had not since June 1953 led to a major challenge to the regime. The economy of the GDR, though lauded as a success story at home and within the communist camp and respected even in the West, was built upon flawed foundations and was unable to provide the standard of living glimpsed nightly by the population on West German television. Heavy dependence upon Western loans, misdirected investment in already outdated high technology, inflexible trade patterns within the Council for Mutual Economic Assistance (CMEA), and cumbersome planning mechanisms marred further by deceit and corruption all contributed to an economy characterized by long but inefficient working weeks. A well-educated and generally hardworking population could not compensate for unreliable old plant and production bottlenecks. The provision of consumer goods was nothing like as dire as in Poland during the 1980s, but choice was poor, quality was low, and there were long waits for motor cars and other major purchases. The obvious deterioration of the physical environment, both through neglect and pollution, contributed nothing to people's sense of well-being. The economic trajectory was also not reassuring: even on the basis of the questionable official figures, growth in net material product declined from 5.5 per cent in 1984 to 2.1 per cent in 1989. It would be mistaken to suggest a simple link between economic slowdown and political protest, although the economic situation restricted the choices available to those at the top in the GDR when the political crisis hit.

Political issues and matters of personal liberty shaped the relatively small dissenting groups of the 1980s, groups which were to provide an important focus for the large-scale protest in 1989. From the beginning of the decade two aspects of militarization were challenged: the stationing of American and Soviet missiles in Europe, and the emphasis on armed preparedness propagated in GDR schools amongst children from a very early age. In January 1986 a small illegal group was founded, the Peace and Human Rights Initiative, the founders of which were intellectuals and artists. They faced harassment and even expulsion from the GDR, but returned to speak out once more in 1989. Another strand of opposition concerned itself primarily with the environmental issue. This was by no means a politically neutral agenda, bearing in mind the GDR's heavy energy dependence on dirty lignite, the over-use of chemical fertilizers in agriculture, and the secretive, largely Soviet-controlled uranium mining in the south of the country. The security forces were even prepared to invade ecclesiastical premises in their 1987 raid on the Berlin Zion church's environmental library. The churches, particularly the Protestant churches, were indeed the only officially permitted alternative forum for debate, and – sometimes against the wishes of the church hierarchy – they came to represent a focus for dissent. Not to be neglected either were those who used the democratic rhetoric and constitutional provisions of the GDR to criticize the regime in practice. In January 1988 and January 1989 the words of the early communist Rosa Luxemburg, murdered in that month in 1919, were taken up by demonstrators: 'freedom is always the freedom of others who think differently'. And in May 1989 unofficial observers attempted to monitor the process of local elections, coming to the unsurprising conclusion that the authorities were deliberately underestimating the growing numbers of those expressing opposition to the official list of candidates of the so-called National Front.

The unofficial peace movement, the environmentalists, the activists within the churches, and the political protesters – amongst whom there was a high degree of overlap – represented nevertheless a very thin stratum of GDR society. Not only that: their ranks were depleted by the voluntary departure or expulsion of many active individuals. Those who remained were under constant scrutiny by the Stasi not only in their purportedly political activities, but in their working, social, private and sexual lives. The spies were not primarily full-time Stasi operatives, but unofficial informers who were often members of the dissenting groups themselves. The writer Sascha Anderson, for example, was thought by his associates to be a mainstay of the alternative cultural scene in the Prenzlauer Berg district of Berlin. Perhaps he was, but he was also a Stasi informant. Similarly, several figures who emerged in the new oppositional political parties of 1989 – Wolfgang Schnur of Democratic Awakening and Ibrahim Böhme of the SPD, for example – were irretrievably compromised by their connections with the Stasi. Church leaders were not immune, although the prominent lay figure, Manfred Stolpe, survived as post-unification Prime Minister of Brandenburg, despite admitted contacts with the security forces.

The Stasi might feel that it was in complete control of potential opposition, but it could not prevent long-term dissatisfaction on the part of the population at large. The particular focus of an individual's or a family's disgruntlement might vary, but the imposition of the tight border and the day-to-day behaviour of the bureaucracy took their toll on people's patience. For the upsurge to come, however, it required extraneous factors, and these were to emerge in 1989.

IV   The revolution of 1989

The process began in Hungary, which had so far progressed along the path of reform that the communist leadership agreed with neighbouring Austria to dismantle the fortifications on the common border from 2 May. This decision affected the GDR because a large number of East German holiday-makers realized the possibility of crossing into Austria and thence to the Federal Republic, where they could claim automatic citizenship. Through the summer, crowds built up in the Hungarian resorts and near the border, swollen by East Germans who had travelled to Hungary not for a holiday but in order to emigrate. They were not at first allowed through the border officially, although illegal breaches did take place, and then – under pressure and financial cajolement from Bonn and against the express wishes of their allies in East Berlin – the Hungarians on 11 September let the East Germans out without hindrance. Their trembling joy and the warm reception they received in the Federal Republic – initially at least – were flashed around the news bulletins of the world. West German television kept the population of the GDR fully informed.

Meanwhile the compound of the Federal German embassy in Prague was occupied by large numbers of would-be emigrants, and smaller numbers ensconced themselves in its Warsaw counterpart and in the Federal German mission in East Berlin. The Federal German Foreign Minister, Hans-Dietrich Genscher, negotiated with East Berlin a resolution of the mounting problem in Prague, and on 30 September personally announced to a rapturous reception outside the embassy that trains would leave Prague for the Federal Republic. Erich Honecker had insisted that they pass through GDR territory – causing violent scenes outside the railway station in Dresden when the local population realized what was happening and tried to get into the station premises – but there was no attempt to prevent the departure of these citizens. Indeed the official GDR response was that this was good riddance, an attitude which further inflamed feelings against the regime.

Escape was but one response to the growing crisis. From September, at the Nikolaikirche in the centre of Leipzig, Monday evening services began to be followed by ever-growing demonstration marches. The participants had a variety of demands: permission to travel outside the GDR, but also freedom of speech and assembly at home. There were those who chanted 'We want out!', but increasingly the marchers declared that 'We are staying here!' In their further assertion that they, and not the party hierarchy, were 'the people' in whose name the GDR existed, the emphasis had shifted to demands for political reform. This was potentially a very dangerous situation. The security forces waded in on many occasions to seize placards and to arrest marchers, but as the size of the demonstrations grew from several hundred to hundreds of thousands the threat grew of armed suppression in imitation of the Chinese. Only narrowly was mass bloodshed avoided on 9 October, although the responsibility for the crucial intercession has been claimed by a number of individuals, least convincingly by SED security secretary Egon Krenz himself.

The instability of population exodus and political protest was compounded by crisis within the SED itself. At the top Erich Honecker was sick with a gall bladder complaint for most of the summer, and it was unclear who, if anyone, was now in charge. Günter Mittag, the Party Secretary for the Economy, was Honecker's nominee, but – complained other members of the Politbüro – he took no action to stave off the deepening crisis. Not only in the Politbüro, but also in the further reaches of the party at district level opinion began to harden that Honecker had reached the end of his career. He took up work again on 25 September, hosted the celebrations of the fortieth anniversary of the GDR on 7 October, and was voted out of office by the Politbüro on 17 October and by the Central Committee the following day.

The anniversary festivity was indeed a crucial juncture, which brought together popular discontent, stirrings within the SED and the influence of Gorbachev. What had been intended by Honecker as a ringing endorsement of the success and stability of the GDR turned into the beginning of its final crisis. There were serious scuffles in Berlin between demonstrators and the security forces, and even the massed uniformed youth of the GDR were more enthusiastic about the reformer Gorbachev than they were about the hard line of the GDR leadership. Honecker looked completely out of touch with reality and was an embarrassment to Gorbachev and to most of the SED Politbüro. Quite what Gorbachev remarked on the eve of celebrations is contested by the eye-witnesses, but his message was clear: there had to be changes at the top. This was an encouragement in particular to Politbüro members Egon Krenz and Günter Schabowski, who conducted behind-the-scenes discussions with most of their comrades. At the meeting of 17 October it was Prime Minister Willi Stoph who interrupted Honecker to propose his dismissal, along with that of Mittag and Propaganda Secretary Joachim Herrmann. Honecker, Mittag and Herrmann in loyal communist fashion joined the rest of the Politbüro in voting in favour of the motion, and Egon Krenz was confirmed next day as new SED General Secretary by the Central Committee.

The ousting of Honecker did not bring the crisis to an end. Rather the reverse: demonstrations for wide-ranging political reforms and against the power of the Stasi

Illustration 22.2   Demonstration in Karl-Marx-Stadt (Chemnitz) on 28 October 1989. Throughout the GDR demonstrators found the courage to protest and demand free elections, freedom of the press and travel, and official recognition of New Forum

took place now in towns and cities throughout the GDR. The Leipzig events dominated, but by 4 November the numbers on the streets in the capital were now the highest yet: estimates began at 500,000. A number of new parties and organizations had been founded in September and October, the most important and broadest of which was New Forum. Krenz and Schabowski meanwhile attempted to present a new face of the SED, the former appearing on television engaging in debates in the street with ordinary citizens and the latter facing the cameras at a nightly press conference. They both stressed that democratic reforms were possible and they promised a new travel law. When this appeared on 6 November it excited nothing but disappointment and contempt, and was rejected next day by a committee of the GDR parliament, the People's Chamber. Events were now moving very swiftly. The Stoph government resigned that day and the Politbüro immediately afterwards on 8 November, opening the way for the Central Committee to elect a new one. For the first time the votes cast for and against candidates were made public, and some did not find favour. An important new face also appeared in the Politbüro: Hans Modrow, the district Party Secretary for Dresden and a man who had been considered for several years as a possible reformist leader of the GDR. He was recommended as successor to Stoph as prime minister, while Krenz continued as effective head of state and General Secretary of the party.

The most exciting events were about to occur. Krenz had arranged for the drafting of yet another travel law, this time making it possible for GDR citizens to venture westward after only routine and short-notice application for an official visa. He hoped thereby – in curious reverse logic to that employed back in 1961 when the Wall was built – to ease the crisis in the GDR by allowing its citizens out. The assumption – broadly correct as it turned out – was that most would return home. In the early evening of 9 November Krenz gave Schabowski, who was departing for his regular briefing of the international press, a summary of the new regulations for him to announce. They were intended to come into force the next day, but Schabowski told those who questioned him that as far as he knew they applied with immediate effect. This was a televised response and the consequences were felt at once in Berlin. Crowds gathered at the border crossing points and demanded to be let through. The mood was generally good-humoured, but the crush of people and the uncertainty of the security forces meant that calamity was possible. Without a clear chain of command any more but showing good sense in an emergency, the border guards opened the barriers and the crowds surged through. On the Western side the wider section of the Wall by the Brandenburg Gate was scaled by revellers. Through the small hours of 10 November Easterners swept into West Berlin and caroused in the cafés of the Kurfürstendamm, while Westerners moved through the bleak dark Friedrichstrasse down to Unter den Linden and a view of the Brandenburg Gate from the other side.

If the effects of this night were to be felt worldwide, its first characteristic was of a divided city coming once more together. The (West) *Berliner Zeitung* on 10 November carried a banner headline of 'The Wall has gone! Berlin is Berlin again!' Its second characteristic was then, perhaps, the window-shopping exodus of the following days, and the alacrity with which Western business set about creating brand loyalty. At the Chausseestrasse crossing point in Berlin, Kaiser's supermarket from the back of a container lorry dispensed free coffee and chocolate bars, packaged in branded carrier bags. At Checkpoint Charlie the youth branch of the West Berlin CDU handed out leaflets declaring 'Unity, Justice and Freedom' and 'Self-determination for all Germans'. Attached was a token for 'one small drink' at McDonald's, generously valid for three days.

Egon Krenz reaped little reward. The political crisis deepened, while the potential economic consequences began to exercise the authorities east and west of the broken Wall. As Krenz began to establish dialogue with representatives of the Bonn government and Modrow installed his new government, the demonstrations continued. It was not going to be possible for the debate to take place solely within the SED. Federal Chancellor Helmut Kohl seized the initiative in late November when he put forward his ten-point plan for German unity, and then in early December pressure from within the SED as well as from without forced Krenz into resignation and brought Modrow into negotiation with a wide range of old and new parties at the so-called Round Table. Events in Berlin were matched by widespread purges of the SED throughout the GDR and the establishment of local round tables.

V Crisis and unification in 1990

From this point evolved a divergence into two political perspectives. On the one hand the democratic renewal of the GDR began painfully to take shape, as New Forum, Democracy Now, Democratic Awakening, the Peace and Human Rights Initiative and other new movements and parties set an agenda for change. The emphasis was as much on social responsibility and justice as on personal freedom; the socialist ideal was still at the forefront, but now in a democratic context. These developments were matched by processes of reform – part idealistic, part opportunistic – within the old parties of the GDR, including the SED, which in December took as its sub-title 'Party of Democratic Socialism'. This appellation of PDS in February supplanted the old name entirely. On the other hand, popular pressure on the streets and diplomatic manoeuvre by some governments of the West were pushing strongly in the direction of German unity, even if at this stage it was considered to be a distant rather than an immediate goal. As the crisis of population loss and economic instability continued, the latter strand of unity began to be the dominant one. The crowds now declared not 'We are the people' as they had done in the autumn, but 'We are one people', and just before Christmas 1989 gave Helmut Kohl an ecstatic welcome in Dresden. Although the British, French and Russians were concerned about the effects of over-hasty moves towards unification, Kohl saw an opportunity to seize the inter-German initiative and behind him from an early stage were the Americans.

Within the GDR the economic situation was running out of control. Production was suffering from a continued haemorrhaging of labour, and West German goods and money were entering the country. Smuggling and an illegal currency market were preventing economic stabilization. The political situation was as confused. Modrow was trying simultaneously to maintain the old power structures while granting concessions, a recipe for further conflict. One example was his attempt to replace the Stasi with a downgraded national security office, which promptly acquired the unfortunate nickname of 'Nasi'. He was forced to back down, but this did not reduce popular anger about the activities of the Stasi, revealed daily in ʳhe press. On 15 January 1990 the Stasi headquarters in Berlin were stormed by protesters, some of whom were probably Stasi operatives anxious to destroy incriminating files. Another example was Modrow's foundation in March of the Treuhandanstalt, a trustee agency originally intended to take over the economic assets of the GDR and maintain the bulk of them in the state sector. Only later did it take on the opposite role of selling enterprises off to the private sector.

The SED-PDS was disintegrating, as members left or were expelled, but the new political movements were just as fractious. New Forum, the largest of the new groupings, failed to seize the initiative as an alternative political party, choosing to remain as a broad loose movement. This helped to open the way into GDR politics for the Federal German political parties, although this would no doubt have been a characteristic of the situation anyway. As the sense of political crisis deepened, the proposed elections to the People's Chamber were brought forward from the original May to 18 March, and the Western CDU, SPD and FDP sought out for themselves appropriate Eastern partners. Helmut Kohl's CDU hedged its bets by forging an Alliance for Germany with the old Eastern CDU, a new conservative German Social Union (DSU) from Saxony, and Democratic Awakening; the SPD joined forces with its new and weak namesake in the East; and the FDP brought together old and new 'liberals' in the League of Free Democrats. New Forum teamed up as Alliance 90 with the much smaller Democracy Now and Peace and Human Rights Initiative, but in doing so failed to make a connection with the Greens environmental lobby or the Social Democrats.

All these groups and parties, plus others, were represented in the new coalition and purportedly non-party government conceded by Modrow on 5 February. The opposition parties had no specific portfolios, however, so there was no sense of real responsibility. The PDS was still perceived as the main obstacle to real reform, but none of the new players could exert much positive influence. They began to lose ground, and the elections of 18 March saw a resounding victory of the Alliance for Germany, spearheaded by the CDU. With 192 seats out of 400, it did not quite reach an overall majority and brought the SPD (88 seats) and League of Free Democrats (21 seats) into government. The PDS – now unacceptable as a coalition partner – survived with 66 seats, but the representatives of the citizens' initiatives which had been at the forefront of the revolution were nowhere, with only 12 seats in the new parliament. On 9 April Lothar de Maizière, leader of the Eastern CDU since November 1989, formed a cabinet dominated by the CDU, but with Social Democrats as Foreign Minister (Markus Meckel) and Minister of Finance (Walter Romberg).

The success of the CDU, which had not been indicated by earlier opinion polls, can be attributed to the efforts of Helmut Kohl's party to promise rapid economic integration of the GDR into the Federal Republic and to the growing international acceptance of the notion of German unity. Already in February it had been agreed in Ottawa that 'Two-Plus-Four' talks would take place, bringing together the two German states and the four former occupying powers, who had important residual rights not only in divided Berlin but also in Germany at large. Margaret Thatcher and Mikhail Gorbachev were still broadly hostile to the rapid creation of a large politically united Germany, but the momentum for an agreement of sorts was hard to stop. The desperate economic situation in the GDR had prompted even Modrow in February to agree to move toward monetary and economic union, and his attempt to create a neutral Germany had been blocked firmly by Kohl. Once the de Maizière government had taken over, Kohl could proceed rapidly with his plans for first economic, then political unity, and he had the full support of US President George Bush.

The appeal of the Deutschemark to the population of the GDR was crucial in the discussions of German unity. It was a lure to large- and small-scale currency speculators and also to those seeking better employment. To the Kohl government it was clear that the current situation had to be stabilized and that it was better to take the Deutschemark to the East Germans than to have them come westwards to the Deutschemark. There remained the question of the exchange rate, however, which must not be allowed to weaken the powerful Federal German currency and awaken memories of the inflation of the early 1920s and late 1940s. In the event, Bonn ignored the advice of the Federal Bank and gave way to pressure from the East German population and its new government. On 23 April – only two weeks after the formation of the de Maizière government – it was announced that a 1:1 exchange rate would apply to East German wages and to the first tranche of private savings. The following day Kohl and de Maizière agreed that 1 July 1990 would be the date of monetary, economic and social union, and less than a month later – on 18 May – the treaty was signed in Bonn which provided the detail. The necessary legislation was moved through the People's Chamber in the GDR and the Bundestag and Bundesrat in the Federal Republic in June. From midnight on 30 June/1 July the inter-German border was open, the currency was shared, and when shops opened in the GDR on Monday, 2 July, West German produce was already in place. Saxon butter had disappeared, and Bavarian butter was on display instead.

The speed of these events should not disguise the considerable but minority opposition to them in both GDR and Federal Republic. In the former it was to be expected that the PDS would object to what it saw as the sell-out of the GDR, but there were those in the other non-coalition parties who saw the opportunities for a non-aligned, democratic and socialist GDR being thrown away in favour of hard-currency consumerism. There was no let-up in the economic melt-down of the GDR, especially after 1 July, when demand for East German produce slumped. Domestic consumers were understandably attracted to new attractively packaged Western goods, and the former export markets of the GDR in eastern Europe fell away drastically. Industrial workers and farmers in the GDR began to protest about their predicament. Meanwhile in the Federal Republic the Social Democrats, led by Oskar Lafontaine, Prime Minister of the Saarland, adopted a strategy towards economic union which managed to antagonize both the western and eastern electorates. Lafontaine correctly accused the Kohl government of underestimating the problems and costs of unification, but gave the impression of trying to sabotage the national cause. At the same time he made the East German working classes feel as if they were regarded as unwanted second-class Germans. There were, to be honest, many West Germans who felt precisely this, but for the trade-union-oriented SPD to take this line was for the party a political disaster in the making.

Kohl's haste in the summer of 1990 must be understood in its international setting.

He knew that the Americans would not tolerate a Germany outside NATO, nor did he wish any such thing himself. On the other hand, he had to have the agreement of the Soviet Union, and if negotiations took too long there was no guarantee that the relatively accommodating Gorbachev would still be in place. It therefore came to him as an immense and astonishing relief when at the meeting of the Chancellor and the Soviet President in the Caucasus in mid-July 1990 the latter agreed to all-German NATO membership. This was not the last hurdle in the way of German unification, but it was the most important one and the subsequent negotiations – though hectic and hair-raising at times, as the accounts by Kohl's main negotiator Interior Minister Schäuble and by Bush's aides Zelikow and Rice attest – could proceed with energy. By this stage the wishes of the GDR government, represented after the mid-August sacking of the SPD ministers by Lothar de Maizière himself, were of little consequence. Kohl's dealings were primarily with the Federal Republic's Western allies and with the Soviet Union. The Poles, anxious about the inviolability of the Oder–Neisse border, were brought in briefly to the Two-Plus-Four meeting in Paris in July, but even their concerns were put off until German unification was in place. On the last day of August the 900-page unification treaty was signed in East Berlin, on 12 September the Two-Plus-Four talks were concluded in Moscow, the following day signatures were appended to a German–Soviet cooperation treaty on Soviet troop withdrawal and German economic assistance to the USSR, and at midnight on 2/3 October 1990 the territory of the GDR became part of the Federal Republic of Germany and Berlin was restored as the capital city.

Two days later 144 representatives of the GDR joined an enlarged Bundestag, pending federal elections in December. Meanwhile, on 14 October the five reconstituted East German federal states (Mecklenburg/West Pomerania, Brandenburg, Saxony-Anhalt, Saxony and Thuringia) held elections, which emphatically confirmed CDU dominance. Only in Brandenburg did the SPD emerge with the largest percentage of the vote. The federal results on 2 December painted the same picture, with the CDU and its Bavarian ally, the CSU, taking 43.8 per cent and the SPD only 33.5 per cent. Exceptionally for these elections the 5 per cent hurdle for getting into the Bundestag had been applied separately to the 'old' and the 'new' federal states, in order to give some recognition of the specific political circumstances in the former GDR, and this meant that the PDS and Alliance 90 (now coupled with the East German Greens) did win seats. The PDS presence, however, limited the advance of the weak East German SPD, which also faced a resurgent East German FDP. Helmut Kohl had a commanding majority in the first parliament of the united Germany. Even in the House of Representatives of the newly united federal state of Berlin, holding its election on the same day, the CDU was the major party, even if without an overall majority.

VI The new Germany adjusts

A historiography of the final phases of the GDR has already begun to emerge, fuelled not least by the availability of East German and to a lesser extent Russian and

American archival sources. Participants in the events – busily producing their memoirs – have themselves had recourse to the documentary evidence which they helped create. In the summer of 1993, for instance, former GDR head of state Egon Krenz was to be seen daily in the reading room of the former SED party archive, working through the Politbüro files of 1980. In the archives of the so-called Gauck Authority, which holds the Stasi files on innumerable individuals, shocking revelations have appeared to those daring to read what colleagues, friends and relations had reported on them. This instant access to the historical record – even greater than that of the immediate post-Nazi period – has not lessened the disputes between participants and historians about the course and interpretation of events. Let two examples here suggest typical areas of debate. The East German historians Armin Mitter and Stefan Wolle have engaged in sometimes sharp exchanges with West German historians not only about the history of the GDR but also about the survival of the historical profession and use of the archives in the new federal states. Their book *Untergang auf Raten* ('Downfall in Instalments') has in turn met with the criticism that it takes selective chunks from the documentary legacy of the GDR in order to chart a steady decline, thereby misrepresenting the historical development of the state and society. Looking at the GDR from a very different perspective, the West German political scientist Jens Hacker has in his *Deutsche Irrtümer* ('German Errors') taken a very critical view of the role played by Federal German politicians and intellectuals in an alleged legitimation of an illegitimate dictatorship in the East.

To complicate matters further, so many aspects of the end of the GDR represent still unfinished business. The after-effects of unification are to be felt most keenly in the 'new federal states', but they influence developments in the old Federal Republic too, and the ways in which they are interpreted depend very much upon attitudes to the old GDR and to the processes of unification itself. To give one example of many, a judgement today on the wholesale reorganization of agriculture in the former GDR since unification is coloured by one's approach to some or all of the following: to the validity of the land confiscation and redistribution of the mid-1940s, to flight westward in the late 1940s and 1950s, to the forced collectivization of 1960, to the Common Agricultural Policy of the European Community/Union since the 1950s, and to the exploitation of market opportunities by West German supermarket chains in the 1990s. Justice is claimed both by those East Germans who have lived and worked on the land for decades and by the West German descendants of former owners expropriated or impelled to flee and leave their property behind.

Such issues make it impossible as yet to make historical judgements about a German unification which is still so recent. At every turn there are surprises and ambiguities as the situation develops. Despite official jubilation and signs of conservative desires now to draw a line under aspects of the German past, many Germans in the west and south of the country felt apathetic or even hostile to the incorporation of the east. Beyond the circulation of unfunny jokes about *Wessis* and *Ossis*, however, antagonism has yet to be significant. Massive unemployment in eastern Germany seemed to threaten social sta-

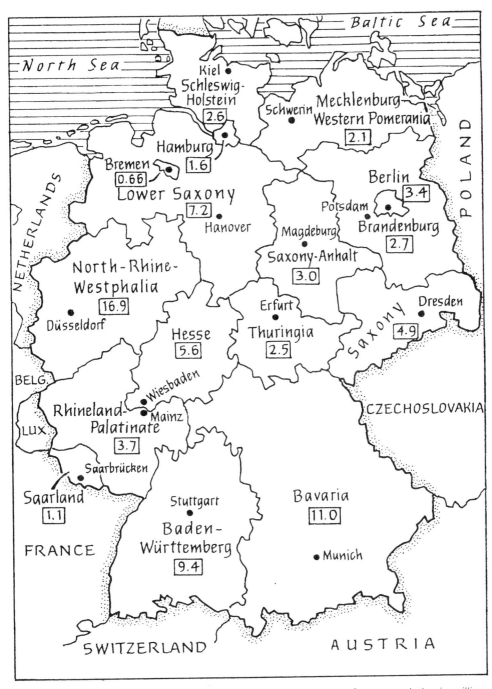

Map 22.1 Germany re-unified 1990. Numbers shown in boxes refer to population in millions

bility and the very coherence of the new Germany, but opinion polls then suggested that most East Germans looked favourably upon unification and saw their living standards rising. There is no doubt that the working-class presence in Germany is now more pronounced, without that yet helping the SPD to revive its sagging fortunes. Just when it seemed in the late 1980s that the extreme right was about to establish itself again as a significant political force in the Federal Republic, its support fell away in West Germany and failed to develop beyond some foul racist gangs in the former GDR emulating those in the West. At the other end of the political spectrum, the PDS seemed doomed to extinction in the 1994 Bundestag elections, when the split 5 per cent rule would no longer apply. In the event it survived, and continued to make impressive local gains as a representative of the social complaints of the East German population. In the economy there has been devastation in many areas of the former GDR, but there are signs that in certain respects the region could emerge with an ultramodern infrastructure. The overall financial costs of unification continue to be immense – giving the lie to facile governmental promises in 1990 – but the German economy, even in a period of less vigorous growth, is more able than any other in the world to cope.

Generally speaking, the old Federal Republic has imposed its structures on the old GDR, not always against the wishes of the latter's population, although some issues such as the abandonment of the more liberal GDR abortion law have proved divisive. There have had to be adjustments on the part of West Germans too, however, some of them uncomfortable. The Bonn region is fearing the economic and social damage of the government moving to Berlin, and other parts of West Germany are seeing important administrative functions being transferred to cities in the east in accordance with federal principles. It is too soon to judge how the incorporation of the relatively small and poor East German federal states will affect the political system, but it is unlikely to remain unchanged. It may be that the federal organs will acquire more power, and almost certainly the political clout of Bavaria and Catholic Germany in general will be diminished. With territorial expansion to the east and the revival of Berlin the emphasis of German concerns will shift more toward central and eastern Europe again. Much will depend too on the proposed monetary and political development of the European Union, which Chancellor Kohl has done much to pursue.

Just as the writing of the history of the GDR has now begun apace, there are too many imponderables to yet have a proper assessment of united Germany. This must wait awhile. The smell of Germany's future in 1997 is as much a blend as it was in 1844, but the components are different and as yet difficult to detect, even with a keen nose.

Select bibliography

Andert, Reinhold and Herzberg, Wolfgang, *Der Sturz: Erich Honecker im Kreuzverhör* (Berlin and Weimar: Aufbau, 1990).

Dennis, Mike, *Social and Economic Modernization in Eastern Germany from Honecker to Kohl* (London: Pinter, 1993).

'German History and German Nationalism after Unification: Seven Historians Give their Views', *Debatte*, 1 (1993).

Glaessner, Gert-Joachim, *The Unification Process in Germany: From Dictatorship to Democracy* (London: Pinter, 1992).

Glaessner, Gert-Joachim and Wallace, Ian, eds., *The German Revolution of 1989: Causes and Consequences* (Oxford: Berg, 1992).

Hacker, Jens, *Deutsche Irrtümer 1949–1989: Schönfärber und Helfershelfer der SED-Diktatur im Westen* (Frankfurt am Main and Berlin: Ullstein, 1992).

von Hallberg, Robert, *Literary Intellectuals and the Dissolution of the State: Professionalism and Conformity in the GDR* (Chicago: University of Chicago Press, 1996).

James, Harold and Stone, Marla, eds., *When the Wall Came Down: Reactions to German Unification* (New York: Routledge, 1992).

Jarausch, Konrad H., *The Rush to German Unity* (Oxford: Oxford University Press, 1994).

Jarausch, Konrad H. and Gransow, Volker, eds., *Uniting Germany: Documents and Debates, 1944–1993* (Providence, RI and Oxford: Berghahn, 1994).

Kolinsky, Eva, ed., *Between Hope and Fear: Everyday Life in Post-Unification East Germany: A Case Study of Leipzig* (Keele: Keele University Press, 1995).

Krenz, Egon, *Wenn Mauern fallen: die friedliche Revolution: Vorgeschichte – Ablauf – Auswirkungen* (Vienna: Neff, 1990).

Larres, Klaus, 'Collapse of a State: Honecker, Krenz, Modrow, and the End of the German Democratic Republic', *European Review of History*, 1 (1994).

Lewis, Derek, and McKenzie, John R. P., eds., *The New Germany: Social, Political and Cultural Challenges of Unification* (Exeter: University of Exeter Press, 1995).

McAdams, A. James, *Germany Divided: From the Wall to Reunification* (Princeton: Princeton University Press, 1993).

Maaz, Hans-Joachim, *Behind the Wall: the Inner Life of Communist Germany* (New York and London: Norton, 1995).

Merkl, Peter H., ed., *The Federal Republic of Germany at Forty-Five: Union Without Unity* (Basingstoke and London: Macmillan, 1995).

Mittag, Günter: *Um Jeden Preis: im Spannungsfeld zweier Systeme* (Berlin and Weimar: Aufbau, 1991).

Mitter, Armin and Wolle, Stefan, *Untergang auf Raten: Unbekannte Kapitel der DDR-Geschichte* (Munich: Bertelsmann, 1993).

Modrow, Hans, *Aufbruch und Ende* (Hamburg: Konkret Literatur, 1991).

Osmond, Jonathan, ed., *German Reunification: A Reference Guide and Commentary* (Harlow: Longman, 1992).

Philipsen, Dirk, *We Were the People: Voices from East Germany's Revolutionary Autumn of 1989* (Durham, NC and London: Duke University Press, 1993).

Pond, Elizabeth, *Beyond the Wall: Germany's Road to Unification* (Washington DC: The Brookings Institution, 1993).

Popplewell, Richard, 'The Stasi and the East German Revolution of 1989', *Contemporary European History* 1 (1992).

Schabowski, Günter, *Der Absturz* (Berlin: Rowohlt, 1991).

Schäuble, Wolfgang, *Der Vertrag: wie ich über die deutsche Einheit verhandelte* (Stuttgart: Deutsche Verlagsanstalt, 1991).

Sinn, Gerlinde and Sinn, Hans-Werner, *Jumpstart: The Economic Unification of Germany* (Cambridge, MA and London: The MIT Press, 1992).

Southern, David, 'Restitution or Compensation: The Open Property Question', *German Politics* 2 (1993).

Wolle, Stefan, 'In the Labyrinth of the Documents: The Archival Legacy of the SED-State', *German History* 10 (1992).

Zelikow, Philip and Rice, Condoleezza, *Germany Unified and Europe Transformed: A Study in Statecraft* (Cambridge, MA: Harvard University Press, 1995).

Part V

Continuities and discontinuities in modern German history

Introduction to Part V: Continuities and discontinuities in modern German history

Mary Fulbrook

The final part considers the broad sweep of German history over the two centuries as a whole. What shifts can be discerned in the paradigms through which Germans themselves perceived their own history? In what ways did the overall shape of society change, particularly in view of that most problematic question for modern German history, the emergence of the conditions for civil society? What were the changing roles of men and women in different social positions in this period? Where should one stand on debates over the conditions for war and peace, which some commentators have controversially seen as intrinsically linked to Germany's allegedly fateful central European geopolitical location? And how were changing notions of German national identity constructed and propagated in this period of remarkably discontinuous political systems? These fundamental questions are addressed in the following chapters, which reflect more broadly on some of the themes and issues which have been adumbrated within discrete periods in preceding chapters of this book.

23

The German tradition of historiography, 1800–1995

Stefan Berger

'Like everything great and good which pleases our national existence, our modern historiography goes back to the beginning of the century – to the unique time of our national renaissance and liberation. Bringing together past and present, the idea of nationality, perceived as a great and growing personality which encompasses all individuals throughout the ages, was born.' In this way Heinrich von Sybel (1817–95) in 1856 connected the rise of historiography as a discipline to the rise of nationalism in Germany. The wars of liberation against Napoleon were, for him, the starting point for the modern way of writing history. By postulating such a rupture of consciousness around 1800, Sybel constructed a particular idea of what constituted a 'modern historiography'. In so doing he excluded modes of writing about history which originated in other traditions than that of the nation, for example much of the historiography of the so-called 'Göttingen school'.

History as an academic discipline critically reconstructing past events originated at the University of Göttingen between 1760 and 1800. Göttingen historians like Johann Christian Gatterer (1727–99), August Ludwig Schlözer (1735–1809) and Ludwig Timotheus Spittler (1752–1810) for the first time formed an intellectual community which defined methodological ground rules for the writing of history distinct from other forms of writing. For the first time professional standards were set in Göttingen which established the discipline of history as a 'science' (*Wissenschaft*). And yet, from Sybel's standpoint, the Göttingen historians could not be counted amongst the 'modern' historians because they wrote predominantly regional, social and economic history rather than national history. Some, using statistical methods, developed an interest in comparing different European societies and in establishing 'types' of development. They investigated processes of industrialization, social inequality and people's standard of living and traced how the idea of political freedom had developed in European society. The rise of the doctrine of nationalism cut short those promising beginnings of a

German social history. According to the dominant historiographical narrative of the nineteenth century, the Göttingen school, with its methodological and conceptual 'naivety', belonged at best to 'pre-history'. There existed without any doubt many traditions of historical writing. Especially in the first half of the nineteenth century, it was by no means a foregone conclusion that the national perspective would come to dominate the historiography in the second half of the nineteenth century – despite the backwards-oriented teleology of Sybel and other Prussian historians. Yet this chapter cannot do full justice to the multitude of sideline and ultimately sidelined historiographical discourses. Instead it chooses to delineate the hegemonic discourse of German historiography which came to rest on the twin pillars of nationalism and historism.

I   The construction of the German national tradition of historiography in the nineteenth century

Both historism and nationalism were not peculiarly German phenomena. They had a European dimension, and one of the most challenging aspects of contemporary historiography is to develop a comparative perspective on alleged national traditions of history-writing. In the course of this chapter, however, I shall have to restrict myself to providing *one* interpretation of the ideas, structures and processes which came to shape the discourse on history-writing in Germany. It happens to be one which I find convincing, but there are other perspectives, some of which will also be alluded to in the following pages. First I want to look at the way in which historism and nationalism merged in Germany to become almost the only accepted way of writing history within the academic discipline – a discipline which to this very day likes to refer to itself as a guild (*Zunft*) with its own entry requirements, controls and codes of conduct.

Historism is a confusing term. Historicism, the far more common term in English, is even more confusing, because the one word refers to two, quite separate sets of ideas. The German language, for once, has been more precise. There *Historizismus* describes a notion, criticized and rejected by Karl Popper (1902–94), that history develops towards a particular end according to predetermined laws. Popper criticized in particular Plato, Hegel and Marx for having a teleological sense of historical development, in which historical events were judged according to whether they fitted certain norms and values which were postulated *a priori* by writers of history: e.g. the idea of freedom for Hegelians, or the classless society for Marxists. *Historismus*, on the other hand, refers to a concept, represented most prominently by Leopold von Ranke (1795–1886), which understands all political order within its own historical context. To understand the nature of any historical phenomenon (be it an institution, be it an idea), the historist argues, one has to consider its historical development, i.e. the changes it underwent over a period of time. Historical epochs, Ranke argued, should not be judged according to predetermined contemporary values or ideas. Rather, they had to be understood on their own terms by empirically establishing 'how it actually was' (*wie es eigentlich gewesen*). It is only with historism in the sense of *Historismus* that I am concerned here.

As it was the towering figure of Ranke who came to symbolize the international reputation of German historiography in the nineteenth century, we shall look to him for guidance as to the meaning of historism. Some of its key elements had already been defined before Ranke by, amongst others, Martin Chladenius (1710–59) and Wilhelm von Humboldt (1767–1835). In particular, Humboldt's hugely influential educational ideal – his insistence that education should be more than functional training and should aim at the development of strong and humane personalities – gave prominent place to the teaching of history. Yet Ranke came to embody historism, largely because he practised what he preached in such superior fashion. He emphasized both 'individuality' and 'development' in history. Every historical phenomenon, every historical epoch and every historical event had its own individuality, and it was the task of the historian to establish its essence. To do this, historians, according to Ranke, had to immerse themselves in the epoch and look at it through the eyes of the time itself. They had, in Ranke's words, 'to extinguish' their own personality. This individualizing approach to the writing of history went hand in hand with a notion of historical development which, according to Ranke, was sanctioned by God's will. This Protestant element in Ranke's historical thinking should be taken very seriously. It made historism inherently conservative by justifying what had historically triumphed and by condemning historical losers. It also robbed historians of any norms and values against which to judge historical events. The major problem with historism was not, as Friedrich Nietzsche (1844–1900) had surmised, its 'antiquarianism', i.e. its alleged lack of interest in the present, but its relativism which often essentially served to legitimate the present.

Ranke and Georg Wilhelm Friedrich Hegel (1770–1831) differed over an inductive or a deductive approach to the writing of history. For Hegel, the interpretation of historical events depended on first conceptualizing the movement of history, i.e. on linking it to specific norms and values, certain ideas whose realization could then be traced in history. For Ranke, in contrast, 'the facts' had to be established before all else. Any conceptualized, normative thinking only got in the way of the historians' task of immersing themselves fully in the period. In the German tradition of historiography Ranke in the end won out, and henceforth historism was profoundly sceptical of any kind of philosophy of history. And yet the great adversaries Ranke and Hegel essentially agreed that history was ultimately meaningful. For Hegel, it was the *Weltgeist*, i.e. the underlying principle of all historical development which assumed different personifications in different periods, but ultimately moved history towards ever greater freedom and rationality. For Ranke, freedom and rationality were normative concepts which he rejected. Yet history revealed to the historian (if only in hindsight) the hand of God in this world.

Ranke's allegedly value-free immersion in a chosen historical period helped to establish the dominance of national history in Germany. Most of Ranke's writings were on the early modern period. Here he concentrated on the history of the 'great' European states. He thought of them as 'thoughts of God' (*Gedanken Gottes*) and was convinced that the states with the strongest moral energies moved history forward. Not so much Ranke, but later generations of historians, had little difficulty in identifying Germany as the morally superior state. Ranke's historism thus mapped out the path followed by subsequent generations of German historians, e.g. their belief that the only true history was the political history of nation states, that the constraints affecting a nation's foreign policy had important repercussions for that nation's domestic politics, and that great personalities were able to shape the nation and its identity. There was much in Ranke's historical thinking to recommend itself to a nationalist historiography, although Ranke himself was at best lukewarm about German nationalism. Yet for the nationalist historians who came to dominate the historiographical discourse in the second half of the nineteenth century, the main problem with Ranke was his insistence on objectivity. This conflicted with their political commitment to creating a unified German nation. Therefore, while nationalist historiography could build on Ranke's historism methodologically, conceptually it had to look elsewhere.

Here, it was especially the political thought of Johann Gottfried Herder (1744–1803) which influenced their conceptualization of a national history. Towards the end of the eighteenth century Herder floated the idea that every people had an essential ethnic core (*Volksseele*, *Volksgeist*) which separated it from all others. A people, he argued, was quasi 'naturally' organized in a nation and each nation had its own spirit and life span. A nation was perceived as an organism, and the task of the historian was to look for its collective identity in history. In presupposing the nation as a collective personality writ large, such organicist thinking necessarily aimed at homogeneity. Any idea of multiple, conflicting and competing identities within a people or a nation was interpreted as the sign of a split personality, of neurosis, of schizophrenia, of illness. If the nation was defined as having a homogenous identity which could be traced backwards in time, this was a recipe for excluding all those elements who allegedly did not fit into the hegemonic discourse of identity. Hence it became fashionable in nationalist circles to use metaphorical language contrasting 'healthy' parts of the nation with 'sick' or 'parasitical' parts which had to be 'cut out'. And yet Herder was not a nationalist. Quite the contrary, he was a cosmopolitan, sceptical of the universalizing and totalizing principles of the Enlightenment, but committed to the peaceful coexistence of different nations and people which had evolved in the course of history and which, he firmly believed, all shared in the basic equality of humanity. It fell to Johann Gottlieb Fichte (1762–1814) to harness Herder's idea of the *Volksgeist* to aggressively nationalist goals. In the context of the 'wars of liberation' against Napoleon he argued that a people finds its true expression only through language and that nations are 'natural' linguistic communities. Fichte ranked nations according to the value of their language, establishing a list of 'worthier' and 'unworthy' nations. Since he perceived German as the original language (*Ursprache*), Germany came top of the list. Both Herder's and Fichte's work is far more complex and ambiguous than these few sentences can allude to, yet German historians were quick to take up the deadly cocktail of ethnic, cultural and linguistic nationalism that *could be* distilled from

Herder and Fichte. Another major proponent of historism, Johann Gustav Droysen (1808–84), for example, argued that the historian's primary task was to establish the peculiar *Volksgeist* of each nation. In Droysen's view, this was shaped by religion, culture and the power of the state.

II Prussian historiography

Especially the power of the state came to fascinate mainstream German historiography. For national-liberal Protestant North-German historians, the strong state was necessary above all to bring about the German nation, to protect and develop it. If their hopes were largely pinned on the Prussian state, the main problem for Prussian historiography was Prussia's illiberalism, its absolutism and its complete lack of constitutionalism. When the concept of the modern nation was invented in Germany at the turn of the nineteenth century, it was an exclusively liberal concept. There was no anti-liberal nationalism, at least not in the first half of the nineteenth century. Nationalism went hand in hand with participatory demands for greater freedom and political rights. This liberal nationalism culminated in the German revolution of 1848 and some of the most well-known national-liberal history professors of the time were amongst the distinguished list of 'revolutionaries': Friedrich Christoph Dahlmann (1785–1860), Droysen, Max Duncker (1811–86), Georg Gottfried Gervinus (1805–71), Karl Welcker (1790–1869), Rudolf Haym (1821–1901), and Georg Waitz (1813–86).

Their central aim in taking part in the revolution was to reconcile the idea of national liberalism with the Prussian state. They wanted to link the idea of freedom to the idea of a powerful state. 1848 had brought a constitution to Prussia, if little else. Although disappointment about the meagre outcome of 1848 was widespread amongst the '48 generation of national-liberal historians, Prussian constitutionalism allowed them to cling to the possibility of uniting the Prussian traditions with their liberal aspirations. Bismarck's unification from above between 1866 and 1871 was interpreted by them as the culmination of German history. They subsequently tended to accept those deficits in liberalism that the new-found nation state still had, in the belief that history had in the long run to be on their side. Prussia-Germany might not yet represent an ideal merger of the liberal and the Prussian traditions since the latter still predominated. In Imperial Germany Prussian historiography once again underlined its commitment to a compromise between Prussian state traditions and liberal principle by adhering to the concept of a 'constitutional monarchy' as the form of government best suited to the needs of the nation. A party government, i.e. a parliamentary government, would mean a weak government. Given that Germany was not yet a consolidated nation and that its geographical position in the middle of Europe (*Mittellage*) meant that it was potentially surrounded by external enemies, it needed strong monarchical government, even if that meant accepting deficits in the liberalization of Germany.

In the classic works of Prussianism like Droysen's 14-volume *History of Prussian Politics* (published between 1855 and 1886) or Heinrich von Treitschke's (1834–96) multivolume *German History* (1879 ff.), progress in German history is generally identified with the Prussian-Protestant mentality. The emphasis placed on Protestantism by Prussian historians ensured conflict with Catholic historians who, before 1866 and in so far as they were nationalists, tended to look to Austria-Hungary rather than Prussia for strong leadership. The competing discourses of 'greater German' and 'small German' conceptions of national history, i.e. the struggle between those who wanted a Germany which included Austria and those who favoured excluding Austria-Hungary from any future German nation state, were a continuous feature of German historiography from the nineteenth century right up to 1945. The 'Prussian mission' in history was as unacceptable to many Catholic historians as it was essential to Prussian historians. For the latter, only Prussia could bring unity to the badly divided nation. Thus they justified the continued expansion of Prussia in the eighteenth century as serving a single purpose: that of unifying Germany. A series of gigantic Hohenzollern kings allegedly singlemindedly pursued the goal of fulfilling the age-old dream of German unity. Prussian historiography underpinned both Prussia's hegemonic position within a united Germany after 1870/71 and Germany's claim to become a world power in the Wilhelmine era.

III   Ranke revival or continuation of Prussianism?

Around the turn of the century, historians increasingly came to criticize Prussianism for its openly one-sided and politicized writing of history. Stressing instead that the historian should be committed to the ideal of objectivity, historians like Max Lenz (1850–1932) and Erich Marcks (1861–1938) aimed at returning to Ranke as the great model for any historian. The nation state, it seemed to them, had been established. Therefore the major aim of Prussianism had been achieved, and now historians could once again write history more dispassionately. However, beneath the surface of this claim to greater objectivity, neo-Rankean historiography provided the essential justification for Germany's *Weltpolitik* under Wilhelm II. In this respect neo-Rankean historiography simply expanded Prussia's mission in Germany to Germany's mission in the world. For this very reason one could argue that neo-Rankeanism not only represents a break with Prussianism but that it also, to a large extent, continued Prussianism.

Many neo-Rankean historians were charmed by the lure of Social Darwinism. They wrote history to establish the superiority of the European race over other races and – more to the point – the superiority of the German people over other European peoples. Ranke's concept of the great powers was put to good use in propping up German ambitions to become the dominant power in continental Europe. His insistence on the importance of 'great men' in history justified the pompous Bismarck cult practised by neo-Rankean historiography. Historians like Dietrich Schäfer (1845–1929) served the 'official nationalism' (Benedict Anderson) by writing semi-official histories of Germany which supported the nationalist and imperialist politics of successive Wilhelmine governments. Above all, this historiography legitimated the state's rigorous stance as the last bulwark against socialism. Even more moderate neo-Rankeans such as Friedrich Meinecke (1862–1954), Hermann Oncken (1869–1945) or Hans Delbrück (1848–1929) found Friedrich Naumann's (1860–1919) merger of social reform and *Weltpolitik* attractive only as a means to create a more powerful state.

Two important challenges to the dominance of the German tradition of historiography came from both within and outside the universities. Three established members of the *Zunft*, Karl Lamprecht (1856–1915), Eberhard Gothein (1853–1923) and Otto Hintze (1861–1940) – notwithstanding Lamprecht's and Hintze's nationalism and both historians' rigorous opposition to the parliamentarization and democratization of Germany – became dissatisfied with historism's sole concern with the political, the individual and the specific. Hence Lamprecht sought to employ ethnic-psychological criteria to explore social history. Gothein, for his part, attempted to introduce cultural history to Germany while Hintze aimed to establish a sociological understanding of the state, using typologies to explore economic, structural and comparative history. The Lamprecht controversy around the turn of the century was a major effort by mainstream German historiography to retain its historist homogeneity, and in the end Lamprecht was defeated. The introduction of social history at German universities was delayed yet again.

Social history was practised very largely only by Marxist historians outside the *Zunft*, e.g. Franz Mehring (1846–1919), Wilhelm Blos (1849–1927), and Gustav Mayer (1871–1948). Thus, for a long time, as Eckart Kehr (1902–33) once remarked, social history and socialist history meant one and the same thing in the German context. Socialists, however, could not become professors in Imperial Germany. They remained to a certain extent excluded from the nation as 'chaps without a fatherland' (*vaterlandslose Gesellen*). The close association between social history and socialist history effectively made it even more difficult for social history concepts to become established at German universities. For the *Zunft* proper the nation and not society remained the guiding principle and leading concern.

IV The German tradition in the Weimar Republic and Nazi Germany

One of the best examples of the continued national apologetic stance of German historiography was the fervour with which leading historians made the defence of the nation against the war guilt clause of the Versailles Treaty their overriding concern after 1918. Delbrück, Hans Rothfels (1891–1976), Hans Herzfeld (1892–1982), Siegfried A. Kaehler (1885–1963) and Wilhelm Mommsen (1892-1966) were only a few of the prominent historians who all cooperated closely with the *Kriegsschuldreferat* set up within the Foreign Office to deal with questions relating to German war guilt. In seeking revision of the Versailles Treaty, they aimed to help re-establish Germany as a major European power again. A young student at the university of Freiburg, Hans Rosenberg (1904–88) clearly perceived that nationalism was still one of the pillars on which the whole discipline rested: 'Many historians . . . were of the opinion that one ought to be a proud nationalist [*stramm deutsch-national*] before becoming a professor'. Apart from a few outsiders like Franz Schnabel (1887–1966) or Walter Goetz (1867–1958) few historians questioned whether the Bismarckian nation state had strong roots in history.

Instead the *Zunft* cultivated a good deal of anti-republican, 'anti-system' sentiment which was powerfully underpinned by the notion of the German *Sonderweg*. According to the 'ideology of the *Sonderweg*' (Bernd Faulenbach) the German nation state was different from and superior to the western European nation states on several accounts. In particular the Prussian idea of the state as standing above society and party politics prevented an endorsement of the pluralism of parliamentary democracy. As far as their own profession was concerned, even the relatively moderate Meinecke insisted that the German historist concept of 'understanding' (*Verstehen*) as the basis for historiography was superior to the various normative approaches of 'Western' historiography. The *Sonderweg* paradigm together with the deep sense of humiliation derived from the 'Versailles complex' only served to strengthen a deeply held belief amongst historians in the merits of authoritarian government, military prowess, and efficient bureaucracy. The Weimar Republic had, in their eyes, betrayed the specific German path and exposed Germany to the alien forces of shallow Westernization and parliamentarization. As such it could win neither the hearts nor the minds of German historians. Even amongst the small band of historians who had turned to republicanism after 1918 (*Vernunftrepublikaner*), most remained deeply attached to the concept of a strong, unified German state. Historians who could be described as committed republicans could mostly be found amongst the younger generation: one thinks here of G. W. F. Hallgarten (1901–75), Kehr, Arthur Rosenberg (1889–1943), Hans Rosenberg, Hajo Holborn (1902–69) and Karl Dietrich Erdmann (1910–90).

It was amongst this latter group that one could find the most powerful questioning of the mixture of nationalism and historism which had come to characterize German historiography. Their challenge, however, was cut short by the Nazis' assumption of power. Most of them were driven into exile. Thus a second opportunity (after Lamprecht and the *Methodenstreit*) to break with the dominant traditions of German historiography, was missed. An explicitly Nazi race-oriented historiography, as personified by Walter Frank's (1905–45) newly found Reich Institute for the History of the New Germany only scratched the surface of the profession's self-understanding. The impact of *Volkshistoriker* such as Hans Freyer (1880–1969), and Gunther Ipsen (1899–1984) has to be taken more seriously. By establishing sociological categories for the writing of history, they were aiming to widen the horizon of historians to encompass social and cultural history. However, their nostalgia for pre-modern community life and their espousal of a crude and blatant racism tainted their conceptualization of social history. After 1945 it could not have a future. Overall, it was the traditional blend of historism and nationalism which served the regime well enough to prevent the Nazis from even attempting any changes from above.

V   The delayed break with the German tradition after 1945

In 1945 – at least in West Germany – the key pillars of German historiography remained intact even amongst the burnt-out ruins of what once had been German universities. In the GDR the break with the German tradition was sharper and more thorough. There the profession was completely transformed between 1948 and 1958. Already the early appointment of committed Marxists such as Jürgen Kuczynski (b. 1904), Alfred Meusel (1896–1960) and Walter Markov (b. 1909) to important academic positions in the Soviet zone of occupation indicated a willingness for change. The small dissident Marxist tradition of German history-writing which had largely been kept outside the universities became the new orthodoxy. It left even less room for alternative discourses than had the earlier orthodoxy. The more traditionalist elements, but also some of those Marxists who found it hard to conform to the dogmatic variant espoused by the SED, were ruthlessly driven out of the universities and out of the country. This decade of GDR historiography witnessed many personal tragedies and a serious dwindling of the number of qualified historians teaching at GDR universities. However, at the same time the drastic change allowed GDR historians to write social and economic history on a scale still unknown in the FRG. In the works of Alexander Abusch (1902–82) and Georg Lukács (1885–1971), for example, the link between historiography and nationalism was abandoned. GDR social history stimulated and provided important impulses to a variety of historical debates, e.g. on class formation, revolution, the origins of the First World War and German fascism. Initially the rejection of the national heritage went so far as to allow only research which concentrated on the so-called 'progressive' traditions in German history, i.e. especially the history of revolution, of the working class and of the labour movement. Only from the 1970s onwards did GDR historiography begin to research the whole of German history again, and the 1980s saw marked efforts to integrate a sense of a positive national identity into the historical consciousness of a self-professed socialist society. Ernst Engelberg's (b. 1909) positive re-evaluation of Bismarck's role in German history was probably the best example of GDR historiography's attempt to legitimate the 'socialist German nation' in the GDR.

The situation in the Federal Republic, by contrast, was characterized by the widespread lament about the 'German catastrophe' (Friedrich Meinecke). A variety of efforts to identify the root causes of the success of National Socialism in Germany rarely followed Meinecke's example and linked it to specific Prusso-German traditions. Instead historians like Gerhard Ritter (1888–1967) routinely referred to the emergence of mass politics in Europe after 1789 as the major reason for Nazism's success. He argued that the positive identification with the national past was all the more necessary in the face of the massive upheaval produced by the Second World War and its aftermath. Uppermost in his mind was the continued link between the generations and their sustained belief in the nation state as a positive value. Therefore a routine distinction between a 'good nationalism' and the National Socialist perversion of it came to characterize German historiography. There was hardly any change either in the personnel of West German historians or the history curricula at German universities. The exiles were never formally asked back and most of them stayed away in any case.

There had been developments after 1945 which opened the door a little towards a revision of the German tradition of historiography. So, for example, genuine moves towards a Europeanization of historical writing took place. And the revival of Catholic historiography went hand in hand with a critical reassessment of the German national tradition by, amongst others, Ludwig Dehio (1888–1963), Karl Jaspers (1883–1969), Karl-Dietrich Bracher (b. 1922), Johann Albrecht von Rantzau (b. 1900) and Kurt Sontheimer (b. 1928). Most importantly, Theodor Schieder (1908–84) and Werner Conze (1910–86) pioneered forms of social history in the 1950s. However, it was the publication of Fritz Fischer's (b. 1908) books on the outbreak of the First World War which flung the door wide open and marked the 'swansong' (W. J. Mommsen) of the older tradition of German historiography. Fischer's books were concerned with foreign policy, and as such they were methodologically hardly innovative. What acted like a bombshell was his conclusion that the First World War should be seen as a first conscious attempt by Germany's ruling elite to create a German-dominated central Europe. By comparing Germany's war aims in the First and Second World Wars, Fischer drew a direct line from the history of Imperial Germany to the Third Reich. Henceforth it was to be impossible to present the history of the Third Reich as the evil exception to an otherwise proud national history. Characteristically, Ritter's review of Fischer's first book ended with him worrying what Fischer's interpretation would do to the continued commitment of future generations of Germans to the nation state.

The political and moral dirt thrown at Fischer for betraying the *Zunft's* consensus was considerable. Funds were withdrawn, suggestions were made about withdrawing his permission to teach at the university, he was slandered as a communist fellow-traveller, and as an anti-nationalist. This showed up yet another tradition of German historical debates which has not entirely lost its validity today: German historians tend to take up a position and then inflexibly reiterate it. Any indication of giving way, of compromising, of incorporating new perspectives is often interpreted as a sign of weakness and linked with an alleged loss of authority. The result is at times a rather underdeveloped and certainly unpleasant culture of historical debate. Add to this the traditionally authoritarian structure of the profession where the advancement of young historians depends on a small circle of almost all-powerful professors, and there is another good reason why historians in Germany are ill-prepared for controversy and debate. There are hardly any permanent positions for young history lecturers. The institutionalization around 1850 of the second major dissertation (*Habilitation*) as the precondition for becoming a professor meant that historians obtain their first permanent post (usually their first professorship) at the age of approximately 35 to 40. Until then, it is of the utmost importance not to offend any of the important professors of the *Zunft*, as any offence immediately reduces the chances of the young historian to get a professorship. Only if the power of the professors to determine the career opportunities of younger historians is broken once and for all, and only if the guild is thoroughly democratized, can there be any hope that a genuine culture of historical debate will emerge in Germany.

In view of that strong authoritarianism prevailing at German universities, it is almost surprising that a number of younger historians took up Fischer's theses with a vengeance. This is explicable only in terms of the general political climate in Germany in the 1960s. The student protest movement was underpinned by a desire to end the politically and morally stifling years of uninterrupted Christian Democratic rule between 1949 and 1966. The trials of Adolf Eichmann in Jerusalem and of Auschwitz SS guards in Düsseldorf in the early 1960s had heightened public awareness of the Holocaust and raised questions about why such acts of barbarity had occurred in Germany. The answer to that question was increasingly sought in German history. The old notion of a German *Sonderweg* was now, to paraphrase Marx, turned from its head to its feet. Historians such as Imanuel Geiss (b. 1931), Hans-Ulrich Wehler (b. 1931) and Jürgen Kocka (b. 1941), who were politically close to the Social Democrats, now began to replace the politics of the nation with the politics of emancipation. Their project was to contribute through the writing of history to the bringing about of a genuine civic society in Germany. The new history which they propagated was that of a critical historical social science. It explicitly rejected the key pillars of the German tradition of historiography, i.e. nationalism and historism. Methodologically it at long last established social and economic history in German historiography. Questioning the individualizing approach of historism, it built on Max Weber's (1864–1920) 'ideal types' and Hintze's 'generalizing methods' in order to put forward a more theoretically informed way of writing history. Exile historians such as Kehr and Rosenberg, some of whom had to be literally rediscovered, served as an inspiration. So, too, did the pioneering efforts of Conze and Schieder. Historians now turned to investigating structures and processes rather than the impact of 'great men'. Particular emphasis was given to explaining the rise of National Socialism in Germany, and the German *Sonderweg* now proved to be an extraordinarily fruitful concept with which to investigate the continuities and traditions that facilitated the rise of radical fascism in Germany. Representatives of historical social science perceived National Socialism and in particular the Holocaust as the nemesis of German history: the result had been the destruction of the German nation. The division of Germany had also brought an end to the profession's national mission. Thus Kocka and Wehler, for example, argued that the time had come for a shift from national history to social history.

Adapting Thomas Kuhn's notion that any scientific progress relies on replacing a set of older explanatory theories (paradigms) by new ones, representatives of historical social science sought to bring about nothing short of a paradigm change. However, it would be misleading to present the significant change that took place in German historiography in the 1960s and 1970s as the emergence of a 'new orthodoxy' which simply replaced the older one. Instead, what emerged in the 1980s was a series of parallel discourses none of which could lay claim to hegemony or dominance. Ultimately the outcome of the break with the national tradition was a pluralization of both the politics and the methodologies of German historiography. Although the older tradition lost its quasi exclusive position, it was far from being dead in the water. Traditional political history continued to be written and was explicitly defended by prominent historians such as Andreas Hillgruber (1925–88) or Klaus Hildebrand (b. 1941). A historism freed of its previous apologetic function of endorsing the nation state found eloquent defenders in Thomas Nipperdey (1927–93) and Hermann Lübbe (b. 1926). In the 1980s historians committed to this older tradition were at the forefront of efforts to strengthen German national identity via the writing of history in the 1980s. These efforts found their erstwhile culmination in the *Historikerstreit* of the mid-1980s. When Jürgen Habermas (b. 1929) attacked the 'apologetic tendencies' amongst historians in the German weekly *Die Zeit* in 1986 it engendered a massive national and international debate which had many facets but which tended to focus on the question of whether or not it was legitimate to write history with the explicit aim of creating national identity.

Quite apart from the continued existence of both historism and nationalism within the mainstream of German historiography, the 'challenger', historical social science, can hardly be described as a homogeneous historical 'school'. The conceptualization of an explicitly political social history, for example by Wolfgang Mommsen (b. 1930), was always quite distinct from efforts by Wehler to write the 'history of society' (*Gesellschaftsgeschichte*). Furthermore, in the 1970s and 1980s, the particular concept of social history defended by Wehler, Kocka and those loosely termed the 'Bielefeld school', relied heavily on modernization theory and the idea of a German *Sonderweg*. It came under increasing criticism from a variety of groups equally determined to get away from the older tradition, yet similarly dissatisfied with the conceptualization of social history associated with the Bielefelders. Some, like Lutz Niethammer (b. 1939) and Alf Lüdtke (b. 1943), turned to the history of everyday life, emphasizing from early on the importance of memory and oral testimony. Others, like Hans Medick (b. 1939) or Richard van Dülmen (b. 1940), began to develop a historical anthropology which was more interested in human agency, the ordinariness of everyday life, *mentalité* and microhistory. The History Workshop Movement made rapid progress in the Federal Republic throughout the 1970s and 1980s, and thousands of lay historians, unattached to the 'guild', began to 'dig where they stood', unearthing a rich stream of local and regional history. Women's and gender history, pioneered by amongst others Karin Hausen (b. 1938) and Gisela Bock (b. 1942), provided new fields of historical investigation and reinterpreted older ones with refreshing new perspectives. A younger generation of British historians of Germany argued in the first half of the 1980s that the idea of a German *Sonderweg* was conceptually flawed and, notwithstanding its earlier importance in inspiring important research into the pre-history of National Socialism, might have reached its sell-by date.

Thus a historical social science based on modernization theory and the idea of a German *Sonderweg*, far from having achieved any kind of hegemony, was already in a defensive position by the mid-1980s. It had boxed itself into a corner and was caught between the older tradition on the one hand and the variety of new developments on the other. And here again, the lack of a genuine culture of historical debate is important in explaining the apparent inability of German historians to build bridges across conceptual, methodological and ideological divides. Hence the 1980s saw the ritual repetition of accusations and counter-accusation between representatives of historical social science and historians of everyday life. It remains ironic that those who freed German history from the chains of historism and nationalism should have been at times so unwilling to accept a pluralism of compatible approaches. No doubt, the misguided notion of a paradigm change – with its inbuilt binary opposition which simply does not allow for multiplicity – contributed to the surprising spasms of mutual intolerance amongst German historians.

Quite apart from the often bitter conceptual and methodological squabbles, the various 'schools' of social history were more or less agreed that the united nation state created by Bismarck in the nineteenth century had been nothing but a fleeting episode. The Federal Republic should best be perceived as a 'state nation' (R. M. Lepsius) rather than a nation state. The prime loyalty of its citizens was not to the nation but to the constitution of the FRG. 'Constitutional patriotism' had replaced the older orientation towards the nation. Nationalism had lost its integrative function after 1945, at least in Western Europe and specifically in Germany. The Germans had successfully developed a post-national identity. That Germans had lived in several different states for most of their history was declared the historical norm, whilst the short period of a united nation state between 1870 and 1945 was perceived as the exception. Some were even talking of an emerging 'binationalism', with the citizens of FRG and GDR both developing specific loyalties to their variants of a German nation state. This is precisely where 1989–90 becomes important.

VI Contemporary trends

The collapse of the GDR in 1989 and reunification of the country in 1990 reinvigorated attempts to renationalize German historical consciousness. A 'new right', incorporating historians like Ernst Nolte (b. 1923), Rainer Zitelmann (b. 1957) and Karlheinz Weißmann (b. 1959), has called for the establishment of a 'self-confident nation'. A triumphant mood reigned after 1990 amongst those who wanted to return to the older tradition of German historiography. The framework for the future writing of national history put forward by new right historians consists broadly speaking of five separate notions, two of which take up arguments prominent in the *Historikerstreit*. First, there was a rejection of the theory of the German *Sonderweg* as a crude form of psychotic anti-nationalism. Second, nationalist historians have continued to marginalize what was essential about National Socialism, namely its extreme racism leading to the Holocaust. Instead they have chosen to foreground the allegedly modern aspects of the Nazi regime. Third, they have argued that a second coming-to-terms with the past, this time with the past of a communist dictatorship, will at long last shift the history of

National Socialism into the background. Fourth, they have begun to portray the history of the old Federal Republic as an unpalatable provincial *Sonderweg* which should at best be quickly abandoned in the pursuit of the alleged new superpower status of the reunified country. Fifth, nationalist historians have been busy re-establishing the 'normality' of the nation state as the 'natural' focus of identity for people at the end of the twentieth century. A stable political system, they have argued, has to rest on a 'healthy' national consciousness. More mainstream liberal-conservative historians like Hans-Peter Schwarz and Klaus Hildebrand have so far refused to put their intellectual weight behind the 'new right'. The latter's tendency to relativize the criminal energies of the Nazi regime and their attempts to de-Westernize the reunified Germany have not met with much of a positive echo amongst more mainstream conservative historians. Yet it should also be noted that conservatives widely share the rhetoric of 'normalization' and 'national identity'. In all five of the issues mentioned above, the borderline between the 'new right' and liberal conservatism has at times become rather blurred.

Furthermore some prominent representatives of historical social science like Kocka and Heinrich August Winkler (b. 1938) have declared their willingness to move back to the nation. Their unwillingness to leave national history to the political right has produced radically different perspectives on the nation from those endorsed by the 'new right'. Any national identity in the new Germany, they have insisted, will have to give a prominent place to the history of National Socialism and to the Holocaust in particular. They have interpreted the revolution of 1989 as the first genuine opportunity since 1848 to link the democratic and national traditions in Germany and to combine a fully Westernized understanding of the nation with the democratic political culture of the old Federal Republic. They have warned against simply returning to the outdated nineteenth-century nationalist myths and the anachronistic concept of the autonomous nation state.

Methodologically the events of 1989–90 brought a revival of classic diplomatic and political history. Despite a spirited defence of structural social history by Kocka, there has been an increasing feeling that 'the wind has changed' (W. J. Mommsen). However, if the particular variant of structural social history pioneered by the Bielefeld school has been put even more on the defensive by the events of 1989–90, this does not automatically mean an unequivocal return to the ideals of historism. On the contrary, historians seem to be experimenting with and adopting an ever wider variety of different methodologies and theories in their approaches to the writing of history. The return to the nation has not been marked by a return to historism. Instead we continue to see a blossoming of eclecticism.

After the conflict between structural historians and historians of everyday life had become rather stale in the 1980s, the most important international methodological debate of recent years has been on post-modern approaches to the writing of history and the so-called 'linguistic turn'. In Germany, post-modernism has not yet found any serious practitioners within the *Zunft*, and it has only been from the early 1990s onwards that post-modern approaches have been discussed in German history journals at all. So far, there has been a tendency to dismiss them because of their alleged extreme relativism and because of their supposed tendency to produce a multitude of arbitrary and ultimately unconnected stories. This in turn would make any effort at synthesis impossible. Whilst there are valid criticisms to be made about the inherent methodological and conceptual shortcomings of some post-modernisms, e.g. their potential for relativism, aestheticism and de-contextualization, their anti-essentialism endorses plurality and increases the historian's wariness of all linear and totalizing accounts of historical development. A post-modern historiography would also undermine efforts to return to a homogeneous national paradigm. Its deconstruction of the 'nation' as one of the nineteenth-century master narratives and its understanding of national identity as a construction which is constantly undermined, challenged and reworked would militate against the re-emergence of essentialist notions of the nation as 'normal' or 'natural'. At long last the 1960s saw the break with the stifling consensus about what constituted 'proper' 'scientific' (*wissenschaftlich*) historical writing. 1989–90 does not have to mean the return to these narrow historiographical conceptions. The 'new right' has made some advances into historiography after 1989, and there is a concerted attempt by conservative historians to renationalize German historical consciousness. However, the methodological plurality and conceptual variety of history writing in contemporary Germany is still a hopeful sign that any *Sonderweg* of German historiography belongs firmly to the past.

Select bibliography

Berger, Stefan, *The Search for Normality: National Identity and Historical Consciousness in Germany since 1800* (Oxford: Berghahn, 1997).

Burleigh, Michael, *Germany Turns Eastwards. A Study of 'Ostforschung' in the Third Reich* (Cambridge: Cambridge University Press, 1988).

Evans, Richard J., *In Hitler's Shadow. West German Historians and the Attempt to Escape from the Nazi Past* (London: I.B. Tauris, 1989).

Fletcher, Roger, 'Recent Developments in West German Historiography: The Bielefeld School and its Critics', *German Studies Review*, 7 (1984), pp. 451–80.

Geyer, Michael, and Jarausch, Konrad H., 'The Future of the German Past. Transatlantic Reflections for the 1990s', *Central European History*, 22 (1989), pp. 229–59.

Iggers, Georg G., *The German Conception of History. The National Tradition of Historical Thought from Herder to the Present*, 2nd rev. edn. (Middletown/CT: Wesleyan University Press, 1983).

Iggers, Georg G., *Marxist Historiography in Transformation. East-German Social History in the 1980s* (Oxford: Berg, 1991).

Lambert, Peter, 'German Historians and Nazi Ideology. The Parameters of the *Volksgemeinschaft* and the Problem of Historical Legitimation, 1930-45', *European History Quarterly* 25 (1995), pp. 555–82.

Lehmann, Hartmut and Melton, James van Horn eds., *Paths of Continuity: Central European Historiography from the 1930s to the 1950s* (Cambridge: Cambridge University Press, 1994).

Lipp, Carola, 'Writing History as Political Culture. Social History versus "Alltagsgeschichte". A German Debate', *Storia della Storiografia* 17 (1990), pp. 66–100.

Maier, Charles, *The Unmasterable Past. History, Holocaust and German National Identity* (Cambridge, MA: Harvard University Press, 1988).

McClelland, Charles, *State, Society and University in Germany 1700–1914* (Cambridge: Cambridge University Press, 1980).

Moses, John A., *The Politics of Illusion. The Fischer Controversy in German Historiography* (London: Allen and Unwin, 1975).

Ritter, Gerhard A., *The New Social History of the Federal Republic of Germany* (London: German Historical Institute, 1991).

Sheehan, James J., 'What is German History? Reflections on the Role of German History and Historiography', *Journal of Modern History* 53 (1981), pp. 1–23.

Weber, Wolfgang, 'The Long Reign and the Final Fall of the German Conception of History: A Historical-Sociological View', *Central European History* 21 (1988), pp. 379–95.

24

The difficult rise of a civil society: societal history of modern Germany

Jürgen Kocka

In the late 1960s and 1970s a new paradigm of German history emerged: history as 'history of society' or 'societal history' (*Gesellschaftsgeschichte*). It never became the dominant paradigm, and it always was extremely varied in itself – not a homogeneous school at all. But in the following years it strongly influenced the work of many historians of modern Germany. It helped to produce interpretations of nineteenth- and twentieth-century German history which emphasized its social dimension, took 1933–45 as a pivotal period, and interpreted the German case against the background of west European developments, by more or less explicit comparison and usually in a critical – or self-critical – mood.

Nowadays the societal perspective on German history continues to be strong, productive and influential. But over the years it has changed, and it has to cope with a new situation. It has broadened by learning from some of its major challengers: gender history from the 1970s on, history of everyday life in the 1980s, and the new cultural history of the 1980s and 1990s. The restoration of a German national state has started to alter the perceptions of historians. The post-modern intellectual currents of the day deeply challenge some of the intellectual convictions on which societal history is built.

Where do we stand now? This essay first sketches some of the debates over *Gesellschaftsgeschichte* as a controversial approach to modern German history. It secondly introduces a possible approach for an eventual societal history of modern Germany: the concept of civil society. The bulk of the essay (sections III–V) presents the basic outline and the major turning points of the development of civil society in Germany from the late eighteenth century to the present, and discusses two topics in slightly more detail: the role of the bourgeoisie and of the working class. This can be justified since the problem of civil society was indeed closely linked to the development of the bourgeoisie and the working class. But there are many other topics and problems which might have been discussed in the context of the history of German civil society. In this short essay, they had to be left aside. 'Bourgeoisie' is used in the sense of the German *Bürgertum*, a concept sometimes translated by 'middle class'. All these concepts are not completely congruent. Again, a choice had to be made.

I Societal history: a changing approach

In the 1960s and 1970s, 'social history' caught the imagination of a young generation of historians. It became a central concept – and a rallying point – of historiographic revisionism. It meant many things at the same time. It gave priority to the study of particular kinds of phenomena, like classes and movements, urbanization and industrialization, family and education, work and leisure, mobility, inequality, conflicts and revolutions. It stressed structures and processes over actors and events. It was attracted by analytical approaches close to the social sciences rather than by the traditional methods of historical hermeneutics. Frequently social historians sympathized with the causes (as they saw them) of the little people, of the underdog, of popular movements or of the working class. Social history was both demanded and rejected as a vigorous revisionist alternative to the more established ways of dominant historiography in which the reconstruction of politics and ideas, the history of events and hermeneutic methods traditionally dominated.

There were two meanings of social history. On the one hand social history was understood as the history of one dimension of historical reality, as history of social structures, processes, practices and meanings – in contrast to political history, economic history, cultural history and other sub-disciplines of similar range. On the other hand social-history was conceived of as an approach to general history studied from a social historical point of view. It is for this second variant of social history that in West Germany the label *Gesellschaftsgeschichte* emerged: history of society or societal history.

Clearly, societal history aimed at including the study of the political system, economic change and cultural patterns as well as the study of the social sphere proper, but by stressing social (and sometimes economic) factors – whatever that meant in detail. The project of societal history aimed at *Zusammenhang* (making connections), at overall structures in a diachronic and synchronic sense. It claimed to reconstruct the relatedness of the different spheres or spaces or dimensions of history, and it intended to conceptualize this interrelatedness as *Gesellschaft* (society). There was a fundamental conviction that one must not dissolve the past into its constituent parts if one wanted to understand it. Societal history wanted to get below the surface, the events, the perceptions, the images – without abstracting from them altogether. It did not just ask 'how?' but also 'why?' Frequently it was hoped that in this way historical knowledge would be attained which would contribute to a better orientation and more enlightened practice in the present. Practitioners of societal history were aware that they could only succeed with such an ambitious project if they were prepared to choose advanced analytical tools: explicit and well-defined concepts, theories and models, sophisticated qualitative and quantitative methods. The neighbouring social sciences were looked at for suggestions and cooperation. There was much methodological and theoretical self-reflexion about the conditions and consequences of what societal history was and did.

Beyond these common traits societal history appeared in very different forms, as one can see if one compares major practitioners of the field in different countries: Hans-Ulrich Wehler in Germany, Eric Hobsbawm in England, Fernand Braudel in France and Charles Tilly in the USA. Different approaches were used: Marxist ideas in or outside the tradition of historical materialism, concepts of modernization, Weberian approaches, theories of social inequality as well as other approaches, frequently eclectic, self-made, *bricolages*. The fully fledged synthesis was the exception, reserved for the masters in the field. More frequent were synthetic sketches, frameworks within which more detailed, monographic studies could then be embedded. Very often it was just the general perspective, the intellectual mood which showed the indebtedness of an article or a book to societal history. It was rare that the programme as a whole could be fully realized.

In the 1960s and 1970s, the main adversaries of societal history were proponents of political history. In Germany they were influential, but their arguments did not carry much weight since most practitioners of societal history did not ignore politics, but rather tried to relate politics to social and economic factors.

Later on, women historians criticized the gender-blindness of societal history which had indeed privileged class and ignored gender as well as other dimensions of social inequality. It did not prove impossible, however, to broaden the parameter of societal history, and historians like Ute Frevert have practiced gender history within frameworks indebted to traditions of societal history (see, for example, Chapter 25). But the relations between class, gender and ethnicity continued to be a classical, not fully resolved issue within societal history.

In the 1980s the most interesting attack came from the proponents of the history of everyday life (*Alltagsgeschichte*). They were suspicious of big analytical concepts like industrialization, class formation, nation-building or urbanization, which were often used by practitioners of societal history. Instead, they sought to reconstruct the world of the past from the viewpoints and with the concepts of the people of the past – a 'historicist' strategy, the built-in difficulties of which had long been criticized by analytical historians inside and outside societal history. Historians of everyday life regarded societal history as overly structuralist and they preferred to study the subjective side: how people of the past experienced, perceived and – perhaps – changed their world. Everyday historians criticized societal history as 'history from above' (which was only partially true), and frequently advocated 'history from below'. They preferred micro-historical studies and they usually neglected – or rejected – societal history's stress on broad context and interrelatedness.

The debate was controversial and interesting; now it is over. I think that it had three results. First, it revealed the built-in limits, weaknesses and contradictions of the history of everyday life if presented as a strict alternative (not a supplement) to societal history. Second, it helped practitioners of societal history to be aware of the indisputable fact that a full reconstruction of the past cannot succeed without attention to perception and agency. For example, to measure and describe patterns of social mobility is only one step; it does not tell us anything about the experiences, values and actions of people in response to social stability or change. As a consequence societal history has become more sensitive to subjective factors. Its practitioners have tried to combine structure and agency, process and experience, with varying degrees of success. But, third, it has become clear that there is and remains a gap and a tension between societal history and the history of everyday life. If one wants to understand *conditions* and *consequences* of perceptions, decisions and actions, if one aims at an understanding of interconnections and synthesis, one cannot do without analytical approaches and one has to reconstruct structures and processes – which are inaccessible or uninteresting to historians of everyday life.

The most productive challenge came from the side of the 'new cultural history' of the 1980s and 1990s (already pioneered in the 1970s). Extremely diverse in itself, practitioners and advocates of cultural history (or sociocultural history) have criticized societal history for neglecting the production and destruction of meaning, processes of signification and de-signification, cultural practices and products, the symbolic aspects of historical reality, language and other forms of communication – i.e. dimensions of history which are woven into all other dimensions as well, and which are present whenever humans relate to each other and to their world. They have a point. German social history (including societal history) emerged by distancing itself from older traditions which had strongly privileged the dimensions of meaning, intentions and actions as well as a fictitious world of 'objective ideas' at the cost of material conditions, social relations as well as of problems of inequality, authority and dependence. German societal history found it necessary to confront and redress an unequal balance, and in this process new imbalances may have emerged, this time at the cost of cultural aspects.

In recent years, impulses from French, English and American cultural history, from cultural anthropology and from the classical writings of Georg Simmel, Ernst Troeltsch, Norbert Elias and again Max Weber were picked up. Reinhart Koselleck's *Begriffsgeschichte* (history of concepts) which has always been open to semantic *and* social history served as a bridge. Anyway, many social historians had already included culture when they had studied the working class, the bourgeoisie, gender relations or family history. Societal history correctly rejects the totalizing claims of some cultural historians who equate culture with the totality of the historical process. It rightly rejects the absolutist claims of some adherents of the 'linguistic turn' who deny the accessibility to historians of anything but texts. But societal history is well on the way towards incorporating cultural historical approaches which pose new theoretical and empirical problems, not as yet fully resolved. In the process, societal history and the forms of its presentation will necessarily change, and it remains to be seen how far this will go.

There are more radical – and less productive – challenges to societal history. Most historiographical work is specialized, monographic and narrowly defined by subject, period and space. There is, of course, nothing wrong with that; on the contrary. This is how much of the advancement of an empirical discipline takes place, as long as specialized research or microhistorical reconstructions are related to broader contexts (which can be constructed in very different ways). But in the last decade or so it has become increasingly common for historians concentrating on the history of specific events, constellations, images or practices to find it either superfluous or even illegitimate to attempt to explicitly situate their specific topic in a broader context. In a certain post-modern mood one favours the decentralization and deconstruction of systematic concepts. Contexts are denounced as chimeras, inaccessible to historians or dull. Fragments are retrieved, traces (*Spuren*) preserved, glimpses produced and partial phenomena reconstructed. Any attempt to reconstruct the glimpses and fragments analytically by relating them to one other and to broader structures, processes and contexts is avoided. So is the explicit use of systematic concepts. The presentation becomes insular though rich, and sometimes confusing. History is dissolved into stories.

Such work can be highly sophisticated and entertaining. Certainly, the house of history has and must have many different halls, rooms and niches. But clearly, such approaches are very far away from societal history with its analytical and synthesizing claims. From the point of view of societal history one is tempted to say that history loses its power of orientation to the present if it is fragmented and departmentalized into unrelated parts. To reconstruct partial phenomena, preserve vestiges and retrieve images is indispensable and deserving, but it cannot replace conceptual labour.

II The dynamics of civil society

Societal history has been practised by German writers in different forms. Modernization theory was used, by Thomas Nipperdey for example, to construct a synthesizing account of German history in the nineteenth and twentieth centuries. Theories dealing with the succession of 'societal formations' in a revolutionary or non-revolutionary way have informed accounts of societal history, not only by authors from the GDR, but also by West German historians such as Reinhard Rürup in his synthesis of the period between 1815 and 1871. There have been attempts to use the concept of a 'class society' for structuring syntheses or frameworks for monographic studies, for example in my own book on World War I *Facing Total War*. Hans-Ulrich Wehler's *Gesellschaftsgeschichte*, which uses a flexible Weberian approach, is so far the most important accomplishment in the field of societal history: three volumes have so far appeared, concentrating on Germany during the 'long nineteenth century' from 1789 to 1914; volume 4 is in preparation.

Recently, some progress has been made with conceptualizing German history from the late eighteenth century to the present in terms of an as yet unfinished (and probably never finishable) process of the birth, the crises, the breakdown and the resuscitation of civil society. Research on the history of the German bourgeoisie (*Bürgertum*) has been intensive over the last one and a half decades, and it has contributed much to the sharpening of the concept *bürgerliche Gesellschaft* or *Bürgergesellschaft* (bourgeois or civil society). (It should be remembered that the German word *Bürger* stands both for 'bourgeois' and for 'citizen'.) Notions and visions of 'civil society' were widely discussed in the late 1980s and early 1990s in east central Europe by dissenting intellectuals who used this tradition to criticize dictatorial communism. An approach built around the concept of 'civil society' could become an important way of conceptualizing and writing German societal history of the last two hundred years in a comparative way.

The concept of civil society which I have in mind emerged as a utopian project in the second half of the eighteenth and in the early nineteenth century. Many different authors have contributed to it in different ways, from Locke, Ferguson and Adam Smith through Montesquieu and the *encyclopédistes* to Kant, Hegel and the liberal theorists of the post-Napoleonic period.

Of central importance was the vision of a modern, secularized society of free and self-reliant individuals who would manage their relations with one another in a peace-

Illustration 24.1   The Thinkers' Club', a caricature on the suppression of freedom of speech. Sign on the wall reads: 'Important question for consideration at today's meeting: how long shall we be allowed to think?'

ful and reasonable way, through individual competition as well as through voluntary cooperation and association, without too much social inequality and without the tutelage of an authoritarian state. For that purpose certain institutional arrangements were needed: the guarantee of individual rights, the protection of the family, markets, an arena for public debate, the nation state, due process of law, constitutional government and parliamentary representation. These demands were intrinsically linked to a new conception of social relations: work, achievement and success – not birth and privilege – should determine the distribution of wealth, status and power. Education should be of the utmost importance. The public use of reason should replace legitimation by tradition. Private and public life should be clearly distinguished. Certain cultural attitudes, norms and practices – including individual self-discipline and cleanliness, strictly defined differences between the sexes, certain aesthetic values and a clear notion of superiority *vis-à-vis* the natural world – should become universal. This was a culture which had been pioneered and emphasized in bourgeois circles, in the emerging *Bürgertum*. At the same time, the project of a civil society claimed universal applicability. In principle it aimed at freedom, equal chances and participation *for all*. In that it reflected its inspiration by ideas of the Enlightenment.

This was its basic contradiction. On the one hand it claimed universal applicability. On the other hand it was intrinsically tied to the very small bourgeois milieu, not only in the sense that this was the social location where it originated, but also in the sense that the bourgeois status – including individual independence due to wealth or position and education – was needed in order to qualify fully as a citizen. Nineteenth-century voting laws made that very clear, and this meant that both the female half of the population and the mass of the lower classes (including those a little bit further up) were virtually excluded from citizenship and from the demands and promises of the project of civil society. Universalist claims versus exclusive reality – it took two centuries to reduce this discrepancy, which was most effectively challenged by the socialist labour movement and Marxist criticism and later on by the feminist movement, and by liberal-democratic reformers throughout the period. All of them basically used the claims and the principles of the model of civil society to criticize the imperfect stage of its realization. Processes of democratization were demanded and pushed through, the welfare state was developed, some steps towards more equality between the sexes were finally achieved. New difficulties, dangers and crises emerged. There were setbacks and breakdowns, particularly during the dictatorships of the twentieth century. In these conflicts and processes the concept of civil society changed. It will have to change further in order to cope with the problems of the present and the future. It has nowhere been fully realized as yet, and its worldwide extension has only begun.

What has been and continues to be a normative concept with political, social, economic and cultural reach, can be reformulated as an ideal-typical concept and used for analytical purposes. How did civil society develop in Germany? What was specific to the German case? What were the decisive turning points?

III   The rise of civil society in Germany, 1800–1918

In Germany, a civil society emerged in three and a half stages between 1800 and the early 1870s. Certainly, there had been preparations in the eighteenth century: capitalism had slowly advanced in both agriculture and industry, some administrative and legal reforms had taken place, in Prussia for example in 1794. But it was in the period between 1800 and 1815–18 that the feudal order in the countryside and the corporate order in the towns were either brought to an end or severely weakened. This laid the legal ground for the dynamics of capitalism in the coming two centuries. Far-reaching educational reforms institutionalized the importance of education which became the other great dynamic force of the time to come. Administrative and constitutional reforms were limited, but not altogether absent; they provided for the eventual political participation of the emerging bourgeoisie and beyond. A national movement began. Directly or indirectly, French influence was decisive. Basically, these were reforms from above in a largely traditional society; popular movements played only a marginal role.

In contrast, popular movements were important in making liberal demands for constitutional reform partly successful in some German regions in 1830–31. A similar constellation – though more dynamic and socially more heterogeneous – appeared in the revolution of 1848–49, which did not just end in defeat but also advanced the cause of civil society: by accelerating the still unfinished business of agrarian reform, by making economic policy more favourable for industrialization, and by establishing constitutional government (though of a rather conservative nature) in the two leading monarchies of the German Federation, in Prussia and Austria.

It was the decade from the early 1860s to the early 1870s which brought the decisive breakthrough. Legal reforms gave the final blow to the surviving remnants of the feudal and corporate order, and loosened the government's encroachment upon society; all kinds of controls and checks were weakened, economic change and social mobilization accelerated. The industrial revolution quickly advanced, social conflicts sharpened, and the labour movement emerged. A German national state was put together under Prussian hegemony, under Bismarck's guidance and with the help of three wars, something the revolution of 1848–49 had sought in a different way, but in vain. And the constitutional question was decided: against full parliamentarization as demanded by the liberals, and in effect maintaining much of the power of the old elites and old institutions; but also against the reactionary demands of many conservatives and in favour of a constitution with some liberal elements. Universal manhood suffrage in national elections – rather democratic for the period – added a further element which was meant by Bismarck to be a weapon against the liberals. This compromise sharply distinguished the German constitutional history of the following decades from the west European model of parliamentary government. Again, radical change had been guided 'from above', but in contrast to his predecessors in 1800–15,

Bismarck had to come to terms with an active sociopolitical movement, the liberals, whose conflict and cooperation with the government deeply influenced the decisions and results of the decade.

By the 1870s, the core elements of a civil society had been established, in a special German way. They were further developed in the phase of the Empire (1871–1918): a capitalist economy, highly dynamic, innovative, increasingly industrialized, and growing; a relatively liberal system of law regulating essential elements of civil society; civil rights, private contracts and family life; a functioning arena of public debate; many voluntary associations and citizens' initiatives; a dynamic system of education and science; competing parties and constitutional government. On the other hand, the *Kaiserreich* was definitely not a parliamentary system. Much political power and cultural influence stayed with the old elites, the nobility, the bureaucracy and the army. Everyday life and public culture were tainted by social militarism and civil bureaucratization. Nationalism grew, became more aggressive, and moved to the right, in close association with growing illiberal moods and movements. On the national level at least, liberalism severely declined. Constitutional reforms got stuck. It needed a war, a humiliating defeat and another revolution to realize parliamentarization, against stiff resistance. The *Kaiserreich* on the whole was a deeply ambivalent and unstable compromise on the difficult path towards civil society in Germany.

IV Bourgeoisie and working class

The rise of civil society was intrinsically linked to the changing class structure, first of all to the changing character and role of the middle class or bourgeoisie (*Bürgertum*). While older historiographical traditions had tended to equate the history of the bourgeoisie with the history of merchants, bankers, manufacturers, industrialists and other business people, in recent years a more balanced view has emerged, which gives full credit to the educated, professional bourgeoisie (*Bildungsbürgertum*) as well, i.e. to educated persons like doctors, professors, ministers, lawyers and other professionals as well as to academically trained administrators and civil servants. These categories – according to contemporary observers and on the basis of understandable criteria – belonged to the bourgeoisie no less than the economic bourgeoisie (*Wirtschaftsbürgertum*), i.e. capitalists, entrepreneurs, managers and the like. What the different segments of the bourgeoisie had in common was not a shared class position in a Marxian sense, but two other factors. First, they shared common opponents. They set themselves apart, in the eighteenth and nineteenth centuries, from the world of aristocratic privilege, unrestricted absolutism and religious orthodoxy as well as, in the nineteenth and twentieth centuries, from those below them, the lower strata, the people, the working class. Second, the different sections of the bourgeoisie shared a common culture, defined by a specific type of family life and unequal gender relations, respect for work and education, emphasis on personal autonomy, achievement and success, by a specific view of the world and a typical style of life in which clubs, associations and urban communication played an important role. It was on those common grounds – common opponents and a common culture – that the bourgeoisie, in spite of its remarkable heterogeneity in most other respects, developed something like a common identity and became a major propagator of progress with an outstanding impact on social, political, economic and cultural change, in eighteenth-, nineteenth- and twentieth-century Europe.

It was not its small size (5–7 per cent of the population, not counting the much larger *petite bourgeoisie* or lower middle class) which made the German bourgeoisie specific; in this respect other European cases were not much different. Nor was it specific to Germany that bourgeois support for and identification with the programme of civil society became much weaker in the late nineteenth and early twentieth century than it had been in the late eighteenth and early nineteenth; everywhere the bourgeoisie became more established, exclusive, conservative and defensive in the course of time. Nor can one hold, in contrast to an older view, that the German upper bourgeoisie was particularly 'feudalized' or 'aristocratized' in the late nineteenth century. In Britain and France the development of a composite elite out of parts of the nobility and parts of the bourgeoisie was more advanced than in Germany.

Rather, besides a high degree of regional and religious differentiation, four specifics of the German bourgeoisie should be mentioned. Relative to the business and economic bourgeoisie the *Bildungsbürgertum* was extremely strong, well-respected and influential in Germany. Inside the *Bildungsbürgertum* the civil servants clearly played a leading role, and this correlated with the strong bureaucratic traditions, inclinations and orientations of the German bourgeoisie in general. The social dominance and the political influence of the German bourgeoisie appears to have been relatively weak if compared with the west, though relatively strong if compared to the east of Europe. And the German bourgeoisie was challenged by a particularly well-developed working class and a remarkably strong labour movement.

In Germany, as in most other countries, the emergence of a working class was closely linked to industrialization which, with marked regional variations, had its breakthrough in Germany in the period between the 1840s and the 1870s, and which further accelerated during the *Kaiserreich* (see Table 24.1). It was the industrialization as well as concomitant migration and urbanization (see Table 24.3) that turned wage labour (which was, of course, a much older institution) and the separation between household and industrial work (again not completely unknown before) into mass phenomena. Relations between workers and employers changed, communication between different types of workers increased, they shared common experiences and learned to articulate common interests, particularly under conditions of tension and conflict with employers, other parts of the bourgeoisie and the authorities. In this constellation, though nourished from different roots (among them old journeymen and artisan traditions) something like a working-class culture emerged, as much influenced by specific living conditions and experiences of dependence and exclusion in the public sphere as by work experience itself, separate from, critical of, but influenced by bourgeois cul-

Table 24.1 German labour force by major economic sectors, 1800–1993 (selected years)

	Agriculture (%)	Industry (%)	Services (%)	Total (millions)
1800	62	21	17	11
1849	56	24	20	15
1875	50	29	21	19
1907	35	40	25	28
1939	25	41	34	36
1970	9	49	42	26
1990	4	40	56	29
1993	3	39	58	36

Note: 'Agriculture' includes agriculture, forestry and fishery. 'Industry' includes crafts, manufacturing, mining and construction. 'Services' includes commerce (*Handel*), traffic and transportation (*Verkehr*) as well as services (*Dienstleistungen*). The figures for 1800 and 1875 relate to the population on the territory of the German Empire of 1871. All other figures relate to the German Empire and the Federal Republic (changing boundaries). The figures for the GDR, 1970: 13 per cent agriculture, 49 per cent industry and 38 per cent services (total labour force: 8 million).

Sources: W. Fischer *et al.*, *Sozialgeschichtliches Arbeitsbuch*, vol. 1 (Munich: Beck, 1982), pp. 52f.; Statistisches Bundesamt, ed., *Bevölkerung und Wirtschaft 1872–1972* (Stuttgart: Kohlhammer, 1977), p. 142; R. Rytlewski and M. Opp de Hipt, *Die Deutsche Demokratische Republik in Zahlen 1945/49–1980* (Munich: Beck, 1987), p. 66; Statistisches Bundesamt, ed., *Statistisches Jahrbuch 1992 für die Bundesrepublik* (Stuttgart: Metzler-Poeschel, 1992), p. 114; Statistisches Bundesamt, ed., *Statistisches Jahrbuch 1995 für die Bundesrepublik Deutschland* (Stuttgart: Metzler-Poeschel, 1995), p. 108.

ture. It was this configuration which made specifically working-class actions and labour organizations possible, to which minorities of workers committed themselves: strikes and protests, cooperatives and friendly societies, unions and workers' parties.

This was a complicated, unfinished process of class evolution, the initial and formative phase of which occurred in Germany in the third quarter of the nineteenth century. It accelerated, spread and deepened in the following decades. As Table 24.2 shows, 55 per cent of the labour force were counted as *Arbeiter* (blue-collar workers) in 1907, only 10 per cent belonged to the category of salaried personnel, and about 20 per cent to the shrinking category of 'self-employed' (the rest were defined as 'family helpers'). By 1907, the industrial sector (including crafts, construction and mining) had become the largest sector, absorbing 40 per cent of the labour force (agriculture 35 per cent, services 25 per cent). In manufacturing and mining (in units with ten or more employees) 120,000 entrepreneurs and managers were confronted by 6.2 million blue-collar workers (and only 615,000 white-collar employees). From 1871 to 1910 the

Table 24.2 German labour force by position (*Stellung im Beruf*), 1882–1993 (selected years)

	Self-employed (%)	Family helpers (%)	White-collar/ salaried (%)	Blue-collar workers (%)	Total (millions)
1882	28	10	6	56	19
1907	20	15	10	55	28
1925	17	17	17	49	32
1933	16	16	17	50	32
1950	14	17	22	47	22
1960	12	10	28	50	27
1970	10	7	36	47	27
1980	9	3	46	42	27
1990	9	2	52	37	29
1993	9	1	53	37	36

Note: The German categories are: *Selbständige, Mithelfende Familienangehörige, Beamte und Angestellte* and *Arbeiter*. As to territorial extension and sources, see note to Table 24.1.

Sources: As in Table 24.1 and Statistisches Bundesamt, ed., *Statistisches Jahrbuch 1981 für die Bundesrepublik* (Stuttgart: Kohlhammer, 1981), p. 95. As to the different categorization in the GDR see Rytlewski and Opp de Hipt, p. 67.

share of the population living in places with fewer than 10,000 inhabitants had fallen from 81 to 54 per cent, the percentage of inhabitants of large towns of more than 100,000 had increased from 5 to 27 per cent (Table 24.3). Such figures only suggest the growing *possibility* of working-class formation. But other evidence points to corresponding changes on the level of attitudes and behaviour as well. On the eve of World War I roughly three million workers belonged to unions, the overwhelming majority of them to socialist or social democratic ones. About 30 per cent of all workers outside agriculture were unionized. Industrial conflict became massive. There were years (1905, 1912) in which about 500,000 workers participated in strikes or became victims of lock-outs, far surpassing earlier figures. In 1912 the strictly oppositional Social Democratic Party won 35 per cent of the national vote; among its 4.25 million voters workers were undoubtedly in the majority. Class language abounded. Class distinctions and tensions structured the social reality of the Empire more than any other fault line of social differentiation or tension. Intermediations and loyalties bridging class divisions were certainly not altogether absent. Nevertheless, on the eve of World War I, German society had become a class society to a much greater extent than ever before.

It would not be correct to assume that the German labour movement was more radical than similar movements in France, Italy or other parts of Europe. Nor, in general, were civil rights, political opportunities, and social chances withheld from German workers to a greater extent than from their counterparts in other European countries.

Table 24.3 German population by percentage size of residential community, 1819–1993 (selected years)

	Less than 2,000	2,000–10,000	10,000–50,000	50,000–100,000	More than 100,000
1819	91		5–6	1–2	1–2
1830	92		5	1–2	1–2
1871	62	19	9	5	5
1890	49	19	12	4	16
1910	35	19	13	6	27
1933	30	18	12	6	35
1950	25	21	17	6	31
1970	19	21	21	7	32
1987	6	20	32	9	33
1993	9	19	31	9	32

Note: The figures for 1819 and 1830 relate to the population of the German Federation without Austria and Luxembourg. All other figures relate to the German Empire and the Federal Republic (changing boundaries). In 1970, 26 per cent of the population of the GDR lived in communities with less than 2,000, 52 per cent in communities with 2,000 to 100,000 and 22 per cent in communities with more than 100,000 inhabitants.

Sources: J. Kocka, *Arbeitsverhältnisse und Arbeiterexistenzen. Grundlagen der Klassenbildung im 19. Jahrhundert* (Bonn: J. H. W. Dietz, 1990), p. 54; Statistisches Bundesamt, ed., *Bevölkererung und Wirtschaft 1872–1972*, p. 94; R. Rytlewski and Opp de Hipt, p. 47; Statistisches Bundesamt, ed., *Statistisches Jahrbuch 1988 für die Bundesrepublik* (Stuttgart: Kohlhammer, 1988), p. 60; Statistisches Bundesamt, ed., *Statistisches Jahrbuch 1995 für die Bundesrepublik* (Stuttgart: Metzler-Poeschel, 1995), pp. 58–9.

Rather, two other specific features of the German situation should be emphasized. First of all, the relative timing was important. Separate workers' parties in Germany were a product of the 1860s. This was early by international standards, related to the early introduction of universal manhood suffrage, and it indicated the limited capacity of German liberalism to reach out, integrate and dominate. The simultaneous emergence of the labour movement, the formation of the national state, and the decisive breakthrough of civil society, should be stressed as specific to the German pattern of development. It may have contributed to a fundamental tension between civil society and nation state on the one hand, and the labour movement on the other. Second, the German labour movement was especially large and well organized, offering a principled opposition on a well-elaborated theoretical basis, derived from democratic thought and Marxist socialism. It was not very disruptive in reality, but did present a vigorous challenge to an inflexible political system and a hierarchical society. Perhaps this was due to a distinct pattern of class formation, perhaps to the impact of surviving feudal and corporate traditions, certainly to the authoritarian and illiberal character of the system of government which combined paternalism with repression and exclusion.

As a consequence, large parts of the German bourgeoisie felt especially challenged and deeply threatened. They became highly defensive and moved to the right, aligning themselves with the old elites and the political status quo. They lost sight of the universalist promises of the as yet unfulfilled project of civil society which were so clearly contradicted by social reality. While the socialist labour movement attacked central elements of this project (particularly the capitalist market economy), it was firmly committed to others: civil rights, equal opportunity, public criticism, democratization. At the end of the nineteenth and the beginning of the twentieth century the project of civil society lost part of its middle-class support, but gained some working-class allies who, however, tended to change the project by claiming its principles for themselves. A similar argument could be made with respect to feminist demands and movements, which were much weaker then, but would become very powerful in the second half of the twentieth century.

Since then the class constellation has deeply changed. While class formation was the dominant trend up to World War I, counter-tendencies gained the upper hand from the interwar period onwards, tending rather to class fragmentation or dissolution. The labour force changed. As Table 24.2 shows, the relative weight of the blue-collar sector has strongly declined. From the 1960s onward, it started to shrink even in absolute numbers. Working-class culture had always been a blue-collar phenomenon, part of the world of skilled manual workers. The shift towards salaried white-collar and professional jobs was bound to change the equation. Working-class culture and institutions suffered deeply under the Nazi dictatorship. Terror and war, the bombing of the cities and the violent reshuffling of German society and culture as consequences of war and defeat, mass migration and population transfer further contributed to the weakening of traditional class structures. Above all, unprecedented economic growth from the 1950s to the 1980s, democratization and the success of the welfare state, the rise of consumerism and mass culture, the changing balance between work and leisure, cultural shifts, the blurring of social inequality patterns and the 'individualization' of life chances, strongly contributed to the erosion of class identifications. This was particularly the case in West Germany: economic growth, consumerism and democratization were less important or entirely lacking in the GDR. But there the abandoning of market principles and dictatorial communist rule resulted in the destruction of the traditional class system in an even more thorough way. The working class has not disappeared in Germany, but the relative importance of class as a factor determining wealth, status and power, belonging and social distance, self-identification and cultural orientation, has strongly declined. Class is much less important today than it was at the start of the century.

Crisis and success, expansion and erosion have characterized the history of the bourgeoisie since World War I. The dissolution of the working class has deprived the bourgeoisie of its major remaining opponent. On the other hand, the distinction between aristocracy and bourgeoisie had already lost most of its legal importance by 1918–19 and subsequently lost any remaining political and social meaning. The aristocracy has lost all of its privileges and ceased to be the powerful ruling elite it had been for many centuries. In a way the bourgeoisie has outlived its opponents; but without them it has also lost part of its identity.

The salaried bourgeoisie outnumbers the self-employed bourgeoisie. Bureaucratization has left its mark. The notion of bourgeois independence has changed. Ever since World War I, the number of servants in bourgeois households has steadily declined; servants had been of the utmost importance to nineteenth-century bourgeois families. Classical education became marginal, giving way to more specialized forms of training, and this change dissolved an important element of cultural unity within the bourgeoisie. The culture of work and thrift, of progress and order that defined large parts of the rising bourgeoisie in the earlier parts of the nineteenth century has largely disappeared. The most central institution of bourgeois culture, the family, has changed tremendously, as a clear separation of gender roles had been essential to it. Gender relations have changed thoroughly. Other influences also had an effect: for example, the changing status of youth, the rise of the media and the multiplication of choices available in modern society. As a result the family has lost many of its nineteenth-century functions and part of its inner cohesion, with disintegrative effects on bourgeois culture. The two German dictatorships (the Third Reich and the GDR) have contributed much to the destruction of bourgeois strongholds, traditions and values.

At the same time, surviving features of bourgeois culture have spread widely to all parts of the upper strata, to a certain extent to the shrinking rural population, to the middle masses that used to be called 'lower middle class' (or *Kleinbürgertum*), and even to parts of the working class. After the end of the Nazi dictatorship and the breakdown of 1945, with the economic improvement and the social reconstruction of the 1950s, there was even something like a partial renaissance of bourgeois values and practices in the Federal Republic. The same may happen in eastern Germany in the years to come, although the removal and destruction of bourgeois structures and traditions in the 40 years of the GDR were much more thorough and lasting than what happened in the 12 years of the Third Reich. Certainly, there continue to be economic and social limits to the spread of bourgeois culture. But bourgeois culture, which always had a built-in tendency towards universalization, has moved far beyond the social group where it originated and which it once helped to define.

The descriptive and analytical power of the concepts 'bourgeoisie' (*Bürgertum*) and 'working class' (*Arbeiterklasse*) is limited in relation to patterns of social inequality and conflict in the present. Certainly the class basis of the project of civil society has been loosened, weakened, eroded. Maybe this is one of the reasons why this project is doing relatively well today.

V   Twentieth-century turning points

The years 1918–19 were a profound turning point in German societal history which started as a dictated reform from above (parliamentarization by order of the army High

Command under the pressure of an inevitable defeat in October 1918), continued as a spontaneous revolution from below (November 1918), and led to fundamental reforms on the one hand, to widespread violence and civil war on the other (1919–20). Certain revolutionary objectives clearly aimed beyond the model of civil society and were partly directed against it, but largely failed: for example, attempts at thorough socialization and experiments with non-representative forms of direct democracy outside a constitutional framework. As things turned out, the revolution advanced the cause of civil society in Germany by leading to a liberal constitution, a parliamentary system, the first really democratic elections (including the suffrage for women), basic social reforms which included new mechanisms of conflict resolution, and an important broadening of the political elite. But in this last respect as well as in others it remained half-hearted. It allowed a considerable (and critical) degree of political, cultural and socioeconomic continuity. Too much of the *ancien régime* survived. At the same time the revolution was disruptive, violent and radical enough to produce deep frustration, hardship and rejection at both extremes of the political spectrum. Both the continuity permitted and the wounds inflicted by the revolution burdened and delegitimized the model of civil society it had brought to life.

There were other burdens, of course: the consequences of a war which had not only ended in defeat but in national humiliation, economic disturbances, hardship and social inequality, inflation and subsequently depression, the widespread ineffectiveness of the new system, insufficient time for mental adjustment. This is not the place to retell the story of the hopes and failures of the Weimar Republic (see Chapter 12, above). It succeeded in realizing the principles of a civil society to an – in Germany – unprecedented extent and laid the foundations for new civil traditions which could be built on eventually, in the FRG. But at the same time the Weimar model of civil society was widely rejected by large parts of the bourgeoisie and the lower middle classes on the right, as well as by the communist part of the working class, while social democracy belonged to its few and increasingly helpless supporters. New radical mass movements with totalitarian ambitions had emerged from World War I, both on the left and on the right. They grew and represented a deadly threat to the reality and the principles of civil society. Lack of acceptance, outright hostility and internal deficiencies reinforced one another: it was a civil society in crisis.

The year 1933 brought the Weimar experiment with civil society to an end, on the basis of a coalition between old upper strata (including large parts of the bourgeoisie) and the new fascist mass movement on the right. There has been much debate about whether 1933 can be seen as a revolution. Perhaps. There has also been a controversial debate on the question of whether the National Socialist period not only brought suppression, terror, war and catastrophe to Germany, Europe and the world, but also – in the long run – some modernization to German society, intentionally or otherwise. Advocates of this view may have a point and are not necessarily apologetic. Modernization can be catastrophic, its meaning is not necessarily positive and often vague. In addition one should not exclude the possibility that actions and processes which are destructive and devastating in the short term can sometimes have liberating and even beneficial effects in the long run (which does not, of course, justify them morally at all).

It is, however, quite clear what 1933 meant with respect to the history of civil society in Germany. It brought a dictatorship into power which was an outright negation of nearly all the principles of civil society. It could build on illiberal and authoritarian, racist, anti-Semitic and imperialistic traditions of German history dating far back into the nineteenth century, i.e. on older deficits of civil society in Germany. They explain why German civil society could not mobilize more forces of resistance against the temptation of fascism. But in many respects, particularly in its most destructive features, German fascism presupposed the disintegration of older structures and traditions. It was something new, it grew out of a totalitarian mass movement born in World War I. The Nazi period brought the 'German divergence from the West' to its epitome. It was the period when the distance between the German bourgeoisie and the project of civil society reached its historical peak. But the dictatorship destroyed a vital and central part of the German bourgeoisie, its Jewish component. In this respect and in other respects it severely damaged not only the model of civil society but also – in spite of bourgeois support for the rise and the rule of National Socialism – the strength, the culture, the principles and the mission of the bourgeoisie. (A similar point has been made with respect to the working class, above. It could also be made with respect to other social groups and institutions, particularly the aristocracy and the army.)

After 1945, the basics of a civil society were reintroduced to West Germany. They were firmly established, and this time they have worked, so far. This is not the place to summarize the history of the Federal Republic of Germany, its difficult start in the post-war years under the influence of the Western Allies, the restructuring of its elites (partly a restoration), its economic success, its slow and painful coming-to-terms with its National Socialist heritage, the successful history of its parliamentary institutions and of its party system which largely broke with older traditions, its early orientation towards the West and later on its cautious reconciliation policy towards the East, the gradual development of an open society and the complicated rise of a relatively liberal culture (with many setbacks), its legitimacy and support among large parts of the population, this time including the upper strata and the bourgeoisie. In the FRG the long and problematic 'German divergence from the West' came to an end (see the chapters in Part IV, above).

Certainly, one must not overlook the dark sides. The legacy of the National Socialist past continued, and continues, to be a heavy burden. The inherent problems of a modern civil society are immense, ranging from intolerable forms of deprivation and inequality to the loss of meaning and the ecological crisis. The future is hard to predict. And Germany was divided. While this may have helped the Federal Republic to solve some of its problems and avoid others, it also meant the loss of the German nation state and, following from that, insecurity as to collective identity and political culture.

The confrontation with communist East Germany may have helped to stabilize the FRG, but it also cramped its political culture and threatened its civility. The division also meant that the eastern part of Germany remained under dictatorial rule, which was certainly different from and less devastating than the previous (Nazi) dictatorship, but again a negation of civil society and, simultaneously, a continuation of old authoritarian and illiberal traditions which the Federal Republic tried to overcome.

Still, despite such limitations and other drawbacks, compared to previous periods of German history and to other countries, the record of the FRG between 1949 and 1990 was relatively successful. At least this holds true with respect to the criteria used in this essay. While much remains to be done, major principles of a civil society were translated into reality by the Federal Republic, more than in any previous period of German history.

The last major turning point within German history – 1989–90 – is sometimes seen as a revision and correction of what the turning point of 1945–9 had brought. According to this view the turning point of 1945–9 primarily led to the loss of the German nation state and started more than 40 years of a new German anomaly, the life of a nation in two states. The turning point of 1989–90 restored the German nation state, though not in its old extension. It brought the German division, together with the division of Europe, to an end. The turning point of 1989–90 thus corrected the decisions of 1945–9. This is how the relationship between the last two German turning points can appear if interpreted from the perspective of the history of the nation state.

In the framework of societal history, however, the picture looks different. From the point of view of the history of civil society, the break of 1989–90 – the revolution in the GDR, its transformation into a movement for unification with the FRG and the accession of the GDR to the FRG – appear to be the completion, not the correction, of 1945–9. It extended the system of the West to the Germans in the East who had opted for it with a large majority. It opened up the opportunity to include the East Germans into a relatively successful development towards civil society from which they had been excluded. Whether and how this will work remains to be seen. It is unlikely that the new Federal Republic of Germany will be just a continuation of the old one. The ability to change peacefully is one of the strengths of civil society.

Select bibliography

Augustine, D. L., *Patricians and Parvenus: Wealth and High Society in Wilhelmine Germany* (Oxford: Berg, 1994).

Berghahn, Volker R., *Modern Germany. Society, Economy and Politics in the Twentieth Century* (Cambridge: Cambridge University Press, 1982).

Blackbourn, D., and Eley, G., *The Peculiarities of German History. Bourgeois Society in Nineteenth Century Germany* (Oxford: Oxford University Press, 1984).

Conrad, Christoph, and Kessel, Martina, eds., *Geschichte schreiben in der Postmoderne. Beiträge zur aktuellen Diskussion* (Stuttgart: Reclam, 1994).

Dahrendorf, Ralf, *Gesellschaft und Demokratie in Deutschland* (Munich: Piper, 1968).

Frevert, Ute, *Frauen-Geschichte. Zwischen bürgerlicher Verbesserung und neuer Weiblichkeit* (Frankfurt: Suhrkamp, 1986).

Iggers, Georg, ed., *The Social History of Politics. Critical Perspectives in West German Historial Writing Since 1945* (Leamington Spa: Berg, 1985), esp. pp. 1–48 (editor's introduction).

Kaelble, Hartmut, *Auf dem Weg zu einer europäischen Gesellschaft. Eine Sozialgeschichte Westeuropas 1880–1980* (Munich: Beck, 1987).

Katznelson, Ira, and Zolberg, Aristide R., eds., *Working-Class Formation. Nineteenth-Century Patterns in Western Europe and the United States* (Princeton: Princeton University Press, 1986), esp. pt. 3: Germany.

Kocka, J., 'Theory and History: Recent Developments in West Germany', *Social Research* XLVII (1980).

Kocka, Jürgen, *Facing Total War. German Society 1914–1918* (Leamington Spa: Berg, 1984).

Kocka, Jürgen, 'German History before Hitler. The Debate about the German "Sonderweg"', *Journal of Contemporary History* XXIII (1988).

Kocka, Jürgen, 'The Middle Classes in Europe', *Journal of Modern History* LXVII (1995).

Kocka, Jürgen, and Mitchell, Allan, eds., *Bourgeois Society in Nineteenth-Century Europe* (Oxford: Berg, 1993), esp. pp. 3–39.

Koselleck, Reinhart, *Vergangene Zukunft. Zur Semantik geschichtlicher Zeiten* (Frankfurt: Suhrkamp, 1979).

Lüdtke, Alf, ed., *Alltagsgeschichte. Zur Rekonstruktion historischer Erfahrungen und Lebensweisen* (Frankfurt: Campus, 1989).

Mooser, Josef, *Arbeiterleben in Deutschland 1900–1970. Klassenlagen, Kultur und Politik* (Frankfurt: Suhrkamp, 1984).

Niethammer, Lutz, *et al.*, *Bürgerliche Gesellschaft in Deutschland. Historische Einblicke, Fragen, Perspektiven* (Frankfurt: Fischer, 1990).

Nipperdey, Thomas, 'Probleme der Modernisierung in Deutschland', *Saeculum* XXX (1979).

Prinz, Michael, and Zitelmann, Rainer, eds., *Nationalsozialismus und Modernisierung* (Darmstadt: Wissenschaftliche Buchgesellschaft, 1991).

Rürup, Reinhard, 'Deutschland im 19. Jahrhundert 1815–1871', in Rürup *et al.*, *Deutsche Geschichte*, vol. III (Göttingen: Vandenhoeck and Ruprecht, 1985), pp. 3–200.

Sieder, R., 'Sozialgeschichte auf dem Weg zu einer historischen Kulturwissenschaft?', *Geschichte und Gesellschaft* XX (1994).

Stern, Carola, and August Winkler, Heinrich, eds., *Wendepunkte deutscher Geschichte 1848–1990* 1994), pp. 317–53.

Tenfelde, Klaus, 'Stadt und Bürgertum im 20. Jahrhundert', in Klaus Tenfelde and Hans-Ulrich Wehler, eds., *Wege zur Geschichte des Bürgertums* (Göttingen: Vandenhoeck and Ruprecht, (rev. edn. Frankfurt: Fischer, 1994).

Wehler, Hans-Ulrich, *Deutsche Gesellschaftsgeschichte*, 4 vols. (Munich: Beck, 1987, 1995).

25

Gender in German history

Ute Frevert

If one considers the question of continuity and discontinuity, of persistence and change during the last 200 years of German history, it is above all the element of change, of discontinuity, that appears to be reflected in the development of gender relations. Encounters between women and men are today decidedly different from what they were around 1900 or 1800. Compared to former times, men and women are raised differently, grow up with differently oriented value systems and design different life-plans. Their 'public' functions and roles have changed just as much as their 'private' experiences and premises. Middle-class women born in the first half of the nineteenth century would hardly understand their great-great-great-granddaughters; they would probably find them much too self-sufficient and tomboyish and lament their lack of 'femininity'. In a similar fashion, men born in the 1890s would, upon seeing their male descendants, throw up their hands in disgust and criticize their 'unmanly' manners. Because gender differences were still sharply contoured during their lifetimes, they would appear to them to have been distorted and eroded beyond recognition.

Contemporaries of the closing twentieth century, however, perceive things differently. We do not find it particularly problematic to differentiate between women and men, even if difficulties occasionally arise in attributing someone to one sex or the other. Not only fashion contributes to one's sense of orientation; men and women go different ways during the course of their lives. Women generally follow different life-plans than men, set other priorities, make other decisions. They are actively supported in this by the society in which they live. Parents, schools, churches, career advisers, the media, advertising – all of them keep a tight grip on the distinctive features of gender and code female behaviour differently from male. Despite undeniable changes in gender relations, these differences between the sexes represent even today a central principle of organization which structures not only the division of labour within society, but the distribution of political and economic power as well.

It is apparent, then, that *gender* as a topic can be treated under both headings: it is 'continuous' as well as 'discontinuous'. In light of this, the chapter attempts to do jus-tice to both perspectives. It inquires into change in gender relations as well as into that which has persisted throughout all changes. It considers the driving forces of these changes and the causes of this persistence. It does this under the premiss that gender is not an unchanging, constantly static category, but rather a sociocultural construct which undergoes permanent adjustment, be it intentional or unintentional. Both women and men, both femininity and masculinity, are affected by the processes of his-torical change and this is valid to an equal extent for their mutual relations. Love, mar-riage, and sexuality – we at the end of the twentieth century have an understanding of these terms different from that valid at the end of the nineteenth, not mention the eigh-teenth, century. Within the public sphere, too, the conventions of gender have shifted unmistakably, without, however, having been eliminated as a formal principle. One must keep this in mind so as not to be taken in by the seemingly dominant dynamics of change.

I   Thoughts on the gender system

As long as modern civil society has existed – initially as a rough draft, but one put more and more frequently into practice since the nineteenth century (see Chapter 24, above) – the respective positions of women and men within its boundaries have been subject to analysis. In 1838, the liberal politician and historian Carl Welcker wrote in the influ-ential, widely-distributed Staats-Lexikon that 'the relations between the sexes are undeniably the most universal and the most important relations within human society'. They coincide with 'the deepest and most important basic elements of the entire struc-ture of society' and are for this reason, although extremely difficult for 'legal and polit-ical theory', also central to it.[1]

Above all liberals found it problematic to define these relations; conservatives had a much easier time of it. The counter-revolutionary draft conceived of society as a cor-porative organism in which households, occupational groups, estates, neighbourhoods, etc., had close ties to one another and acted interdependently. Political representation was not regarded as a right of the individual, but rather a matter of the corporation, that is, for example, of the family. Even though the representatives were, in general, male, women were to consider themselves to be represented to an equal extent because they could make their influence felt within the bounds of the corporation.

In contrast, the political theory of liberal constitutionalism found itself confronted with massive gender troubles. Liberals envisioned society not as an amalgamation of households and corporations, but rather as a marriage of convenience between indi-viduals. In their capacity as citizens, these individuals entered into direct, personal relations with civil society; in both the political and the legal sense, they represented only their own person.

These persons had freed themselves to a large extent from the classifications and restrictions of the *ancien régime*. Consequently, their union, too, followed different rules and took on a new shape. Modern civil society as it had been launched by the American and French Revolutions was guided by the governing principles of freedom, equality and brotherhood. Gender was contained within the semantics of this programme, as nineteenth-century nations all conceived of themselves as associations of free and equal brothers – sisters went unmentioned. Neither in France nor in Germany, where this development came at a later date in the form of a defensive modernization strategy, did it occur to anyone to extend the concept of active citizenship to women.

As a rule, civil society's intellectual innovaters and pragmatists did not explain why a citizen could only be of the male sex. For them, it was a matter of course, as it were. The first demands for a justification of this implicitly presupposed principle came from feminists and conservatives. Beginning in the 1830s, then with increasing frequency after the 1860s, liberal politicians and political scientists in Germany took up the challenge and mounted arguments which sought to explain the exclusion of women from civil society in a convincing manner.

In the final analysis, all of these arguments were based on the assumption that men and women were fundamentally different sorts of human beings. Nature, it was stated time and again, had destined them for different functions and, for that reason, had provided them with different physical and mental attributes. To the same extent that the male physique differed from the female, the respective mental disposition of each sex was unlike that of the other. If Woman represented the principles of beauty, love, and modesty, then Man embodied power, courage, and severity. He was, as it was phrased in 1785, 'driven by nature to rule, whereas Woman, who is aware of her weakness, tends to obedience'.[2] Women belonged to the dependent, men to the independent, self-reliant sex. As a logical consequence, women found their life-purpose in the care of others, while men excelled in personal ambition, healthy egoism, and the active will to create. The central domain of the female sex was the private sphere of the family, whereas men were responsible for public life, for economic and political industriousness.

As of the late 1800s, legions of writers, theologists, pedagogues, and above all medical doctors contributed to the elaboration upon and the scientific proof of this anthropology of gender. The political discourse of the nineteenth century greedily took up their arguments and wove them into the theory and practice of civil society. Among both conservatives and liberals, it was said that the state was necessarily male – political offices could only be occupied and administered by men. Furthermore, men alone were entitled to represent society through the passive and active right to vote. In contrast, women were to keep their distance from public differences of opinion and renounce the 'rough life of men' in favour of the intimate world of the family. Their nature did not qualify them for 'logical reasoning' and 'methodical dialectic', but rather for 'irritability and passion', both of which, according to male authors, were qualities which could only serve to harm the state.

'The state for the man, the family for the woman' – such was the concise and self-confident summary of the mood of the times to be found in *Meyers Konversations-Lexikon* of 1894. This division of labour between the sexes was considered modern and reasonable; a society organized according to this schema was merely following the intention and interests of nature itself and would, as a consequence, engender the best of all possible worlds. Conversely, attempts to shake up this division of labour were judged to strive against the course of nature and were ridiculed. That women and men fulfilled different purposes (family vs. employment) and occupied different spheres (private vs. public) reflected 'unchangeable natural conditions'. To want to alter these conditions and 'to blur the difference between the sexes in all of life's external relations' was, according to the *Brockhaus* encyclopedia in 1898, 'enduringly impossible'.

The women's movement, which came into the public eye in the 1860s, chimed in with this credo. Although there were indeed women, among them the lone warrior Hedwig Dohm, who formulated radical demands for equality, the greater part of all women held to the motto that women were equal to men in worth, but not in nature. Helene Lange, one of the leading figures of the bourgeois women's movement, said at the beginning of the twentieth century that women embodied a specifically 'feminine culture', which she equated to a great extent with motherliness, with the selfless, self-sacrificing care of others. The highest aim of the women's movement was to foster this culture in order to ensure its decisive influence on society as a whole. Equipped with feminine-motherly moral concepts, women were to round off to perfection the 'one-sided male creations' of the 'great culture-systems' and counteract the destructive faults in their development. The far-reaching imaginativeness of this concept lay in the fact that the feminine essence was to heal not only the husband, exhausted from his public duties, but the entire 'modern world'.

Despite such ambitious impulses to rescue the world, the feminist movement did not challenge the premiss that women were to find their primary purpose within the family. Only unmarried women without children were supposed to realize their 'spiritual motherliness' in the public sphere, be it as teachers, doctors, lawyers, social workers or politicians. The opening of such careers, as well as of the corresponding educational opportunities, was among the most important aims of the early women's movement.

Middle-class feminism's increasing success after the turn of the century was thanks not only to its convincing arguments but also to its pronounced nose for publicity. Without the readiness of influential circles of male society to acknowledge and to reflect upon these arguments, the 'women's question' would not have been dealt with in encyclopedias, at conferences on social policy, or at church and party conventions. That such openness could be awakened in the face of great resistance can in essence be attributed to the social proximity of those who brought attention to the problem with those who accepted it as a problem. The women who were engaged in the feminist movement were the wives, daughters, sisters and cousins of men who belonged in one way or another to the societal Establishment, who moulded and represented public opinion.

Not least due to social grounds of consideration, this Establishment proved itself willing to meet female demands for better educational and career opportunities. However, support was always offered solely under the premiss that such opportunities would only be taken advantage of by unmarried women. The conventions of gender as such had to be protected from profound alteration. Consequently, the political sphere was closed to women until 1918 – in this the bourgeois parties were absolutely unwilling to compromise. As one could still read in the 1911 *Handbook of the German Conservative Party*, women 'only have use for the right to vote in respect of one individual' – meaning their future husbands.

After the revolution of 1918 had made short work of the male political monopoly, it seemed that the gender system, at least in the political and legal form it had been given during the nineteenth century, was going to falter decisively. 'The world is a different place', claimed the writer Frank Thiess in 1929, 'since women have become active in parliaments, in welfare organizations, in schools, in social policy, and in hospitals.' Under the surface as well, he continued, 'revolutionary things' were happening: 'Within marriage, in the mutual relations of the sexes, a hidden theatre of war has gradually come to be in which a dogged and bitter struggle is being carried out to this day.'[3]

The delight in experimentation during the Weimar Republic, which had brought accusations of 'feminization' from conservative German nationalists, was brought to an abrupt end in 1933. In order to prepare and wage the great manly war of the races and nations, the National Socialists had to smother the smaller war between the sexes. They envisioned a gender system which would once again clearly separate the 'small' world of women from man's 'wide world'. Whereas men were to take reponsibility for politics, war and employment in the public sphere, women should attend to family, household and race. 'The first, best, and most appropriate place for a woman', claimed Propaganda Minister Josef Goebbels in 1933, 'is in the family, and the most wonderful task that she can undertake is to provide her country and people with children.' Hitler put it even more clearly in 1934: 'Every child she bears is a battle she fights for the existence or non-existence of her people.'

As mothers of future soldiers women, too, participated in the war between the races. Nevertheless, the male contribution was clearly held to be more important than theirs. At the heart of the *völkisch* state – and the National Socialists left no doubt in this matter – stood the warrior-like man. He chose a wife with the intention of fathering manly, warrior-like offspring; in the eyes of the state and the national community, only by these means did he confer honour and worth upon her. The soldierly man was the measure of all things; only in relation to him was woman worthy of any notice whatsoever.

When the male state of the Third Reich collapsed in 1945, it left behind considerable gender trouble. Immediately thereafter, a new wave of reflection on how women's roles (but less so those of men) were henceforth to be defined set in. Whereas the German Democratic Republic, pursuing political and economic motives, sought to take the matter of gender equality seriously, the Federal Republic of the 1950s initially experienced a powerful renaissance of inherited gender stereotypes. Not until the New

Illustration 25.1 Election poster by the NSDAP: 'Women! Save the German family, vote for Adolf Hitler!'

Feminism of the 1970s had caused elemental turmoil in these stereotypes, did gender discourse profit from any innovative impulses. The movement protested vociferously against the precept, unchallenged up to this point, that women existed primarily for husband and children and were only to seek work within the family. Instead, it argued in favour of a primarily open model – neither women nor men should be hindered through premature assumptions about their so-called essence in the autonomous planning and realization of their goals in life. In this sense, the only possible conception of equal rights was to grant all people, regardless of gender, the opportunity for self-realization.

As a consequence, equal rights were not the ultimate political goal of second-generation feminists, but rather a kind of vehicle, a necessary formal prerequisite to the fundamental reorganization of gender relations in accordance with individual free will and behaviour. This complex left completely open the question of how men and women would act toward one another. In any case, it would no longer be appropriate to speak of a set gender 'order' in view of the extensive disintegration of traditional stereotypes and dualities.

II Interjection

Even though reflection on gender relations towards the end of the twentieth century is new and at the same time disorderly, challenging previous formal categories, this does not mean that these relations can be lived out in just as new and disorderly a fashion. There was, and there still is, an irrevocable difference between reflection and action, between theory and practice. Nevertheless, even pure thought does not take place in a vacuum, but is constrained by concrete human needs, problems and the given range of possibilities.

Therefore, when feminists of the 1970s sounded the bell for gender trouble and introduced disorder into honed patterns of thought, this did not yet signal a widespread new social practice. But it did indicate that new expectations for the future had been formulated, and allows the historian to conjecture that these expectations were based on a change in experience. Without the modernizing spurts of the 1960s and 1970s, so the theory goes, innovative concepts of gender relations would have been neither thinkable nor communicable. The New Feminism undoubtedly profited from the sense that society was capable of new departures, from the expansion of the educational system and the certainty of economic growth. In this reform-friendly atmosphere, in which the West German election slogan 'No Experiments' could be replaced by a call to 'Risk More Democracy', it was also possible to problematize the structural inequality affecting gender relations in a new, radical way.

Previous changes and innovations in society, economy, or politics had affected thought on gender policy in a less fundamental way. The concept of a natural gender difference had outlived all waves of modernization in the nineteenth and early twentieth centuries, even though societal consequences of this difference had been conceived of in dissimilar fashion. The first women's movement had cleaved to the idea of the polarized 'characters of the sexes', too, and had limited itself to calling for concessions in order that feminine nature might unfold under a wider range of possibilities.

This restraint can be explained in that women of that time actually did have different experiences from men, that the male and female worlds appeared to be sharply divided from one another, making border-crossing hardly feasible. The cultural production of gender polarity was so powerful and ubiquitous that it did not leave room for alternatives. Only with the weakening of this polarity during the years after the First, but above all after the Second World War, could other expectations germinate, awakening further-reaching hopes for change. Only the convergence of male and female spheres of experience in a demilitarized, education, consumption, and service society in the throes of democratization permitted a new conception of gender relations.

III Gender and class

At this point, a more differentiated argumentation becomes necessary. In view of our previous discussion of the production of gender polarity, said to have captivated people of the nineteenth century and to have constrained alternative thinking, one must add by way of correction that this cultural model was primarily accessible to the upper and middle strata of the population. The lower classes and the bulk of the rural population had only heard tell of such a thing and led their lives according to other rules.

In fact, the dividing line between the male and the female sphere was much less sharply drawn in non-bourgeois strata. Although they knew differences between male and female work, behaviour, and life-plans, the sexes affected each other differently and much less rigidly in these elements of the population. For example, in rural areas, which after all were inhabited by almost half of the German population at the end of the nineteenth century, a continuous, strict division between a female 'interior' and a male 'exterior' was not to be observed. Although farm women were primarily responsible for household management and for work in garden and barn, it was a matter of course that they, too, helped in the fields at harvest time. The great importance of their contributions to the income of the family farm becomes evident in the fact that women as a rule sold vegetables, fruit, eggs and poultry at a weekly market in town. In this way, they were able to furnish a considerable part of the family's cash income. However, this admittedly important economic function did not ensure an absolute equality of rank between the sexes. Instead, a long tradition of the low estimation of women and a patriarchical law of property and inheritance saw to it that the husband had a greater say in things than did his wife.

In those parts of society, however, in which there was nothing to own or to inherit, male authority appears to have been less well grounded. In the rural sub-strata of peddlers and cottagers, just as among the homeworkers and hired hands, a strict gender-specific division of labour was largely unknown. At this level of society, men, too, did housework, which would have been unthinkable in farm families. Furthermore, a survey on female farm workers in the early twentieth century demonstrated that women administered the family's cash income for the most part independently. 'It is the custom in the country that the husband gives his money to the wife and she gives him pocket money if he wants to go out occasionally. All the rest is purchased by the woman.'[4]

As long as the General Legal Code of 1794 was valid in the Prussian provinces, such an arrangement would not have been at all legal. Instead, according to the letter of the law, all monies that a woman earned through employment outside the home passed automatically into the possession of her husband, although she was unable to claim a right to his income as her own personal property. Only with the Civil Legal Code of 1900 was this regulation annulled, taking into account an economic development which was transforming women, too, albeit in a much slower and more limited fashion than men, into salaried workers. In working-class families in which both partners were gainfully employed, both incomes flowed into a common till – to which the husband apparently helped himself much more frequently than did the wife. It was not unusual that the husband retained a good part of his pay for his personal need for tobacco, alcohol and pleasures, while the wife used the entirety of her income, which was as a rule smaller, for the support of the family.

Illustration 25.2 Women working in a tobacco factory, *c.* 1840

Among urban workers, women additionally held full responsibility for children and household, which role they were obliged to fill from childhood on. It was the daughters, and not the sons, who had to take care of the younger siblings, who helped their mothers with the housework, and who lent a helping hand with darning and sewing. After girls completed elementary school, their lives continued to be family-orientated. At this point they generally aspired to enter 'into service', that is to take on a position as a maid in a bourgeois household. Particularly the better-off skilled workers, the so-called labour aristocrats, preferred to have their daughters acquire the art of solid household management in this way than to send them as unskilled workers to the factory. Whereas their sons completed apprenticeships, parents considered an education which would qualify girls for a career to be wasteful. Their future career would be, it was claimed on all sides, that of mother and housewife and for this they were best prepared through employment under a bourgeois master and mistress. Future husbands appreciated the abilities acquired there and it was common knowledge that many workers 'will only take a factory girl as a wife if she has also spent some time in service and learned something of housekeeping and farming'.[5]

In 1907, the employment statistics designated 1.57 million women as being in 'domestic service', a sector of the economy occupied almost exclusively by women. These were predominantly young, unmarried women who lived in the households of their masters and mistresses. As soon as they married, they were obliged to give up their positions, for their new family status was not reconcilable with working conditions which required of them a full availability not to be measured in hours. However, it was very seldom that the wish of these young women – in accordance with the example set by their bourgeois mistresses – to live within their own marriage free of material worries, no longer burdened by the need for employment outside the home, and able to concentrate exclusively on children and household, was granted. If they married a worker, they could be certain that his earnings would barely be sufficient to satisfy the needs of the family for housing, food and clothing. Not only in the families of unskilled workers was it customary that women 'earned a little on the side'. Even under conditions in which men brought home a higher salary, women as a rule were compelled to find a way to earn additional income.

It was relatively unusual that they went to work in the factory in order to do this. Although married female industrial workers numbered almost half a million in 1907, factory work was the domain of young, unmarried women. Wives with small children preferred work within the home, which they could combine more flexibly with their familial duties. By sub-letting parts of their living quarters, serving as cleaning women to bourgeois families, or leasing a small tract of land on which they could plant vegetables and potatoes, women managed to bring home additional cash and food.

Some women were able to open a small shop or, provided that they had learned a trade, set up their own workshops for the completion of semi-finished industrial products. Primarily in the confectionary and textile industries, but also in the retail and catering trades and in cleaning, income statistics record a great number of

Table 25.1 The employment of German women and men, 1882–1994
(a) 1882–1933

	1882		1895		1907		1925		1933	
	Million	%	Million	%	Million	%	Million	%	Million	%
Women										
Percentage employed[1]		37.5		37.4		45.9		48.9		48.0
Total employed	5.54		6.58		9.49		11.48		11.48	
Total employed by economic sector:										
*Agriculture	2.53	45.6	2.75	41.9	4.6	48.4	4.97	43.3	4.65	40.5
*Industry/Artisan	1.13	20.4	1.52	23.1	2.1	22.2	2.99	26.0	2.76	24.0
*Trade/Transport	0.30	5.4	0.58	8.8	0.93	9.8	1.56	13.7	1.96	17.1
*Domestic service/Admin./Military	1.47	26.5	1.55	23.5	1.57	16.6	1.36	11.8	1.25	10.9
*Free Profess.	0.12	2.1	0.18	2.7	0.29	3.0	0.60	5.2	0.86	7.5
Total employed by status:										
*Self-employed	—	—	1.1	16.8	1.09	11.5	0.89	7.8	0.93	8.1
*Family worker	—	—	1.16	17.6	3.18	33.5	4.13	36.0	4.15	36.1
*Civil servant/white collar	—	—	0.16	2.4	0.37	3.9	1.46	12.7	1.71	14.9
*Worker	—	—	4.16	63.2	4.85	51.1	5.0	43.5	4.69	40.9

Men

	Total	%	Total	%	Total	%	Total	%	Total	%
Percentage employed[1]		95.5		95.0		95.2		95.3		93.9
Total employed	13.42		15.53		18.6		20.53		20.82	
Total employed by economic sector:										
*Agriculture	5.7	42.5	5.54	35.7	5.28	28.4	4.79	23.3	4.7	22.6
*Industry/Artisan	5.27	39.3	6.76	43.5	9.15	49.2	10.49	51.1	10.29	49.4
*Trade/Transport	1.27	9.5	1.76	11.3	2.55	13.7	3.68	17.9	4.0	19.2
*Domestic service/ Admin./Military	0.26	1.9	0.22	1.4	0.17	0.9	0.04	0.2	0.02	0.1
*Free Profess.	0.92	6.8	1.25	8.1	1.45	7.8	1.53	7.5	1.81	8.7
Total employed by status:										
*Self-employed	—	—	4.47	28.8	4.41	23.7	4.12	20.1	4.28	20.6
*Family worker	—	—	0.91	5.9	1.11	6.0	1.3	6.3	1.16	5.6
*Civil servant/ white collar	—	—	1.67	10.7	2.51	13.5	4.08	19.9	3.91	18.7
*Worker	—	—	8.48	54.6	10.57	56.8	11.03	53.7	11.47	55.1

[1] Of the population of employable age.

Table 25.1 *continued*
(b) 1939–1980

	1939[2] Million	%	1950[3] Million	%	1961[3] Million	%	1970[3] Million	%	1980[3] Million	%
Women										
Percentage employed[1]		49.8		44.4		48.9		49.6		52.9
Total employed	12.8		8.49		9.93		9.59		10.48	
Total employed by economic sector:										
*Agriculture	4.93	38.5	2.85	33.6	1.96	19.7	1.25	13.0	0.73	7.0
*Industry/Artisan	2.98	23.3	2.4	28.3	3.28	33.0	3.26	34.0	3.11	3.1
*Trade/Transport	1.69	13.2	1.18	13.8	1.88	18.9	1.93	20.1	2.2	2.2
*Service sector	3.2	25.0	2.06	24.3	2.82	28.4	3.16	32.9	4.44	42.4
Total employed by status:										
*Self-employed	0.82	6.4	0.64	7.6	0.73	7.3	0.57	5.9	0.50	4.8
*Family worker	4.64	36.3	2.6	30.7	2.19	22.0	1.52	15.8	0.83	7.9
*Civil servant/white collar	2.04	16.0	1.81	21.3	3.41	34.3	3.99	41.6	5.86	55.9
*Worker	5.3	41.4	3.43	40.4	3.61	36.3	3.51	36.6	3.29	31.4

Men

Percentage employed[1]										
Total employed	22.9	95.6	15.01	93.5	16.9	93.5	17.03	91.1	17.16	86.4
Total employed by economic sector:										
*Agriculture	3.73	16.3	2.34	15.6	1.62	9.6	1.16	6.8	0.76	4.4
*Industry/Artisan	11.45	50.0	8.1	54.0	9.63	57.0	9.95	58.4	9.39	54.7
*Trade/Transport	3.71	16.2	2.57	17.1	2.75	16.3	2.74	16.1	2.66	15.5
*Service sector	4.01	17.5	1.98	13.2	2.89	17.1	3.18	18.7	4.36	25.4
Total employed by status:										
*Self-employed	4.12	18.0	2.78	18.5	2.52	14.9	2.28	13.4	1.87	10.9
*Family worker	1.1	4.8	0.65	4.3	0.47	2.8	0.29	1.7	0.14	0.8
*Civil servant/white collar	5.7	24.9	3.03	20.2	4.61	27.3	5.31	31.2	6.78	39.5
*Worker	11.97	52.3	8.56	57.0	9.29	55.0	9.15	53.7	8.37	48.8

[2] Territory of 31/12/1937.
[3] Federal Republic of Germany.

Table 25.1 *continued*

(c) 1987–1994

	1987[3]		1994[4]	
	Million	%	Million	%
Women				
Percentage employed[1]		60.7		65.8
Total employed	10.53		14.49	
Total employed by economic sector:				
*Agriculture	0.54	5.1	0.48	3.3
*Industry/Artisan	2.7	25.6	3.18	21.9
*Trade/Transport	2.22	21.1	3.15	21.7
*Service sector	5.07	48.2	8.28	57.1
Total employed by status:				
*Self-employed	0.8	7.6	0.86	5.9
*Family worker	0.88	8.4	0.4	2.8
*Civil servant/ white collar	5.81	55.2	9.79	67.6
*Worker	2.63	24.3	3.44	23.7

Men

Percentage employed[1]				
Total employed	16.66	91.0	20.25	88.5
Total employed by economic sector:				
*Agriculture	0.65	4.0	0.71	3.5
*Industry/Artisan	8.38	50.4	10.45	51.6
*Trade/Transport	2.68	16.2	3.42	16.9
*Service sector	4.84	29.4	6.4	31.6
Total employed by status:				
*Self-employed	1.72	10.4	2.43	12.0
*Family worker	0.91	5.5	0.09	0.4
*Civil servant/ white collar	6.77	40.9	8.89	43.9
*Worker	7.07	42.7	8.84	43.7

[1] Includes the former GDR.

Sources:

Klauder, Wolfgang, 'Wirtschaftliche und gesellschaftliche Bedeutung der Frauenerwerbstätigkeit heute und morgen,' in Karl Schwarz, ed., Frauenerwerbstätigkeit – Demographische, soziologische, ökonomische und familienpolitische Aspekte – Deutsche Gesellschaft für Bevölkerungswissenschaft 26. Arbeitstagung vom 19. bis 21. Februar in Gosen bei Berlin (1992).

Presse- und Informationsamt der Bundesregierung, ed., Gesellschaftliche Daten 1982 (1982).

Röger, Werner, Frauenerwerbstätigkeit und Strukturwandel in der Bundesrepublik Deutschland (1991).

Statistisches Bundesamt, ed., Bevölkerung und Wirtschaft 1872–1972 (1972).

Statistisches Bundesamt, ed., Bevölkerung und Erwerbstätigkeit, Fachserie I. Reihe 4.1.1., Stand und Entwicklung der Erwerbstätigkeit 1994 (Ergebnisse des Mikrozensus) (1995).

Müller, Walter et al., Strukturwandel der Frauenarbeit 1880–1980 (1983).

Petzina, Dietmar et al., Sozialgeschichtliches Arbeitsbuch III (1978).

self-employed women. However, their businesses were more often than not small, employing only very few workers beyond the immediate family, if any at all.

Women married to owners of artisanal or service concerns stepped into the position behind the counter. Particularly in the grocery trade, a form of gender-specific division of labour was (and is) widely predominant in which that which the husband produced was sold by the wife in the shop. Retail trade and many restaurants were also dominated by the very conditions which the authors of the Civil Code must have had in mind when they automatically attributed to women 'work within the husband's business'. This work was officially documented by the employment statistics – along with the occupational categories of the 'self-employed', 'workers', 'salaried employees and civil servants', these cited 'assisting family members', who, as a rule, were of the female sex and found in the agricultural, artisanal and retail sectors of the economy.

It is not difficult to conceive of the fact that all these women were hardly able to lead a 'bourgeois' family life with the division of labour between household and the public sphere that went along with it. This does not rule out the possibility that they from time to time may have dreamt of the advantages of a true bourgeois existence. They longed for successful social advancement, at least for their daughters, like that of Jenny Bürstenbinder, a Treibel by marriage, in Theodor Fontane's famous novel *Frau Jenny Treibel*. Jenny Treibel, who as a child had still glued paper cones in her parents' dry-goods shop, no longer stood behind the counter as the wife of a distinguished businessman. Instead, she personified her spouse's riches and arranged advantageous marriages for her sons.

It was exactly this apparent absence of work among women that distinguished middle-class lifestyle from all others. The bourgeois household could live from the income of the male provider and, as a consequence, could afford to free women for non-material pursuits. Even if an array of work-intensive household and representational duties were concealed behind their demonstrative idleness and many (lower) middle-class women even sewed and knitted articles for sale in secret, they stubbornly attempted to project the appearance of female leisure. In the nineteenth and the early twentieth century, the paid employment of middle-class women was almost scandalous. Certainly the wives and daughters of businessmen, civil servants or the self-employed could commit themselves to the care of the poor in volunteer positions and organize charity bazaars. But to tailor a professional career out of such activities and to allow oneself to be paid for it would not have been at all befitting of one's social status.

Only those women who remained unmarried were permitted to look about for suitable employment opportunities. Instead of watching their lives slip away as barely tolerated 'old maids' in the households of married siblings or cousins, or serving as governesses, they increasingly preferred to build up a self-sufficient existence financed through a career of their own. It gradually became the practice in middle-class families to prepare daughters for such an eventuality and not only to give them a dowry, but also career training along the way. After the universities had bowed to the massive pressure of the feminist movement and had opened their gates to women as well, more and more 'young ladies' acquired academic degrees. The number of registered female students increased from 1,896 in the winter term 1911–12 to 20,256 twenty years later.

Yet it was still more customary for middle-class families to finance a son's university studies than those of a daughter. The latter generally had to content themselves with a non-academic teacher's education, if they did not want, after a short-term course of study at a trade school, to join the ranks of female white-collar workers. Into this career, which had recorded the highest rates of growth since the turn of the century, flocked young women from *petit bourgeois* and working-class families as well, for whom the extremely dependent life of a servant no longer represented a desirable perspective.

Although it had originally been filled by men who sheltered it jealously from women, the corps of white-collar, salaried positions was accessible to both sexes by the twentieth century. The reorganization of the economy and the expansion of the service sector that went along with it were reflected in the employment statistics in an

Table 25.2 The education of German women and men, 1900–1994

(a) Students receiving secondary education providing qualification for higher education

Year	Total	Male		Female	
		Number	%	Number	%
1900[1]	176,269	—	—	—	—
1906[1]	227,349	—	—	—	—
1911	604,900	392,697	64.9	212,221	35.1
1913[1]	275,165	—	—	—	—
1921/22	720,030	475,047	66	244,983	34.0
1926	822,609	551,322	67.1	271,287	32.9
1931/32	778,440	530,578	68.2	247,862	31.8
1935	673,975	428,861	63.6	245,114	36.4
1939	733,793	482,566	65.8	251,227	34.2
1942	717,400	454,828	63.4	262,572	36.6
1950	620,488	369,460	59.5	251,028	40.5
1954	763,462	456,054	59.7	307,408	40.3
1958/59	855,000	510,000	59.6	345,000	40.4
1965/66	958,000	563,000	58.8	395,000	41.2
1969/70	1,352,000	764,000	62.5	588,000	37.5
1972/73	1,567,000	851,000	54.3	716,000	45.7
1976[2]	1,928,582	994,111	51.2	943,471	48.5
1980[2]	2,135,222	1,064,801	49.9	1,070,621	50.1
1985[2]	1,765,296	873,324	49.5	891,972	50.4
1990[2]	1,566,605	761,495	48.6	805,110	51.4
1992[2,3]	2,067,483	956,591	46.3	1,110,892	53.7
1994[2,3]	2,166,277	993,974	45.9	1,172,303	54.1

[1] The only educational statistics in the *Statistische Jahrbücher für das Deutsche Reich* from the years 1903 to 1911 pertain exclusively to the *Volksschulen*.
[2] *Gymnasium* and night-*Gymnasium*, not including *Gesamtschule*.
[3] Including the new states of the Federal Republic of Germany.

(b) University students

Year	Total	Male		Female	
		Number	%	Number	%
1902[1]	35,875	—	—	—	—
1908[1]	47,253	—	—	—	—
1911	55,118	52,654	94.6	2,464	5.4
1914[2]	79,511	75,198	92.5	4,313	7.5
1920[2]	115,633	106,957	92.5	8,676	7.5
1925	59,645	52,866	88.6	6,779	11.5
1928/29	82,526	69,951	85.0	12,305	15.0
1934/35	68,043	57,053	83.8	10,990	16.2
1940[3]	38,285	31,366	81.9	6,919	18.1
1943	52,346	27,337	52.2	25,009	47.8
1950	73,783	58,345	79.1	15,438	20.9
1955	84,525	65,263	77.2	19,262	22.8
1961	173,163	134,034	77.4	39,130	22.6
1965/66	267,000	207,000	77.5	60,000	22.5
1969/70	375,472	263,672	70.0	111,800	30.0
1974/75	601,370	387,111	64.6	214,259	35.6
1979/80	711,258	439,184	61.7	272,074	38.3
1984/85	912,940	539,303	59.9	373,637	40.9
1989/90	1,017,003	592,185	58.2	424,818	41.8
1992/93	1,245,183	706,824	56.8	538,359	43.2
1994/95	1,126,011	631,154	56.1	494,857	43.9

[1] The figures do not distinguish according to gender.
[2] Students attending *Wissenschaftliche Hochschulen* (universities; polytechnical universities; schools of veterinary medicine, agriculture, forestry, trade, physical education, mining; not including paedagogical institutions and academics or academies of art or music.
[3] First trimester 1940.

Sources:
Führ, Christoph, *Zur Schulpolitik der Weimarer Republik, Darstellung und Quellen* (1972).
Hochschulverwaltungen, ed., *Deutsche Hochschulstatistik, Sommerhalbjahr 1928* (1928).
Hohorst, G., Kocka, J. and Ritter, G. A., *Sozialgeschichtliches Arbeitsbuch II, Materialien zur Statistik des Kaiserreichs, 1870–1914* (1978).
Länderrat des Amerikanischen Besatzungsgebiets, ed., *Statistisches Handbuch von Deutschland, 1928–1944* (1949).
Petzina, D., Abelshauser, W. and Faust, A., *Sozialgeschichtliches Arbeitsbuch III., Materialien zur Statistik des Deutschen Reichs, 1914–1945* (1978).
Reichsstelle für Schulwesen, ed., *Wegweiser durch das Höhere Schulwesen des Deutschen Reichs, Schuljahr 1935* (1936).
Reichsstelle für Schulwesen, ed., *Wegweiser durch das Höhere Schulwesen des Deutschen Reichs, Schuljahr 1939, 5. Jahrgang* (1940).
Statistisches Bundesamt, ed., *Statistisches Jahrbuch für die Bundesrepublik Deutschland 1952* (1952).
Statistisches Bundesamt, ed., *Die Frau im wirtschaftlichen und sozialen Leben der Bundesrepublik* (1956).
Statistisches Bundesamt, ed., *Die Frau in Familie und Beruf* (1970).
Statistisches Bundesamt, ed., *Die Frau in Familie, Beruf und Gesellschaft* (1975).
Statistisches Bundesamt, ed., *Bildung im Zahlenspiegel 1978* (1978).
Statistisches Bundesamt, ed., *Bildung und Kultur, Fachserie 11, Reihe 4.1, Studenten an Hochschulen, Wintersemester 1992/93* (1995).
Statistisches Bundesamt, ed., *Bildung und Kultur, Fachserie 11, Reihe 1, Allgemeinbildende Schulen 1994* (1996).

enormous increase in the share of white-collar jobs. Women above all profited from this change.

As a consequence, a cross-section of female employment figures in the twentieth century demonstrates a more modern profile than that of men: while in 1990 almost 60 per cent of all women were employed as white-collar workers and only 28 per cent as industrial workers, the respective percentages for men amounted to 33 per cent vs. 44 per cent. In contrast, during the first industrial revolution in the nineteenth century, it had been the men who were the first to be caught up in the change in economic structure. While men had been open to the new, modern form of salaried work, women had followed in their paths only after some period of time, in much lower numbers, and distributed themselves in branches with less promise for the future.

A closer look at the allegedly so modern female employment structure characteristic of the twentieth century reveals that it, indeed, holds its perils. For one thing, the majority of female white-collar workers was confined to lower salary and qualification levels; at the top of the managerial pyramid, women were to be found working for the most part in the reception room and hardly ever in the corner office. Furthermore, the total rate of female employment still lies far below that of men: in 1990, 82.7 per cent of all 15- to 65-year-old men in the states of the pre-1989 Federal Republic were employed, compared to 58.5 per cent of the women of the same age (in the states of the former German Democratic Republic, the rate of female employment was at that time over 80 per cent). The GDR, where, thanks to the presence of extensive daycare facilities, married women with children were also part of the workforce, offers a sharp contrast to the case in the former Federal Republic. Here, many mothers preferred an additional part-time employment which allowed them to combine work outside the family. The clear readiness of women to limit their involvement in a career in favour of the family, or even to put it aside for a period of time, had a direct effect on their chances for advancement and their level of pay. In addition, it is well known that women's careers are not exactly supported by their superiors who more often than not are male.

IV   Interjection

It has become quite clear up to now that the very apparent class differences in male and female lifestyles have diminished continuously and increasingly during the course of the twentieth century. If the bourgeois model of gender relations emphasizing polarity had for a long time been accessible only to the middle and upper classes, it eventually succeeded in staking a claim in wider sections of the population. The generally accepted life pattern in which men supported their families with income and women were exclusively occupied with the care of household, husband and children could only first become predominant in the 'levelled middle-class society' of the early Federal Republic. It was only at this time that real wages reached a level which could support a family. Additional alleviation was provided by the fact that family size shrank appreciably, so that there were only very few couples who raised more than two children. Furthermore, it had become the practice in all sectors of the population that women pursue a career before marriage, save their earnings, and with these means finance the founding of their own households.

Can one speak, then, of a gradual domination of the bourgeois way of life or a de-proletarization of gender relations in the twentieth century, above all in its second half? Two limitations appear to be unavoidable. The first one concerns the German Democratic Republic. There, completely different signals were sent by the forced integration of all women into the job market, which was one of the government's political goals. In the case of a country where 90 per cent of all women between the ages of 16 and 60 were part of the workforce in 1989, one cannot speak of 'bourgeois' gender relations. For GDR women, a career consistently played a much more important role than for their sisters in the Federal Republic. Occupational training and further education enjoyed high status, which manifested itself in the higher proportion of skilled women workers and qualified white-collar women workers. Although even in the GDR, men held better jobs and were overrepresented in leadership positions, gender differences in the employment sector were less strongly pronounced than in West Germany.

The incomparably higher rate of female participation in the labour market did not change the fact that housework and care of the family continued to be considered women's responsibility in the GDR. It was a matter of course that only women took advantage of the 'baby year', and it was perfectly clear that women stayed at home when sick children needed care. Government policies and the media supported this behavioural orientation and kept the dualistic gender code alive.

Despite all this, that code did not affect the society of the GDR quite so powerfully as it did in the Federal Republic where it moulded the relations between men and women for a much longer time and to a greater extent But here, as well, a closer look hardly seems to confirm the hypothesis of an increase in bourgeois behaviour patterns. Herein lies our second limitation to this notion. Even if the 'bourgeois nuclear family', with its role models of the fatherly provider and the motherly housewife, became societally dominant, the gender polarity originally linked with it had been in many ways broken down and weakened. Even if women to this day continue to show a stronger orientation towards the family than do men, the world of 'male' experience was and is by no means strange to them, although their life-plans place greater emphasis on children and family and their lives are less centred around a career.

For approximately the last 100 years, the strict separation of male and female spheres presupposed by the bourgeois gender model has been increasingly disintegrating. To the extent that women have been integrated into the labour market – at first during certain distinct periods, but continuously since the 1970s – that their participation in further education has grown, that the rate at which they complete university education has increased, new realms of experience previously dominated by men have opened up to them. An alignment of male and female biographies has taken place at every level of income and in all groups of the population.

This alignment could come about more easily due to the fact that the family sphere, the place in which the genders now as then intersect, has clearly decreased. With the size of the average household at 2.3 people (1990) and dramatically reduced 'fertility rates', household and children today require a smaller investment of time and energy. Even when one takes into account that hygiene and educational standards have risen appreciably in the last few decades, this qualitative intensification has been more than neutralized by the possibility of easier consumption and better infrastructures. Women fill the role of housewife and mother, if at all, for only for a relatively short period of their lives. In general, they interrupt their career path merely for a few years or even try to combine family and career in the form of part-time employment.

As a consequence, the concept of radically separate gender worlds has lost its material basis. The dividing-line has become permeable, but the chance to cross this line has been and still is taken almost exclusively by women. They have conquered schools, universities, and jobs which, for a long time, had been accessible only for men. The independence won in this fashion has put them in a position from which they can change their private relations with men, as well. The 'moral double standard' which had the nineteenth and a great part of the twentieth century within its grip has been a thing of the past for the last few decades. Above all since the development of 'the Pill', women have been able to live out their sexuality as autonomously as men have always done. The fear of an unwanted pregnancy that ruins one's reputation has become anachronistic, and sexual relations before and outside of marriage are no longer a male privilege. In addition, the readiness to change life-partners or to end an unhappy marriage has increased enormously. The divorce rate rose from 1.5 per cent of all marriages between 1881 and 1885 to 32 per cent between 1986 and 1990 (in the GDR 37 per cent). Within this context it has been above all women who file for divorce.

All this demonstrates the extent to which the female way of life has become more similar to that of men, even though up to now, it still shows many particularities of its own. Conversely, a similar equalization of male lifestyles with female ones is hardly to be registered. Despite all the talk in the media about 'new fathers' and 'new men', men have remained astonishingly loyal to traditional predetermined roles. This becomes clear as much through opinion polls as through concrete behavioural patterns – from choice of name at marriage to the division of work within the family. Although men today concede to women a much greater range of actions with which they can experiment than twenty years ago, their concept of their own role has proven to be highly inflexible. Work and breadwinning is for them today as earlier the point from which the world of male identity and social convention is set in motion. The doctrine that women are primarily responsible for children and family is as good as never contradicted from the male perspective. Although men, too, have been granted the opportunity to take a paternity leave after the birth of a child since 1986, this offer is hardly ever taken up – only 1.4 per cent of all applications for maternity and paternity leaves come at this time from fathers.

V   Gender and politics

Nonetheless, men have changed, albeit not so clearly and irrevocably as women have. As early as the Weimar Republic, contemporaries had observed this change and had commented on it both critically and approvingly. Men, it was said at the end of the 1920s, were increasingly being moulded into 'social, cooperative creatures'. They were shedding their wild, raw, violent nature and orienting themselves more according to fatherly, protective values than to warlike, destructive ones. This change manifested itself in as immediate a fashion as their physical appearance: 'The manly beard is frowned upon, it is held to be uncultivated, if not offensive and obscene. The cutaway and the worthy male frock coat have disappeared entirely. Men's clothing has become lighter and brighter. Wide, baggy knickerbockers are appearing increasingly often on the streets and, from a certain distance, the split in the material is invisible; these pants are the equivalent of the rudiments of the modern women's skirt.'[6]

What was nearly entirely absent from the street scenes of the Weimar era was the military uniform, which, before the war, had been the most beloved and erotic male piece of clothing. During the nineteenth century, men in uniform were held to be particularly masculine, just as the army conceived of and presented itself as the 'school for masculinity'. Due to general military conscription, introduced in Prussia in 1813–14, all men between the ages of 20 and 23 were potential students of this institution. Above and beyond the divisions of social class, military service was among the experiences during the formative years which had the greatest consequences. Here not only military technical qualifications and nationalistic consciousness were drilled, but also a manly attitude and a manly way of thinking.

The army's social prestige, booming since the 1860s, and its great public presence ensured that this habitus did not fall into oblivion in civil life. Furthermore, almost three million men belonged to veterans' associations, which kept the memory of war and military service alive and carried it over into civilian existence.

Men could only share these memories with other men, with fathers, brothers, friends. Women were excluded from the military, bellicose realm of experience – only since 1975 have there been female officers and soldiers in the German army. These women are employed exclusively in medical duty and the musical corps, and this solely on a voluntary basis. Although the extension of compulsory military service to women started to be a topic of public discussion in 1996, most people still hold the military to be a genuinely male field of activity, from which women should be excluded to the greatest possible extent. They are only to be tolerated, apart from medical duty and as musicians, in the army's administration, but by no means in combat units.

This attitude has survived the centuries, but the societal relevance of the military has changed. Whereas before World War I it was a highly regarded institution with a reputation and influence beyond compare, it retreated to the margins of society after the Second World War. Even in the GDR, which adapted the Prussian military tradition to a much greater extent than did the former Federal Republic, the *Nationale Volksarmee* was unable to develop a social nimbus, despite varied incentives as well as means of compulsion. Consequently, the influence of the military on the socialization of its recruits and the formation of a masculine disposition was reduced here, too.

As early as the Weimar era, during which general military conscription was abolished, this loss of prestige served as a civilizing factor for the male 'gender character'. If the war had, as the writer Arnolt Bronnen put it in 1929, 'forced millions of men onto the masculine side of their beings', this side suffered considerable damage to its aura in the wake of military defeat and the massive reduction of the army. At first, it seemed that this development would not be lasting, for the increasing strength and presence of paramilitary groups since the late 1920s signalled the beginning of an about-face which was to be pursued with the greatest energy and single-mindedness after 1933. However, after 1945, the 'Military' as the motto of masculine behaviour had finally served out its usefulness. Even the reintroduction of general military conscription during the 1950s could not alter this fact.

Gender polarity had thus lost one of its most important supporting pillars. Far into the twentieth century, the impregnation of the masculine with military ideals had served to mark sharply the line of division from the feminine. Just as the male body underwent a certain preparation based on toughness, discipline and bearing, male social behaviour, too, was formed according to norms such as companionship and obedience to authority. Moreover, a man entered into a special relationship with the state during his time in the army. He provided the greatest service he could conceive of, sacrificed many years of his life to it, perhaps even his body and soul. In this way, he qualified as a true citizen who had proven himself to be worthy of his political rights.

Before 1918, this link between voting rights and military service was a favourite argument with which women's claims to political equality were dismissed. Since women made no personal sacrifices for the state, they consequently did not deserve to participate in active politics. Alone the Social Democrats, who had given up their resistance to voting rights for women at the early date of 1891, pointed out that, after all, it was women who gave birth to the future soldiers. In view of the high mortality rate among mothers, they could be regarded as sacrificing two lives for the state, that of their sons and their own.

This objection did not succeed in convincing the opponents of the female vote. Because women did not shed their blood for the 'Fatherland' in a direct way, claimed the conservative court chaplain Adolf Stoecker in 1903, they could not 'make the great decisions concerning the life of the state or partake of the councils in Parliament, where these decisions are made'.[7] Even after the male monopoly on politics had been done away with in 1918–19 (along with general military conscription), the argument associating military service with the vote continued to show up in German-nationalist, conservative circles. Only the thorough and extensive devaluation of things military after 1945 undercut its practical basis in any lasting way.

Regardless of this, the prejudice that politics is a man's business survived until the most recent past. Whereas in the nineteenth century, women were prevented from political activity by means of a legal ban and police repression, they avoided it more or less of their own free will in the twentieth century. On the one hand, they tended to vote just as frequently as did men and did not demonstrate party preferences visibly different from those of men. The sexes diverged when it came to the more radical political currents, in which women showed less interest than men. At the time of the Weimar Republic, proportionately fewer women voted for the Communists and the National Socialists. In today's Federal Republic, too, parties to the left and right of the political spectrum find less female approval.

On the other hand, despite these similarities, women actively participate in politics to a much lesser extent than men. At the beginning of the 1990s, at most one third of all registered members of the political parties were women. This maximum was reached by the Greens, whereas the Christian Democratic Union had only a quarter female members and the Christian Social Union a mere 15 per cent. The Social Democrats, who have been recruiting women since the beginning of the twentieth century, were able to increase their percentage from 15 per cent in 1946 to 27 per cent in 1991.

In view of this relatively limited membership percentage, it is not surprising that women have been underrepresented in parliamentary bodies. Often, their level of participation here was even lower than their party membership quota because the parties preferred to nominate male over female candidates. At last, in the late 1980s, this problem was confronted, as female party members, initially among the Greens, then in 1988 among the Social Democrats, and gradually in the Christian Democratic Union as well, began to demand special quotas for women. At the same time, the presence of female parliamentarians in the Bundestag had risen from not quite 10 per cent in 1983 to over 26 per cent in 1994. In addition, one no longer needs a magnifying glass to identify female ministers in the federal and state governments.

Experience has shown that women have only been able to carry through with improvements in their political, economic, and legal status when they themselves have become involved in these causes. For example, the simple article on gender equality in the Bonn federal constitution (Basic Law) of 1949 was only included upon the initiative of women members of the Parliamentary Council and after massive pressure by women's interest groups. The liberal abortion regulations, too, as well as the numerous reforms in social and gender parity policies since the mid-1970s would never have come into being without the emergence of the feminist movement within, as well as outside, parliament.

As early as the Weimar era, women members of parliament and of the parties had above all fought for concerns of women's and family policy. Social, educational and health policies were among the departments they favoured. This did not change in either the Federal Republic or the GDR. The results have been considerable:

relatively generous legal protection of mothers-to-be and new mothers, improved pension regulations, programmes to sponsor women in higher education and in the non-academic occupational training system, as well as a family and surname code which considers men and women to be equal in these apparently highly sensitive areas of the civil code.

For the last 20 years, federal policy has no longer come to a halt at the point of ending discrimination against women and creating equality in the letter of the law. To a large extent in response to pressure from women themselves, it has begun carefully to pave the way for a new social contract between the genders, to create incentives for social change, to encourage innovation. In this matter, there are grave institutional as well as mental barriers to be overcome. Among these barriers is, above all, an occupational system which is geared to an average male worker with constant, lifelong availability. This institutional framework is supported and strengthened by tenacious mental dispositions which characterize men in particular.

Whether the conversion of the predominant gender system, sustained during the last 100 years above all by women, will be continued in the future will depend not least upon whether the attempt to animate men to greater flexibility and 'modernity' succeeds. Here, too, the saying holds that 'women's work is never done'.

Translated from German by Polly Kienle.

Notes:

1. Welcker, Carl, 'Geschlechtsverhältnisse', in *Staats-Lexikon oder Encyklopädie der Staatswissenschaften*, vol. VI (1838), p. 629.
2. Quoted in Ute Frevert, *'Mann und Weib, und Weib und Mann': Geschlechter-Differenzen in der Moderne* (Munich: C. H. Beck, 1995), p. 48.
3. Huebner, Friedrich Markus, ed., *Die Frau von Morgen wie wir sie wünschen* (1st edn, 1929; 2nd. edn Frankfurt: Insel, 1990), pp. 141–2.
4. Elly zu Putlitz, *Arbeits- und Lebensverhältnisse der Frauen in der Landwirtschaft in Brandenburg* (1914), pp. 26–7.
5. Quoted in Ute Frevert, *Women in German History* (Oxford: Berg, 1988), p. 92.
6. Huebner, *Die Frau von Morgen*, pp. 81–2; Frevert, *'Mann und Weib'*, pp. 33–4.
7. Quoted in Frevert, *'Mann und Weib'*, p. 121.

Select bibliography

Bock, Gisela, and Thane, Pat, eds., *Maternity and Gender Policies: Women and the Rise of the European Welfare States, 1880s–1950s* (London: Routledge, 1991).
Bridenthal, Renate, Grossmann, Atina, and Kaplan, Marion, eds., *When Biology Became Destiny – Women in Weimar and Nazi Germany* (New York: Monthly Review Press, 1984).
Fout, John C., ed., *German Women in the Nineteenth Century* (New York: Holmes and Meier, 1984).

Frevert, Ute, *Women in German History* (Oxford: Berg, 1988).

Frevert, Ute, '*Mann und Weib, und Weib und Mann*'. *Geschlechter-Differenzen in der Moderne* (Munich: C. H. Beck, 1995).

Joeres, Ruth-Ellen B., and Maynes, Mary Jo, eds., *German Women in the Eighteenth and Nineteenth Centuries* (Bloomington: Indiana University Press, 1986).

Kolinsky, Eva, *Women in West Germany: Life, Work and Politics* (Oxford: Berg, 1989).

Koonz, Claudia, *Mothers in the Fatherland – Women, the Family, and Nazi Politics* (New York: St Martin's Press, 1987).

Moeller, Robert G., *Protecting Motherhood: Women and the Family in the Politics of Postwar West Germany* (Berkeley: University of California Press, 1993).

26

German war, German peace

Charles S. Maier

I The issue of German militarism

When Chancellor Helmut Kohl and Secretary Erich Honecker met at Moscow in March 1985, they solemnly declared that 'war must never again emanate from German soil – let peace alone emerge!' For the Chancellor, the lofty promise had the virtue of entailing no concrete commitments, while for his East German counterpart it testified to his state's importance and legitimacy. Seemingly so innocuous, the joint pledge itself was a reminder that Germany had had a long reputation as a source of international conflict and violence. Prussian militarism was a byword even before Mirabeau observed that Prussia was not a state with an army, but an army with a state. The martial reputation continued until the Allies of 1945 abolished the German army and its General Staff. After 200 years, the German military vocation was to be ended.

Germany had been devastated by the disastrous Thirty Years War, when Frederick William, the Great Elector embarked on a 48-year reign of repeated military activity and diplomatic reversals, contesting Polish overlordship of Prussia, the Swedish hold in the southern Baltic, and then the invasions of Louis XIV, securing subsidies and slices of territory (though never as much as hoped for). Just as important, he subdued the estates and urban patriciates and laid the foundations for absolutism by using his military revenue agencies as the wedge of the centralizing state. His son Frederick extracted the title of King in Prussia (the Hohenzollern holding outside the Empire) for joining the grand alliance against Louis XIV during the War of the Spanish Succession. The next Hohenzollern, Frederick William I (1713–40), devoted unceasing effort to building the Prussian army and uniting civil and military revenue administrations, while his son in turn, Frederick II or Frederick the Great, devoted his long rule to seizing and holding Silesia and perfecting his bureaucracy and his army. Thus for over a century the tenacious long-lived Hohenzollern rulers developed a military capacity that was proportionally unmatched in Europe. A population of approximately 2.5 millions before 1740 could field 80,000 soldiers; Frederick the Great's expanded kingdom that grew from about 3.6 (after Silesia's addition) to about 5 million could finally muster about 200,000. These forces were deployed astutely, often with strategic and tactical brilliance. With the monarch's geopolitical independence, his alacrity in switching sides, and an administration built to extract money and manpower for war, Prussian military power became a major resource in central Europe, a key element in balancing either Habsburg or French armies. The presence of the Prussian armies displaced the military arenas of Franco-Imperial contention deep into south central Germany and offset Saxon Austrian combinations; they also kept the Russians out of the West. Prussian armed potential was not sufficient initially to stand alone against Austria or France, but it could provide the decisive edge as part of an alliance, each one of which was repeatedly auctioned off for territorial titles, reconfirmations of conquest, or subsidies for military effort. By the mid-eighteenth century, in fact, Prussian troops under Frederick were dominating the central European theatre.

Key to the remarkable development in Prussia was a political organization designed to extract taxes and mobilize military labour service with greater single-minded efficiency than the French or Austrians. Of course, the personal capacities of the monarchical line, single-mindedly and sometimes brutally trained for war, also helped. The incautious wagers of adversaries played an important role; Frederick I benefited from the suicidal crusade of Sweden's Charles XII against Peter the Great. Despite brilliant victories early in the Seven Years War, Frederick II came close to defeat at the hands of the Russians and his exhausted state and army were finally saved only by the death of his personal nemesis, the Russian empress, Elizabeth. Luck helped; pluck was necessary; continuous organization of state and army was the indispensable basis for success.

To sustain and mobilize Prussia's military assets required a concentration of fiscal power in the hands of the monarchs. Tax resources had to be extracted from town merchants and the provincial landowners, and the Great Elector began the process of browbeating the squires who directly controlled peasant power and local agricultural output. The monarchs husbanded the resources of the extensive royal lands and forests even as they ratcheted up the taxes on non-domain land and on the town dwellers of the realm. The provincial estates lost their power, and their stubborn leaders were periodically thrown into prison. From the mid-seventeenth to mid-eighteenth century they became the servants of the regime, not its rivals, gaining as a sort of compensation increased judicial and administrative control over their peasant tenants and enhanced recognition as a privileged caste.

The implicit bargain revealed that for all their subjection of local privileges and opposition, the monarchs still needed their agricultural elite. Along with the civil servants supplied by town patricians and the children of the Protestant clergy, the nobility furnished bureaucrats and officers. Had the Junkers persisted in a surly *fronde*, the state would have quickly degenerated. And although the 'soldier king', Frederick William, sought to offset aristocratic influence by turning to qualified commoners for his more technical military branches, such as ballistics and the artillery, Frederick II reversed this policy and tightened the collaboration with the nobility, who alone – so he remained convinced – had the innate capacity to command.

The ruling elite of Prussia, the Junker squirearchy, served either as officers or civil servants, and often both successively over the course of their active lives. This emerging process of bureaucratization fascinated the historians of state-building several generations ago, and Walter Dorn (*Competition for Empire*) and Sidney Fay (*The Rise of Brandenburg-Prussia to 1786*) and later the German émigré Francis Carstens (*The Origins of Prussia*) contributed some of the clearest brief outlines in English, following upon the pioneering explorations of Otto Hintze who patiently edited the kingdom's massive archival resources as the *Acta Borussica*. At the same time that the monarch and his servants moved to centralize the extraction of fiscal resources, they exploited the local jurisdictional privileges of the nobility to mobilize manpower. The so-called canton system rested on a symbiosis of private and public power that reinforced the aristocracy's local judicial and police authority and upheld their capacity as estate owners to extract private rents and labour services, even as it placed the peasants' liability for public military service under the landlords' role as army officers. The historian Otto Büsch has most revealingly reconstructed these interconnections of local government, agrarian economy, social caste and military recruitment in his 1962 study of *Militärregime und Sozialleben im alten Preußen*. The viability of the system – so we have learned from the recent researches of William Hagen – rested not only on the degree of social control that it might bring to bear, but upon the continued economic vitality of the peasant village economy. Despite the labour exactions and rents, agricultural productivity allowed the peasant villager, even if legally servile, to sustain a modicum of prosperity.

After Frederick the Great's death in 1786, the intense social discipline of the regime came undone. The remnants of his military-political regime crumbled against the armies of the French Republic and Empire. The 'cabinet' government of civil servants developed earlier, who met under the king's supervision and administered a mix of territorial and functional agencies, could not control the far larger, wealthier but fiscally strapped state once the brilliant, workaholic, and long-reigning monarch disappeared. The battlefield catastrophes of 1806 and a treaty that cost the state its western territories prodded an effort at reform and mobilization of national energies. Emulation of France suggested that participation and citizenship had to replace the reliance on obedience, command, and extraction of resources that had fallen into disrepair. While civilian reformers sought to establish a free peasantry, to enhance municipal self-government and the authority of the state ministers, and to reinvigorate higher education, Generals Boyen, Gneisenau and Scharnhorst reforged the army after the battlefield catastrophe of Jena. They opened its officer corps to commoners, encouraged volunteers, and established a system of conscription that assigned draftees first to the active army and then to longer-term reserve obligations. Even though Napoleon limited the size of his defeated foe's army, the reformers managed to re-establish Prussian organizational potential so that the state might join the Russians and then Austria and Britain

Illustration 26.1   The giant Krupp cannon at the Paris World Exhibition, 1867

in the anti-Napoleonic coalition of 1813–15. Half a century later, William 1, first as regent, then as king, renewed the monarch's stolid and soldierly devotion to his army, forced reforms that lengthened national service, undermined the liberals' effort to make the army more of a militia, and then, under the guidance of Bismarck and his generals, deployed his force brilliantly in the three rapid wars of unification.

Did this heavy reliance on military assets amount to militarism? In one sense yes: the key chapters in Prussian development depended upon military prowess and military wagers; soldiers were integral to statesmanship. The monarchs gave pride of place to their armed forces; the officer corps developed a highly corporate sense of allegiance. Prussian and later German policy-makers repeatedly gambled on war, or actions they understood would quickly result in war, to achieve national goals. Taking advantage of the precarious succession of Maria Theresa to the Habsburg domains, Frederick II seized Silesia at the outset of his regime. Between 1864 and 1870, Bismarck and his collaborators, the War Minister Albrecht von Roon and the Chief of Staff, Helmut von Moltke, exploited one easy war, against the Danes, and then provoked two risky ones, first against the Austrians, then against the French, to establish Prussia as the armature of a reconstructed German federal nation. Bismarck went to the brink in 1875 and 1887 at least in part to re-establish his domestic leadership at home. The mercurial

Kaiser William II (1888–1918), who delighted in his military functions and regalia, ratified the provocative naval expansion programme and demonstrations of armed force, including the dispatch of gunboats to Moroccan waters in 1905 and 1911. Some members, at least, of the German General Staff, including the younger Moltke, seriously contemplated pre-emptive war against Russia in 1905 and 1912; and the army command was ready for the decisive test when they believed it necessary at the end of July 1914. For four long and terrible years, Germany sustained its own forces and those of its partners against the numerically preponderant *entente* forces on eastern, western, and Italian fronts.

Generals and admirals, of course, can be cautious as well as daring; they are reluctant to squander or sometimes even to risk their military resources. Admiral Tirpitz fretted that his fleet was not ready in 1914; and the commanders of the restricted professional army stipulated by the Versailles Treaty of 1919, and even of the rapidly expanding Wehrmacht after 1935, worried about taking on France and her allies prematurely. But by this time, they were serving under a civilian leader who imposed the most expansionist German military programme ever conceived. Adolf Hitler, moreover, envisaged national life in terms of perpetual warfare against adversaries – some of whom he thought contemptible, others highly dangerous and some both at once. The German dictator, who took over the direct command of the Wehrmacht in 1938, managed repeatedly to confirm his confidence in success until the end of 1941. It was not really surprising that by the time the United States finally entered World War II, Germany's hard-pressed opponents did not finely distinguish between a cautious Prussian military tradition and a racialist and reckless Nazi populism. The two were apparently highly compatible components of 'German militarism'.

If, however, militarism implies the decisive influence of officers over civilian administration, then Germany was rarely militarist in the sense, say, that nineteenth-century Hispanic lands were. There were no *pronunciamentos* and no military rulers. Neither did the officer corps gradually subordinate civilian governance, as happened in Japan during the 1930s. On the other hand, the armed forces did achieve a decisive voice at particular junctures; they argued for the annexation of Alsace-Lorraine in 1871 and prevailed against a more sceptical Bismarck. Most notoriously, the stalemate of World War I led the civilians to abdicate policy-making to the Supreme Command (*Oberste Heeresleitung*), that is, to Generals Hindenburg and Ludendorff, who ultimately blamed their failure to secure victory precisely on the civilians who had so loyally followed their prescriptions. Under the weak Weimar Republic that emerged from the defeat of 1918, a reduced officer corps also retained control over many key decisions concerning budgets, policy planning and force levels. Social Democrats deferred to generals to demonstrate their bona fides as patriots and sound politicians. Hitler finally would circumscribe the influence of the military elite – but more to overrule their caution than to limit their dreams. All in all, the armed forces' command played only a sporadic role in explicit policy-making after national unification. Their counsels were sometimes divided and sometimes overruled. It might be retorted, however, that throughout modern German history, military prestige remained so dominant a background factor that the army did not have to assert an explicitly political role. Indeed, by the end of the nineteenth century, not only did the monarchs feel their soldiers remained the chief bulwark of the regime, but significant numbers of the educated middle classes tended to identify with military goals, and indeed served as officers. Such a major trend of national development has long aroused the critical attention of historians. Alfred Vagts, transplanted to Connecticut from Germany and married to the daughter of Charles Beard, the great dissenting American historian and political scientist, traced what he clearly beheld as the fateful proclivity toward militarization of policy in his pre-war *History of Militarism*. Gerhard Ritter, the conservative anti-Nazi historian, who followed the important episodes of strategic thinking and civil military relations in the magisterial volumes of *Staatskunst und Kriegshandwerk* acknowledged how the Prussian reliance on the military that he had once accepted as viable had come to appear tragic and catastrophic. Most recently Stig Forster (*Ver doppelte Militarismus*, 1985) has argued that the domestic and external missions assigned to the army increased militarism but undermined effectiveness.

Despite historians' emphasis on the 'feudal' or reactionary attributes of the Prussian-German army, it is not certain that it evolved into significantly more closed a professional caste or enjoyed greater prestige than, say, its French counterpart. The flashing sabres of French *gardes républicaines* also evoked a strong popular resonance. Military brass bands in France played 'Sambre and Meuse' as pervasively as German army musicians – with their picturesque *Schellenbäume* (the 'trees' of small brass bells suspended from ox horns, which had been originally copied from Turkish instruments) – tootled Frederick the Great's *Hohenfriedberg March*. Almost every war that Prussians or Germans entered involved French troops as well. Indeed the army provided an emperor in France. Nonetheless, after General Boulanger's irresolute drive to become a new Bonaparte at the end of the 1880s, the prestige and power of the French army became a function of partisan politics: the right reaffirmed the mission of the army and defended its General Staff even when the frame-up of Dreyfus became clear, while the left sought to roll back its influence and purge the opponents of the Republic. In Germany, the civilian forces who wanted to limit military appropriations and military influence just never achieved an equivalent electoral success. And since Germany had a powerful, dynastic chief executive who felt that his uniformed role was critical – whereas after 1870 (or, at the latest, 1877) France did not – German military enthusiasms generated more powerful institutional and policy consequences than French patriotic fervour.

Why, it might be finally asked, did not the armies of the Habsburg and Russian empires assume equal political ascendancy? This is a difficult question but one whose necessarily speculative answer can prove revealing. As traditional empires built territorially upon the centuries-long military expansion of the state frontier, these states necessarily incorporated a massive army presence. But while the monarch in both states was surrounded by officers, and the military remained one of the most conspicuous social corps, neither army was so associated with the nineteenth-century historical achievements of its regime. After the great commanders of the early eighteenth century passed from the scene, Austrian armies lost repeatedly – in four successive trials of war during the Napoleonic period, to Napoleon III in 1859 and, devastingly, to the Prussians in 1866. While an aristocratic, clannish army dominated court society, it could not claim the same role in creating the modern Habsburg state. Budget restrictions later compelled cutbacks in conscription and limited modernization. The Hohenzollern dynasty rested on its military; the Habsburgs on their complex territorial checks and balances. So too, the Russian armies of the nineteenth century – still a bulwark of authority at home – remained a mediocre military force, their reputation resting less on strategic brilliance than the force of number. The Russians and Austrian armed forces were, in effect, a force for conservation, but not for modernization and modern state creation. Prussia's and then Germany's military, in contrast, became active participants in building the modern state and encouraging its technological development. They contributed military intellectuals and organizers of complex rail and supply systems. They did not have to overcome the bureaucratic inertia that suffused the older empires. In this respect, the German (and Japanese) armed forces served a technocratic political and developmental function that was often at odds with their social values.

II Two metanarratives

Given the army's central role in the rise of Prussia, the formation of the German Empire, and the two world wars, historians have sought to account for the recourse to military power and to warfare that seemed so central to German history from the Great Elector to the Führer. Two major theories have been advanced to explain this Prussian/German military vocation, and its success. The more venerable attributes Germany's recourse to military action as a result of the country's middle-European geographical site. It is in effect a demand-driven theory of German militarism. External circumstances – *die mitteleuropäische Zwangslage*, the central European vise – call forth an internal response. As the land of the 'middle', without protective frontier barriers, the German states, it is argued, were menaced from *tous azimuts*. No Channel, no Pyrenees allowed the Germans to develop unthreatened. In the Thirty Years War and the succeeding decades, first imperial troops, then the Swedes ravaged the north German plains and towns. From Richelieu to Louis XIV and after, the French had pressed continually at the Palatinate or the Rhine. Jealous Habsburgs allegedly worked to humiliate the aspiring kingdom and change the delicate central European equilibrium. Prussia with its disparate territories and long, ragged frontiers, hostage in both the northwest and in the east, was continually threatened.

According to this model, the Hohenzollern state developed to cope with this continuing menace. There was no leisure for parliamentary evolution; the monarch had to subordinate the estatist privileges of the aristocracy to the primacy of raising money and troops. Frederick II battled armies to west and east in the Seven Years War: a long, lonely and heroic passage of arms that Prussian historians liked to recall during the harsh days of World War I and World War II. Neither Frederick, nor other Germans, wanted these confrontations – so the scenario – but they had to accept the geographical cards dealt by destiny. Indeed this narrative is usually written in a sombre minor key; harsh necessity or history seems to compel the German fate. Even Otto Hintze, the clear-sighted historian of Prussian institutions and feudal elites, provided a popular version during the First World War (*Die Hohenzollern und Ihr Werk*) emphasizing the thankless commitment to duty on the part of the monarchical line. Here, as in other accounts, Prussian redemption results from heroic and often lonely commanders, whether the 'great' elector, Frederick William, or the selfless, weary Frederick II, or the heroes of 1806–15, Scharnhorst, Gneisenau, and Boyen, or Bismarck and Moltke in the 1860s, Hinderburg and Ludendorff in 1914, and finally the Führer himself (at least as scripted by Goebbels).

Of course, the narrative incorporates an apologia: Germany is always surrounded, perpetually encircled, provoking hostile combinations at different periods among conspiring Austrians, superficially 'civilized' French, the huge mass of Russians, and the calculating materialistic British. Given the balance of power, not all these powers are continuous enemies, but usually three of the four are. Frederick the Great's seizure of Silesia (justified by *raison d'état*) makes Austrian enmity a constant for half a century, and the Habsburgs will be abetted in turn by the British, the French, and for a time the Russians. Striking back at Paris or Vienna, Prussia manages at least to defeat Dresden, just as, endeavouring to tranquillize St Petersburg, it manages to swallow Poznan, Thorn, and briefly Warsaw. Other German powers, notably Saxons and Bavarians in the eighteenth and nineteenth centuries, play lackey parts in these great coalitions, anxious to reverse the rise of Berlin and making common cause with larger enemies until they are defeated *en passant*. It is not that Frederick wilfully chooses an expansionist role; it is thrust upon him as the condition of Prussian viability. But within half a century Napoleon and Alexander will meet on their famous raft at Tilsit to ratify the halving of Prussia; Metternich will veto the Prussian-supported claims of German nationalists at the Congress of Vienna; and another century thereafter, England will weave together the *entente* that frustrates Germany's legitimate imperial energies.

To survive as a nation state, according to this narrative line, requires moving up the territorial food chain: Leopold von Ranke builds his narratives around the international relationships in which the great powers are embedded; Heinrich von Treitschke can organize his narrative of German national emergence around this 'truth' with bluster and bravado in the late nineteenth century, whereas Friedrich Meinecke, who analyses the ideas behind national assertion, coats the Darwinian homily in the sombre tones of historicist inevitability in the 1907 dialectic of *Weltbürgertum und Nationalstaat*. Even contemporary Germany's greatest historian of international relations, the late Andreas Hillgruber, who so unsparingly analysed Hitlerian ambitions, re-evokes the tragic prevail-or-perish metanarrative of Germans and Russians in his essay, *Zweierlei Untergang: Die Zerschlagung des deutschen Reiches und das Ende des europäischen Judentums*. The historiographical trope thus does not yield easily: it continually tempts by its exculpatory thrust, its great minor key tragic mood music, its theodicy of Prussian-German expansion, its emotional identification with selfless heroes. It is a historiographical approach that often tends to psychologize: mind-sets are sometimes attributed to landscapes, a connection made by Hegel and Spengler, but also Montesquieu and non-German theorists. Still, it comes as second nature to German conservatives, and it does produce a historiography that is dense but grand, less Wagnerian than Brahmsian in its tonalities.

Nonetheless, this interpretive tradition raises some harsh questions. Why is Germany more destined for militarism by its geographical situation than, say, Poland, similarly poised between powerful neighbours and unprotected by natural frontiers? Or is it just that either Germany or Poland must be divided as a condition of European equilibrium? (Indeed between 1795 and 1990 (1919–39 excepted) one or the other of the two countries remained partitioned: it is a long time since Europe has seen both countries endeavouring to exist simultaneously as undivided national states in the European middle.) Most generally, have geographical factors (at least in the era before atomic weaponry) so compelled historical outcomes? Are leaders and their peoples so helpless before the circumstances of territory?

The contemporary updating of the scenario, in fact, diverts the focus from territory *per se* and toward the supposedly objective contraints of the international system. It borrows from the 'realist' tradition of international relations in which national communities are trapped in a Hobbesian war of all against all and the absence of a common sovereign imposes rivalry and competition on every state. But even if the historian (following Thucydides in effect) accepts this realist analysis, it cannot explain differing national policy responses. If all statesmen must cope with an overarching atmosphere of endemic insecurity, how can this universal condition account for Germany's specific military adaptation? If the historian wishes to emphasize the exogenous sources of Prussian-German militarism, then 'realism' or neo-realism in international relations theory does not discriminate sufficiently.

Finally, of course, the experience of the Third Reich sets a further intellectual challenge to the geopolitical scenario. Plausible though it might be even to encompass the First World War, the geographical metanarrative cannot really account for the National Socialist vision of *Lebensraum*, the plans for the depopulation of eastern Europe (including the extermination of the Jews), and the quasi-racial war in the east of 1941 to 1945. The Nazis may themselves have believed the geographical metanarrative and may have been convinced Germany required vast conquests, but even most German historians did not accept the Nazi justifications once Germany lost the war. Nonetheless, if Nazi aggression and conquest could not be assimilated to the apologetic history of geographical determinism, was it simply to be excluded as an aberration from the development of the military state before 1918? Did it not suggest that the recurring recourse to militarism and the power of a state machine designed for the deployment of raw power might derive from some terrible imbalance within German society? The National Socialist experience thus compelled consideration of the second metanarrative: the *Primat der Innenpolitik* and, in particular, the supposedly peculiar German combination of industrial modernization with archaic militarist values.

This other major tradition of historical explanation has been critical, not apologetic, fixed upon social structures and not geographical conditions, and analytical rather than narrative. It endeavours to persuade by relentlessly exposing the material interests and ideological convictions of German elites, whereas the first tradition depends upon the pathos of a dramatic story-line in which harsh external circumstances compel a military response. But the second tradition will not take war or national military vocation as a product of tragic necessity or of an environment that seems to transcend human agency. Instead it analyses the recourse to military solutions as a product of the persisting, indeed archaic, feudal inequalities within Prussia and later the Reich. By the late nineteenth century, so it explains, German militarist policies tend to arise from the frozen sociopolitical cartel between the new industrialists and old Junkers, the lords of rye and iron respectively.

This analysis has come to be known as the *Primat der Innenpolitik* or the primacy of domestic policy, a phrase chosen to contrast with Ranke's *Primat der Aussenpolitik*. According to its proponents, instead of domestic political and social alignments flowing from the dictates of Germany's difficult geostrategic situation, foreign policy emerges as a result of divisions within society. The analysis was implicit in Marxian and left-liberal critiques of the Bismarckian state; Schumpeter's 1918 essay on the sociology of imperialism (English version: *Imperialism and Social Classes*) and Thorstein Veblen's World War I tract, *Imperial Germany and the Industrial Revolution* adumbrated some aspects, while Eckart Kehr elaborated the most intriguing case study in his 1930 analysis of turn-of-the-century fleet expansion as a product of political horse-trading among Junkers, industrialists and Catholic politicians (*Schlachtflottenbau und Parteipolitik*) – a work influenced by Charles Beard's approach to American constitution-making and earning Kehr the opprobrium of the contemporary German historical establishment. The approach was revived in recent decades by Hans Ulrich Wehler's study of *Bismarck und der Imperialismus* (1969), and has tended to characterize the studies generated by what was somewhat misleadingly labelled the 'Bielefeld school', that is by Wehler and his Bielefeld colleagues of the 1970s. These critical historians believed in turn that they were reimporting into German historiography the social science approaches of Marx and Weber (eventually leavened by Hintze), such as Kehr had pursued four decades earlier; and they also appealed to the work of the émigré historian Hans Rosenberg, whose 1958 study *Bureaucracy, Aristocracy, Autocracy: The Prussian Experience* emphasized how the Prussian administrative polity arose from a status-conscious elite that claimed the resources of legal expertise.

The 'primacy of domestic politics' might thus seem to have owed much to the American or British sojourns of its German authors. Historians sympathetic to the focus on internal elites tended to feel that only outside the constraining pressure of

German history faculties – which continued to discourage dissenting approaches through the 1950s – might critical historians find the breathing space to assimilate Marxian and Weberian analytical approaches. Of course, such an account oversimplifies the development of a critical historiography. Conservative historians in the 1950s and early 1960s nurtured students interested in social history. And Fritz Fischer, after all, did not develop his major thesis of annexationist elites in the United States, but in the German archives. The social science categories that the critical historians pressed into service were originally German and only thence taken into American exile. Still, the collaboration with Anglo-American social scientists does seem to have helped German historians to crack the dominant paradigms that had interpreted militarism and the recourse to war as fateful products of geopolitical necessity.

In contrast to the first tradition, this analytical approach can be envisaged as a supply-side history of military and foreign policy. It argues that the sharply stratified social structure of Prussia encouraged the very military and political outcomes that reinforced the original hierarchies. The East Elbian Junkers cultivated war and command, not because the international environment compelled this military dedication, but because their soldierly vocation justified their continued role at court and in the provincial estates and county assemblies, their spirit of exclusivity and caste, and their continued ascendancy over town dwellers, commoners, and of course their peasant draftees. A century and a half later, industrialists pursued expansionist policies that justified their domination of capitalist enterprises and their control over a growing proletariat. The elites of 'rye and iron' had an interest in policies of confrontation.

Gradually, so the account goes, the 'feudal' and military aristocracy's values penetrated the bourgeoisie, who sought to assimilate themselves into the landed elite. The French wars opened the officer corps to commoners; later in the century, bourgeois university students could achieve coveted reserve officer status by a year of service. The habits of military command and bureaucratic ranks pervaded industrial organizations; the passage of commoners through conscription gave drill sergeants the chance to inculcate the values of the fatherland and patriotic obedience among youth otherwise susceptible to democratic values and socialist ideologies. Consequently the German Empire embarked on its imperial career with the social habits of the feudal dynastic state coupled with a dynamic industrial plant.

Logically enough, the focus on domestic inequality as the source of a proud and retrograde militarism appealed to historians of the left. It ascribed Germany's aggressive behaviour to a long, indeed 'pre-modern' or 'feudal' tradition. It suggested that the absence of revolution at home allowed Germany to become an increasingly intolerable neighbour. Finally it connected Hitler's expansionism to a long tradition of aggression rooted in the power of Germany's elites. While Hitler himself and Nazi ideology might have derived from populistic sources, the military (and their industrialist authoritarian allies) had long fought democracy and helped install Hitler in power to protect their interests. The second metanarrative seemed to account for Germany's final war.

III   Germany's constitutions, Europe's treaties

Must we choose between these two grand explanations for the conditions of German war and German peace? Can we not – as many historians in fact do – attempt to synthesize them, or agree that internal and external impulses can interact to reinforce each other, that is, drop the effort to assert the 'primacy' of one approach or the other? Or can we actually test the two approaches and measure their respective explanatory values? The difficulty is that each one is designed to account for all outcomes, indirectly if not directly, such that both are totalizing. No single case can be used to disprove one or the other explanatory model. Documentation of relevance can be cited for both the *Primat der Innenpolitik* and the *Primat der Aussenpolitik*. Indeed the adherence that the respective approaches have commanded has tended to depend as much on the historian's political orientation as on the data intrinsic to the events being researched. Not surprisingly, in light of general political trends, many historians have retreated from the confident approaches of the 1960s and early 1970s, which stressed social-scientific analysis and the causal primacy of domestic inequality. War and peace no longer seem easily derived from domestic divisions. The economic impact of contemporary 'globalization' has sensitized historians and social historians to the apparent fact that the international system as such generates forces, whether in the realm of economics or security or culture, that impinge on nations from outside their borders. Hence the temptation to rehabilitate the *Primat der Aussenpolitik*.

At the same time, however, some political theorists have proposed, in effect, a reformulation of the *Primat der Innenpolitik*. Democracies, they have argued, do not go to war against each other. To be sure, the number of paired democratic states that might have had the sort of conflicting interests and proximity that normally would make war plausible has been very limited. Nonetheless, the idea, classically expounded in Kant's essay on *Perpetual Peace*, that a world of republics would not engage in war, has enjoyed a revival. Woodrow Wilson had made a similar claim during 1918, when he argued that so long as the German system allowed the emperor some residual uncontrolled power, genuine peace would remain out of reach. Wilson's argument hastened the German abdication crisis of November 1918. It was not an implausible idea, and indeed the fact that post-war Germany has proved a peaceful state gives retrospective strength to the argument.

Both analytical paradigms have thus been persuasively updated. The international system does generate as a system pressures that impinge on states from outside any one state's borders: statesmen must make real and momentous decisions about external policy. On the other hand, national elites do develop their historically peculiar defences of privilege and inequality. It is less that the German *Sonderweg* was a myth than that every country has its own exceptionalism. And every major country probably runs its own special 'plantation' where full rein can be given to impulses of oppression and marginalization. Britain had Ireland and the Empire, the United States had an imported slave race, Germany eventually had the folks next door. In the final analysis the two metanarratives are complementary.

But I think it also useful to focus on a third circumstance that has been important for the German experience of interstate relations. The successive major German states have perhaps been special in Europe in having their constitutional settlements so integrally connected with changes in the international status of the German lands. German constitutions in effect emerge out of major international upheavals and peace settlements. These international settlements in turn shape key domestic alignments and institutional structures. Conversely, when Germans have the autonomy to order their domestic system relatively untrammelled by foreigners, as in 1871 and 1933, the arrangements they institute have had profound international consequences.

In what sense, it will be asked immediately, is this unique? Carrying through a French Revolution in the 1790s embroiled Europe in war, and the defeat of French regimes in 1870 and 1940 swept away the constitutions in being. A constitution for united Italy depended upon international events. The size and structure of the Polish Commonwealth – both when it has existed and when it has been absent – reflected the rivalries of the powerful neighbours around it; indeed precisely when Poles sought to reform their institutions, whether in 1791 or 1956 and 1980, they triggered foreign countermeasures or at least powerful threats. The emergence of other east European and middle Eastern states had to wait on the collapse of older empires. Defeat in war and revolutionary changes of regime have generally been twin outcomes in the twentieth century.

My argument is that in the case of Germany the relationship between international and domestic settlements may, in effect, be even more intimate, and is, in any case, more sustained. The structure of German national institutions has itself been the stake of peace-making. Constitutions and international systems are created as two sides of the same German coin, and remain as such for as long as either prevails. Over the centuries, Swedish, Austrian and French, British and Russian, Anglo-American and Soviet rivals have helped to configure, and in turn have had their own aspirations configured by the alignment of German domestic forces: the balance between Catholics and Protestants, Prussian centralizers and non-Prussian federalists, authoritarians and liberals – categories of conviction and ideology that sometimes (but never more than imperfectly) overlap with particular social groups, such as 'feudal' landowners, town elites, and urban or rural working families. German constitutions and the European international system have been interconnected for 300 years.

The reason is not geography, but the ambiguous sovereignties that characterized the Holy Roman Empire since the late Middle Ages. Most famously, the Treaties of Westphalia of 1648 regulated the external obligations of the Holy Roman Empire and its internal structure. The treaties allowed more than 300 units to claim most of the attributes of 'sovereignty' – indeed the concept of sovereignty was virtually defined to explicate the peace settlement – even while embedding these units in the confederal imperial structure. Westphalia linked such constitutional ideas as the power of princes and estates, the balance of religious forces, the rights of appeal and the jurisdiction of courts, with the fragmented and weak imperial entity that corresponded to the interests of the contending powers: French, Habsburgs and Swedes. Apologists for the system, then and since, have praised its almost paralytic checks and balances; however, they protected princes and states, not individual subjects.

Bonaparte and the Habsburgs together abolished the residual institutions of the Holy Roman Empire, but only after the internal rivalries between Prussia, Bavaria and Austria grew more intense than the imperial institutions could accommodate. Napoleon grouped the western mid-size states (smaller than Austria and Prussia) in the Confederation of the Rhine, and each of these states engaged upon a French-modelled modernization of institutions to rationalize the medieval constitutions they had hitherto depended upon. So too, the Vienna Settlement of 1815 connected both an effort at Austro-Prussian balance with a conservative constitutional settlement: the resulting German Confederation was an effort to keep the French from dominating central Europe, while letting Metternich ensure that estatist and non-nationalist concepts dominated internal politics. Bismarck's North German Confederation and German Empire threw over this settlement; the constitution proclaimed, in effect, at Versailles in the moment of victory no longer had to incorporate a system of international checks and balances inscribed in internal politics. Nonetheless, by the close of the 1870s – with the so-called 'second founding of the German Empire' – Bismarck committed Germany to a fundamental alliance with a state, Austria-Hungary, whose own internal structure was hostage to all the currents of international rivalries and emerging ethnic rivalries. Despite the ostensible freedom of action of the German Empire, fundamental political orientations depended upon international alignments and vice versa.

By constitution I do not mean just a written charter of institutions and rights, but the major historical constraints that bind a country and determine underlying options for policy or the legitimacy of its government. In nominal terms the Weimar Constitution codified a republican state with advanced social democratic and liberal institutions. But as the product of an international defeat that brought down the Empire, Weimar politics never overcame the political divisions arising out of peace treaty issues. Signed six weeks before the Constituent Assembly promulgated the constitution, the strictures of the Versailles Treaty became, in effect, part of the German constitutional settlement. Versailles required renunciations of military sovereignty (a limited army and demilitarization of the Rhineland) and a decades-long reparation settlement. No German could judge the Weimar regime independently of the international climate in which it had emerged; and thus the regime could never really overcome the bitter difference between those willing to accept the international limitations (at least provisionally) and those determined to throw them off. The regime created between 1933 and 1935 by Adolf Hitler, from the Law for the Protection (in fact, abolition) of the Constitution to conscription and the Nuremberg Laws, established not only a monstrous internal order, but overthrew the international framework Germany had had to accept from 1919 to 1924. Finally, we can recall that the two German constitutions of 1949 presupposed the division of the state (despite the Grundgesetz declaration to the contrary) and the preponderant voice of occupying powers over the development of

internal affairs. The entry of West Germany into the North Atlantic Alliance lifted virtually all those formal restrictions for the larger half of the former nation state, but
made certain that the respective constitutional orientations of the two German
republics remained in line with their respective international communities. And while
the 1990 settlement removed the remaining foreign constraints on German constitutional autonomy, that very settlement rested on extensive treaty frameworks emerging
from the 'Two plus Four' negotiations, including a German-German agreement, a
final settlement by the four occupying authorities of 1945, and a Conference on
Security and Cooperation in Europe (CSCE) ratifying act.

The point is that German constitutions have never been created purely as German
internal covenants. They have always incorporated the claims of powerful outsiders, or
they have been statements about independence from the outsiders. Neither the North
Americans of 1787, nor the British of the late seventeenth century and afterward, nor
the French have had to craft their institutions under such intimate interference. In this
sense Germany has always been in the middle – but less the middle geographically than
the middle institutionally. Remaking German institutions has meant remaking the
treaty settlements that patched together the efforts at European equilibrium. German
constitutions were European covenants.

Such interdependence did not *per se* imply that Germany must develop a peculiarly
military vocation. But it did mean that war and peace issues were likely to emerge
repeatedly around and within the German territories. It was rare, at least in the eras
before nuclear deterrence cast a shadow, for renegotiations of the European balance to
occur without war. As Europe lurched, usually through major warfare, from one international system to another, Germany has changed constitutions and regimes. Regime
changes in Germany have entailed international adjustments. Thus the underlying
power alignments within Germany – whether the balance between the major confessions from 1520 to 1648, or among the major territorial princedoms from 1618 to
1870, or between its liberals and its clericals and conservatives from 1815 to 1933, or
between its social classes from 1878 to 1960 – have had international settlements as a
major hostage. And vice versa: the balance between Vienna and Paris; or Vienna, Paris,
London and St Petersburg; or Paris, London, and Berlin; or finally Washington and
Moscow has been a crucial factor in determining how confessions, classes, parties, and
social forces have been equilibrated within German institutions. Even had there been
no German 'militarism,' no Junkers, or conversely even had there been natural barriers in the west and the east, German outcomes would have been intimately connected
with war and peace issues. And first the Prussian, then the German state developed the
capacity to play a decisive role in pressing and resolving military confrontations.
Capacity lagged at times, but it certainly caught up under gifted leaders.

After more than three centuries, Germany, while dominant in the middle of Europe,
need not compel the outcomes of war and peace. The German constitution has, so to
speak, been repatriated or re-naturalized, brought home to Germany; it is no longer
intertwined with broader security regimes. Then, too, a German military class has

ceased to exist; the military is at most a vocation and not a caste. And even Germany's geographic centrality no longer seems terribly consequential in an era of global trade alignments, US preponderant power, or the growing importance of Asia. Maintaining German fragmentation or division has ceased to be an aspiration for major international actors; the last nostalgic velleities disappeared during 1990. Conversely, German statesmen emphasized that their own ambitions did not extend beyond unification. With that double acceptance, German issues no longer remain a source of conflict and German territory no longer a site of conflict. It is hard to envisage a war between European states, although violence and civil strife are sadly present. Germany will doubtless have to play a role in a wider web of international negotiations and disputes – probably more than many of its citizens wish, but Honecker and Kohl probably had it right: Germany will no longer be a source of war.

Select bibliography

Almost every history of warfare, the German military, and indeed German national development could be cited as bearing on the topic taken up in this essay; here I mention only a few that seem particularly relevant, and I omit military history. I have cited some leading works in the text above. On the problems of military and society, see Gordon Craig's masterly synthesis, *The Politics of the Prussian Army, 1640–1945* (1955); Otto Büsch, *Militärsystem und Sozialleben im alten Preußen* (1962), stressing the interaction of landed society and military recruitment; for the Empire see Hans-Ulrich Wehler's formative works, including *Das deutsche Kaisserreich* (trans. *The German Empire*), and Stig Förster, *Der doppelte Militarismus: Die deutsche Heeresrüstungspolitik zwischen Status-Quo-Sicherung und Aggression 1890–1913* (1985); and for the period after World War I, see the still riveting John W. Wheeler-Bennett, *The Nemesis of Power: The German Army in Politics, 1918–1945* (1953). Gerhard Ritter's *Staatskunst und Kriegshandwerk. Das Problem des 'Militarismus' in Deutschland*, 4 vols. (1958–68); English-language edition: *The Sword and the Scepter. The Problem of Militarism in Germany* (1969–73), is a monumental and deeply felt work about the militarization of policy and society. Michael Geyer's *Deutsche Rustungspolitik 1860–1980* (1984) stresses the impact of the modern armaments process since the mid-nineteenth century as a driving force in shaping the civil–military balance; it was no accident that the book was written at the very height of the Cold War arms race. For studies that emphasize the primacy of internal policy, besides Eckart Kehr's study of German naval building, see his essays collected in Hans-Ulrich Wehler, ed., *Der Primat der Innenpolitik: Gesammelte Aufsatze zur preußisch-deutschen Sozialgeschichte im 19. und 20. Jahrhundert* (2nd edn, 1976) and Wehler's own *Deutsche Gesellschaftsgeschichte*, 3 vols. to date (1987–95); also Fritz Fischer, *Griff nach der Weltmacht* translated as *Germany's Aims in the First World War* (1967), as well as Fischer's volume on the preceding period: *War of Illusions: German Policies from 1911 to 1914* (1975); also Volker R. Berghahn, *Germany and the Approach of War in 1914* (1973). See also Berghahn's *Militarism 1861–1979* (1981). A brief but suggestive outline of war and diplomacy is provided by Andreas Hillgruber, *Germany and the Two World Wars*, trans. William C. Kirby (1981). The historians of the Federal Republic's military history archive in Freiburg, including Wilhelm Deist, H.-E. Volkmann, Manfred Messerschmidt and others, have contributed mightily to documenting the recent German military record, including the four-volume collaborative history, *Das Deutsche Reich und der Zweite Weltkrieg* (1979–82). For construction of a 'democratic' army after the Second World War, see Donald Abenheim, *Reforging the Iron Cross: The Search for Tradition in the West German Armed Forces* (1988). For the general issue of militarism, the older comparative study by Alfred Vagts, *A History of Militarism: Civilian and Military* (1937) and Samuel P. Huntington, *The Soldier and the State: The Theory and Politics of Civil-Military Relations* (1957) still repay reading.

For military intellectuals see Michael Howard and Peter Paret's edition of Carl von Clausewitz's *On War* (1976) as well as Paret's study of *Clausewitz and the State*. On the later formative military thinkers, see Arden Bucholz's two studies: *Hans Delbrück and the German Military Establishment* (1985) and *Moltke, Schlieffen, and Prussian War Planning* (1991) and the essays in Edward Meade Earle, ed., *Makers of Modern Strategy* (1953). For some general recent studies of the international context for German war and peace see Paul W. Schroeder, *The Transformation of European Politics 1763–1848* (1994); and David Kaiser, *Politics and War: European Conflict from Phillip II to Hitler* (1990).

27

The national idea in modern German history

John Breuilly

The view that peoples and the territories they inhabit are national and should be independent is the most important political idea of modern times. This is particularly the case with Germany, a new nation state and one in which an extreme form of nationalism temporarily held sway. The national idea continues to shape the present and our understanding of German history. Indeed, the very notion that the history of a certain region in central Europe is best understood as 'German history' testifies to the centrality of the national idea. However, terms like 'national', 'nation' and 'nationalism' are used in different and conflicting ways which cause confusion. In this brief survey I will begin with ideas elaborated by intellectuals, move on to the political uses of the national idea and then its impact on the bulk of the population. I divide the story into three parts – before, during and after the nation state period of 1871–1945 – with a short epilogue on the reunification of 1989–90 and subsequent developments.

I Before the nation state, 1800–1871

The only institution which political writers could identify as German in 1800 was the Holy Roman Empire of the German nation. In the late eighteenth century some intellectuals advocated reforms to strengthen the Empire, though as a coordinating institution, not a sovereign territorial state. After the collapse of the Empire this imperial idea underpinned Napoleon's Confederation of the Rhine. It continued to inform such features of the Confederation established in 1814–15 as the Austrian Presidency, plans for an army and partial restoration of the privileges of former imperial nobles.[1]

However, this idea was palpably failing in the political sphere because of the impact of Napoleon and the attitude of the larger German states which collaborated with Napoleon in dismembering the Empire. Only Austria, the major German power and representative of the imperial idea, constantly fought Napoleon, going so far as to

Illustration 27.1 *Outpost Duty* by Georg Friedrich Kersting (1815): a contribution to the patriotic myth of the war of liberation against the French

invoke German patriotism in the war of 1809. After defeat in that war Austria retreated to a conservative and dynastic policy under Metternich. Prussia made peace in 1795 and benefited from the destruction of small imperial states. The reform movement after the disastrous war of 1806–7 included German patriots but they were a minority within a minority. Once Napoleon's *grande armée* collapsed in Russia, Prussia abandoned its alliance with France. Other German states followed suit and Austria, after mediation attempts, joined the anti-Napoleonic alliance. These new allies now fought what has been dubbed a 'war of national liberation'. However, the states used the idea of 'Germany' as it suited them.

The dismemberment and destruction of the Empire, along with the impotence and egoism of individual German states, provided the background to the elaboration of an a-political, even anti-political national idea.

> The German Empire and the German nation are two different things. The glory of the Germans has never been based upon the power of its princes. Separated from the political sphere, Germans have established their own values. Political defeats could not undermine those values (Schiller, 1804)[2]

For Schiller this cultural ideal was to be realized through such projects as a National Theatre and making German a major literary language. A cynic might discern compensation for Napoleon's triumphs but this cultural idea continued to exert intellectual attraction after 1815. Beyond the 'high culture' of Schiller, Herder had argued that language shaped identity and divided humanity into nations, though he did not draw political conclusions from this and condemned powerful territorial states like Prussia as 'mechanical'. Such ideas could be politicized as when von Arndt declared the German Fatherland was wherever the German tongue was heard and advocated a single monarchical state based on this *Volk* or Fichte argued that German was a precious language whose purity must be preserved against French pollution by state action.[3]

This politicized version of the cultural ideal inspired some people to action. Patriotic volunteers fought in the war of 1813–15. Gymnastic societies propagated an ideal of 'Germandom' as healthy, serious and masculine, counterposing this to the stereotype of an effete, cynical, cosmopolitan, frivolous French. This patriotic movement had at best some tens of thousands of supporters, little military significance and no clear, let alone practical political programme or organization.

Most studies of national ideas do not extend beyond intellectual and political history. But nationalist intellectuals and politicians claim to be the representatives of the nation. What did 'normal Germans' think about nationality in the Napoleonic period? This is a difficult if not impossible question to answer as most people do not leave indirect, let alone direct evidence about their thoughts and feelings for historians to consider. I can only offer some speculative comments.

Most 'Germans' in 1800 lived in small states. Society was organized along a hierarchy of local privilege. Only small groups like civil servants and university teachers enjoyed privileges on a wider geographical scale. Combined with limited mobility, literacy and communications, this meant that most people probably thought in local and status terms. Incorporation into a larger state could broaden their experience, especially if the state acted against privilege and local autonomy. Usually those capable of collective action opposed such policies, sometimes invoking a patriotism informed by nostalgia for a more fragmented and less powerful Germany, a desire to return to the rule of their own former prince or bishop. There was widespread anti-French feeling, partly due to living in states under direct French rule or the rule of one of Napoleon's family, but mainly due to the more widespread burdens imposed by Napoleon's continual warfare. Insofar as such resentments were channelled into wider positive loyalties, these were religious and monarchical.

The Confederation with its Austrian Presidency was a pale shadow of the old Empire. The new states were preoccupied with integrating enlarged territories and resisted Confederal interference. Positive aims such as an army foundered as states refused to relinquish command. The Confederation was used to repress liberal and national movements whose significance it overrated. Ironically this repression made the Confederation more effectively national than the old Empire. At the same time the Confederation discredited the imperial idea by appearing as anti-national and operating on behalf of existing states, especially the two dominant states of Austria and Prussia. The imperial idea as celebrated in romantic depictions of medieval German greatness appeared hopelessly at odds with reality.

In other respects the romantic understanding of societies as organic cultures had a deeper intellectual impact. The idea that humanity consisted of national cultures was elaborated through the cultivation of 'folk' music, in romantic art and the history of art, the scholarly study of folklore and language, and in historical study. Intellectuals like Leopold von Ranke, Wilhelm and Alexander von Humboldt in their respective disciplines of history, linguistics and anthropology extended this approach to other cultures. Similar ideas can be found elsewhere in Europe but in Germany, lacking a political centre, this idea of unity as cultural was especially strong. Educated townsmen founded many associations dedicated to promoting national art and music. Some states encouraged this national idea. The Bavarian monarchy was devoted to the construction of great national monuments such as the Valhalla at Regensburg. Writers, painters and musicians claimed status as national artists. By the 1830s Goethe and Schiller had been transformed into national icons, Goethe experiencing this idolatry in his own lifetime. All this predisposed educated elites in Germany to equate culture with nationality though not necessarily to draw political conclusions from this perception.

A more political use of the national idea developed rather differently. Some states, notably Prussia, had promised their subjects a constitution following victory over Napoleon. Some of the smaller states did grant constitutions in the early post-war years. One of the clauses in the agreement establishing the Confederation stipulated that states should enact constitutions. However, Prussia failed to honour its promise, the constitutions promulgated provided limited rights to assemblies mainly elected on

Illustration 27.2   *Gothic Cathedral at the waterside* by Karl Friedrich Schinkel (1823), a copy of the 1813 painting by Wilhelm Ahlborn. Celebration of Germany's medieval past was a significant component in early-nineteenth-century articulations of the national idea

the basis of estate divisions, and the Confederal stipulation was for constitutions guaranteeing traditional privileges. This was challenged by a modern constitutionalism based on equality and liberty.[4]

This liberalism could acquire a national character in various ways. Some liberals argued that constitutional progress was only possible in large territorial states. As the Confederation repressed liberalism, liberals concluded that Confederal reform was a necessary condition of state reform. Some democrats[5] went further and identified the nation with the 'people', the nation state with a state based on popular sovereignty. Germany was defined not as cultural unity or imperial restoration but as a politically transformed Confederation. At the same time, the idea of Germany as an advanced culture functioned as a background assumption amongst liberals who considered it unworthy that so progressive a nation be subject to the arbitrary rule of princes.

These liberal and democratic ideas informed the most significant national oppositions of the post-1815 period. The *Burschenschaften* were effectively suppressed from 1819. Their romantic sensibility, insofar as it was given political expression, turned to support other 'national liberation' struggles such as the Greek war against the Ottoman Empire and the Poles who rebelled unsuccessfully against Russian rule in 1831. Especially prominent in this were educated circles in the south and west of Germany where enlarged states like Prussia, Bavaria, Baden and Württemberg included regions very distinct from those of their core territories. Unable to envisage imperial restoration, patriots looked towards a stronger national authority as a way of escaping state control. Such ideas could take a democratic form as in the festival held in the Palatine town of Hambach in 1832. Such opposition threatened to spread beyond educated groups.

Renewed repression following Hambach made national opposition impossible. Exiled liberal and democratic nationalists commanded support amongst émigré communities but little within Germany. There was some political relaxation in the 1840s which enabled a limited revival of national movements. Liberals from the Rhinelands and southwestern states drew up a programme in October 1847 which looked to the *Zollverein* to lead the way. Democrats meeting in Offenburg in September 1847 listed a series of political demands in the name of the 'German people'. But there were nothing like political parties at regional, let alone state or national level.

For most Germans after 1815 the national idea remained remote and unimportant. The Articles of Confederation had intimated otherwise. Article 18 declared that subjects of the Confederation should be able to purchase real estate anywhere in the Confederation, emigrate to other states without being taxed, enter government service in another state, and enjoy press freedom. Press freedom and many other liberties were suppressed in 1819. Freedom of emigration meant nothing without a corresponding freedom of immigration and governments refused entry to 'foreigners' from other German states. States increasingly enforced fiscal, military and other claims which implied statewide citizenship. In 1842 the Prussian state introduced a law defining state membership which was linked to other laws relaxing rights of internal migration and poor relief outside the locality to which a person belonged. Similar measures to impose common territorial rules were passed in other states. However, so long as there was limited migration, poor relief remained a communal obligation (Prussia in 1842 was exceptionally advanced in this regard), there were few political or legal rights associated with citizenship, and there was little incentive for states to define who were their citizens.

If state citizenship mean little, German citizenship meant nothing. German nationality had no legal basis. The Confederation defended incumbent regimes. Some business and educated groups developed contacts across state boundaries to influence *Zollverein* policy or establish a newspaper but this was very limited. Some confessional and regional minorities looked to national authority for protection against their state but found it difficult to ally with one another. People who migrated across state boundaries such as journeymen resented being treated as aliens and felt a national solidarity in exile. But most people lived their lives within state boundaries and did not expect civil rights. In a negative way, as in 1840, a wave of anti-French feeling could still sweep through the German lands. The national idea informed the culture of many educated Germans. There were limited liberal and democratic oppositional movements. However, most popular protest did not touch upon national questions and German society remained socially and geographically fragmented, even within individual states.

These states encouraged a broader sense of identity through the processes of state-building. They could promote German identity positively through cultural policies and negatively through the repression of national movements. However, none of the states before 1848 favoured greater national unity. This was obvious in the case of the multi-national Habsburg Empire and the smaller states whose interests so clearly conflicted with a strong national authority. It was also true of Prussia. The establishment of the *Zollverein* has been interpreted as Prussia leading the way to unification. However, initial motives were commercial and fiscal, and the *Zollverein* was opposed by many liberals because it strengthened princes.[6] Economic nationalists like Friedrich List argued that the liberal tariff policies of the *Zollverein* were detrimental to the construction of a strong national economy. The Prussian monarchy accepted its subordination to Austria and pressed for little more than a larger say in the Confederation. Its resistance to constitutionalism, as in its confrontation with a Prussian United Diet in 1847, meant rejection of the dominant form of political nationalism, that is liberal nationalism. There were already in the 1830s writers like Droysen and Pfizer who looked to Prussia for a lead on the national question and by the 1840s liberal nationalists could see the *Zollverein* as a foundation on which to build. But none of this elicited positive reactions from Prussia.

1848 witnessed an explosion of political action and organization. The general acceptance of the cultural ideal of nationality amongst educated Germans, and the attraction of liberal and democratic forms of nationalism to the political activists who quickly took the lead in the wake of popular disturbances, meant that many of the petitions drawn up in early 1848 demanded a national parliament. Prominent liberals and democrats pushed the project forward against paralysed states and a discredited Confederation. The resultant elections constituted the greatest popular political event to date, as millions of men voted for a national parliament. For a moment the idea of German citizenship acquired a concrete meaning, even if individual states organized the elections and varied greatly in how they did this.[7]

The parliament which met in Frankfurt am Main from May 1848 was dominated by liberal, educated bourgeois. For them Germany consisted of the states of the Confederation. Their main concerns were to create a stronger national authority in place of the present Confederation and a common system of rights and obligations throughout Germany. All this gave a special flavour to the meaning of terms such as 'Germany' and 'German'. The constitution drawn up by the parliament defined a German as a citizen of *the* German state. In turn, a citizen of the German state was anyone who was a citizen of *a* German state. If nationality is defined as citizenship of the nation-state, then in the Imperial Constitution of 1849 German nationality is state citizenship, not culture or language or direct membership of the nation state.

Beyond this liberal and federalist consensus there was much scope for disagreement. One extreme minority wanted a democratic unitary republic; another a minimal national authority. Some in the moderate majority looked to Prussia, others to Austria for a lead. This was the basis of the smaller/greater German division rather than different conceptions of 'where' the German nation was to be found. Some wished to expand German boundaries in certain border zones but others opposed them. A few democrats desired war, preferably with Russia, but in order to mobilize and unite Germans rather than make territorial gains. The image some historians have painted of a bellicose nationalism at work is misleading. There were numerous differences and many long debates which have led historians to portray the parliament as a contentious and ineffectual collection of academics, a 'Professors' Parliament'.

This is harsh criticism. The parliament had to work with rather than against states, as it lacked a civil service, an army and popular loyalty. Whether it could have built up popular support which would have given it leverage in negotiations with states is debatable. Even where liberals sympathetic to the national idea were in power in individual states, they resented making concessions to Frankfurt and were preoccupied by issues at the level of the individual state.

German states in 1848 concentrated on restoring order, even when liberals were in power, and upon programmes of state reform. Frederick William IV did declare in March 1848 that Prussia would 'go forth into' Germany but it is not clear what he meant and the phrase has little relevance to actual Prussian policy through the rest of 1848. The Frankfurt parliament, after delaying action on the political problem raised by Austro-Prussian dualism in the hope that the course of the revolution would make things clearer (e.g., by undermining the Habsburg Empire), eventually turned to Prussia for leadership. However, this was not because there was a 'pro-Prussian' majority in the assembly but was the product of complex calculations and compromises.

By the time Frederick William IV rejected the offer of the imperial crown, only democrats who supported the democratic rather than the national or imperial features of the constitution were prepared to fight for it. Their repression permanently weakened democratic nationalism. Pro-Austria liberals left the assembly when it voted to exclude Austria. Most remaining deputies left when ordered to by their governments. In 1849–50 Prussia tried to draw northern and central German states into a closer union but backed down as soon as Austria opposed it. Pro-Prussian deputies from the Frankfurt parliament cooperated with this limited national policy pursued by Prussia in 1849–50 but withdrew from active politics by 1851.

For most Germans the national issue rapidly lost its allure during 1848. The electorate of May 1848 sent educated bourgeois to Frankfurt to deal with the abstruse national question while returning people like themselves to state parliaments to take up 'practical' questions like land reform. Some states promulgated the Basic Rights of the Imperial Constitution but the whole constitution was soon set aside. Changes in legal rights were made at state level, the most important being peasant emancipation laws. So too were new political rights such as those granted under the Prussian constitution of 1848. Not only did nothing concrete emerge from Frankfurt, but discussion of ways of unifying Germans created hostility. Businessmen who wanted protection were not interested in a low tariff *Zollverein*. Guildsmen opposed to state interference with communal autonomy would hardly welcome national interference. There was probably less support for national unity by the end of the revolution than at the beginning. The 1848 revolutions demonstrated that categories such as the 'people', the 'citizens' or the 'loyal subjects' invoked by democrats, liberals and conservatives, were fictions. German society was riven by conflicts which the revolution had brought out into the open.

All this stimulated political intellectuals to revise their understanding of the national question. The sense that popular or elite opposition lacked the power and the smaller states and Austria lacked the inclination to advance the national idea was strengthened by the failure of national projects in 1848. Some liberals came to see Prussia as the only possible instrument of unification, even if not a very promising one. Others looked to the *Zollverein* for a material conception of nationality, a vision of economic progress and integration promoting a stronger sense of national identity and compelling states to pool their sovereignty. In these ways national ideas associated with western Germany and Catholic Austria, with culture, empire and federalism gave way to ideas focused on northern Germany, Protestantism, a powerful state and a modernizing economy. Nevertheless, the dominant assumptions were still that Austria was part of Germany, that the nation state should be liberal, if not democratic, and that states should enjoy considerable autonomy.

However, after Prussia dropped even the limited national policy of 1849–50 there was little political support for such thinking. In the 1850s Prussia sought at most parity with Austria in the restored Confederation, as during the crisis sparked off by the war between Austria and France in 1859. Even in 1862, with Bismarck in power, there was no sudden change. Austria and Prussia acted together against Denmark in 1864 and incurred the wrath of the national movement for their refusal to support the Duke of Augustenburg. Both Austria and Prussia flirted with Confederal reform but in opportunist and sporadic fashion. Other states discussed reform but their own interests were too much at variance to produce practical results.

The dominance of counter-revolutionary politics in the 1850s has meant that histories of the national idea which focus on intellectual and political history see this as a decade of stagnation. Yet this period also saw the beginning of an economic boom which greatly increased internal migration and was associated with improvements in transportation (most dramatically through railway-building), greater literacy, urban growth and improved communications. All this pushed governments into agreements on matters like cross-border migration. A more national society was taking shape, especially in northern and central Germany, just as national movements were being suppressed. In this context the *Zollverein* came to take on a national importance and Prussian dominance of it ensured that Austria was excluded from membership. This could only strengthen the plausibility of those liberals who argued in terms of Prussian leadership and economic progress as the way forward.

Political liberalization from the late 1850s provided the exponents of this version of the national idea with new opportunities of organizing and mobilizing support. A national movement resurfaced in the late 1850s, drawing upon a wide network of cultural movements which were especially strong in Protestant parts of Germany. Constitutional reforms meant liberal parties could be formed. These liberal nationalists, less worried than in 1848 about democratic challenges and organizing within rather than against state institutions, dominated the national movement. Democrats were compelled, if they were to be effective, to work within liberal-dominated organizations. As for nationalists who favoured a pro-Austrian, federalist and greater German approach, they were much more weakly organized and supported. Often their chief concern appeared to be anti-Prussian rather than a desire to realize an alternative national ideal.

Nevertheless, pro-Prussian liberal nationalists had no more impact on policy-making before 1866 than any other component of the national movement. Both Prussia and Austria made occasional bids for national support between 1862 and 1866 but it was a fairly minor consideration. The national movement watched helplessly as the two leading German states went to war in 1866.

The national movement only came into its own from 1867 when Bismarck set about organizing Prussian gains in a form which could command elite and popular support.[8] He allied himself with the chief exponents of the national idea as Protestant, economically progressive and centred on Prussia – the National Liberals. Prussia declared it had no intention of annexing the south German states and respected the territorial integrity of Austria. It sought to draw the south German states into its orbit by constitutional and economic methods. Yet it became increasingly apparent up to 1870 that these policies did not persuade south Gemans who remained fearful of what they saw as Prussian and Protestant dominance.

The same policies proved very effective in the north and centre. In the North German Confederation the integrating measures pushed through by the National Liberals worked with the grain of increased social and geographical mobility. A law on freedom of movement between member states went much further than anything previously and created the basis for national citizenship. Prussia, aided by national liberal support in other states, pushed through this policy based on its state membership law of 1842. This was to become the basis for German citizenship in the Second Empire. As more people moved across state boundaries and enjoyed common rights in different states, so nationality, in terms of membership of a national state, took on an everyday significance.

Nevertheless, there were many who did not accept this new version of the national idea. Radical nationalists opposed what they saw as greater Prussia. Loyalists in the smaller German states, Catholics and left-liberals in Prussia variously advocated greater federalism, closer links to Austria and greater constitutional and parliamentary power. Even into the 1860s national political festivals still celebrated a vision of Germany which was not subject to one centralizing source of power. Those in power denounced these programmes and values as anti-national. The uneasy combination of liberal nationalism and Prussian power dominated by 1870. To this the 1870–71 war added strong anti-French sentiments and a pride in military achievement which strengthened pro-governmental nationalism. How far it had created a more enduring national consensus is another matter, especially as south Germans and Catholics were suspicious of a national idea focused upon north Germany and Protestantism.

The stress on the national character of what had been achieved in 1870–71 would push the new state into directions not intended by those who had created it. There was no question of the Second Empire simply being a greater Prussia. The assumption of the imperial title upset supporters of the Hohenzollern and other dynasties. The idea of a dynasty above its subjects had helped maintain Polish loyalty in Prussia. The conversion of that dynasty into a national institution broke with such supranational rule. There was an uneasy mix of dynastic and national values, symbolized in the adoption of a flag which was neither Prussian (black and white) nor German (black, red and gold) but a compromise (black, white and red). Even that sat uneasily with the renewed stress on federalism occasioned by the entry of the south German states into the Second Empire. This was not peculiar; other nation states also displayed uncertainty in their choice of national symbols. However, the sudden and violent creation of Germany and its rapid rise as a major power meant that this failure took a peculiar form and that the national idea would be used in many different ways to force changes in the new nation state.

II   In the nation state, 1871–1945

However difficult to define, the Second Empire had now come into existence, the product of a national war against France which had a profound impact on its institutions and self-image. As it reached increasingly into the lives of all Germans, so the very existence of this state stimulated new versions of the national idea.

Burkhardt shrewdly and gloomily predicted that there would soon emerge historical schools which interpreted the foundation of the Second Empire as the natural end to all history.[9] There were apologists who argued that 1871 was the culmination of, not a break with, earlier traditions, a glorious and inevitable fusion of culture with power, though this sat uneasily with celebrating the Second Empire as the creation of genial figures, above all Bismarck. War and genius were adopted as the symbols of the new state in the absence of consensus on a more comprehensive national idea. The anniversary of Sedan became the major political festival. Monuments to Wilhelm I and Bismarck quickly sprang up after their deaths.[10] Opportunism, enthusiasm and the very human tendency to come to terms with success all induced people to forget or ignore the extent to which the new state differed from what they had wanted or envisaged. A middle-class monarchism took shape which focused on new monuments and festivals such as those associated with the great statue of Hermann erected in the Teutoborger forest.[11] There was a shift to a nostalgic and passive tone in these festivals. Parades replaced processions and participants replaced contemporary dress with historic costumes. This suggests a turning away from activist liberal nationalism towards monarchical and authoritarian nationalism. There was little celebration of the one genuinely new, national institution, the Reichstag, which was portrayed instead as a source of factionalism and opposition. Nor was the constitution – a pragmatic, not an inspirational document – made into a symbol of national loyalty.[12]

A dynamic view of the national idea shifted from domestic to foreign affairs, as in the agitation for a powerful navy. The navy was modern, based on new technologies of steam power, steel construction and gunnery. It was not associated with Prussian military traditions based on the army. The idea of Germany as a world power lacked tradition. For bourgeois nationalists this was an advantage, a task for the imperial government rather than the states which might divert attention from internal divisions. The Reich could become its own justification; the bid for world power, the next stage in the forward march of Germany. Politics as a struggle between nation states was projected from Europe on to the world. Within Europe the break with the dynastic alliance with Russia in 1890 signalled a greater stress on the national idea.

Political struggle was nationalized. Germans were struggling with Russians, British and other nations for their rightful 'place in the sun' and assuming their share of the 'white man's burden'. The idea was elaborated by vulgarizing and redirecting Darwin's principle of natural selection to society and politics. This altered notions of struggle associated with capitalism and traditional power politics. Economic competition shifted from the individual to the nation; the objective of struggle from profit or prestige to that of survival. 'Old' nations like Britain and France blocked the rise of 'young' nations like Germany. Russia was now opposed less as an enemy of progress – the basis of mid-century democratic and liberal nationalist hostility – and more as a powerful national rival and leader of Slav interests.

This also transformed the imperial idea. The traditional idea of a 'greater Germany' had meant a Germany which included Austria as part of a cultural and imperial tradition. This idea was originally used to criticize the Reich. For the new pan-Germans within the Reich, this state was itself an empire and the core of something more. 'Greater Germany' meant an alliance with Austria as a fellow German power (not a fellow dynasty), the extension of Reich power into other areas of German settlement, the creation of a broader hegemony in Europe and the expansion of an overseas empire – all justified by the 'needs' of the ethnic community. The ideology of one ethnic or racial nation dominating others challenged that of a plurality of culturally defined nations occupying distinct territories. In place of an optimistic idea of progress developed the fatalistic, even pessimistic assumption of history as unending struggle from which one could not withdraw but only win or lose.

There was a domestic aspect to this. Authoritarian nationalism had condemned as anti-national those who did not share the political loyalties or culture of the elites which held power. This could lead to persecution on grounds of belief (socialists, Catholics) or language (Poles). Even if that hardened rather than overcame conflict, in principle it implied a chance for persecuted groups to convert to the values of authority. If, however, Poles were treated as an inferior race, no such resolution of the conflict was possible.

The same logic applied to anti-Semitism. Traditional anti-Semitism as religious discrimination implied that religious conversion could lead to assimilation. Liberal and cultural conceptions of nationality envisioned assimilation not through religious conversion but by making religion a private matter separate from public affairs and national culture. Jewish liberals advocated assimilation through emancipation against Christian anti-Semites and traditional Jews defending their communal culture against dissolution. The prominent role of emancipated Jews in political and economic affairs stimulated outbursts of anti-Semitism in periods of economic difficulty. This anti-Semitism was taken up in a radicalized, racial form which made Jewishness a matter of descent, not religion or culture. As the national idea ceased to be informed by a broader religious, cultural or political value system, it became an end in itself. A large literature developed elaborating ethnic and racial ideas in a great variety of ways. This literature and these radical right nationalist movements provided the soil in which what is known as *völkisch* nationalist ideology could grow.[13]

For some time Bismarck stood aloof from these new versions of the national idea. He had little interest in colonial acquisitions; he valued an alliance with Russia as much as with Austria; he saw both in dynastic rather than national terms; and he declared Germany to be a 'satiated' power. With his departure, however, more ambitious views of the national idea could be used for a variety of purposes. Some of these were domestic; some concerned exploiting favourable international conditions to Germany's advantage; some were motivated by a more thorough-going expansionist nationalism. Whatever the mix of reasons, the result was that by 1912 Germany was allied only with Austria against Britain, France and Russia and was pursuing ambitious policies both in and beyond Europe.[14]

This was a marked change from the situation in 1871 and cannot be explained purely in terms of the rise of more aggressive nationalist ideas. We also have to consider the politics of nationalism and the impact of the national idea upon the bulk of the population.

The empire was originally a weak institution superimposed upon the states. It rapidly acquired power in such fields as welfare, tariffs and navy-building. These and other developments led to the establishment of new ministries and other agencies. Imperial institutions needed financing. The imperial government set the pace in policy-making for the individual states. A powerful civil service took shape to support imperial ministries. State institutions declined and took on a more defensive character. The Bundesrat failed in its role of steering imperial government and this came to fall to the chancellor. As popular opinion and mass politics increased in importance and legislation was needed to authorize and finance new imperial tasks, the Reichstag become a vital part of national government.

The National Liberal Party dominated the Reichstag in the 1870s. It accepted the nation state in its current form, though wanting to make it more unitary and increase the power of parliament. As the party declined relative to other parties it shifted to a defence of existing institutions against mass politics. Reformist nationalism[15] was left to various left-liberal factions. National Liberals allied with conservatives in defence of the political status quo although the imperial government was compelled to expand its powers in ways which altered the nature of politics.

The Catholic Centre Party and the Socialist Party emerged as the most popular parties. These were labelled 'anti-national' by states and governmental parties, though most Catholics and workers accepted the nation state. Their more inclusive versions of the national idea were marginalized by opponents who stressed their supranational confessional and class loyalties. There were, however, very great differences and conflicts between the two parties, with the socialists much less ambiguous about the democratic reforms they wished to see implemented in order to make the state truly national.

A third nationalist position was right-wing but also radical. Ideas of expansion abroad and campaigns against enemies of the nation at home (Jews, Catholics, socialists, non-Germans) were pressed in a populist and *völkisch* manner by agitational organizations such as the Navy and Army Leagues, the League against Social Democracy, the Colonial and the Pan-German Leagues which had considerable influence within conservative and liberal parties. Though monarchical and loyalist, these radical nationalists criticized the authoritarian and elitist institutions of the Second Empire. Amongst these radical groups nationalism came to be preached as a 'political religion'.

We cannot assume that the national ideas taken up by political movements necessarily reflected the values of most Germans. Germany was still far from democratic. Most people had little active interest in politics and in 1871 still lived in the countryside. Germany was a federal state. Even if people looked beyond their locality, it was to the individual state which controlled income and property taxes, provided education, and generally regulated most everyday affairs.

Yet there is much to suggest that national identity came to mean more to more people. Germany industrialized under the Second Empire. There was massive east–west migration and large-scale urbanization. Germans moved around much more and long-range migration was increasingly within rather than beyond Germany. Mass schooling and literacy meant Germans increasingly read and experienced the same things. More Germans joined political parties, trade unions and other interest groups which extended their horizons.[16] A sense of common culture was promoted through the standard language of mass circulation newspapers, periodicals and books. From being the medium of communication this could also come to be regarded as something which bound people together.

There were also distinct institutional changes which promoted a sense of nationality. All German males from their twenty-fourth birthday could vote in Reichstag elections and by 1912 well over 80 per cent did so. By 1873 German citizenship rights had been codified, building upon state citizenship and the Prussian law of 1842. People increasingly were subject to the same obligations such as those of military service. They also began to acquire common rights such as those associated with Bismarck's welfare legislation.

As the national state reached increasingly into people's lives, so more people acquired an interest in the actions of that state. Oppositional movements focused on particular regions gave way to national parties of opposition. Catholic and working-class voters might oppose the Hohenzollern monarchy but it was for the *German* Centre Party and the *German* Socialist Party that they voted. And even though in opposition, these voters participated in some way in politics and derived some advantages from imperial welfare measures and other policies, as well as from the generally increasing standards of living. Even if many Germans rejected the way the nation state was run and felt mistreated by that state, nevertheless they could not but see themselves as belonging to one nation and one state.

This sense of identity had an exclusive aspect. Those citizens of the Reich who did not share in the common culture, such as Danish or Polish speakers, felt themselves increasingly alienated from this state. Germans who emigrated to the USA might maintain cultural links but lost political ties as they acquired American citizenship. Most Austrian Germans, though grateful for the protective alliance with the Reich, lived a political life oriented to Vienna and the maintenance of a multi national Empire. The small pan-German movement in Austria was clearly an Austrian, not a Reich form of German nationalism. Being German was increasingly a matter of both ethnicity and membership of the Reich. This was most vividly expressed in the 1913 Citizenship Law. The Reichstag had agitated for such a law for some time, partly because of differences between states on such matters as naturalization procedures, partly because of the problems of defending German interests abroad and dealing with the onset of large-scale labour immigration into the Reich. The law did not reflect the majority view of the Reichstag which would have favoured a more liberal procedure for immigrants to acquire German citizenship. Instead the law hardened the prevailing practice of *ius sanguinis* (the law of blood) which made citizenship a matter of inheritance. Germans who went abroad would continue to be Germans, as would their children; non-Germans who moved into Germany would not be German citizens and neither would their children. Strictly speaking this was not an ethnic law and had never been intended or used as such by the individual German states. However, in the Reichstag debates the ethnic element was stressed. German culture, German nationality, German citizenship were all oriented to the existence of the Reich. The Second Empire, rather than being the product of one version of the national idea, was turning into its principal creator.

By the time war broke out in 1914 the national idea and its identification with the interests of the Reich had become an end in itself for many Germans. A collection of essays published by some academics on the 'ideas of 1914', justifying Germany's position in the war, makes this clear. The national idea dominated. Germany was surrounded and threatened by enemies. Her system of government was defended as one uniquely suited to Germans; not a model for other countries. The national idea was counterposed to the universalist values propagated by 'the west' although these were also denounced as hypocrisy concealing self-interest. The demand for German hegemony in central Europe and an overseas empire, even if justified as necessary forms of defence, turned the national idea into little more than one of power wielded on behalf of the ethnic or racial nation.

The deeds of the Third Reich have sensitized us to such intellectual trends. However, race ideas were still largely implicit and confined to a small part of the political spectrum. (It is important to distinguish the doctrine of race from a broader ethnic conception of nationality, although they were often confused in practice. Ethnicity is a cultural concept, even if cultural definitions are linked to race ideas. Strictly speaking the race idea has no cultural content at all.) For most conservatives the national idea meant the status quo, an authoritarian conception of politics and culture; for moderate liberals it meant power and progress, science and education. There were many who regarded themselves as patriots but believed the Fatherland would only be truly national when subjected to a liberal or democratic or socialist transformation, and who only supported a war of defence. It was the broader consensus that the nation state was worthy of loyalty and was threatened from outside which explained the great unity at the beginning of the war.

The outbreak of war brought a temporary truce between these different groupings. The government insisted it was fighting a war of defence and appealed to the patriotism of the opposition parties. William declared he no longer recognized parties, only Germans. The political process was closed down through self-imposed and governmental censorship, the suspension of elections and the drift of power to the army. By 1917 strains between the different national values were re-surfacing. Left-liberals, Centre Party and socialist deputies argued for peace negotiations on the basis of no annexations, whereas the right, coordinating under the umbrella of the new Fatherland Party, pressed ambitious war aims. The collapse of the war effort swept the right from power and the end of the war was negotiated by the oppositional parties. Under unpromising conditions they tried to project their national values on to the Weimar Republic.[17]

War in 1870–71 had involved a large number of soldiers and helped create national solidarity. That was as nothing compared to the intensity of the national experience Germans underwent in the First World War. Every aspect of life was subordinated to the pursuit of victory. The obligation to perform military service became the duty to die for one's country after 1914 and the Auxiliary Service Law of December 1916 extended the power of military discipline to the whole of society. Propaganda was intense. Almost all surviving Germans lost family and friends to the war and suffered deprivation. That did not necessarily make nationalists of them and many welcomed peace even at the cost of defeat. Nevertheless, the sense that Germans were members of a national community was immeasurably strengthened by the experience of war.

Defeat had the same impact. The loss of Alsace-Lorraine and Danish and Polish territories made Germany ethnically more homogenous as well as subjecting it to ethnic German immigration from lost territories. The defeat of right-wing nationalism, both governmental and radical, meant that the opposition parties which had advocated a more defensive and liberal conception of nationality played the central role in the foundation of the Weimar Republic. The removal of the dynasties which had provided the basis of the federalist system made it easier to adopt a unitary constitution and national symbols such as the black, red and gold flag (though not for all institutions and in the face of right-wing hostility) and a national anthem. For the first time German citizenship was defined directly in terms of membership of the German state, not indirectly through membership of a member state. To the intense national experience of war was added the growth of mass consumption and leisure, enhanced through new media like film and radio, which contributed to the formation of mass culture.[18] In many ways Weimar was Germany's first 'real' nation state and national society.

For the first time women were officially included in the nation. Women could now vote in parliamentary elections. Political citizenship was no longer an exclusively male province. In theory women could also stand for elections but there were still many obstacles before that happened on a significant scale (though some women deputies represented the German Democratic and the Communist parties). Women were regarded as 'passive' citizens, their citizenship amounting to the right to choose between male politicians and to help the nation in their capacities as wives and mothers. Furthermore, women continued to be formally excluded from other kinds of citizenship. *Ius sanguinis* decreed that the inheritance of citizenship passed through the father, not the mother (though illegitimate children could inherit citizenship through their mother). Women, especially married women, still did not enjoy equality before the law with men. Nevertheless, women mattered as voters, played a more active role in the developing consumer culture, and began to acquire new legal rights through the expanded welfare state provisions which related to the family. Some of the aggressively masculine features of radical right-wing denunciations of the Weimar Republic may be related to this limited entry of women into the public sphere.

This was just one example of how Weimar was a much divided state and society, originating in military defeat and revolution, punctuated by violent attempts at its overthrow from left and right, and in which new capacities for mass organization could intensify conflict rather than express unity. Many accepted the Weimar constitution pragmatically rather than regarding it as an embodiment of the national idea. Others regarded it as an alien, Western imposition which betrayed the national ideal. Partly Weimar was the least objectionable arrangement, acceptable to the Allies as a liberal democracy, to the left as preferable to monarchical or authoritarian rule, and to the right as preferable to communism, as well as providing scope for old elites to defend their interests. This negative consensus helps explain the capacity of Weimar to resist violent attempts at its destruction between 1919 and 1923.

Weimar also demonstrates vividly that a common, even intense, sense of nationality does not of itself produce unity. Almost all Germans were agreed that the peace settlement was unjust and should be revised. However, there was no consensus on how to set about revision and how to manage internal problems. Political intellectuals sketched out a wide variety of alternative national ideals such as monarchical restoration, national bolshevism, a corporate state, government by experts, military rule and various *völkisch* fantasies. None of these commanded much popular support and without mass appeal no political idea had any chance of success. Pragmatic elites concentrated on manipulating Weimar institutions to their own advantage.

One idea that perennially fascinated people across the political spectrum was that of the leader of genius. Bismarck had established the tradition in Germany but in the mass society of Weimar such a leader must also be a man of the people. The idea neatly combined the mass base of democracy, the authoritarianism of monarchy, and nationalism. In Max Weber's prescient typology, as well as traditional authority (the Hohenzollern monarchy) and legal-rational authority (republican Weimar) there was the third possibility of charismatic authority.

National Socialism did not offer a new ideology. It drew from an amalgam of nationalist ideas, above all *völkisch* creeds with which Hitler had been familiar since his early days in Vienna.[19] For Hitler Germany had only been experienced as the peacetime Second Empire during 1913–14 and thereafter only as mobilization and war followed by demoralization and peace. Hitler's visceral hatred of Weimar and all those he held responsible for creating it – the Allies, communists, socialists, cowardly bourgeois and, above all, Jews – was exceptional and could never attract more than minority support. Even after he had accepted the electoral route to power and had unified the radical right by 1928, his movement remained on the fringe until the depression years. More powerful, conventional conservative nationalists criticized Weimar but were implicated in operating its institutions.

When Weimar was subject to the greatest economic crisis Western capitalism has known, parliamentary democracy was placed on the defensive and tough deflationary policies adopted which were massively unpopular.[20] What made Hitler attractive was that he did not try to offer a coherent institutional or policy alternative. For Hitler politics was about willpower in the eternal race struggle. Institutions and policies were subordinate to this struggle. The image of energy and will was what the National Socialist movement sought to convey, even while it incorporated interests and issued numerous promises. The distinctively national elements of Hitler's ideology, race struggle and imperialism, were played down in the last years of Weimar. Germans were not much concerned with them but were attracted to the idea of the great leader, the political genius who would find and impose solutions to the domestic crisis which were beyond the reach of ordinary mortals and fallible institutions. Above all, the idea of a

Volksgemeinschaft (national community) appealed to a longing to overcome the only-too-obvious divisions within German society, even if if meant very different things to different people. Hitler could also exploit the new possibilities of mass media to bring home this message vividly to Germans. It did not appeal as much to those raised in alternative national traditions, such as the oppositional socialist and Catholic movements. It was regarded with the same pragmatism as Weimar itself by many elite Germans (including those who took the crucial decisions which brought Hitler to the office of chancellor). It may often have been an act of desperation rather than faith which led many to vote for Hitler. Nevertheless, to those who had no faith in institutions, charisma could appear the only answer.

The very idea of the Third Reich as the leader state (*Führerstaat*) embodied this anti-institutional view of politics and nationality. Intellectuals, especially lawyers, tried to square the circle by offering legal and institutional rationales for the idea of charismatic power, just as they tried to provide rational definitions and bureaucratic procedures for applying the race idea to such matters as citizenship. Yet the inherent irrationality of notions of charisma and race meant they coexisted uneasily with the would-be rationality of law-making and bureaucratic procedures.[21]

With Hitler's assumption of power the idea of race ceased to be one component of nationalist rhetoric and became a deadly obsession to be taken to a iscientifici and practical conclusion. Armed with race science one could categorize people racially and measure the health of individual members of a race. These ideas were expressed in a pervasive symbolism and propaganda.

Hitler understood history as race struggle, above all between the Aryan and the Jew. The principle of natural selection was returned, in vulgarized and unrecognizable form, to its biological origins. One key to victory in the unavoidable struggle was racial empire. Picking up on older themes of Germany as encircled and hemmed in, Hitler argued that Germany must carve out 'living space' in eastern Europe. To the anti-Russian and anti-Slav traditions was added a virulent anti-communism. In the conquered lands, non-Germans would be replaced by German settlers or reduced to slaves.

Politics as organized conflict over control of the state was abolished in the Third Reich and replaced by secretive struggles between different interests under the arbitration of Hitler. Exponents of liberal and democratic versions of the national ideal were silenced or exiled. To begin with there was a good deal of influence on the part of a conservative nationalism aiming at revision of Versailles, the build-up of military power and the re-establishment of authoritarian rule. The regime drew upon the bureaucratic and managerial skills of established elites for the effective implementation of policies, tending to make these elites feel that they could maintain some control over Hitler and the National Socialist movement.

They were wrong. A process of radicalization pushed aside this authoritarian nationalism, reaching its apogee after 1941 when war with the USSR unleashed new levels of violence and provided exponents of race empire, exploitation and genocide with opportunities to implement their ideas. As the war turned against Germany, this radicalized the domestic situation where the regime had hitherto displayed some caution in pushing ideological aims too far when they conflicted with popular values. By the end of the war the national idea had become literally murderous, justifying the mass killing not only of those defined as non-German but also of those Germans who were deemed unworthy, biologically or ideologically, of membership of the race.

The Third Reich projected itself as the 'national community' (*Volksgemeinschaft*) which did not recognize divisions within the nation. Institutions embodying such divisions like trades unions and political parties were abolished. The language of class was forbidden and replaced by a language of *Volk* defined in racial terms and insistently hammered home through festivals, symbols and propaganda.

It is difficult to estimate the impact of this. No-one could openly reject regime propaganda and remain at liberty. People lacked the means, let alone the inclination, to consider alternatives. Yet inequalities persisted and it seems likely that many Germans, especially the less well off or powerful, regarded the imagery of community with indifference or scepticism. The regime could give a racial twist to earlier traditions of prejudice but it is debatable how far it could actually alter values, especially of those who were adults by 1933. Some did commit themselves enthusiastically to the racial idea and were crucial to its implementation. Others adapted more traditional national values to the racial idea, sometimes as opportunists, sometimes by radicalizing those values.

Perhaps the normal response, however, was to project existing values upon the Third Reich. Hitler was the 'good German' who provided essential leadership in a state whose institutions – monarchical or republican, authoritarian or democratic – no longer worked. The early policies of rearming, withdrawing from the League of Nations and de-militarizing the Rhineland fulfilled the national desire to undo Versailles. The suspension of parliamentary liberties and the suppression of labour and left-wing organizations was necessary for the restoration of strong government, and was vindicated by overcoming the economic crisis. Even where Hitler went further – annexing Austria and the Sudetenland – one could appeal to the tradition of 'greater Germany', the military alliance of 1914–18 and Austrian and Sudeten German resentment of Versailles. Internally race policy was directed mainly at the small Jewish minority and had little impact on most Germans. Eugenics policy affected more Germans. Even then, aspects such as support for large families was welcome. Where a policy like euthanasia did offend traditional Christian values, there was greater uneasiness and even, on occasion, resistance.

The regime had unprecedented control of communications, yet anxiously monitored passive resistance to its values. At every crisis fear of war was palpable and most Germans took pleasure in foreign policy triumphs only after a fairly bloodless victory was assured. There was little enthusiasm for war in September 1939.

The racial state began to acquire an everyday meaning with the conquest of large parts of Europe. Huge numbers of foreign workers were shipped into Germany;

Germans wielded immense power over non-Germans in large parts of occupied Europe. Germans had few qualms about exploiting foreign workers who were stereo-typed according to ethnic traditions. More controversial is the extent of knowledge, acceptance and involvement in the imprisonment and murder of millions of Jews and others, most of which took place in occupied eastern Europe.

The 1871 Reich had established the norm of the German nation state. Although the new state had been challenged by alternative conceptions of the national idea at the outset, by 1914 these had either faded away or been transformed into pressures for reform within existing boundaries. Amongst bourgeois minorities the national idea came to be projected abroad and to take on an ethnic quality which challenged both reformist and conservative nationalism. In 1914 the idea of a war of defence created a fragile unity between these different national values though the ravages of war and the revelation of conflicting war aims had destroyed that unity by 1918.

War and the mass society and politics of Weimar made national identity something 'natural'. Germans might disagree violently over what national identity meant but they did so as Germans. The Third Reich, and in particular Hitler's charismatic power, could build on that ethnic consciousness though it only converted a minority to its racial and imperialist version of ethnic nationality. The sense of nationality as some-thing natural was not based on biology, propaganda, high or folk culture but on com-mon experiences within an industrial economy and single state. That sense of identity could persist detached from and available to a very wide range of values.

III   After the nation state, 1945–1989

The defeat of the Third Reich and the suicide of its leader apparently discredited not only the charismatic and racial versions of the national idea but the national idea *per se*. By dividing Germany and seeking structural and attitudinal reform, the Allies – though in very different ways – hoped to root out these ideas along with whatever had sus-tained them.

In the zone of Russian occupation which became the German Democratic Republic (GDR) the socialist idea was proclaimed as successor to the national idea. Nevertheless, the constitutions of 1949 and of 1968 both refer to the German Democratic Republic as being 'a socialist state of the German nation' and this nation appears to be implicitly understood as the ethnic German *Volk*. However, German cit-izens of a socialist state had more in common with citizens of other socialist states than with German citizens of a capitalist state. Article 6 of the 1968 constitution, for exam-ple, asserts that in the GDR militarism and Nazism have been destroyed and that the GDR is bound indissolubly to the USSR and other socialist states. If there was a national history of significance it was the history of the 'toiling masses', their exploita-tion and their conflicts with the ruling classes and the way in which a communist party had eventually led these masses to socialism. The GDR wanted to claim sole legiti-macy as a successor German state after 1945. It remained committed to reunification, a commitment given special political salience in 1952 when Stalin flirted with the idea, but one which only made sense as part of Soviet policy and under communist auspices. In reality the GDR turned away from West Germany and stressed its new, non-historical, international socialist credentials.[22]

There were some significant changes later. The turn from the West became definitive with the building of the Berlin Wall in 1961. The development in the early 1970s of a more stable relationship between the two German states induced the GDR to take up the idea of being 'one state, one nation'. Article 1 of the 1974 constitution deleted the phrase 'socialist state of the German nation' and substituted that of 'socialist state of workers and peasants'. Article 6 now referred to the *Volk* without the prior term 'German'. In the 1980s the GDR also tried to appropriate aspects of German history when 'bourgeois' or even 'feudal' figures could be seen playing a key role in progressive events, e.g., Luther and the Reformation, Frederick the Great and Prussian advancement, Bismarck and unification.

It is difficult to work out the impact of this on GDR citizens. Some three million people who left the GDR for West Germany up to 1961 were clearly not convinced. (This leaves aside those who left the Russian zone between 1945 and 1949.) That alone indicates that many East Germans looked to West Germany as a potential home. However, 'identity' is not simply a matter of conscious choice but also of the habits that are developed within a society and a state. In that sense specific forms of GDR identity undoubtedly did take shape over 40 years, though how far these were explicitly 'national' is almost impossible to gauge.

By contrast, the new Austrian republic was a state without an 'idea'. Understandably rejecting the German as well as the imperial tradition it had little but the neutral pursuit of stability and prosperity to recommend it. Obviously in subsequent years its institutional success and stability has generated appropriate senses of identity but rather distant from those to do with ideas of German nationality.

The three German zones of Western occupation which became the Federal Republic of Germany (FRG), like the GDR, officially subscribed to the national idea. The preamble to the Basic Law of 1949 declared this had been enacted by the German people of the constituent *Länder* who were also acting 'on behalf of those Germans to whom participation was denied' and who called upon 'The entire German people ... to achieve in free self-determination the unity and freedom of Germany'.[23]

Who were the German people? They were the citizens of the German state. Citizenship was acquired by descent under the terms of the 1913 law. That law and the constitutional claim to speak for other Germans was projected on to the territory of Germany of 31 December 1937. (For this and the following see Article 116 of the Basic Law: 'Definition of "German", regranting of citizenship'.) The Basic Law also offered refuge to 'Germans' who were forced out of their homes in such countries as Hungary, Czechoslovakia and the USSR. These *Volksdeutsche* had suffered terribly in the mass migrations of the war period and the Federal Republic felt an obligation to offer them refuge from the prospect of continued suffering. The official national idea therefore went even beyond the *ius sanguinis* terms of the 1913 law and acquired an explicitly ethnic component. So long as Germany was a land of ethnic Germans and the only immigrants were from the GDR or communities of dispossessed ethnic Germans this could appear as an expansive rather than a restrictive view of nationality.

This expansive character, however, was linked to the idea of the Federal Republic as a provisional creation, a nucleus for the development of liberal democracy within all Germany and available to all Germans. Thus it complemented rather than contradicted the strong desire to identify Germans and their values with those of the 'west'. The constitution granted the liberal-democratic catalogue of rights to its citizens and the FRG was generous in its openness to those seeking asylum. The national idea was to be so thoroughly grounded in Western values that there could be no question of unifying with other German territories at their expense. The stress on the federalism of the FRG and the need to integrate the FRG into supranational institutions such as the European Community and NATO played down the sovereign nation state as the supreme object of loyalty and identity.

All this, later accompanied by *Ostpolitik* which implied recognition of the GDR, stimulated conservative anxiety about the 'de-nationalization' of West Germans. Except for an extremist minority, the racial or ethnic ideal could not be invoked. Instead conservatives only had the cultural idea of German nationality to underpin unification demands beyond the justification of extending liberal democracy. By the late 1980s some conservatives argued that intellectuals should help instil national pride, for example by stressing the positive features of German culture and history. Against this liberals insisted that political loyalty be grounded only in the state's acceptance of the universal values of liberal democracy and that the consequences of diverging from those values which had been so marked a feature of modern German history be kept constantly in the public mind.

Political elites in both German states were preoccupied with economic recovery and the construction of state institutions, under constraints imposed by the occupying powers. Under Adenauer the FRG pursued integration into the West through supranational agreements. Refugees from eastern Germany ensured that the claim to represent all Germans and the refusal to recognize as valid boundaries such as those with the GDR and of the GDR with Poland continued to be asserted. During the Cold War such policies did not create problems with allies. Conservative nationalist rhetoric coexisted with pro-Western and anti-unification policies. When unification ideas were advanced, for example by left-wing neutralists (encouraged by appropriate shifts in Soviet policy) they were quickly combated by the insistence that unity could only come through integration into the FRG and the West. Meanwhile, except when Soviet policy forced it to flirt with unification, the GDR concentrated on building a 'socialist nation'.

By the early 1960s pursuit of this policy justified the Berlin Wall and harsh border controls. This reinforced the FRG claim that it, rather than the government of the GDR, represented the interests of ordinary Germans in the GDR, although the *de facto* acceptance of the Iron Curtain meant that this was given little practical expression. In the FRG *Ostpolitik* was intended to provide the basis for such practical support and to help dismantle Cold War tensions. Conservative nationalists were troubled that this involved recognition and even support of the GDR and could disengage the Federal Republic from the broader Western alliance. However, the policy fitted in with the *de facto* acceptance of the division of Europe and of coexistence. When the Christian Democrats returned to power in 1982 much of *Ostpolitik* had become bi-partisan. The dilemma was clear. If one accepted pragmatically the division of Europe and Germany, the only way the two parts of the 'divided nation' could be brought closer together was by cooperation between regimes. However, that helped the GDR regime and could involve a refusal to support its domestic opponents. The alternative of appealing beyond the regime to the 'German people' it misruled only made sense if one believed that communism would collapse and such appeals could help bring that about. Few believed that in 1989.

Most Germans after 1945 were concerned with survival. How deeply they had been conditioned by the ideology of the Third Reich and how far they subsequently turned away from such ideas are much debated questions. Ethnic consciousness remained an important part of experience, if only because Germany was a land of immigration and the first wave of immigrants into the FRG were German refugees from other parts of Europe. Later labour migrants from countries such as Greece and Turkey were culturally distinct, placed at the bottom of society and, even after long-term residence, could not easily become German citizens. At first such workers were treated as temporary workers regulated by the Ministry of Labour. However, long-term settlement (if anything increased through restrictive policies which deterred such people from making visits home) created a multicultural society with many second- and third-generation immigrants. At this point the combination of *ius sanguinis* and special concessions to ethnic Germans could appear illiberal and restrictive. Even when naturalization procedures for second- and third-generation immigrants were relaxed, as in the *Auslandergesetz* of 1990, they required renunciation of existing citizenship. This has meant a very slow naturalization rate. The 1990 law established various conditions such as lack of a criminal record and years of residence and was associated with an increased supervision of immigrant behaviour. Furthermore, attempts to integrate these long-term residents has been hindered by fresh anxieties concerning rising unemployment amongst Germans, refugees from eastern Europe and the subsequent tightening up of Germany's generous law on political asylum.

Behind the suspicion of dual citizenship one can discern the idea that nationality is more than a matter of legal rights and duties but is a matter of a common culture and descent and that someone from outside that community must make a special commitment to be accepted. This requirement of a special commitment in itself inhibits the possibility of a multicultural and civic conception of nationality taking root and reduces the prospects for the kind of social integration which might persuade large numbers of long-settled immigrants to make such a commitment.

Yet despite this implicit view that nationality was a matter of a common culture and history there was little serious attempt in the period immediately after 1945 to ground such a sense of community upon any serious engagement with German history or culture. Germans in the GDR never confronted the crimes of the Third Reich which were attributed to a capitalist society in crisis, all traces of which had been removed in the socialist society. For some time there was little discussion of the issue in the FRG. By the 1960s a new generation of Germans demanded more openness about the past, expressed not just in academic historical inquiry but in television drama and film. Amongst younger Germans the national idea exerted less appeal than amongst their French or British counterparts. Contemporary American culture rather than German culture or history exercized the most influence upon these Germans.

Until the building of the Berlin Wall there had been a good deal of East to West movement, facilitated by FRG policy that citizens of the GDR were automatically citizens of the FRG. The wall altered the nature of contacts. The GDR permitted visits to the East which sustained family connections and earned the regime hard currency. Economic subventions from the West – personal, governmental and business – increased. West Germans were assuming responsibilities over and influence in East Germany. East Germans could not but be aware of this supportive relationship, notwithstanding official declarations. More indirect contacts with the West, for example, through the reception of Western television programmes, reinforced the belief that West Germans enjoyed a superior lifestyle, both in terms of material prosperity and freedom. As West Germans identified with the West, East Germans turned away from identity with the wider socialist bloc and saw themselves as deprived in relation to their fellow nationals in the West.[24]

IV   Epilogue: in the new nation state, 1989 to the present

The collapse of Soviet power in east-central Europe left other communist states to fend for themselves. In every country except the GDR changes were made within the existing territory of the state. In the GDR the national idea was crucial to unification with the FRG and the abandonment of indigenous institutions.[25]

The standing commitment of the FRG to its 'fellow German citizens' meant the option of emigration instead of dissent or reform was available. The desire to join with western Germany undercut movements for internal reform. The crisis of the GDR was initiated by a rush to the West, first of all through other communist states and then, after 9 November 1989 and the opening of the Wall, directly into West Germany.

The speed of collapse forced the FRG into direct action, stimulated by concern that the Soviet Union might not remain aloof for long. By early 1990 electioneering in the GDR had been taken over by West German parties. Soon after that came economic unification through the 1:1 convertibility of currency. Finally, the procedure in the Basic Law enabling individual *Länder* outside the present FRG to accede to the republic was adopted. The national idea had apparently carried all before it.

On closer inspection it appears that East Germans were as much concerned with unification as a fast route into the West as with union with fellow nationals. West Germans saw themselves extending aid to deprived fellow nationals. There was an ethnic component to this but the values stressed were those of liberal democracy. Unification had as much to do with the general process of communist collapse and westernizing reform as with specifically national values. It was not national values which mattered so much as the sense that common nationality was a basic fact.

Unification has imposed great economic costs on West Germans and psychological and economic burdens on East Germans. West Germans and East Germans have become aware of how different they are, even if the 'fact' of common nationality apparently united them.[26] At the same time the faltering of the European idea and reactions against various kinds of non-German immigrants (all too easily lumped

Illustration 27.3   An African woman gestures in protest as she stands in front of a burnt out asylum seekers home in the northern German town of Lübeck that was set on fire in an apparent anti-foreigner arson attack early Thursday, 18 January 1996. At least nine people died and 55 others were injured in the fire

together into one simple category of 'the foreigner') might negatively promote a sense of ethnic unity, especially if the economic problems of unification are overcome. (If they are not there will continue to be a tension within the ethnic national idea focused on the cultural distinction between *Ossis* and *Wessis*.) This could be reinforced by an emphasis on national pride and that Germany should no longer feel inferior to her neighbours. Opposing these trends are those who wish to continue with the European commitment and move towards a concept of 'citizenship nationality' which can integrate long-term residents who are not ethnic Germans. Representatives of these values reject what they see as the resurgence of nationalism, including a more apologetic reading of German history. In all these ways people are likely to become more self-conscious about the national idea, to realize that it is a matter of values, and conflicting values at that, rather than something natural which is beyond questioning. How these conflicting values will shape German politics and society, only the future will tell.

Acknowledgement

I am grateful to Ian Kershaw and Dieter Langewiesche for comments on a draft of this essay.

Notes:

1. For further details see Chapter 2 by Whaley.
2. Quoted in Michael Hughes, 'Fiat justitia, pereat Germania? The Imperial Supreme Jurisdiction and Imperial Reform in the Later Holy Roman Empire', in J. Breuilly, ed., *The State of Germany: the National Idea in the Making, Unmaking and Remaking of a Modern Nation-state* (London: Longman, 1992), p. 31.
3. For more detail about such ideas see Chapter 5 by Freidrich.
4. For more detail see Chapter 3 by Clark.
5. I use the term 'democrats' where many would use the word 'radical'. This is to avoid confusion with the term 'radical nationalist' used later on in the essay which refers to right-wing views.
6. See the Chapter 4 by Lee.
7. For more detail see Chapter 6 by Siemann.
8. See above, Chapter 7, on German unification.
9. See Chapter 23 by Berger for just this kind of historical writing.
10. For the political functions of art see Chapter 10 by Jefferies.
11. Hermann or Arminius was mythologized as a leader of German resistance to Roman imperialism; the Teutoborger forest was the site of his greatest battlefield success.
12. For Bismarckian Germany see Chapter 8 by Lerman.
13. The term *völkisch* is difficult to translate. It refers to a stress on the 'people' (*Volk*) but more in an ethnic, even racial sense than in a democratic sense.

14. For the period after 1980 see Chapter 11 by Lerman.
15. I use the term 'reformist nationalism' to refer to those who regarded themselves as patriots but believed that the Second Empire would only be a truly national state following a number of liberal and/or democratic reforms.
16. For further detail see Chapter 9 by Berghahn.
17. For further details see Chapter 11 by Lerman and Chapter 12 by Bessel.
18. See Chapter 14 by Harvey.
19. For further detail see Chapter 15 by Stephenson.
20. For further detail see Chapter 13 by Ferguson.
21. For further detail see Chapters 16 and 17 by Kershaw and Stargardt.
22. For more details on the GDR see Chapters 19 and 21 by Allinson and Carter.
23. For more details on the FRG see Chapters 18 and 21 by Roseman and Carter.
24. Judgements about popular opinion in the GDR must be more tentative than for the FRG where there was a free press, elections and opinion surveys. The new research now being undertaken on the history of the GDR will provide us with a more detailed and accurate picture.
25. For more detail see Chapter 22 by Osmond.
26. See Chapter 20 by Fulbrook.

Select bibliography

Generally: Breuilly, ed., *The State of Germany: the National Idea in the Making, Unmaking and Remaking of a Modern Nation-state* (1992) (essays for the whole period in chronological order); M. Hughes, *Nationalism and Society: Germany 1800–1945* (1988); H. James, *A German Identity 1770–1990* (1989); J. Sheehan, 'What is German History? Reflections on the Role of the Nation in German History and Historiography', *Journal of Modern History*, 53/1 (1981), pp. 1–23. In German: O. Dann, *Nation und Nationalismus in Deutschland 1770–1990* (3rd ed., 1996).

On nationalism as an intellectual movement, including its myths and ceremonies, see G. L. Mosse, *The Nationalization of the Masses* (1975) and *The Crisis of German Ideology* (1966). Most histories of German political ideas include a section on nationalism understood in this sense.

On nationalism as a political movement for the first part of this period: J. Sheehan, *German History, 1770–1866* (1989); O. Dann and J. Dinwiddy, eds., *Nationalism in the Age of the French Revolution* (1988); E. N. Anderson, *Nationalism and Cultural Crisis in Prussia, 1806–1815* (1939). For 1848–9, apart from D. Langewiesche in Breuilly, *The State of Germany*, see the contrasting views of F. Eyck, *The Frankfurt Parliament 1848–49* (1968) and L. Namier, *1848: The Revolution of the Intellectuals* (1944). For unification see Chapter 7. For radical nationalism in the Second Empire see G. Eley, *Reshaping the Right: Radical Nationalism and Political Change after Bismarck* (1980); R. Chickering, *We Men Who Feel Most German: A Cultural Study of the Pan-German League, 1886–1914* (1984). The literature on 1919–45 is too vast to cite; for the whole period to 1990 I simply refer to J. Breuilly, *The State of Germany*.

On nationality as citizenship: R. Brubacker, *Citizenship and Nationhood in France and Germany* (1992) and Brubacker, ed., *Immigration and the Politics of Citizenship in Europe and North America* (1989). See also A. Fahrmeir, 'Nineteenth-Century German Citizenship: A Reconsideration', *Historical Journal*, 3 (1997) and J. Breuilly, 'Sovereignty and Boundaries: Modern State Formation and National Identity in Germany', in M. Fulbrook, ed., *National Histories and European History*, (1993), pp. 94–140. On nationality as experience and opinion there is relevant material in I. Kershaw, *Popular Opinion and Political Dissent in the Third Reich: Bavaria 1933–1945* (1983) and M. Steinert, *Hitler's War and the Germans: Public Mood and Attitude dur-*

ing the Second World War (1977). For post-1945: M. Fulbrook, 'Germany for the Germans: Citizenship and Nationality in a Divided Nation', in D. Cesarani and M. Fulbrook, eds., *Citizenship, Nationality and Migration in Europe* (1996). For problems concerning citizenship since 1990: S. Green, 'Integration durch Staatsangehörigkeit: Die Ausländerpolitik der Bundesregierung, 1955–1995', in H. Timmermann, ed., *Nation und Europa* (1997); D. Thränhardt, 'Die Reform der Einbürgerung in Deutschland', in *Einwanderungskonzeption für die Bundesrepublik Deutschland*, edited through the Friedrich-Ebert-Stiftung (1995), pp. 63-116.

The most recent bibliographical guide in English is D. Buse and J. C. Doerr, *German Nationalism: A Bibliographic Approach* (1985). More recent is H.-U. Wehler, ed, *Bibliographie zur neueren deutschen Sozialgeschichte* (1993), especially pp. 391–5.

Chronology: Germany, 1800–1990

1799	Coup brings Napoleon to power as First Consul in France.
1801	Austria makes peace with France.
1802	Britain makes peace with France.
1803	France gains the left bank of the Rhine; the larger German states receive compensation on the right bank, resulting in the destruction of many small states.
1804	Francis II, Holy Roman Emperor, assumes title of Francis I, Emperor of Austria; Napoleon crowns himself Emperor.
1805	Bavaria and Württemberg become kingdoms. Third war of coalition (including Austria, Britain and Russia) against France. French victories over Russia and Austria (Austerlitz). French naval defeat at Trafalgar. Peace of Pressburg: Austrian territorial losses.
1806	End of Holy Roman Empire. Napoleon establishes the Confederation of the Rhine. Fourth war of coalition pits Prussia, Russia and Britain against France. French victories over Prussia (Jena and Auerstadt). With Berlin Decree Napoleon initiates blockade of Britain.
1807	Peace of Tilsit between France and Russia ends war. Prussia reduced to rump state; her lost territory is used to form Grand Duchy of Warsaw in the east and Kingdom of Westphalia in the west. Stein appointed First Minister in Prussia and begins process of reforms with the October Edict emancipating the peasantry. Napoleon tightens blockade with Milan Decree and founds an order of imperial nobility.
1808	Stein dismissed on Napoleon's insistence; Spanish uprising against Napoleon.
1809	Fifth war of coalition (Austria and Britain against France). Austrian defeat (Wagram) leads to further territorial losses and to appointment of Metternich as Austrian Chancellor.

1810	Napoleon marries Marie-Louise, daughter of Francis I. Hardenberg appointed Prussian Chancellor.
1811	Prussia joins military alliance with France.
1812	June: Napoleon invades Russia. French retreat begins in October. Yorck, the Prussian general, signs agreement with Russian army in December (Convention of Tauroggen).
1813	March: Prussia declares war on France. Austria declares war on France in August. October: France defeated in 'Battle of the Nations' at Leipzig.
1814	March: Allies enter Paris. May: first Peace of Paris. Peace Congress convened in Vienna agrees territorial settlement of German lands.
1815	March: Napoleon lands in France. June: Napoleon defeated at Waterloo. Final Act of Congress of Vienna. German Confederation established. Otto von Bismarck born.
1817	German Students' Associations (*Burschenschaften*) organize nationalist festival at Wartburg.
1818	Constitutions granted in Baden and Bavaria. Hegel appointed Professor at the University of Berlin.
1819	Murder of Kotzebue by a nationalist student in March leads in September to proclamation of the Carlsbad decrees by the German Confederation to enforce political restrictions on the German states. October: Prussia signs first trade treaty (with Schwarzburg-Sonderhausen).
1820	Vienna 'Final Act' establishes greater control of Confederation over affairs of individual states.
1823	Provincial diets established in Prussia.
1826	Start of publication of *Monumenta Germaniae Historica*, edited by Stein and intended to cultivate a love and knowledge of German history through the publication of medieval documents.
1830–1	Revolts in Hesse, Brunswick and Saxony lead to granting of constitutions.
1832	Nationalist festival in Hambach. Death of Goethe.
1833	Establishment of *Zollverein* (German customs union).
1834	Launch of Young Germany movement.
1837	Hanoverian constitution of 1833 suspended by new king.
1840	Frederick William IV becomes King of Prussia. 'Rhine crisis' with France.
1841	Friedrich List publishes *National System of Political Economy* advocating a programme of economic protectionism and nationalism.
1842	Consecration of Cologne Cathedral in presence of Frederick William.
1847	Meeting of the Prussian United Diet in Berlin.
1848	Outbreak of revolution in the German lands, other territories of the Habsburg Empire and elsewhere. German National Assembly convenes in Frankfurt in May; Prussia goes to war with Denmark over issue of Schleswig-Holstein; a truce agreed in August. December: Franz Joseph

becomes Emperor of Austria. The Prussian National Assembly is dissolved and Frederick William issues his own constitution.

1849   April: Frederick William IV rejects offer of hereditary emperorship of Germany under terms of constitution drawn up by German National Assembly. Spring and early summer: counter-revolution, including use of Prussian and other troops against rebels in smaller states, Habsburg troops in Italy and Hungary, and Russian troops in Hungary.

1850   March: Frederick William IV summons a German parliament to Erfurt. July: peace agreed between Prussia and Denmark. November: Prussia backs down over Hesse-Cassel, abandons its 'Erfurt Union' plan and agrees to accept the authority of the Confederation. December: Austrian Chancellor, Schwarzenberg, abandons plan to include all of Habsburg Empire in Confederation.

1851   Confederation formally restored; Bismarck appointed first Prussian ambassador to Federal Diet.

1852–3   Formation of Germanic National Museum in Nuremburg.

1853   *Zollverein* renewed for a further 12 years. Austria unable to form Austro–German customs union and has to settle for commercial treaty with *Zollverein*.

1854–6   Crimean War signals final breakdown of the 1814–15 alliance system: Austria neutral but anti-Russian; Prussia neutral.

1858   Agreement between France and Piedmont to act against Austria. William appointed Regent in Prussia.

1859   War of France and Piedmont against Austria. Austria cedes Lombardy to Piedmont; Piedmont later cedes Savoy and Nice to France. The German National Association (*National Verein*) established. Bismarck appointed Prussian ambassador to Russia.

1860   Prussian Minister of War, Albert von Roon, introduces military reforms into Prussian parliament.

1861   Death of Frederick William IV; William I (Wilhelm I) becomes King of Prussia.

1862   September: Bismarck recalled from his recent appointment as Prussian ambassador to France and appointed Minister-President in midst of constitutional conflict. October: Bismarck delivers his 'blood and iron' speech.

1863   March: Denmark incorporates Schleswig. October: German Diet votes for action against Denmark. December: Hanoverian and Saxon troops enter Holstein.

1864   February–July: War of Austria and Prussia against Denmark. By Treaty of Vienna (October) Denmark cedes Schleswig and Holstein to Austria and Prussia. November: Confederation agrees Prussian and Austrian forces should remain in sole charge of Schleswig–Holstein.

1865   August: by terms of Convention of Gastein, Austria and Prussia occupy and administer Holstein and Schleswig respectively. October: Napoleon III and Bismarck meet at Biarritz.

1866   January: renewal of *Zollverein* on low tariff basis which ensures continued exclusion of Austria–Hungary. April: secret three-month alliance between Prussia and Italy. June: start of war of Italy and Prussia against Austria. July: Prussian victory at Königgrätz. August: Treaty of Prague – Austria agrees to her exclusion from Germany. October: Treaty of Vienna – Austria cedes Venetia to Italy. Prussia annexes Schleswig–Holstein, Hanover, Hesse-Cassel and Frankfurt. The North German Confederation established.

1867   February: Constitution agreed for North German Confederation, including a lower house (Reichstag) elected by universal manhood suffrage. May: Bismarck acts to block French acquisition of Luxembourg. July: customs agreement between Confederation and the south German states.

1868   Establishment of a customs parliament.

1870   July: Hohenzollern candidacy (for the throne of Spain) made public; outbreak of war of Prussia and other German states against France. September: German victory at Sedan and Paris placed under siege. October: capitulation of French fortress of Metz.

1871   January: German Second Empire proclaimed at Versailles – William becomes German Emperor. March: first imperial Reichstag convenes and agrees a constitution in April. May: Treaty of Frankfurt by which France cedes Alsace and Lorraine to Germany and agrees to pay a large war indemnity. July: beginning of the *Kulturkampf* (the campaign against Catholics).

1872   June: expulsion of Jesuits from Germany.

1873   May Laws increase power of Prussian state over education and appointment of clergy.

1873–4 End of the economic boom ushers in a period of reduced growth and price deflation.

1875   Pius IX condemns German government for persecution of Catholics. Formation of the Reichsbank. 'War in Sight' crisis.

1878   Bismarck shifts policy: introduces anti-socialist law following two assassination attempts on William I. Reichstag elections weaken the largest party, the National Liberals.

1879   Bismarck meets a papal envoy of the new Pope, Leo XIII. Bismarck able to form new parliamentary coalition with one section of the National Liberal party along with conservative deputies. Introduces a general protective tariff.

1882   May: Germany, Austria–Hungary and Italy form Triple Alliance. December: Colonial League formed.

1882–4 A period of active colonial policy by Bismarck.

1884   Reichstag elections held with great emphasis by Bismarck on colonial issues.

1887	February: 'cartel' elections to Reichstag leading to majority for the governmental parties (Free Conservatives, Conservatives, National Liberals). June: Reinsurance Treaty with Russia.
1888	March: Death of William I. Short reign and death of his son, Frederick, in June leads to the accession to the Prussian crown and German emperorship of Frederick's son, William II.
1890	February: Reichstag elections undermine the Bismarckian 'cartel' majority; anti-socialist law not renewed. March: Bismarck resigns and General von Caprivi appointed Chancellor. June: the Reinsurance Treaty with Russia is allowed to lapse.
1891	Formation of Pan-German League.
1893	Formation of Agrarian League in response to a series of bilateral treaties reducing grain tariffs.
1894	January: formation of Franco–Russian alliance. October: Caprivi resigns as Chancellor and is replaced by Prince von Hohenlohe.
1896	William II congratulates President Kruger of the Boer Republic on the failure of the Jameson Raid.
1897	Conservative reconstruction of government with three key appointments: von Tirpitz as Secretary for the Navy; von Miquel as Prussian Minister of Finance; and Bernard von Bülow as Secretary for Foreign Affairs.
1898	March–April: breakdown of Anglo-German talks on resisting Russian expansion in the Far East. April: passage of first Navy Law through the Reichstag; formation of the Navy League. June: Reichstag elections produce poor results for the right. September: Fashoda crisis between Britain and France.
1899	Anglo-French agreement on Africa.
1900	June: second Navy Law. October: Bernard von Bülow becomes Chancellor.
1902	Britain and Japan sign defensive alliance. Implementation of a new protective tariff.
1903	Reichstag elections see major socialist party success.
1904	Formation of Entente Cordiale between Britain and France. Commercial treaty between Germany and Russia. War between Russia and Japan.
1904–5	Naval defeats in Russo-Japanese war precipitate crisis and revolution in Russia.
1905	February–July: First Moroccan crisis.
1906	January–April: Algeciras Conference settles Moroccan crisis. February: Britain launches its first Dreadnought in response to German navy building. June: third Navy Law.
1907	January: Reichstag 'Hottentot' elections see socialist setback and a parliamentary majority (the 'Bülow bloc') of pro-colonial parties against Centre Party and SPD. Naval talks between Britain and Russia lead to agreement. June–October: Germany rejects disarmament proposals at The Hague. July: Triple Alliance renewed for six years.

1908	The *Daily Telegraph* affair. October: Austrian annexation of Bosnia-Herzegovina. Fourth Navy Law.
1909	March: collapse of 'Bülow bloc'; June: final defeat of the financial reform programme that had led to collapse. July: Bülow resigns and is replaced as Chancellor by von Bethmann-Hollweg.
1910	Failure of scheme to reform Prussian three-class franchise for elections to the lower house (Landtag).
1911	Second Moroccan crisis.
1912	February: Haldane mission to Germany fails to end naval race. March: new Navy Law published along with an Army Bill. First Balkan War. Reichstag elections: SPD becomes largest party with 110 seats and over one-third of the popular vote.
1913	Second Balkan War. June: Army Finance Bill to pay for massive expansion of army. France also passes an Army Bill to expand its army.
1914	28 June: assassination of Archduke Franz Ferdinand of Austria leads to the July crisis. Austrian ultimatum to Serbia issued on 23 July. The first declaration of war was Austria on Serbia (28 July). Seven further declarations of war by 12 August saw a general state of war in Europe. On 4 August, in a demonstrative display of national unity, all the parties in the Reichstag vote for war credits. September: first battle of Marne halts German advances into France; Russian defeat at the Masurian Lakes. Falkenhayn replaces Moltke as German Commander-in-Chief. November: Hindenburg appointed Commander-in-Chief on the eastern front.
1915	February: Germany declares blockade of Britain. War on western front settles into pattern of inconclusive trench warfare.
1916	February: battle of Verdun. July: battle of the Somme. August: Hindenburg appointed Chief of General Staff with Ludendorff as Quartermaster-General. December: Auxiliary Service Law.
1917	February: revolution in Russia. April: USA declares war on Germany; William II promises universal suffrage for Prussian elections. July: Bethmann-Hollweg replaced as Chancellor by Michaelis; mutiny in German navy; Reichstag passes motion in favour of peace. October: Bolshevik seizure of power in Russia leads in November to opening of peace negotiations between Russia and Germany. December: hostilities suspended on eastern front; Michaelis replaced as Chancellor by Hertling.
1918	January: strikes in Berlin. March: Brest-Litovsk treaty between Russia and Germany gains territory in the east and provides basis for a renewed offensive on the western front (March–April). July: third and last German offensive on western front. September: the Army Command admits the war is going badly and calls for an armistice; Hertling replaced as Chancellor by Prince Max von Baden. October: Germany requests armistice from President Wilson of USA; dismissal of Ludendorff; William agrees to the

appointment of a chancellor based on a Reichstag majority and a democratic reform of the German constitution; sailors' mutiny. November: revolution; abdication of William II; armistice signed; proclamation of a republic under the SPD leader, Ebert. December: Reich Congress of Workers' and Soldiers' Councils in Berlin; foundation of KPD.

1919   January: Spartacus rising, murder of Karl Luxemburg and Rosa Liebknecht; election of a National Assembly. February: Ebert elected President; formation of 'Weimar coalition' government (SPD, Centre, DDP). June: signing of Treaty of Versailles. August: Weimar constitution proclaimed.

1920   March: Kapp–Lüttwitz *putsch*. March/April: communist uprisings. June: Weimar coalition loses its majority in the general election, SPD goes into opposition.

1922   Treaty of Rapallo between Germany and USSR.

1923   January: occupation of the Ruhr by French and Belgian troops; passive resistance by Germany. Summer: peak of great inflation. November 9: Hitler Beer Hall *putsch* in Munich. New currency, end of inflation.

1924   Hitler imprisoned in Landsberg; writes *Mein Kampf*. Dawes Plan to deal with reparations.

1925   Death of Friedrich Ebert; election of General Field Marshall von Hindenburg as President. Locarno Treaty.

1926   Berlin Treaty with the USSR. Germany enters the League of Nations.

1928   Grand Coalition (SPD, Centre, DDP and DVP) under SPD Chancellor Müller.

1929   Young Plan on reparations. Death of Foreign Minister Stresemann. Wall Street Crash inaugurates economic depression.

1930   Collapse of Müller cabinet, replaced by minority government under Brüning. French troops leave Rhineland. NSDAP make big gains in September elections.

1931   Harzburg front formed.

1932   Hindenburg re-elected President after second ballot. Resignation of Chancellor Brüning; formation of minority government under von Papen. SPD government in Prussia overthrown; in the July general election, NSDAP becomes largest party in Reichstag. Hitler refuses offer of vice-chancellorship. November: NSDAP loses votes in general election; resignation of von Papen. December: General von Schleicher appointed Chancellor.

1933   January: Schleicher resigns; Hitler appointed Chancellor on 30 January, heading a mixed cabinet. February: Reichstag burnt, state of emergency declared. March: NSDAP still fail to gain overall majority in general election, but parliament passes Enabling Act after the 'Day of Potsdam'. Dachau founded. March/April: beginnings of dismantling of *Länder* powers. April: organized boycott of Jewish shops and businesses. May: independent trade unions banned, replaced by DAF; burning of Jewish and other banned books on Unter den Linden. June and July: all parties except NSDAP banned or disbanded. July: Concordat with the Vatican. October: Germany leaves League of Nations.

1934   January: Reichsrat (upper house of parliament) and federal system abolished. June: SA (Sturmabteilung) is beheaded, and key politicians (including Schleicher) assassinated in the 'Röhm *putsch*', or 'night of the long knives'. August: death of Hindenburg; army swears oath of allegiance to Hitler, who becomes 'Führer and Reich Chancellor'.

1935   January: Saar plebiscite; returns to the Reich. September: Nuremberg Race Laws.

1936   March: German troops march into demilitarized Rhineland. August: Olympic Games in Berlin. October: Four-Year Plan announced, under Goering; treaty with Italy, forming 'Berlin–Rome Axis'. November: pact between Germany and Japan.

1937   November: Hitler harangues army leadership ('Hossbach memorandum').

1938   Purge of army leadership (Blomberg, Fritsch). March: *Anschluß* with Austria. September; Munich Treaty; Sudentenland ceded from Czechoslovakia to Germany. November 9: organized pogrom against Jews in *Reichskristallnacht*.

1939   March: German invasion of Czechoslovakia; establishment of Protectorates of Bohemia and Moravia; Memel territory returned to Reich. August: non-aggression pact between Germany and USSR ('Hitler–Stalin pact'). September: Germany invades Poland; Britain and France declare war on Germany. Euthanasia programme officially begins. German *Blitzkrieg* campaigns.

1940   April: occupation of Denmark; invasion of Norway. May: German invasion of Belgium, the Netherlands, Luxembourg and France. June: Franco–German ceasefire.

1941   June: Germany attacks USSR; special units (*Einsatzgruppen*) round up and murder Jews in USSR. August: euthanasia programme officially terminated. Autumn: beginning of organized killing of selected Jews taken from ghettos in Poland; first use of gassing in vans at Chelmno. December: Japan bombs American fleet at Pearl Harbor; Germany declares war on USA; Hitler accepts Brauchitsch's resignation and assumes personal command of the army in the field.

1942   January: Wannsee Conference to coordinate the 'final solution' under Heinrich Himmler. Founding of the extermination camps of the 'Reinhard Action' (named after Heydrich); extension of Auschwitz with the construction of the extermination centre at Birkenau. June: successes for Axis forces in North Africa under General Rommel. Autumn: successful Allied counter-offensive in Africa.

1943   January: Casablanca Conference between Roosevelt and Churchill, demanding unconditional surrender of Germany. German army defeated at Stalingrad. July: Allies land in Italy. Mussolini deposed. Summer/ autumn: Allied bombing raids on Germany. November/December: Teheran conference.

1944   Allies land in northwest France. July 20: failure of 'July Plot' to assassinate Hitler.

1945   January–April: Allied armies advance and occupy Germany from west and east. February: Yalta Conference. April: death of Roosevelt. Hitler marries Eva Braun and commits suicide in his Berlin bunker. May: German sur-render; winding up of short-lived Dönitz government. Allied occupation begins – four occupation zones. July/August: Potsdam conference. September: land reform in Soviet zone.

1946   April: amalgamation of KPD and SPD to form SED in Soviet zone. September: Byrne's speech in Stuttgart. October: Nuremberg war crimes trials end. December: USA and Britain agree to form Bizone.

1947   January 1: Bizone comes into effect. February: state of Prussia officially dis-solved. March/April: Moscow Foreign Ministers' Conference. Truman doctrine about 'roll-back of communism' enunciated. June: Marshall Plan announced; Munich Prime Ministers' Conference; establishment of Economic Council of Bizone. November/December: London Foreign Ministers' Conference.

1948   March/April: Six-Powers Conference in London; recommendation to set up separate West German state. June: currency reform in western zones; Berlin blockade begins. September: establishment of parliamentary council in Bonn.

1949   May: lifting of Berlin blockade; West Germany's Basic Law announced. August: election of first West German parliament. September: Theodor Heuss (FDP) elected President, with Konrad Adenauer (CDU) as Chancellor. October: establishment of the German Democratic Republic; Wilhelm Pieck as President, Otto Grotewohl as Prime Minister, Walter Ulbricht retaining effective power as leader of the ruling SED.

1950   February: Ministry for State Security founded in GDR. June: start of Korean War.

1951   Treaty on European Coal and Steel Community signed in Paris.

1952   March: first Stalin Note proposing reunification. May: German Treaty signed in Bonn; European Defence Community treaty signed in Paris; five kilometre border zone cleared in GDR. July: SED pronounces the 'building of socialism' in the GDR; creation of the *Bezirke* to replace the *Länder*. Collectivization of agriculture begins.

1953   March: death of Stalin; 'New Course' announced. June: uprising with widespread strikes and demonstrations in GDR is suppressed by force. July: ceasefire in Korea.

1954   Treaty of Paris signed, allowing West Germany to join NATO, following

French rejection of EDC. *Jugendweihe* (secular youth ceremony) introduced in GDR as part of SED campaign against the churches.

1955   Paris Treaty comes into force; ending of Occupation Statute for FRG, which becomes a member of NATO. Founding of the Warsaw Pact, of which the GDR is a member. October: plebiscite in Saarland.

1956   National Peoples Army (NVA) founded in GDR. Stalin cult denounced at XX Congress of the CPSU. Uprisings in Poland and Hungary, but not in GDR.

1957   January: Saarland joins Federal Republic. March: Treaty of Rome establishes European Economic Community (EEC). September: CDU/CSU win absolute majority in Bundestag election.

1958   Khrushchev's Berlin Ultimatum.

1959   July: Heinrich Lübke (CDU) elected President of FRG. November: SPD Bad Godesberg Conference renouncing radical rhetoric.

1960   Collectivization of agriculture speeded up in GDR. Wilhelm Pieck dies and is replaced by a new collective head of state, the Council of State.

1961   August: Berlin Wall erected.

1962   GDR announces compulsory conscription. Cuban crisis. 'Spiegel affair' in West Germany.

1963   Franco-German Friendship Treaty signed in Paris. Adenauer resigns, Ludwig Erhard (CDU) elected Chancellor. First agreement on transborder travel West Berlin/GDR. New Economic System (NÖS) introduced in GDR.

1964   *Bausoldatenerlass* in GDR allows alternative military service as construction workers without bearing weapons.

1966   FDP leaves West German government over budget differences: 'Grand Coalition' of CDU/CSU and SPD formed under Kurt-Georg Kiesinger (CDU) as Chancellor.

1968   Student demonstrations in West Germany. Bundestag passes Emergency Decree. GDR adopts new constitution enshrining leading role of SED. Warsaw Pact troops invade Czechoslovakia and suppress 'Prague Spring'.

1969   Gustav Heinemann (SPD) elected West German President. A major watershed in West German politics is crossed with the formation of the SPD/FDP coalition government under Chancellor Willy Brandt (SPD).

1970   Brandt (SPD) and Willi Stoph (SED) meet in Erfurt and Kassel. August: German–Soviet Non-Aggression Pact signed in Moscow. December: German–Polish Treaty signed in Warsaw. Winding up of New Economic System in GDR.

1971   Ulbricht replaced by Erich Honecker as SED leader in GDR. Signing of Four Powers' Agreement on Berlin. Brandt receives Nobel Peace Prize.

1972   Failure of CDU/CSU attempt to unseat Brandt's government by a constructive vote of no confidence. Bundestag ratification of Moscow and Warsaw Treaties. SPD/FDP coalition government re-elected with a clear majority. Signing of Basic Treaty between GDR and FRG.

1973   Basic Treaty ratified by Bundestag. GDR and FRG become members of the United Nations. World oil crisis.

1974   Brandt resigns and is replaced by Helmut Schmidt (SPD). Walter Scheel (FDP) elected Federal President. GDR revises its constitution to build up the concept of a 'GDR nation'.

1975   Helsinki Final Act of Council for Security and Cooperation in Europe (CSCE).

1976   Exile of Wolf Biermann to West Germany, followed by protests from East German intellectuals. Self-burning of Pastor Brüsewitz in GDR.

1977   Terrorist attacks and assassinations (Buback, Ponto, Schleyer) by Red Army Faction in FRG.

1978   Church/state agreement in GDR.

1979   Karl Carstens (CDU) elected Federal President. Decision to deploy nuclear missiles on German soil. Soviet invasion of Afghanistan. Second world oil crisis inaugurates a further period of economic difficulties.

1982   FDP leaves governing coalition over budget differences and votes in Helmut Kohl (CDU), in a constructive vote of no confidence, as Chancellor of a coalition between the FDP and the CDU/CSU.

1984   Erich Honecker's attempted visit to FRG cancelled.

1985   Mikhail Gorbachev becomes Soviet leader. Kohl and US President Reagan meet over SS graves at Bitburg.

1987   Honecker makes an official visit to FRG. Olof Palme Peace March in GDR. Stasi raid on *Umweltbibliothek* (Environmental Library) in East Berlin.

1988   January: Mass arrests by Stasi at Luxemberg/Liebknecht demonstration in East Berlin.

1989   East German dissidents observe falsification of May election results. Summer: Hungary begins to dismantle its border with Austria; refugee crisis as East Germans flee west. September: foundation of New Forum; Monday demonstrations in Leipzig. October: Gorbachev visits Berlin for GDR 40th anniversary and warns Honecker that it is time to reform; Honecker is deposed and replaced by Egon Krenz; demonstrations grow all over GDR. November: Politburo resigns; Berlin Wall opened on 9 November; Kohl announces 'Ten-Point Plan' for German unification on 28 November. December: SED renounces its claim to leadership. Formation of interim Round Table government.

1990   'Two-plus-Four talks' take place to consider international aspects of the reopened German question. March: elections in GDR bring in conservative-dominated coalition government. July: currency union with West Germany. October 3: unification of Germany by means of accession of newly recreated East German *Länder* to Federal Republic of Germany. December: Kohl re-elected Chancellor of united Germany.

Notes on the contributors

Mark Allinson is Lecturer in German at the University of Bristol. His Ph.D. thesis was on popular opinion in Thuringia, 1945–1968, and his research interests include the politics and society of the GDR and modern Austria.

Stefan Berger is Lecturer in Modern German History at the University of Wales, Cardiff. He has recently published *The British Labour Party and the German Social Democrats, 1900–1931* (1994; German transl. J. W. H. Dietz Nachf., 1997), *The Force of Labour* (1995) and *The Search for Normality: National Identity and Historical Consciousness in Germany Since 1800* (1997). He is currently working on the relationship between nationalism, ethnicity and labour in Britain and Germany, and he is also writing a history of German social democracy in its international context from 1870 to the present.

Volker Berghahn is J. P. Birkelund Professor of European History at Brown University, Providence, RI. His recent publications include *Otto A. Friedrich, Ein Politischer Unternehmer, 1902–1975* (1993); *Imperial Germany, 1871–1914* (1995); and (ed). *Quest for Economic Empire* (1996).

Richard Bessel is Reader in Modern History at the Open University and co-editor of the journal *German History*. His publications include *Political Violence and the Rise of Nazism: The Storm Troopers in Eastern Germany, 1925–1934* (1984); *Germany after the First World War* (1993); (ed.) *Life in the Third Reich* (1987); (ed.) *Fascist Italy and Nazi Germany: Comparisons and Contrasts* (1996); and (ed. with Ralph Jessen) *Die Grenzen der Diktatur. Staat und Gesellschaft in der DDR* (1996).

John Breuilly is Professor of Modern History at the University of Birmingham. His main interests are in nationalism, modern German history, and comparative urban and cultural history in modern Europe. His recent publications include: *The Formation of* *the First German Nation-State, 1800–1871* (1996) and (co-ed. with G. Niedhart and A.D. Taylor) *The Era of the Reform League: English Labour and Radical Politics 1857–1872* (1995).

Erica Carter is Research Fellow in German Studies at the University of Warwick. Her most recent publication is *How German is She? Post-war West German Reconstruction and the Consuming Woman* (1997). She is currently researching popular German cinema of the 1930s and 1940s.

Christopher Clark is a Fellow and Lecturer in Modern European History at St Catherine's College, Cambridge. He is the author of *Politics of Conversion. Missionary Protestantism and the Jews in Prussia 1728–1941* (1995).

Niall Ferguson is Fellow and Tutor in Modern History at Jesus College, Oxford. His recently published *Paper and Iron: Hamburg Business and German Politics in the Era of Inflation* (1995) was shortlisted for the *History Today* Book of the Year award. He has also written numerous articles on nineteenth- and twentieth-century financial history, including an influential critique of Keynes's *Economic Consequences of the Peace*, and he is currently writing a history of the Rothschilds.

Ute Frevert is Professor of Modern History at the University of Konstanz, Germany. Her publications include *Krankheit als politisches Problem 1770–1880* (1984); *Frauen-Geschichte* (1986; English edn 1988); (ed.) *Bürgerinnen und Bürger* (1988); Ehrenmänner. *Das Duell in der bürgerlichen Gesellschaft* (1991; English edn 1995); '*Mann und Weib, und Weib und Mann*' (1995); (ed.) *Militar und Gesellschaft im 19. u. 20. jh.* (1997).

Karin Friedrich is Lecturer in History at the School of Slavonic and East European Studies, University of London. She is currently working on early modern urban history (Poland and Prussia) and on the history of political ideas and national identity. Her *The Other Prussia: Poland, Prussia and Liberty, 1454–1772* will soon be published.

Mary Fulbrook is Professor of German History at University College London. Her publications include *Piety and Politics: Religion and the Rise of Absolutism in England, Württemberg and Prussia* (1983); *A Concise History of Germany* (1990); *The Divided Nation: Fontana History of Germany 1918–1990* (1991); *The Two Germanies 1945–1990: Problems of Interpretation* (1992); *Anatomy of a Dictatorship: Inside the GDR, 1949–1989* (1995); (ed.) *National Histories and European History* (1993); and (ed. with David Cesarani) *Citizenship, Nationality and Migration in Europe* (1996).

Elizabeth Harvey is Lecturer in History at the University of Liverpool. Her publications include *Youth and the Welfare State in Weimar Germany* (1993); (ed. with Jennifer

Birkett) *Determined Women: Studies in the Construction of the Female Subject, 1900–1990* (1991) and (ed. with Lynn Abrams) *Gender Relations in German History* (1996). She is currently carrying out research on women's involvement in National Socialist Germanization policies in the 'German East'.

Matthew Jefferies is Lecturer in German History at the University of Manchester. He is the author of *Politics and Culture in Wilhelmine Germany. The Case of Industrial Architecture* (1995) and other publications on German cultural history. He is currently continuing his research in this area, and writing a biography of the German–American architect Peter J. Weber (1863–1923) for the Art Institute of Chicago.

Ian Kershaw is Professor of Modern History at the University of Sheffield. He was elected a Fellow of the British Academy in 1991; he is also a Fellow of the Royal Historical Society. Publications on German history include: *Der Hitler-mythos. Volksmeinung und Propoganda im Dritten Reich* (1980); English version: *The 'Hitler Myth'. Image and Reality in the Third Reich* (1987); *Popular Opinion and Political Dissent in the Third Reich: Bavaria, 1933–45* (1983); *The Nazi Dictatorship. Problems and Perspectives of Interpretation* (1985; 3rd edn., 1993); *Hitler. A Profile in Power* (1991); (ed. with Moshe Lewin) *Stalinism and Nazism: Dictatorships in Comparison* (1997); and (ed.) *Weimar. Why did German Democracy Fail?* (1990).

Jürgen Kocka has held the chair for the History of the Industrial World at the Free University of Berlin since 1988. He became a permanent Fellow at the Wissenschaftskolleg zu Berlin (Institute for Advanced Studies) in 1991. He is co-editor of the journal *Geschichte und Gesellschaft: Zeitschrift für Historische Sozialwissenschaft* (since 1975) and editor of a series *Kritische Studien zur Geschichtswissenschaft* (since 1972). Publications include *Unternehmensverwaltung und Angestelltenschaft am Beispiel Siemens 1847–1914* (1969); *Facing Total War. German Society 1914–1918* (1984); *White Collar Workers in America 1890–1940* (1980); *Les employés en Allemagne 1850–1980* (1989); *Arbeitsverhältnisse und Arbeiterexistenzen. Grundlagen der Klassenbildung im 19. Jahrhundert* (1990).

Robert Lee is the Chaddock Professor of Economic and Social History at the University of Liverpool. He has published widely on the demographic, economic and social history of Germany. His publications include (ed. with Pat Hudson) *Women's Work and the Family Economy in Historical Perspective* (1990); (ed. with Richard Lawton) *Urban Population Development in Western Europe from the Late-Eighteenth to the Early-Twentieth Century* (1989), and *The Population Dynamics and Development of Western European Port Cities* (1997); (ed.) *German Industry and German Industrialisation. Essays in German Economic and Business History in the Nineteenth and Twentiety Centuries* (1991); (ed. with Eve Rosenhaft) *State, Social Policy and Social Change in Germany 1880–1994)*. He is currently completing two projects on the demographic and socio-economic development of Bremen and Stralsund in the nineteenth century.

Katharine A. Lerman is Senior Lecturer in Modern European History at the University of North London and her publications include *The Chancellor as Courtier: Bernhard von Bülow and the Governance of Germany 1900–1909* (1990). She is currently writing a book on Bismarck and researching into the genealogy and position of women within the imperial German ruling elite.

Charles S. Maier teaches Modern European History at Harvard University where he is Krupp Foundation Professor of European Studies and Director of the Center for European Studies. His publications include *Recasting Bourgeois Europe: Stabilization in France, Germany and Italy in the Decade after World War I* (1975); *In Search of Stability: Explorations in Historical Political Economy* (1987); *The Unmasterable Past: History, Holocaust, and German National Identity* (1988); and, most recently, *Dissolution: The Crisis of Communism and the End of East Germany* (1997).

Jonathan Osmond is Professor of Modern European History at the University of Wales, Cardiff. He is author of *Rural Protest in the Weimar Republic: The Free Peasantry in the Rhineland and Bavaria* (1993) and editor of *German Reunification: A Reference Guide and Commentary* (1992). His current research is on the rural social history of the Soviet Zone and GDR.

Mark Roseman is Senior Lecturer in Modern History at Keele University. He has written widely on post-war West Germany and the Third Reich. His publications include *Recasting the Ruhr (1945–1958): Manpower, Economic Recovery and Labour Relations* (1992), and he has edited *Generations in Conflict: Youth Revolt and Generation Formation in Germany 1770–1968* (1995).

Wolfram Siemann is Professor of Modern and Contemporary History at the University of Munich. His recent books include *Die deutsche Revolution von 1848/49* (1996); *Gesellschaft im Aufbruch: Deutschland 1849–1871* (1996); *Vom Staatenbund zum Nationalstaat Deutschland 1806–1871* (1995); (ed. with Ute Daniel) *Propaganda. Meinungskampf, Verführung und politische Sinnstiftung 1789–1989* (1994).

Nicholas Stargardt is Lecturer in Modern European History at Royal Holloway College, University of London. He has written *The German Idea of Militarism: Radical and Socialist Critics, 1866–1914* (1994), as well as essays on theories of nationalism. He is currently working on the history of childhood in modern Germany, including children's art in the Holocaust.

Jill Stephenson is Reader in History at the University of Edinburgh. She is the author of *Women in Nazi Society* (1975), *The Nazi Organization of Women* (1981) and numerous articles and essays on women in twentieth-century Germany and Württemberg in the Second World War. From 1986 to 1996 she was joint editor of *German History: The Journal of the German History Society*.

Joachim Whaley is a University Lecturer in German and Fellow of Gonville and Caius College, Cambridge. He is the author of *Religious Toleration and Social Change in Hamburg, 1529–1819* (1985) and is currently working on a study of early modern Germany.

Index